ECONOMICS AND THE LAW, SECOND EDITION

ECONOMICS AND
THE LAW, SECOND EDITION

FROM POSNER TO POSTMODERNISM
AND BEYOND

Nicholas Mercuro and Steven G. Medema

PRINCETON UNIVERSITY PRESS   PRINCETON AND OXFORD

Library of Congress Cataloging-in-Publication Data

Mercuro, Nicholas.

Economics and the law : from Posner to postmodernism and beyond /
Nicholas Mercuro and Steven G. Medema.—2nd ed.
p.   cm.
Includes bibliographical references and index.

ISBN-13: 978-0-691-12572-5 (pbk. : alk. paper)
ISBN-10: 0-691-12572-4 (pbk. : alk. paper)
1. Law and economics.   I. Medema, Steven G.   II. Title.

K487.E3M468 2006
340'.115—dc22   2006041599

British Library Cataloging-in-Publication Data is available

This book has been composed in Times Roman

Printed on acid-free paper. ∞

pup.princeton.edu

Printed in the United States of America

1   3   5   7   9   10   8   6   4   2

To the memory of Aaron Director

Contents

Preface

WHEN PETER DOUGHERTY, our editor at Princeton University Press, asked us if we were willing to prepare a second edition of *Economics and the Law*, the first thing we did was to reexamine the reviews of the first edition that appeared in various economic and legal journals. Given the positive reception accorded to the first edition, the feeling that we could do some things a little better than we had the first time around, and, some of the new and interesting developments taking place in Law and Economics, we agreed to go forward with the writing of a second edition. Our intent was that the new edition would remain true to the scope and purposes of the first edition but also take account of the evolution of the field in the eight years since the book was originally published. As such, this second edition of *Economics and the Law* has maintained both its basic structure and its original purpose—to provide the reader with a concise overview of the dominant schools of thought that make up the field of Law and Economics.

Those familiar with the first edition will notice that we have made several changes for this new edition. First, we have expanded the discussion of the New Haven and Modern Civic Republican approaches and combined them with a new discussion of the Austrian school of law and economics in a chapter entitled, "Branching Out." Second, we have added a chapter exploring the law and economics literature on social norms, which has become an integral part of all of the schools of thought in Law and Economics. The chapters on the Chicago approach to law and economics, public choice theory, institutional law and economics, and the new institutional economics have been expanded, and each includes a substantive "At Work" section that presents applications of that particular school of thought. Finally, we have eliminated the postmodern chapter, "Critical Legal Studies," which appeared in the first edition. Our decision to do so was based on the premise that if one includes Critical Legal Studies, there is really no rationale for excluding additional and complementary chapters on Critical Race Theory, Feminist Jurisprudence/Law and Economics, and the work of the Rights-Based Theorists from the realm of philosophy, all of which have some bearing of modern-day jurisprudence. To include them would have taken us too far afield from our original purpose. The sum total of these changes has led to a new subtitle for the book: *From Posner to Postmodernism and Beyond*.

As with any project like this, we owe a great deal of thanks to a great many people. We would like to express our gratitude to all those who took the time to provide a careful reading of selected chapters and suggested very worthwhile changes to drafts of this second edition or its predecessor. These include

Susan Rose-Ackerman, Peter Boettke, Thráinn Eggertsson, Ross B. Emmett, Harry First, Dub Lane, Gary Libecap, Bill Lovett, Robin Paul Malloy, Cindy Person, Warren J. Samuels, A. Allan Schmid, Mark Tushnet, Mark D. White, and Gerald Whitney, and several anonymous reviewers. Kyle Reynolds did yeoman's work in organizing the entire reference list as well as cross-referencing each and every text citation with that list. We implicate none of these individuals in the final product.

Steven Medema would like to thank the Dean of the College of Liberal Arts and Sciences and the Department of Economics at the University of Colorado at Denver for research support during the writing of both editions of the book, and Carol for her endless patience throughout the past year. Nicholas Mercuro gratefully acknowledges the faculty and the former Dean of Tulane Law School, John R. Kramer, for affording him the opportunity to teach "The Economics of Legal Relationships" course annually at the law school, as well as the many Tulane law students who, over the six years he taught the course, asked many probing questions that forced a valuable rethinking and reformulation of many of the ideas contained in this book. He also acknowledges the support given to him at Michigan State University College of Law and James Madison College.

Finally, we would like to thank all of the people at Princeton University Press for encouraging us to go forward with this undertaking and for all of the support they have provided along the way. Sophia Efthimiatou, Jill Harris, and Tim Sullivan did a great job in shepherding the book through the publication process. Chris Brest did a masterful job preparing the figures, and Linda Truilo's copyediting saved us from sins of commission and omission too numerous to mention. We are also grateful to Rose Carmellino for her efforts in compiling the index. Finally, particular thanks go to Peter Dougherty, an editor sui generis, a source of endless patience and encouragement, and a good friend.

Nicholas Mercuro
East Lansing, Michigan

Steven G. Medema
Denver, Colorado

ECONOMICS AND THE LAW, SECOND EDITION

CHAPTER 1.

The Jurisprudential Niche of Law and Economics

> It is somewhat surprising that so conspicuous a truth
> as the interaction of economics and law should have
> waited so long for recognition—a recognition by no
> means universal. Some of those who question it
> maintain the independence and self-sufficiency of
> law, while others maintain that of economics. In
> reality law and economics are ever and everywhere
> complementary and mutually determinative.
> *(Fritz Berolzheimer 1912, p. 23)*

INTRODUCTION

"LAW AND ECONOMICS" can be defined as the application of economic theory—primarily microeconomics and the basic concepts of welfare economics—to examine the formation, structure, processes, and economic impact of law and legal institutions. Various schools of thought compete in this rich marketplace of ideas,[1] including the Chicago approach to law and economics, public choice theory, institutional law and economics, and the new institutional economics. The primary purpose of this book is to provide the reader with a concise overview of the dominant schools of thought within Law and Economics.[2] We also provide an overview of the principal contours of the New Haven school, modern civic republicanism, and Austrian law and economics, as well as review the burgeoning area of social norms and law and economics, each

---

[1] The metaphor of "the marketplace of ideas" is attributed to Justice Oliver Wendell Holmes, in his dissent in *Abrams v. United States*, where he wrote,

But when men have realized that time has upset many fighting faiths, they may come to believe even more than they believe the very foundations of their own conduct that the ultimate good desired is better reached by free trade in ideas—that the best test of truth is the power of the thought to get itself accepted in the competition of the market, and that truth is the only ground upon which their wishes safely can be carried out. (250 U.S. 616, 630 (1919))

[2] Throughout this book we use "Law and Economics" (capital "L" and "E") as an eclectic title to refer to all of the schools of thought discussed here. These are identifiable, coherent schools of thought that, in our opinion, deal explicitly with the interrelations between law and economy.

of which places significant emphasis on the interrelations between law and economy.

We are presenting these schools of thought as both competing and complementary perspectives on, or approaches to, the study of the development and the reformulation of law and to the examination of the interrelations of legal and economic processes generally.[3] As such, this material is of fundamental importance not only for those working in the fields of economics and law, but also to those in the contiguous fields of political science, philosophy, and sociology.[4] It must be underscored from the outset that we are trying only to describe the ideas central to each school of thought. No attempt is made to critique the schools or the ideas contained therein. We are also well aware of the pitfalls of trying to describe the essential elements of a particular school of thought when there are continuing, and occasionally acrimonious, disputes within and between these schools. Our response, in short, is that the benefits of identifying the schools of thought as presented here exceed the costs of expressed misgivings by those few within each school of thought who object to or refuse categorization. The reception given to the first edition of this book would seem to validate this approach.

There are a wide variety of measures that document the continued expansion in the number of scholars interested in exploring and understanding the interrelations between law and economics.[5] First, there is the relatively recent establishment of the American Law and Economics Association, the Canadian Law and Economics Association, the European Association of Law and Economics, the Israeli Association of Law and Economics, the Australian Law and Economics Association, and the Latin American Law and Economics Association. As recently as 2003, the Portuguese, the Scandinavian, and the Greek Law and Economics Associations held inaugural conferences. Second, there are a number of leading publications dedicated to publishing the scholarly contributions to this field, including journals such as the *Journal of Law and Economics; Journal of Legal Studies; American Law and Economics Review; Journal of Law, Economics & Organization; Public Choice; Constitutional Political Economy; International Review of Law and Economics;* and the *European Journal*

---

[3] The second edition of this book, like the first, builds on and extends the discussion in Mercuro and Medema (1995). Another much more brief description of several of these schools of thought can be found in Parisi (2005).

[4] For a discussion of contiguous disciplines, see Coase (1978), Lazear (2000), and Radnitzky and Bernholz (1987).

[5] It was recently observed by Harris (2003, p. 660) that "law and economics [is] the most successful school of jurisprudence of the second half of the twentieth century and whose influence in law schools is still on the rise." See also Landes and Posner (1993, 1996). Throughout this book, all references or parenthetical citations to Posner are to Richard A, Posner; references or parenthetical citations to Eric Posner's work are identified as E. Posner.

of Law and Economics. In 2000, the five-volume *Encyclopedia of Law and Economics* came into print, edited by Boudewijn Bouckaert and Gerrit De Geest (2000). There are also four research annuals—the *Supreme Court Economic Review, Research in Law and Economics, The Economics of Legal Relationships*, and *New Horizons in Law and Economics*—devoted to the field, and a wide variety of traditional economics journals and law reviews now regularly publish Law and Economics articles.

The extent and significance of this literature is reflected in the *Journal of Economic Literature*'s formal recognition in 1991 of Law and Economics as a separate field within its classification system for the discipline of economics. The Association of American Law Schools Directory began listing Law and Economics as a separate subject area in 1988–89.[6] A third indicator is the existence of a number of programs in Law and Economics within the major law schools, including Harvard University, Yale University, Columbia University, Stanford University, George Mason University and the University of California-Berkeley; the very active working paper series at these schools; and the host of "law and economics" websites now available.[7] Fourth, in the past decade, we have witnessed the establishment of the European Union's Erasmus Programme in Law and Economics;[8] the recent French initiative, the European School of New Institutional Economics;[9] and the *Erasmus Law and Economics Review*, an online journal described as a "new, open and free communication interface between lawyers, academics and economists."[10] Finally, for the past twenty-six years Henry G. Manne, the former Dean of the George Mason University School of Law, and his successors have organized and hosted Law and Economics workshops for judges and law professors, and for economists. Taken together, these programs have had over one thousand professors and judges in attendance.[11]

[6] Interestingly, before the 1931–34 edition of the *Index to Legal Periodicals*, legal-economics articles were categorized under the designation "Political Economics"; from 1935 through 1987 they were found under the subject heading "Economics"; since 1988 they have been listed under the two headings, "Economic Jurisprudence" and "Economics" (there is no designation "Law and Economics" in the Index).

[7] A good place to start is with the Sixteen Law and Economics websites found at Findlaw: http://lawecon.lp.findlaw.com/index.html.

[8] See http://www.frg.eur.nl/rile/emle/.

[9] See http://www.esnie.org/en/home/index.php.

[10] See http://www.eler.org/modules.php?op=modload&name=News&file=article&sid=1&mode=hread&order=0&thold=0&POSTNUKESID=4fd74406cd79cdd97f0a5fc9ddc3927d.

[11] This information is contained in the 1995 program brochure for Law and Economics Center's Institute for Law Professors, Law and Economics Center, George Mason University School of Law, Arlington, Virginia. Available at http://www.law.gmu.edu/lawecon/Programs.htm. This education program has generated some debate in the U.S. Congress with regard to those who receive public funding to attend. This debate is chronicled by Staff Reporter in the *Wall Street Journal* (2000, p. 26).

THE PRESENT SITUATION IN LEGAL-ECONOMIC SCHOLARSHIP

Although the seeds of contemporary Law and Economics go back at least a century,[12] it is only in the past five decades that it has emerged as a substantial and important body of thought within both economics and law. During this time, Law and Economics has developed within, and in part because of, a somewhat uncertain and unsettled atmosphere within jurisprudence. What once existed as prevailing legal doctrine derived from conventional political and legal theory still exists, but law no longer develops in a self-contained, autonomous manner. Rather, most professors now recognize law as "a multi-dimensional phenomenon—historical, philosophic, psychological, social, political, economic and religious" in its inspiration and implications (Packer and Erlich 1973, p. 56). Furthermore, almost all American legal scholars, judges, and lawyers hold an instrumental view of the law—instrumental in the sense that legal rules are adopted so as to promote some goal, be it equality, justice, fairness, or efficiency.[13] Regardless of whether one believes law is used to promote these goals, it *does* have wide-ranging impact, and the assessment of these impacts necessitates the use of tools and ideas from disciplines outside of legal theory proper.

Today, the law is being analyzed from an incredibly diverse set of perspectives, including Law and Economics, critical legal studies, rights-based theory, feminist jurisprudence, and critical race theory, all of which claim to have something worthwhile to say as to the origin, legitimacy, and development of the law. The outward turn of law thus far has generated no consensus-type movement toward a new and stable foundation for the law (Minow 1987). We now stand at a point where legal study embodies a plethora of competing and often mutually exclusive points of view. To use Alan Hunt's (1987, p. 7) metaphor, "[T]he glacier that is law has fractured into numerous pieces, and its replacement (if there is to be one) remains to be determined." Perhaps the present situation is best summed up in the comment that legal scholarship has been "left with a plethora of explanatory frameworks, [and] a dearth of criteria for choice among them" (Note 1982, p. 1976).

The unsettled nature of legal theory and the relationship of law to economics did not arise in a vacuum. Rather, it is partially the outcome of 1) the development of the "Law" in "Law and Economics"—in particular, the various

---

[12] In fact, one can go back much further than this, to Adam Smith, whose work *Lectures on Jurisprudence* (1978) and *The Wealth of Nations* (1937 reprint) is, in some respects, well within the tradition of Law and Economics.

[13] As Kornhauser (1984, p. 366) stated, "Everyone debates what law ought to be while quietly adhering to instrumentalism. The adherence to legal instrumentalism . . . has largely been implicit in traditional legal studies." On this point, see also Summers (1981). We recognize that this belief is not universally held among legal scholars. On the idea that law maintains its autonomy and has its own internal, coherent logic, see, for example, Weinrib (1995).

evolving perspectives from which one can analyze the prevailing legal relations governing society—and 2) the development of the "Economics" in "Law and Economics"—particularly as embodied in the work of neoclassical microeconomists since Alfred Marshall. While Law and Economics has had an impact on both the legal and economic disciplines, there is no doubt that it "was institutionalized as a discipline in law schools rather than in economics departments," where it is just another branch of applied microeconomic theory rather than a disciplinary philosophy as it is in law. The result is that, by "analyzing legal rules and providing prescriptions for legal reforms, law and economics scholars could participate in the major areas of discourse within legal academia. They could even demonstrate the power of their coherent and rigorous theory over the confused intuitions of other legal scholars" (Harris 2003 p. 664).[14]

In the next section of this chapter, we will examine briefly the path that brought law and legal theory to its present situation. This will be followed by a brief characterization of the relevant concepts of economic efficiency variously employed by legal-economic scholars.[15] We will then present a description of the stages of choice and the underlying logic of Law and Economics, followed by a section that highlights some of the fundamental differences in methodology and modes of reasoning between economics and the law.

THE "LAW" IN "LAW AND ECONOMICS"

The Three Fundamental Questions

Before we begin our outline of the history of American jurisprudence, it is useful to bear in mind that the several legal theories described here, as well as the schools of thought constituting Law and Economics, try, each in its own way, to provide answers to three fundamental and interrelated questions:

1. What is the law?
2. Where does the law come from and how does it acquire its legitimacy?
3. What should the law be?

The distinctive elements of the various approaches to law, including the several schools of thought within Law and Economics, as well as their similarities emerge quite clearly when examined against the backdrop of these questions, and we shall allude to the questions throughout our discussion.

---

[14] Nonetheless, (as we described earlier) it is interesting to observe that while in 1991 the *Journal of Economic Literature* formally recognized Law and Economics as a separate field within its classification system of the discipline of economics, the legal system has yet to revise its classification system accordingly.

[15] The two appendices to this chapter provide a detailed analysis of the primary concepts of economic efficiency.

The Nature of Common Law

Common law, as it has evolved from the English royal courts of centuries past to present-day America, consists of the doctrines and principles developed gradually by judges and used as the foundation for judges' decisions. The history of this common law jurisprudence has at its roots a search for moorings, for a set of interpretive and adjudicatory principles in which to ground law's legitimacy and authority, and, thereby, to justify judicial decisions. Once those moorings were set in place, they provided a firm, albeit evolving, basis upon which to guide the law's development. During the Middle Ages, the interpretation of law was guided by theological considerations, as law claimed to stand as divine revelation or the will of God. From the time of the Renaissance until the middle of the nineteenth century, this idea received a somewhat more secular cast, as law was said to be grounded in ultimate principles or ideas, such as natural law.

Sir William Blackstone, writing in the late 1700s and early 1800s, suggested that the common law can be interpreted as a mass of custom and tradition, manifested in judge-made maxims.[16] These so-called maxims of the common law symbolized the broad guidelines which could be considered to underlie and direct legal decision-making. As observed by one commentator, "[T]hese maxims were the essential core of the common law, woven so closely into the fabric of English life that they could never be ignored with impunity" (Sommerville 1986, p. 96). This concept of "maxims" points to the enduring idea that "the heart of the common law is not comprised of specific rules or procedures, but rather of broad notions which, while difficult to systematize, nonetheless remain, as foundational doctrines, woven into the fabric of life" (Cotterrell 1989, p. 24). Whereas some commentators began to observe a surface chaos in these accumulated judicial decisions, supporters of classical common-law thought continued to argue that there remained an internally coherent, unified body of doctrines and principles making up the substrate of common law. The emphasis on the more malleable doctrines and principles of common law, as opposed to the more rigid rules and procedures of statutes, was intended to convey the notion that the common law remained flexible, that it retained the dynamic character needed in legal decision-making in modern society. Indeed, within the United States, at least, the period between the Revolutionary and Civil Wars witnessed a movement "to frame general doctrines based on a self-conscious consideration of social and economic policies" that would meet the needs of the time (Horwitz 1977, p. 2).[17]

---

[16] This discussion of the common law is based largely on Cotterrell (1989, pp. 21–37).

[17] See also Duxbury (1995, p. 9).

A Very Brief Overview of the History of Legal Theory to the Mid-Nineteenth Century

If one were to go back in time and look at the various legal theories that have attempted to provide answers to our three fundamental questions, the obvious starting point is with the theory of natural law. Early natural law theory has proved somewhat problematic to describe. As Alexander Passerin d'Entrèves has observed, this difficulty is due in part to the fact that "many of the ambiguities associated with the concept of natural law can be ascribed to the many ambiguities of the concept of nature that underlies it."[18] Most conceptions of natural law share the idea that the sources of natural law are other than of human invention. Further, the precise connection between positive law and morality varies depending upon which version of natural law one embraces.

There are two prominent conceptions of natural law: one is based on reason and the "nature" of man, while the other is based on reason in relation to God. The first of these conceptions, reasoned natural law, argues that natural law denotes a system of rules and principles for the guidance of human conduct that can be discovered by the rational intelligence of man. Simply put, the idea is that there exist certain principles of human behavior and conduct that await an unearthing or discovery by human reasoning. These principles have as their source the basic inclinations inherent in human nature and are thought to be absolute and immutable. Reasoned natural law, once discovered, dictates that all man-made law must conform to these principles—hence, not only "life" according to nature, but "law" according to nature. Rules of positive law that conflict with the principles of natural law would be deemed invalid. Thus, natural law, so conceived, exists independent of prevailing systems of social control peculiar to any one people, including enacted law, except where informed by natural law. From this vantage point, the law and legal norms derive their legitimacy from the facts that they are (i) discernable through human reasoning and (ii) derived from the ethics of right reason.

The second conception, consistent with the first, also argues that law stands above and apart from the activities of human lawmakers. It substitutes a supreme being for human nature, however, holding that the law is divinely inspired by God. Thus, rules and principles are revealed as the expressed will of God, with reason as the vehicle for divine instruction. Secular laws are deduced from the divine law of God (Cataldo et. al. 1973, p. 28). Whether the legitimacy of the natural is said to rest with "reason" or "divine inspiration," natural law theorists argue that individuals in society have a moral obligation to make and obey law consistent with these overarching natural law principles.

---

[18] d'Entrèves's assessment is contained in Doherty (2001, p. 144).

Against this metaphysical approach came the positivist scientific attitude toward the law, circa 1820–30. The postivist attitude was born out of the success of the natural sciences in the nineteenth century and the attempts by the social sciences, as well as the law, to apply the methods of the natural sciences.[19] Not surprisingly, proponents of positivism rebelled against the concept of natural law in all its forms. Theirs was an effort to separate the questions as to what the law is from questions of what the law ought to be. The unifying principles here were that laws are social facts or phenomena that can (and should) be studied systematically, and that the substance of law should have some sort of empirical grounding.

The positivists were led by John Austin,[20] and he was later joined by the continental positivist Hans Kelsen.[21] Austin, responding to Blackstone's assertions (discussed earlier), sought to understand what he termed the "science of law"—law *as it is*. His focus was on positive law: the human laws laid down by, or on the authority of, political superiors (typically focusing on executive orders and legislation, not judge-made law). In Austin's jurisprudence, the law is what is set forth by the commands of the sovereign and, in this regard, was seen as an instrument of state power. Austin set out to organize and logically relate the elements of law and, in so doing, to systematize the law and thereby clarify the reasoning contained in it. To this end, he asserted that since law was a human artifact, (i) it was able to be studied in a systematic and scientific way, and (ii) its substance should be empirically grounded. Through this effort he hoped to locate the concepts through which law could be scientifically understood and thereby maintain a strict separation between questions regarding the morality of the law from questions of what the law is.[22]

Kelsen, on the other hand, rejected Austin's view that law was a command of the sovereign. Against this, in his *Pure Theory of Law*, Kelsen set forth a systemic approach where by law was seen as a system of rules. At its base was the "Grundnorm"—the base norm requiring that individuals in society should act in accordance with constitutional prescriptions. Kelsen then built on this foundation a hierarchy or pyramid of rules, exclusive of ethical, political, and social considerations, which were to be enforced through the coercive sanction of the base norm.[23]

---

[19] See, for example, Bodenheimer (1974, chs. 1–7).

[20] Austin's more important works include *Lectures on Jurisprudence or The Philosophy of Positive Law* (1885) and *The Province of Jurisprudence Determined* (1861).

[21] Kelsen's more important works include *General Theory of Law and State* (1945) and *The Pure Theory of Law* (1967).

[22] Cotterrell (1989, p. 56).

[23] H.L.A. Hart (1961) is considered one of the foremost contemporary legal positivists. Unfortunately, space does not allow for a complete discussion of Hart's classic work, *The Concept of Law*, nor of the contributions made by the late-twentieth-century positivists such as Ronald Dworkin and Joseph Raz.

As noted, the positivists as a group actively distanced themselves from the natural law advocates, who they thought confused legal norms and moral ideas. This is reflected in the positivists' assertions that (i) law is the command of the sovereign and nothing more, or owes its origins to the "Grundnorm"; (ii) law exists only to the extent that it is capable of being enforced; and (iii) ethics, politics, morals, and customs are outside of the domain of jurisprudence. Positivism has had a mixed history, and it attracted both advocates and critics. Some thought that positivism was useful, but limited—its impact attenuated by the very nature of the undertaking. Hilaire McCoubrey and Nigel D. White (1999, p.156), assessing the impact of the work of the positivists, observed that "pure theory [of the positivists] may be considered both interesting and useful within its own appointed context, but that context is severely constrained." Others have found it more influential. For instance, Hayman, Levit, and Delgado (2002, p. 80) suggest that "[m]uch of the teaching in law schools at the cusp of the twenty-first century is still rule-centered. American society believes in the rule of law—law that is written, public, and interpreted impartially by the courts. As Frank Michelman (1995, p. 1298) has pointed out, "[W]e are all to some degree positivists now."

Doctrinalism

The second half of the nineteenth century witnessed the development of a second movement attempting to mimic the methodology of the natural sciences—doctrinalism, which is concerned with the law as it is, apart from reference to the religious and/or metaphysical principles of earlier eras. Law here is not a search for the principles of some natural or divine law, but rather a scientific enterprise that "takes as its starting point a given legal order and distills from it by a predominately inductive method certain fundamental notions, concepts, and distinctions" (Bodenheimer 1974, p. 95). It is, as Julius Stone (1950, p. 31) has said, primarily concerned with "an analysis of legal terms, and an inquiry into the *logical* interrelations of legal propositions."

It was Christopher Columbus Langdell, Dean of the Harvard Law School, who, within American law, perhaps came to be most closely associated with this view.[24] Langdell was appointed Dean of Harvard Law School in 1870 by Charles W. Elliot, the new president of the university. Elliot was a chemist and mathematician by trade. While at Massachusetts Institute of Technology he had developed a textbook–laboratory method of teaching chemistry that allowed students to replicate past experiments and thereby induce general principles from these experiments on their own. Langdell was brought to Harvard

---

[24] See, for example, Langdell (1871). The following discussion of Langdell draws on Friedman (1973, pp. 530–36); see also Grey (1983); and for additional background see Chase (1979).

to emulate this pedagogical method in the law school, and his response was to establish the case method within American legal education and promote the use of this method as necessary for teaching law as a science. Thus was born the case-study approach to legal education. Langdell saw law as a set of principles or doctrines that were imbedded in legal cases and could be revealed through the study of case history. Given this, he considered the judicial opinion to occupy a place of preeminence in law, as the corpus of judicial opinions embodied "a handful of permanent, unchanging, and indispensable principles of law" (Posner 1990, p. 15) that revealed themselves in different guises in different cases. These doctrines, he believed, could be mastered only through the careful and exacting study of cases, and the task of legal reasoning thus became that of discerning the doctrines from the judicial opinions. As Hayman, Levit, and Delgado (2002, p.158) note, "Langdell's case study method emphasized the formal connections (inductive and deductive) between rules of law and case holdings, and helped reenforce the notion of law as a self-contained system—a science—in which decisions flowed necessarily from a limited number of discoverable and foundational concepts or doctrines." Because of this emphasis on the evolution of legal doctrine from opinions, Langdell had little use for those areas of law that arose from other sources, such as statutes and the Constitution.

Langdell, says Lawrence M. Friedman (1973, p. 535), believed that law was "a pure, independent science" whose data consisted solely of legal cases. From this body of knowledge it was possible to render decisions in new cases through the use of syllogistic reasoning from the precedential principles set forth in previous like cases. Inherent within this perspective is the idea that judges neither make nor create law; they interpret and apply it. In deciding cases, "the judge expresses part of the total, immanent wisdom of the law (a wisdom existing only in one's mind) which is assumed to be already existent before the judge's decision. The judge works from within the law and thus from within the repository of the experience of the community over time— a community imbued with its own culture and customs" (Cotterrell 1989, pp. 25). It is the judge's discernment of the community's culture and customs over time that lends both authority and legitimacy to the common law. To the extent that the common law is seen to be residing in the community and not the political arena, the emergent legal order comes to command the highest respect. If instead the judge was thought to have *made* the law—that is, had imposed the law on the community as if he were a political ruler or the servant of one—his authority would be undermined. Inasmuch as a judge's authority is based on his being a representative of the community, he is thereby able to *state* the community's law—not *make* the community's law (Cotterrell 1989, p. 27).[25]

---

[25] We will return to the issues of judges "making law."

Perhaps nowhere is the doctrinalist ethos better characterized than by William W. Fisher, Morton J. Horwitz, and Thomas A. Reed (1993, p. vii) in the introduction to their book *American Legal Realism*:

> Properly organized, law was like geometry. . . . Each doctrinal field revolved around a few fundamental axioms, derived primarily from empirical observation of how courts had in the past responded to particular sorts of problems. From those axioms, one could and should deduce—through noncontroversial, rationally compelling reasoning processes—a large number of specific rules or corollaries. The legal system of the United States . . . did not yet fully conform to this ideal; much of the scholars' energies were devoted to identifying and urging the repudiation of rules or decisions that disturbed the conceptual order of their respective fields. But once purified of such anomalies and errors, the scholars contended, the law would be "complete" (capable of providing a single right answer to every dispute) and elegant.

This doctrinal method served to legitimate judicial decisions through the logical power of the inductive process and the weight of jurisprudential history. In the process, says Friedman (1973, p. 535),

> the new method severed the cords, already tenuous, that tied the study of law to the main body of American scholarship and American life. Langdell purged from the curriculum whatever touched directly on economic and political questions, whatever was argued, voted on, fought over. He brought into the classroom a worship of common law and of the best common-law judges. Legislation he disdained; illogical decisions he despised. All this he cloaked with the mantle of science. He equated law absolutely with judges' law; and judges' law was narrowed to formalism and abstraction.

Law, under this approach, was self-referential, consisting of a set of legal doctrines and objectively inferable rules and procedures logically applied. Law thus became both formal and insular. Jurisprudence consisted only in an established body of legal doctrine, a set of principles in which judicial discretion was minimized, and where ethics, social and economic conditions, politics, ideologies, and the insights of disciplines outside of the law had no proper place.

Friedman (1973, p. 536) suggests that the attraction of Langdell's method was that it served the needs of the profession at that time: "It exalted the prestige of law and legal learning; at the same time it affirmed that legal science stood apart, as an independent entity, distinct from politics, legislation, and the man on the street." The professional belief in the lawyer's monopoly of legal practice was reaffirmed by law's status as a profession that required a rigorous, formal education. The bar association movement, which entrenched the professionalization of the law, arose at the same time as Langdell's movement, and the two fed off each other. Whole subject areas in the present law school

curriculum—for example, contracts, torts, and property—have had their boundaries fixed and are distinguished from each other by their respective common
law principles. Indeed, today much of legal education and legal scholarship
consists of the exposition and systematization of legal doctrines and principles, together with the legal rules and procedures that emanate therefrom, as
well as the techniques required to apply them.

Moving Away from Doctrinalism

One can see the appearance of an influential reaction against doctrinalism already in the late nineteenth century. The first major strand of this scholarship
has been classified as "sociological jurisprudence" and included such notable
contributors as Oliver Wendell Holmes, Jr., Roscoe Pound, and Benjamin Cardozo. Sociological jurisprudence was a reaction against both the formalism
of doctrinalism and the traditional concepts of natural or objectively determinable rights.[26] These writers claimed that law cannot be understood without
reference to social conditions, and thus that insights from the other social sciences should be integrated into the law. Law, here, was not seen as an autonomous discipline. Rather, they said, judges should be aware of the social
and economic conditions that affect the path of law and that result from the legal decision-making process and should employ the tools necessary to enhance such awareness (Bodenheimer 1974, pp. 12–21).

Pound was considered the leader of sociological jurisprudence (Paton and
Derham 1972, p. 22) and a strong advocate of reforming law by taking social
reality into account. Pound attacked the tradition of Langdellian legal science
and its inherent tendency to transform law into some form of "mechanical jurisprudence." To Pound, law was a social phenomenon that ultimately translated
into policy; his quest was to examine "law in action" not dwell on the topic of
law in books. He saw law as "a form of social control, to be adequately employed in enabling just claims and desires to be satisfied." Moreover, it needed
to "be developed in relation to social needs," which in turn meant "relying on
the social sciences in studying the place of law in society" (Hampstead and
Freeman 1985, p. 564). To this end, Pound advocated the use of the metaphor
of engineering to guide the reform of law. Specifically, by viewing law as a
means for reconciling or balancing conflicting interests, Pound advanced the
concept of "social engineering" to help build an efficient legal structure for society, thereby maximizing satisfaction and minimizing friction and waste. His

---

[26] As Duxbury (1995, pp. 10, 32–64) has aptly noted, however, neither these scholars nor the
Realists who followed them were totally able to shed formalistic elements from their thought. Nor
did they necessarily attempt to do so. Holmes, for example, saw an important role for logical
analysis within legal thinking.

was a system that relied on a fair balancing of interests, recognizing that there were different levels or planes of interest—individual interests, public interests, social interests—within which conflicts took place. By engaging in the scientific exercise of examining and balancing conflicts on the same level (his version of social engineering), the legal system would ensure neutrality and serve the ends of justice and fairness. Of course, there would be instances when disputes were accompanied by assertions of new interests. In these cases, it would be impossible to examine conflicts at the same plane or level. These conflicts would, according to Pound, have to rely on his notion of "jural postulates," which are akin to the presuppositions of legal reasoning upon which society was based. Pound's idea of social engineering, while attractive to the progressive lawyers in America (White 1972, pp. 1004–5), was actually more descriptive of a neutral process—captured in his argument for the fair balancing of interests—than prescriptive of pragmatic reform. The thrust of his approach was to argue that law should be shaped by social ends, but not to advocate any particular ends (Wigdor 1974, p. 230).

Cardozo, for his part, emphasized the need for judges to be attuned to social realities and, while not rejecting the role of analytic processes in jurisprudence, believed that "considerations of social policy loom large in the art of adjudication" (Bodenheimer 1974, p. 121). His prescription for judicial reasoning entailed not only articulating the directive force of a principle, but, when principles were in conflict, to understand precisely how judges choose among them—"a jurisprudence of realism tempered by principle" (Duxbury 1995, p. 217). For Cardozo, both judicial decision-making and the path of law are necessarily influenced by subjective elements of instinct, belief, conviction, and views as to social need. That is, he recognized that judges are at times swayed by their prejudices. Although precedent was important for Cardozo, he believed that when it conflicted with the greater interests of justice or social welfare, the latter should carry the day (Bodenheimer 1974, p. 121).[27]

Holmes (1923, p. 1), like Cardozo, emphasized the limits of doctrinalism, but went further than Cardozo, insisting that the "law does not consist of a deduction from principles of ethics or admitted axioms but is instead prophecies of what the courts will do in fact" (Hayman, Levit, and Delgado 2002, p. 159). In discounting the role played by logical reasoning in jurisprudence, Holmes argued, "The felt necessities of the time, the prevalent moral and political theories, intuitions of public policy, avowed or unconscious, even the prejudices which judges share with their fellow men, have a good deal more to do than the syllogism in determining the rules by which men should be governed." Law, in his view, expresses the will of the dominant interests in society. Holmes, says Richard A. Posner (1987a, p. 762), "pointed out that law is a tool for achieving social ends, so that to understand law requires an understanding

---

[27] See also Hall (1947).

of social conditions." He also believed that judges need to be acquainted with the historical, social, and economic aspects of the law (Bodenheimer 1974, p. 123).[28] These ideas are also reflected in Pound (1954, p. 47), who saw law as "a social institution to satisfy wants" and the history of law as "a continually more efficacious social engineering." These pragmatic and socially attuned conceptions of law set the stage for an even more pronounced reaction against doctrinalist thinking—Legal Realism.

Before turning our attention to Legal Realism, we need to point out that the advocates of the formalist, doctrinal approach did not simply roll over and play dead in the face of criticism leveled by the advocates of sociological jurisprudence Doctrinalism remained alive and well at Harvard and then, in 1923, academics banded with judges and lawyers to form the American Law Institute in an effort "to project the scientific study of law into the very center of professional life" (Ackerman 1974). This project took the form of publishing Restatements of Law that would provide a clear statement of common law principles for use in guiding and evaluating judicial decisions. These Restatements, however, served a role beyond simply clarifying fundamental common law principles. As Bruce Ackerman (1974) has pointed out,

> [T]hey also served the ideological and economic interests of the dominant elements of the profession. The fundamental legal principles of the Common Law of the 1920's were permeated with the laissez-faire philosophy. Their clear articulation would serve as a bulwark against the forces for change which threatened the economic interests of the dominant members of the law profession as well as their larger conception of the nature of the good society. Indeed, even the institutes' choice of subjects suitable for restatement reflected the limited legal concern of the nineteenth-century state enshrined both by classical economics and by Social Darwinism. The Institute tried, for example, to clarify the law dealing with contract, property, tort and the intergenerational transfer of wealth, but lavished no similar concern upon areas like economic regulation or family law where the Common Law did not reflect a coherent policy.

All of this, then, was aimed toward the end of promoting and facilitating free enterprise, the fluid operation of which, it was believed by large numbers of academics and judges alike, would maximize social welfare.

The Legal Realist Challenge

The most influential of the challenges to doctrinalism was the Legal Realist movement, which reached its zenith in the 1930s. The Realist movement was part of a more general response to formalism and logical reasoning during the

---

[28] See also Holmes (1897, p. 469).

early part of the twentieth century, a time when American intellectual life was impacted by "a more empirical, experimental, and relativistic attitude toward the problems and guiding assumptions" of the various scholarly disciplines (Purcell 1988, p. 359). The Realists, following the work of Holmes and others within sociological jurisprudence, sought to turn law outward to make it attuned to the social realities of the day. In doing so, they affected both the process of legal education and the intellectual life of the law (Friedman 1973, p. 591).[29]

The reverence for the traditions of the law, so central within doctrinalism, held little sway among the Realists. The divergence between the law as written into books and the law as it operates in fact was relentlessly pursued. The Realists rejected the existence of objectively determinable rights; the use of rigid legal rules, categories, and classifications; appeals to the authority of the past—citations, eminent jurists, and classic treatises; and the logic of reasoning from precedent. The Langdellian system, in all of its manifestations, was thus an anathema to the Realists. Karl Llewellyn (1934, p. 7), a leading Legal Realist, suggested that the role of legal rules within the lawmaking process was far less important than generally assumed, and that the "theory that rules decide cases seems for a century to have fooled, not only library-ridden recluses, but judges." In a similar vein, Jerome Frank asserted that, contrary to the logical cloak in which they are enveloped, judicial decisions are largely informed by "emotions, intuitive hunches, prejudices, tempers, and other irrational factors" (Bodenheimer 1974, p. 125). The judge, rather than the logic of the law, was the central factor in the resolution of legal cases. Law was seen not as a set of rules, but as what judges actually do. The logic of precedent, according to the Realists, was seriously flawed. The use of precedential reasoning was essentially the determination as to whether the decision in an earlier case could be applied in straightforward fashion to the facts of the case at hand. The human factor underlying this form of judicial decision-making was apparent to the Realists: such decisions inevitably entailed a choice as to the relation between the facts of one case and another, a choice that was necessarily determined by subjective value judgments rather than by logic (Mensch 1990, p. 22). It is from this view of things that we get the caricature that legal decision-making has less to do with logic, rules, and precedent than with what the judge ate for breakfast.[30] Because decisions rested on the judge's conception of right and wrong, social, political, and economic considerations became important variables.[31]

---

[29] It should be noted that there is no settled position as to the boundaries and contours of Legal Realism. For surveys of various issues related to the Realist movement see Fisher, Horwitz, and Reed (1993) and Duxbury (1995, ch. 2).

[30] See Minow (1987, p. 93).

[31] Rubin (1996, p. 1395) wrote that " the realists maintained that general legal principles do not exist: law is always the creation of some specific lawmaker, whether legislator, administrator, or judge, and it usually reflects the policy predilections of that lawmaker."

Furthermore, the constant change of law, perhaps most strikingly in response to the industrial revolution, belied the claim that law was certain, fixed, and logical. The formalist approach used inductive reasoning with an exclusive focus on data from past common law cases to establish legal doctrine, and then, through deduction and syllogistic reasoning, to apply the law. The Realists countered with an emphasis on developing legal theory through inductive scientific principles based on a wider range of data and observations—on real-world phenomena—on what they saw as a "true" science of law.[32] Gary Minda (1995, p. 31) offers a similar characterization of the Realists, asserting that, with their view of law as social science, they were not that different from the traditional Langdellian theorists who argued for law's scientific character.

Along with the idea that law cannot be a logical, self-contained discipline came the prescription that it should cease all pretensions of being so, and that law should become more overtly attuned to the social ends that it necessarily serves. The Realists held a strong instrumentalist conception of law; for them, law was, and had to be seen as, a "working tool" (Friedman 1973, p. 592). This demanded an understanding of the relationship between law and society and of the way that results—economic, political, and social—followed upon legal decisions. Every legal decision was understood to have social, ethical, political, and economic implications, and the Realists maintained that these should be recognized and explicitly dealt with by judges, not hidden behind a veil of logical reasoning. The corollary was that to understand these implications better, it is necessary to explore the interrelations among law and the other social sciences, including sociology, psychology, political science, and economics.

Of particular import for present purposes is the Realist interest in using economics to understand and to guide the development of law.[33] The Realists argued that the importance of the interrelations between economics and the law can be seen in the twin facts that legal change is often a function of economic ideas and conditions, which necessitate and/or generate demands for legal change, and that economic change is often governed by legal change.[34] Llewellyn pointed to a number of ways in which law influences economic conditions, including its role in providing a foundation for the economic order, its influence on the operation and outcomes of the competitive market process (particularly through the structure of law pertaining to property, contract, and credit, and through restrictions placed by law on the competitive process), and the influence of taxation, social welfare legislation, and public enterprise on production and distribution.[35]

[32] The Realist quest for a "true" science of law is described in Duxbury (1995, pp. 79–82).

[33] For surveys of the intersection between Realism and economics, see Samuels (1993) and Duxbury (1995, ch. 2).

[34] See, for example, Llewellyn (1925), Litchman (1927), and Holdsworth (1927–28).

[35] See Llewellyn (1925, pp. 678–81) and the discussion in Samuels (1993, pp. 247–48).

Given the important interdependencies that they saw between law and economy, it is not surprising that Realists such as Llewellyn considered economic analysis a useful tool for understanding law and legal change and for devising laws that would improve the social condition. Indeed, Samuel Herman went so far as to assert that "[t]he law of a state never rises higher than its economics" (Herman 1937, p. 831), and expressed the hope that " 'a disciplined judicial economics' might become 'a realistic and tempered instrument for solving the major judicial questions of our time' " (Samuels 1993, p. 263, quoting Herman 1937, p. 821). Whereas the Realists found certain aspects of neoclassical economics, such as marginal analysis, useful, it was with the Institutional economics of Thorstein Veblen and John R. Commons, rather than with neoclassical economics, that the Realists found a close affinity. This affinity turned very much on the pessimism reflected within both Realism and Institutionalism regarding laissez-faire legal-economic policy and the inequalities of power and position that were masked under the laissez-faire emphasis on individual liberty.[36] From the Realist-Institutionalist project came numerous studies that attempted to probe the linkages between law and economy, and, in the process, to inform legal and economic thinking and decision-making.

The Need to Fill the Void

Although Legal Realism largely spelled the end of doctrinalist excesses, it never became established as the dominant view of law. Its sputtering existence, if not its demise, was followed, in the 1940s, by a renewed belief in the autonomy of law, this time in the form of the legal-process movement—a movement that ran roughly from 1940 to 1960 and emphasized that certain principles of process were neutral, and hence immutable.[37]

The main exponents of the legal-process approach were Lon L. Fuller (1940), Henry M. Hart and Albert M. Sacks (1958), and Herbert Wechsler (1959). Like the Realists, the legal-process school viewed law as dynamic and policy-oriented. To this end, Hart and Sacks drew on the earlier works of Fuller to establish the interconnectedness of human beings and the usefulness of law in establishing a community. For them, law had a purpose: the state was there to advance society's collective goals. Hart and Sacks argued, "Law is a doing of something, a purposive activity, a continuous striving to solve the basic problems of social living" (1958, p. 166).

---

[36] For a discussion of the links between Realism and Institutionalism, see Duxbury (1995, pp. 97–111), Medema (1998), and Rutherford (2003, 2004). A discussion of the Institutionalist position, which traces its roots to this earlier era, is found in chapter 4.

[37] See, for example, Monahan and Walker (1990, p. 28), Woodward (1968), and Duxbury (1995, ch. 4).

Unlike the Realists, however, proponents of the legal-process approach generally advocated a return to the view of law as an autonomous discipline, with law's legitimacy and objectivity now preserved by focusing on the process and institutions by which the law evolved. This marked a major point of departure from previous theories of law that looked to other foundations to justify preservation of the autonomy, morality, and legitimacy of law. The focus of the legal-process approach was on procedure—on what Hart and Sacks (1958, p. 4–5) termed the "principles of institutional settlement"; and on what Wechsler (1959, p. 17) termed "neutral principles." With this as their focus, legal process scholars tried to avoid the implicit nihilism of the Realists by offering a theoretical alternative to formalism.[38] Its central principle was that each institution of government possesses a distinctive area of competence such that specific tasks can be assigned to that institution without reference to the substantive policies involved. Because it has no substantive implications, it does not commit the error of the formalists by placing legal principles above the political process. As Rubin (1996, p. 1396) describes it, "The legal process school reconstituted the prior separation between law and politics, not by positing transcendent legal principles, but by identifying a separate and politically established legal realm in which reasoned argument prevails." Thus, against debates over whether a particular decision conformed to principles of natural law or the scientifically based principles of doctrinalism, the legal-process approach argued that law's legitimacy was embedded in neutral, institutional structures and legal procedures—that is, within the very *process* by which the society had chosen to govern itself. If a decision is purposive and the result of an established, accepted, neutral legal process, the outcome was said to be legitimated.[39]

By the end of the 1950s, we witness a tension created by two divergent trends. On the one hand, there was a continuing focus on legal process, together with an ongoing doctrinalist legacy: legal education largely consisting of studying, analyzing, and critiquing authoritative texts—opinions, statutes, and legal rules—with an eye on process. On the other hand, one cannot ignore the impact the Legal Realists had in cracking the edifice of doctrinalism; and, with the edifice cracked, a void had been created for others to fill. As Edmund Kitch (1983a, b), among others, has noted, it was the Legal Realists who created an environment that was more receptive to the introduction of economics into the law school curriculum.

This tension led to yet another breakdown in the belief in law's autonomy—whether grounded in natural law, doctrinalism, or legal process—beginning in the early 1960s. Posner (1987a, pp. 765–73) suggests several reasons for this.

[38] This discussion draws on Rubin (1996, pp. 1395–98).

[39] There are certain commonalities between this idea and the constitutional approach to Law and Economics advanced by James M. Buchanan and others, which is discussed in chapter 3.

First, this period witnessed the end of the political consensus in the United States that was so prominent in the 1950s. As Owen Fiss (1986, p. 2) has put it, the potential "death of law" is derivative of the turmoil of the 1960s, from which came a "rejection of the notion of law as a public ideal" and of "adjudication as the process for interpreting and nurturing a public morality." Second, the "boom" in disciplines complementary to law, such as economics and philosophy, gave rise to efforts by practitioners within these other disciplines to branch out into new areas, especially law. Third, there was a collapse of confidence in the ability of lawyers to solve the major problems of the legal system on their own. Fourth, there was a feeling that there was little new to be said in law, from the traditional autonomous perspective. Fifth, the increasing prestige and authority accorded to scientific modes of inquiry, and thus the relative decline in the prestige and authority accorded to the ostensibly nonscientific method of legal analysis, pushed legal scholars to adopt more "scientific" modes of analysis. Finally, statutes and the Constitution were becoming increasingly important relative to common law, and the legal profession quickly found out that the tools for interpreting statutory and Constitutional issues and documents were simply inadequate. That is, lawyers trained in the traditional legal method to analyze the underpinnings of case law had few, if any, skills to explore the underpinnings of statutes or the Constitution. This caused legal scholars to look elsewhere—outward—for interpretive principles.

This rebirth of the disillusionment with the idea of law as an autonomous discipline, and the search for other bases on which to ground legal analysis[40]— the setting for which had in fact been established by the Realists—has resulted in the growth of numerous "law and _____" movements over the past thirty years. These movements have sought to bring the insights of sociology, Continental philosophy, literary theory, anthropology, feminist studies, Marxism, and, of particular importance here, economics, into legal studies. Each of these projects represents an attempt to turn law outward and has, in its own way, sought to answer the three fundamental questions we laid out earlier—in particular, in positing a basis on which to found law's legitimacy. In doing so, each sought, overtly or not, to fill the void left by Legal Realism. The plethora of ideas and the zeal of their advocates has made legal analysis highly politicized and interwoven with the social sciences and humanities (Minow 1987, p. 79).[41] No longer is law seen as being able to, on its own, generate results that constitute objective truth—to state what the law is, to discern its basis for legitimacy, or to say what the law should be. The earlier consensus regarding how to think about and to resolve important legal questions has all but disappeared.

---

[40] Again, we note that this tendency is by no means universal among legal scholars. See Weinrib (1995).

[41] See also Gordon (1990, p. 413).

THE "ECONOMICS" IN "LAW AND ECONOMICS"

Against the idea that law can be understood only through the use of the traditional legal doctrinal concepts based on justice and fairness, economics counters that our understanding can be enhanced—even supplanted, according to some—by economic concepts, including the criteria of economic efficiency. As such, the "Economics" in "Law and Economics" consists primarily (but, as will become clear in subsequent chapters, by no means exclusively) of neoclassical microeconomics and welfare economics, where the operative organizing concepts are Pareto efficiency in exchange, Pareto efficiency in production, and Kaldor-Hicks efficiency (i.e., wealth maximization). We want to underscore the point that not all the schools of thought presented here give equal credence to these various criteria of efficiency, and it certainly is not without dispute across schools of thought, or even within them, as to how much emphasis one ought to give to these concepts. Nonetheless, their important place within the Law and Economics literature necessitates an understanding of these concepts. Toward that end, we provide a brief overview of neoclassical efficiency analysis at this point, leaving a more extensive discussion to the two appendices to this chapter.

The Circular Flow of Economic Activity and the Concept of Efficiency

The intellectual construct that depicts the ideal workings of the *economy* is that of perfect competition. The purely competitive, perfectly functioning market has the following characteristics: (i) a large number of buyers motivated by self-interest and making the choices they expect will maximize their utility; (ii) many sellers, also motivated by self-interest, and acting to maximize their profits; (iii) individual buyers and sellers are unable to exert any control over market prices and are thus price takers; (iv) prices serve as the guideposts for decision-makers in the market to (among other things) communicate scarcity; (v) products are standardized (i.e., homogeneous); (vi) there are no barriers to entry or exit, which means that consumers and producers are free to enter or leave all product and factor markets; (vii) all buyers and sellers are fully informed as to the terms of all market transactions; (viii) resources are held in private property with all rights defined and assigned; and (ix) prevailing laws and property rights are fully enforced through the state.

The interrelations and flows inherent in a perfectly competitive economy are best depicted in a circular flow diagram such as figure 1-1. Here the privately owned, scarce (in the sense that their supply is limited relative to the demand for them) factors of production—land, labor, and capital—are allocated through factor markets to firms that, in turn, produce goods and services to

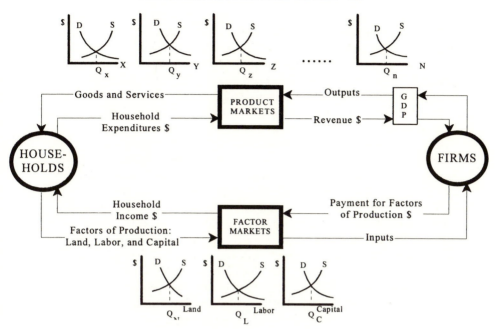

FIGURE 1-1. Circular Flow Diagram

satisfy the demands of consumers. In evaluating the outcomes of this process, economists are primarily concerned with allocative efficiency—that is, with (i) the extent to which the allocation of inputs within the productive process results in the production of the combination of outputs that best satisfies the economic wants and desires of the individuals in society, and (ii) the extent to which the allocation of these outputs across individuals in society generates the highest possible level of social well-being.

If all factors of production and all goods and services are bought and sold in perfectly competitive markets, the outcome generated can be shown to be efficient. That is, under the assumptions outlined earlier and given an initial assignment of rights to resources, the optimal amounts of land, labor, and capital good—no more, no less—will be allocated to the production of each and every commodity (X, Y, Z, . . .), resulting in the optimal output of each (Q_x, Q_y, Q_z . . .). Such efficient outcomes are said to be *Pareto optimal*, by which we mean that resources cannot be reallocated so as to make one individual better off without making someone else worse off. Formally, this concept is embodied in the first optimality theorem of welfare economics, which states that, barring major problems with information, enforcement, public goods, and externalities, a purely competitive, perfectly functioning market will achieve a

Pareto-efficient allocation of society's scarce resources.[42] Graphically, this concept is depicted in the product market and factor market supply and demand diagrams within figure 1-1, where *all markets have cleared*—the quantity demanded for each commodity and factor of production equals the quantity supplied. This concept deserves closer scrutiny in that it subsumes much and is fundamental to understanding the concept of efficiency.

From society's perspective, the efficient level of any activity is attained when that activity is engaged in up to the point where marginal social benefit (MSB) is just equal to marginal social cost (MSC). Assuming that the market sector is society's sole means of social control for the allocation of society's scarce resources, all decisions are made by individual consumers and producers attempting to maximize utility and profits, respectively. The effect of this maximization process is that producers and consumers make their choices based on a weighing of marginal benefits and costs—that is, comparing the additional benefit from engaging in another unit of an activity with the additional cost of doing so. For an efficient outcome to be achieved through the market, it is necessary that the four conditions set forth in table 1-1 be fulfilled for each commodity.[43] These conditions ensure that private calculations of benefits and costs are in line with society's calculations, so that the efficient outcome is achieved. If these conditions are not met, we have a situation of market failure. A brief, but closer, look at each of these four conditions is necessary to understand fully the meanings of efficiency and market failure and their ultimate significance for Law and Economics, and, indeed, all disciplines that assert an interest in the efficient allocation of resources.

- Marginal Social Benefit (MSB) = Marginal Private Benefit (MPB) means that the incremental benefits to society from a consumer's individual, private market transaction are not any different than the incremental benefits that the consumer personally receives from undertaking a particular market transaction. That is, there are no positive or negative externalities in consumption.
- Marginal Private Benefit (MPB) = Product Price (P) means that the price an individual pays for a particular amount of a specified commodity is equal to the marginal benefit received from the last unit purchased.
- Product Price (P) = Marginal Private Cost (MPC) means that the market price of the commodity is equal to the marginal private cost of producing the good.
- Marginal Private Cost (MPC) = Marginal Social Cost (MSC) means that the incremental cost society incurs from a firm's private production of a commodity

[42] The literature identifies this as the duality theorem, which demonstrates that a perfectly competitive economy will yield an efficient allocation of resources. This is concisely explained in Feldman (1980, pp. 1–4; 47–58); see also Pindyck and Rubinfeld (1992, p. 584).

[43] This tabular approach to depicting the efficiency conditions is based on Wonnacott and Wonnacott (1979, pp. 178–94).

TABLE 1-1

For Good X

MSB = MPB
  MPB = P
    P = MPC
      MPC = MSC
Thus, MSB = MSC yields a Pareto-efficient allocation of resources.

is not any different from the incremental cost that the individual firm incurs in undertaking the production of that commodity. That is, there are no positive or negative externalities in production.

The simultaneous satisfaction of these four conditions will ensure that marginal social benefit equals marginal social cost for each and every commodity. In more elementary terms, the market demand curve will reflect MSB and the market supply curve will reflect MSC, and thus the market equilibrium (demand = supply) will be efficient (MSB = MSC). The significance of this condition, and its relation to Pareto optimality, is best illustrated by examining the situation when it does *not* hold.[44]

In figure 1-2, where the marginal social benefits and costs associated with good X are depicted, consider first an allocation of resources such that the quantity X_1 is produced. Notice that, at this point and from it up to X*, marginal social benefit is greater than marginal social cost. Given this, the allocation of additional resources to the production of good X will generate incremental social benefits in excess of the incremental social costs, thus enhancing society's welfare. This increase in net social benefits is available up to X*, beyond which the costs to society of additional units of good X exceed the gains. At X*, then, MSB = MSC and society is said to have achieved a Pareto-efficient allocation of those resources devoted to the production of good X. At any level of output less than X*, where MSB > MSC, there will be a *persistent underallocation of society's scarce resources* to good X.

Second, consider an allocation of resources to good X that generates an amount X_2 of the good. Here, and at all points between X* and X_2, marginal social cost exceeds marginal social benefit. By reducing the level of resources allocated to the production of good X, and thus the amount of good X produced, the costs saved by society exceed the benefits lost, thereby increasing social welfare until we reach X*, where MSB = MSC. Thus, beyond X*, such as at X_2, MSB < MSC, and we now have a *persistent over-allocation of society's scarce resources* to the production of good X.

[44] For a graphical analysis of the implications of violating each of the four conditions, see appendix 1.

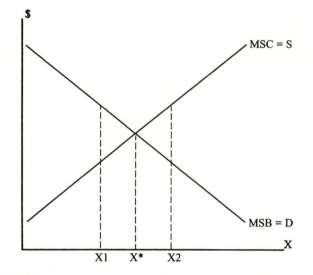

FIGURE 1-2. Marginal Social Benefit = Marginal Social Cost

Finally, let us look at the outcome X* itself. Any reduction in the level of output below X* generates a loss of social benefit in excess of the reduction in social cost, and any increase in output beyond X* generates social costs in excess of social benefits. Thus, it is not possible to move away from X* without making someone worse off. At X*, then, society is said to achieve a Pareto-efficient allocation of resources.

Under the conditions postulated, an exchange will take place only when the parties to the transaction believe that they will benefit by going ahead with the transaction. When no additional exchanges can be made, the economy has reached a situation where each individual in it cannot improve his or her situation, or welfare, without diminishing the welfare of another. Once an economy has arrived in this state—when no one can be made better off without someone else being made worse off—Pareto optimality has been attained. If all markets are perfectly competitive, society achieves a Pareto-optimal allocation of resources throughout the entire economy. Again, the important point to be underscored is that when supply (S) equals demand (D) for each commodity, all benefits and all costs are accounted for; that is, MSB = MSC for all commodities in the economy, and the resulting outcome is Pareto efficient.

It must be noted that each Pareto-efficient solution is contingent upon an initial and unique assignment of rights to resources, within which subsequent market activity takes place. That is, each initial assignment of rights yields a unique set of supplies and demands, a unique bundle of goods and services

produced and consumed, and hence a unique Pareto-efficient allocation of resources—a state of the economy that is sometimes called *maximum social welfare* (MXSW). Thus, rights assignment #1 (some arbitrary, initial distribution of rights) can be shown to yield a Pareto-efficient allocation of resources $MXSW_{\#1}$; similarly, a different rights assignment, #2, can be shown to yield an alternative Pareto-efficient allocation of resources $MXSW_{\#2}$; yet another rights assignment, #3, can be shown to yield $MXSW_{\#3}$; and so on. Hence, as will become evident in the Edgeworth box analysis provided in appendix 2 to this chapter, there are an infinite number of Pareto-efficient states of the economy, each contingent upon the initial assignment of rights, and each of which is noncomparable to the others in terms of efficiency. The only way one can compare these states is to engage in making interpersonal comparisons of utility—and the positivistic stance of economics is to avoid economic criteria that invoke such comparisons.

Although the attainment of a Pareto-optimal state for the whole economy is predicated upon some initial distribution of rights to assets that exist, the analysis says nothing about the justice or fairness of that initial starting point. Within neoclassical economics, this is an issue of distribution—an ethical problem—not one of efficiency. Given the infinite number of Pareto-optimal states, we require additional criteria based on political precepts and/or moral considerations to state a preference for one state of MXSW over another. Thus, as Allen V. Kneese (1977, p. 19) has pointed out, "An exchange economy . . . will achieve an *optimum optimorum*—the best of all possible (economic) worlds—if the prevailing income distribution is ethically ideal—a judgement which, in western liberal societies, can be made legitimately only through the political process."

Finally, with respect to table 1.1, the market sector will fail to generate a Pareto-optimal outcome (i.e., fall short of providing a state of MXSW) if any one of the four conditions is not met for any one of the goods produced in the economy. Deviations or departures from the basic structural characteristics of the purely competitive market, the existence of externalities or public goods, the absence of private rights or the failure to perfectly enforce them, or, under some conditions, the existence of open-access resources, may drive a wedge into any one or more of the four basic equalities. As a consequence, the overall condition for Pareto efficiency (MSB = MSC) will not be met, in which case there exists market failure. All economists recognize that, in reality, there are a variety of factors and forces at work in any market economy that create such inequalities, and, in many respects, it is this recognition, together with a desire to find remedies to instances of market failure, that is at the core of old and new Law and Economics.[45]

---

[45] The distinction between the old versus the new Law and Economics is discussed in Posner (1975, pp. 757–61).

The Compensation Principle

It is generally recognized that there are few policies, however creatively structured, whose effects leave no one worse off, as required by Pareto efficiency.
Typically, legal change creates winners and losers.[46] Thus, if the Pareto criterion were the basis for policy evaluation, no legal change could ever pass
muster. As a consequence the compensation principle was formulated as an alternative to the restrictiveness of the Pareto criterion. Its various formulations
were part of an attempt to see how much can be said about general welfare as
a consequence of legal change without resort to interpersonal comparisons
(Blaug 1978, p. 625). The compensation principle is often termed *Kaldor-
Hicks efficiency* or, as formulated and popularized by Posner, *wealth maximization*. It should also be noted that the compensation principle, beyond
being the analytical equivalent to Posner's *wealth maximization*, also serves as
the theoretical basis of the economics of benefit-cost analysis.

The compensation principle holds that a change from one state to another
(brought on, for example, by legal change) that favors some individuals at the
expense of others can be said to result in an unambiguous improvement in society's welfare—with almost the same force as the Pareto principle itself—if
those who gain from the change could hypothetically compensate the losers
for their losses and still be better off themselves.[47] In the simplest of terms,
the compensation principle holds that a change constitutes an improvement if
the gains to the winners exceed the losses to the losers—a basic benefit-cost
concept. A simple historical example of the compensation principle, one often
cited in the literature, is that of the discussion in nineteenth-century England
regarding the repeal of the Corn Laws. The original Corn Laws prohibited the
importation of (cheaper) foreign wheat to England, and thus had the effect of
generating artificially high prices for wheat. This benefitted farmers at the
expense of the bread consumers. It was argued by Nicholas Kaldor (1939)
that if those who had benefited from the repeal of the Corn Laws (the consumers) were so much better off that they could have afforded to compensate
the farmers for their loss, and yet still be in a better position than before a

---

[46] We use the expression "legal change" here and elsewhere to denote any change in law, or implementation of new laws, coming through judicial, legislative, bureaucratic, or executive action.

[47] The line of literature that comprises the core elements of compensation principle analysis includes the works of E. Barone (1908, translated into English in 1935), Nicholas Kaldor (1939),
John R. Hicks (1939), and Tibor Scitovsky (1941-2). Kaldor-Hicks efficiency—the so-called
compensation principle in economics—implies that society should adopt those legal changes
leading to results whereby (i) income could have been redistributed after the change in the law so
as to make everyone better off than before, and (ii) it was not possible to improve welfare before
the legal change took place simply by redistributing income. A straightforward analysis is provided in Price (1977); a more detailed explanation is presented in Feldman (1980, pp. 138–49).

change in the law, then the repeal of the Corn Laws represented an increase in welfare for the country as a whole, even if the compensation was not actually paid.

The concept of the compensation principle was consciously developed without any requirement that the compensation actually be paid. In an attempt to maintain a positivist stance with respect to the evaluation of legal-economic policy, the idea was that it would be enough to show that a policy generated gains sufficiently large *to potentially* compensate the losers. The requirement to actually pay the losers was thought to be purely distributional—within the realm of normative, political decision-making and thus beyond the scope of the more positive thrust of the economic compensation principle as formulated. Simply put, the fact that there existed net gains to be distributed was thought to be proof enough that the change increased economic welfare. Throughout the literature it was clear that if the losers are actually compensated by the gainers, the scheme would essentially revert back to the Pareto principle. It likewise was recognized, however, that if the potential compensation was not in fact paid, labeling the change an improvement requires an implicit acceptance of the prevailing distribution of income, inasmuch as the compensation payments are a function of both willingness and ability to pay. Thus, without the actual payments (i.e., the revealing of preferences) we are perilously close to making interpersonal comparisons of utility.

Joe B. Stevens (1993, pp. 48–49) offers a simple example concerning a proposal to institute a program of tax-funded college scholarships that is useful for understanding the compensation principle. In figure 1-3, suppose that, before such a program is set in place, the economy is at point A, with the utility of the taxpayers at T_0 and the utility of the college students at S_0. Once the tax-funded college scholarships are set up, the outcome of the program would place society at, say, point B. Students would be better off because of the scholarships, but at the same time the taxpayers would be worse off because they have to pay for the scholarships (implicitly assuming higher incomes yield greater utility and lower incomes yield lower utility). Once at B, however, the potential exists for the gainers (the students) to compensate the taxpayers sufficiently to return them to point C, at which point the students are better off and the taxpayers no worse off. One could even conceive of a situation where the taxpayers were yet further compensated (in the potential sense), taking us to, for example, point D, where both students and taxpayers would be better off than before the program was undertaken.

These twin concepts of efficiency and the compensation principle are the operative economic concepts within Law and Economics. Both are used extensively and must be understood to grasp the logic underlying Law and Economics, and to assess the impact of legal change made at any one of the three stages of choice—the subject to which we now turn.

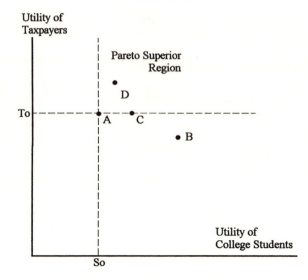

FIGURE 1-3. Compensation Example

THE STAGES OF CHOICE IN CONTEMPLATING LEGAL CHANGE

Today, much of the conventional study of law is organized around modern doctrinal principles and concepts drawn from legal and political theory. The view of law as comprised of the totality of constitutional law, administrative law, procedural law, criminal law, and especially the common law of torts, property, and contract is probably most familiar to law students. Each of these areas of law, as well as the underlying common law principles and doctrines are transmitted from generation to generation in varied forms of legal scholarship including restatements, casebooks, law review articles, and classroom lectures. Law is, in part, the outcome of a complex, multilayered process whose evolution reflects morally based values and social norms, and a long tradition of political and legal thought and analysis. In contemplating whether or how to change the law, and assessing the potential consequences thereof, it is sometimes helpful to alter the vantage point and focus on the various stages of choice from which legal change emanates. To this end, we will focus on three stages of choice: the *constitutional stage*, the *institutional stage*, and the *economic impact stage* (see figure 1-4).

The constitutional stage of choice deals with society's social contract—the laying out of the fundamental behavioral rules that bind people together, rules that are subject to both reinterpretation and incremental revision. The essential point to be understood is that whatever governmental and nongovernmental

institutions come to characterize a society, and whatever policies flow from them, they owe their existence, development, and legitimacy to the initial choices made at the constitutional stage. That is, the provisions of the constitution, together with the rule of law, provide the authority for the political and legal institutions that emanate from them and thus lend legitimacy to their respective decisions. Changing the constitution is one mechanism by which to make policy, though it is not used very often because of its rather blunt, imprecise nature.

Once the constitution is framed, it provides the basis for the emergence of a broad assemblage of political-legal-economic institutions that will more directly affect the allocation of resources in society. The structuring of these institutions constitutes the institutional stage of choice. This stage involves the (re)structuring of political-legal institutions through the adoption or revision of the *working rules* and *legal doctrines*. The working rules are the complex set of rules that give rise to the institutional decision-making processes in the executive branch, the legislature, across government agencies, departments, and commissions (i.e., the "bureaucracy"), and the judiciary. These rules help shape the character of life in society. More often than not, the decision-making processes of an institution are formally worked out by the institution itself in developing its own working rules, such as departmental or agency by-laws. Likewise, common law doctrines and principles emerge over time as the judiciary decides cases and produces judge-made law. The policy decisions at this stage of choice are subtle but nonetheless do have an impact on the allocation of resources. As in the case of constitutions, the working rules and legal doctrines that undergird political/legal institutions are not set in stone, but rather they are themselves a response to economic needs and, as such, can and do undergo structural revisions.

Legal-economic policy also entails issuing executive orders, passing new statutes, or altering existing statutes, and (re)writing government rules and regulations. The focus here is on altering the *legal relations governing society*: the rights structures that underlie the mixed-market economy, which is comprised of four sectors: a market sector, a public sector, a communal sector, and a sector with open-access resources.[48] Making changes to the legal relations governing society involves making choices at the *economic impact stage of choice*. As elaborated in the following paragraphs, the scope and character of each of these four sectors, or systems of social control, is contingent upon the extant rights structure: the private property rights of the market sector, the status rights of the public sector, the communal property rights of the communal sector, or open-access resources in the open-access sector.

---

[48] The four rights regimes are presented in Bromley (1991) and Mercuro (1997), and are used in passing in both Burger and Gochfeld (1998) and Ostrom, Burger, Field, Norgaard, and Policansky (1999).

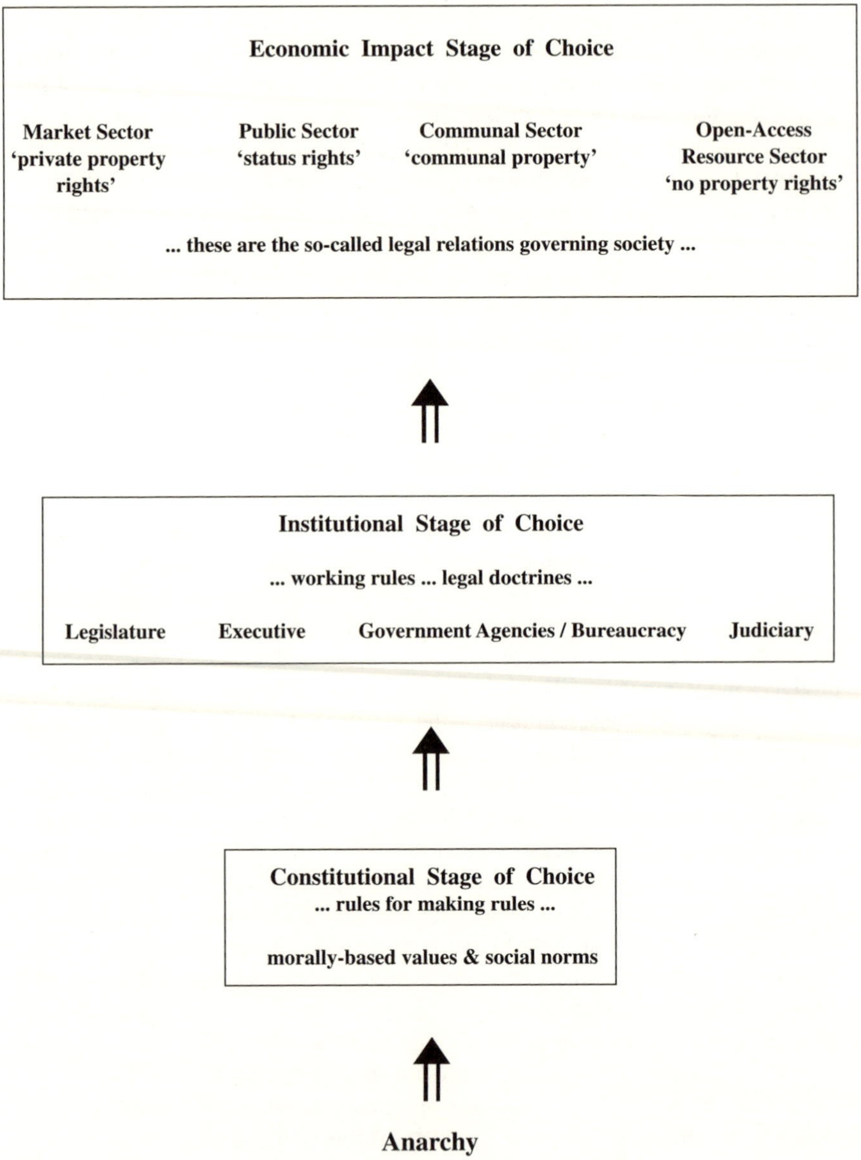

Economic Impact Stage of Choice

Market Sector 'private property rights'	Public Sector 'status rights'	Communal Sector 'communal property'	Open-Access Resource Sector 'no property rights'

... these are the so-called legal relations governing society ...

⇑

Institutional Stage of Choice

... working rules ... legal doctrines ...

Legislature   Executive   Government Agencies / Bureaucracy   Judiciary

⇑

Constitutional Stage of Choice
... rules for making rules ...

morally-based values & social norms

⇑

Anarchy

FIGURE 1-4. Three Stages of Choice

Market Sector

When individuals in a society, acting through their rule-making institutions, choose to use the market as the preferred system of social control, they must first use the state to define, assign, and enforce a structure of private property rights. Once this is accomplished, it is possible for the individuals to enhance their welfare further by specializing and engaging in exchange through trade or realigning the use of resources in production.[49] This process of trade is conventionally viewed as a purely voluntary endeavor and, as characterized here, is at the core of market sector activity. The voluntary nature of this market process is such that no individual will engage in a trade that leaves him worse off, the final allocative outcome will be arrived at once all the gains from trade have been exhausted in both exchange and production. Thus, given a set of defined private property rights and some initial distribution of these rights, and barring problems with information, enforcement, public goods, and externalities, one can expect that the market outcome will provide a Pareto-efficient allocation of resources.[50]

Public Sector

In the public sector, resources are allocated via the establishment of status rights by governmental entities, including legislatures, agencies, commissions, and boards. Status rights are defined as rights established by the government's pronouncements of specific eligibility requirements for individuals to use goods, services, or resources and are taken to be exclusive and nontransferable.[51] With the public sector as the system of social control, the emergent structure of status rights has a direct impact on the allocation of society's scarce resources. Unlike the market-sector resource allocations, however, there are no spontaneous mechanisms within the public sector for ensuring that government decision-makers will formulate policies that are economically efficient. This problem is partially offset by the extent to which public-sector decisions are based on benefit-cost calculations. In such cases, public-sector decisions can be said to approach a Kaldor-Hicks efficient allocation of resources.

Communal Sector

Common-property resources are those where private property is owned by a group of co-owners.[52] Under communal ownership a group of individuals has the rights to use and transfer the resource, and typically a management group oversees the manner in which a common property resource can be used and

[49] The former involves a move from "off to on" a contract curve in commodity space, the latter a move from "off to on" a contract curve in input space. See appendix 2 of this chapter.

[50] Again, this is the duality theorem as described at note 42.

[51] The original formulation of status rights was provided by Dales (1972, pp. 152–54).

[52] Bromley (1991, pp. 25–31); see also McCay (1996).

reserves the right to exclude nonmembers. Depending upon the group rules used to manage the resource, communal property can result in an efficient allocation of resources.

Open-Access Sector

Finally, the open-access sector is that sector wherein rights to commodities or resources are owned by no one, which is to say there are no property rights attached to the resource. As a consequence, these resources are equally available to all, and thus will belong to the party (or parties) to first exercise control over them. The resulting open-access allocation will be efficient only if supply of the resource should exceeds demand at a zero price. If supply, however, does not exceed demand at a zero price and society nonetheless retains the resource in open access (by not attaching any property rights to it), there is no method to exclude individuals from using the resource, and the resource will be depleted or overused.[53]

Typically, Western industrialized societies are structured so that resources are allocated, and the character of life is determined by all four of these sectors or systems of social control. The final combination of sectors selected is a result of individuals working through a pluralistic government to advance their individual and /or group interests, with the relative scope and content of each being the result of the collective determination of those who prevailed in choice-making processes within the political-legal-economic arena.

THE LOGIC OF LAW AND ECONOMICS

Public-policy debates typically revolve around the question, "In what direction shall we change the law?" Law and Economics provides a systematic way to think about this question. The underlying logic inherent in the conceptual model portrayed in figure 1-4 is that much of public policy involves altering the *law*, for example, through (i) a constitutional amendment, (ii) a change in a working rule that alters the decision-making process by which judicial, administrative, or legislative decisions are reached; (iii) a change in a legal doctrine within common law adjudication; (iv) a change in the definition or assignment of private property rights; (v) the altering of a status right (i.e., an administrative eligibility requirement) by the executive branch, the legislature, or some government agency or department; (vi) expanding or diminishing the scope of communal rights; or (vii) transferring rights to resources heretofore held as open access to either private, status, or communal property. The belief is that the goals of public policy will not be realized by changing the law

---

[53] This was the essence of the seminal article by Garrett Hardin (1968).

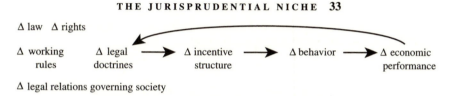

Δ law   Δ rights

Δ working   Δ legal ⟶ Δ incentive ⟶ Δ behavior ⟶ Δ economic
  rules   doctrines   structure   performance

Δ legal relations governing society

FIGURE 1-5.

willy-nilly or in an ad hoc manner, but by structuring and adopting those laws, rights, rules, and doctrines for which there is a known nexus between the said change in law and the desired outcome (see figure 1-5).

The view that public policy has no singular origin is reflected in Judge Rendlen's statement in *Eyerman v. Mercantile Trust Co.*, "Public policy may be found in the Constitution, statutes, [working rules], and judicial decisions of this state or the nation."[54] From the vantage point of Law and Economics, one must understand that a change in the law will alter the incentive structure confronting individuals and groups in society. This change in incentives will alter behavior, and that new behavior will ultimately and systematically affect economic performance. Much of positive Law and Economics tries to describe the exact nexus between policy options and their outcomes, with economic performance being measured or evaluated in terms of Pareto efficiency in exchange and production, and Kaldor-Hicks efficiency.[55] That nexus is captured in what has been termed the legal-centralist approach, which focuses on the central role of law in making policy.

Changing law, whether by changing the rights, rules, or doctrines, alters the incentives confronting individuals in society and thereby alters their behavior; in the aggregate, the new behavior results in a different economic performance. The reverse link in figure 1-5 attempts to depict the fact that as economic performance unfolds, as consumer demand shifts, as technologies change, as new resources are discovered and/or old ones move toward depletion, and as competition ensues, the economy changes over time. In a dynamic economy, new economic circumstances will invite new calls for additional changes in law and new policy initiatives.

Of course, the logic of causation between Law and Economics just described is really more complex than the legal-centralist approach indicates. Economic performance is not only driven by the incentives promulgated by the state-sanctioned law, but is also impacted by changing technology and by social norms. The role of technology and social norms in creating incentives

[54] *Eyerman v. Mercantile Trust Co.* 524 S.W. 2d 210, 217 (1975).

[55] This approach, being quite systematic as compared to what lawyers "do," led Bruce Ackerman (1984, p. 22) to ask, "When they speak so resonantly of 'public policy,' do lawyers have the slightest idea what they're talking about?"

and thereby affecting behavior and performance has come in for increasing attention in recent years and is the subject of chapter 7.

MODES OF REASONING IN ECONOMICS AND LAW:
DIFFERENCES IN EMPHASIS

A proper appreciation for the insights gained from a synthesis of economics and the law requires keeping in mind that there are differences in the methodologies employed by the two disciplines—as well as differences in the modes of reasoning that they use. In many respects these differences form the basis for a mutual scepticism on the part of economists and lawyers, and there is plenty of this scepticism, and even hostility, running in both directions. At times this occurs because understanding is accompanied by rejection, but more often it occurs because the nature of the other's approach is simply *not* understood. We recognize that little can be done beyond persuasion to resolve the former problem. The purpose of this section is to address the latter, and to explicate the differences that center on (i) the level of analysis from which the impact of legal change is assessed, (ii) inductive and deductive reasoning, (iii) *ex post* versus *ex ante* thinking, (iv) positive and normative approaches in both economics and the law, and (v) the emphasis given to the allocation of resources, as opposed to their distribution. We will also discuss (vi) the myth that "judges don't make the law." It is our belief that a fuller understanding of these differences between lawyers and economists will shed more light on the ongoing attempts by the various approaches to legal analysis to answer the three fundamental questions regarding the law.

Levels of Analysis: Naming and Framing

One of the most difficult issues in legal-economic policy-making is trying to decide upon the appropriate level from which to analyze the impact of policy. What typically transpires under the legal-centralist approach is that a regulation or piece of law is culled out for investigation from an arbitrarily chosen configuration of law and subjected to some version of efficiency analysis. Much more is involved here, however. As we noted in our discussion of compensation theory, it is recognized throughout Law and Economics that in fashioning legal-economic policy or in a court ruling, the final determination of rights between competing interests will, inevitably, result in someone gaining and someone losing. That is, almost all legal change will bring about a unique stream of benefits and costs to the respective parties of interest.

The vehicle of analysis that will be used here to explicate the issue of "the choice of level of analysis" is the takings issue as it arose in *Pennell v. City of*

San Jose.[56] The case deals with a 1979 rent-control ordinance adopted by the City of San Jose, California, that included a so-called "tenant hardship provision." In this case, the U.S. Supreme Court Justices were required to determine whether the "harm to tenants" provision of this rent-control ordinance constituted a taking of private property without just compensation under the Fifth and Fourteenth Amendments to the U.S. Constitution.[57] We begin with a brief outline of the facts of the case.[58]

In 1979 the City of San Jose, California, enacted a rent-control ordinance stipulating that a landlord may annually set a "reasonable rent" comprised of an increase of as much as 8 percent, plus an increment based on seven factors that are subject to review by the mediation hearing officer. If a tenant objects to a greater than 8 percent increase in rent, a hearing is required before the hearing officer to determine whether the landlord's proposed increase is reasonable under the circumstances. Of the seven factors to be considered, the first six factors were described by the court to be *objective* in that they were derived from (i) the history of the premises, (ii) the physical condition of the units, (iii) any changes in the provided housing services, (iv) the landlord's costs of providing an adequate rental unit, (v) the cost of debt servicing, and (vi) the prevailing status of the rental market for comparable housing. Application of these first six factors resulted in an objective determination of a reasonable rent increase. The seventh factor included in the ordinance was termed the "tenant hardship provision," which, in part, read as follows:

> In the case of a rent increase, which exceeds the standard set [in the ordinance], with respect to such excess and whether or not to allow same to be part of the increase allowed . . . the Hearing Officer shall consider the economic and financial hardship imposed on the present tenant(s). . . . If the Hearing Officer determines that the proposed increase constitutes an unreasonably severe financial or economic hardship . . . he may order that the excess of the increase . . . be disallowed. (*Pennell v. City of San Jose* 485 U.S. 1, 5–6 (1988))

It was the potential denial of the incremental rent increase on grounds of the tenant's financial hardship that was at issue in this case. Richard Pennell (owner of 109 rental units) and the Tri-County California Apartment House Owners Association sued in Superior Court of Santa Clara County seeking a

---

[56] *Pennell v. City of San Jose*, 485 U.S. 1 (1988).

[57] The Fifth Amendment to the U.S. Constitution states, "[N]or shall private property be taken for public use without just compensation." While cases regarding regulatory takings are not new, the U.S. Supreme Court case that firmly established them as a distinctive class was *Penn Central Transportation Company v. City of New York*, 438 U.S. 104 (1978).

[58] The facts of this case are taken directly from the *U.S. Supreme Court Reporter*. This section draws directly from the case as reported. Our purpose in so stating this is to avoid what otherwise would be excessive citations within this brief review of the case.

declaration that the ordinance was, on its face, constitutionally invalid inasmuch as application of the tenant hardship clause violated the takings clause of the Fifth and Fourteenth Amendments. Pennell and Tri-County argued that the potential reduction (solely attributable to the application of the provision regarding the tenant's hardship), from what otherwise would have been a *reasonable* rent increase based on the other six specified *objective* factors, constituted a taking in that it transferred the landlord's property to individual hardship tenants.

The Superior Court of California found the provision to be a taking and entered a judgment on behalf of Pennell and the association. The California Court of Appeal affirmed the lower court's ruling. The Court of Appeal's decision was, however, subsequently reversed by the Supreme Court of California, which found that the ordinance was not in violation of the takings clause. The case was then appealed to the U.S. Supreme Court.

The U.S. Supreme Court, in restating the facts of the case, noted that the ordinance made it mandatory to consider the hardship to the tenant.[59] That is, under conditions specified in the ordinance and when requested by an aggrieved party, the hearing officer was required to consider the economic hardship imposed on the present tenant. If the proposed increase constituted an unreasonably severe financial or economic hardship, then the officer could order that some or all of the excess of the increase (beyond 8 percent) be disallowed, although the officer was not required to do so.

While it had been stipulated that the tenant hardship clause had never been relied upon to reduce a tenant's rent, the U.S. Supreme Court still went forward and considered the substantive merits of the case. In deciding for the City of San Jose, the court's majority clearly recognized that price regulation was a legitimate goal within the context of the police powers of the state. Specifically, it found the purpose of the ordinance—that of preventing unreasonable rent increases caused by the city's housing shortage—to be legitimate. Justice Rehnquist (108 S.Ct. 849, 1988 at 858) named and framed the issue broadly, insisting that it was merely just another form of price regulation that, like others, served a protective function: "we have long recognized that a legitimate and rational goal of price or rate regulation is the protection of consumer welfare"; "a primary purpose of rent control is the protection of tenants"; and "one purpose of rent control is to protect persons with relatively fixed and limited incomes, consumers, [and] wage earners . . . from undue impairment of their standard of living." Furthermore, the majority of the court found the ordinance to represent a rational attempt to accommodate the conflicting interests of protecting tenants from burdensome rent increases and at

---

[59] Chief Justice Rehnquist delivered the opinion of the court. Justice Scalia, joined by Justice O'Connor, concurred in part and dissented in part. Justice Kennedy did not participate in the decision of the case.

the same time ensuring that landlords were guaranteed a fair return on their investment. In so finding, the U. S. Supreme Court affirmed the California Supreme Court's ruling that a taking had not occurred. It ruled that the ordinance, which so carefully considered both the individual circumstances of the landlord and the tenant before determining whether to allow an additional increase in rent over and above certain amounts that are deemed reasonable, when so named and framed, did not, on its face, violate the Fifth and Fourteenth Amendments' prohibition against the taking of private property for public use without just compensation.

In his dissent, Justice Scalia disagreed with the Court's majority finding and named and framed the question quite differently. Instead of looking broadly at the legality of price regulation, he focused in on the single "harm to tenant's" provision. While he did not go so far as to agree with an *amici* claim asserting that any and all rent control programs are, in and of themselves, a taking (108 S.Ct. 849, 1988 at 857 at note 6), Scalia concluded that the individual tenant hardship provision of this rent-control program did indeed effect a taking of private property without just compensation. Scalia maintained that the bounds of excessive versus reasonable rent increases were properly set by the first six objective factors alone, and he then framed the issue by concentrating on the one single provision and named it accordingly. That is, he argued that the tenant hardship provision served a different purpose, that being a "poverty program for poor tenants." He contended that putting the burden of resolving a public problem—poverty—on one class of individuals—landlords—constituted a taking because it forced a small group of private individuals to bear a burden that should have been borne by the public at large, as is typically done through social welfare programs.

This is a useful case because it so clearly illustrates that the analysis of legal-economic policy or legal decision-making necessitates "picking up a camera," so to speak, to frame the issue. That is, the contrasting visions makes clear that the selection of the level of analysis has implications for understanding court rulings and in analyzing legal-economic policies. Donald Schön (1979, pp. 264–65) has labeled this process "naming and framing," and describes the process and its effects as follows:

> Things are selected for attention and named in such a way as to fit the frame constructed for the situation. . . . Through the processes of naming and framing, the stories make . . . the "normative leap from data to recommendations, from facts to values, from 'is' to 'ought.' " It is typical of diagnostic/prescriptive stories such as these that they execute the normative leap in such a way as to make it seem graceful, compelling, even obvious.

It is clear that the majority of the court framed the issue more broadly than did Justice Scalia. For them, the package of provisions was just another instance of legitimate price regulation that protected people and hence did not constitute a

taking. In the way that Justice Scalia framed the issue, this single provision constituted another poverty program that placed a burden on landlords, and hence worked as a taking.

Naming and framing is part of determining the "appropriate" level of analysis. The choice is made by isolating and focusing on a particular facet of law, which in turn determines what is at issue, and at the same time places it against a legal relief that determines what constitutes the appropriate (read "legitimate") background law—that which is not (or should not be) in dispute. In legal argument, the parties of interest, in attempting to make their case, will select a level of analysis that best suits their interests and try to convince the court accordingly. In like manner, the judge, in deciding the case, will set forth his or her rationale for deciding the case at one level of analysis or another. In so doing, the court's ruling in a case is significantly advanced by subjectively couching the issue—naming it and framing it—at the level of analysis that helps legitimate the argument and the decision. In simple terms, the level of analysis chosen partly serves as the predicate for the court's ruling. One key to understanding case analysis and court decisions is first to uncover the subtle choices made in arguments by the respective parties to the dispute and/or the judge as they selectively decide what is at issue and what is appropriately relegated to the status of legitimate background law. This naming and framing process shapes one's vantage point and thus, ultimately one's conclusion as to what the law should be.

One can approach the case from any one of several levels of analysis (see figure 1-6). First, in the narrowest context, one can concentrate on a single provision of an ordinance. That is, following Scalia, one can cull out this one provision (here, the tenant hardship provision) and subject it to legal-economic scrutiny while leaving the other provisions of the ordinance and rent control programs as part of background law. In doing so, one can expect to see a clear pattern of benefits *and* harms emerge. It is these concentrated harms that provide a litigant a potential claim for a taking and/or a judge's rationale for deciding it was a taking. This observation is perfectly consistent with the appellants' contention that "the provision accomplishes a transfer of the landlord's property to individual hardship tenants" (108 S.Ct. 849, 1988 at 856), and it was clear to Scalia that this one isolated provision would serve to benefit one party of interest (the tenants) over the other (the landlords). Thus, from the dissenting minority's vantage point, the ordinance (if ruled constitutional), in one sense, "takes" from the landlords. A ruling declaring the ordinance unconstitutional (opposite the Rehnquist majority), however, would have the effect of taking from the tenants to and for the direct benefit of the landlords. The court had no way of making a ruling that did not result in a "giving" while simultaneously, in some form, constituting a "taking."

From a slightly broader perspective, one could examine the "harm to tenants" provision as but one facet of the city's rent control program, a program that was at that time part of San Jose's (indeed, California's) housing policy. From this broader level of analysis that focuses on rent control programs

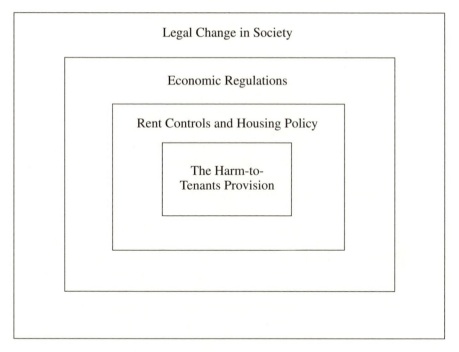

Legal Change in Society

Economic Regulations

Rent Controls and Housing Policy

The Harm-to-
Tenants Provision

FIGURE 1-6.

and housing policy in general, it would have required a certain selective perception—a particular normative frame—to single out this one harm to tenants provision as *the one* causing a taking. San Jose and California's housing policy is a maze of (i) federal and state public tax and expenditure programs, (ii) state and local housing regulations, and (iii) a vast array of municipal building and other codes. Each of these programs and policies has its own differential stream of economic benefits and costs—impacts that benefit some parties at the expense of others. None of them provides only benefits; all involve some costs, the latter of which could provide a potential claim for a taking. From the vantage point of this broader relief, the loss to landlords due to the "harm to tenants" provision becomes blurred. The argument to legitimate a taking claim looks much more arbitrary and raises the question, Why pick on this one provision when there are so many other California rent control programs and housing regulations and policies from which to choose? One could have instead gone after the entire rent control program,[60] or gone after one of the many other regulations that constitute California housing policy. Indeed, one can frame it even more broadly and couch the argument in terms of the entire spectrum of "economic regulations" in the United States.

[60] As mentioned earlier, this indeed was the argument of one *amici* party asserting that all rent control programs constitute a taking.

As is evident in this case, it was at this somewhat broader level of analysis that the U.S. Supreme Court's majority decided the case. The majority of the court thought this rent control program to be part of settled jurisprudence; it was treated as background law for which there was no good reason to rework at this time. For the majority, the rent control program was just one more facet of a long-recognized, legitimate program of price or rate regulation; it was a program that served to protect the welfare of consumers. All this ran contrary to Scalia, who "framed" the issue differently, "named" it a "welfare and/or poverty program," and came up with the opposite conclusion. Again, the point here is that the chosen level of analysis partly serves as the predicate for the court ruling—the naming and framing process shapes one's vantage point and thus, one's conclusion as to what the law should be.

Finally, one could frame the "harm to tenants" provision in the broadest context possible, as just one, singular instance of legal change across society. That is, the "harm to tenants" provision can be seen as merely one legal change (or public policy) alongside all those legal changes related to national transportation policy, education policy, energy policy, environmental policy, and so on. Viewed from this perspective, one sees that since, in modern government, legal change is ubiquitous, so too are the differential economic benefits and the economic burdens—the latter each potentially a taking (Samuels and Mercuro 1979, 1980). This is not to suggest that all legal changes are part of a zero-sum game. We do contend, however, that few legal changes are win-win situations; and further, we pragmatically contend that the vast majority of legal changes are win-lose situations, where the gains to the winners may or may not exceed the losses to the losers. The fundamental point here is that in modern mixed-market economies, society is constantly redetermining rights between competing sets of interests. The inevitable result is that some will gain and some will lose. Since rights are continually being created and re-created against this background, against this legal relief, there will be a vast number of losers who will (and must) for fiscal reasons go uncompensated.

Thus, with respect to the question, "In what direction shall we change the law?" in Law and Economics the questions to be answered are (i) Who will have rights?" and (ii) Whose losses will be compensated? As demonstrated earlier, these questions may be answered differently depending, in part, upon the level of analysis chosen—on how the legal change is framed and how it is named. The level at which the analysis is conducted drives the results generated by making some elements of the analysis central and fundamental while others are pushed into the background. Given the win-lose nature of legal-economic policy, and given the motivations of plaintiffs who are prepared to contend that a cost brought on by a legal change constitutes a taking, a deeper understanding of the fundamental issues in such cases is garnered by appreciating how the parties of interest and the judge name and frame the issue. That is, we need to understand from which level of analysis the discourse is being

conducted, and, ultimately, on what basis legal policy and court decisions are being argued and decided.

Inductive and Deductive Thinking in Economics and the Law: Tendencies, Not Absolutes

Most legal-economic scholars would agree with the observation that a major difference between economics and the law is that in economics the emphasis is on the use of *deductive* thinking while the law tends to emphasize *inductive* thinking. For example, it is not uncommon to read statements such as the following:

> Perhaps because [the economist] is trained to think deductively from general models more than inductively from particular cases, [he] is likely to be more mindful than the lawyer of the effects of legal rules on social organization and behavior and, in turn, the effects of the behavior on legal rules. (Gelhorn and Robinson 1983, p. 251)

In a similar vein, Minda observed that

> [w]hile Langdell [read "advocates of formalism"] believed that students could learn to discover fundamental principles by the inductive process of analyzing cases, Posner [read "economists"] believes that students can learn to deduce unifying characteristics by applying economic analysis to legal problems. (Minda 1978, p. 441)

That is, it is commonly believed that in economics, the focus of inquiry is on model-building under particular assumptions, and drawing logical deductions from the generalized observations; lawyers, in contrast, are said to think inductively, relying on the doctrines and principles drawn from particular cases and then applying them to the case at hand under the doctrine of *stare decisis*.

The methodological point to be understood here is that, in spite of these either-or caricatures, both economics and the law engage in both inductive *and* deductive thinking. Where they differ is in the emphasis each gives to these two modes of reasoning. Economics does employ inductive analysis—the process of observing regular patterns of behavior from raw data and distilling or drawing generalizations, principles, or theories from those observations— including, at times, the development of assumptions on which deduction is based. What emerges from this inductive process are "abstract" models, often, though not always, mathematical in form. Much of what economists "do," and therefore why they tend toward *deduction*, is to use these abstract models to reason from their assumptions / models to conclusions. That is, they first empirically test hypotheses (models that purport to describe reality) against real-world data to assess the validity of their economic models. If the empirical

testing suggests that the models are useful, economists then draw logical deductions from the core principles of the models to explain consumer and producer behavior and to formulate economic policy.

In law, and the formalist approach to law in particular, the emphasis is on induction, but here, too, there is an element of deductive analysis. First, formalism, the belief that one can obtain the right or correct answers to legal questions by engaging in formal legal analysis, entails the careful reading of cases and legal texts from which one can induce certain fundamental doctrines and principles. This approach asserts that law achieves its autonomy, not from some external source, but from the fact that there exists a handful of permanent, unchanging, indispensable doctrines and principles embodied in the many thousands of published judicial opinions. This handful of doctrines and principles is thought to be extensive enough to cover all imaginable cases and thereby forms an intelligent, coherent system of law. As with economic principles, the overarching legal principles and doctrines were (and are) uncovered through a process of induction. Second, but also significantly, law achieves its "scientific" status (i.e., determinate and systematic results) by way of a hierarchal *deductive* structure. Within this hierarchal structure, the rules and/or legal directives are deducible from the foundational principles and doctrines; that is, the rules are applied to factual situations to deduce consistent and correct legal outcomes.[61] The essence of this approach is captured by Posner:

> [T]he formalists had reconceived law as an inductive science. . . . The reports of appellate decisions were the data from which the principles of the common law could be *inferred*—principles such as that a promise is not legally enforceable unless supported by consideration, or that liability in tort requires proof of blameworthy conduct. Once these principles were brought to light the correct outcome of a case could be *deduced*. Thus the principles could be used both to show that outliers in the sample of appellate cases from which the principles had been derived had been decided incorrectly and to guide the decision of new cases. Although . . . these principles did not have divine backing, they had something almost as good—the power of scientific induction and the verdict of time. (Posner 1990, p. 15; emphasis added)

It is in this sense that we read assessments, such as Posner's, that "[j]udges more often reason upward from particular cases and argument rather than downward from some overarching principles" (Posner 1999, p. 115).

The foregoing discussion should make it evident that there are elements of both inductive *and* deductive thinking in economics and in law and that the

---

[61] This perspective is not much different than Judge Learned Hand's characterization of Joseph Beale, the then-young Harvard law professor who was a "true" Langdellian and who, according to Hand, preached that "Adequate diligence would reveal eternal 'principles of justice' from which specific rules could be readily deduced" (Gunther 1994, p. 49).

distinction is one of relative emphasis—economics emphasizing deduction, the law emphasizing induction. Neither is exclusively an inductive or deductive undertaking, and, as a consequence, one must logically expect elements of both inductive *and* deductive thinking to be evident throughout our survey of the schools of thought constituting Law and Economics.

Ex Post versus Ex Ante Thinking

Another significant difference between economists and lawyers is that, in many respects, lawyers see the law as a set of rules and procedures whereas economists see the law as a system for altering incentives. That is, lawyers typically take a retrospective or *ex post* view, while economists take a prospective or *ex ante* view.

The lawyer typically comes to a problem after the dispute has arisen, and hence a particular pattern of benefits and costs has already been incurred by the parties. Once a conflict or dispute arises and a factual inquiry begins, the choice of legal remedy involves looking backward—engaging in syllogistic reasoning to apply legal principles that have been distilled from the decisions in past cases. Hence, the issue for the court is to apply the appropriate doctrines and thereby reallocate the pattern of benefits and costs—for example, to make someone "whole" once again. In this regard, it is natural that judges should focus on questions of justice, fairness, and equity to reach a decision in that they are putting in place a remedy that affects the welfare of the parties directly involved (Veljanovski 1996, p. 38).

The economist, on the other hand, takes a prospective, rather than a retrospective, view. Part of the reason for preferring the ex ante approach stems from the perceived ambiguities inherent in ex post, syllogistic reasoning. As Henry Hansmann (1983, p. 226) once described the problem, "Law students are taught to be good at making, and at defeating, arguments to the effect that one fact situation looks like another and therefore should be treated similarly. In making such 'looks like' arguments almost anything goes,"and "the criteria for evaluating such arguments have been vague." In contrast to this, as Cento Veljanovski (1996, p. 38) has observed, "The economist's factual inquiry starts well before the dispute or conflict arises, when both parties had the opportunity to reorganize their activities so as to minimize the possibility of a dispute, and the costs and harm that it would inflict." In this way, economists are not directly concerned with the effect of the decision on the welfare of the parties to a dispute, as with the aforementioned judge following ex post analysis, but with the wider repercussions of the legal remedy to be imposed and, in particular, with the incentives created (or altered) for potential litigants who are apt to find themselves in similar circumstances in the future. To an economist, the application of the law—the selection of legal rules and legal directives

deduced from the core doctrines and principles—is seen as a mechanism or device to create or alter incentives that will help individuals reduce harm and use resources more efficiently. As Veljanovski (1996, p. 39) goes on to say,

> Lawyers are concerned with the aftermath of the general conflict of interests and activities which inevitably occurs in society. The economist is concerned with the effect that rules have on behavior *before* the mishap. The economist normally thinks of altering and tilting the incentives confronting individuals. In short, to quote Professor Lawrence Friedman, "The basic idea of economic theory is that the legal system is a giant pricing machine. . . . When laws grant rights, or impose duties, they make behavior of one sort or another cheaper or more expensive."

In his book, *Law's Order*, David Friedman (2000, p. 11) makes the same point:

> In any particular law case it looks as though what is at stake is how the legal system will deal with this particular set of events, all of which have already happened. From that backward-looking point of view it is often hard to make sense out of existing law. The reason is not that law does not make sense but that we are facing in the wrong direction. . . . Legal rules are to be judged by the structure of incentives they establish and the consequences of people altering their behavior in response to those incentives.

Frank H. Easterbrook (1984b, pp. 4–5) brings all of this out very nicely in his description of the U.S. Supreme Court as a regulator. "The Court," he says, "regulates the operations of government," and today's Supreme Court Justices "are more sophisticated in economic reasoning, and they apply it in a more thoroughgoing way, than at any other time in our history." His description of the court's role in resolving disputes is instructive vis-à-vis the arguments set forth by Veljanovski and in highlighting the differences between ex post thinking and ex ante thinking. Easterbrook focuses on the role of judges with respect to (i) dispute-resolution and (ii) rule-creation, noting that these two "functions of the Court tug the Justices in different directions." Like Veljanovski, Easterbrook (1984b, p. 5) argues that, on the one hand, the "dispute resolution is backward looking, an exercise in apportioning gains and losses given the occurrence of some known injury or conflict." Thus, in dispute resolution it is the principles of justice and fairness and ex post thinking that are at center stage. On the other hand, Easterbrook (1984b, p. 5) observes that "rule creation is forward looking, and a rule knows not its subjects"; it "thereby induc[es] people to become informed or change their positions" via its effect on incentives, future behavior, and performance.

This then places the judge in situations where he is torn between "doing justice" in the case at hand and applying a rule that creates additional benefits for people who can alter their behavior in the future. The implications are clear to Easterbrook:

It is nonetheless startling how often these arguments collapse to claims about "fairness," which in the law almost always means some appeal to an equitable division of the gains or losses among existing parties given that certain events have come to pass. Fairness arguments are *ex post* arguments, and few lawyers or judges are comfortable arguing about or deciding a case without invoking the ideal of fairness. Who is for unfairness? (1984b, p. 11)

He goes on to point out, however, that "judges who look at cases merely as occasions for the fair apportionment of gains and losses almost invariably ensure that there will be fewer gains and more losses tomorrow" (Easterbrook1984b, pp. 10–11). The point "is not that creating incentives for future conduct should be the Court's sole objective in adjudicating legal disputes, but that the Court is bound to send the wrong signals to the economic system unless the Justices *appreciate the consequences of legal rules for future behavior*" (p. 11; emphasis added).

In trying to understand the jurisprudence of the court, "[t]he first line of inquiry, then, is whether the Justices take an ex ante or an ex post perspective in analyzing issues. Which they take will depend, in part, on the extent to which they appreciate how the economic system creates new gains and losses; those who lack this appreciation will favor 'fair' treatment of the parties" (Easterbrook 1984b, p. 12). Perhaps the lesson to be taken from these remarks by Easterbrook, Friedman, and Veljanovski is that one must be aware of both ex ante and ex post considerations that are at work in legal reasoning and in the impact of legal decisions, and that there are real dangers in taking a one-sided view.

Positive versus Normative Legal-Economic Analysis

As our three fundamental questions illustrate, Law and Economics has both positive and normative components, and, in the evaluation of legal-economic problems and arguments, one must be careful to distinguish between positive and normative analysis.

Positive Legal-Economic Analysis and Efficiency

Positive legal-economic analysis describes what is, and there are two strands of this analysis in Law and Economics. One strand attempts to provide a description of the factors and forces governing the determination of economic welfare in society. It involves describing the interrelations between the economy and government and the ongoing reconstruction of the economy vis-à-vis government with some focusing on the evolution of property rights, others on the emergence of the state, while still other emphasizing the concepts of power, coercion, and the necessity of choice. The second branch involves applying economic theory and the tools of econometrics to estimate the direct

and indirect impacts of alternative legal doctrines, legal rules, and property rights. Most often, such studies describe the actual impacts of legal change—impacts brought on by (i) a legal-institutional change over time under a specified legal regime (i.e., within a given nation or state or local jurisdiction), or alternatively, (ii) cross-sectional empirical studies that compare one legal regime (i.e., nation or state or local jurisdiction) to another where one significant difference between them is the imposition of a particular legal arrangement. The impacts are then compared across a variety of outcome dimensions, including, often, economic efficiency.[62]

Work in the *positive* realm of Law and Economics is less controversial than that in the normative area.[63] In the positive realm, answers are sought to such questions as, Does the rule of negligence in force induce those who can undertake precautionary activities at the lowest cost to do so? To what extent does the law of contracts facilitate or inhibit the movement of resources into areas where they are most highly valued? Do environmental regulations or the application of common law nuisance rules generate benefits (through pollution abatement) in excess of their costs? Do the judicial and/or legislative processes facilitate efficient legal change? And so on. These are very typical questions for an economist to ask, but here they are applied to legal issues. In this respect, the analysis is no different from the traditional economic analysis of the efficiency of alternative market structures, farm subsidies, minimum wages, capital gains taxes, and tariffs on imports.[64] Even in its positive, descriptive form, however, efficiency analysis is not without controversy. One particular concern is with the question of whether, and to what extent, the use of economic concepts such as efficiency drives the way we think about the law. It has been argued that the very enterprise of applying economics to law, even in a descriptive manner, shapes legal thought and language by determining what we look at and therefore what we see. The efficiency analysis of law tends to frame the law a certain way and thereby frames law's objectives (Johnston 1990; Schön 1979). Simply put, how can one regularly labor through precise analyses of the efficiency of laws X, Y, and Z and then not think of efficiency as an objective of law? In this regard, some have argued that the positive efficiency analysis of law constitutes a filter that sifts out other important

---

[62] Economic efficiency is not the only output category used in Law and Economics. Other performance criteria are suggested in Mercuro (2001).

[63] Nonetheless, there are some who find the attempt by positive economics to emulate the work in the natural sciences and to downplay the works of philosophy and legal theory as disconcerting. Thus, we see Cooter and Ulen (1988, p.12) suggesting that, "Infatuated by the model of natural science, economists tend to regard theories of ethics [as related to law] worked out over several thousand years of debate as insubstantial." The result, they suggest is that "[l]ike prophets in the desert, this conceit insulates economists from the mainstream of legal theory."

[64] These topics really fall within the bounds of Law and Economics, as broadly defined here.

influences on the law. Steven N. S. Cheung (1980, p. 3) once described the ease of shifting from the positive to the normative as follows:

> To accept or to deny the desirability of a public policy necessarily involves "normative" value judgements on whether it *should* (or should not) be adopted. Economic efficiency, on the other hand, can be defined in "positive" terms concerned with whether a certain activity *is* (or is not) efficient. The transition from positive analysis to normative argument on policy requires only the inference that efficient allocation of resources is desirable to society. This inference is easy to draw and, to most economists, easy to accept.

Yet, to the extent that this "filtering" process is true of economics and efficiency, it is also true of any other approach to law.

One response to this critique is that while "law and economics helps to illuminate and enrich our understanding of the law . . . as an instrument of analysis which inevitably shapes the legal world it analyzes, the economic model alone is not enough: It must be enriched by a broader understanding of the social and cultural context within which law and economics operates" (Johnston 1990, p. 1221). Criticisms notwithstanding, incorporating positive legal-economic analysis into traditional legal education has had a discernable impact.[65] By employing the tools of economics, positive legal-economic analysis promotes a causal reasoning and a consistency that provides a greater clarity of the issues being analyzed and thus a potentially more powerful foundation for legal argumentation.[66] Many, and perhaps most, practitioners of Law and Economics would not argue that it is the *only* approach, but they would insist that it should be *one* of the perspectives brought to bear on legal-economic questions.

Normative Legal-Economic Analysis and Efficiency

Normative Law and Economics deals with what should be; it is the arena in which legal policy is debated and formulated. As described earlier, the shift from the positive realm to the normative is quite subtle, particularly for those in Law and Economics who advance efficiency as the sole or dominant criterion for evaluating legal issues. The primary question on the normative front concerns the desirability of selecting one law over another based on the efficiency criterion; that is, to what extent should efficiency be the or one of the

---

[65] As Lessig (1999, p. 105) has stated, "We are all law-and-economists now."

[66] As Mark White, however, has pointed out in comments on an earlier draft of this chapter, "[O]ne could argue that positive economics provides a great clarity of some of the issues that are relevant to a particular court case, mainly issues of efficiency and cost, but it does not provide that same clarity on other important issues such as justice, rights, etc. In other words, the issues that economics deals with, it deals with well, but not everybody would agree that these issues are the most important ones to be analyzed."

criteria employed in selecting among alternative legal rules? The normative use of the efficiency criterion may take two forms: a "first-order" rule, in which efficiency is the goal or one of several goals in making legal-economic policy, and a "second-order" rule, in which efficiency is used to determine the means by which noneconomic goals are pursued.[67] The use of the first-order rule will yield the optimal or efficient level of an activity—one that maximizes net benefit to society. For example, the efficiency norm would suggest that the level of pollution allowed by law be that level which is efficient, promoting abatement so long as $MSB_{abatement} = MSC_{abatement}$. The use of the second-order efficiency norm would suggest that once society has determined on, say, ethical grounds or for political reasons the appropriate level of pollution reduction, this reduction should be carried out in the least-cost manner.

The use of efficiency as a criterion for legal decision-making raises questions beyond those that arise on the positive side.[68] One is over the defensibility of labeling as an improvement instances where gains do exceed losses but losers are not compensated, as with wealth maximization. Many critics argue that the wealth maximization criterion reifies the existing distribution of wealth—that is, that wealth maximization favors those who already have the wealth—and consequently that the invocation of the efficiency norm merely serves to reinforce the existing power relations within the economic system and makes the market system the arbiter of rights. One sees this criticism within Institutional law and economics (see chapter 4 of this book), and even Posner (2001b, pp. 102ff), the Chicago school's foremost exponent, has recognized the legitimacy of this issue. Another question concerns the issue of whether efficiency should play any role at all in the determination of what constitutes justice. This quickly became the arena of one of the most widespread arguments regarding the Law and Economics movement. Whereas Posner (1981), for example, has argued eloquently that efficiency is moral and comports with the dictates of justice, others are equally adamant in their views that the use of the efficiency criterion in making law is antithetical to the idea that law should reflect some sense of justice.[69]

Avery Katz has suggested that part of the source of the difficulty over locating the jurisprudential niche of efficiency in legal theory lies in the culture clash between economics and law: "Within their own culture," he says, "economists can safely restrict their attention to means—that is, to efficiency—knowing that some other actor or institution will see to the content of ends.

---

[67] The first-order rule is consistent with solving an unconstrained maximization problem, whereas the second-order rule is consistent with solving a constrained maximization problem.

[68] Apart from questions as to the uniqueness of any such efficiency judgments, the criticisms raised against the use of such efficiency norms come primarily from moral philosophy See, for example, the articles in the "Symposium on Efficiency as a Legal Concern," *Hofstra Law Review* 8 (1980): 485–972.

[69] For example, see Coleman (1988); this debate will be more fully explored in chapter 2.

Lawyers may not feel they can abdicate responsibility for these other goals, and citizens and public officials surely cannot adopt such an approach" (1996, p. 2264). Katz is correct. Economists frequently make normative pronouncements on questions related to, say, taxes or with regard to tariffs on imports. Although economists are sometimes questioned on other grounds—perhaps distributional—generally they have been given a voice, if for no other reason than that such questions are generally acknowledged to be on the economists' home turf. Yet, the more widespread application of the efficiency criterion to areas such as the Constitution, the making of common law rules, the internal workings of the political process, and social theory generally, represents a vast extension of the application of the economist's toolkit into areas where many believe it does not belong, at least in the normative sense.[70]

Law is not simply a set of commands; it is a set of principles for ordering society. The open question here is thus one of whether efficiency is the, or one of the, principles to be used in determining the basic ordering of society. If it *is* to be one of the principles employed, then the ancillary question becomes that of the appropriate weight to be given to it when it conflicts with other ethical or political principles. This is a question that remains to be worked out within Law and Economics, within law generally, and within society at large. Even if one holds to the view that efficiency should play no role at all in the making of legal-economic policy, this does not vitiate the fact that there are choices to be made among competing ends, that trade-offs accompany these choices, that certain of these tradeoffs are economic, that legal rules have economic consequences, and that an understanding of economics is thus an important component of understanding the impact of law. In sum, questions about the normative side do not negate the import of positive Law and Economics.

It should be evident by now that many issues remain to be resolved, both within Law and Economics and between economics and the law and legal theory generally, in deciding the proper domain of efficiency analysis. It is beyond dispute that the emphasis on efficiency as a positive descriptor and as a legal norm, evidenced particularly within the Chicago-oriented approaches, has caused much of the hostility toward Law and Economics.[71] Even within Law and Economics, the various schools of thought are not all in agreement on several efficiency-oriented issues. First, there is ongoing disagreement over the degree to which one should use efficiency as the single-value policy touchstone. A second point of contention concerns how much to rely on a framework of analysis that stresses the importance of individual preferences, extolls

---

[70] On advocating the use of the efficiency criterion, see Kaplow and Shavell (2002).

[71] Most critics of the economic analysis of law identify Law and Economics almost exclusively as Chicago law and economics; hence the critics' hostility toward efficiency is concentrated on Chicago.

the virtues of voluntary exchange in production and consumption, and dwells on the alleged inefficiencies induced by many collective interventions in markets.[72] And a third issue that is often raised is whether, and if so on what basis, Law and Economics should concern itself with normative legal policy-making, as opposed to maintaining an exclusively positive focus. All of this adds up to a decidedly unsettled role for efficiency—in both its positive and normative applications—across the schools of thought that make up Law and Economics. That each school of thought has its own take on these issues will become clear in the chapters that follow.

A Change in Law Affects Both Allocation and Distribution

While some Law and Economics scholarship relies almost exclusively on the criteria of efficiency to assess outcomes of legal change, other strands of this research attempt to describe both the allocative *and* distributional impacts of alternative legal structures and working rules. There is no easy means, however, of serving, let alone satisfying, these two masters:

> Our task would be so much easier if efficiency could be rigorously defended as the only and ultimate objective. Instead we face two all-too-often opposing objectives, efficiency and equity. It must be remembered that the ultimate goal is what economists like to call *social efficiency,* which requires trading off resource allocation efficiency against distribution of income. . . . Legal rules must be concerned about both efficiency and income distribution. . . . Guidelines given by economic theory require two successive steps—first, income should be redistributed in the most desirable manner; second, resources should be allocated in the most efficient manner, preferably in response to competitive forces. An effort must thus be made to agree on a subjectively preferred income distribution and it must be followed by an effort to attain allocative efficiency. The formulation of prudent legal rules would have to proceed by considering both goals, not just allocative efficiency—a formidable task. (Hirsch 1988, p. 6)

It is clear from the thrust of the "economic side" of Law and Economics that the efficiency with which resources are allocated consequent to legal change is a major concern. Indeed, much of the economic theory brought to bear on analyzing legal change focuses directly on the relative efficiency of the allocation of resources. On the other hand, from the "law" side, the traditional concerns are often with questions of distribution under the guise of legal doctrines

---

[72] These are points raised by Trebilcock (1983, pp. 289–290) in his discussion of some of the Canadian objections to any analysis that maintains an exclusive reliance on using efficiency as sole criteria for judging legal change.

built on the precepts of justice and fairness. What remains to be sorted out is what sort of roles efficiency and distributional analysis should play in Law and Economics. If the world were as simple as that described by the perfectly competitive market, then all we need do is to set in place the just and fair initial property rights structure and, barring problems with information, enforcement, public goods, and externalities, the market would provide us with an efficient allocation of resources—the *optimum optimorum*.[73] Life is not that simple, however. Legal-economic policy, and thus legal change, is a continuous process in modern, mixed-market economies, and markets themselves never quite manage to satisfy the requirements of perfect competition. The effect is that judges and policymakers must continually make choices among competing goals.

The major reason for the emphasis on efficiency within Law and Economics is that mainstream economics takes as one of its primary goals the assessment of the efficiency of economic outcomes. As a glance at almost any text in economic theory will tell you, economists tend to believe that making distributional judgments is a matter for the politicians, not for the economists. What the economist offers, rather, is an assessment of the relative efficiency of various states of the world. One might well ask how a discipline that pays so little attention to distribution would come to achieve such prominence in a discipline, such as law, where distributional issues (in various guises) have traditionally played such a central role. Reuven Brenner's (1980) assessment as to why the economic approach to the study of law has dominated other social science approaches is instructive here. First, he says, economics has a received paradigm, a mature, uniform framework built on first principles that each legal-economic analyst knows and can confidently assume the other contributors to know; that is, they have a common takeoff point from which to extend ideas and theories. Brenner argues that the other present-day social science paradigms lack such uniformity and broad acceptance within their own disciplines and therefore require each social science observer of law to start anew building his or her own theory from its foundations.[74] Second, Brenner contends that part of the success of the economic approach owes to its predictions

---

[73] See quote from Kneese at page 25.

[74] Of all the other social sciences, sociology has perhaps come under the most significant criticism by mainstream economists and many within Law and Economics. In describing what he terms a "sociologically enriched law and economics," Ellickson says that "[it] continues to resemble what sociology is today: a field without a paradigm. This failure of theory leads to a lessening of scholarly interest" (Ellickson 1998, pp. 551–52). He goes on to argue that "sociology itself has long suffered from terminological disagreements, which helped prompt Arthur Leff to characterize it as a swamp" (Ellickson 1998, p. 549). It was the French mathematician and scientific genius Henri Poincaré (1952; 1908c, pp. 19–20) who once observed that "[n]early every sociological thesis proposes a new method which, however, its author is very careful not to apply, so that sociology is the science with the greatest number of methods and the least results."

being more consistent with the facts than the predictions of other theories of social sciences—that is, that economics has better predictive power.[75] Whether Brenner is correct or not, it seems that this perception is widely held, and this has no doubt helped economics gain an upper hand in the wider social science marketplace of ideas—perhaps most notably, via its incursion into the field of political science in the form of public choice theory.[76] Brenner's point is further brought home by the growing number of schools of thought in Law and Economics and the increasing number of new journals, national and international associations, and other trappings of professional success. Given its success, economics was well placed to fill the void that existed in law in the 1960s. And with its inherent emphasis on efficiency, it becomes clear why, from the "economics side," the allocation of resources is at center stage within Law and Economics.

The situation is very different for the legal doctrines built on the concepts of justice or fairness. From the "law side," fairness and justice, as evidenced in most of the conventional teachings of law, are directly related to distribution and thus put it at center stage. Whatever hold that doctrines based on justice and fairness may have over the legal academy, they appear to hold less and less sway for many of the legal scholars regularly contributing to Law and Economics. Indeed, one of the common themes of some of those contributing to Chicago law and economics is that "economic principles are encoded in the ethical vocabulary that is a staple of judicial language, and that the language of justice and equity that dominates judicial opinions is to a large extent the translation of economic principles into ethical language" (Landes and Posner 1987, p. 23). This tension will likely persist as long as there remains a traditional legal realm and a group of economists doing law. Our purpose here is not to argue the merits of whether law should incorporate more or less economics—we think it *will* include more, but that's not the point! The purpose of this section is simply to demonstrate that for a variety of reasons, due in part to what both economics and law bring to the table, no consensus exists on how to combine systematically and formally issues of allocation and distribution.

The reality appears to be that, although Hirsch's admonition (appearing at the beginning of this section) to consider both allocation and distribution is widely accepted in principle, it is most often honored only in the breach; thereafter one moves quickly (speed depending upon how brazen) into a detailed analysis of efficiency considerations. There is as yet no consensus within Law and Economics as to how we are to undertake a systematic analysis that formally includes a combined description of allocation and distribution, to say nothing of what rules should be adopted to judge among outcomes on a combined basis—the relative weights to be given to efficiency vis-à-vis distribution. Much remains to be done, and many questions remain.

---

[75] This is consistent with the argument in Posner (1987a).

[76] See the discussion in chapter 3.

The Myth That Judges Don't Make Law

There continues to be a popular myth within certain quarters, including among some journalists, politicians (particularly during times when judicial appointments are being reviewed), and, to perhaps a lesser extent, among those in the economics profession, that "judges do not make the law; legislators make the law, judges interpret the law." This myth continues in the face of clear evidence to the contrary. Those working in Law and Economics seem largely to have jettisoned this myth, as evidenced by the ubiquitous use of the phrase "judge-made law" by legal-economic scholars across all schools of thought. The thrust of the argument that follows is that while it is clear that the legislature can change (read "make") the law, and that government agencies and departments can change (read "make") the law, judges, too, are an integral part of the this process as they refashion common law doctrines and decision rules. In this regard judges do indeed *make* the law! As David Friedman (2000, pp. 3, 104) has correctly observed, "[M]uch of the law is a creation not of the legislatures but of judges, embedded in past precedents that determine how future cases will be decided. . . . One of the startling discoveries that students make in the first year of law school is how much of law is created, modified, and in some cases later repealed, entirely by judges." A casual listening to debates surrounding federal judicial appointments suggests that observers have yet to make this same "startling discovery."

The common law is replete with examples demonstrating that judges "make the law." This does not require a unique or nuanced interpretation of existing cases; it simply requires an understanding of the judges' written word. A synoptic review of three cases should make the point.

Rosenberg v. Lipnick

Charlotte Rosenberg, the plaintiff, brought an action in the Probate Court against the executors of the estate of Perry Rosenberg, her deceased husband.[77] Mrs. Rosenberg was seeking to have an antenuptial agreement that had been executed by her and her late husband invalidated, and thereby have the court declare that she was entitled to her statutory share of his estate and a widow's allowance.

In February of 1958, the then fifty-eight-year-old plaintiff met the then sixty-nine-year-old Perry Rosenberg. Both were gainfully employed; the plaintiff was a widow, the defendant a widower; each had children by previous marriages. After a courtship of approximately eighteen months, Rosenberg proposed marriage and told the plaintiff that he would like her to sign an antenuptial agreement. Charlotte Rosenberg took the agreement to her brother, a practicing attorney. After some discussion, they reached an agreement that

---

[77] *Rosenberg v. Lipnick*, 389 N.E.2d 385 (1979). Text edited from the case as reported.

upon her husband's death, Charlotte Rosenberg would accept $ 5,000 from Perry Rosenberg's estate; Perry Rosenberg surrendered any claim against her estate in the event that he survived her.

On the plaintiff's motion, the action was referred to a master. The master made findings of fact and concluded that the agreement was valid and that the plaintiff was not entitled to a statutory share of the estate or to a widow's allowance. The probate court judge confirmed the master's report and entered judgment for the defendants. Both the master and the judge relied on the settled law of the state—the Wellington decision—which had remained undisturbed law in the Commonwealth of Massachusetts for over a half-century. Under the rule of *Wellington v. Rugg*, 243 Mass. 30 (1922), a plaintiff seeking invalidation of an antenuptial agreement could not prevail in the absence of proof that her deceased husband either misrepresented or fraudulently concealed the extent of his assets prior to execution of the agreement. That is, in Massachusetts, the court held that a husband's simple failure voluntarily to disclose the value of his property prior to executing an antenuptial agreement was not sufficient to invalidate the antenuptial agreement.

Rosenberg filed an application for direct appellate review, asking the Supreme Court to overrule *Wellington* and hold that (i) an antenuptial agreement that fails to make a full and fair provision for the wife is not enforceable if the husband failed to disclose his assets prior to execution of the agreement, and (ii) the representatives of the husband have the burden of proving full and fair disclosure.

The Massachusetts Supreme Court noted that the rule in *Wellington v. Rugg* runs clearly contrary to Rosenberg's argument. *Wellington* holds that nothing short of proof of fraud will invalidate an antenuptial agreement, irrespective of the unfairness of the agreement's provisions. Accordingly, the Supreme Court ruled that the master found that the plaintiff had failed to establish that the decedent either misrepresented or fraudulently concealed the extent of his assets prior to execution of the agreement. In light of the master's finding, which the judge confirmed and which was supported by the record, the plaintiff could not prevail under the *Wellington* rule. The court affirmed the judgment for the defendants and then stated,

> [W]e have reviewed this case for error under the law as it existed in 1959. We have discerned none and thus affirm the judgment for the defendants. However, we take this opportunity to delineate new rules that shall apply to antenuptial agreements executed after the publication date of this opinion. . . . Although we agree that the *Wellington* principles should be abandoned, we do not think it wise to act retroactively.

The court went on to change the law, observing that Massachusetts stood alone in requiring the party seeking invalidation of an antenuptial agreement to show fraud. The court argued that the burden is not on either party to inquire

but on each to inform, for it is only by requiring full disclosure of the amount, character, and value of the parties' respective assets that courts can ensure intelligent waiver of the statutory rights involved.

Molitor v. Kaneland Community Unit District No. 302

Thomas Molitor, the father of Peter Molitor, brought an action against Kaneland Community Unit School District for personal injuries sustained by his son Peter when the school bus in which he was riding left the road, allegedly as a result of the driver's negligence.[78] The bus hit a culvert, exploded, and burned. Mr. Molitor's son sustained severe, permanent burns and injuries as a result of the defendant's negligence. Molitor asked for a judgment in the amount of $56,000. The Kaneland Community Unit School District entered a motion to dismiss the complaint on the ground that a school district is immune from liability for tort. The Illinois Appellate Court affirmed the decision of the trial court ruling again on behalf of the school district.

The case then went before the Supreme Court of Illinois. In his brief to the court, Molitor recognized the rule established by the court in 1898 that a school district is immune from tort liability, and then asked the court either to abolish the rule in toto, or to find it inapplicable to a school district (on a variety of different grounds). The Illinois court recognized that it was squarely faced with a highly important question: in light of modern developments, should a school district be immune from liability for tortiously inflicted personal injury to a pupil thereof arising out of the operation of a school bus owned and operated by said district?

The court noted that, while it had adhered to the old immunity rule in the past, it had not reconsidered and reevaluated the doctrine of immunity of school districts for over fifty years. During these years, however, the subject had received exhaustive consideration by legal writers and scholars in articles and texts, almost unanimously condemning the immunity doctrine. In the end, the Supreme Court of Illinois made new law in concluding that the rule of school district tort immunity is unjust, unsupported by any valid reason, and has no rightful place in modern-day society. In its consideration, the court noted that the school district strongly urged that if said immunity was to be abolished, it should be done by the legislature, not by the court. To this, the Supreme Court of Illinois stated,

> With this contention we must disagree. The doctrine of school district immunity was created by this court alone. Having found that doctrine to be unsound and unjust under present conditions, we consider that we have not only the power, but the duty, to abolish that immunity. . . . "We closed our courtroom doors without

---

[78] *Molitor v. Kaneland Community Unit District No. 302*, 163 N.E.2d 89 (1959). Text edited from the case as reported.

legislative help, and we can likewise open them." *Pierce v. Yakima Valley Memorial Hospital Association*, 43 Wash.2d 162 (1953) at 178. We have repeatedly held that the doctrine of *stare decisis* is not an inflexible rule requiring this court to blindly follow precedents and adhere to prior decisions, and that when it appears that public policy and social needs require a departure from prior decisions, it is our duty as a court of last resort to overrule those decisions and establish a rule consonant with our present day concepts of right and justice (at 95).[79]

Sommer v. Kridel

The issue raised in this case was whether an apartment rental contract is binding on both parties, thereby not requiring the owner of the apartment unit to try to mitigate damages by re-renting the unit in the event a renter wants to 'back out' of the contract.[80] On March 10, 1972, the defendant, James Kridel (the renter), entered into a lease with the plaintiff, Abraham Sommer, to rent an apartment; Sommer was the owner of the "Pierre Apartments" in Hackensack, N.J. The term of the lease was for two years starting May 1, 1972. Although the defendant had expected to begin occupancy around May 1, his plans were changed. He wrote to Sommer on May 19, 1972, explaining,

> I was to be married on June 3, 1972. Unhappily the engagement was broken and the wedding plans canceled. Both parents were to assume responsibility for the rent after our marriage. I was discharged from the U.S. Army in October 1971 and am now a student. I have no funds of my own, and am supported by my stepfather. In view of the above, I cannot take possession of the apartment and am surrendering all rights to it. Never having received a key, I cannot return same to you. I beg your understanding and compassion in releasing me from the lease, and will of course, in consideration thereof, forfeit the two month's rent already paid. Please notify me at your earliest convenience.

---

[79] In *Pierce v. Yakima Valley Memorial Hosp. Ass'n*, 260 P.2d 765, 178-180 (1953), the court stated,

As one writer has said: "The courts which have granted immunity to charitable organizations appear to have usurped the legislative function of declaring public policy and making changes in the law in accord therewith. It would be strange for these same courts to sit back and wait for the legislatures to reverse the value judgments the courts have made. (38 *Columbia Law Review* 1485, 1489)". . . . [H]aving previously undertaken this function, and having now concluded that our court-declared policy is no longer valid, there seems to be no compelling reason why we must wait for legislative action. We closed our courtroom doors without legislative help, and we can likewise open them. . . . It is our opinion that a charitable, nonprofit hospital should no longer be held immune from liability for injuries to paying patients caused by the negligence of employees of the hospital. Our previous decisions holding to the contrary are hereby overruled.

[80] *Sommer v. Kridel*, 378 A.2d 767 (1973). Text edited from the case as reported.

Plaintiff did not answer the letter. In September 1973, Sommer did rent the heretofore empty apartment and then sued Kridel demanding $7,590, the total amount due for the period from the beginning of the lease until he rented it. Kridel filed an amended answer to the complaint, alleging that the plaintiff breached the contract and failed to mitigate damages and accepted defendant's surrender of the premises. The trial judge ruled in favor of Kridel; thereafter the Appellate Division reversed and ruled for Sommer, concluding that the lease had been drawn to reflect "the 'settled law' of the State of New Jersey."

The Supreme Court of New Jersey noted that the Appellate court had relied on the fact that

> the weight of authority in this State supports the rule that a landlord is under no duty to mitigate damages caused by a defaulting tenant (see *Joyce v. Bauman*). . . . This rule has been followed in a majority of states and has been tentatively adopted in the American Law Institute's Restatement of Property. Nevertheless, the court observed that while there is still a split of authority over this question, the trend among recent cases appears to be in favor of a mitigation requirement.

The Supreme Court of New Jersey observed that the rule is based on principles of property law that equate a lease with a transfer of a property interest in the owner's estate. Under this rationale, the lease conveys to a tenant an interest in the property, which forecloses any control by the landlord; thus, it would be anomalous to require the landlord to concern himself with the tenant's abandonment of his own property. The Supreme Court of New Jersey then made new law, however, holding that

> [The] antiquated real property concept which served as the basis for the preexisting rule, shall no longer be controlling where there is a claim for damages under a residential lease. Such claims must be governed by more modern notions of fairness and equity. . . . We now reverse and hold that a landlord does have an obligation to make a reasonable effort to mitigate damages in such a situation We therefore overrule *Joyce v. Bauman* to the extent that it is inconsistent with our decision today.

In his biography of Oliver Wendell Holmes, G. Edward White (1993, p. 487) writes that one of the three themes that dominated American jurisprudence in the twentieth century was "the belief that judges 'make' rather than 'find' the law." We see this theme clearly expressed in the court's contention that

> [O]urs is not a closed system of existing precedent. The law is not such a formal system at all. We [the United States Supreme Court] are not, as a court of last resort, absolutely bound by our own decisions. We legitimately made the law in question and can legitimately change it. *Courts must make law.* Indeed courts are

major policy makers in our system of government. We must be wary of petrifying the common law into a rigid system, utterly behind the times and totally at odds with the progress of science and social change. (quoted in Duxbury 1995, p. 48; emphasis added)[81]

This issue remains an area of continuing dispute within modern-day jurisprudence. No set of facts will lay it to rest. It is a act that is replayed year after year, most often coming to the forefront in the course of legislature's review of nominations for federal judges. Parties of interest will emphasize one side of the dispute or the other depending upon their own ideology and the ideas of the judge under scrutiny. . . . The myth will persist.

CONCLUSION

Law and Economics has developed along several paths over the last past several decades. First, some work has been devoted to positive description of the development of the law and legal institutions—for example, looking at the question as to whether law has exhibited an efficiency logic in its development over time. Second, the normative component complementary to this first line of literature has sought to recommend, based primarily on efficiency criteria, certain changes in law—those that would tend to promote efficient outcomes. Third, a great deal of effort has been devoted to describing what is transpiring in those areas of the law that directly impact the allocation and distribution of society's scarce resources. Fourth, attempts have been made to explicate what is going on in the decision-making processes where law and economics are intricately intertwined, not mutually exclusive. The operative concept here is the legal-economic nexus, and, in this descriptive realm, the government and the economy are instruments available to whomever can get into a position to control and use them. The legal-economic nexus is the arena of power and power play—the social location of the processes in and through which resources are allocated and distributed. Finally, some in Law and Economics have begun to explore the role of changing social norms and their systematic impacts on economic performance. Social norms appear to matter in legal analysis for many reasons: (i) norms sometimes control individual behavior to the exclusion of law, (ii) norms and law may work together to influence behavior, and (iii) norms and law can influence each other. The logic of Law and Economics makes it clear that the structure of rights, rules, doctrines, values,

---

[81] The source of this quote remains in question. It is cited twice in the legal literature, first by Neil Duxbury (1995, p. 48) and then by Neil Andrews (1998)—both citing the same source: *Southern Pacific Co. v. Jensen*, 244 U.S. 205, 221 (1917) (Holmes J. dissenting). It is not from *Southern Pacific*, and, as of this writing, we are still unable to locate the original source. Nonetheless, it restates the underlying philosophy of our discussion here.

social norms, as well as technology all influence behavior, and thus economic performance.

The scholarship emanating from the field of Law and Economics is a product of a diverse group of scholars who contribute to this increasingly rich marketplace of ideas. None of them comes to the marketplace without their particular way of thinking about economics or the law. They all bring with them their own tendencies and biases regarding the naming and framing of the issues, the role of efficiency in describing and prescribing law, the use of inductive and deductive thinking, how to balance *ex post* versus *ex ante* thinking, positive and normative vantage points, the "proper" role of judges in American jurisprudence, and the degree to which social norms should be included in the analysis. Each school of thought has its own unique perspective, and views are by no means homogeneous even *within* particular schools.

To this end, we have undertaken to write this book based on our belief that each of the schools of thought surveyed here has important things to contribute to the analysis of legal-economic policy. Our goal is to provide the reader with a concise overview of just what each of these schools of thought is attempting to convey. To that end we describe the intellectual origins, identify some of the main contributors, outline the respective principles and ideas as well as the dominant modes of analysis within each school of thought, and present examples of the approach in action. In doing so, we hope to provide a fuller understanding of the relationships between the formation, structure, and processes of law and legal institutions and their impact upon the performance of the economy—and, with this understanding, perhaps work to reduce any tensions brought on by other, more diverse ways of thinking about the law.

The Theory of Market Failure

But even in the most advanced States there are
failures and imperfections. . . . [T]here are many
obstacles that prevent a community's resources from
being distributed among different uses or
occupations in the most effective way. The study of
these constitutes our present problem. That study
involves some difficult analysis. But its purpose is
essentially practical. It seeks to bring into clearer
light some of the ways in which it now is, or
eventually may become, feasible for governments to
control the play of economic forces in such ways as
to promote the economic welfare, and, through that,
the total welfare, of their citizens as a whole.
(Pigou 1932, pp. 129–30)

BEFORE EXPLORING each of the four conditions spelled out in table 1-1 (reproduced here as table A-1 for convenience), one should keep in mind that (i) since
the market participants (consumers and producers) use market prices as the
guideposts from which to make choices, and (ii) since they take only those actions that maximize their respective utility and profit, the outcome associated
with each market will be at that level of output where MPB = MPC, that is, the
markets yields *private-private* solutions. Also, it should be noted that in an extended discussion of market failure associated with each condition, implicitly
one is bringing to the forefront the question of the role of government (beyond
the minimalist idea of defining, assigning, and enforcing rights) in designing
policies to rectify the underlying causes of market failure. With these two
points in mind, we now turn to an examination of these four conditions.

CONDITION #1

With respect to condition #1 shown in table A-1, Pareto efficiency requires that
marginal social benefits be accounted for, while utility maximization in a market economy assumes that the consumers consider only private benefits. Thus,
achieving condition #1, MBS = MPB, would be consistent in those instances

TABLE A-1
For Good X

MSB = MPB
    MPB = P
        P = MPC
            MPC = MSC
Thus, MSB = MSC yields a Pareto-efficient allocation of resources.

---

where all social benefits will be accounted for in the market sector by the activities of individual consumers. The meaning of this condition can be intuitively grasped by considering what occurs when an individual consumes a steak for dinner. The incremental benefit society acquires by this private action is probably not much different than the incremental benefit that the individual acquires in eating the steak—the individual benefits by so much and, as the individual is a member of the society, society benefits by that same incremental amount.

There are many situations, however, in which society's incremental benefits differ from the benefits acquired by an individual when that individual undertakes certain types of market transactions. Instances where the benefits accruing to society exceed the benefits gained by an individual in a market transaction include such transactions as (i) having the family go to a private doctor to have their children inoculated for contagious diseases, (ii) a family purchasing smoke alarms for their apartment, or (iii) families seeing that students acquire higher education (assuming here that all higher education is only privately provided). In each of these cases, not only does the individual acquire a marginal private benefit (MPB), but, in each instance, there also is an external benefit (XB) conferred on others (those who are not part of the transaction). These examples can be depicted in figure A-1 where MBS equals the summation of the private consumption benefits (MPB) plus the external benefits accruing to other members of society as a result of the private consumption decision (XB), thus, MBS = MPB + XB.

As is evident from the material presented in the text, from society's standpoint, the optimal or efficient allocation of society's resources would be where MSB = MSC, that is, where X_0 units of good X are produced at price P_0. Consumers and producers in the market, however, make decisions with regard to *private* benefit assessments (along MPB) resulting in a solution where MPB = MPC [= MSC]. This market outcome corresponds to a non-optimal, persistent underallocation of resources at point X_1 at price P_1, where it is observed that the price consumers are willing and able to pay (along MSB) is well in excess of P_1 and at a quantity that violates condition #1, since at X_1 MSB > MPB. From this, we observe that, in an effort to arrive at a more efficient level of production, the government often gets involved in the inoculation of children, distributing smoke alarms, and providing resources for public universities.

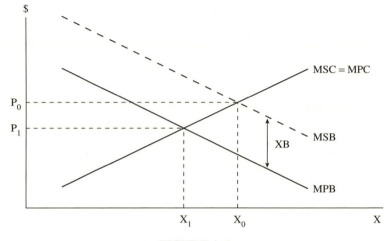

FIGURE A-1.

CONDITION #2

Condition #2, MPB = P, states that the price an individual consumer is willing to pay to acquire a good reflects perfectly his private marginal benefit derived from the good. In fulfilling this condition, each individual is maximizing his utility. Furthermore, these prices are the ones that will guide producers to allocate greater or lesser amounts of resources to the production of various goods and thereby take into account the private benefit assessments of the consumers.

It is difficult to imagine violations of this condition for consumers in the market for final goods and services. Monopsonists in resource markets (i.e., a single buyer or association of buyers with some control over the factor price) do, however, violate this condition. An example of a monopsonistic firm in the labor market is depicted in figure A-2. This example requires some redefinitions as we shift to the labor market. In the labor market, price (P) is now the price of labor (P_L)—the wage rate, W. MPB, the private gain to the firm from hiring another worker, is represented as the marginal revenue product to the firm from employing that additional unit of labor. This MRP_L is analytically equivalent to MPB and is assumed here equal to MSB. MSC becomes MSRC, society's marginal resource cost, and represents the true opportunity cost incurred by society in supplying additional units of labor in a monopsonistic labor market (as such, MSC is the supply of labor curve). And finally, MPC = MPRC represents the private marginal expense to the firm in acquiring additional units of labor, the firm's private marginal resource cost. From society's standpoint, the efficient solution would dictate that the firm hire L_0 laborers (where MSB = MSC) and pay wage rate W_0. Here, the price of labor equals the mar-

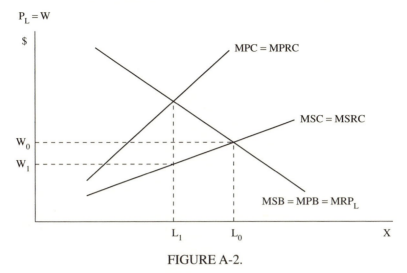

FIGURE A-2.

ginal revenue product to the firm ($W_0 = MRP_L$. In terms of condition #2, table A-1, this corresponds to meeting the condition $P = MPB$.

In making its decision on how many laborers to hire the firm, however, will consider only the private cost of hiring additional laborers (i.e., move along MPRC) and will continue to hire labor as long as MRP_L exceeds MPRC up to L_1 laborers, where $MPRC = MRP_L$. At L_1 the firm will pay wage rate W_1, the minimum price necessary to induce that supply of labor onto the market. Thus, the market solution under monopsony generates a persistent underallocation of resources, as $W_1 < MRP_L$—a violation of condition #2, $P = MPB$, in table A-1. From this, we observe that in an effort to arrive at a wage that approximates the competitive wage (higher than that which would prevail in an otherwise monopsonistic industry), labor laws are passed and enforced by the state in an effort to provide labor unions a countervailing force against monopsony power.

CONDITION #3

Condition #3, $P = MPC$, states that the price received by a producer perfectly reflects the marginal private cost of producing the good, that is, the market price equals the opportunity cost of using the resources needed to produce the good. In fulfilling this condition, each firm would be maximizing its profits under perfect competition.

Recall that in a perfectly competitive market each firm acts as a "price taker," which means that it perceives that it has no control over product price.

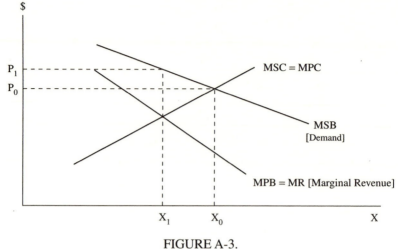

FIGURE A-3.

Each firm, within a limited range, can sell as much or as little of the good as it wants at the prevailing market price. As a result, the marginal revenue (MR) of one additional unit sold is equal to the market price (i.e., $MR = P$). Since profit-maximizing firms will always produce at a level of output where their private marginal cost of the next unit is equal to the marginal revenue of that unit ($MPC = MR$), and since in a perfectly competitive industry ($MR = P$) firms will produce at an output level where price is equal to marginal private cost, condition #3, $MPC = P$, is thus met.

Violations of condition #3 occur in cases of imperfect competition where firms, to some extent, exert control over the market price (figure A-3). Typically, this is what transpires in various degrees in the market structures of pure monopoly, oligopoly, and monopolistic competition. Firms in these market structures typically face a downward sloping demand curve, which implies that the marginal revenue of the next unit sold (the firm's MPB curve) is less than the price for each quantity produced and sold ($MR < P$). As depicted in figure A-3, efficiency would dictate that X_0 units be produced and sold at price P_0, where $MSB = MSC$. The firm, however, acting privately to maximize its profits, will move along its marginal revenue curve and produce that output that equates marginal revenue (MR) to its marginal private cost (MPC), and produce X_1 units and charge price P_1 (along the demand curve). As a result, the profit maximizing firm with market power sufficient to affect price will systematically underallocate resources and produce at a level of output where price exceeds marginal private cost; that is, since $P > MR$ and the firm produces that level of output where $MR = MPC$, consequently $P > MPC$, a violation of condition #3. From this, we observe that in an effort to arrive at a more

efficient level of production, the government (through the Federal Trade Commission and / or the Antitrust Division of the U.S. Justice Department) often gets involved in enforcing antitrust laws. In other instances, the government may decide, for reasons of necessity and convenience, to regulate the industry by limiting new entrants and/or price.

CONDITION #4

Finally, since Pareto efficiency requires that all marginal social costs be considered, and profit maximization assumes that the producers consider only private costs, then condition #4, MPC = MSC, describes those market transactions whereby all social costs will be accounted for in the market sector by the activities of individual producers.

The fulfillment of condition #4 can be illustrated by the example of the organic farm that avoids the use of any nonorganic fertilizers, pesticides, or rodenticides. The implication is that the marginal social costs incurred by society is precisely equal to the sum of the all of the marginal private costs incurred to produce the farm products, that is, there are no external costs. Violations of condition #4—the case of external costs or negative externalities—can come about due to (1) the external costs associated with the existence of open-access resources, (2) technological interdependencies, or (3) interdependencies due to the location or proximity of individuals. Typically, the class of negative externalities associated with the violation of condition #4 includes such phenomena as air, water, and noise pollution.

Exploring this in some detail, firms make their output decisions on the basis of the costs of production that result from the purchase of privately owned factors of production, which then is expressed by the firm's marginal private costs (MPC). In cases where the firm, however, utilizes an unowned, open-access resource—perhaps it emits water effluents into an unowned river or emits semi-toxic air emissions in the unowned air—the production of a good also entails costs that are not borne by the firm but are borne by other producers or consumers in the society, yielding an external cost of XC (see figure A-4).The marginal social cost, MSC, equals the sum of the marginal private cost plus the external cost, MSC = MPC + XC. From society's standpoint, the efficient allocation of resources would coincide with the production and consumption of X_0 units of good X at price P_0, where MSB = MSC.

The perfectly competitive firm, however, will maximize profits by considering only private costs, moving along MPC, resulting in a level of output at X_1, where [MSB =] MPB = MPC. This corresponds to a non-optimal, overallocation of resources at point X_1 at price P_1, well below society's marginal cost of producing X_1, where it is observed that MSC > MPC, a violation of condition #4. From this, we observe that in an effort to arrive at a more efficient level of

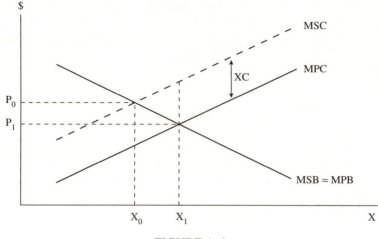

FIGURE A-4.

production, the government attempts to internalize the heretofore negative externalities through the imposition of taxes or to regulate the industry using the standards approach (through its U.S. Environmental Protection Agency, the U.S. Department of Interior, as well as federal and state anti-pollution statutes and regulations).

ADDITIONAL SOURCES OF MARKET FAILURE

There are two other notable sources of market failure, one concerning information, the other concerning the enforcement of rights. Both the lack of full information for market participants and the incomplete enforcement of rights can drive a wedge into any one of the equalities given by the four conditions specified in table A-1.

Information

Recall that one of the basic assumptions of a purely competitive, perfectly functioning market is that all consumers and producers have perfect information over all facets of all market transactions. If the requirement of perfect information is not met, however, then conditions arise that can serve to drive a wedge into the equalities given presented in table A-1 and especially in conditions #2 and #3, and thereby prevent the market from attaining a Pareto-optimal outcome. For example, if a consumer is not fully informed as to the actual benefits to be derived from the acquisition of additional units of a good, then the price he is willing to pay for the good will likely be at variance with

the benefits received. That is, MPB ≠ P here, since the purchase was based on an incorrect or incomplete assessment of benefits due to a lack of full information.

The impact of the lack of full information can be beneficial or detrimental to the consumer. If the specific impact on the consumer was to his benefit, then MPB may exceed P, as, for example, in the case of an unanticipated discovery of oil on the site of a newly acquired vacation home. If the impact was to his detriment, in contrast, then MPB may be less than P. An example might be the unknown side-effects of medications. In either case MPB ≠ P, which precludes the attainment of a Pareto-efficient outcome.

In like manner, a producer who lacks perfect information, say with respect to market demand, scarcity of resources, or technology, is likely to make output decisions that are at variance with the actual costs incurred, resulting in P ≠ MPC. If the actual market demand for a producer's product, and therefore the market price, is not fully known due to a lack of perfect information, then the true market price may be greater or less than the producer's assessment of that price. In either case, P ≠ MPC, which prevents the attainment of a Pareto efficient solution.

Enforcement of Rights

The complete governmental enforcement of rights is another of the basic assumptions of purely competitive markets. For example, the full enforcement of rights pertaining to contracts is one of the prerequisites for the smooth functioning of purely competitive markets. Once private property rights are defined and assigned, then the subsequent lack of protection of the rights underlying the market sector can drive a wedge into any one of the four conditions and thereby prevent the market from attaining a Pareto-optimal outcome. A simple example of the impact on allocative efficiency as a result on nonenforcement of rights as related to each of the four conditions will make this apparent.

The lack of enforcement of rights leading to a violation of condition #1, MSB = MPB, can be illustrated by the case of an individual who, for his own fishing enjoyment, stocks his private lake with fish. If anti-poaching or trespass laws are not enforced, then MSB > MPB. Condition #2, MPB = P, will be violated if laws that allow for the establishment of unions to countervail monopsony power are not enforced; as a result, $MRP_L > W$ (i.e., MPB > P). Condition #3, P = MPC, will be violated if antitrust laws go unenforced (i.e., P > MPC). Finally, condition #4, MPC = MSC, will be violated if environmental or nuisance laws that prohibit firms from discharging smoke into the air are not enforced (MPC < MSC).

Efficiency Concepts in Law and Economics

> Economists draw on many different forms of
> [efficiency], such as efficient production, efficient
> exchange, Pareto efficiency, national income
> maximization, wealth maximization, and utilitarian
> efficiency. Most economists move easily from one
> form to another, but the subtle shifts in significance
> are lost upon noneconomists.
> *(Cooter 1982b, p. 1263)*

EFFICIENCY: EDGEWORTH BOX ANALYSIS

THREE principle concepts of efficiency are employed within, and are indeed central to the study of, Law and Economics—efficiency in exchange, efficiency in production, and Kaldor-Hicks efficiency. This appendix provides a detailed overview of these three concepts.[82]

Efficiency in Exchange

CONSUMER CHOICE

Consuming units are assumed to derive utility (or satisfaction) from the consumption of goods and services, and to make their consumption choices rationally so as to maximize utility. For present purposes, we assume two individual consumers, A and B, and two goods, X and Y, which the individuals take to be imperfect substitutes. All the analysis, however, generalizes to any number of consumers and goods.

The behavior of individuals A and B is assumed to conform to four axioms:

1. Completeness: An individual either prefers one bundle of X and Y—bundle 'R'—to a different bundle of X and Y—bundle 'S'; prefers bundle 'S' to bundle 'R'; or is indifferent between holding bundle 'R' or bundle 'S'.

---

[82] The graphical analysis regarding general equilibrium theory and welfare economics is consistent with its usual treatment in standard intermediate price theory textbooks, such as Pindyck and Rubinfeld (1992). The original graphical formulation was by Francis M. Bator (1957); we have generally followed the presentation by Gould and Ferguson (1980). A more advanced treatment is contained in Feldman (1980).

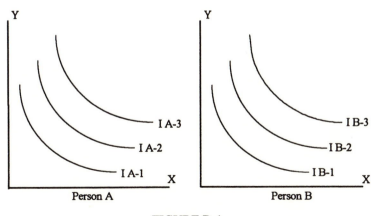

FIGURE B-1.

2. Transitivity: An individual who prefers bundle 'R' to bundle 'S', and prefers bundle 'S' to bundle 'T', will prefer bundle 'R' to bundle 'T'.

3. Dominance: Given bundle 'S' with a specified amount of X and Y, if bundle 'R' contains more of good X and no less of good Y (or contains more of good Y and no less of good X), then the individual will prefer holding bundle 'R' to bundle 'S'.

4. Solipsism: An individual's preference ranking is defined over the commodity bundles that he consumes and is not influenced by the commodity bundles allocated to other individuals.

Given these four choice axioms, the relationship between the quantities of goods X and Y consumed and an individual's level of utility can be described with a family of indifference curves. An indifference curve is defined as a locus of points showing combinations of X and Y that yield the same level of utility to the consumer. A family of indifference curves for person A, such as that shown in figure B-1, describes higher ordinal levels of utility as you move to the northeast; IA-3 is associated with a higher level of utility than IA-2, and IA-2 is associated with a higher level of utility than IA-1. In a like manner, a family of indifference curves for person B describes higher ordinal levels of utility as you move to the northeast; IB-3 is associated with a higher level of utility than IB-2, and IB-2 is associated with a higher level of utility than IB-1.

All indifference curves are negatively sloped, do not intersect, are mathematically dense, and are convex to the origin. The convexity property of an indifference curve is a direct corollary of the principle of diminishing marginal rate of substitution. The marginal rate of substitution of good X for good Y ($MRS_{of\ X\ for\ Y}$) measures the number of units of Y that an individual is, *subjectively*, willing to relinquish per unit of X gained so as to maintain a constant level of satisfaction or utility. An individual's indifference curve for two goods

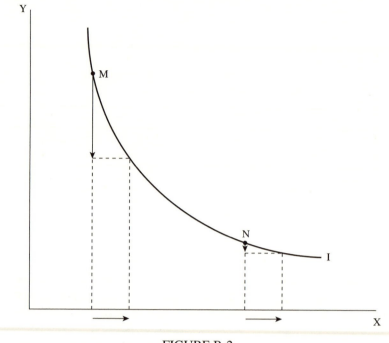

FIGURE B-2.

that are imperfect substitutes is convex because as the individual acquires additional units of X (starting at a point such as M in figure B-2 and moving down along an indifference curve), the individual will be willing to give up less and less Y to obtain an additional unit of X while maintaining the same level of utility. That is, as the consumer moves toward N, holding more X relative to Y (utility constant), the consumer will be more and more reluctant to give up Y to secure an additional unit of X.

A's marginal rate of substitution of X for Y (denoted MRS-A$_{\text{of X for Y}}$) is given by the slope of a line tangent to any point on an indifference curve. As one moves down the indifference curve toward N, the slope of a line tangent to points on the indifference curve becomes smaller and smaller (in absolute value terms), and thus the convex indifference curve is merely the graphical manifestation of the *principle of the diminishing marginal rate of substitution.*

EQUILIBRIUM AND EFFICIENCY IN A PURE EXCHANGE MODEL

Assuming that there exist given amounts of goods X and Y in the economy, Edgeworth box analysis can be used to examine exchange relations in the

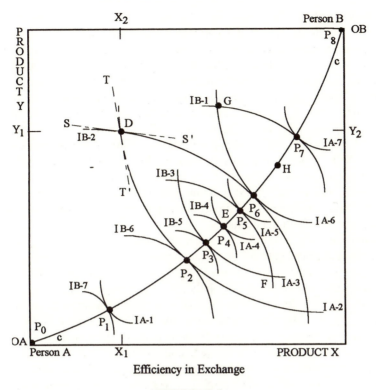

Efficiency in Exchange

FIGURE B-3.

economy.[83] The given amounts of X and Y determine the dimensions of the Edgeworth box in figure B-3, and the points within the box illustrate all possible allocations of X and Y between persons A and B. Individual B's family of indifference curves is rotated so that its origin is now situated in the northeast corner (0_B). Consequently, B's utility is enhanced as he comes to rest on inverted utility curves further to the southwest. The origin of individual A's family of indifference curves (0_A) is maintained at its initial position in the southwest corner, and A's utility is enhanced as he comes to rest on utility curves further to the northeast.

Persons A and B are each assumed to start out with an initial endowment of X and Y, such as depicted by point D. Thus, person A is starting out with X_1 and Y_1 (a lot of Y as compared to X), which places A on indifference curve I_{A-2}. Likewise, person B starts out with X_2 and Y_2 (a lot of X as compared to Y),

<hr />

[83] The following discussion of consumer and producer equilibrium is presented in the context of a pure exchange model. For a treatment of these issues in a competitive market framework, see, for example, Boadway and Wildasin (1984) and Pindyck and Rubinfeld (1992).

which places B on indifference curve I_{B-2}. Given these initial endowments, we can see from the diagram that A prefers all points northeast of I_{A-2} (since they lie on higher indifference curves and thus make A better off), and, for similar reasons, B prefers all points southwest of I_{B-2}. It is clear, then, that at point D potential *gains from trade* exist. Graphically, the region for realizing this potential is the *trading lens*—the lens-shaped region demarcated by the two indifference curves I_{A-2} and I_{B-2} passing through point D. Any point in the area within this lens makes *both* A and B better off than they are at point D. Thus, in a pure exchange model, the individuals will find it advantageous to exchange X for Y, or Y for X, so as to enhance their respective utilities. Persons A and B can contract and recontract—exchanging X for Y, and Y for X, respectively, and, in the process, continuously groping toward higher levels of utility—say, from D to F, and finally coming to rest at E, a point from which no further gains from trade exist.

The underlying reason for this spontaneous (re)contracting to exhaust the gains from trade lies in the differing subjective $MRS_{of\,X\,for\,Y}$ for persons A and B at point D; that is, at D, person A's $MRS_{of\,X\,for\,Y}$ is high (as graphically depicted by the high slope of TT'), indicating that person A is quite willing to give up a lot of Y for an additional unit of X. Alternatively, at D, person B's $MRS_{of\,X\,for\,Y}$ is low (as graphically depicted by the lower slope of SS'), indicating that person B is simultaneously quite willing to give up a lot of X for an additional unit of Y. Herein lie the potential gains from trade. The individuals contract and recontract, and only fully exhaust the gains from trade once they arrive at a point where their respective marginal rates of substitution are equal—here, point E. As compared to point D, and *given the same amount of X and Y in the economy*, at point E both individuals have increased their utility by consuming bundles of X and Y different than their initial endowment. Person A is now at utility level I_{A-4} and person B at utility level I_{B-4}. More generally, at E it is said that the economy has attained a *general equilibrium of exchange* where there is no incentive for further trade.

Notice that at this point, A's indifference curve is tangent to that of B, indicating that A's $MRS_{of\,X\,for\,Y}$ = B's $MRS_{of\,X\,for\,Y}$. Furthermore, any move away from this point will put either A or B (or both) on a lower indifference curve—that is, it will reduce the utility of one or both of them. Point E is said to be Pareto optimal: There is no movement from this point that can make one person better off without making someone else worse off. All this is brought together in the condition for efficiency in exchange, which states that an exchange equilibrium is Pareto efficient if A's $MRS_{of\,X\,for\,Y}$ = B's $MRS_{of\,X\,for\,Y}$. Thus, since at point E the marginal rate of substitution between every pair of goods is the same for all parties consuming both goods, *efficiency in exchange* obtains.

Whereas the initial endowments reflected in point D lead to an efficient equilibrium at point E, a different set of endowments will likely generate a

different trading lens and, subsequently, a different negotiated equilibrium point (such as that reflected in the movement from point G to point H in figure B-3). The locus of all tangency points between A's and B's indifference curves—points such as P_0, P_1, P_2, P_3, P_4, P_5, P_6, P_7, P_8—is depicted by curve cc, and is known as the *contract curve*. The exchange equilibrium point on the contract curve that is ultimately realized is partially a product of the distribution of initial endowments between persons A and B, as well as their respective bargaining skills. The contract curve is an *optimal* locus in the sense that if the individuals are located at some point not on the contract curve, one or both individuals can be made better off, and neither suffer a loss, merely by exchanging goods and moving to a point on the contract curve. *Thus, conceptually, a movement from a point off the contract curve to a point on the contract curve is efficiency enhancing.* Consequently, once on the contract curve, any movement from that point will influence aggregate utility. If the movement is along the contract curve, it must result in benefiting one party at the expense of the other; alternatively, if the movement is off the contract curve, then the utility of both persons will be diminished. Neither such movement can be efficiency enhancing. Being at a point on the contract curve—an exchange equilibrium—constitutes what is termed a *Pareto optimum.*

Formally, a Pareto-optimal state is one from which any change makes at least one individual worse off, regardless of whether or not others are made better off in the process. Alternatively, an economy is not in a Pareto-optimal state if there exists a potential change that will make some people better off and will not make anyone worse off. Consequently, every outcome that is represented by a point on the contract curve is said to be *Pareto optimal*; the contract curve is a locus of Pareto optimality.

THE POINT UTILITY POSSIBILITY FRONTIER

Given the total endowment of X and Y and the family of indifference curves for persons A and B, there exists a point utility possibility frontier that illustrates the utility levels for persons A and B associated with the set of Pareto-optimal outcomes along the contract curve. As such, the frontier lies in a different space—not one of goods X and Y, but in utility space depicting the utility of person A and the utility of person B (see figure B-4).

As described earlier, the contract curve, cc, is comprised of the locus of all tangency points between person A's and person B's indifference curves and thus is the locus of Pareto-optimal points such as P_0, P_1, P_2, P_3, P_4, P_5, P_6, P_7, P_8. Let us plot each of these points in utility space, beginning with P_0. This point represents a *possible* state of the economy such that there is zero utility for person A and person B attains the highest level of utility possible. At the

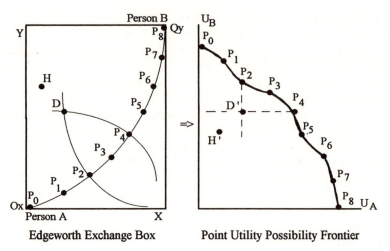

Edgeworth Exchange Box   Point Utility Possibility Frontier

FIGURE B-4.

other extreme, P_8 represents zero utility for person B while person A attains the highest level of utility possible. In a like manner each remaining point, P_1, P_2, P_3, and so forth, on the contract curve cc has a corresponding point in utility space, with more utility for A and less for B as we move northeast along the contract curve, reflecting the fact that, as we do so, A has a larger share of X and Y, and B a smaller share.

Several points should be noted regarding the point utility possibility frontier and its relationship to the contract curve:

- All points along the contract curve and all points on the point utility possibility frontier are Pareto-optimal efficient points.
- With respect to point D in the Edgeworth box, all points in the lens are Pareto superior (someone can be made better off and no one made worse off); in a like manner, all points to the northeast of D′ (in utility space) are Pareto superior to D′.
- With respect to point D, all points such as H, to the northwest of D, are Pareto inferior (one or both individuals are made worse off); similarly, all points to the southwest of D′ (e.g., H′) are Pareto inferior.
- With respect to any one point on the contract curve or the point utility possibility frontier, say, P_5 (in each diagram), all other points along the contract curve or along the point utility possibility frontier are, respectively, Pareto noncomparable.
- With respect to D, all points outside of the lens (exclusive of those to the northwest of D) are Pareto noncomparable; all points to the northwest and southeast of D′ are Pareto noncomparable.

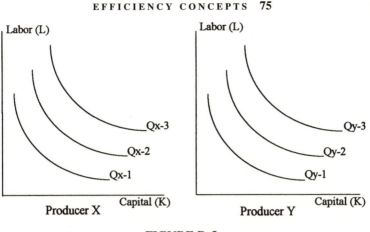

FIGURE B-5.

Efficiency in Production

PRODUCER CHOICE

Producing units make choices with respect to the acquisition and use of society's scarce resources and are assumed to produce commodities with the goal of maximizing profits. For our purposes, we assume only two producers—one producing X (Producer X) and the other producing Y (Producer Y)—and two factors of production—labor (L) and capital (K)—which are imperfect substitutes for each other. The analysis generalizes to any number of producers and inputs.

The relationship between the amount of inputs used and the level of output generated by a producer can be described with a family of isoquants. An "isoquant" is defined as a locus of points showing combinations of labor and capital inputs that can be used to produce a specified level of output of a particular commodity under the unchanging, prevailing technology. In figure B-5 we show a family of isoquants for each producer depicting cardinally measurable higher levels of output as you move to the northeast. For Producer X, Q_{x-3} is associated with a higher level of output than Q_{x-2}; likewise, Q_{x-2} is associated with a higher level of output than Q_{x-1}. Similarly, a family of isoquants for Producer Y depicts higher levels of output as you move to the northeast: Q_{y-3} is associated with a higher level of output than Q_{y-2}, and Q_{y-2} is associated with a higher level of output than Q_{y-1}.

All isoquants are negatively sloped in their efficient range, do not intersect, are mathematically dense, and are convex to the origin. The convexity property of the isoquant is a direct corollary of the principle of diminishing marginal rate of technical substitution ($MRTS_{of\ K\ for\ L}$)—the producer's isoquant is convex because of this technical regularity embodied in the law of variable proportions for factors of production that are imperfect substitutes. From one vantage point,

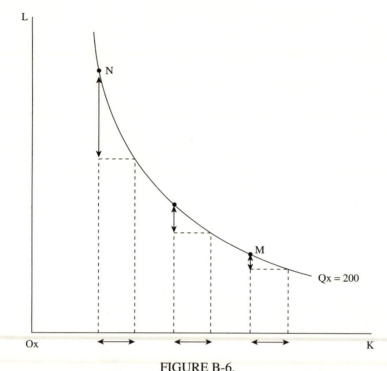

FIGURE B-6.

as we move from N to M down along the isoquant depicted in figure B-6, the marginal rate of technical substitution of capital for labor indicates the number of units of labor that can be released (under the prevailing technology) as a result of employing an additional unit of capital while maintaining the same level of output. That is, as we move from N to M down along the isoquant, in order to maintain the production of 200 units of X, for each additional unit of capital employed the producer would be forced to release less and less labor.

Perhaps a more intuitive description of the marginal rate of technical substitution of capital for labor can be captured by starting at a point such as M, and moving up along the isoquant toward N. From this vantage point the $\text{MRTS}_{\text{of K for L}}$ measures the number of units of labor that must be acquired (under the prevailing technology) for each additional unit of capital released so as to maintain the same level of output. Thus, starting at point M and moving toward N, progressively larger incremental units of labor would be needed to maintain a constant level of output ($Qx = 200$) as additional, incremental units of capital are released.

The $\text{MRTS}_{\text{of K for L}}$ is given by the slope of a line tangent to any point on an isoquant curve. As one moves down the isoquant from N toward M, the slope of

a line tangent to the points on the isoquant curve gets smaller and smaller (in absolute value terms). Thus, the convex isoquant is merely the graphical manifestation of the *principle of the diminishing marginal rate of technical substitution*.

EQUILIBRIUM AND EFFICIENCY IN PRODUCTION

Assuming there exists a given amount of labor and capital in the economy, an Edgeworth box can be formed (see figure B-7), the dimensions of which are determined by the given amounts of L and K.[84] The points within the box illustrate all possible allocations of L and K between the production of X and the production of Y. The Producer Y's family of isoquants is rotated so that its origin is now situated in the northeast corner (O_y), and, consequently, the levels of output of Y are higher as he produces on inverted isoquants further to the southwest. Producer X's family of isoquants is maintained at its initial position in the southwest corner (O_x), and the output of X is higher as he produces on isoquants further to the northeast.

Producers X and Y are each assumed to start out with an initial endowment of L and K such as that depicted by point J, where Producer X is starting out with K_1 and L_1 (employing a large amount of labor as compared to capital) on isoquant Q_{x-200}, and Producer Y is starting out with K_2 and L_2 (employing a large amount of capital as compared to labor) on isoquant Q_{y-150}. These producers will find it advantageous to realign their resource use by exchanging L for K, or K for L, so as to increase their respective levels of output. It is clear that, at point J, potential gains from trade exist with respect to the realignment of resource use. Graphically, the region for realizing this potential is the lens-shaped region demarcated by the two isoquants Q_{x-200} and Q_{y-150}—those isoquants passing through point J. Any point within this lens enables both producers to increase output relative to point J, and thus they will find it advantageous to exchange L for K, or K for L, so as to increase their respective outputs. The producers can contract and recontract—continuously groping toward higher levels of their respective outputs—until they reach a point beyond which no further gains from trade are possible, such as point G.

The underlying reason for this spontaneous contracting and recontracting to exhaust the gains from realigning resource use lies in the differing $MRTS_{of\ K\ for\ L}$ for each producer. At J, Producer X's $MRTS_{of\ K\ for\ L}$ is high (as graphically depicted by the high slope of UU′), which means that, by using an additional unit of capital, a relatively large amount of labor can be released by Producer X. Alternatively at J, Producer Y's $MRTS_{of\ K\ for\ L}$ is low (as graphically depicted by the low slope of VV′), and, by using an additional unit of labor, a relatively large amount of capital can be released by Producer Y.

---

[84] The following analysis is parallel to the Edgeworth box discussion of consumer exchange, mentioned earlier.

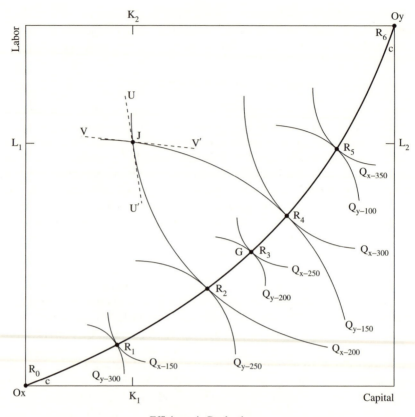

Efficiency in Production

FIGURE B-7.

Herein lie the potential gains from the realignment of resources use. By shifting labor out of the production of X and into Y and, with the trade, simultaneously shifting capital out of the production of Y and X, *using the economy's same fixed resource base*, both outputs can be increased by moving to point G—here, to Q_{x-250} and Q_{y-200}. More generally, at G it is said that the economy has attained a *general equilibrium of production*.

Notice that, at point G, the producers' isoquants are tangent to each other, indicating that Producer X's $MRTS_{of\ K\ for\ L}$ = Producer Y's $MRTS_{of\ K\ for\ L}$. Furthermore, any movement away from point G will result in a reduction in output for one or both producers. That is, point G is said to be Pareto optimal, in that there is no reallocation of inputs that can make one producer better off without making the other worse off. All this is brought together in the condition for efficiency in production, which holds that a production equilibrium is

efficient if Producer X's $MRTS_{of\ K\ for\ L}$ = Producer Y's $MRTS_{of\ K\ for\ L}$. Thus, since at point G, the MRTS between every pair of inputs is the same for all producers producing both goods, *efficiency in production* obtains.

Whereas the initial endowments reflected in point J lead to an efficient equilibrium at point G, a different set of endowments will likely generate a different trading lens and thus a different negotiated equilibrium point. The locus of all points of tangency between the producers' isoquants—such as R_0, R_1, R_2, R_3, R_4, R_5, R_6—is depicted by curve *cc* and is again termed the *contract curve*. The point on the contract curve that is ultimately realized is a product of the distribution of the initial input endowments among the two producers. The contract curve is an *optimal* locus in the sense that if the producers are located at some point not on the contract curve, merely by realigning the use of resources and moving to a point on the contract curve, more of either commodity can be produced while not reducing the other, or the production of both commodities can be increased. *Thus, conceptually, a movement from off the contract curve to a point on the contract curve is efficiency enhancing.* Consequently, once on the contract curve, any movement off it will diminish aggregate output, whereas any movement along the contract curve must result in an increase in the output of one product but at the expense of the other. Neither such movement can be efficiency enhancing. Once again, being at a point on the contract curve—a production equilibrium—constitutes a *Pareto optimum*: efficiency in production.

THE PRODUCTION POSSIBILITY FRONTIER

Given the total endowment of L and K and the family of isoquants for the production of commodities X and Y, we can construct the *production possibility frontier*. The production possibility frontier (also termed the "transformation curve") is defined as the locus of points showing the maximum attainable output of one commodity for every possible volume of output of the other commodity, given the fixed resource base of labor and capital and a fixed technology. As such, it shows the maximum combinations of outputs that can be produced given society's resource endowment. The frontier lies in a different space, not one of inputs—labor and capital—but in commodity space for goods X and Y (see figure B-8).

As described earlier, the contract curve is comprised of the locus of all tangency points between the isoquants of Producer X and Producer Y, and thus is the locus of Pareto-optimal points such as R_0, R_1, R_2, R_3, R_4, R_5, R_6. Let us plot each of these points in commodity space, beginning with R_0. This point represents a *possible* state of the economy such that all of society's scarce resources are devoted to the production of Y and none to X. At the other extreme, R_6 represents zero production of good Y and all resources devoted to the production of good X. In like manner, each remaining point on the contract

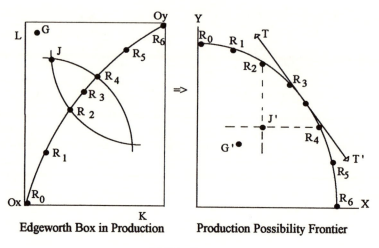

Edgeworth Box in Production   Production Possibility Frontier

FIGURE B-8.

curve cc—R_0, R_1, R_2, R_3, and so on—has a corresponding point in commodity space, with more inputs devoted to the production of good X and less to Y as we move northeastward along the contract curve. The slope of the production possibility frontier (or transformation curve) is the *marginal rate of transformation of x into y* ($MRT_{X \text{ into } Y}$) and indicates the number of units by which the production of Y must be decreased to expand the output of X by one unit. Thus, the $MRT_{X \text{ into } Y}$ is given by the slope of TT' at any given point.

Several observations should be made regarding the production possibilities frontier and its relationship to the contract curve:

- All points along the contract curve and all points on the production possibility frontier are Pareto optimal points.
- With respect to point J, points in the lens are Pareto superior; in a like manner, all points to the northeast of J' are Pareto superior.
- With respect to point J, all points such as G to the northwest of J are Pareto inferior; similarly, all points to the southwest of J' (e.g., G') are Pareto inferior.
- With respect to any one point on the contract curve or on the production possibility frontier, say, R_5 (in each diagram), all other points along the contract curve or along the production possibility frontier, respectively, are Pareto noncomparable.

Welfare Economics: Attaining Maximum Social Welfare

TWO LEVELS OF INFINITY

As previously noted, given both the level of technology and the resource endowments of labor and capital, a multiplicity (in fact, an infinite number) of Pareto-efficient production points along the contract curve in input space exist

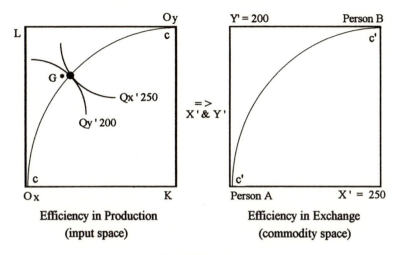

Efficiency in Production   Efficiency in Exchange
(input space)   (commodity space)

FIGURE B-9.

(see *cc* in figure B-9). Select any point among the infinite along cc, say G*. This point is associated with a particular bundle of commodities X and Y (i.e., $X' = 250$ and $Y' = 200$). This bundle of X and Y, in turn, yields the dimensions of the adjoining Edgeworth exchange box in commodity space. This Edgeworth box has its own infinite number of Pareto equilibrium points (along $c'c'$). To appreciate the manner by which welfare economics attempts to resolve these two levels of infinity—that is, how it determines the optimal allocation of inputs and outputs for society given the infinite number of efficient production and exchange equilibria—one must understand the three marginal conditions for an economy's attaining a state of *maximum social welfare*.

The three conditions to attain maximum social welfare are

1. Marginal Condition for Exchange: For the economy to attain a Pareto-optimal state, the marginal rate of substitution ($MRS_{of X for Y}$) between any pair of consumer commodities must be the same for all individuals who consume both commodities.

2. Marginal Condition for Factor Substitution (Production): For the economy to attain a Pareto-optimal state, the marginal rate of technical substitution ($MRTS_{of K for L}$) between any pair of inputs must be the same for all producers who use both inputs.

It should be clear from the preceding analysis that the inherent gains from trade incentives within a perfectly competitive equilibrium will ensure that the first and second conditions will be met.

3. Marginal Condition for Product Substitution: For the economy to attain a Pareto-optimal state, the marginal rate of transformation ($MRT_{X into Y}$) must equal the common marginal rate of substitution ($MRS_{of X for Y}$) in exchange for

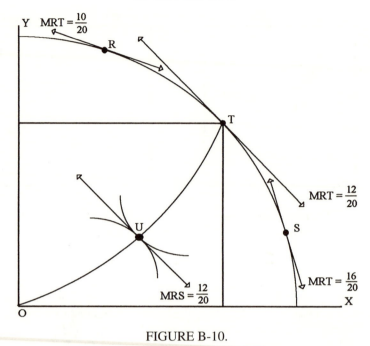

FIGURE B-10.

every pair of commodities and for every individual who consumes both—that is, $\text{MRT}_{X \text{ into } Y} = \text{MRS}_{\text{of } X \text{ for } Y}$. This latter condition needs some elaboration.

The third condition states that the MRT must equal the common MRS for both parties for both goods. The underlying market forces take the consumers' preferences as data and respond accordingly. Suppose, following figure B-10, that consumers arrive at an equilibrium at U, where the common $\text{MRS}_{\text{of } X \text{ for } Y} = 12/20$ and (for whatever reason) the economy finds itself on the transformation curve producing at point R with MRT = 10/20. Here, MRS > MRT. The MRS indicates that consumers are willing to give up 12 units of Y to get an additional 20 units of X, whereas the MRT indicates that an additional 20 units of X can be produced at a cost of only 10 units of Y. Given this, consumers will be better off if resources are shifted from the production of Y into the production of X. Market forces will thus *transform* Y into X until MRT = MRS. Similarly, if instead MRS < MRT (as at point S), then consumers will be better off if resources are reallocated from the production of X into the production of Y, and market forces will this time *transform* X into Y until MRT = MRS. Thus, if MRS is not equal to MRT, it is possible to reallocate society's resources so as to make at least one person better off without making anyone worse off, until MRT is brought into equality with MRS. At this point, no further reallocations can be made without harming at

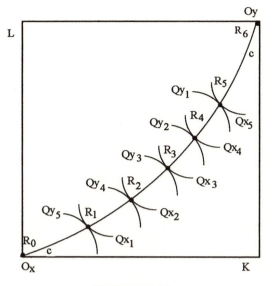

FIGURE B-11.

least one party, and thus MRS = MRT is the third condition necessary for the existence of a Pareto-efficient allocation of resources within society.

THE GRAND UTILITY POSSIBILITY FRONTIER

Whereas the point utility possibility frontier shows the maximum attainable utility for A and B given the endowments of goods X and Y in the economic system, the grand utility possibility frontier (GUPF) allows us to illustrate the maximum attainable utilities for A and B when the production of X and Y can vary (subject to the economy's resource constraint). To generate the GUPF, we continue to assume a given technology and a given amount of labor and capital, thereby determining the dimensions of the Edgeworth box in production in figure B-11.

Along the contract curve cc the second marginal condition is fulfilled. Going from input space to commodity space (plotting all the points along cc into commodity space) yields the transformation curve (i.e., the production possibility frontier) depicted in figure B-12 (where points $R_0 \rightarrow R_6$ are in a one-to-one relationship in both diagrams).

By selecting any point on the transformation curve, say R_4, and drawing horizontal and vertical lines to each axis, one can generate an R_4-specific Edgeworth exchange box with dimensions $0X_4$ and $0Y_2$, together with its own contract curve c_4c_4. All the points along c_4c_4 are Pareto optimal, indicating

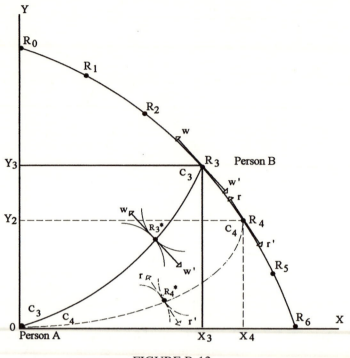

FIGURE B-12.

efficiency in exchange and thus fulfilling the first marginal condition. At point R_4 on the transformation curve (Person B's origin), the $MRT_{X \text{ into } Y}$ is given by the slope of the transformation curve; specifically, at R_4, $MRT_{X \text{ into } Y}$ = the slope of rr'. Given the selection of point R_4, the third marginal condition will be satisfied at a point along the c_4c_4 contract curve, R_4^* where, as indicated, the $MRT_{X \text{ into } Y}$ equals the common $MRS_{\text{of } X \text{ for } Y}$ for persons A and B.

Moving from the interior commodity space to utility space, one can now plot the point utility possibility frontier uniquely associated with *point* R_4 (hence its name). As we see in figure B-13, plotting c_4c_4 into utility space yields the point utility possibility frontier c_4c_4, which includes point R_4^*, corresponding to R_4^* in figure B-12. As should be clear from the foregoing analysis, point R_4^* is the only one along c_4c_4 that meets all three marginal conditions for the economy attaining a state of maximum social welfare.

To develop the grand utility possibility frontier, it is necessary to return to figure B-12 and conceptually select another point along the transformation curve, say R_3. One can now generate an R_3-specific Edgeworth exchange box with dimensions OX_3 and OY_3 together with its own contract curve c_3c_3. As

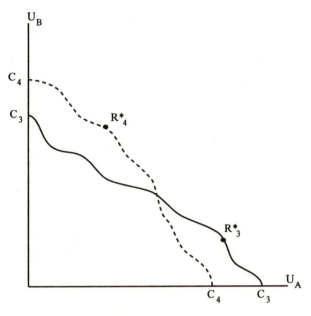

FIGURE B-13.

before, all the points along c_3c_3 are Pareto optimal, representing efficiency in exchange and thus fulfilling the first marginal condition. At point R_3 on the transformation curve, the $MRT_{X \text{ into } Y}$ is the same as the slope of the transformation curve (specifically, at R_3, $MRT_{X \text{ into } Y} =$ the slope of ww'). Given the selection of point R_3, the third marginal condition will be satisfied at a point on the new c_3c_3 contract curve, R_3^* where the $MRT_{X \text{ into } Y}$ will again equal the common $MRS_{\text{of X for Y}}$.

Moving from the interior commodity space to utility space, we can now plot another point utility possibility frontier uniquely associated this time with point R_3. Plotting c_3c_3 into utility space yields the point utility possibility frontier c_3c_3 with its unique point—R_3^* (see figure B-13). Like R_4^*, R_3^* meets all three marginal conditions for the economy attaining a state of maximum social welfare. This process is repeated over and over by selecting each and every point on the transformation curve, generating a corresponding point utility possibility curve, and thereby yielding a collection of unique R^*-ed points—each of which meets all three efficiency conditions. Connecting all the R^*-ed points generates the *grand utility possibility frontier* (GUPF) in figure B-14, an infinite locus of all Pareto-optimal points, each one representing states of the economy that fulfill all three marginal conditions necessary for an economy to attain a state of maximum social welfare.

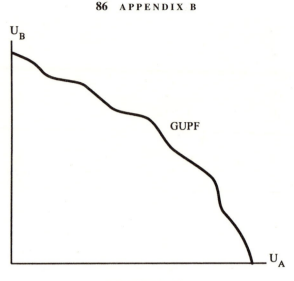

FIGURE B-14.

CLOSING OUT THE ANALYSIS: SOCIAL WELFARE FUNCTIONS

Given the infinite number of states of the economy that fulfill all three conditions for attaining maximum social welfare, in an attempt to close out the analysis, the existence of real-valued social welfare functions was postulated to give a basis upon which to choose among these optimal points.[85] Two types of social welfare functions were contemplated: social welfare contours in utility space and social indifference curves in commodity space. In either case, a social welfare function would have to be formulated, recognizing that political and/or ethical considerations must be made explicitly and imposed either through a collectivity or through a dictator. The social welfare function implies the existence of an ordinal ranking of alternative utility levels achieved by the various members of the community (in our case, persons A and B). Thus the concept of a real-valued social welfare function is somewhat analogous to that of indifference curves: The idea of a family of indifference curves for an individual is conceptually aggregated into a family of social welfare contours for the society (SWC_1, SWC_2, SWC_3, etc.) as depicted in figure B-15. Each social welfare contour defines a politically determined, subjective trade-off between the utilities of persons A and B. As society moves to the northeast, each social welfare contour represents a higher level of societal welfare.

---

[85] A detailed discussion of real-valued social welfare functions (also known as Bergson-Samuelson welfare functions) is provided by Mueller (1989, pp. 373–83). For the original formulations, see Bergson (1938) and Samuelson (1947, ch. 8; 1955; 1956).

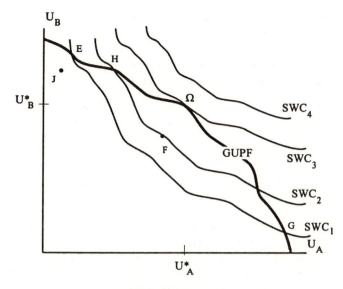

FIGURE B-15.

Of the infinite number of Pareto-optimal points making up the grand utility possibility frontier (GUPF), Ω is the only point that has unequivocal prescriptive significance. It is not merely Pareto optimal; given the social welfare function and the political and/or ethical considerations subsumed in it, this point is also uniquely associated with maximum social welfare. In this regard, Pareto optimality (or efficiency) is said to be a *necessary* but not a *sufficient* condition for an economy's attainment of a position of maximum social welfare. The three marginal conditions yield only the Pareto-efficiency requirement; alone they do not guarantee a social welfare maximum. For the latter, an explicit social welfare function (derived solely from political/ethical considerations) is needed to attain, in the words of Kneese, the *optimum optimorum*.

Points to note:

- If the SWF is known, we could not maximize utility at Ω without simultaneously achieving efficiency in both exchange and production.
- In accordance with the first optimality theorem, a perfectly competitive market may achieve efficiency, which can lead the economy to attain a point on the GUPF but not necessarily at Ω; perfectly competitive markets may instead have the economy come to rest at such points as H, G, or, indeed, anywhere along the GUPF.
- Certain moves can worsen social welfare but increase efficiency and vice versa. For example, a move from F to G in figure B-15 represents a gain in efficiency (a move from off to on the GUPF) but a loss in social welfare (from SWC_2 to SWC_1). Likewise, a movement from J to F (although neither Pareto superior

nor Pareto efficient) does enhance social welfare as compared to the move from J to E, which is Pareto efficient but reflcts a lower level of social welfare as compared to the inefficient F.

- Note that, given the existence of a social welfare function, the selection of Ω encompasses efficiency in exchange and production and yields:

  1. a unique distribution of utility for persons A and B ($U_A{}^*$, $U_B{}^*$);

  2. a particular X, Y aggregate output combination on the production possibility frontier;

  3. a unique output allocation of commodities X and Y for person A and person B; and

  4. a unique allocation of labor and capital for the respective production of each commodity, X and Y.

- Finally, it must be observed that without reference to a social welfare function, exclusive reliance on market solutions (under the conditions specified for perfect competition) will enable the economy to attain some point on the GUPF, barring problems with information, externalities, and public goods. If society is not satisfied with that particular outcome, then the theory of welfare economics proffers the following:

  > [The] observation . . . that the market mechanisms might produce a good (Pareto-optimal) result, but not the very best result, motivates the second basic theorem of welfare economics. Suppose someone . . . concludes that of all the Pareto-optimal distributions of goods possible in an economy, distribution X is the very best, the ideal of the optimal. The second basic theorem says that, with minor modifications involving transfers of cash among various people, the competitive market mechanism can be used to reach X. That is, X can be achieved via the interplay of profit-maximizing firms and/or utility-maximizing individuals. Consequently, it is unnecessary to have a huge bureaucracy to decide who gets what in the economy. (Feldman 1980, pp. 3–4)

In summary, a Pareto optimum—being on the GUPF—can be interpreted as a state of the economy from which it is impossible to improve anyone's welfare, in the sense of moving a person to a position that (s)he prefers—either by "transforming" commodities through the realignment of resources in production, or by "trading" commodities in exchange—without impairing someone else's welfare. To the extent that a policy is set forth that conforms to the Pareto principle—that is, someone is being made better off and no one made worse off—it both provides the underlying rationale to go forward with a public policy or legal change and is consistent with the thrust of Pareto, providing the recommendary force without the necessity of making interpersonal comparisons of utility and thereby avoiding the ambiguities involved in evaluating changes in welfare. Although the notion of a social welfare function was thought to serve to close out the analysis, it was largely put to rest by the work

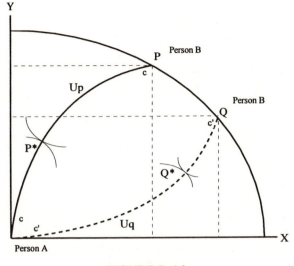

FIGURE B-16.

of Kenneth J. Arrow (1951), who demonstrated that there are no rules for collective choice—a social welfare function, even one with apparently reasonable and widely accepted conditions—that yields a complete and transitive, unambiguous ranking of social preferences. As an alternative to this search for global efficiency, the compensation principle offers a more piecemeal approach to evaluating legal change.

THE COMPENSATION PRINCIPLE: KALDOR-HICKS EFFICIENCY

The graphical analysis of the compensation principle is typically undertaken using point utility possibility curves,[86] and as such does not search for a globally efficient solution associated with the GUPF. Instead, it is more modest in that it is piecemeal and attempts to compare and evaluate (in as unambiguous a manner as possible) two different states of the economy brought on by the promulgation of a government policy or legal change.

For diagrammatic simplicity, it is assumed throughout that a government policy or legal change will take society (persons A and B) from a point such as P (the starting point) in figure B-16 to a point such as Q (the ending point) along society's transformation curve for commodities Y and X. The analytical concern is with the two associated point utility possibility frontiers, U_p and U_q.

[86] The analysis can also be carried out by reference to the Scitovsky community indifference curves in output space. For example see Rowley and Peacock (1975, pp. 46–51).

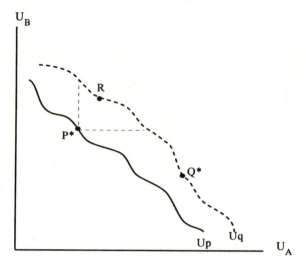

FIGURE B-17.

Thus, in figure B-16, before the government promulgates its new policy or institutes the legal change, the economy is at point P, with U_p as the relevant contract curve cc.

Subsequently, once the government policy or legal change is in effect, the economy comes to rest at point Q with U_q as the relevant contract curve c'c'. It should be clear that the thrust of the compensation principle is the attempt to assess whether going forth with the legal change resulting in situation Q and contract curve U_q, together with a new distribution of welfare depicted as Q* (which is to the benefit of person A at the expense of person B), is or is not unambiguously preferable to maintaining the existing situation P and contract curve U_p together with the P* distribution of welfare (this initial situation being to the benefit of person B vis-à-vis person A).

In assessing a movement from P to Q, and as we go from commodity space to utility space, there exist four possible cases to be analyzed, each depending upon the relative positioning of the point utility possibility curves before versus after the legal change.[87]

• Case 1: The two point utility possibility curves U_q and U_p do not intersect, and U_q lies wholly outside of U_p as in figure B-17. This case yields an unambiguous result. Clearly if the legal change results in a movement from P* to Q*, total utility rises and person A's gain exceeds the loss of person B. Consequently, person A is in a position to compensate person B for agreeing to the change. The graphical test is whether there exists a Pareto-superior point (a

---

[87] These four cases are variously presented in Price (1977, pp. 19–30). For an alternative graphical treatment, see DeSerpa (1988, pp. 468–72).

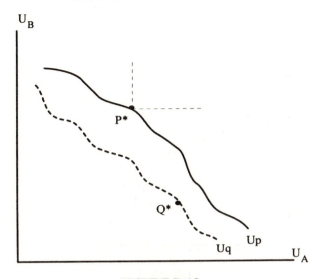

FIGURE B-18.

point such as R to the northeast of P*) along U_q. In this case, with the legal change, in economic state Q, person A would potentially be able to compensate person B (along U_q) to a point such as R, where both would be better off than under the economic state observed in state P along U_p. The compensation principle would recommend going ahead with the government policy or legal change.

• Case 2: The two point utility possibility curves U_q and U_p do not intersect, and U_p lies wholly outside U_q as in figure B-18. This case also yields an unambiguous result. Clearly, if the legal change results in a movement from P* to Q*, total utility falls and person A's gain does not exceed the loss of person B. Consequently, it is impossible for person A to compensate person B for agreeing to the change. Again, the graphical test is whether there exists a Pareto-superior point (a point to the northeast of P*) along U_q. As there is not, in this case, person A would not potentially be able to compensate person B (along U_q), and the legal change resulting in economic state Q should be foregone, since neither person could be made better off without the other being made worse off. The compensation principle would recommend maintaining the economic state associated with P.

• Case 3: The two point utility possibility curves U_q and U_p intersect with P* and Q* as shown, respectively, in figure B-19. This case represents the Kaldor compensation principle as originally formulated, together with the inherent paradox and ambiguity. The movement to Q can be shown to be preferable to the initial state of the economy P. For example, if the legal change results in a movement from P* to Q*, and person A's gain exceeds the loss to

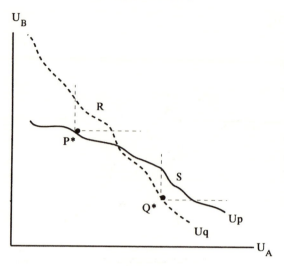

FIGURE B-19.

person B, person A is in a position to compensate person B to agree to the change. Once again, the graphical test is whether there exists a Pareto-superior point (a point to the northeast of P*) along U_q. Here, as in Case 1, there is— point R. With the legal change to Q, person A would potentially be able to compensate person B (along U_q) to a point such as R, where both would be better off than under the economic state observed in state P. The compensation principle thus would recommend going ahead with the contemplated government policy or legal change.

Suppose, however, that once at Q*, we again employ the Kaldor criterion using the graphical test to determine whether there exists a Pareto-superior point, this time a point to the northeast of Q* along U_p. It can be observed that, indeed, such a point does exist, namely, point S. Thus, in going from Q back to P, person B would potentially be able to compensate person A (along U_p) to a point such as S, where both would be better off. Therein lies the paradox. In this case, with the original legal change, from P to Q, the compensation principle (as proffered by Kaldor) would recommend going ahead with the change in government policy. Once the change is instituted and the economy is in state Q, however, the compensation principle would then recommend reverting back to the initial policy associated with P. Under this welfare criterion, each state can be shown to be superior to the other.

• Case 4: The two point utility possibility curves U_q and U_p intersect with P* and Q*, respectively, as shown in figure B-20. This case represents the Hick's formulation of the compensation principle, which states that Q is superior to P if the loser cannot compensate the winner for forgoing the gains from the legal

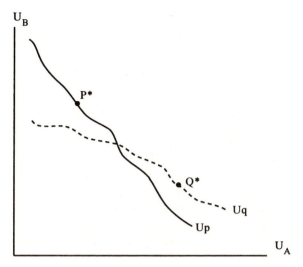

FIGURE B-20.

change. Note that, in figure B-20, person B's loss is not sufficient to compensate person A, the gainer, into forgoing the legal change. Thus, the *Hicks* compensation principle would recommend going ahead with the legal change. This, however, raises another potential ambiguity. Notice that in contemplating a policy change that would transform the economy from P^* to Q^*, person A cannot compensate person B for accepting the change. That is, this policy change does not meet the *Kaldor* test (i.e., there are no points to the northeast of P^* along U_q). Thus, the Hicks and Kaldor tests can give contradictory answers to the question of whether a given policy change will increase social well-being.

It is generally recognized, following the work of Tibor Scitovsky (1941–42), that it is only when both Kaldor's and Hick's conditions are satisfied that a legal change can unambiguously be judged an improvement. Thus, the modern-day formulation of the compensation principle is as follows: A change may be judged to improve society well-being if and only if both the gainers from the change could compensate the losers for their losses and remain better off themselves, *and* the losers could not have compensated the gainers to forgo their gains without being themselves worse off than in their original position.[88]

---

[88] See, for example, Price (1977, p. 23).

CHAPTER 2

Chicago Law and Economics

A second meaning of "justice," and the most
common I would argue, is simply "efficiency." When
we describe as "unjust" convicting a person without
a trial, taking property without just compensation, or
failing to require a negligent automobile driver to
answer in damages to the victim of his carelessness,
we can be interpreted as meaning simply that the
conduct or practice in question wastes resources.
(Posner 1975, p. 777)

INTRODUCTION

WHILE the roots of Law and Economics go back at least to Adam Smith and Jeremy Bentham,[1] it came of age as an intellectual discipline within economics and law in the 1960s and 1970s through the work of such notable figures as Ronald H. Coase, Guido Calabresi, Henry Manne, Gary Becker, and Richard A. Posner.[2] The work of these scholars—of whom Posner as professor, scholar, and judge is perhaps the foremost exponent—forms the core of the Chicago approach to law and economics, an approach that has attracted a large following and has come to dominate scholarship within the economic analysis of law. For the purposes of this discussion, the Chicago school is deemed to encompass most of the scholarship falling under the umbrella of "mainstream law and economics," as reflected in the pages of, for example, the *Journal of Law and Economics*, the *Journal of Legal Studies*, the *American Law and Economics Review, Research in Law and Economics*, and many of the major law reviews.[3]

This having been said, the history of law and economics at the University of Chicago begins well before the birth in the 1960s of the "new law and economics" that is now synonymous with the Chicago school label. The distinction that

---

[1] For Smith, see his *Lectures on Jurisprudence* (1978); on Bentham, see Posner (1998a; 2001b ch. 1).

[2] Coase, Calabresi, Manne, and Posner were honored as the "four founders" of law and economics at the Plenary Session of the American Law and Economics Association on May 24, 1991. Coase and Becker have been awarded the Nobel Prize in economics.

[3] This is also the approach to law and economics that is reflected in the major texts in the field, including Posner (2003), Cooter and Ulen (2004), Hirsch (1999), Shavell (2004), and a comprehensive casebook by Barnes and Stout (1992).

is often made between the "old" and "new" Chicago law and economics within the Chicago oral tradition is part folklore and part fact,[4] and, to appreciate the nature of this distinction, it is useful to mention a few of the highlights of this earlier era of economics and law. As will become evident, although some of the early history and subsequent success of Chicago law and economics is attributable to scholars in the Department of Economics at Chicago, much of the credit owes to the intellectual edifice provided by the faculty of the law school.[5]

The Law School

As we noted in chapter 1, the Realist-Institutionalist interaction of the 1920s and 1930s did a great deal to bring law and economics together. A similar interaction, but with a distinctly different flavor, commenced at nearly the same time at the University of Chicago. Within the law school, the origins of Chicago law and economics can be traced back to the latter part of the 1930s, when the faculty, under the deanship of Wilber Katz, instituted a four-year interdisciplinary legal studies curriculum that included courses in economics and accounting (Katz 1937). In 1939, the law school appointed its first economist, Henry Simons, to the faculty. Simons had been a lecturer in the Department of Economics and was a former student of Professor Frank Knight, who was in many respects the father of the modern price-theoretic tradition of Chicago economics (Kitch 1983a, p. 167).[6] Simons's appointment to the law school was the culmination of many episodes of political infighting between Frank Knight and Paul Douglas within the Department of Economics. Douglas—a strong proponent of Keynesian thinking and advocate of government intervention in the economy—and others within the economics department fought both Simons's promotion and tenure. As a result, Simons was ultimately appointed to the law faculty to teach a course titled "Economic Analysis of Public Policy" (essentially a course in applied microeconomics for lawyers), and, in 1945, he was promoted to full professor and became the first economist granted tenure by the law school. By the mid-1940s, Simons

---

[4] The use of the "old" and "new" terminology is evidenced in Posner (1975, p. 759) and Kitch (1983a) and is explored more fully in the following section.

[5] This brief survey of the Chicago school of law and economics prior to 1960 draws on the work of Reder (1982), Duxbury (1995, ch. 5), Kitch (1983a), and Coase (1993); see also Hovenkamp (1995) and Medema (1998, 2007a).

[6] Frank Knight's students included, among others, Milton Friedman, James M. Buchanan, Aaron Director, and George Stigler, all of whom, with the exception of Director, have received the Nobel Prize in Economics. Gary Becker was a student of Jacob Viner, another stalwart in the economics department in the early days of the Chicago school and later a professor at Princeton, where Becker did his undergraduate work. Becker then went on to become a professor at the University of Chicago and was later awarded the Nobel Prize in economics.

had established himself as a contributing, but by no means seminal, figure at the headwaters of the Chicago law and economics movement,[7] and his view that law should be structured so as to promote competitive markets reflected the perspective that has come to be associated with Chicago law and economics. His tenure at the law school helped to lay a solid foundation and provide a receptive environment for the then-emerging field of law and economics.

Simons helped to ensure the continuity and growth of Chicago law and economics through his role (together with Friedrich A. Hayek and financial backing from the Volker Fund) in bringing to the law school the individual most responsible for firmly establishing the law and economics tradition at Chicago, Aaron Director. Director was a student of Frank Knight, had been a member of the economics faculty in the early 1930s, and had authored articles that had a distinct Chicago price-theoretic flavor.[8] After being away for a short time, Director returned to the University of Chicago in 1946. Simons urged the law school to have Director assume the directorship of a university center (affiliated with the law school) dedicated to undertaking "a study of a suitable legal and institutional framework of an effective competitive system" (Coase 1993, p. 246), and he was appointed to that position in 1946. Director also took over responsibility for teaching the course on "Economic Analysis of Public Policy" from Simons, who died in the summer of 1946.

Subsequent to his law school appointment, Director was invited by Edward Levi to collaborate in the teaching of the antitrust course. Director continued teaching the course throughout his time at the law school, and it was during this period that the Chicago approach to antitrust law began to emerge as a distinct body of thought. Antitrust had long been an area of law particularly open to the influence of economic ideas, and it was through his teaching in this course that Director, armed with the tools of price theory, had an especially formidable impact on both Chicago law students and a number of his colleagues. Director's students included Robert H. Bork, John S. McGee, Henry Manne, Edmund Kitch, Bernard H. Seigan, and Wesley J. Liebeler; colleagues who were impacted included Ward Bowman and Lester G. Telser. Director's antitrust students, many of whom went on to very successful careers as economists in their own right, speak of the "conversion" that they experienced in this class.[9] Levi would teach a traditional antitrust course for four days each

[7] In his review of the history of law and economics at Chicago, Coase stated that "[w]hat can, I think, be said with confidence is that Simons . . . played little or no part in the development of the ideas which make up the modern subject of law and economics" (Coase 1993, p. 242). Simons' work on tax law, however, is very worthy of note in this context, and Posner continues to cite it in his discussion of tax law in his *Economic Analysis of Law*. See, for example, Simons (1934, 1938, 1948, 1950) and the discussion by Groves (1974).

[8] See, for example, Director (1933).

[9] This "conversion" is openly discussed throughout "The Intellectual History of Law and Economics" conference as recounted by Kitch (1983a).

week, and then Director would come in on the fifth day and, using the tools of price theory, show that the traditional legal approach could not stand up to rigors of microeconomic analysis. As Posner points out,

> The "kinked demand curve," "workable competition," "cut-throat competition," "leverage," "administered prices," and the other characteristic concepts of the industrial organization of this period had this in common: they were not derived from and were often inconsistent with economic theory, and in particular with the premises of rational profit maximization. They were derived from observation, unsystematic and often superficial, of business behavior. Director's approach was the opposite. He explained tie-ins, resale price maintenance, and other business behavior described in antitrust cases not by studying the practices but by looking for an explanation for them that squared with basic economic theory. (Posner 1978, p. 931)

The result was, as Liebeler put it, "We learned that there was a system of analysis [price theory] that (1) was quite relevant to the stuff we talked about in law school and (2) was much more powerful than anything that the law professors, than anything Ed Levi had to tell us" (quoted in Kitch 1983a, p. 183).[10]

Director taught his students that the appropriate goal for antitrust law was the promotion of efficiency. Reflecting the emphasis within the Chicago tradition on the efficacy of the competitive system, monopoly was viewed as occasional, unstable, and transitory—a potential outcome of the competitive process, but one that would soon be removed (in effect if not in existence) by competitive pressures. Given this, rigorous antitrust enforcement was thought to be unnecessary, and, even when monopolies were shown to generate long-term inefficiencies, the governmental cure was thought to be often worse than the disease, owing to the inefficiencies of government. The past several decades of legal-economic scholarship bear witness to Herbert Hovenkamp's (1986, p. 1020) comment that "the Chicago School has done more for antitrust policy than any other coherent economic theory since the New Deal. No one . . . can escape [its] influence on antitrust analysis." Indeed, and as we will show later in this chapter, the Chicago school has become so firmly established within this area that it can claim a partial victory in what Eleanor Fox (1987a) has called the "battle for the soul of antitrust."[11]

Director's impact at the law school, however, went far beyond antitrust: he was the prime mover in the early professionalization of Chicago law and

---

[10] The transcript of the conference indicates that, over the course of time, Professor Levi also became converted (Kitch 1983a). Indeed, in 1951 Director and Levi (1951, p. 282) wrote, "We believe the conclusions of economics do not justify the application of the antitrust laws in many situations in which the laws are now being applied."

[11] See also Fox (1981).

economics. Director formally established the nation's first law and economics program (derivative of the school's antitrust project), which maintained visiting fellowships for law and economics scholars, set in place the workshop in the law school (an arena of vigorous debate over issues of current research, already an established tradition within the economics department), and, in 1958, founded the *Journal of Law and Economics*. Throughout his tenure at Chicago, he imparted a persuasive message to the students—that regulation was the proper function of markets, not government. This message was one that often resulted in legal reasoning losing out to economic analysis and was, to the students of law, "a message which was at once both unfamiliar and yet quite understandable" (Duxbury 1995, p. 344).

Kitch, a Chicago-trained lawyer (1961–64) and later the director of the Law and Economics Program at Chicago, describes the thrust of law and economics at the Chicago law school during this era in terms that make it seem like a perfectly natural activity for law school professors to pursue—a view, in fact, very consistent with the rationale behind the Legal Realists' blending of economics and law:

> The interest . . . in economics did not come out of any anti-interventionist thinking. It essentially came out of the idea that the legal system is going to be doing this now [i.e., impacting the economic system] and that means we need to learn how to do it right and maybe economists know something about how to do it right. . . . There is a great legitimacy given to the idea that government is going to be doing these things and we in the law schools should try to help the government do it right. (Kitch 1983a, pp. 175–76)

Indeed, this was the very perspective motivating much of the work of one of the other major founders of Chicago law and economics in this early period, Ronald H. Coase.

Coase was educated at the London School of Economics and served on the faculty there from 1935–51, when he emigrated to the United States. He held appointments at the Universities of Buffalo and Virginia before moving on to the University of Chicago Law School in 1964. Although Coase is most closely associated with the Chicago school, his seminal article, "The Problem of Social Cost," which is the cornerstone of Chicago law and economics literature (see pp. 107–19), was actually written several years before he arrived at Chicago. One of Coase's major reasons for going to the law school was to assume the editorship (with Director) of the *Journal of Law and Economics*, and he describes his motivation in going to Chicago as follows: "I don't think that I would ever have come to the University of Chicago had it not been for the existence of the *Journal of Law and Economics*. That's what I wanted to do. I wanted to get what Aaron had started going for the whole profession—and when I say the profession, I mean the economics profession; I have no interest in lawyers or legal education" (Coase, quoted in Kitch

1983a, p. 192). That someone so avowedly indifferent to legal education became such a major figure in the evolution of the economic analysis of law is itself an interesting episode in the history of ideas (Medema 1994, 1998)—but then, Coase could not have anticipated that the influence of his insights in "The Problem of Social Cost" would be at least as great on legal scholarship as on economics.

The Economics Department

Although the events in the law school laid the foundation for the development of law and economics at Chicago, a full understanding of what transpired also necessitates an appreciation of the scholarship generated by the faculty of the Department of Economics, both before World War II and thereafter. Especially with respect to economic method, there were really two Chicago schools of thought, roughly divided in time by the war (Duxbury 1995, p. 367; Reder 1982; Emmett, forthcoming).[12] The perspective of the prewar Chicago school is evidenced in the scholarship of Frank Knight, Jacob Viner, Paul Douglas, and Henry Schultz, who were themselves by no means of a homogeneous perspective. In simple terms, proponents of the early Chicago approach generally accepted the propositions that had been at the heart of economics since the publication of Adam Smith's *Wealth of Nations* (1776)—within a liberal democracy, the rational pursuit of economic self-interest by economic actors was taken as given, competition was seen as inherent within and intrinsic to economic life, and market-generated outcomes were said to be generally superior to those resulting from government interference with the market mechanism. Although these propositions (the latter two in particular) were being increasingly called into question within the profession at large during the 1930s, their continuity within the Chicago tradition served (and continues to serve) to set the Chicago perspective apart from much of the rest of the economics profession.

From this group, it was Knight who had the most impact on what has come to be known as Chicago law and economics. While his writings were a significant force, his greatest influence came through the perspective that he imparted to his students—most importantly, for present purposes, Milton Friedman, George Stigler, and Director. Knight's interest and strength did not lie in the use of formal mathematical and quantitative tools, but rather in the economic way of thinking and in applying this way of thinking to the development of

---

[12] For wide-ranging discussions of the Chicago school of economics, see Bronfenbrenner (1962), Coats (1963), Miller (1962), Samuels (1976), Reder (1982) and Emmett (forthcoming). It should be noted that, even today, the Chicago school is not nearly as homogeneous as some would make it out to be.

economic ideas and to the tearing down of what he saw as false theories that were becoming increasingly fashionable within economics (Reder 1982, pp. 4, 6).

The next generation of Chicago economists kept one foot in this camp but also moved beyond it. As Duxbury (1995, p. 368) has pointed out, whereas the earlier generation of Chicago economists "had grasped and applied certain of the basic insights of Adam Smith . . . [p]ost-war Chicagoans were more intent on elaborating and extending these insights." In line with this, the new generation undertook to demonstrate, in formal terms, the detailed nexus between competitive markets and efficient outcomes. The nature of these price-theoretic undertakings was necessarily abstract and typically ahistorical, largely relying on positive, empirical research and mathematical analysis, all very much in keeping with broader movements within neoclassical economics at the time, and toward which Knight, ironically, had been rather hostile.[13] In this sense, then, as Reder (1982, p. 6) has noted, "Knight contributed to the formation of their minds but did not influence the direction of their research." Following the lead of Friedman and Stigler, postwar Chicago economists, buttressed by their empirical research, emphasized the efficacy of the competitive market system, arguing for less government intervention, fewer wealth redistribution policies, reliance on voluntary exchange with a concomitant reliance on the common law for mediating conflicts, and an across-the-board promotion of more private enterprise—which, based on the evidence provided by their empirical research, would facilitate a more efficient allocation of resources.

Exploding the Boundaries: Becker and Posner

There is no doubt that the economic analysis of law—Chicago law and economics—has been the most successful of economists' imperialistic forays into other disciplines, though their move into political science in the form of public choice theory, too, has had major influence on the "invaded" field (see chapter 3 of this book). Coase's "The Problem of Social Cost" (1960) and Calabresi's "Some Thoughts on Risk Distribution and the Law of Torts"

---

[13] James M. Buchanan, a Chicago-trained economist and also a Nobel Prize winner, has not been reluctant to castigate the methodological thrust of "economic science" as practiced in the 1980s and exemplified by many of the positivists working within the Chicago tradition. His reference to "economic science" is purely pejorative, and he argues that the modern economists' focus on tools and mathematical prowess has rendered them illiterate as to fundamental ideas and principles of economics and, further, has turned them into "ideological eunuchs." Most academic programs in economics, he says, are "now controlled by rent-recipients who simply try to ape the mainstream work of their peers in the discipline . . . and they seem to get their kicks from the discovery of proofs of propositions relevant only for their own fantasy lands" (Buchanan 1986, pp. 14–15).

(1961) raised many issues for both economists and lawyers; in particular, they revealed both the economic nature of many of the questions of legal analysis—that legal rules and decisions across many traditional fields of law beget both benefits and costs, and thus are amenable to analysis in efficiency terms—and the potential for the application of economic analysis to the law.[14] The intellectual direction and concerns of both the law school and the economics department transformed the academic landscape at Chicago, as the institutionalization of Chicago law and economics and the growing imperialism of the science of economics moved forward. This idea began to stimulate economic analyses of legal questions in the areas of property, contract, and tort law. Then, in 1968, came Becker's pathbreaking economic analysis of criminal behavior and criminal law. By the early 1970s the new law and economics had emerged as a recognized field of inquiry, best marked, perhaps, by the publication of Posner's *Economic Analysis of Law* (1972).

Becker's contribution to the Chicago school during this era is of particular import for the development of the economic analysis of law. Seizing upon the idea that economics is the science of choice, Becker employed the Chicago price-theoretic framework to explain choices across a broad range of nonmarket behavior, including racial discrimination in labor markets (Becker 1957); criminal behavior and law enforcement (Becker 1968); the organization of the family (including marriage and divorce), the decision to have children, and the division of labor within the household (Becker 1976); altruism (Becker and Barro 1988; Becker and Murphy 1988a); and addictive behavior, including drug use (Becker and Murphy 1988b; Becker, Grossman, and Murphy 1991). These works illustrate Becker's distinct approach to the economic analysis of law and typifies, perhaps better than any other scholarship, what has come to be known as the "economics imperialism."[15]

Posner received his LL.B. from Harvard Law School in 1962, and the period following his graduation was spent in Washington, first clerking for Supreme Court Justice William J. Brennan, Jr., and then working in the Kennedy and Johnson administrations. Posner was appointed associate professor of law at Stanford in 1968, and it was there that he came into contact with Aaron Director, who exposed him to the economic approach to analyzing legal rules. Posner moved on to the University of Chicago Law School in 1969. Since 1981, he has served as a judge on the U.S. Court of Appeals for the Seventh Circuit, including as Chief Judge from 1993 until 2000. During his tenure on the court, Posner has continued both to teach regularly at Chicago and to publish at a prolific rate.

---

[14] See Grembi (2003) on the distinction between the respective contributions of Coase and Calabresi; see also Posner (2005) and Hylton (2005) for discussions of Calabresi's role in the development of the economic analysis of law.

[15] On economic imperialism, see Brenner (1980), Posner (1993a), and Lazear (2000).

It would surely not be an overstatement to rank Posner among the foremost legal scholars of the second half of the twentieth century. For if, as both its advocates and critics acknowledge, the law and economics movement ranks as the most significant development in jurisprudential analysis during this period, Posner, as the leading presence in this movement in scholarship and on the bench, deserves much of the credit.[16] His *Economic Analysis of Law*, now in its sixth edition, served both to develop the field well beyond the classical applications to property, contract, tort, and criminal law, and to present the subject matter in a way that facilitated its integration into the law school curriculum. He has taken on issues as diverse as sex, aging and euthanasia, the AIDS epidemic, law and literature, sexually transmitted diseases, the Clinton impeachment proceedings, the Supreme Court's role in the 2000 Bush-Gore election, cloning, homosexuality, surrogate parenting, religious freedom, and adoptions, as well as a vast array of more traditional topics spanning virtually every area of law and jurisprudence—all these analyses being infused, in some cases to a greater extent and in other cases to a lesser extent, with an underlying economic flavor. If Becker opened the floodgates to an economic analysis that touches on all areas of life, it was Posner who took this approach and ran with it to the far corners of the legal arena.

FUNDAMENTAL BUILDING BLOCKS OF THE CHICAGO APPROACH

The defining characteristic of the Chicago approach is the straightforward application of microeconomic (or price-theoretic) analysis to the law.[17] As such, this approach is grounded in the following premises: (i) individuals are rational maximizers of their satisfactions in their nonmarket as well as their market behavior; (ii) individuals respond to price incentives in nonmarket as well as market behavior; and (iii) legal rules and legal outcomes can be assessed on the basis of their efficiency properties. Along with (iii) comes a two pronged normative prescription; first, that legal decision-making should promote efficiency, and, second, that in formulating public policy, decision-makers should rely heavily on markets. Each of these premises will be discussed in turn.

The Rational Maximization of Satisfaction

The assumption that economic agents are rational maximizers—that is, they make purposeful choices so as to pursue consistent ends using efficient means[18]—stands as a cornerstone of modern economic theory. Under this view,

---

[16] For a further discussion of Posner's contributions see Medema (2007b).

[17] See Ulen (1989).

[18] Note that this definition of rationality does not imply the necessity of conscious deliberation.

individuals are assumed to have a set of preferences that are complete, reflexive, transitive, and continuous. Given these conditions, it can be shown that consumer preferences can be represented by an ordinal utility function,[19] based on which, assuming that individuals are perfectly able to process all relevant information about the alternatives available to them, they can rank all possible outcomes according to their relative desirability. Consumers will then choose to consume the bundle of goods/activities that maximizes utility. Similarly, firms are viewed as profit maximizers, with the result that the level of output produced, the price charged, the composition of inputs and of payments thereto, the contracting practices of the firm, and so on are those that will maximize the firm's profits.

The rational maximization assumption has straightforward implications for the individual choice process. As was made clear in appendix A to chapter 1, individuals will engage in additional units of an activity as long as the additional benefit derived from another unit of that activity is greater than or equal to the additional cost—that is, as long as marginal benefit is greater than or equal to marginal cost—whether that activity is the consumption of goods, production, or the supply of labor. Thus, for example, the decision as to how many apples to consume comes down to an evaluation of whether the additional benefit from each additional apple consumed is greater than or equal to the cost, in terms of the best foregone alternative to consuming that apple. In the present context, decisions regarding unlawful activity (e.g., to breach a contract, to take precaution against breach, to engage in potentially tortious conduct, or to engage in criminal behavior) become a matter of comparing marginal benefits with marginal costs. From this perspective, those who break the law are not essentially different from the rest of the population; they simply have different preferences, opportunity costs, and constraints and engage in "illegal" activities because these are the activities that maximize their net benefit. Some commentators have challenged this idea on the grounds that individuals do not have full and complete information—but information, too, is a good, additional units of which are consumed only as long as marginal benefit is greater than or equal to marginal cost. Thus, as the price of information rises relative to the associated marginal benefit, so too does the optimal level of ignorance.[20] This, in fact, is part of the economic rationale for the failure to specify fully all contingencies in a contract, or the failure to fully abate pollution or eliminate all crime.

The "rational" individual of economics contrasts, of course, with the "reasonable" individual of traditional legal theory—an individual who is socialized into the norms and conventions of a community, and whose behavior corresponds to these norms. The law is said to reflect these norms and conventions, and thus is obeyed by reasonable individuals. Those who engage in

---

[19] See Kreps (1990, ch. 2) and Varian (1992).
[20] See Stigler (1961).

"illegal" activities are seen as unreasonable in that they have violated these norms and conventions. In contrast, the economic approach says that behavior can be (and usually is) rational, even when it conflicts with these social norms (Cooter and Ulen 1988, pp. 11–12).[21]

Legal Rules as Prices

The idea that individuals are rational maximizers implies that they respond to price incentives: consumers will consume less of a good as its price rises and producers will produce more of a good as its price rises (all of this, ceteris paribus).[22] Within the legal arena, legal rules establish prices, such as fines, community service, and incarceration, for engaging in various types of illegal behavior. The rational maximizer, then, will compare the benefits of each additional unit of illegal activity with the costs, where the costs are weighted by the probability of detection and conviction.

The adjustment of the level of illegal activity, be it tortious acts, breach of contract, or criminal behavior, thus becomes a matter of adjusting the prices reflected in the legal rules. To reduce the amount of such activities, one simply raises their price through the imposition of higher fines or greater jail time by an amount sufficient to induce the desired degree of behavioral change. As Posner (1983, p. 75) has said, "The basic function of law in an economic or wealth maximizing perspective is to alter incentives." This is the core of what was termed "legal centralism" in the discussion of the "logic of law and economics" in chapter 1. An increase in the price of engaging in an illegal activity will induce individuals to reduce or even eliminate their involvement in such activity, and what illegal activity remains will be that for which the marginal benefits to these individuals continue to exceed even the higher marginal cost.

The predictions derived from this are very straightforward. The imposition of liability on polluting firms will raise the price of pollution and induce the firm to reduce the level of pollution as long as the marginal benefits (e.g., foregone damage payments) from doing so exceed the marginal cost of pollution abatement. Similarly, the institution of higher damage payments for negligence in tort (e.g., punitive damages, pain and suffering, etc.) will induce potential tortfeasors to take additional precaution to prevent the occurrence of a tort. In addition, higher fines and longer jail terms will reduce the amount of crime.

---

[21] The influence of social norms will be explored in chapter 7.

[22] As Becker (1976, pp. 151–58) has shown, however, we may expect an increase in price to lead to a reduction in quantity demanded even when people are not rational.

Efficiency

The third defining characteristic of the Chicago approach to law and economics is that legal decision-making and the evaluation of legal rules should be grounded in economic efficiency.[23] As Posner (1990, p. 382) has put it, "The economic task from the perspective of wealth maximization is to influence [individuals] so as to maximize [their] output." One criterion employed is Pareto efficiency—that a course of action is efficiency-enhancing if at least one person can be made better off without making anyone else worse off. The Pareto criterion is generally recognized to be quite limited as a guide to legal decision-making because of the ubiquity of losses due to legal change. The impossibility and/or prohibitive cost of compensating all of these losses make it virtually impossible to conceive of alterations in legal rules that *would* satisfy the Pareto criterion. As such, the use of the Pareto criterion would forever perpetuate the status quo. The standard definition of efficiency employed in Chicago law and economics is Kaldor-Hicks efficiency, or wealth maximization: A legal change is efficiency-enhancing if the gains to the winners exceed the losses to the losers[24] or, alternatively stated, if the wealth of society (as measured by willingness to pay) is increased.

An example will easily demonstrate this efficiency concept in action. Suppose that a firm dumps chemicals into a stream, the effect of which is to reduce the property values of downstream landowners by a total of $1 million. Suppose further that the downstream landowners file suit seeking a permanent injunction against this dumping. If the downstream landowners have no way of preventing the damage, but the firm could eliminate the damage by installing a filtering device at a cost of $600,000, efficiency would dictate that the firm install the filter, since the cost of abatement is less than the damage from the chemical discharge. Thus, the injunction should be granted, which in turn would induce the firm to install the filter, increasing societal wealth by $400,000. Suppose, however, that due to the nature of the damage and the technology available, the downstream landowners could, in fact, eliminate the damage themselves for a cost of $300,000. In this case, efficiency would dictate a denial of the injunction, as the landowners could eliminate the harm at a lower cost than could the firm, and would in fact do so if the injunction were denied, since the gain from doing so ($1 million) exceeds their cost ($300,000).

The Chicago school's reliance on efficiency is in part due to the belief that it is a legitimate and important goal for legal-economic policy, but it also reflects their concern as to what can "come in" under the name of "justice" or "fair-

---

[23] See appendices to chapter 1.

[24] Thus the winners could, hypothetically, compensate the losers for their losses and still be better off, creating a hypothetical (or potential) Pareto improvement.

ness," neither of which has a unique definition that commands universal acceptance. As a consequence, Chicagoans are skeptical of the motives of those who invoke its use, and it is not unusual to read characterizations of the concepts of justice or fairness such as "A suitcase full of bottled ethics from which one freely chooses to blend his own type of justice" (Stigler 1972, p. 4), or, "Fairness is a vagrant claim applied to any value that one happens to favor" (Areeda 1978, p. 21). The purported objectivity of the efficiency criterion makes it the preferred alternative to the ambiguities inherent in using justice or fairness, in the eyes of its proponents. In like manner, markets—readily capable of generating efficient outcomes—are viewed as the preferred system of social control.

The view of efficiency as justice is what many of the critics of the Chicago approach to law and economics find so troubling.[25] Posner (1992, p. 27), however, has argued both that efficiency is "perhaps the most common" meaning of justice and that "a moral system founded on economic principles is congruent with, and can give structure to, our everyday moral intuitions" (Posner 1983, p. 84).[26] At one point, Posner (1983, p. 89) attempted to ground the ethical basis for a rule of wealth maximization in the principle of consent, which he describes as "an ethical criterion congenial to the Kantian emphasis on treating people as ends rather than as means, in a word, on autonomy." The notion of consent employed by Posner here is based on ex ante compensation. The connection between consent and ex ante compensation lies in the idea that individuals would consent to wealth maximization as a criterion for establishing common law rules of adjudication as long as there is a sufficient probability that they will benefit (i.e., be net winners) from the application of such rules in the long run, even though they may be losers from the application of a particular rule. It thus is not necessary to compensate those who lose from the application of a particular wealth-maximizing decision rule, because these individuals have garnered ex ante compensation in the form of the greater wealth (lower costs) that accompanies the adoption of these wealth-maximizing rules.[27]

Posner has also suggested that wealth maximization, which he sees as blending certain elements of the utilitarian tradition and Kantian tradition (the latter with its emphasis on human respect and autonomy) is superior as an ethical concept to both utilitarianism and Kantianism. First, he says, "the pursuit of wealth, based as it is on the model of the voluntary market transaction, in-

---

[25] See, for example, the *Hofstra Law Review*, "Symposium on Efficiency as a Legal Concern" (1980), especially Coleman (1980); see also Dworkin (1980), Kronman (1980), and Michelman (1978).

[26] Posner does, however, rule certain wealth-maximizing ideas out of bounds; see Posner (1983, chs. 3 and 4) and Posner (1990, pp. 374–87).

[27] For an elaboration of these ideas, see Posner (1983, pp. 88–115). See also Mercuro and Ryan (1984, p. 125).

volves greater respect for individual choice than in classical utilitarianism" (Posner 1983, p. 66). Second, economic liberty "can be grounded more firmly in wealth maximization than in utilitarianism" (p. 67). Third, "the wealth-maximization principle encourages and rewards the traditional 'Calvinist' or 'Protestant' virtues and capacities associated with economic progress" (p. 68). Finally, wealth maximization "provides a firmer foundation for a theory of distributive and corrective justice," along with a firmer commitment to the principle of rights than is evident in utilitarian and Kantian thinking (p. 69).

Posner has since overtly moved away from the attempt to ground wealth maximization in moral philosophy. The strongest argument for wealth maximization, he says now, is pragmatic: "We look around the world and see that in general people who live in societies in which markets are allowed to function more or less freely not only are wealthier than people in other societies but have more political rights, more liberty and dignity, are more content . . . so that wealth maximization may be the most direct route to a variety of moral ends" (Posner 1990, p. 382). Posner's perspective here is consistent with the larger Chicago school aversion to concepts, such as justice and fairness, that are grounded in moral philosophy.[28] That is, Posner's position here is not the result of any sort of weakened commitment to efficiency but rather to any defense of efficiency based in moral philosophy.

The three features of the Chicago approach to law and economics that we have just laid out here—rational maximization, legal rules as prices, and the efficiency criterion—are all reflected in what some would call *the* cornerstone of the economic analysis of law: the Coase theorem and its corollary, which we shall call "the Coase lesson."

The Coase Theorem

We noted earlier in this chapter that the Chicago approach to the analysis of common law rules received its impetus from Coase's contribution in "The Problem of Social Cost" (1960). The traditional legal and economic approaches to harmful effects are similar in that each seeks to label one party (A) the cause of the harm and the other (B) the victim. From a legal perspective, then, the question is whether A should be liable for the harm it causes to B, with various common law rules available to resolve the liability issue under different conditions. Coase took the discussion in a different direction by pointing out that, while it is traditional to think of externality issues in terms of these conventional notions of causation—for example, the polluting factory *causes* damage to the surrounding neighborhood—the problem, in reality, is reciprocal in nature. That is, while it is true that there would be no harm to B

---

[28] See also Posner (2003) and Medema (2007b).

(the members of the neighborhood) absent A's pollution, it is equally the case that there would be no harm to B if B were not located in the vicinity of A. Looking at matters from a cost perspective, A's pollution imposes costs on B, but for B to be free from pollution (through A's abatement) imposes costs on A (the costs associated with abatement). As Coase points out, the real legal *and* economic question is, "[S]hould A be allowed to harm B or should B be allowed to harm A?" "The problem," he says, "is to avoid the more serious harm" (Coase 1960, p. 2). This approach contrasts starkly with the unidirectional notions of causation and the attendant decision rule implication, as reflected in, for example, the past doctrines of "first-in-time" or "coming to the nuisance" as heretofore enunciated in traditional tort and property law.[29] It is also in marked contract to the Pigovian approach to externalities in economics, where taxes, subsidies, or regulations are used to alter the behavior (i.e., abate the activities) of the party "causing" the externality.[30]

Coase then went on to suggest that, beyond being reciprocal in nature, externalities are also amenable to efficient resolution without government tax or regulatory measures being imposed—at least if markets operate without frictions. This requires that three conditions be met. First, rights over the resources in question must be fully specified. That is, some party must have legal control over those resources; if there are no rights over said resources or those rights are incompletely defined or unassigned, market-oriented solutions are all but precluded. Second, legal rights must be alienable: if rights cannot be exchanged, the processes envisioned here are rendered inoperative. The final assumption is that transaction costs, including the costs of acquiring information, are zero.[31] When these conditions are met—that is, when the exchange or market process is frictionless—all that is necessary is that the government decide liability one way or the other, in effect granting one party the right to act or the other party the right to be free from the action of the first party. Once these rights are defined and assigned, the parties are then free to trade the rights, and will do so if it is in their self-interest—ultimately, to an efficient solution. A simple example will illustrate this idea at work.

Suppose that a rancher (R) and a farmer (F) occupy adjoining parcels of property. If the rancher puts more than ten head of cattle on his property, the cattle tend to wander onto the farmer's property and do damage to the crops. Suppose further that the rancher's profits and the value of damages to the farmer's crops associated with various quantities of cattle, are as given in

[29] For example, Epstein (1973) challenges the notion of reciprocity.

[30] The term "Pigovian" derives from the influence of Cambridge economist A. C. Pigou (1920) in developing the neoclassical approach to the analysis of externalities—an approach that was elaborated and extended by a host of others in the middle third of the twentieth century.

[31] These will later be explored more fully. The implication of this is that all agents have full and complete information regarding benefits, costs, etc.

TABLE 2-1

Q_R (head of cattle)	Π_R (total profit to rancher)	$M\Pi_R$ (marginal profit to rancher)	TD_F (total damage to farmer)	MD_F (marginal damage to farmer)	NSB (net social benefit)
10	100	—	0	—	100
11	106	6_{11}	1	1_{11}	105
12	111	5_{12}	3	2_{12}	108
13	115	4_{13}	6	3_{13}	109
14	118	3_{14}	10	4_{14}	108
15	120	2_{15}	15	5_{15}	105
16	121	1_{16}	21	6_{16}	100
17	120	-1_{17}	28	7_{17}	92

table 2-1. If the government (legislature or the court) determines that the ranchers are *not liable* for the damages caused by their wandering cattle, this rancher will raise sixteen head of cattle, as that is the quantity that gives him the highest profit, $121. In deciding how much to produce, the rancher has no incentive to take into account the damages that his cattle cause to the farmer. Note that net social benefit (of $109) is maximized at $Q_R = 13$.

Observe that the sixteenth head adds only $1 to the rancher's profit while simultaneously causing $6 in damage to the farmer's crops. The farmer will be willing to offer (bribe) the rancher up to $6 to have fifteen cows rather than sixteen.[32] Of course, the rancher will be willing to reduce herd size to fifteen for any payment in excess of $1. Any payment from the farmer to the rancher between $6 and $1 will make both parties better off. Additional bribes by the farmer to the rancher will continue to make both parties better off. For example, for the fifteenth cow, the additional profit to the rancher is $2 and the marginal damage is $5; and for the fourteenth cow, the marginal damage to the farmer still exceeds marginal profit to the rancher. A reduction in herd size from thirteen to twelve, however, reduces damage to the farmer by $3 while reducing the rancher's profits by $4. Given this, the farmer will not be willing to offer the rancher an amount of money sufficient to get him to reduce his herd size to twelve. Thus, when the rancher is not liable, the farmer will be willing to offer the rancher an amount sufficient to induce him to limit his herd size to thirteen. This is exactly the herd size where net social benefit is at its highest level, $109.

Now suppose instead that the government decides to make the ranchers liable for the damages caused by their wandering cattle—that is, our farmer has the right to be free from harm. This means that the rancher cannot expand his

---

[32] The use of the would "bribe" in discussing these payment is entirely nonpejorative.

herd size beyond ten cows unless the farmer agrees to allow him to do so. Obviously, $Q_R = 10$ is below the efficient herd size, $Q_R = 13$. Notice however, that the addition of the eleventh cow increases the rancher's profit by $6 while causing only $1 in damage to the farmer. The rancher will thus be willing to pay up to $6 to increase herd size to 11, while the farmer will accept any payment in excess of $1 to agree to this. Any payment from the rancher to the farmer between $6 and $1 will make both parties better off. Likewise, the twelfth and thirteenth cows increase the rancher's profits by more than they increase damage to the farmer's crops, so the rancher will be able to bribe the farmer to allow him to increase herd size to thirteen. The fourteenth cow, however, adds only $3 to the rancher's profits while increasing damage to the farmer by $4; hence, the rancher will not be willing to offer the farmer an amount sufficient to convince him to allow herd size to expand to fourteen. This time, when the rancher is liable, we see that the herd size is thirteen, just as it is when the rancher is *not* liable.

Thus, whether the government, through its definition and assignment of rights (i.e., liability), decides that the rancher has the right to allow his cattle to roam freely or the farmer has the right to be free from damage caused by roaming cattle, we end up, through the bargaining process, with the same solution—a herd size of thirteen, $6 worth of crops destroyed, and the highest net social benefit attainable = $109. This result has come to be known as the Coase theorem. The theorem has been stated in numerous ways over the years, but a statement that closely follows the spirit of Coase's own discussion is,

> *If rights are fully specified and transaction costs are zero, parties to a dispute will bargain to an efficient and invariant outcome regardless of the initial specification of rights.*[33]

The Coase theorem guarantees not only the attainment of the efficient outcome but also that the efficient outcome will be reached in the most efficient fashion. Suppose, for example, that an alternative to reducing herd size is to install a fence, and that a fence that eliminates damage can be installed by the farmer at a cost of $6, or by the rancher at a cost of $8. Of course, if a fence is to be installed, both the rancher and farmer would prefer that the other party install and pay for it. If the rancher is not liable for damage caused by his

---

[33] See Medema and Zerbe (2000) for a litany of statements of the Coase theorem, as well as a fairly comprehensive survey of the vast literature on the theorem. Other surveys include Zerbe (1980), Cooter (1982a), Medema (1994, chapter 4; 1995), and Farber (1997). One of the most controversial aspects of the Coase theorem is what is known as the invariance proposition—that the *same* efficient outcome will be reached regardless of the initial assignment of rights. It is widely accepted that the presence of income effects is sufficient to invalidate the invariance claim; that is, *an* efficient outcome will be reached regardless of the assignment of rights, but these efficient outcomes will not give *identical* allocations of resources. This issue is dealt with in detail in the surveys cited in this note.

cattle, then the farmer would choose to install the fence for $6, resulting in zero damage to his crops. He would prefer to incur the $6 cost as it is cheaper than either bribing the rancher to reduce herd size down to zero, which would have cost him at least $21 ($\Sigma = \$6 + 5 + 4 + 3 + 2 + 1$), or bribing the rancher at least $8 to install the fence. Once the fence is in place, the rancher will then maintain a herd size of sixteen.

If instead the rancher is liable and the farmer has the right to be free from damage, then the rancher will bribe the farmer to install the fence, because the $6 cost is cheaper than either installing the fence himself for $8 or the bribe that he would need to pay the farmer in order to expand his output. Indeed, for the same $6 the rancher would be able to bribe the farmer to allow a herd size only equal to thirteen ($\Sigma = \$1 + 2 + 3$). With the availability of this cheaper alternative, once the rancher bribes the farmer $6 to install the fence, the rancher will once again be able to maintain a herd size of sixteen. Thus, no matter to whom the right is initially assigned, the farmer's land gets fenced and the rancher has a herd size of sixteen. Recalling that damage associated with any herd size is zero when the fence is installed, the net benefit to society of any given herd size is rancher profit minus the $6 fencing cost. As such, net social benefits are maximized where profits are maximized, so efficient herd size here is sixteen—the exact result reached by the parties themselves, regardless of the initial assignment of rights.

The Coase theorem can also be depicted graphically, as reflected in figure 2-1.[34] Here, $M\pi_R$ shows the marginal profit to the rancher of additional head of cattle, while MD_F shows the associated marginal damage to the farmer. Assume that the three conditions outlined earlier—all rights fully specified, alienable rights, and the zero transaction costs—are satisfied. If the government determines that the rancher is *not liable* for the damages caused by his wandering cattle, the rancher will produce a level of output Q_3, where his marginal benefits are exhausted and his profits maximized. Because $MD_F > M\pi_R$ at Q_3, there exists scope for a mutually beneficial bargain between the rancher and the farmer such that the rancher will agree to reduce the size of his herd. That is, the farmer is willing to pay the rancher an amount up to MD_F to reduce the herd size, and the rancher is willing to accept any payment greater than $M\pi_R$ to do so. Given that $MD_F > M\pi_R$ between Q_3 and Q^*, the farmer will bribe the rancher to reduce his herd size to Q^*. That is, because it is in the interest of both parties to bargain, and because all parties have full and perfect information and face zero costs of transacting, they will bargain until the gains from exchange are exhausted—here, at Q^*.

If the government instead makes the rancher liable and the farmer is entitled to be free from the harm caused by the rancher's activity, the rancher will be

---

[34] The figures in this section are designed for a more general discussion and are not intended to reflect the numbers in the previous table.

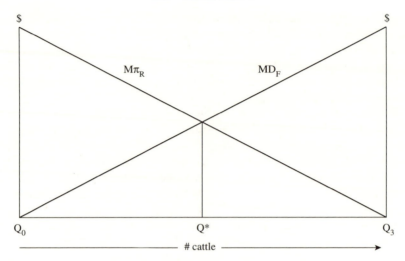

FIGURE 2-1. Cattle Rancher and Farmer

forced to maintain Q_0 cattle unless he can induce the farmer to agree to let him undertake some non-zero amount if this activity. Since $M\pi_R > MD_F$ at Q_0, there is scope for a mutually beneficial bargain whereby the rancher compensates the farmer for damage done. Furthermore, because $M\pi_R > MD_F$ between Q_0 and Q^*, the rancher will bribe the farmer to allow him to increase his herd size to Q^*, at which point the gains from trade are exhausted. Thus we see, diagrammatically, the thrust of the Coase theorem: it does not matter to which party the rights are initially assigned—that is, whether the rancher is or is not liable for the damage caused by his straying cattle. As long as the government defines and assigns the right, one way or the other, the parties will bargain to an efficient and invariant level of output, Q^*.

The Coase theorem is one of the most debated, most powerful, and most misunderstood concepts in the entire legal-economic literature. Literally hundreds of articles have been written on the theorem, attempting to prove, disprove, test (experimentally or empirically), praise, or denigrate it.[35] To understand the theorem and its implications properly, there are three simple facts to keep in mind.

First, the Coase theorem is correct. Period. *All* supposed disproofs and refutations of the theorem involve violations of one or more of the theorem's underlying assumptions—usually that of zero transaction costs.[36] Second, the world that we live in bears little correspondence to the world assumed by the

---

[35] Again, much of this literature is discussed in Medema and Zerbe (2000).
[36] See as well as Medema and Zerbe (2000).

Coase theorem.[37] The world of zero transaction costs is one in which there are no frictions, no imperfections—where, in particular, all parties have full and complete information. It is a world in which, as Coase (1988, p. 15) has remarked, "[E]ternity can be experienced in a split second." Of course, Coase concludes from this that, among other things, analyzing a world of zero transaction costs is akin to "divining the future by the minute inspection of the entrails of a goose" (1981, p. 187). The Coase theorem simply tells us that, under certain conditions, the form of legal rules does not affect the allocation of resources. It is a starting point for analysis—a useful fiction, if you will. A look at the world around us tells us not only how unrealistic those conditions and assumptions really are, but also that much insight into economics and the law can be gained by looking at the consequences of relaxing those assumptions—the thrust of the "Coase lesson," which we explore in the next section. Third, the Coase theorem undergirds the strong philosophical argument that can be made for efficiency as the criterion for legal rule-making. The logic here is both simple and persuasive, and it is related to Posner's consent-based argument presented earlier. The Coase theorem tells us that parties will bargain to the efficient outcome regardless of how rights are initially assigned if transaction costs do not preclude said bargaining. This, then, is the outcome that agents would choose voluntarily if they were able to do so. Given this, why should the judge not assist them in doing so by imposing that outcome—the efficient outcome—when transaction costs preclude bargaining to it? So, you see, the Coase theorem—a purely positive depiction of life in a world without transaction costs—provides the underpinnings for a normative law and economics based upon the efficiency criterion. Against those who would argue for the moral/ethical/philosophical bankruptcy of Chicago law and economics, the theorem, with its roots in voluntary agreements among affected parties, provides a strong rebuttal.[38]

The Coase Lesson

We have already emphasized that the Coase theorem's results hinge crucially on the assumptions that all rights are fully specified and alienable, and that the costs of transacting are zero. The assumption that transaction costs are zero is far more restrictive, and certainly more controversial, than the others. The most simple and obvious notion of transaction costs encompasses the costs of negotiating, monitoring, acquiring information, and enforcing contractual

---

[37] In fact, Coase pointed to the unrealistic nature of the zero transaction cost assumption already in "The Problem of Social Cost" (1960).

[38] There are certain important commonalities between this idea and the catallactic approach that undergirds public choice theory and constitutional economics (see ch. 3 and Buchanan [1983]), as well as with the analysis by Rawls in *A Theory of Justice* (1971).

agreements.[39] The most important subset of transaction costs, in terms of the implications for the allocation of resources, is information costs. Costly information and the resulting informational asymmetries give rise to the specter of strategic behavior, which, as many commentators have shown, negates the operation of the theorem's mechanisms.[40] In fact, however, all of these costs are significant. Thus, a more accurate definition is, "Transaction costs are the costs of establishing and maintaining property rights" (Allen 1998, p. 108).

A moment's thought makes clear how violation of the zero-transaction-costs assumption impedes bargaining to the efficient solution. First, sufficiently large transaction costs will preclude bargaining altogether. That is, if the costs associated with the bargaining process, gathering information, and so forth are greater than the expected gains from bargaining, no one has any incentive to bargain over rights once the court has rendered its decision on liability (or rights in general). Second, even if transaction costs are not so high so as to preclude bargaining, the marginal cost of additional negotiations may exceed the marginal benefit beyond *some* point, with the result that the final allocation of resources *will*, in fact, depend on to whom the rights are initially assigned. We can see the result in figure 2-2. The point to be emphasized here is that, given the presence of transaction costs, parties will bargain over rights so long as the expected gains from the bargain exceed the expected costs, which include the costs of transacting.

Continuing with our example of the rancher and the farmer, $M\pi_R$ and MD_F remain as defined above, and we will assume initially, for convenience, that marginal transaction costs (MTC) are constant and equal for both parties—that is, $MTC = MTC_R = MTC_F$—and that both parties will simultaneously incur these costs regardless of to whom the government assigns liability. The fact that both parties will incur transaction costs requires us to adjust $M\pi_R$ and MD_F by the amount of the transaction costs, which provides us with the two parties' respective bargaining curves, BC_R and BC_F.[41] The diagrammatic impact of the simultaneous imposition of transaction costs depends on whether or not the cattle rancher is liable for the damage caused by his straying cattle.

Suppose that the government were first to determine that the rancher was *not* liable for the damages caused by his wandering cattle. In the absence of some agreement between the rancher and the farmer, the rancher would maintain Q_3 cattle. We can see in figure 2-2 that when the rancher is not liable, the presence

[39] For useful treatments of the concept of transaction costs, see Dahlman (1979), Allen (1991, 1998), and Medema and Zerbe (2000).

[40] For example, the rancher may take advantage of informational asymmetries by attempting to overrepresent his net marginal benefit and the farmer by overstating his marginal damage—in both cases toward the end of inducing the other party to pay a larger bribe.

[41] In the discussion up to this point, marginal damage and marginal profits illustrate the parties' willingness to pay or the minimum payment that they are willing to accept to bring about a change in herd size. The presence of transaction costs affects willingness to pay and willingness to accept within the bargaining process, causing them—and thus the parties' bargaining curves—to differ from those in the zero-transaction-costs case by an amount equal to the size of the transaction costs incurred.

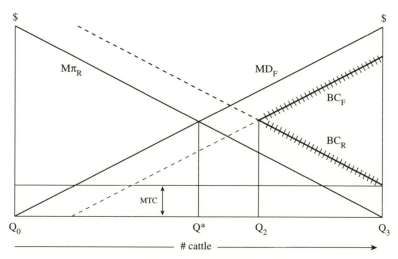

FIGURE 2-2. Rancher Not Liable

of transaction costs causes the rancher's bargaining curve, BC_R, to lie above the $M\pi_R$ and the farmer's bargaining curve, BC_F, to lie below MD_F. Thus, starting at Q_3, the farmer will have to initiate the bribe to get the rancher to reduce herd size, but the maximum bribe that the farmer is willing to pay will now be reduced owing to the presence of transaction costs the farmer must now incur. The farmer bargains down along the hatched segment of the BC_F curve. At the same time, the rancher will agree to reduce the herd size only if the bribe from the farmer (hatched segment of BC_F) covers both the reduction in his marginal profits and his costs of transacting. Thus, starting at Q_3, the rancher bargains up along the hatched segment of the BC_R curve, and the resulting bargaining solution is at herd size Q_2. That is, when transaction costs are positive, symmetric, and simultaneously incurred by both parties, the bargaining process will result in a herd size of $Q_2 > Q^*$ if the government determines that the rancher is *not* liable.[42]

Alternatively, when the rancher *is* liable, the rancher will have to initiate the bribe to induce the farmer to move away from Q_0. As we see in figure 2-3, when the rancher is liable the presence of the transaction costs causes the rancher's bargaining curve, BC_R, to lie below $M\pi_R$ and the farmer's bargaining curve, BC_F, to lie above MD_F. The maximum bribe that the rancher is willing to pay is reduced by the presence of the transaction costs that he must now incur. Thus, starting at Q_0, the rancher will bargain down along the hatched segment of the BC_R curve. At the same time, the farmer will agree to

---

[42] Of course, as previously described, if transaction costs are sufficiently high, no alteration of output will take place because the expected costs of bargaining will exceed the expected gains.

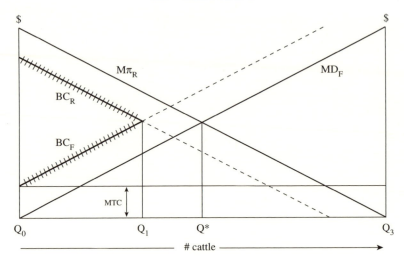

FIGURE 2-3. Rancher Liable

allow the rancher to increase the size of his herd only if the bribe from the rancher (hatched segment of BC_R) covers both the marginal damages of the wandering cattle to the farmer and the farmer's costs of transacting. Thus, the farmer bargains up along the hatched segment of the BC_F curve. The resulting equilibrium herd size is Q_1.[43] The results (Q_1, Q_2) that diverge from the optimum (Q^*) are efficient in the presence of transaction costs, since the costs of movement away from such points exceed the benefits.[44] The upshot is that, in the presence of any of the various types of costs associated with the transacting process, there is no unique optimal outcome. Instead, the outcome ultimately reached will be a function of the initial assignment of rights and the relative magnitude of transaction costs.[45] We call this the "Coase lesson":

[43] Note that if marginal transaction costs are increasing, the divergence between Q_1 and Q^* or between Q_2 and Q^* will be even greater.

[44] These positive transaction-costs-bargaining results are efficient in the Paretian sense—that is, all gains from trade have been exhausted, given the level of transaction costs, but the result is not efficient in the globally wealth-maximizing sense. See Buchanan (1983).

[45] Of course, income effects, endowment effects, and so on—implicitly assumed to be zero throughout this discussion—will have a similar influence on equilibrium outcomes, pushing them away from Q^* and, potentially, exacerbating the divergence already caused by the presence of transaction costs. On income effects, see, for example, Mishan (1967, 1971). Endowment effects exist when having or not having a right influences one's valuation of it—that is, causes a divergence between the amount that one is willing to pay to acquire a given right and the amount that one is willing to accept to give up that right. See, for example, Kahneman, Knetsch, and Thaler (1990). For a survey of the literature dealing with divergences between willingness to pay and willingness to accept, see Hoffman and Spitzer (1993). Many of these issues are discussed in Medema and Zerbe (2000), and they are also part of the subject matter of the new "behavioral law and economics."

The assignment of legal rights to one party or another impacts the allocation of resources and thus has clear efficiency implications. Moreover, depending on the assignment of rights (e.g., deciding that the cattle rancher is or is not liable for damages caused), the outcome may be in direct contradiction with the outcomes generated by policies reflecting uni-directional notions of causation prevalent in the past doctrines within traditional legal theory of property and tort law and the Pigovian approach to externalities in economics.

Now let's consider the economic impact of asymmetric transaction costs, which has further implications for the Coase lesson. Here we make two assumptions. First, we assume that the transaction costs incurred by the rancher are greater than those incurred by the farmer ($MTC_R > MTC_F$). Second, for expositional simplicity, we are assuming that once the government assigns the right to one party, say the farmer, then the other party, the rancher, would have to bear the entire burden of the rancher-specific transaction costs; hence, under this rights structure, the farmer would not incur any transaction costs.[46]

We begin by considering the case where the rancher is not liable for the damages caused by his straying cattle, as shown in figure 2-4. Thus, the farmer must incur the transaction costs, resulting in a bargaining curve BC_F, where BC_F is the farmer's marginal damage from additional head of cattle adjusted for transaction costs. In this case, the bargaining process will begin at Q_3. Through incremental bribes paid by the farmer (down along the hatched segment along BC_F) to the rancher in excess of the rancher's marginal benefits (up along the hatched segment along $M\pi_R$), the farmer will be able to bribe the rancher to get the rancher to reduce herd size. The bargaining will proceed to the point where $M\pi_R = BC_F$, yielding a herd size of Q_2. Here then we see that the existence of transaction costs precludes the bargaining process from yielding the wealth-maximizing solution Q^*.

Alternatively, if the farmer is granted the right to be free from trespass damage (i.e., the rancher is liable), then the rancher incurs all of the transaction costs. In figure 2-5, BC_R depicts the marginal benefits of additional units of herd-size expansion to the rancher adjusted for transaction costs. The rancher's willingness to pay is thus reduced by the amount of the transaction costs incurred when the farmer is granted the right by the government. This time bargaining will begin at Q_0. Through incremental bribes by the rancher (down along the hatched segment of BC_R) that are in excess of the farmer's marginal damages (up along the hatched segment of MD_F), the rancher will bribe the farmer to allow him to enhance the size of his herd. The bargaining will

---

[46] We could generalize the example by assuming that both parties simultaneously incur transaction costs, but that the transaction costs facing one party are larger than those facing the other. However, making what is quite clearly an unrealistic assumption here—that only one party at a time bears transaction costs—makes for a greatly simplified graphical treatment, as seen below.

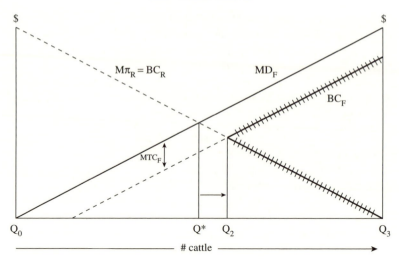

FIGURE 2-4. Rancher Not Liable

proceed to the point where $BC_R = MD_F$ yielding a herd size of Q_1. Once again it is clear that the existence of transaction costs does not allow the bargaining process to yield the wealth-maximizing, Q^*. Inasmuch as Q_2 is closer to the efficient solution Q^* than is Q_1, however, the normative implication for government policy is that the efficiency-enhancing rights structure associated with Q_2 is said to be preferred to the alternative rights structure associated with Q_1.

As noted earlier, the assumption that only one party actually incurs costs within the transacting process is unrealistic and made here only for expositional convenience. It is more likely that both parties will simultaneously incur costs, and probably not of the same magnitude. Moreover, it may well be that the sum of transaction costs across parties varies greatly with the assignment of rights. One party may be more difficult to locate or deal with, particularly if given the rights in question, and the transacting process may thus be smoother—that is, less costly—if the other party is assigned these rights instead. Ceteris paribus, if, in making legal decisions, we are going to use up some of society's scarce resources by incurring transaction costs, then the "Coase lesson" suggests that the courts should structure rights in a way that minimizes the amount of resources used up so that society can use the "saved" resources for other, more highly valued activities.

It follows that if efficiency is considered an important value in determining the law, in general, courts should attempt to assign rights in such a way as to minimize the sum of all costs associated with the externality, including transaction costs. It should be clear that this may very well generate remedies opposed to those that would be reached if courts subscribed to the more traditional uni-directional notions of causation prevalent in either the "first-in-time"

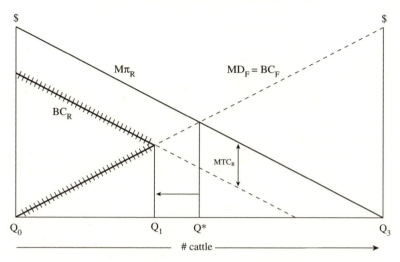

FIGURE 2-5. Rancher Liable

and "coming to the nuisance" rules of the traditional legal theory of property and tort law, or the Pigovian approach to externalities in economics—all of which would act to protect the victim-farmer and restrain the harm-causing rancher. Here, in contrast, the rancher is instead given the right.

The economic logic that underpins the Coase lesson is that a wide range of benefits and costs can, and usually do, attend alternative assignments of rights. That is, no matter what one's view of the normative import of efficiency, law does have important efficiency implications, and these include the costs associated with transacting over rights. The logic of this reasoning is inherent in Coase's approach where he states,

> The problem which we face in dealing with actions which have harmful effects is not simply one of restraining those responsible for them. What has to be decided is whether the gain from preventing the harm is greater than the loss which would be suffered elsewhere as a result of stopping the action which produces the harm. In a world in which there are costs of rearranging the rights established by the legal system, the courts, in cases relating to nuisance, are in effect, making a decision on the economic problem and determining how resources are to be employed. (Coase 1960, pp. 27–28)

Coase also argued that, as he put it, "the courts are conscious of this" and that judges "often make, although not always in a very explicit fashion, a comparison between what would be gained and what would be lost by preventing actions which have harmful effects" (Coase 1960, p. 28). This, in turn, stimulated legal-economic scholars to examine the extent to which legal outcomes of the past may reflect efficiency concerns.

The Efficiency of the Common Law

While many within law believe that the common law is a grouping of largely separate fields of analysis, each with its own set of judge-made legal rules and doctrines, the Chicago approach to law and economics suggests that the common law as a whole is unified by an underlying economic logic.[47] Perhaps somewhat ironically, the literature on the efficiency of the common law bears more than a passing resemblance to doctrinalism and, in certain respects, functions as an attempt by the Chicago school to return to formalism and to autonomous legal thought—here, organized around the doctrine of efficiency. Posner makes this very point:

> Many economic analysts of law, such as myself, are very interested in cases, and when we use economics to reconcile and to distinguish cases, we are carrying on the tradition of the doctrinal analysts. But insofar as we are trying to use modern economic concepts in this task, we fall into the category of positive analysts who use social science. . . . The positive analysts such as myself resemble traditional doctrinal analysts in believing that there really are rules of law—that the law is not wholly a matter of judicial discretion, as the more extreme Legal Realists believed. We use economics to inquire to what extent the common law is a coherent system of rules concerned with promoting efficiency. (Posner 1981, p. 1115, 1120)

As noted before, the idea that judges' decisions in common law cases seem to evidence an underlying economic logic was first raised within the Chicago tradition by Coase in "The Problem of Social Cost" (1960, p. 8–15, 19). The efficiency hypothesis has subsequently been probed in numerous studies by Posner and others who purport to describe the common law's economic logic.[48] As Posner (1987b, p. 5) defines it, the economic theory of the common law (broadly conceived to include all judge-made law) "is that the common law is best understood not merely as a pricing mechanism but as a pricing mechanism designed to bring about an efficient allocation of resources, in the Kaldor-Hicks sense."

There are three threads to the argument that the common law tends toward efficiency. The first is that the institutions of the common law have been designed to promote efficiency by fostering market transactions through contract. This approach uses the expected utility maximization model to provide insight into the issue of pretrial settlement versus formal adjudication and has been analyzed in the contexts of civil, criminal, labor, and antitrust cases. The

---

[47] See Cooter (1985).

[48] The first Chicago study that advanced the efficiency hypothesis in-depth was Posner (1972b). See also Rubin (1977), Priest (1977), and Goodman (1978). An overview of the efficiency theory of the common law can be found in Cooter and Ulen (2004, ch. 10) and Posner (1992, chs. 8, 19–21). Landes and Posner (1987) present an extensive analysis of the efficiency theory of the common law as applied to the area of torts.

issue facing each party is that of settlement versus adjudication, and each party's decision is assumed to turn on which course of action gives them the higher expected utility, given their resource constraints and their subjective probability estimates of prevailing should the case go to trial.

Let's look at the working of this process in the context of a civil case. Assume that both parties agree that the judgment, if the defendant is found liable, will be $100,000 and that the probability of the plaintiff prevailing is 0.40.[49] Suppose further that the plaintiff's trial costs are $20,000 and the defendant's trial costs are $10,000. The plaintiff's expected gain from going to trial is thus $20,000 ($100,000 × 0.40 − $20,000) and the defendant's expected loss is $50,000 ($100,000 × 0.40 + $10,000). Given that the plaintiff's expected gain from a trial is $20,000, she will be willing to settle out of court for any amount greater than this. Similarly, the defendant, with expected costs of $50,000 associated with going to a trial, will be willing to settle for any amount less than $50,000. There is thus a $30,000 range within which a settlement can occur, and if the transaction costs associated with the bargaining process are relatively low, it can be expected that the parties will reach a mutually agreeable settlement within this range.[50]

This same type of analysis can be extended to criminal law and issues surrounding settlements in criminal cases. In a criminal case, the defendant weighs his expected sentence (including the probability of conviction) against the sentence offered in the plea bargain. The prosecutor, whose utility may be defined to include the number of convictions, weighted by the severity of the sentences, will consider the expected sentence (again, weighted by the probability of conviction) in determining what, if any, terms to offer in a plea bargain. If there exist expected gains to both parties from a settlement, then there will be a range of sentences within which a settlement may be reached.[51]

Numerous factors affect the issue of settlement versus trial, and many of these have been introduced into the economic models describing this process. These include differential bargaining costs across disputants, differences in their respective attitudes toward the risks associated with the adjudicatory outcome, and different estimates of the probability of prevailing at trial. Moreover, the various methods by which the legal costs of going to trial are allocated between the litigants (e.g., the standard U.S. method versus the English Rule) have been analyzed in an attempt to explain the trial settlement pattern under each method.[52]

---

[49] Of course, this analysis generalizes as to the differing expectations of judgment value and differing subjective probabilities of prevailing at trial between plaintiff and defendant. The assumed symmetry within this example serves only to simplify the discussion.

[50] The reader should be able to see the parallels between this idea and the Coase theorem in the allocation of mutual gains from trade through the bargaining process.

[51] See, for example, Landes (1971).

[52] See, for example, Gould (1973) and Shavell (1982).

The second theory offered in support of the efficiency hypothesis is that common law *judgments* will tend to mimic the efficient result of a free market, because inefficient legal rules are likely to be more frequently and more intensively (in the sense of resources expended) challenged in court than are efficient ones. The reason for this is that inefficient rules generate higher expected judgments for the challenging parties, and thus individuals will be willing to spend more time, money, and effort in challenging inefficient rules than they will in challenging efficient ones. This is apparent when one recognizes that the overturning of inefficient rules generates both a greater quantity of total wealth and a redistribution of wealth, whereas the overturning of efficient rules *decreases* total wealth at the same time that it redistributes it (Cooter and Ulen 2004, pp. 436–43; Posner 1990, p. 360). Alternatively, parties may seek some form of alternative dispute resolution, such as arbitration, if judicial decisions continue to promote inefficient allocations (Posner 1992, p. 535). As a result, we can expect to see inefficient rules overturned more frequently, thus increasing the stock of efficient rules over time.

When this idea is combined with the logic of the trial-settlement model, the underlying rationale for the economic theory of the evolution of the common law, as evidenced, for example, in the work of Paul H. Rubin (1977) and George L. Priest (1977), becomes quite clear. Rubin describes it as follows:

> The presumed efficiency of the common law and the decision to use the courts to settle a dispute are related. In particular, this relationship will occur because resorting to court settlement is more likely in cases where the legal rules relevant to the dispute are inefficient, and less likely where rules are efficient. Thus, efficient rules may evolve from in-court settlement, thereby reducing the incentive for future litigation and increasing the probability that efficient rules will persist. In short, the efficient rule situation noted by Posner is due to an evolutionary mechanism whose direction proceeds from the utility maximizing decisions of disputants rather than from the wisdom of judges. (1977, p. 51)

Rubin goes on to point out,

> If rules are inefficient, parties will use the courts until the rules are changed; conversely, if rules are efficient, the courts will not be used and the efficient rule will remain in force. An outside observer coming upon this legal rule would observe that this rule is efficient; but this efficiency occurs because of an evolutionary process, not because of any particular wisdom on the part of judges. (1977, p. 55)

That is, efficiency will tend to obtain regardless of what motivates the judges' decisions. That having been said, Rubin (1977, p. 55) also notes that "intelligent judges" may cause the path to efficiency to be a bit shorter than it would be otherwise.

Priest's model builds on the notion that inefficient rules impose higher costs on parties than efficient rules. As a result, the value of overturning an

inefficient rule tends to be higher to the parties than the value of overturning an efficient one, and thus inefficient rules will, on average, lead to more litigation than efficient ones. As a result, the common law has a tendency toward efficiency because the lower probability of relitigation means that efficient rules are more likely to survive than inefficient rules. Priest goes further, asserting that (i) even if judges were actively hostile to the concept of efficiency in their decision-making and/or (ii) (going beyond Rubin) even if both parties do not have a continuing interest in precedent, the ongoing process will result in a tendency toward the efficiency of the common law.

In summary, for both Rubin and Priest, the efficient rule situation noted by Posner is due to an evolutionary mechanism whose direction proceeds from the utility-maximizing litigation decisions of the disputants rather than from the wisdom of judges (Rubin 1977, p. 51).[53]

John Goodman's "differential investment" approach takes the analysis a step further than Rubin and Priest, attempting to set out specific reasons *why* inefficient rules will be overturned. Goodman assumes that judges are amenable to persuasion by the litigants appearing before the court and are completely unbiased with respect to efficiency, and that any increase in legal expenses by either party will increase that party's probability of securing a favorable judgment. Since the economic stakes are higher under inefficient rules, the party on whom liability initially rests has a greater incentive to spend a larger amount on litigation expense here than under efficient rules. The additional expenditures on litigating inefficient rules thus increase the likelihood that such rules will be replaced by efficient ones. Goodman (1978, pp. 394–95) describes this as follows:

> A model of an adversary proceeding is proposed in which the probability that a particular litigant will win a favorable decision depends upon the efforts of both litigants to influence the court and upon the weight of judicial bias. Since parties before the court have an obvious interest in the decision, they have incentives, not necessarily equal, to affect that decision through efforts that incur legal costs— expenses for legal research, factual investigation, forensic talent, and so forth. The fundamental assumption made throughout is that any increment in legal expenses . . . will induce an increment, however small, in the probability . . . of winning a favorable decision. . . . Even if the weight of past precedents favors inefficient solutions, the side with the greater economic stake in the issue will still have a higher probability of winning any succeeding case so long as the ratio of his economic stake to his opponent's exceeds . . . the ratio of legal expenses by the two litigants that must be maintained in order to insure that they both have the same probability of winning.

---

[53] More recently, Rubin (2005a) advanced what he has termed the "macro" argument (inspired by Hayek) for explaining the efficiency of the common law to complement the previously advanced "micro" (evolutionary) models.

The third, most strongly held, rationale for the efficiency of the common law lies in the view that judges—implicitly or explicitly—select legal rules that generate efficient outcomes. Simply stated, the hypothesis is that the development of the common law, especially the law of torts, can be explained *as if* the goal was to maximize allocative efficiency—that is, *as if* the judges who created the law through decisions operating as precedents were trying to promote efficient resource allocation. As Posner puts it, "The hypothesis is not that judges can or do duplicate the results of competitive markets, but that within the limits set by the costs of administering the legal system (costs that must be taken into account in any effort to promote efficiency through legal rules), common law adjudication brings the economic system closer to the results that would be produced by effective competition—a free market operating without significant externality, monopoly, or information problems" (1983, pp. 4–5).[54] "It is," says Posner (1990, p. 356; emphasis in original), "*as if* the judges wanted to adopt the rules, procedures, and case outcomes that would maximize society's wealth."

Posner (1992, p. 252) suggests that economic logic pervades the common law and that, in general, when transaction costs are low the common law gives incentives for individuals to "channel their transactions through the market," whereas when transaction costs are high, making market allocation infeasible, "the common law prices behavior in such a way as to mimic the market." The instances where law and economics scholars have found common law rules comporting with the dictates of efficiency are far too numerous to detail here, but a few examples will suffice to illustrate the point. The law of property structures property rights in such a way as to promote value-maximizing exchange. Tort law, through the application of the Learned Hand formula, promotes the taking of cost-justified precautions. The doctrine of impossibility in contract law places liability on the party who could most easily anticipate or insure against the unforeseen contingency. Other examples are found in admiralty, expectation damages, assumption of risk, and the application and nonapplication of punitive damages.[55]

Chicago law and economics does not have a clearly delineated model of judicial behavior or motivation in decision-making. Yet, there is a more-or-less general theme that judges have in mind the overall well-being of society—a concept incorporating numerous social values—in resolving cases. Utility maximization is sometimes rejected as a motivating force for judges on the grounds that judges almost never have any personal stake in the case at hand, and that the judicial system has been designed to insulate judges from significant economic incentives. Posner (1993b) has questioned this view, arguing

---

[54] The Posnerian distinction between the efficiency properties of common law and those of statutory law has been challenged by Rubin (1982). See also the essays in Hirshleifer (1982).

[55] See, for example, Posner (1992, part II), Posner (1990, ch. 12), Cooter and Ulen (2004), and Landes and Posner (1987).

that judges, like everyone else, are rational utility-maximizers, where the utility functions of judges are primarily a function of income, leisure, and judicial voting. In fleshing out the implications of this utility function in the context of the institutional structure within which judges make decisions, Posner is able both to explain certain aspects of judicial behavior and to offer testable predictions that arise from the model.

While the actual motivation underlying judicial decision-making is open to debate, it remains the case that judges are, at times, called upon to "legislate" (Posner 1993b, p. 40). Whereas societal well-being entails both efficiency and distributional considerations, Posner (1990, p. 359) suggests that "prosperity" (i.e., wealth maximization) is a goal "that judges are especially well equipped to promote," while judges can do little, if anything, to promote the redistribution of wealth.[56] Moreover, says Posner (1990, p. 359), judges wish to avoid controversy, and wealth maximization "is a relatively uncontroversial policy." Because the cases at hand are unrelated to judicial self-interest, and/or because it is difficult to rationalize the judge's personal considerations as to "deservingness" within the context of a judicial opinion, the judge is "[a]lmost by default . . . compelled to view the parties as representatives of activities," and "[i]n these circumstances it is natural that he should ask which of the competing activities is more valuable in an economic sense" (Posner 1992, pp. 523–24).

Critics have often maintained that the common law reflects no overt economic logic or phraseology; yet, the proponents of the efficiency theory suggest that the underlying economic logic is clear, even if judges usually do not speak the language—that judges employ language other than efficiency to explain efficient arrangements (Cooter and Ulen 2004, p. 440). Posner (1992, pp. 254–55) even goes so far as to suggest that these efficient doctrines simply reflect common sense, and that whereas the articulation of these doctrines in formal economic terminology lies beyond the capacity of most judges, the commonsensical intuition does not. Against those who suggest that efficiency is not a value that would enter into the judge's decision-making calculus, Posner (1992, p. 255) responds that justice is often "a version of efficiency" and maintains that efficiency "has always been an important social value," especially during the laissez-faire period of the nineteenth century, when the common law received much of its modern shape.[57]

It must be underscored that acceptance of this view—in any or all of its manifestations—that the common law is efficient serves as an ideological barrier to the general promotion of statutory law. That is, it serves to denigrate the

---

[56] See also Posner (1992, p. 255).

[57] Cooter and Kornhauser (1980) examined the evolution of the common law through a Markov chain analysis. They demonstrated that regardless of (i) differential litigation rates, (ii) whether initial liability rules are efficient of inefficient, or (iii) how judges choose rules in making decisions, there is a positive probability that any given rule, efficient or inefficient, will persist in the long run. That is, we can expect to see *some* inefficient rules persist over time.

role of the legislative process—the means by which statutes are passed—on the grounds that statutes have no corresponding mechanism to ensure efficient outcomes (this will be explored in chapter 3).[58] Thus, the logic underlying the Chicago efficiency theory of the common law generally follows the following contour: Whenever the market falls short of providing an efficient allocation of resources due to externalities or some other form of market failure, one can rely on the common law and damage measures, which, the theory's proponents contend, have been demonstrated to be comprised of rules and doctrines that produce efficient results, to give the market a gentle nudge in the direction of maximum social welfare. In general, given the existence of some form of market failure, society need not rely on the legislative branch to adopt regulatory statutes or bureaucratic mechanisms to remedy these problems; all one needs to do is rely on the common law to generate the efficient outcome.[59]

CHICAGO LAW AND ECONOMICS AT WORK

We have seen that the "positive" side of the Chicago approach to law and economics is concerned with assessing the degree to which common law and other legal doctrines comport with the dictates of economic efficiency. When law is seen to depart from the dictates of efficiency, or when new legal issues present themselves, the concern is with fashioning and adopting efficient legal rules to guide judicial decision-making—the *normative* side of law and economics. The goal of this section is to describe how the Chicago school uses the elements of Chicago price theory to make normative legal choices to decide "what the law should be."

The Formulation of Efficient Legal Rules—A General Discussion

The starting point for analyzing instances where the common law departs from the dictates of economic efficiency is with the assertion by Coase (1960, p. 2) that situations of harm are reciprocal in nature. Examples are present throughout the fields of property, contract, and tort law, and so the concept

---

[58] Stearns (1998, p. 715) describes the evolving role of the Chicago school over time: "While early Chicago School scholars employed economic analysis to *explain* then-existing institutions and rules, a new generation of law and economics scholars employed the same tools to *challenge* the alleged inefficiencies of the expanding regulatory state."

[59] Halper (1993, pp. 230–31) describes the same notion as follows: "The Chicagoans argue that outcomes legitimate the superiority of the market as a form of collective decision-making—the market is the most efficient means to allocate resources. . . . [S]tate intervention in the market is warranted only to correct market failure, . . . the common law, effectively the outcome of the day-to-day interactions of market participants, orders the market more efficiently than statutory law, the artificial creature of the legislative state."

applies generally. Under the reciprocal view of harm, the problem of causation becomes much more open-ended than under the traditional legal or Pigovian approaches.[60]

One can see an excellent example of the reciprocity concept in action in Landes and Posner's (1983, p. 110) description of the economics of causation in tort:

> If the basic purpose of tort law is to promote economic efficiency, a defendant's conduct will be deemed the cause of an injury when making him liable for the consequences of the injury would promote an efficient allocation of safety and care; and when it would not promote efficiency for the defendant to have behaved differently, then the cause of the accident will be ascribed to "an act of God" or some other force on which liability cannot rest. In this view, the injurer "causes" the injury when he is the cheaper cost avoider; not otherwise.

The contrast between the economic approach and the traditional measures of "cause-in-fact" (where, in order for a plaintiff to sue, a defendant must have caused the harm) and "proximate cause" (where remote actions may have been the cause of harm and thus causation becomes a matter of degree) is apparent, but the most interesting characteristic of the economic approach here is that "causation becomes a result rather than a premise" within the economic analysis of torts (Landes and Posner 1983, p. 110).

We have already seen that, in a world of zero transaction costs, rights will end up in their highest-valued uses because all mutually beneficial bargains can and will be costlessly struck by rational maximizing individuals.[61] Given such a situation, the judge will not need to be concerned about efficient rights assignment, as the same efficient outcome will be reached regardless of the judge's decision.[62] Indeed, attempts by judges to engage in social engineering will inevitably be fruitless because rights, regardless of how they are initially assigned, will always end up in their highest-valued use. Consider the earlier example of the polluted stream, where the pollution discharge causes $1 million in damage to downstream landowners. The polluter can prevent the damage by installing a filtering device at a cost of $600,000, whereas downstream landowners could eliminate the damage at a cost of $300,000. Efficiency clearly dictates that the pollution be eliminated, since the damage is greater than the cost of abatement, and that the optimal way of abating the pollution is for the downstream landowners to undertake the abatement. The Coase theorem tells us that, no matter how rights are initially assigned, this is exactly the

---

[60] It also constitutes an excellent example of the effects of the "naming and framing" process discussed in chapter 1.

[61] This is analogous to movements from positions off contract curves to positions on contract curves in the Edgeworth Box analysis of microeconomic theory. See appendix B to chapter 1 and Varian (1993, pp. 484–507).

[62] Again, this is subject to the qualifications dealt with in note 42.

solution that will obtain, with the actual distribution of the gains from this exchange depending on the relative bargaining power of the two sides.

While the pollution example provides a useful context for understanding the legal-economic resolution of a combined property and tort disputes, the approach is also applicable to contract law. Suppose that A signs a contract with B which stipulates that A will sell her house to B for $200,000. After this contract has been signed, C enters the picture, offering to pay A $210,000 if A will sell to him. A then breaches her contract with B and sells the house to C for $210,000. Here, it is clearly efficient for A to breach the contract with B and sell to C instead, since C values the house more highly than does B. Suppose next that B files suit against A for breach of contract, asking that the contract be enforced according to its terms. If the court rules against B, then C retains the house—the efficient result obtains. If instead the court finds in favor of B, the house is transferred from C to B, resulting in an inefficient solution. Just as in the pollution example, however, this is not the end of the story. If C values the house at $210,000 and B only at $200,000, then C will be willing to offer B any amount up to $210,000 for the house. B, who values the house at $200,000, will be willing to accept any amount greater than that to give up the house. Thus, a mutually beneficial bargain will be struck, and the efficient result—C owning the house—will obtain. In a world of zero transaction costs, we thus get the efficient result regardless of the initial assignment of rights—that is, whether or not the court rules on behalf of A or on behalf of B. Coase (1960, p. 10) recognized this, observing that "[w]ith costless market transactions, the decision of the courts concerning liability for damage would be without effect on the allocation of resources." In recounting a judicial ruling in a land-use case, he then almost went on to chide the judges by stating,

> It was of course the view of the judges that they were affecting the workings of the economic system—and in a desirable direction. Any other decision would have had "a prejudicial effect upon the development of land for residential purposes." . . . The judges' view that they were settling how the land was to be used would be true only in the case in which the costs of carrying out the necessary market transactions exceeded the gain which might be achieved by any rearrangement of rights. (p. 10)

Otherwise, the parties would bargain to an efficient use of the land. "But of this" he says, "the judges seem to have been unaware" (p. 10).

The problem, of course, is that the real world is, at least for the most part, a world of positive transaction costs. As discussed earlier, these costs may at times may be sufficiently high to preclude bargaining all together,[63] resulting in what may be called a legal "fly-paper effect"—the right sticks where it hits. Here, the court's decision on behalf of one party or the other will directly

---

[63] More specifically, where transaction costs exceed the economic surplus from a bargain.

determine the final resting place of the right and thus will impact the efficiency of the end state. The goal of efficiency in Chicago law and economics manifests itself in the normative prescription—the Coase lesson—that rights should be assigned in a way that maximizes the wealth of society.[64]

Acknowledgment of the fly-paper effect requires an approach that constitutes what has been called "mimicking the market" and involves assuming a hypothetical zero-transaction-costs world, as in the Coase theorem. The question then becomes one of ascertaining where, in a zero-transaction-cost world, the ultimate resting place of the right will be. By engaging in this type of inferential analysis, courts can attempt to discern the efficient outcome that would have resulted from the market-like machinations of the Coase theorem. By assigning rights in such a way as to achieve this result, the courts can accomplish the goal of wealth maximization. Thus, in a dispute over terms or provisions that are missing from a contract because positive transaction costs made it uneconomical, ex ante, to specify fully the contract over all states of the world, the task of the judge is to attempt to infer which party would have accepted liability for the contingency at issue in a world of costless bargaining. Since it can be inferred that the party accepting liability would have been the one who could have done so at least cost, the efficient decision would be to place ex post liability on that party. The same logic explains why, if the gains from a breach of contract exceed the costs of breach, then the court should allow the contract to be breached.

Law of Torts

The evidence for the efficiency of the common law is thought to be particularly prevalent in the field of tort law, although, as we have noted, much of the literature purports to offer evidence supporting the view that common law doctrines of property and contract also promote efficiency. In the Chicago analysis of tort law, the subtle transition from positive description of efficient common law evolution to normative remedy prescription is easy to discern: if

---

[64] Thus, in terms of the pollution example, since the least-cost method of reducing pollution is for the downstream landowners to abate that pollution, the efficiency criterion would dictate that the polluter be given the right to pollute. As we saw, this would induce the landowners to undertake abatement since the alternative is sustaining $1 million in damage. Of course, the optimal amount of pollution may be some intermediate amount, as opposed to all or nothing. In this case, a property rule will not give the optimal result when transaction costs preclude bargaining. As Calabresi and Melamed (1972) have pointed out, efficiency would dictate the use of a liability rule in such a situation, since the polluter would then pollute only as long as its benefits from additional pollution exceed its costs (as measured by compensatory damages), thereby engendering the optimal outcome. Similarly, referring back to the example from contract law, the court should, from an efficiency perspective, allow A to breach her contract with B and sell to C, since, in doing so, the house is placed in a higher-valued use.

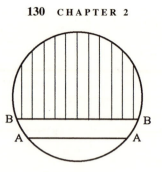

FIGURE 2-6.

society has an array of liability rules from which to pick, rules that may, for example, lead to a reduction in accidents or to the abatement of pollution, then the economic logic suggests choosing the least-cost alternative.

This line of reasoning was originally presented by Calabresi in "Some Thoughts on Risk Distribution and the Law of Torts" (1961), coincidentally at about the same time Coase authored "The Problem of Social Cost."[65] The analysis of efficient liability rules is based upon three suppositions: (i) that all losses can be expressed in monetary terms, (ii) that the quantity of undesirable activities can be reduced by devoting more of society's scarce resources to precautionary or preventive activities, and (iii) that those individuals who are potentially involved in harmful activities are sensitive to cost pressures (Burrows and Veljanovski 1981, p. 11). The aim of efficiency-based tort law is to use ex post damage awards to replace what may be termed "ex ante unfeasible agreements" that would have occurred had market transactions been possible (that is, if transaction costs were sufficiently low).

The economic logic of this approach can be expressed in three simple steps. First, let figure 2-6 represent all the costs associated with, say, automobile accidents (including the actual damages suffered by victims, litigation expenses, legal administrative costs, enforcement costs, etc.) before the government attempts to reduce society's costs of accidents. Assume that the government first installs traffic signals and stop signs, with the net savings to society being the area beneath line AA. Now assume, additionally, that the government erects costly median barriers, again with some net savings, this time equal to the area ABBA. The area above line BB represents the residual costs of accidents, or, as they are commonly referred to, the *interaction damage costs*. It is these costs that are the focus of the literature on economics of liability rules.

The economic approach to the analysis and selection of liability rules can be viewed as one method by which risks in society are determined to be either

[65] We will explore Calabresi's approach more fully in chapter 6 in the section on the New Haven school.

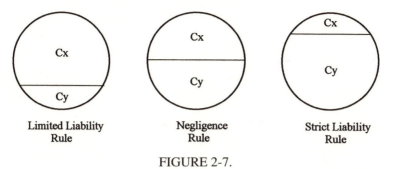

FIGURE 2-7.

background risks, with the costs borne by the victim, or, alternatively, *compensated risks*, which arise from tortious acts and whose costs are borne by the injurer. The primary focus of the economic approach to liability rule formulation is to develop a standard of liability that minimizes the sum of interaction damage costs with full recognition that the selection of a specific liability rule will determine which actions will be considered background risks (and go uncompensated) and which will be deemed compensated risks. Focusing only on the interaction damage costs—the area above the line BB in figure 2-6, now replicated three times and equal to each of the three circles in figure 2-7—we can easily describe the two facets of the problem.

First, in each panel of figure 2-7 let C_x represent all costs borne by victims, because the liability rule chosen considers the risks associated with these interaction damage costs to be background risks. In a like manner, in each panel of figure 2-7 let C_y represent all compensable costs borne by the injurers, because the liability rule chosen considers the risks associated with these interaction damage costs as tortious and not part of society's background risks. It is evident that the liability rule which is chosen will determine the extent of noncompensable background risk vis-à-vis that of compensable risk. Consider, for example, three hypothetical liability rules. With a limited liability rule, most risks are considered background risks, and most injurers are not liable for the damages caused—that is, the victims bear most of the costs. At the other extreme, where injurers are held strictly liable, most risks are considered compensated risks and thus the injurers are liable for most of the damages caused. Perhaps somewhere between the two lies a third liability rule, a negligence rule, that establishes a system under which injurers are liable for the damages only if they are negligent (i.e., at fault). The first fundamental point illustrated here is that the legislative or judicial choice of one liability rule over another results in a different distribution of interaction damage costs for society. It is only for expositional purposes that the three circles have the same area (i.e., represent the same interaction damage costs). Indeed as stated earlier, the thrust of the economic approach to liability rule formulation is to develop a standard of liability that minimizes the sum total of interaction damage costs.

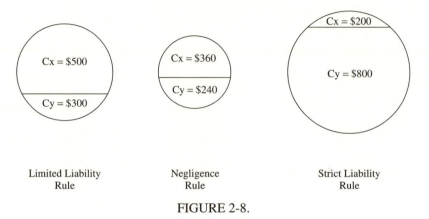

Limited Liability   Negligence   Strict Liability
Rule   Rule   Rule

FIGURE 2-8.

Figure 2-8 illustrates the efficiency consequences of the choice of one liability rule over another. The sizes of each of the three circles—indicating the sum of interaction damages costs, arbitrarily sized, for each rule—are purposely different to convey the notion that there would be no reason to believe that all rules would result in identical interaction damage costs. For example, the third circle, which illustrates a hypothetical strict liability rule, depicts both the distribution of costs—80 percent of which are borne by the injurers, and only 20 percent of which are uncompensated and thus borne by the victims—and the total size of the interaction damage costs, here equal to $1,000. The second circle, by way of contrast, illustrates the situation for the rule of negligence, which yields a different distribution of costs (40 percent being borne by the injurers and 60 percent of the costs going uncompensated and thus being borne by the victims), with the total interaction damage costs equal to $600. In comparing these two rules, the economic approach would suggest adopting the negligence liability rule on the grounds that it allocates risks, alters incentives, and thereby affects behavior so as to minimize the sum cost to society ($600, clearly less than $1,000). Similarly, and also on efficiency grounds, the negligence rule is preferred to the limited liability rule (the first circle, where most costs go uncompensated and thus borne by the victims as part of background risks), since the limited liability rule results in total interaction damage costs of $800, as compared to $600 under the negligence rule. It should be noted that the explicit adoption of the least-cost solution carries with it the implicit adoption of the specific distribution of risk that goes along with the chosen rule. This is an important point of departure between the Chicago school and the traditional justice-fairness approach inherent in conventional tort law. Whereas the justice-fairness approach is concerned with the distribution of the costs associated with risk (i.e., the question as to where *within* the circles one draws the line separating compensable risk from background risk),

the Chicago approach to law and economics is concerned with minimizing the total costs associated with risk (that is, choosing the smallest circle), the distribution of the costs being irrelevant except as it affects the total cost.

Before exploring one of the most notable examples of these ideas entering case law, it is important to understand the nature of the concept of negligence as used in common law. Consider the following quote by Chief Justice Rosenberry in *Osborne v. Montgomery* (234 NW 2nd 372, 378–380 [1931]), which provides a general outline as to what constitutes a negligent action:

> Every person is negligent when, without intending to do any wrong, he does such an act or omits to take such precaution that under the circumstances present he, as an ordinarily prudent person, ought reasonably to foresee that he will thereby expose the interest of another to an unreasonable risk of harm. In determining whether his conduct will subject the interests of another to an unreasonable risk of harm, a person is required to take into account such of the surrounding circumstances as would be taken into account by a reasonably prudent person and possess such knowledge as is possessed by an ordinarily reasonable person and to use such judgement and discretion as is exercised by persons of reasonable intelligence and judgement under the same or similar circumstances.

What the court determines is or defines as "reasonable" is the driving force in separating background risks from compensated risks in society. While one can argue that this determination should be made on the basis of moral and ethical considerations, the Chicago approach to law and economics suggests the use of the efficiency criterion—that society select the rule that minimizes costs and live with the accompanying risk distribution.

Interestingly, however, the injection of economic thinking into the legal concept of negligence did not originate with the Chicago school. Rather, it was introduced by Judge Learned Hand in his decision in *United States v. Carroll Towing Co.*[66] In his ruling, he gave explicit formulation to the standard that the courts had applied throughout the period that the negligence standard flourished (as in *Osborne v. Montgomery*)—and he did so in economic terms. This formula has come to be known as the Hand negligence formula—the injurer is liable for accident damages if the expected accident costs (the probability of an accident occurring times the victim's accident costs) are greater than the costs that the injurer must bear to avoid the accident. Otherwise, the injurer is not negligent and the victim bears the damages. Hand stated that the matter of liability turns on the minimization of expected costs:

> Possibly it serves to bring this notion into relief to state it in algebraic terms: if the probability be called P; the injury, L; and the burden, B; liability depends

---

[66] *United States v. Carroll Towing Co.*, 159 F.2d 169 (1947). Not all agree as to the jurisprudential significance of the Hand rule; for instance, see Wright (2003).

upon whether B is less than L multiplied by P: i.e., whether B is less than PL. (*United States v. Carroll Towing Co.*,1947, at 173)

A simple numerical example will help explicate the workings of the Hand rule and the incentives it creates for potential injurers. Following Hand's notation, let L be the costs of accidents borne by the victims and let B be the potential injurer's costs of avoiding accidents. Let P be the probability that the accident will occur if no avoidance is taken and P′ be the probability that the accident will occur if some avoidance activities are undertaken. Let L = $1000, B = $500, P = .8, and P′ = .2.[67] Again, if P × L > B, then the injurer would be ruled negligent and thus liable for the damages caused. In this case, the Hand formula asserts that the injurer should be liable because expected accident costs, $800 (.8 × $1000), are greater than the costs of avoidance, $500. Since he would be liable for injuries caused in these circumstances, the potential injurer will engage in accident avoidance measures and thereby reduce the probability of accidents from .8 to .2.

The economic rationale for the Hand rule is that it minimizes expected costs (i.e., the sum of accident and avoidance costs). That is, by undertaking avoidance activities, the potential injurer reduces the probability of accidents to .2, resulting in expected accident costs equal to $200, which when added to the avoidance costs of $500 sums to a total of $700. If the Hand rule was not in force and injurers were therefore ruled not liable in these situations, then our prospective injurer would not engage in avoidance activities, leaving expected accident costs at $800 and, given his lack of undertaking any avoidance measures, the avoidance costs would be zero, for a sum total of $800. Inasmuch as the $700 expected cost associated with undertaking avoidance activities is less than the $800 expected costs in the absence of avoidance, adherence to the Hand formula dictates that the injurer should be liable, thereby forcing avoidance measures and minimizing the expected costs associated with accidents.

Consider an alternative case where the simple Hand formula would indicate that the injurer should not be held liable. As before, let L = $1000, P = .8 and P′ = .2, but now assume that B = $900. Since the expected accident costs of $800 (.8 × $1000) are less than the costs of avoidance, $900, the injurer should not be held liable. Here, then, the Hand rule would make the victim bear the costs. The efficiency consequences of this application of the Hand formula parallel those in the previous example. Since injurers are not liable here when avoidance is not cost-justified, potential injurers will refrain from any accident avoidance activities in those circumstances. In the present example, expected accident costs are $800 (.8 × $1000) and avoidance costs are equal to zero for a total expected cost of $800. Note that if the courts had not followed the simple Hand formula and injurers were ruled liable, then, in

---

[67] Note that P and P′ need not sum to 1.

these circumstances, the potential injurers still would not engage in avoidance activities. The reason is undertaking avoidance results in expected accident costs of $200 (.2 × $1000) plus avoidance costs of $900, for a total expected cost of $1100. The potential injurer will choose the option with the lower expected cost, which here means foregoing avoidance activities.

The Hand formula has been seized upon by those opposed to suggestions that the determination of negligence should be based on moral and ethical considerations. As Posner wrote, "Characterization of the negligence standard as moral or moralistic does not advance analysis. . . . Negligence is an objective standard. . . . To characterize the negligence concept as a moral one is only to push inquiry back a step" (Posner 1972a, pp. 31, 32). The more general contrast between the Chicago law and economics and the justice-fairness perspectives is seen in the following statements by Richard Posner and Richard Epstein—the latter of whom was a long-time critic of Chicago law and economics[68]—in their debate over the rule of strict liability. Speaking from the law and economics perspective, Posner (1973, p. 221) argued that "[s]ince the efficient use of resources is an important although not always paramount social value, the burden, I suggest, is on the authors to present reasons why a standard that appears to impose avoidable cost on society should nonetheless be adopted. They have not carried this burden." Epstein (1973, p. 152), in contrast, contends,

> Once it is admitted that there are questions of fairness as between the parties that are not answerable in economic terms, the exact role of economic argument in the solution of legal questions becomes impossible to determine. It may well be that an acceptable theory of fairness can be reconciled with the dictates of economic theory in a manner that leaves ample room for the use of economic thought. But that judgment presupposes that some theory of fairness has been spelled out, which, once completed, may leave no room for economic considerations of any sort.

In essence, Posner is claiming that the goal of legal decision-making should be efficiency, and that the burden rests with the advocates of the justice-fairness approach to demonstrate why fairness considerations should dominate efficiency. Epstein argues from the opposite pole, setting up fairness as the goal and stating, in a sense, that the burden rests with the advocates of the economic approach to show why efficiency considerations should dominate fairness.

TORT REFORM

To a large extent, this is the very logic that underlies the ongoing impetus for tort reform in the United States. To place the issue in perspective, a milestone was reached in 1990: for the first time, the number of new cases filed in state

[68] He is now a fellow traveler.

courts topped 100 million. Advocates of tort reform, like the former Vice President Dan Quayle, have argued that "the costs of the civil justice system amount to a self-inflicted competitive disadvantage" (Jost 1992, p. 435). By the year 2000, the President's Council of Economic Advisers figured that "excessive tort costs" amounted to a $650 "litigation tax" on the economy for every person in the United States. With the Republicans winning both the U.S. House and Senate in 2002, they promised to follow up on the tort reform initiatives that they tried to push through in the 1990s.[69] The rhetoric has heated up even further. In his 2003 State of the Union address, President Bush said, "No one has ever been healed by a frivolous lawsuit"—to which the Trail Lawyers Association responded, "True, but neither has anyone been healed by tort reform" (Karp 2003, p. 1). The result is that for the past decade we have witnessed tort-reform advocates demonizing trial lawyers, while trial lawyers simultaneously argue that the tort reformers are turning their backs on those who have suffered damages and deserve to be made whole once again.[70]

An understanding of the theory reflected in the three different-sized circles enables one to gain some insight into the positions of those who argue for the efficient reform of tort law on the one hand and those who want to focus on using the rules based on justice and fairness on the other. It also brings into sharper relief much of the political rhetoric between the conservative Republicans, who advocate tort reform along lines consistent with Chicago-school thinking, and the liberal Democrats, who echo the fairness claims of the trial lawyers, whose interests liberal Democrats tend to represent. J. M. Balkin explains why the Chicago approach to law and economics has found such a warm reception among conservative academics (1987, pp.1454–55). In his article, he describes the close nexus between American conservatism and the Chicago approach to law and economics, and their corresponding "relatively individualistic" positions in regard to legal-economic policy in general and tort law in particular. It is this "relatively individualist" approach that is, he says, at the root of the advocacy of tort reform by the Chicago school—an approach that tends to limit the defendant's liability, or deemphasizes the defendant's responsibility for an injury to the plaintiff. On the other side of the argument over tort reform are those who adopt what Balkin terms the "relatively communalist" position, an alternative approach that tends to expand the defendant's liability, emphasizes the defendant's responsibility to others, and oftentimes serves a redistributive function. The relevant point here is that, for the

---

[69] This is documented by Coyle (2002).

[70] While the American Tort Reform Association (ATRA) was formed in 1986 to represent hundreds of U.S. and foreign corporations in their bid to overhaul civil liability laws at the state and national levels, much of the early efforts in tort reform came from Vice President Dan Quayle, as head of President Bush's Council on Competitiveness, established in 1989. The Council also assigned then-Solicitor General Kenneth Starr the task of developing a plan to overhaul the country's civil liability laws.

Chicago school, the higher levels of duty in tort law become superfluous because they waste societal resources on administrative costs, whereas the relatively individualist rules—those that lower standards of liability—are preferred based on efficiency considerations. Chicago advocates of the individualist approach take the additional step of denying that liability rules are an efficient method for redistributing income and make the further point that their effects on this front are often unpredictable.

Recall from our hypothetical example that each circle (in figure 2-8) represents all the costs associated with, say, "generic" accidents, including the actual damages suffered by victims, litigation expenses, legal administrative costs, enforcement costs, and so forth, after the government had taken certain obvious actions to reduce some of the most obvious costs. Also, keep in mind that the costs associated with generic accidents are, on the reverse side of the ledger, an income entry for those who collect the fees: the bigger the circle, the greater the costs to one group, hence the larger the income earned by the other. Once the two major parties to the dispute over tort reform are identified—the Chamber of Commerce on one side and the Association of Trial Lawyers of America on the other—their positions emerge. Generally, the argument goes something like this: The trial lawyers want to have the smallest possible share of damages treated as part of life's background risks; hence, they argue that we should rely on the principles of justice and fairness and advocate a rule of law more along the lines or in the direction of strict liability. This is clearly the very rule that increases costs and hence incomes—including incomes of the trial lawyers.

The position of the Chicago-efficiency tort reformers and, in particular, the Chamber of Commerce, is that there are a host of efficiency-enhancing reforms that the legislature should set in place. These would reduce the sum of the costs borne by society owing to generic accidents (and with it, of no concern to them, the incomes of trial lawyers). As a consequence, they advocate a package of reforms that they believe would, when taken together, yield the smallest circle of costs, as reflected in the more limited liability rule—all this, of course, independent of the concepts of justice and fairness advocated by the trial lawyers.[71]

In actuality, tort reforms have been difficult to set in place, in part because

---

[71] The ultimate validity of each of the parties' positions, is partly an empirical question related to the actual differences in the costs under each liability rule and what portion of costs get translated into trial lawyer incomes. In mid-2003, a report on the economics of the litigation of tort claims was issued by the Center for Legal Policy—Manhattan Institute (2003) titled "Trial Lawyers Inc.: A Report on the Lawsuit Industry in America 2003." The report found that in the United States, total costs for tort litigation now exceed $200 billion annually (approximately 2 percent of the nation's GDP), with trial lawyers getting about $40 billion a year. In addition, the study found that the trial lawyers' revenue has grown at about 9 percent per year over the past three decades.

they are seen as a national problem but one with little federal jurisdiction. The federal courts handle only a small portion of the nation's caseload; it is the individual states that carry the bulk of the cases. Thus, federal initiatives for tort reform typically confront states' rights barriers and force the reformers to go state by state to win approval of their reforms. Since 1991, tort reform advocates have set up dozens of tax-exempt groups in at least eighteen states to get out their "lawsuit abuse" message in the media in an effort to influence legislation, the judiciary, and jurors. As of May 2003, tort reform packages including some or all of the provisions described here have been introduced in seventeen states and tend to contain some or all of the following provisions:

> Abolishing joint and several liability—the longstanding principle, which requires losing defendants in tort suits to pay all the damages regardless of their level of fault. Restrictions on venue to keep plaintiffs from seeking the friendliest courts. Legislation to allow trial court evidence on so-called collateral sources of compensation, such as medical insurance. An outright ban on punitive damages, though in practice caps are often imposed as a compromise. Restrictions on noneconomic damages such as pain and suffering. Caps on appeal bonds. And the allowing of appellate challenges to class action certification. (Ballard 2003, p. 1)

Thus far, judges have not clamped down on plaintiffs' lawyers as much as the Chamber of Commerce would like, and Congress has failed to deliver meaningful tort reform. Individual states sputter along taking incremental steps—some succeeding in obtaining liability caps, eliminating various causes of action, and implementing procedural rules making it much harder to sue wrongdoers. Many times, however, their reforms are challenged as unconstitutional by members of the Association of Trial Lawyers of America, with varying results.

The Law of Contracts: Efficient Breach

The economic analysis of contract law provides a unique perspective on the rules, distinctions, categories, and boundaries of the evolving legal doctrine of contract law.[72] From an economic perspective, the major thrust of contract law is to facilitate the accomplishment of the goals of the contracting parties—and to do so efficiently (Goldberg 1989, p. x). Contract law concerns the structuring of contracts, the negotiation of settlements among the parties of interest in a dispute over their asserted legal rights, rules governing arbitration, and, in a lawsuit, the defenses of breach of a contract. If the contracting parties took the

---

[72] Comprehensive treatments of the economics of contract law include Craswell and Schwartz (1994), Cooter and Ulen (2004, chs. 6, 7), Goldberg (1989), Kornhauser (1986), Kronman and Posner (1979), and Posner (1992, ch. 4).

time and incurred the costs to incorporate explicitly into the contract terms that deal with every type of nonperformance under every possible circumstance, there would be no occasion for the courts to prescribe remedies. Obviously, however, from an economic standpoint, it is too costly to negotiate and draft contracts that provide for every conceivable contingency, and this makes disputes unavoidable. In Coasean terms, the problem is one of transaction costs, and thus, as A. Mitchell Polinsky (1989, p. 27) describes it, "Contract law can be viewed as filling in these 'gaps' in the contract—attempting to reproduce what the parties would have agreed to if they could have costlessly planned for the event initially." Thus, contract law has a clear economic justification.

Obligations that arise consequent to a contract are influenced by the answers given to two questions. The first has to do with the circumstances under which an otherwise binding promise would be excused, and the second concerns the issue of what legal consequences flow from breaching a contract. For our purposes here, legal rules of contract can be divided into two distinct classes. In one class are the so-called *immutable rules*, those that govern even if the parties try to contract around them. The other class consists of the so-called *default rules*, which parties can contract around by prior agreement; these are the rules that fill the gaps in incomplete contracts (Craswell and Schwartz 1994; Ayres and Gertner 1989). The assessment of default rules and the legal consequences that flow from breach constitute a major line of literature of the economics of contract law and are the focus of the present discussion.

It may seem odd at first glance to think of a breach of contract as a "good" thing. Yet as Robert Cooter and Thomas Ulen (1988, p. 290) have observed, "One of the most enlightening insights of law and economics is the recognition that there are circumstances where breach of contract is more efficient than performance." They go on to define efficient breach as follows: "the breach of a contract is more efficient than performance of the contract when the costs of performance exceed the benefits to all parties" (Cooter and Ulen 1988, p. 290). The major thrust of the literature, then, is to analyze and assess rules according to the extent to which they promote efficient breach. As with much of Chicago law and economics, doing so requires a return to Pareto efficiency and therefore to Coase. Markets and contracting are not costless processes; thus, following the Coase lesson, contracts should be structured to approximate the efficient outcome by providing incentives for value-maximizing conduct. The ubiquitous reliance on Coasean thinking throughout the economics of contract law is evidenced in Craswell and Schwartz's (1994, p. 54) assertion that "[w]henever a remedial rule requires conduct that seems inefficient, you should consider whether the party who would lose the most from that inefficiency will be able to pay the other party to abandon his or her insistence on the inefficient remedy."

If a party breaches a contract and the court determines that (i) the contract has been validly formed, and (ii) performance will not be excused, then a remedy for the breach must be determined. For our purposes here we will consider

only three options, two of which—legal relief and equitable relief—are court-determined and the third of which—liquidated damages—is not court-determined, but structured by the contracting parties themselves.

1. *Legal relief*: This remedy consists of court-imposed money damages and is the remedy most often imposed by the court. Legal relief can take one of three forms:

Expectation damages: award the victim of breach an amount of money that leaves him in a position identical to the one he would have been in if the contract had been completed according to its terms.

Reliance damages: award the victim of breach an amount of money that puts him in the same position he would have been in if he had not entered into the contract in the first place.

Restitution damages: award the victim of breach an amount of money equal to any benefits (e.g., payments) he has provided to the breaching party.

2. *Equitable relief (specific performance)*: Although not used often, equitable relief is the second court-determined remedy that can be imposed, and is termed "specific performance." Specific performance protects the potential victim's right to performance by ordering the breaching party to perform the contractual promise. That is, the court essentially protects the victim's right with the equivalent of a property rule.

3. *Liquidated damages*: Unlike the first two remedies—legal relief and equitable relief—that are imposed upon the parties by the court, the third remedy—liquidated damages—is imposed by the parties themselves. The liquidated damage remedy awards the breached-against party an amount of money agreed to by the parties at the time of contract formation (Polinsky 1989, pp. 64–65).

The economic analysis of breach of contract asks, at the most basic level, whether and under what conditions the expectation, reliance, restitution, specific performance, and liquidated damages remedies for breach of contract are efficient alternatives to a fully specified (ergo, Pareto-efficient) contract. Putting it slightly differently, the goal, from an efficiency perspective, is to employ the legal remedy that at once prevents inefficient breach and at the same time induces breach when breach is efficient. Each of the remedies mentioned can be examined with this in mind, and we shall do so in the context of a simple example.

Suppose that Acme Autos has a car for sale at a price of $12,000. Fred is willing to pay up to $15,000 for the car, signs a contract with Acme to purchase the car at the $12,000 price, gives Acme a down payment of $5,000, and agrees to return in three days to make the remaining payment and take possession of the car. Shortly thereafter, Fred goes to Parts Unlimited—an auto parts dealer, where he purchases new wheels and tires for this car during their going-out-of business sale, spending a nonrefundable $800 in the process. Not

long after Fred leaves Acme, Jim arrives and offers Acme $13,000 for the car—an amount equal to the value that *he* places on owning it. Setting to one side for the moment the issue of damages, Acme will wish to breach its contract with Fred in order to sell the car to Jim, since it can realize an extra $1,000 from the transaction. Since Fred, however, values the car at $15,000, whereas Jim only values it at $13,000, such a breach would be inefficient, because it would place the vehicle in a lower-valued use. With this as background, we can now examine the effect that the various remedies described earlier would have on Acme's potential breach of the contract with Fred.

EXPECTATION DAMAGES

An expectation damages remedy makes the victim as well off as if the contract had been performed. Thus, if Acme went ahead and sold the vehicle to Jim, an expectation damages remedy would require Acme not only to refund Fred his $5,000 down payment, but also pay Fred $3,000 (the surplus from the transaction that Fred lost due to the breach). Thus, under the expectation damages remedy, Acme would decide not to breach the contract since the gain from selling to Jim ($1000) is less than the damages Acme would have to pay to Fred ($3,000). If, on the other hand, Jim had offered Acme $20,000 for the car, a decision by Acme to breach would be efficient, since Jim values the car more highly than Fred. That is, Acme would breach its contract with Fred and sell to Jim, since the gain from selling to Jim ($8,000) exceeds the damages that they would have to pay to Fred ($3,000). More generally, under the expectation damages remedy, Acme will refrain from breaching its contract with Fred for any amount less than $15,000 and will breach its contract for any amount greater than $15,000.

From the vantage point of economics, the expectation damages remedy encourages efficient breach and discourages inefficient breach. The economic reasoning here is straightforward and can be generalized. The expectation remedy requires the breaching party to pay damages equal to the value of the good or resource to the victim of the breach. If some other buyer enters the arena and values the good or resource more than the initial buyer, then it is efficient for that third party to acquire the good—that is, efficiency dictates that goods and resources should gravitate to their highest-valued uses. Consequently, if the parties anticipate that the court will impose an expectation damages remedy, the seller will have an incentive to breach in order to obtain the higher offer, pay the victim his expectation damages, keep the surplus, and thereby end up better off—with no one made worse off. On the other hand, if a prospective buyer who did not value the good as much as the initial buyer entered the arena, the expectation remedy would appropriately and efficiently discourage the breaching of the contract.[73]

---

[73] On the limits of expectation damages, see Goetz and Scott (1983).

RELIANCE DAMAGES

Reliance damages place Fred in the same position as he was in prior to signing the contract, and as such compensate him for expenditures undertaken in reliance on the contract. Recall, in this case, Fred had made a nonrefundable $800 expenditure on wheels and tires, and thus, under a reliance damages remedy, Acme would be forced to compensate Fred in the amount of $800, plus refund his $5,000 down payment.

It should be apparent that the reliance damages remedy provides an incentive for inefficient breach. With Jim's offer of $13,000, Acme can gain an additional $1,000 by selling the car to Jim, and, since Acme must compensate Fred only an amount of $800, this provides Acme with an incentive to breach the contract. Since Fred, however, places a higher value on the car ($15,000) than does Jim ($13,000), this breach is inefficient—resources would not be gravitating to their highest-valued use. More generally, reliance damages do not internalize to the potential breacher the full cost of the breach to the victim (i.e., the "price" of breaching is inefficiently low) and, as a result, can lead to breaches where the social costs are in excess of the social benefits.

RESTITUTION

Under the restitution damages remedy, the breacher need only return to the victim any monies received from the him—here, Fred's $5,000 down payment. Given this, Acme will breach its contract with Fred and sell to Jim, and, indeed, would do so at any price in excess of $12,000. As with reliance damages, restitution damages do not internalize all costs of breach to the potential breacher, and, as a result, give rise to the potential for inefficient breach.

Thus, among the monetary remedies, only expectation damages, by internalizing the full cost of his actions to the potential breacher, act simultaneously to discourage inefficient breach and to promote efficient breach.[74]

SPECIFIC PERFORMANCE

Specific performance involves an order by the court that the contract be completed according to its terms. Thus, in the context of our example, the court would order Acme to sell the car to Fred for $12,000. As such, specific performance eliminates the possibility of inefficient breach here. It might be argued, however, that specific performance will have the effect of preventing efficient breaches. For example, if Jim had offered $20,000 for the car, then the court's

---

[74] There are two additional efficiency issues that arise in the discussion of the appropriate form of damages. These relate to the effect of the damage remedy employed on (i) the potential breacher's incentive to undertake precaution against breach and (ii) the potential victim's incentive to undertake expenditures in reliance on the contract. For a discussion of these issues, see Cooter and Ulen (1988, ch. 7).

requirement of specific performance, by awarding the car to Fred, would generate an inefficient outcome. Yet, in such a situation there exists a subsequent exchange that would exhaust the gains from trade. Jim would presumably also be willing to pay Fred $20,000 for the car, and Fred, valuing the car at $15,000, would be willing to part with it at the $20,000 price. Thus, unless transaction costs are prohibitive, we would expect that the specific performance remedy would, through subsequent transactions, generate the efficient outcome, and that the difference between specific performance and expectation damages (previously shown to be efficient) will be purely distributional. That is, under specific performance, Fred will capture the gains from Jim's greater willingness to pay, whereas, under expectation damages, Acme will capture those gains.

Based on this, it has been argued that courts should rely more heavily on specific performance as a remedy for breach.[75] This is particularly true if the good is one for which the value of performance to the victim is difficult for the court to discern with certainty. If, for example, the victim places a very high subjective value on the good in question (a value much higher than others would place on it), the court, in questioning whether the victim is accurately revealing his preferences, may well award insufficient damages. Under a specific performance remedy, however, the breacher will have every opportunity to negotiate with the victim and pay him his full value if he is to consent to the breach. More generally, since valuations are more likely to be accurately reflected through the bargaining process than through court-stipulated damages, specific performance offers a greater potential for an efficient resolution of the dispute than do monetary damages as long as transaction costs are low; conversely, monetary damages are to be preferred when transaction costs are high.[76]

LIQUIDATED DAMAGES

Liquidated damages clauses are inserted into the contract by the parties themselves during the contract-formation process and specify the damages that one party must pay to the other in the event that the contract is breached. Nonetheless, courts have traditionally been unwilling to enforce such clauses when the specified damages appear to be overly burdensome or punitive (that is, appear to exceed compensation for the harm caused to the victim). The economic approach, however, places these damages in a somewhat different relief. Since rational maximizing agents will agree only to a contract that both believe to be in their interests, these clauses would seem to be efficient; otherwise, the parties would not have agreed to their inclusion in the first place. There are two important reasons why maximizing agents might agree to such terms. First, the potential victim might place a very high subjective value on performance

---

[75] See, for example. Cooter and Ulen (2004, pp. 259–60) and, more generally, Schwartz (1979).

[76] This is parallel to the argument made by Calabresi and Melamed (1972), discussed earlier.

of the contract—much, much higher than the average person. The high level of liquidated damages specified in the contract may thus reflect the high subjective value placed on performance by the victim, and, in a sense, insurance against nonperformance. Alternatively, the potential breacher may be willing to insert such a clause as a quality signal to attract customers. In either case, the clause is mutually beneficial ex ante and thus, from an efficiency perspective, should be enforced.[77]

We hope this brief review makes it clear that Chicago law and economics provides novel and interesting theoretical insights into the field of contract law. It must be noted, however, that the substantial impact that the Chicago approach to law and economics has had in the areas of torts and antitrust (see discussion later in this chapter) has not carried over to the realm of contracts. In an attempt to discern the influence of economic analysis on contract law, Eric Posner (2002, p. 35) recently reviewed all state and federal court opinions in contract disputes that cited an economics article appearing in either a major law review or a faculty-edited journal since 1980. He found that only twenty-three such opinions were issued, four of which discussed the article and the rest of which only cited it. He also found that the notes to the Restatement (2nd) of Contracts contained only a handful of references to economic ideas.[78] It seems safe to conclude that, while the economic analysis of contract law remains a major feature in the law and economics academy, its impact on the law remains fairly negligible.

Antitrust Policy

It has been said that, of all the fields of law, Chicago law and economics has had its greatest impact on antitrust.[79] Antitrust policy had gone through a remarkable evolution since its inception in the late 1800s.[80] The earliest cases (in the late 1800s to early 1900s) relied primarily on common law rules. Throughout most of the first half of the twentieth century, antitrust was a blend

---

[77] On the economics of liquidated damages, see, for example, Goetz and Scott (1977), Cooter and Ulen (2004, pp. 251–54), and Polinsky (1989, pp. 63–65).

[78] Beecher-Monas (2002) argues that a number of the influential judges who espouse the tenets of law and economics and rational choice theory in contract law are wrong-headed, and he suggests that their analysis of contract doctrine needs to be amended in light of the findings of behavioral economics and evolutionary game theory.

[79] Thus, it is not all unusual to read comments such as, "Since the 1980s, the Chicago School model of antitrust has reigned as the predominant approach of both the courts and the agencies" (Jacobs 1995, p. 219). Duxbury (1995, p. 349) observed that "[T]here exists very little in the way of contemporary antitrust theory which has not been inspired to some degree by Chicago economic analysis." Lande contends, "[T]he dominant paradigm today is that the only goal of the existing antitrust laws is to increase economic efficiency" (1990, p. 258).

[80] This brief history is retold in many places; we have relied on Hovenkamp (1985).

of statutory law and the judge-made law of the U.S. Supreme Court and Appellate Courts. In the early part of the twentieth century, the courts adopted the "rule of reason" approach; later, in the mid-1900s, Edward Chamberlin and Joan Robinson's economic theory of monopolistic competition served as a partial basis for deciding cases. This was followed by J. M. Clark's theory of workable competition, which was later endorsed by the Attorney General's National Committee to Study the Antitrust Laws. In the 1950s and 1960s, antitrust policy was driven by the so-called liberal school, as reflected in the decisions of the Warren Court. While some suggest that the inclusion of economic thinking into antitrust policy is a relatively recent phenomenon, the very economic nature of the problem means that the formulation of antitrust policy has, to various degrees, always incorporated some form of economic thinking. Indeed, as Hovenkamp (1985, p. 217) has pointed out, "Only an extreme form of historical myopia will admit . . . [that] economic theory had nothing useful to say about antitrust policy until the 1970s."

THE SETTING FOR CHICAGO ANTITRUST

To appreciate fully the contribution of the Chicago school to antitrust analysis, it is important to understand the economic and legal milieu from which it arose. In economics, antitrust has long been a part of the field of industrial organization, while in law it is the legacy of the New Deal–liberal school, where the prevention of industrial concentration was pursued for political and social reasons.

Early industrial organization theory argued that the way to understand industrial policy was to utilize the *structure-conduct-performance paradigm*. In the simplest of terms, this approach stated that the structure of an industry (number of firms, industrial concentration, technology, etc.) would affect the behavior of market participants (that is, the conduct of individual firms with respect to pricing decisions, levels of advertising, investment in research and development, etc.), and consequently, market performance (taking into consideration both the levels of profits and social welfare).[81] Some who utilized this paradigm argued that to attain the desired economic performance, antitrust policy should concern itself with the "structure" of the industry under question. These were the so-called "structuralists."[82] The structuralists tended to view large firms and

---

[81] A typical presentation of the structure-conduct-performance approach can be found in Scherer (1970, pp.1–7). For a concise review of this paradigm and its relation to antitrust law, see Carstensen (1983). Some proponents of the Chicago school often suggest this approach is of little value, for example: "Today it is hard to find an economist who believes the old structure-conduct-performance paradigm" (Easterbrook 1986, p. 698). An interesting recent application of the structure-conduct-performance paradigm, however, is contained in Michael R. Baye's *Managerial Economics and Business Strategy* (2002), now in its fourth edition.

[82] Baye (1997 [2nd ed.], p. 262) terms this approach "the causal view," where it is taken to mean that the market structure "causes" firms to behave in a certain way. The distinction between the structuralists and the behaviorists is described by Scherer (1970, pp. 6–7).

mergers with suspicion and explained a variety of business practices as being motivated by monopolistic intent. The antitrust remedies they offered typically involved changing the structure of the industry through legislative, judicial, and/or administrative actions—actions that would deconcentrate the industry.[83] It is with this approach that we typically associate the term "trust-busters."

There were others who countered that emphasis on the structure of an industry was misleading, and that the concern should be with the "behavior" of market participants, regardless of market concentration. These were the so-called "behaviorists."[84] They deemphasized structure and instead probed structure-conduct and conduct-performance associations, thereby emphasizing the intermediate behavioral links. In doing so, they were able to set out an antitrust policy agenda that drew attention away from market structure and, by implication, from firm size and concentration, to focus instead on pricing behavior and economic rationales for horizontal or vertical integrations and merger activity. In so doing, they helped to create a perspective on antitrust policy that proved conducive to the Chicago approach.

The distinction between the structuralists and the behaviorists is not purely academic. One of the arguments for aggressive enforcement of the antitrust laws—pre-Chicago school—was partly based on the emphasis on structure and the associated relationship said to exist between high concentration in market sectors and resultant lessening of competition. Merge this economic thinking with the New Deal–liberal school concerns regarding (i) the political ramifications of bigness of firms and of fewness of competitors and (ii) the socioeconomic impacts of high concentration on the small businessperson and the consumer, and one can then come to appreciate more fully the legal-economic environment surrounding the rise of the Chicago school.[85] This economic structure–socio-political approach to antitrust policy came to be known as the New Coalition[86] and served as the basis for a variety of legislative and

---

[83] A sampling of the scholarship underlying this general approach includes the work of Mason (1937, 1957), Kaysen and Turner (1959), and Bain (1956).

[84] Baye (1997, pp. 262–63) characterizes the behaviorists as part of the so-called "feedback critique."

[85] Hovenkamp (1985, pp. 218, 219) correctly observed the following:

Despite all that has been said about the lack of sophistication or even the hostility toward economics manifested by Warren Court and Eisenhower administration antitrust policy, that policy was in fact very much informed by academic economists. The price theory and industrial organization that dominated the academic study of economics in the 1960s *were simply quite different* from the dominant economic ideology of the 1980s. . . . [Antitrust policy reflected] the academic thinking of the 1960s, in which product differentiation, industrial concentration, barriers to entry, and large firm dominance *rather than* tacit collusion were the principal areas of economic concern for the competitive process. (emphasis added)

[86] This term is employed by Fox (1987a, p. 917). White (1992, pp. 1055–57) labeled them the "Modern Populist School." In fact, there is no single broadly accepted moniker for this approach—that said, we stay with the "New Coalition."

administrative initiatives to reduce concentration levels in selected industries. Eleanor M. Fox and Lawrence A. Sullivan's characterization of the "two central concerns" of antitrust in this period makes all of this very clear:

> The first was political—distrust of bigness and of fewness of competitors as well as a policy preference for diversity and opportunity for the unestablished. The second was socioeconomic, especially as seen from the vantage point of the small businessperson and the consumer. Antitrust set fair rules for the competitive game. What mattered was getting a fair shot as an entrepreneur, and having choice and receiving a fair deal as a consumer. Antitrust was not a tool for increasing aggregate national wealth (sometimes called or equated with allocative efficiency). While a more efficient allocation of resources would probably result from competition as compared with more direct government intervention or blatant laissez-faire, improved resource allocation was never a norm for antitrust, nor a condition precedent to antitrust enforcement. In order to get to the jury, neither the government nor a private plaintiff was expected to show that a particular enforcement action would achieve efficiency. What they had to show was that the competitive process was being harmed. (Fox and Sullivan 1987b p. 944)

This approach to antitrust wove its way into policy and ultimately into the courts; in fact, the U.S. Supreme Court incorporated these very ideas into their case opinions. For example, we read from *United States v. Von's Grocery Co.* (384 U.S. 270, 274–275 [1966], at note 7), quoting Judge Hand, who was reviewing the policy of the antitrust laws and other laws designed to foster small business in *United States v. Aluminum Co. of America* (148 F.2d 416 (1945)):

> Throughout the history of these statutes it has been constantly assumed that one of their purposes was to perpetuate and preserve, for its own sake and in spite of possible cost, an organization of industry in small units which can effectively compete with each other.

More to the point, from *Northern Pacific Railway Co. v. United States* (356 U.S. 1, 4 (1958)), the court wrote:

> The Sherman Act was designed to be a comprehensive charter of economic liberty aimed at preserving free and unfettered competition as the rule of trade. It rests on the premise that the unrestrained interaction of competitive forces will yield the best allocation of our economic resources, the lowest prices, the highest quality and the greatest material progress, while at the same time providing an environment conducive to the preservation of our democratic political and social institutions.

While this is representative of much of the pre-Chicago thinking about antitrust policy in the U.S. Justice Department, the Federal Trade Commission, and the U.S. courts, a different approach had begun to evolve at the University

of Chicago beginning in the 1940s. This early, pre-Chicago work exploring the interaction between economics and the law has been labeled "old law and economics"—a label given to those fields of law that were, by their very nature, inherently concerned with both economics and the law (for example, public utility regulation, corporate law, federal taxation, labor law, and, of course, antitrust).[87] Thus, the interest of Director and others at Chicago in the area of antitrust, described in chapter 1, is not novel; the novelty, rather, lies in the challenge that this new "Chicago view" posed to the traditional structure-conduct-performance paradigm and the policies derived therefrom. It is safe to say that, as a result of the efforts of Director and his disciples, by the 1980s, antitrust academia, the antitrust bar, and the federal judiciary were becoming populated with people who had made serious efforts to learn about price theory and industrial organization (Hovenkamp 1985, p. 216).

THE CORE THEORY OF CHICAGO ANTITRUST

The Chicago approach to antitrust is predicated on four propositions.[88] First, neoclassical price theory (microeconomics) is the most useful social science to explain and understand antitrust issues, and hence should be the science used in formulating antitrust policy. The idea is that linking antitrust policy to the Chicago price-theoretic approach would largely remove antitrust policy from politics and set it on a scientific course.[89] Proponents of the Chicago approach argue that the concept of efficiency explains many of the phenomena that the New Coalition–liberal school described as anticompetitive or exclusionary.

Second, efficiency should be the sole goal of antitrust policy; wealth distribution is not an economic concern.[90] The use of efficiency provides the enforcement authorities with simple quantitative tests by defining anticompetitive behavior solely in terms of price and output. Relying exclusively on the efficiency criterion frees courts from the need to hazard qualitative judgments about the political ramifications and the socioeconomic impacts of high

---

[87] Whereas the "new law and economics"—the application of economic theory (primarily microeconomics and the basic concepts of welfare economics) to examine the formation, structure, processes, and the economic impact of law and legal institutions—begins in 1960 with the work of Coase and Calabresi.

[88] In describing the contours of the core theory of the Chicago school of antitrust, we have, owing to their clear exposition, relied heavily on two sources—Hovenkamp (1985) and Jacobs (1995); our description is a synthesis of portions of these two works. Three of the more significant books outlining the Chicago approach to antitrust are Bowman (1973), Posner (2001a), and Bork (1993); see also Gerhart (1982).

[89] The argument that economics is indeed a science and one that can (and should) be used as the basis for antitrust policy is set forth in Bork (1993, p. 8).

[90] See Hovenkamp (1985, p. 229).

concentration on the small businessperson and the consumer, judgments typically invoked by advocates of the New Coalition–liberal school.[91]

Third, the legislative history of the antitrust laws allows the judiciary to decide antitrust cases in a manner consistent with the goal of efficiency. The Chicago school also asserts, however, that judges are ill-equipped to identify and understand the true sources of a broad array of market imperfections. Consequently, they argue that judicial enforcement should proceed cautiously and with greater reliance on the market (as opposed to the courts) as the regulator; that is, their contention is that the market punishes inefficiency faster than the machinery of the law.[92]

Finally, the simplicity and clarity of the Chicago school approach to antitrust would enable firms to predict more accurately the legal consequences of important business practices, and would thereby promote capital investment and generally facilitate private ordering.[93]

With this as its foundation, the Chicago school constructed a relatively simple analytical framework from which to fashion antitrust policy. This policy holds, contrary to the New Coalition–liberal school, that antitrust enforcement should punish only inefficient conduct. The contention is that

> the focus of the antitrust laws . . . should instead be on: (1) cartels and (2) horizontal mergers large enough either to create monopoly directly, as in the classic trust cases, or to facilitate cartelization by drastically reducing the number of significant sellers in the market. . . . [T]his implied a breathtaking contraction in the scope of antitrust policy. (Posner 1978, p. 928)

More specifically the Chicago approach contends that markets are competitive and tend toward efficiency, even if they contain a relatively small number of sellers. Market imperfections are typically thought to be transitory. Thus, if a monopoly does exist, the problem tends to be self-correcting in that the higher profits of the monopolist would attract new firms into the market and thereby erode its monopoly position. Closely associated with their position on monopoly is the belief that barriers to entry (apart from those erected by government) tend to be more imagined that real and that this allows resources to flow into any market where there is an above-normal rate of return. They also argue that economies of scale are far more prevalent than suggested by the New Coalition–liberal school, as a result of which many more industries than commonly thought should be allowed to operate at fairly high concentration levels.

---

[91] As Fox (1987b, p. 945) described it, "In [the Chicago school's] intellectual universe, antitrust is embodied in a reductionist paradigm: antitrust concerns the functioning of markets; microeconomics is the study of the functioning of markets; therefore, antitrust is microeconomics. The potential and desired effect of markets is the efficient allocation of resources; therefore, the sole purpose of antitrust is to prevent inefficient allocation of resources."

[92] This is one of five "beliefs" of the Chicago school as described by Fox (1987b, p. 957).

[93] On this point, see Jacobs (1995, p. 231) and Easterbrook (1984a, p. 14).

For the Chicago school, given that producers strive to maximize profits, almost all competitively ambiguous business behavior is explained as a drive for greater efficiency. So-called exclusionary practices are generally understood by firms not to be in their long-run interests, and thus, if such practices do exist in particular market settings, they must be more efficient than alternative legal arrangements. As Jacobs (1995, p. 229) observed, "This framework . . . permits courts to interpret commercial behavior coherently, efficiently, and free of political bias. Since price theory views firms as profit-maximizers, it regards conspiracies as inherently unstable, monopoly markets as self-correcting, and entry barriers—except for those imposed by government regulation—as inadequate to prevent the flow of capital to profitable markets."

In all this, the Chicago school of antitrust evidences a strong preference for a market as free as possible from state interference in all of its manifestations. Unless a powerful reason exists for interfering, the state should avoid doing so inasmuch as each intervention may cause other unintended economic distortions and redistribute wealth, which was not part of its intention. On this point the Chicago school is unambiguous—it rejects wealth redistribution through antitrust enforcement as an appropriate role for the state and attempts to restore the state to the position of neutral umpire, which it held in the classical model.

The Chicago school's ascendancy to its dominant position in antitrust in the 1980s was greatly aided by two political factors. First, there was a shift to the right on the U.S. Supreme Court in the 1970s, as the retirements of Chief Justice Warren, Justices Black, Harlan, Fortas, and Douglas led to the appointment, by Presidents Nixon and Ford, of Harry A. Blackmun, Warren E. Burger, William H. Rehnquist, Lewis F. Powell, Jr., and John Paul Stevens.[94] Then, upon his election in 1980, President Ronald Regan appointed William Baxter as his first Assistant Attorney General to take charge of the Antitrust Division, and James C. Miller III as head of the Federal Trade Commission.[95] These two appointments were fundamental in assisting President Reagan in implementing his promise to reduce government's size, scope, and role in business.

The judicial, political, and administrative environments could not have been more accommodating to Chicago school ideas. Baxter was unequivocal in setting forth the standards that he would apply as the Justice Department's chief antitrust enforcer; the same can be said for Miller at the FTC. As characterized by Stoll and Goldfein (1999, p. 3), under Baxter,

> Criminal enforcement proceedings would be limited to cases presenting conduct proscribed by the rule of per se illegality, the use of which would be appropriate

---

[94] Of these, Blackman and Stevens are the two least Chicago-oriented.

[95] Miller is associated with "the Virginia school" of public choice analysis, which shares certain philosophical commonalities with the Chicago school and is discussed in chapter 3.

only in those instances involving cartel-type behavior. Consistent with his con-sumer welfare standard, civil actions challenging horizontal and vertical restraints would be limited to situations where there was a potential for substantial output re-strictions. In this vein, he turned his back on enforcement of the Robinson-Patman Act because there was no threat of higher consumer prices [nor were there] reduc-tions in output. Regarding enforcement of §2 of the Sherman Act, Baxter's view was that as long as a firm was pursuing some legitimate competitive goal the firm's conduct should not be challenged, even if it held a dominant market position.

This became known as the "Baxterization" of the Antitrust Division.[96]

Furthermore, by the late 1980s, several opinions of the United States Supreme Court strongly suggested that antitrust authorities and the courts had come a long way in adopting the ideas being advocated by members of the Chicago school.[97] The Chicago school also had an immediate impact with its influence on the revisions to the Department of Justice Merger Guidelines, to which we now turn.

ANTITRUST MERGER GUIDELINES INCORPORATE THE CHICAGO APPROACH

Shortly after becoming assistant attorney general in charge of the Antitrust Division, Baxter announced that the division would undertake to review and revise its merger guidelines. The new guidelines were to replace an earlier set that had been issued by the Justice Department in 1968 under then Assistant Attorney General Donald Turner, the first Ph.D. economist to lead the antitrust division and architect of the 1968 guidelines. Early indications were that the division believed that some loosening of the 1968 guidelines was appropri-ate. On June 14, 1982, the Antitrust Division issued its long-awaited Merger Guidelines and the Federal Trade Commission (FTC) issued its own "State-ment Concerning Horizontal Mergers." The merger guidelines described the criteria and process by which the Antitrust Division would analyze the com-petitive impact of proposed mergers and, consequently, the basis upon which it would decide whether to challenge them under the antitrust laws. The FTC simultaneously issued a statement on horizontal mergers, announcing that it would give "considerable weight" to the Justice department's guidelines in making its own enforcement decisions.

The 1982 Merger Guidelines were considered a "revolutionary leap for-ward." They were drafted in the light of the then-recent Supreme Court merger decisions, as well as economic studies of antitrust issues—many of which em-anated from the Chicago school. The new guidelines were intended to evidence a much greater economic logic, relying primarily on the Chicago notions of

[96] This moniker is largely attributed to Victor H. Kramer (1981).

[97] Two U.S. Supreme Court cases that illustrate the impact of the Chicago school on judicial thinking are *Continental T. V., Inc. v. GTE Sylvania Inc.* 433 U.S. 36 (1977) and *Matsushita Elec-tronic Industrial Co., Ltd. v. Zenith Radio Corp.* 475 U.S. 574 (1986).

economic price theory, largely to the exclusion of legislative concerns that resulted in the passage of the antitrust laws (Stoll and Goldfein 2002, p. 3).[98] The
guidelines began with an explicit statement of their underlying theme:

> Mergers should not be permitted to create or enhance "market power" or to facil-
> itate its exercise. A sole seller (or "monopolist") of a product with no good substi-
> tutes can maintain a selling price that is above the level that would prevail if the
> market were competitive. Where only a few firms account for most of the sales of
> a product, those firms can in some circumstances coordinate, explicitly or implic-
> itly, their actions in order to approximate those of the monopolist. . . . Although
> they sometimes harm competition, mergers generally play an important role in a
> free enterprise economy. . . . While challenging competitively harmful mergers,
> the Department seeks to avoid unnecessary interference with that larger universe
> of mergers that are either competitively beneficial or neutral. (Blumenthal 2000,
> p. 11)

The stated theme explains the guidelines' emphasis on horizontal mergers and
the abandonment of approaches to vertical and conglomerate mergers es-
poused by the 1968 guidelines.

The new guidelines consisted of five basic elements. First, markets, each
consisting of a group of products and a geographic area, would be defined for
each product of each of the merging firms by analyzing the ability of buyers
to substitute to other products and/or to substitute to the same product produced in other areas. That is, a market would consist of a group of products
and an associated geographic area such that (in the absence of new entry) a
hypothetical, unregulated firm that made all the sales of those products in that

---

[98] It should be noted here that some questioned the basis upon which Baxter set forth the 1982
(and thereafter, the 1984) Department of Justice Merger Guidelines. As background, Baxter and
Bork were members of the Neal Committee of 1968, the committee that came up with recommendations for legislation to break up so-called concentrated industries (quite consistent with the pre-
Chicago, New Coalition thinking). Bork consistently dissented from this effort, describing it as ille-
gitimate from its inception and specious from the outset (see Rowe—in panel discussion—1985,
p. 31). Baxter, on the other hand, went along with what can only be termed a policy of large-scale
industrial deconcentration, based on the premise of the report that rested on oligopoly theory. For
Bork and other members of the Chicago school who rejected the traditional theory of oligopoly of
the day, the merger guidelines promulgated in 1968, 1982, and then 1984 were deemed to be without foundation, because their explicit premise rested on the economic oligopoly model—a model
that provided the only coherent rationale undergirding the notion of high concentration and market
share levels and one they thought to be legally suspect. Baxter's response to this was simply that
the position he took "*does* rest on an oligopoly theory, but it is not *that* oligopoly theory. It is a theory that says firms are always tempted to fix prices, to raise prices if they can. Usually, it's very,
very difficult; they may try but they can't coordinate, it falls apart. But, if a certain set of conditions
is met, it becomes more nearly feasible; if products tend to be homogeneous and the number of
firms tend to be small. The criteria that show up in the Merger Guidelines represent a sort of pro-
phylactic approach to conspiratorial collusion" (Baxter—in panel discussion—1985, p. 34).

area could increase its profits through a small but significant and nontransitory increase in price above prevailing or likely future price levels. Under the new guidelines, a market would be considered an analytical construct consisting of a product and an area, not a group of sellers or buyers or both. Thus, the market definition issue would turn on the question, "If the merging firms perfectly coordinated their actions, could all present and potential sellers of the product in the area profitably raise prices?" The premise here is that if, absent regulation, the sole seller of a product in an area could not raise prices profitably above prevailing or likely future levels, then the merger of two sellers of that product in that area could not enhance market power meaningfully.

Second, the guidelines include as "competitors" in a market not only present sellers of the relevant product in the relevant area but also sellers of other products who could quickly and economically, in response to a small but significant and nontransitory increase in price, begin to sell the relevant product in the relevant area using existing facilities.

Third, market shares would be assigned to each of the present competitors in the market according to particular geographic area based on consumption in the area as well as some consideration for production or capacity to produce in that particular geographic area.

Fourth, while the size distribution of firms is to be examined, the primary analytical procedure set out in the 1982 guidelines is somewhat different than the previous procedure, although the two basic ingredients—concentration and market shares—remain unchanged. Concentration would be measured not by reference to traditional four-firm concentration ratios, but instead on the Herfindahl-Hirschman Index (HHI). Under the new guidelines, there would be three sets of rules for gauging whether the Justice Department would challenge a particular merger, and these rules would be based on different levels of market concentration as determined by the HHI, which would result after the proposed transaction is completed. In essence, the shares of the merging firms were to be examined to determine whether the merger would significantly increase the likelihood of collusion. The guidelines also list many other factors that affect the ease and profitability of collusion, including the nature of the product and its manner of trade, the availability of information about competitors, and the existence of substitutes not included in the market.

Fifth, entry conditions are examined to determine whether collusion by present competitors would be profitable. It was clear that the premise of the guidelines was that high concentration poses little threat to competitive market performance if entry is very easy. The guidelines indicate that the department is unlikely to challenge mergers in markets into which entry is so easy that incumbents would be unable profitably to raise price to a significant extent and for a significant period of time.

The significance of these revisions to the Merger Guidelines is profound, as reflected in Stoll and Goldfein's (2002, p. 3) assertion:

> No policy document issued by the antitrust agencies has been more enduring or far-reaching. . . . Its analysis is as dynamic and vital as the economy to which it is applied and it must be acknowledged that anything less may have unnecessarily impeded the efficiency of the economy, restricted the efforts of American business to compete internationally and, thus reduced the well-being of American consumers.

The new guidelines established the presumption that the "larger universe of mergers [is] either competitively beneficial or neutral" (Stoll and Goldfein 2002, p.3).

The impact on merger activity during the Reagan administration was significant. In 1980, the reported value of mergers was $33 billion; in 1988, $266 billion, an increase of over 700 percent—it turned out to be one of the greatest merger movements in our history. One cannot say definitively that there was a direct causal connection between Chicago-school thinking and the merger wave of the late 1970s through the mid-1980s. A large part of it was conglomerate in nature and, truth be told, no school had a good theory to deal with such mergers. Nonetheless, it is safe to say that the pervasive influence of the Chicago school—with its view that mergers are typically efficiency-enhancing and beneficial to consumers—certainly provided an atmosphere conducive to, if not a "green light" for, those seeking mergers. In the final analysis, the concepts underlying the 1982/1984 guidelines are now so well accepted that even non-Chicago enforcers of antitrust use them. As written and enforced, they do not curtail corporations from engaging in mergers on a scale unthought of thirty years ago.

In summary, during the late 1970s and early 1980s, largely due to what was transpiring at Chicago, economic theory began to play an ever-increasing role in antitrust thinking generally and in merger enforcement in particular. The Chicago law and economics movement posited that the antitrust laws were essentially economic in their underpinnings and that their primary objective should be to increase efficiency and thereby reduce consumer welfare loss. This perception of the objectives of the antitrust laws caused a reformulation of the antitrust enforcement policy, and the use of economic justification has largely supplanted all other considerations as the basis of antitrust enforcement in the merger area. The concepts of increased concentration of resources and trends toward such increases, and their purported impact on economic performance, which for so long acted as the catalyst for merger enforcement, no longer trigger government challenge (Stoll and Goldfein 2002, p. 3).

That having been said, the evolution of antitrust is by no means complete. Stringent opposition to the Chicago school still exists and has had some influence on recent litigation. Yes, it is now generally accepted that economics is

essential to a proper fashioning of antitrust policy, but the Chicago approach is not the final word, according to many. It is commonly recognized that monopolization is not something that can be ignored; that exclusive dealing and predatory pricing can still be a problem; that the tying problem persists; and that we do need to worry about exclusionary practices (in part because of information asymmetries). Finally, serious concerns over policies affecting innovation and mergers still present challenges to antitrust policymakers. In all this, it is clear that the Chicago school has been at work in the field of antitrust law, in and through both the courts and the Antitrust Division. Perhaps Hovenkamp (1985, p. 283) sums it up best when he states, "The Chicago School of antitrust analysis has made an important and lasting contribution to antitrust policy. The School has placed an emphasis on economic analysis in antitrust that will likely never disappear."

CHAPTER 3

Public Choice Theory

Public choice is the study of the political market.
Essentially it is economic methodology applied to
political science.
(Johnson 1991, p. 12)

INTRODUCTION

PUBLIC choice theory is defined as the economic analysis of nonmarket decision-making—a body of theory that treats individual decision-makers as participants in a complex interaction that generates political outcomes. It is also defined more narrowly as the application of economic analysis to political decision-making, including theories of the state, voting rules and voter behavior, apathy, party politics, logrolling, bureaucratic choice, policy analysis, and regulation.[1] As such, it constitutes an approach to Law and Economics that focuses predominately on the creation and implementation of law through the political process—the demand for law and the supply of law, if you will—as opposed to the more judicially focused, common-law-oriented nature of Chicago law and economics. Over the past few decades, public choice analysis, like Chicago law and economics, has made substantial inroads into the conventional paradigms of both economics and political science. David Skeel (1997, p. 648) even contends, "By many yardsticks, public choice is the single most successful transplant from the world of economics to legal scholarship." Reflecting its focus on the interaction between politics and law, public choice offers its own distinct perspective on our three fundamental questions about the law.

The development of public choice theory stems in part from the dissatisfaction among economists and some political scientists with the state of the field of political science in the middle of the twentieth century. During the first half of that century, economics had begun to construct coherent, systematized, integrated models of the private sector, including models that described the

---

[1] For more extensive analyses of the topics and ideas covered here, see Buchanan and Tollison (1972, 1984), McLean (1987), Mueller (1989, 2003), Buchanan (1986), Johnson (1991), Farber and Frickey (1991), Stearns (1997), and Tullock, Seldon, and Brady (2002). We also call the reader's attention to two public choice symposium issues of major law reviews: *Virginia Law Review* 74 (March 1988): 167–518 and *George Mason Law Review* 6 (1998): 709–1012.

nexus between competitive markets and economic welfare. These models set out the conditions for market success and, just as important, the sources of market failure and the resultant inefficiencies. It also generated prescriptive governmental remedies to confront such failures. In doing so, economic theory either explicitly or implicitly assumed a government able to efficiently remedy market failures, levy taxes, supply public goods, and so on. As Coase (1964, p. 195) pointed out, however, there appeared to be an imbalance in the theory of economic policy: "we find a category 'market failure' but no category 'government failure.'"

Political science was of little help here. Having never developed comparable systematized, integrated models of the public sector, political science had no mechanism to identify and deal with potential public-sector failures and the resultant inefficiencies.[2] Mancur Olson (1966, pp. 3–4), who was simultaneously a founder and sympathetic critic of public choice analysis summed up the situation in an appeal to the Social Science Research Council for support for the then-fledgling public choice movement. Economists, he said, had "been working with considerable success for more than a century and a half to explain how well or how badly markets function in various circumstances, [but] they have barely begun to consider how governments or other types of organization will perform these functions." He went on to observe that political scientists had "neglected to master certain scholarly methods of extraordinary importance," and only rarely used deductive modeling techniques and statistical testing. The result, he said, was that "those political problems that are logically too complex to be feasibly capable of solution unaided by common sense, and which demand properly theoretical or mathematical modes of thinking, have not usually been studied," and, moreover, the methods used by political scientists made sophisticated quantitative analysis virtually impossible. As Johnson (1991, pp. 3–4) put it, "[M]ost political scientists devoted their efforts to political and philosophical history, political institutions, political power, data collection and surveys, and to a seemingly endless search for morally and socially correct government policies that would achieve the 'common good.'" James Buchanan, recipient of the 1986 Nobel Prize in economics, in part for his contributions to the theory of public choice, has suggested that this view of the state "proved to be highly conducive to very rapid growth in the size and scope of the public or governmental sector" (1975a, p. 171). A second, less controversial but equally significant consequence was that it left a void in the theory that was ultimately filled by public choice analysis.

The scholars who pioneered public choice analysis suggested that, at the most general level, private and public sector activities parallel one another: in

[2] Johnson's (1991, pp. 3–4) commentary on this period reflects a similar view of the situation: "[T]he emerging profession of political science did not view the political market [or public sector] as a clear alternative to the private market."

the private sector, individuals reveal and satisfy their preferences through the price mechanism of the market, whereas, in the public sector, individuals reveal and satisfy their preferences through collective decision-making that takes place under the aegis of the state. The major differences between the two sectors center on the institutions—the choice mechanisms—employed in each to allocate society's scarce resources in the attempt to satisfy individual or group preferences. By placing the analysis of private and public sectors under a common paradigm, public choice scholars were able to analyze government processes in the same way that economists had long analyzed market processes. In doing so, they were able to develop theories of government success and failure on a par with the more familiar orthodox economic theories of market success and failure.[3]

Public choice theory traces its roots to the analysis of voting rules in the eighteenth and nineteenth centuries. Of particular import here are Charles de Borda's analysis of the impact of simple plurality voting; Marie Jean Antoine Nicholas Caritat—Marquis de Condorcet on, among other things, plurality voting; Pierre-Simon, Marquis de LaPlace's examination of weighted voting schemes; and Charles Dodgson's—a.k.a. Lewis Carroll, of *Alice in Wonderland* fame—work on the theory of elections. The late nineteenth and early twentieth centuries brought Knut Wicksell's contributions to the analysis of tax and expenditure policies (a major source of inspiration for Buchanan), Eric Lindahl's early development of the theory of public goods, and the Italian public finance tradition, which explicitly incorporated government behavior into its analysis of public goods provision and taxation (Buchanan 1960, Medema 2005). The real explosion, though, came in the middle of the twentieth century, both as public finance scholars branched out beyond government tax and expenditure policies in an effort to explore voting theory, and via the publication of a number of seminal works that played an important role in the development of the field:

- a series of articles by Duncan Black in the late 1940s, culminating with his path-breaking book *The Theory of Committees and Elections* (1958), which probes the question of how committees reach decisions when agreement among all members is not possible;
- Anthony Downs's *Economic Theory of Democracy* (1957), which recast political parties as acting analogously to profit-maximizing firms;
- Mancur Olson's *The Logic of Collective Action* (1965), which set forth various theories of interest group behavior, describing the factors that enable one interest group to prevail over another;
- political scientist William H. Riker's *The Theory of Political Coalitions* (1962), which suggested that groups act to ensure minimally winning coalitions;

[3] On this point, see Buchanan (1975a, p. 171) and Medema (2003).

- Gordon Tullock's *The Politics of Bureaucracy* (1965), Anthony Downs's *Inside Bureaucracy* (1967), and William Niskanen's *Bureaucracy and Representative Government* (1971), which looked at the bureaucrat as another utility maximizer;
- Kenneth Arrow's, *Social Choice and Individual Values* (1951), which explored the impact of voting rules on social welfare; and
- Paul Samuelson's many contributions to the theory of public goods (1955), which set out the conditions necessary for efficient provision of collectively consumed good and the circumstances under which underprovision could occur in the market (extending some of the earlier ideas of Lindahl in the process).

Each of these works contributed in various ways to creating the background against which public choice analysis emerged.

While the modern public choice theory has this vast array of roots, the formal inception of the public choice "school" can be marked with the establishment, in 1957, of the Thomas Jefferson Center for Studies in Political Economy at the University of Virginia by James M. Buchanan and Warren Nutter. Buchanan had been a student of Frank Knight at the University of Chicago, and his work during the 1950s, very much influenced by is reading of Wicksell, had been directed toward putting the theory of public finance on more sophisticated political foundations. A subsequent series of conferences on issues in nonmarket decision-making organized by the center led to the founding of the Public Choice Society (initially under the title "Committee on Non-Market Decision-Making") in 1963. In 1966 an economic journal titled *Papers on Non-Market Decision Making* was established under the editorship of Gordon Tullock. Two years later, the journal's name was changed to *Public Choice*, and it became the formal journal of the Public Choice Society. In 1969, following a period of controversy at the University of Virginia, Buchanan and Tullock moved their operations to Virginia Polytechnic Institute and established the Center for Study of Public Choice. In part because of the center's extensive program of visiting scholars from around the world, the internationalization of public choice came rather quickly, as evidenced by the formation of the European Public Choice Society already in 1972.[4] Then, in 1982, the center shifted its entire operations to George Mason University, where it continues to operate today.[5] In point of fact, however, public choice has diffused itself throughout the economics and political science professions, and, as with Chicago law and economics, scholars operating under its umbrella can be found in universities and law schools across the United States and, indeed, the world.[6]

---

[4] The Japanese Public Choice Society was formed a little over two decades later, in 1996.

[5] George Mason also has a thriving law and economics program which reflects the influences of public choice, Chicago, and Austrian perspectives.

[6] Surveys of these events can be found in Medema (2000), Mitchell (1988), as well as in the articles appearing in the symposium on the Virginia Tech years, which appeared in the *American Journal of Economics and Sociology* 63, no. 1 (2004), and was also published as Pitt, Salehi-Isfahani, and Eckel (2004).

THE METHODOLOGY OF PUBLIC CHOICE

The methodology of pubic choice theory involves three different, but related, elements: (i) the selection of the stage of choice under scrutiny, the options being the constitutional stage of choice and the institutional stage of choice; (ii) whether one is engaged in positive analysis or normative prescription; and (iii) whether one adopts the homo economicus approach or a catallatic approach. Each will be explored in the following pages.

Stages of Choice

The economic analysis of collective decision-making processes has evolved to the point where it now consists of several strands, only two of which will be dealt with here.[7] The first of these concerns the constitutional stage of choice—the establishment of the rules of the game—where the social contract, or constitution, that sets out the rules governing collective choices is decided upon. This is sometimes referred to as "constitutional economics," or "constitutional political economy." The other branch centers on the institutional stage of choice and involves the economic analysis of political and governmental processes, including the activities of the executive branch, legislatures, and politicians, as well as of voting procedures and bureaucracies.

Positive and Normative Public Choice

As with Chicago law and economics, public choice theory has both positive and normative components.[8] The positive branch of public choice assesses the impact on political outcomes and the associated implications for economic efficiency of voting behavior, political behavior, the legislative process, bureaucratic decision-making, and the regulatory process. This analysis, in turn, serves as input into the normative analysis of the rules governing political

---

[7] A third major strand is axiomatic social choice theory, which, owing to space limitations, we will not explore here. This literature is an outgrowth of the theory of welfare economics and the literature on real-valued social welfare functions. Given the many difficulties in formulating real-valued social welfare functions, social choice theory sets forth various sets of axioms (based on specified value judgments) and attempts to determine the results of various collective choice processes (typically various voting schemes). For a concise review of the literature on real-valued social welfare functions and axiomatic social choice theory, see Mueller (2003, chs. 23, 24). As it has developed, social choice theory has become increasingly mathematical and abstract. On this latter point, see Mitchell (1982, pp. 98–101).

[8] For a concise, critical review of both the positive and normative elements of public choice theory, see Farber and Frickey (1991).

operations and behavior, including the design of efficient constitutions and other proposals for legislative and regulatory reform. Our discussion here will be largely confined to the positive branch of conventional public choice theory and the normative aspect of constitutional economics.

Homo Economicus and Catallaxy

Public choice analysis also embodies elements of two separate, but in some ways complementary, methodological approaches—homo economicus and catallaxy. Both the economics of the political process and constitutional economics utilize elements of homo economicus and catallactic methodologies. The economic analysis of the political process, however, relies much more heavily on the methodology of homo economicus. The methodology of constitutional economics, in contrast, is heavily catallactic, in that it emphasizes the development of rules for making rules at the constitutional stage of choice—rules for channeling the calculus of consent to produce an efficient constitution.

HOMO ECONOMICUS

The homo economicus approach is simply the standard maximizing paradigm of microeconomics,[9] where individuals in both political and economic arenas are assumed to behave as if they are maximizing utility. Agents' utility functions, then, include variables associated with the political process and political outcomes. The argument here is that the individuals who act in the political context are the same individuals who act in the market context and are likely to be similarly motivated—to make choices that maximize their utility—in both arenas.[10] In this respect, its underlying methodology and perspective are similar to that of the Chicago school's economic analysis of law and economic imperialism generally: probing the implications of the idea that agents are rational utility maximizers in all areas of life. It was Gordon Tullock who brought the hard-nosed homo economicus perspective to the Virginia tradition. Tullock and others showed how this approach is readily amenable to the positive analysis of a wide range of political behavior—for example, voting behavior under alternative voting systems; politicians, political parties, and political activity; the legislative process; bureaucratic activity and the regulatory process; and the implications of all of this for political-legal-economic outcomes.

[9] Buchanan (1986, p. 25) has also referred to this as the "maximization-scarcity allocation-efficiency" paradigm.

[10] This is explored more fully in the section titled "Methodological 'Closure.'"

CATALLAXY

"Catallaxy" is a term suggested by Frederick A. Hayek and is derived from the earlier idea of "catallactics," the nineteenth-century science of exchanges. Within the catallaxy approach, the concepts of spontaneous coordination and spontaneous order take center stage over the principle of maximization, and the emphasis shifts from simple to complex exchanges. That is, the focus is on all processes of voluntary agreements among persons—not only those in the more familiar economics arena, but also now extended to those in the political arena.[11] The market and the democratic state are looked on as social institutions, each of which serves to aggregate individual preferences. As Buchanan and Tullock (1962, p. 19) described them, "The market and the State are both devices through which co-operation is organized and made possible."

The central thrust of the catallactic approach, as advanced by the Virginia school, is to take individual decision-makers as the basic unit of analysis, but, in recognition of the fact that political outcomes are the result of interactions of large numbers of individuals, to view both politics and the political processes in terms of the exchange paradigm and develop models that reflect this (Buchanan 1986, pp. 20–21). Because the exchange relations in the political arena are governed by the set of extant political rules, one branch of the catallaxy approach directs attention to the development of these rules of the game—constitutions, as it were—via *processes* of exchange, trade, agreement, and contract. For Buchanan (1975a, p. 53), contractarian public choice theory constitutes a "genuine theory of law" and, as such, allows him to assert that, once so conceived, "there are no lines to be drawn at the edges of 'the economy' and the 'polity,' or between 'markets' and 'governments,' between 'the private sector' and the 'public sector'" (1986, p. 20). In catallaxy, "the state cannot be conceived as some community embodiment of abstract ideals which take form over and beyond the attainment of the individuals" (Buchanan 1975a, p. 68).

The positive branch of catallaxy applies the public choice paradigm at the level of simple exchange within well-defined rules. At the most basic level, this approach is concerned with the constitutional stage of choice, where the basic rules of collective order are resolved, whereas, at a more intermediate level, the discussion concerns the determination of the structure of government institutions (Buchanan 1975b, p, 228). Much of the positive literature within catallaxy attempts to describe how differences among people are reconciled under the prevailing political institutions. Specifically, it tries to describe more accurately and thereby enhance our ability to differentiate between those institutional arrangements that bring individuals' self-interest and the general

---

[11] The concept of catallaxy is described in Buchanan (1986, pp. 19–27).

welfare into harmony and those institutional arrangements that leave them in conflict (Gwartney and Wagner 1988, p. 8). On the normative side, these insights are then used to offer prescriptions regarding existing rules, outcomes, and possibilities for reform.[12]

Public Choice versus Political Science

The foregoing discussion also gives us strong hints as to what public choice is *not*. Specifically, public choice theory rejects two basic tenets of conventional political science. First, it rejects the organic conception of the state in favor of a methodological individualist approach. That is, public choice theorists forcefully argue that "the state is not an organic body apart from the collection of individuals comprising it" (Johnson 1991, p. 11). Second, it rejects the view that government officials, be they legislators, regulators, or bureaucrats, seek to act for the common good or in the public interest, blindly taking orders from superiors (Gwartney and Wagner 1988, p. 7).[13] Public choice theory is, as Buchanan (1984a, p. 11) has put it, "[T]he avenue through which a romantic and illusory set of notions about the workings of governments and the behavior of persons who govern has been replaced by a set of notions that embody more skepticism about what governments can do and what governors will do, notions that are surely more consistent with the political reality that we may all observe about us." The argument is not only with conventional political science, however. Public choice also rejects the role of government inherent in neoclassical welfare economics—a role that would have the government ever ready and able to intervene to enhance social welfare by ensuring that public goods are supplied in ideal quantities, and that externalities are internalized in a cost-effective manner, or to see to it that the use of open-access resources is limited to a socially optimal level. In public choice the government is not seen as an impartial referee nor as an omniscient corrector of market failures. Far from being "the impartial referee who sets the by-laws by which the economic 'game' in the market is played," government, as Arthur Seldon (1991, p. x) has observed, becomes "a powerful participant in the game, much more powerful than the individuals or firms and other 'players.'" Because of this, the "notion of government as the impartial chair or referee is a myth of conventional political

---

[12] These ideas are more extensively dealt with later, in our discussion of constitutional economics.

[13] Skeel (1997, p. 649) puts all of this quite bluntly: "If nothing else, public choice cast cold water on this perspective and offered a much more sober view of the political process." Buchanan (1987, p. 226) went to far as to assert that "[t]here exists . . . no 'public interest' as such in a society of freely choosing individuals."

science."[14] Against this received political theory, public choice theory characterizes each legislator, regulator, and bureaucrat as having his or her own preferences, interests, and goals and making choices accordingly.

There is one further distinction to be made between public choice—particularly its catallaxy variant—and conventional political science, a distinction that centers on the question of power and who should incorporate power into their analysis. Whereas catallaxy views politics and the political process in terms of a complex, voluntary exchange paradigm, the focus of political science is on the nonvoluntary relationships among individuals involving power and coercion. Buchanan stresses that the catallaxy approach of public choice theory does not imply or suggest that the power elements of political relationships should be squeezed out of what is transpiring in the field of politics or within the political process. Indeed, he argues that this is (or should be) the realm of the discipline of political science. In this regard, Buchanan calls upon the discipline of political science to concentrate more attention on political power arrangements and for economics (public choice theory) to concentrate more attention on constitutional choice and market-like arrangements (1986, pp. 20–22).

Methodological "Closure"

We have noted that public choice theory offers a challenge to the neoclassical economics' view of government as an efficient vehicle for remedying market failure. In this sense, public choice theory's concern with the political process can be viewed as an "opening up" of the conventional neoclassical economic paradigm. At the same time, however, it also represents a "closing up" with respect to methodology. Each of these points deserves some elaboration.

As evidenced in the appendices to chapter 1, the role of government in neoclassical economics is that of an exogenous force rather than active participant. Its role of defining property, assigning rights to resources, and enforcing trades is taken as given; the focus of neoclassical analysis is on trading goods and commodities and the realignment of the use of resources—on the gains from trade in consumption and production. In all this, the political process is typically taken as given; that is, the government is viewed as a black box, so to

---

[14] Not only is it seen as a myth, indeed, the notion that the government can act in the common good or in the public interest is also, in part, viewed as responsible for the breakdown of the moral order of society: "Those who have promoted the extension of government's role under the folly that some national interest exists have, perhaps unwittingly, aided in the effective breakdown in the moral order" (Buchanan 1986, p. 117). For more on the role of dissatisfaction with political theory as a driving force behind the development of public choice analysis, see Medema (2000).

speak. Yes, there is an extended role for government when the market fails—to step in from its otherwise exogenous location and rectify the instances of market failure (through regulation or control)—but otherwise it remains like a referee, observing the action passively until a violation occurs. Moreover, there is no model of the government process. Government is simply assumed to be able to efficiently accomplish the necessary regulatory activities. Public choice "opens up" the economic analysis by incorporating the political process and political actors into the analysis as prominent players in the determination of aggregate economic outcomes. It does so through the formal application of economic analysis to such subject matters as the theory of the state, voting rules and voter behavior, party politics, logrolling, bureaucratic choice, and regulation.

Yet, public choice theory can also be understood as a movement toward "closure" in that, from the methodological perspective, it represents a movement toward the analysis of closed systems (Buchanan 1972a). In contrast to neoclassical economics, where the political institutions, political decision-makers, and thus political decisions are perceived as *exogenous* to economic activity, in public choice theory the political institutions, political decisions, and especially the political decision-makers are endogenous. Rational, utility-maximizing individuals do not act solely in the marketplace where goods, services, and factors of production are exchanged and, through the exchange process, exhaust the gains from trade. These same individuals also participate in the political decision-making processes, and do so with a view to enhancing their utility.[15] As with the analysis of market exchange, where the focus is on utility-maximizing movements within Edgeworth Boxes from positions off contract curves to positions on them in both exchange and production, the motive for agreement in political exchange is assumed to be the pursuit of self-interest, which leads to mutual gains in the division of the surpluses from trade that are available—this time, through political participation. Consequently, society's scarce resources are allocated by both the marketplace *and* the political process—by the same individuals acting in several separate capacities. Buchanan has described this methodological movement toward closure as follows:

> The critically important bridge between the behavior of persons who act in the marketplace and the behavior of persons who act in political process must be analyzed. The "theory of public choice" can be interpreted as the construction of such a bridge. The approach requires only the simple assumption that the same individ-

---

[15] Johnson (1991, p. 13) describes the prevailing mind set as follows: "Previously social scientists and political commentators assumed a curious dichotomy in human motivation where self-interest ruled supreme in all transactions within the private market but self-sacrifice predominated in the individual's relationship to the state."

uals act in both relationships. Political decisions are not handed down from on high by omniscient beings who cannot err. Individuals behave in market interactions, in political-governmental interactions, in cooperative-nongovernmental interactions, and in other arrangements. *Closure of the behavioral system,* as I am using the term, means only that analysis must be extended to the actions of persons in their several separate capacities. (Buchanan 1972a, p. 12, emphasis added)[16]

The consequences of this have been summed up nicely by Fred McChesney and William Shughart (1995, p. 10), who, in discussing the fundamental differences between private choices and public choices, observed that "[d]ifferent outcomes emerge not because public choices are guided by motives different from those guiding private choices, but rather because in private markets self-interested producers and consumers make choices that mainly affect themselves, while in political markets self-interested voters and politicians make choices that mainly affect others."

CONVENTIONAL PUBLIC CHOICE THEORY: THE ECONOMICS OF POLITICS

Conventional public choice theory attempts to develop a logical, positive, consistent theory linking individual behavior to collective action. This literature reflects an attempt to understand and explain the political, legislative, and bureaucratic outcomes that can be expected to follow from the rational utility-maximizing behavior of those engaged in the political, legislative, and bureaucratic choice-making processes under the extant set of constitutional rules governing these processes, as well as the implications of this for government and overall economic performance. As James Gwartney and Richard Wagner (1988, p. 7) describe it, "Public choice analysis is to governments what economic analysis is to the markets. In both cases, the outcomes will reflect the choices of individuals and the incentive structure which influences those choices. In the political arena, the major players are the voters, politicians, and the bureaucrats." Reflective of this market metaphor, much of this analysis focuses on the demand for and supply of "law" through the political process rather than the courts. Here, voters and lobbyists are demanders and, within the representative democracy context, politicians/legislators and bureaucrats function as the supply side.

---

[16] Buchanan (1986, pp. 23–24; 1988, p. 7) traces the roots of this movement toward closure to the work of Knut Wicksell as well as to that of a group of Italian public finance scholars of the late nineteenth and early twentieth centuries, including Antonio De Viti De Marco, Amilcare Puviani, Mauro Fasiana, and Matheo Pantaleoni. See also Buchanan (1960) and Medema (2005).

The Demand for Public and Political Goods and Services

The literature dealing with the demand side of the political marketplace focuses on the analysis of the voting mechanisms and criteria that should be used to pass laws or structure policy.[17] This applies both to direct democracy, where individuals vote on ballot initiatives, and to representative democracy, where individuals vote on political candidates and those political candidates, as legislators, vote on various forms of legislation. This demand-side analysis takes two forms: the positive description of the effects of alternative voting rules within direct democratic and legislative processes, and the normative determination of the appropriate baseline voting rules for society associated with the constitutional stage of choice, where the basic "rules of the game" are being framed.

UNANIMOUS CONSENT

One option for managing collective choices is, of course, to rely on the rule of unanimous consent. The origins of the public choice approach to the unanimity rule dates to the work of Knut Wicksell (1896) and his analysis of the unanimity rule for the provision of public goods. The rule requires that each decision authorizing a government expenditure be accompanied by a related tax bill to finance that expenditure and, further, that the joint expenditure-tax package be passed with unanimous consent.[18] Subsequent work by Lindahl (1919) and others has revealed that by the proper apportioning of benefits and burdens, unanimous consent can in fact be obtained. The attractiveness of the unanimity rule is that it is the only rule that ensures that legal changes constitute movements to a state where *everyone* is better off; if someone will be made worse off by the proposed law, rule, or new regulation under consideration, that person can vote against it and thus prevent its passage. Those who advocate the use of the unanimity rule tend to base their case on the underlying belief that a state that acts only on the basis of voluntary unanimous consent is, by definition, neutral, noncoercive, and hence legitimate.[19]

In spite of its seemingly attractive efficiency properties, the unanimity rule has two important difficulties associated with it. First, it is very costly, in

---

[17] An extensive discussion of alternative voting rules can be found in Mueller (2003, chs. 4–9).

[18] The central portion of this work appears as "A New Principle of Just Taxation," in Wicksell (1967).

[19] The most straightforward application of this is in the context of public goods. By adjusting individuals' tax shares ("Lindahl prices") to reflect the value that these individuals place on the public good in question, one can obtain unanimous consent on the provision and finance of the efficient amount of the public good.

terms of time and other resources, to design a proposal that will command unanimous consent, particularly given that people have different tastes and preferences. Second, by requiring complete unanimity for legislation to be approved, this rule gives individuals an incentive to engage in strategic behavior—to hold out, threatening to veto the proposed law, rule, or regulation unless additional benefits or a smaller share of the costs are apportioned to them. These various costs could well exceed the gains resulting from the legislation itself. Given these (and other) obstacles, it is unlikely that many new laws or rules, or changes in existing ones, will ever be passed under the unanimity criterion. Put another way, by giving a single voter the veto power, the unanimity requirement tends to perpetuate the status quo.

THE OPTIMAL MAJORITY

If unanimity is problematic, the question then becomes, with what rule do you replace it? That is, what is the optimal voting rule for a society to adopt? Here we find an immediate tendency to turn to some form of majority rule. Majority rule, however, fails to guarantee that only proposed laws, rules, or new regulations that are Pareto superior (i.e., make no one worse off and at least one person better off) will be passed into law. It also allows a majority to redistribute society's scarce resources to itself from a minority. The theoretical underpinnings for this view also owe to the work of Wicksell, who recognized that simple majority voting could result in the majority passing bills that concentrate benefits onto themselves while either placing the tax burden on a minority or thinly spreading it across the entire base—of which the beneficiaries constitute only a part. This has led some critics to question the legitimacy of majoritarian legislation on the grounds that statutes passed by simple majority rule are inconsistent with so-called neutral principles of law—a view reflected in John Ferejohn and Barry Weingast's contention that "[d]emocracy—understood as rule by the people or its representatives—is fundamentally at odds with the rule of law" (1992, pp. 567–68).[20] This view has led Louise Halper (1993, p. 231) to characterize the public choice paradigm as an "anti-majoritarian movement [that] seeks to show that legislative majorities are unable to produce law that is coherent, consistent, intelligible, or in a large sense, purposeful." In her depiction of public choice, we have a dismal (political-economic) science in which "not only is the legislative process flawed, but legislation itself is the factional attempt to utilize the state's coercive power for private, and generally redistrib-

---

[20] On this point, Buchanan and Tullock (1962, p. 96) argue that the "majority rule has been elevated to the status which the unanimity rule should occupy," and that "many scholars seemed to have overlooked the central place that the unanimity rule must occupy in any normative theory of democratic government," Elsewhere, Buchanan (1991, pp. 35–36) describes his own efforts in advancing contractarian public choice as defending "constitutional limits on majority voting" and as having "justified bounds on the exercise of majoritarian democracy."

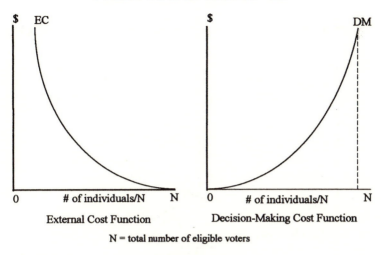

FIGURE 3-1.

utive ends." All of this, of course, is categorically at odds with what is perceived to transpire in the neutral, noncoercive, voluntary workings of the market sector. It is also totally at odds with the traditional view of the political process that one finds in conventional political science.

Of course, under our democratic system a legislative majority can always pass any laws whose scope and effects are not forbidden by the constitution, and, since the constitution does not speak to efficiency, there would be no reason to expect that the resulting laws would be efficient.[21] Thus, given the inherent propensity toward inefficiency under majority rule and the fact that such a large proportion of laws and associated rules and regulations are generated through a majoritarian process, it is not surprising to hear calls, such as that by Buchanan (1975a, p. 169), for serious consideration of "a genuine constitutional change."

Recognizing that all voting rules are costly, the quest for public choice was to identify those voting rules that would generate efficient political outcomes. Buchanan and Tullock began by defining the costs associated with various voting rules, focusing on the sum of (i) the *external costs of decision-making*

---

[21] This is essentially the point made by Halper (1993 p. 233), who observed that there is an inherent presumption "central to our constitution, that majority rule, however hemmed about by checks and balances, is the engine of the state created by the framers of the document. That presumption provides some legitimacy for state action that is inefficient, in the sense of producing outcomes different from those to be realized in a perfectly-functioning market. The majority may approve whatever the constitution does not forbid, and the constitution does not speak of efficiency."

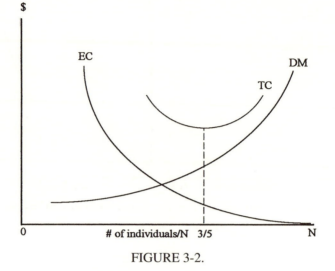

FIGURE 3-2.

(EC)—the costs borne by those who disapprove of a decision—and (ii) *the decision-making costs* (DM)—the bargaining costs associated with making a decision (see figure 3-1). EC decreases as the number of voters required to pass a proposal (N) increases, since fewer and fewer costs can be imposed on external parties as we consider adopting decision rules that come closer and closer to the unanimous consent requirement. Obviously, then, unanimity would be the efficient rule if DM were zero, as it minimizes EC. DM, however, is an increasing function of N, since it becomes increasingly costly to bring more and more individuals into the decision-making process as we consider adopting decision rules that come closer and closer to the unanimous consent requirement. The sum of these external and decision-making costs (TC in figure 3-2) reflects the total cost of imposing any particular consent requirement. Such is the perceived magnitude of DM that even those who are most predisposed to unanimity—including Wicksell, Buchanan, and Tullock—have argued that efficiency dictates something less that unanimity.

The goal from an efficiency perspective, then, is determining the voting rule that minimizes the sum of these costs. This occurs at three-fifths of the electorate in figure 3-2. We do not, however, expect that the cost-minimizing majority is likely to be the same across issues, given that EC and DM themselves tend to vary from issue to issue.[22] The task at the constitutional stage of choice—where the rules of the game are determined—is thus to decide, for

---

[22] The fact that one voting rule will not be optimal for all categories of issues is taken up by Mueller (2003, p. 74–76).

each specific category of public policy, the decision rule that will minimize the sum of these two costs. The optimal share of the votes required for a proposal to be adopted occurs at the minimum point on the U-shaped cost curve TC. In departing from the unanimous consent requirement and selecting the "optimal majority" rule, society, in effect, selects the most efficient rule (Buchanan and Tullock 1962, pp. 43–84), accounting for all costs associated with the voting process. It is in this sense that a "rationally"—or perhaps more accurately, "economically"—constructed constitution will allow for specific collective decisions to be made that do not meet the strict Pareto criterion. That is, while collective decisions can be made that do not meet the strict unanimous consent requirement, when viewed from a broader perspective—the constitutional stage of choice—a collective choice as to which voting rule to employ does attain a legitimated status. It does so because, although the decision may not be Pareto-efficient (here requiring only, say, a three-fifths vote instead of unanimous consent), the decision will have been made based on a rule that, a priori, minimizes the sum of the external costs and the decision-making costs to society and thereby has the virtue of being cost-minimizing. As such, it attains a legitimated status by advancing an economically constructed constitution.

SIMPLE MAJORITY RULE

While it may or may not be the optimal majority, the most widely known and widely used voting rule is simple majority voting, where each voter casts a single vote for a proposition or candidate, and the outcome is determined by which proposition or candidate receives more than 50 percent of the votes cast. The majority rule raises both efficiency and distributional issues.

Majority rule is thought to be relatively efficient in those instances where the electorate is asked to vote (up or down) on a single proposition or where a relatively efficient system was initially in place to narrow the field down to two candidates, particularly in societies wishing to avoid costly, time-consuming decision processes. The majority rule, by creating losers, however, guarantees outcomes that violate the Pareto criterion. In fact, simple majority rule will not guarantee Kaldor-Hicks efficient changes, wherein the gains to the winners exceed the losses to the losers. The problem is that a simple one-person, one-vote system does not allow individuals to register the intensity of their preferences for or against a legislative proposal. For example, although a legislative proposal may pass with 70 percent of the vote, that 70 percent of the electorate may gain less than the 30 percent who voted against the proposal lose. One way to get around this would be to allow the selling of votes. This practice is illegal but mechanisms to facilitate similar processes do exist and are explored more fully in the section on logrolling.

By virtue of the fact that it creates losers, redistribution is inevitable under the simple majority rule. Indeed, majority rule creates incentives *for* redistribution.

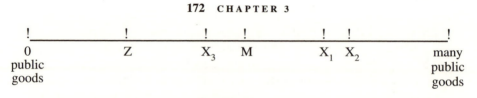

FIGURE 3-3.

Any majority coalition has an incentive to place as large a share of costs as possible on those who lose from the measure in question. In the limit, the winning coalition can redistribute costs away from itself up to the point where the share of the vote going to the proposal falls to 50 percent plus one.

MEDIAN VOTER THEOREM

Perhaps the most significant implication to arise from the public choice analysis of simple majority voting is the median voter theorem. The median voter model assumes, not unreasonably, that all voters can rank their positions on a scale—for example, over a range from extreme liberal to extreme conservative or from none of some public good to a large quantity of that public good.[23] The effect is that all voters can be placed along a spectrum such as that in figure 3-3. The voter who lies exactly in the middle of this spectrum, in the sense that there are equal numbers of voters on either "side" of him, is the median voter (Mr. M). The median voter theorem states that, under certain conditions, election outcomes—laws passed by citizens and legislatures, and those elected to office—will reflect the outcomes preferred by the median voter.

Suppose that this spectrum in figure 3-3 is over the quantity of public goods such as national defense, running from none on the left to very large levels of defense spending on the right, and that there are two ballot proposals for national defense provision, one at level X_1 and another at level X_2 (ignoring X_3 for the moment). Suppose further that point Z represents the position of some voter, Ms. Z. While neither proposition very accurately reflects Ms. Z's preferred level of national defense, she will vote for X_1 because it embodies a level of national defense that is closer to her preferred level than is X_2. More generally, proposal X_1 will be preferred by all voters to the left of X_1 and by half of those between X_1 and X_2. By the same reasoning, proposal X_2 will be favored by all voters to the right of X_2 and the other (right-hand) half of those between X_1 and X_2.

It should be obvious that X_1 will win the election. More to the point, whichever proposal can capture the median voter will win the majority vote. In this case, by capturing the votes of Mr. M and all those to the left of him, proposal X_1 is assured of victory. As such, an even smaller level of national

[23] See Black (1948a, 1948b, 1958) and Mueller (2003, pp. 85–93, 231–32).

TABLE 3-1

	Small	Medium	Large
Fred	1	2	3
Bob	2	3	1
Ralph	3	1	2

defense, such as X_3, could prevail over both X_1 and X_2 since it lies closer to the preferences of the median voter than either of the other options. The strategy for those proposing ballot initiatives or legislation is thus to design their proposal so that it reflects the preferences of, and thus captures the vote of, the median voter. Likewise, vote-maximizing politicians will adopt the program preferred by the median voter so as not to be "outflanked" by an election opponent.

It is interesting to note how the median voter idea helps us to understand the significance of the choice as to the size of the majority required for voter approval. Under a supramajority voting rule, where, say, two-thirds of the vote is needed to pass a ballot initiative or legislation, a greater proportion of the electorate must have their interests served to secure a law's passage. This implies that different allocations of benefits and costs are necessary under supramajority as against what would be required under a simple majority scheme. Smaller majorities allow for greater concentration of benefits and greater spreading of costs.[24] The size of the fraction of voters that must be captured to secure passage can thus drastically affect how ballot initiatives and legislation must be designed.

CYCLING

The outcome of a given vote will, in fact, reflect the preferences of the median voter if voters do not have multi-peaked preferences—in simple terms, if individual voters do not prefer both extremes to the middle ground.[25] A simple example will illustrate how multi-peaked preferences can cause problems with simple majority voting (see table 3-1).

Suppose that there are three voters, Fred, Bob, and Ralph, and that they have to vote over levels of national defense provision. The numbers reflect their preferences, with "1" being first preference (giving the individual the most utility among the options under consideration) and "3" being least. Thus, Fred prefers a small national defense; a medium-sized defense would be his

[24] This does not mean that simple majority and supramajority rules always generate different outcomes. Even under simple majority, distributions of costs and benefits are often such as to garner substantial majorities in favor of legislation.

[25] There is an abundance of literature on the issue of multi-peaked preferences and their implications for voting. Mueller (2003, ch. 5) provides a detailed discussion.

utility

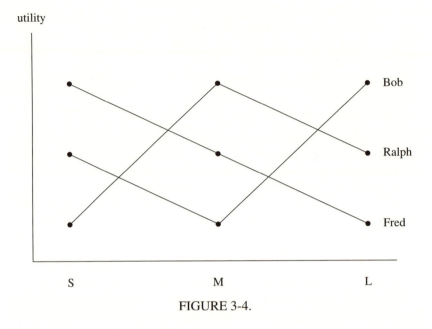

FIGURE 3-4.

second choice; and a large defense his third choice—and analogously for Bob and Ralph. In a pairwise vote, if the choice were between small and medium levels of defense, Fred and Bob would vote for small, while Ralph would vote for medium; thus, small would win (i.e., small beats medium). If the choice were between medium and large, medium would win, as it is favored by Fred and Ralph (i.e., medium beats large). Now, if small beats medium, and medium beats large, we would expect that, by transitivity, small would beat large. Notice, however, that while Fred prefers small to large, Bob and Ralph prefer large to small, and thus large wins. This is the standard representation of cycling, where there is no one outcome that can be said to be unambiguously preferred to the other two, in the sense of commanding majority support over both of them. The outcome of the series of votes will thus depend on the order in which the votes are taken.

This cycling problem is caused by the nature of Bob's preferences—specifically, that he prefers the two extremes to the middle ground. This phenomenon, which is known as multi-peaked preferences, and its contrast with the preferences of Fred and Ralph is illustrated in figure 3-4. Here the sketches of Fred's and Ralph's preferences have single peaks, whereas that of Bob is double-peaked. If instead Bob's preferences were single-peaked, the cycling problem would disappear. More specifically, if all voters have single-peaked preferences, there *is* a unique majority outcome in which the median voter's preferences carry the day.

The fact that political outcomes depend on the order of the voting process when some voters have multi-peaked preferences has implications for control over the voting process, or agenda-setting. With the large increases in federal and state legislation over the past three decades together with the rise of the modern administrative state, agenda setting has become an increasingly important topic in public choice theory. Indeed, as Riker (1993, p. 1) has observed, "Agendas foreshadow outcomes: the shape of the agenda influences the choices made from it. . . . [M]aking agendas seems just about as significant as actually passing legislation." Thus, in a very real sense, the legislative and bureaucratic agendas, when creatively manipulated, can, and oftentimes do, become the path to the final choice.

McKelvey and Schofield (1986) had previously demonstrated that agenda setting is a powerful device used to restrict the alternatives to be considered. From this vantage point the process of agenda formation can be viewed as a whittling-down process that Riker (1993, p. 2) describes in a hypothetical political discourse: Assume there is some feasible set of political issues potentially "on the table" for discussion. The first stage of restriction involves the use of constitutional barriers, government directives, and rhetorical and heresthetical maneuvers. Exercising a combination of these options serves to admit some issue from the feasible set to be considered while excluding others. At the second stage, politicians can maneuver to form a set of admissible alternatives to the temporarily fixed set established during stage one. Finally, politicians put in place a formal set of procedures (voting rules) for choosing one alternative over the others. This sequential narrowing of alternatives—the agenda—leads to the final choice.

Thus, agenda control assumes a great deal of import in these contexts in that those who control the order of voting can, in effect, predetermine the outcome. In the above small-medium-large example, if votes were conducted sequentially and small wins the contest against medium, medium against large, and large wins the vote against small, large would be the winner of that particular sequence of votes. Now suppose that we begin with small versus large, which large wins. A second round between medium and large is won by medium. Medium then takes on small, and small wins. Small, then, is the winner of that particular sequence of votes. Thus, if those controlling the agenda prefer "small," they can structure the order of votes so that small wins, and likewise for any other preferred outcome.

LOGROLLING

The problem of the inability of voters to register the intensity of their preferences affects both direct and representative democracy, and is evidenced with regard to preferences for or against candidates, ballot initiatives, and legislation, including regulations and tax-expenditure proposals. One way to overcome

this problem is through logrolling, or vote trading. Vote trading is technically illegal in the United States; nonetheless, logrolling is a common phenomenon that takes place during each and every legislative session. This is politics as exchange-catallaxy at the institutional rather than constitutional level. As Tullock has noted, "In the U.S. Congress logrolling is fairly open and above-board. Although the bulk of the negotiations takes place in committee sessions, cloakrooms, and congressional offices, there is no particular secret as to what is actually going on. People realize that the art of legislation involves bargaining, haggling, and efforts made to sweeten deals" (Tullock, Seldon, and Brady 2002, p. 30). Its greater prominence in legislative voting than in direct democracy is reflective of the lower transaction costs associated with organizing these trades in a legislative context, where numbers are far smaller, legislators are concentrated, and interaction is much more regularized and extensive than in direct democracy.

What happens in the logrolling process is that representative A agrees to vote for a bill that representative B wants passed, in return for B's vote on A's favored piece of legislation. Legislators who are in the minority on an issue about which they feel strongly may, through logrolling, be willing to trade their votes on other issues about which they feel less strongly in exchange for the votes of others legislators and, in the process, construct a majority coalition in favor of their preferred issue. From an efficiency perspective, logrolling is a two-edged sword: It allows efficient proposals that would not otherwise command a majority, in fact, to do so; however, it also allows for the passage of inefficient proposals that would not otherwise be adopted. A simple example will help make clear the issues and problems associated with logrolling.

Assume that the legislature operates under a system of simple majority rule, and that there are two bills under the legislature's consideration—Initiative I, "the farmers' bill," and Initiative II, "the environmental enhancement act." Assume further that there are three legislators—Urban Bob, Farmer Frank, and Environmental Earl. Table 3-2 shows the respective utilities derived by Urban Bob, Farmer Frank, and Environmental Earl under the two bills.[26] As we can see from the table, Urban Bob has no interest in either initiative. Indeed, he feels that the passage of either initiative will result in a loss of 200 utils of welfare.[27] Farmer Frank is an advocate of Initiative I, but, like Urban Bob, is opposed to Initiative II. Environmental Earl, on the other hand, is an advocate of

---

[26] The utils gained by our three legislators, Bob, Frank, and Earl, may be thought of as coming in the form of gains or losses in welfare to their constituents, which in turn translate into gains or losses in votes come election time.

[27] This could be because Bob's constituents' tax share outweighs their gains or because the rules flowing from the farm and environmental legislation negatively impact his urban constituents' utility.

TABLE 3-2

	Initiative I, "the farmers' bill"	Initiative II, "the environmental enhancement act"
	voter / representative	(measured in utils)
Urban Bob	−200	−200
Farmer Frank	+600	−200
Environmental Earl	−300	+500

Initiative II, but, also like Urban Bob, is opposed to Initiative I. Under simple majority rule, neither initiative gets passed since Urban Bob and Environmental Earl's negative votes would defeat Initiative I and Urban Bob and Farmer Frank's negative votes would defeat Initiative II.

Farmer Frank and Environmental Earl have an incentive to work a trade—that is, to engage in logrolling. Farmer Frank will agree to vote for Environmental Earl's favored Initiative II if, and only if, Environmental Earl promises to vote for Farmer Frank's favored Initiative I. (Of course, this assumes promises are considered binding.) If they logroll, Farmer Frank will then end up with a net gain of 400 utils (+600 − 200 = +400) and Environmental Earl with a net gain of 200 utils (+500 −300 = +200). Once the votes are traded and cast, Initiatives I and II both pass, to the net benefit of Farmer Frank and Environmental Earl. Meanwhile, Urban Bob's welfare is decreased by 400 utils. Thus, we can see that logrolling leads to the passage of both initiatives and a net increase in welfare of 200 utils.[28]

What public choice analysis reveals here is that, under simple majority rule and without the opportunity to engage in logrolling, those who have less intense preferences for various initiatives as measured by the expected utility gain or loss (such as the Urban Bobs of the world) are often able to dominate an election. Environmental Earl and Urban Bob would jointly defeat Initiative I, and Farmer Frank and Urban Bob would jointly defeat Initiative II. Logrolling, by way of contrast, allows individual voters or representatives (the Farmer Franks and the Environmental Earls) a mechanism to trade off their weaker preferences against their more strongly held ones.

In this example, prohibiting logrolling would deny the community a Kaldor-Hicks efficiency-enhancing opportunity. But this, however, is not

[28]
Urban Bob	− 400
Farmer Frank	+ 400
Environmental Earl	+ 200
Net	+ 200

always the case. As Mueller (2003, p. 106) points out, logrolling "also imposes externalities (utility losses) on the nontraders who would have been better off in the absence of trading, and, if these are large, they can outweigh the gains to the traders, lowering the community's net welfare." To see this, suppose that the passage of either initiative leaves Urban Bob with a loss of 400 utils each, rather than just 200. Both initiatives will still pass if logrolling is possible, but, from an efficiency standpoint, the community will be made worse off. Frank and Earl gain 600 utils between them, but Bob loses 800, leaving a net change in social welfare of -200 utils. That is, logrolling allows for the passage of Kaldor-Hicks inefficient proposals that would not otherwise be adopted.

There are two other objections to majority-rule logrolling cited in the public choice literature, and these, like the inefficiency issue, are a reflection of public choice's recurrent emphasis on "government failure." First, by enabling various interest groups to trade votes, one can reasonably anticipate a proliferation of passed initiatives. Here the public choice literature focuses on the usual suspects: tariff bills, tax loopholes, and, of course, everyone's favorite: pork-barrel public projects. "Pork," in the popular view, is the term used to catagorize an undefinable set of public projects that have been funded in the home district of a legislator other than one's own; from a public choice perspective, it is the sum of all of the "inefficient" public projects and programs passed and funded due to logrolling. As emphasized in the public choice literature, it virtually goes without saying that the logical outcome of government-project proliferation brought on by logrolling leads to increased government spending (which may take the form of deficit spending) and hence, larger and larger government. Second, since the initiatives that are passed must be financed from taxes, it should be clear from the previous example that Farmer Frank's and Environmental Earl's two passed initiatives are partly financed by tax revenues received from Urban Bob's constituents (assuming that all citizens are taxpayers). The extent of the redistribution is of course dependent upon each party's general tax obligation.[29] Thus, not only does logrolling allow for the passage of initiatives that are sometimes (read "often") inefficient and therefore encourage overspending by the government, but it also allows the beneficiaries of legislation to spread the associated expenditure burden onto other parties.[30]

[29] Additional sources of problems related to logrolling include the possibility of individuals or representatives strategically misrepresenting their preferences—bluffing as to voting intentions or outright cheating—and thereby causing unstable coalitions. The implicit assumption of the theory of logrolling has long been that vote-trading agreements are honored. Scholars working in the New Institutional Economics tradition have recently called this into question, as we shall see in chapter 5.

[30] While there are some in public choice that look more favorably on some of the outcomes associated with logrolling, the more-often expressed assessment of legislative logrolling goes something like the following: "[O]ptimistic descriptions of how the legislative process functions stands in sharp contrast to most of the majority rule–logrolling literature" (Mueller 1989, p. 94).

OTHER VOTING RULES

While simple majority and supra-majority rules are standard fare in the electoral process, there are other direct-democracy voting rules that offer alternative mechanisms for translating the preferences of individual citizens into a single, collective choice.[31] These voting rules can be applied to decisions regarding, or choices among, political propositions such as with respect to the supply of a public good, or candidates seeking office. The evaluation of these voting rules derives from the pioneering work of Duncan Black, who established the criterion for an efficient voting system. Simply put, this criterion is that "[t]he entire preference ordering of voters must be presented and the alternative or candidate with the highest standing on the voters' preference ranking is called the efficient candidate or alternative" (Johnson 1991, p. 168). Five such rules are described briefly here.[32]

In the *single vote plurality system*, each voter casts one vote for a proposition or candidate, and the winner is the proposition or candidate that receives the most votes—even if its share of the votes is less than 50 percent. The single vote plurality is considered fairly inefficient because the candidate elected or the winning proposition might not reflect the preferences of the majority of the voters. Consider a race of three candidates—one extreme left, one center left, and one center right. Suppose further that the preference ordering of 55 percent of the electorate is grouped on the left, say with 15 percent extreme left and 40 percent center-left, while the center-right had 45 percent support. By Black's criterion, a candidate from the left side of the spectrum would represent an efficient outcome. Yet with the distribution of the vote as stated here, under the rule of single vote plurality, the center-right candidate (with 45 percent) will be the winner—an inefficient outcome.[33]

A second option is the *single vote primary* (double election), and there are two variations of this rule. One, sometimes labeled the "open primary," involves the presentation of all alternatives or candidates to the voters in a first election. The two candidates with the greatest pluralities then run off against each other in the second election. Many U.S. cities use this rule to elect their mayors. A variation on this voting rule is used in the United States for presidential elections. Here, some designated groups (typically the two major political parties, as well as, in most election cycles, any number of minor parties), nominate their respective candidates according to their own internally

---

[31] This brief section describing six voting rules is a summary and synthesis that borrows directly from Johnson (1991, pp. 166–79).

[32] Three rules not included here are the exhaustive majority system (also known as the Condorcet criterion); the weighted ranking vote, first suggested by Borda; and the point distribution method.

[33] The analysis would be the same if the vote was between an array of propositions rather than a group of candidates.

established mechanisms. The candidates who emerge from this nominating process then compete in a general election, with the candidate with the plurality of votes winning the election.[34] This rule is subject to the same inefficiency problems as the single vote plurality. In fact, the alert reader will note that this problem is, in effect, what happened in the 2000 U.S. presidential election, where the votes on the left were divided between Al Gore and Ralph Nader, allowing George W. Bush to prevail in the election. An additional significant source of inefficiency under this rule is that the internal mechanisms for nominating a candidate in the first round may inadvertently eliminate the most efficient alternative.

The *alternative vote* is a mechanism that, while requiring more counting iterations (not voting iterations), does produce a more efficient outcome than any of the aforementioned rules. Under this scheme, each individual votes by ranking the candidates, say, in the case of four candidates, first, second, third, and fourth. If the initial vote count indicates that one candidate receives a minimum of half-plus-one first place votes, that candidate is immediately elected. If not, the candidate with the fewest first place votes is eliminated with all of the votes cast for him now allocated across the remaining three candidates based on their second choice votes previously registered on those ballots. This elimination process continues until one candidate receives more than fifty percent of the total vote.

A fourth rule is the *exhaustive primary system*. Again, assume that there are four candidates. Under this scheme, in the first round of elections, each voter is given three votes to cast and must cast one vote for each candidate except the one that is least acceptable. The candidate receiving the fewest votes in the first round is eliminated. A second round of voting ensues where each voter is now given two votes. Again each voter casts one vote for each candidate except the one that is least acceptable. The candidate receiving the fewest votes in this round is eliminated, and so on. Once only two candidates remain, with each voter having one vote, the candidate receiving the most votes in this final election is the winner. Beyond the need for costly, multiple, iterative elections, this option introduces the potential for additional inefficiency by opening the door to strategic voting. For example, consider an election with eight candidates, and suppose that for one particular group of voters, A is their preferred candidate and B their second choice. These voters, however, feel that if it comes down to a vote for A versus B in the final election, B may in fact win. In this case, they have an incentive not to include B on any of their initial iterative ballots in an attempt to eliminate B before getting to the final vote.

Finally, we have the *approval voting* scheme. Under approval voting every voter can vote for each candidate that he approves of—indeed, can vote for all

---

[34] This discussion excludes any discussion of the role and function of the U.S. electoral college.

the candidates if he believes all are acceptable. The candidate with the most votes wins the election. While considered more efficient than simple plurality, it, like the exhaustive primary system rule, is open to problems of strategic voting. That is, in our four-candidate illustration, a group of voters who prefer A to B but find both of them acceptable may not vote for B to increase the likelihood of A securing more votes than does B.

REFERENDA

For individuals and groups in society who prefer direct democratic processes to representative ones or do not feel that the "representative" process accurately and effectively translates their preferences into policy, the referendum represents an important mechanism to express their political preferences on issues about which they feel strongly. The referendum allows citizens to bypass involvement of political representatives and vote directly on a political initiative. The referendum process can take a variety of forms—four of which we will note only briefly here to give the reader a sense for the thrust of the literature.[35]

For example, let's take the case of an environmental bottle-deposit bill. The *direct referendum* process is used to enact legislation that the government has not yet addressed or considered. This method involves voters using the petition process to get the bottle-deposit bill put on the election ballot, and, if it secures a sufficient number of votes (usually a simple majority), it becomes law.[36] While the direct referendum bypasses the legislature completely, three other types of referenda are part of the overall legislative process rather than substitutes for the representative government. These referenda vary depending on the status of a given legislative initiative. The *obligatory referendum*, for example, requires that only those legislative initiatives that are antecedently approved by a referendum can become law. Thus, if heretofore "environmental statutes" were designated as coming under the rules of the "obligatory referendum," before the legislature can move forward to pass a bottle-deposit bill (or any other environmental statute), a bottle-deposit bill must first be passed in an obligatory referendum. The second is the *approval referendum,* used to pass muster on a bill which has already been voted on by the legislature. So, if a bottle-deposit bill has been passed by the legislature, then a subsequent approval referendum can either approve or disapprove (if the latter, then thereby negate) the legislation. The third is the *popular initiative,* a referendum vote on legislation that has been submitted to the legislature, but which the legislature has not yet taken up. Thus, if a popular initiative passes for a bottle-deposit

[35] These various types of referenda are discussed in Butler and Ranney (1978, 1994); see also Walker (2003).

[36] This form of referendum is very widely used in state and local politics in the United States.

bill, this would require that the legislature act on the bill one way or the other. Each of these schemes represents an alternative way for individuals in society to register directly their preferences on political issues or legislation and, thereby work to influence or (as in the latter case) bypass the intricate workings and nuances of representative government.

The Supply of Public and Political Goods and Services

The analysis of the supply side of the political market under representative democracy brings into play many of the same voting rules issues that we dealt with under direct democracy, but is also concerned with the behavior of politicians and of the bureaucrats who are charged with implementing the programmatic goals contained in legislation.[37] For example, some models within this branch of public choice theory focus on the behavior of voters in selecting and supporting legislators; other models look at the behavior of political parties and legislators during political campaigns; others focus of the behavior of legislators while in office; and still others look at the behavior of bureaucrats and their relationship to the legislators. The primary goals of the analysis here are to model political behavior accurately and to analyze the efficiency properties of the outcomes of the political process. As we alluded to at the beginning of this chapter, the theory that emerges from this analysis is one of government failure, leading Farber and Frickey (1991, pp. 22, 2) to describe public choice as "a jaundiced view of legislative motivation" with very explicit implications: "If the descriptions of public choice scholars are correct, certain normative conclusions seem inevitable, and those conclusions are generally not happy ones."[38]

REPRESENTATION IN A DEMOCRATIC SYSTEM

The electoral mechanism employed in the United States to select representatives at state and federal levels is one legislator per district for a given size regional population.[39] An alternative method for expressing the wishes of the

---

[37] For a synoptic review of the nature of the analysis of politicians, see Reisman (1990, pp. 56–60), Hayes (1981, pp. 98–126), and Riker and Ordeshook (1973, pp. 272–305).

[38] Judge Abner Mikva, a U.S. Circuit Court Judge, U.S. Court of Appeals for the District of Columbia, and former Illinois state legislator, offered an even more stinging assessment: "Not even five terms in the Illinois state legislature—the last vestige of democracy in the "raw"—nor my terms in the United States Congress, prepared me for the villainy of the public choice literature" (Mikva 1988, p. 167).

[39] Obviously, this is not the case for state and national senates, where seats are not tied to population numbers. As will become clear, however, the issues pointed to in this section are even further magnified in the senate context.

TABLE 3-3

Four Regions	North	South	East	West	Representatives Holding Office
Red Party	40,001	40,001	40,001	40,001	4
Green Party	40,000	40,000	40,000	40,000	0

public is multiple–proportional representation. The one-legislator-per-district method gives no voice to the losers, whereas the multiple–proportional representation, which elects a certain number of representatives from a single district, does. We will briefly discuss and compare the single-member district approach with the multiple–proportional representation.

The underlying rationale for the single-member district approach is that individuals in a particular district have a set of common preferences, and those preferences can be expressed by a single representative most familiar with the wishes and desires of the individuals in the district. This rationale notwithstanding, single-member representation is open to a variety of problems that can be clearly seen in the following two simple examples.

Assume that we have two parties, the Red Party and the Green Party, and that the state comprises four regional districts—North, South, East, and West. All districts are of comparable size. If the voters in each region are fairly evenly split in the support of party programs, there is a distinct possibility that, under single-member representation, there will be a wide variance between the number of elected representatives from each party and the actual political preferences of the individuals within the state. That is, we can envision a situation, as in table 3-3, where one party gets just over one half the votes but garners 100 percent of the representatives' seats. Here we can see clearly that while the individuals within this state are pretty much divided down the middle as between the programs being offered by the Red Party and the Green Party, the Red Party has four elected representatives and the Green Party has none.

Alternatively we can envision a situation, such as in table 3-4, where one party gets a large majority of the votes cast. Here, the Green Party receives almost 60,000 more than the Red Party. Nonetheless, under single representation, the Green Party remains a minority Party in the number of representatives' seats held. In both of these instances, single-member representation opens the door for inefficient outcomes in the form of legislation that does not reflect the preferences of a large share of the population. In the latter case, in fact, we see that a minority can impose its will on the majority.

A system of proportional representation, where multiple–proportional representatives are elected from each district, can help society get around the problems that beset single-member representation. The idea behind this approach is to have multiple representatives from each of the four regions, with

TABLE 3-4

Four Regions	North	South	East	West	Total Votes	Representatives Holding Office
Red Party	40,001	40,001	40,001	10,000	130,003	3
Green Party	40,000	40,000	40,000	70,000	190,000	1

the party composition based on the proportion of votes received within the region. This, it is argued, would better reflect the spectrum of political views both within each region and across the state, thereby yielding outcomes that are more efficient than those associated with single-member representation.[40]

POLITICIANS AND VOTERS

At center stage in the analysis of politicians are the concepts of the self-interested legislator and the rationally ignorant voter. Politicians, both as candidates for office and as sitting legislators, are assumed to make decisions that maximize their utility, which, in turn, is a function of factors such as votes, power, and political income. In public choice theory, then, legislators are motivated not by a desire to enhance the public interest or the common good, but to win reelection. In a nutshell, and reflecting Downs' (1957, p. 28) contention that "parties formulate policies in order to win elections, rather than win elections in order to formulate policies," politicians are assumed to be vote maximizers. This literature has developed along two lines. One group of models assumes that legislators act to maximize their appeal to their constituents, who are assumed to vote based on their own economic self-interest.[41] The other group of models, originating with the work of Mancur Olson (1965), assumes that legislators vote for those programs or laws that are most responsive to the desires of special interest groups—for example, major financial supporters, those energizing effective publicity, or those providing politically meaningful endorsements—thereby enhancing their prospects for (re)election.[42]

Voters, meanwhile, are assumed to exhibit rational ignorance. Under majority rule, voters have little reason to invest the time, money, or energy that is required to cast a well-informed vote because they know that there is only the slightest of chances that their vote will be decisive in any given election. One implication of this is that many individuals choose not to vote at all; for them,

[40] There are several variations of proportional representation that we do not explore here. A concise review of both the single transferable vote system and the party list system are provided in Johnson (1991). On issues related to modeling the legislature see Shepsle (1985).

[41] See for example, Weingast, Shepsle, and Johnsen (1981), Shughart and Tollison (1986), and Faith and Tollison (1983).

[42] See Stigler (1976), Peltzman (1980), and the discussion of "interest group theory" below.

taking the time to vote just doesn't pass the benefit-cost test. In fact, one might ask why individuals vote at all. Even among those who, for reasons of duty or interest, do vote, given the high probability that the outcome of an election will be unaffected by whether a voter makes an informed choice or simply chooses on the basis of an existing, albeit, low level of knowledge, it is sensible (rational) for voters to remain uninformed on many candidates and/or issues. Beyond some point, the costs of acquiring additional information outweigh the benefits—that is, it is rational to be ignorant.[43]

The analysis of voting rules in our discussion of direct democracy also has extensive applications to the context of representative government. Under a two-party democracy, the size of the legislative majority necessary for the passage of a proposed law, whether a simple majority—50 percent-plus-one—or a supra-majority of, say, two-thirds, is extremely significant because it influences both the likelihood of a law's passage and the specific form that the law will take. That is, the voting rule that governs decision-making in a representative government will have a profound effect on the answers given to our fundamental questions about the law.

We have already seen that electoral outcomes tend to reflect the preferences of the median voter, with the effect that candidates will attempt to position themselves in such a way as to capture the median voter's vote. This has interesting implications for primary systems as against general elections. The low incentive to vote results in very low voter turnouts in most primary elections. Those who *do* turn out tend to be those with very strongly held views—often those occupying the more extreme positions rather than the middle ground. As such, the "median voter" who has to be appealed to in a primary election is a vastly different voter than the median voter of the general election. The result is that the candidates emerging from the primaries often have relatively extreme views, and these candidates must then attempt to reposition themselves toward the middle in the general election in an effort to capture the support of the median voter, and hence the election.

The public choice literature has gone well beyond median voter theory to explore a variety of variables that impact the legislative process. Some of the models incorporate the candidate's platform, the opposition's platform, and the level of campaign expenditures. With respect to the direction and levels of campaign contributions, two variables have been analyzed: (i) the expected benefits to the contributors from the candidate's victory as measured by the positions the contributors expect the candidate to take on issues, and (ii) the expected impact of the campaign contributions on the outcome of the election as measured by the closeness of the election. There is a vast empirical literature examining these issues that is far too extensive to be explored here. Suffice it to say that proponents of public choice theory collectively, affirmatively,

---

[43] See Mueller (2003, ch. 14) for a survey of this literature.

and unambiguously argue that "this literature demonstrates that the vote-maximizing and profit-utility-maximizing assumptions lead to models with predicative content" (Mueller 1989, p. 215).

THE BUREAUCRACY

Once the ballot initiatives are approved or the legislation is passed, we come to the part of the supply function that includes the task of implementing the programmatic goals contained therein. This task falls to the bureaucracy. Public choice theory uses the rational actor model in an attempt to shed light on the bureaucratic decision-making process and its political-economic consequences.[44] Most pre-public choice discussions of bureaucracy were inspired by the work of Max Weber (1947), whose contributions to political sociology provided the early foundation for the political science and public administration analyses of politics and the bureaucracy. Weber, one of the founders of modern sociology, "built the foundation for much of modern [pre-public choice] analyses of politics, social stratification, and bureaucracy" and "stressed the idealized operation of a bureaucracy in a democracy" (Johnson 1991, p. 282). Weber's theory linked the behavior of politicians with the bureaucracy. That is, it was predicated on what some might characterize as the romantic belief that politicians were going to be elected by knowledgeable, informed, public-spirited voters and that those same politicians would pass legislation for the common good to further the public interest. Knowledgeable, informed, public-spirited bureaucrats would then objectively carry out the policy of the elected government in a manner that was as cost effective as possible. With the development of the public-choice-theoretic approach to the behavior of political agents, this perspective was largely undermined.

The role of the bureaucrat takes on importance because of the bifurcated motives or incentives underlying bureaucratic behavior. Bureaucrats have relatively weaker incentives to consider the social welfare implications of the institutions that they serve—in the case of government bureaucrats, the public interest[45]—and relatively stronger incentives to improve their own positions within the bureaucracy in which they work.[46] Besides this, gaps often exist in legislation; that

---

[44] See Niskanen (1971, 1973) and his more recent treatment (1994); see also Mueller (2003, chs. 16, 17), Johnson (1991, ch. 10), Tullock, Seldon, and Brady (2002, ch. 5), and Reisman (1990, pp. 61–62). In spite of a rather well-developed body of theory dealing with bureaucratic behavior, Skeel (1997, p. 653) has argued, "Public choice theorists have had far more difficulty modeling bureaucrats' and judges' behavior, as compared to legislators and private economic actors, due to the absence of a compelling theory as to what bureaucrats and judges maximize."

[45] Corporate bureaucrats face similar incentive issues regarding the firm's profits.

[46] Typically, the argument is *not* that bureaucrats are idle, lazy, and inefficient; the problem, rather, centers on the question of incentives. Of course, the notion that bureaucrats are idle, lazy, and inefficient just adds additional fuel to the anti-big-government fire.

is, legislation specifies certain goals but may not be fully specific with respect to implementation. These gaps may well be intentional, as legislators defer the difficult political choices to the bureaucrats in order not to overly damage their chances for reelection. In any event, much of the gap-filling falls to the bureaucrats, though it occasionally falls to judges. The ambiguous bureaucratic motives and the often substantial scope for bureaucratic discretion in implementation allows for the possibility of an extensive divergence between the legislative intent reflected in the political-choice process and the final impact of that legislation. As a result, to gain a more complete understanding of the implementation of legislation by bureaucrats, it becomes necessary to analyze and understand the role of the incentives facing, and the resulting actions of, bureaucrats, as well as the problems relating to information with respect to costs and evaluation of bureaucratic output. Also at issue are the interrelationships among the various bureaus of the government, the bureaucracy and the surrounding special interest groups, and the bureaucracy and the legislature.[47]

The public choice analysis of the bureaucracy was pioneered by Tullock, Downs, and Niskanen. While their models have some subtle differences, they essentially argue that bureaucrats will make institutional decisions with a view to maximizing their utility—subject to the constraints that they face. The bureaucrat's utility is assumed to be a direct function of things like "salary, perquisites of the office, public reputation, power, patronage, output of the bureau, ease of making changes, and ease of managing the bureau." As Niskanen notes, "All except the last two are a positive function of the total budget of the bureau during the bureaucrat's tenure" (1973, p. 22). Hence, the model suggests that in maximizing their utility, bureaucrats will make those choices that will maximize their bureaus' budgets.

In effect, bureaucrats are modeled as entering into a competition with other each other for funding from the relevant funding source, be it local, state, or a unit of the federal government. The greater their budget, relative to that of other bureaucrats, the higher their position in the bureaucratic pecking order and, thus, the greater their utility. The problem here is that bureaucratic budget maximization is akin to revenue maximization in the producer context. Budget maximization, like revenue maximization, takes no account of the opportunity costs of "production" and leads to an overproduction of output, relative to the efficient level. In simple economic terms, bureaucrats will not produce at an efficient level of bureaucratic output Q_E—where marginal social costs equal marginal social benefits—but will find every way to increase their cost base and client base and produce a level of output Q_0, where the *total private* costs equal the *total private* benefits (see figure 3-5).

Given that higher costs mean a larger budget, there is also little incentive to economize on the costs of what is supplied—hence, not only might an

---

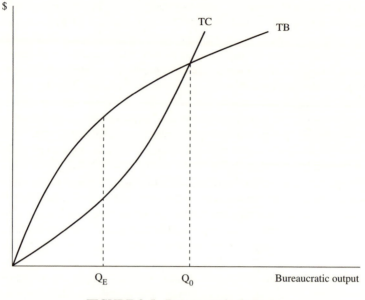

FIGURE 3-5. Bureaucratic Output

unneeded (from an efficiency perspective) building be constructed, but it might be constructed with two-thousand-dollar toilet seats rather than the fifty-dollar variety. That is, public choice theory suggests that utility-maximizing "bureaucrats confront a perverse incentive structure that will lead to both high per unit costs and a rate of output for which the marginal value of the bureau's output is less than its cost" (Gwartney and Wagner 1988, p. 16). The driving force behind bureaucratic inefficiency, then, is the inconsistency between the bureaucrat's utility-maximization process and the maximization of social welfare. The situation is nicely described by Niskanen (1971, p. 38),[48] who suggests that while a manager in a profit-seeking firm will strive to produce output level Q_E (and perhaps be given a bonus for his efforts), if a manager of a bureau or an agency produced Q_E instead of Q_o, he would probably "receive a citation and a savings bond, a lateral transfer, the enmity of his former colleagues, and the suspicion of his new colleagues."

How are bureaucrats able to accomplish this? Legislators are one factor in the overproduction of bureaucratic services. Reelection implies catering to voters, and many of these voters will be aligned with particular interest groups interested in maximizing their gains from government. Because those interest groups tend to be served by specific bureaucracies, legislators become sup-

---

[48] This is also the source of figure 3-5.

porters of those bureaucracies, perhaps by helping to enhance their budgets or reducing the extent of legislative oversight. To make matters worse, legislators lack the incentive and effective ability to curb the inefficient and wasteful performance of government bureaus. Several reasons for this are typically identified in the public choice literature: (i) bureaus do not have an easily identifiable index of performance (i.e., no bottom line or quantifiable unit of output), (ii) biased information regarding performance (i.e., information on a bureau's performance is typically acquired from the bureau), (iii) the fact that, for political reasons, inefficient performance rarely terminates the operation of a bureau, and (iv) the bureaucrats and their clients can form powerful coalitions, thereby forming interest groups capable of influencing political decisions.

A second factor is bureaucratic agenda control. We have seen in our discussion of logrolling how agenda control can be used to secure a preferred election outcome when voter preferences are multi-peaked. Bureaucrats, too, have the power to control the voting agenda in certain contexts, and this can be used to generate a higher budget. Consider the example presented by Romer and Rosenthal (1982), where a local school board is the agent that puts funding referenda on the ballot. We would expect such election results to reflect the preferences of the median voter if there was political competition—but, as a monopolist, the school board can propose a budget greater than that favored by the median voter, and, if the alternative is sufficiently unsatisfactory, secure passage of that larger budget. As Buchanan (1984a, p. 19) notes, this is not limited to the referendum context: "the bureaucracy can manipulate the agenda for legislative action for the purpose of securing outcomes favorable to its own interests. The bureaucracy can play off one set of constituents against others, insuring that budgets rise much beyond plausible efficiency limits."

Proponents of public choice theory believe that this type of utility-maximizing model can better describe what is going on in bureaucracies and will ultimately out-predict the public interest–oriented model of political science.[49] Even while the empirical evidence is not as extensive here as in other areas of public choice, it is obvious that all of this fits very well with the popular view of government bureaucracy as wasteful and inefficient. It thus should come as no surprise that the public choice theory of the bureaucratic choice process reflects these same themes. Nor is the dissatisfaction with the prevailing bureaucratic process confined to those promoting minimalist government. As Gwartney and Stroup point out, "In the past, criticism of bureaucratic decision-making arose primarily from sources seeking to reduce the size of government . . . in recent years, advocates of public sector action have often been at the forefront of those charging that the bureaucracy has failed to carry

---

[49] Hence, it is not at all unusual to read the following: "Models based on the assumption that bureaucrats are attempting to maximize their own well-being rather then the public interest seem to have very considerable predictive value" (Tullock, in Tullock, Seldon, and Brady 2002, p. 54).

out legislative intent and has been insensitive to the needs of the average citizen (Gwartney and Stroup 1980 p. 451).

The question of what can be done about the bifurcated motives of bureaucrats and the economic waste associated with the overproduction of their services takes us into the realm of normative public choice. While recognizing that bureaucrats typically act in their own interests, there is a continuing quest to design bureaucratic institutions that would align bureaucrats' interests with those of society as a whole and thus lead them to make choices more consistent with social welfare. Based on their empirical findings in analyzing the size and role of the bureaucracy, public choice scholars have proffered a variety of recommendations that they believe will improve the performance of existing bureaucratic institutions with an emphasis on enhancing the efficiency of decision-making processes through incentive alignment. For example, Niskanen (1973, ch. 4) suggests that we should find ways to foster competition among bureaus, revise the reward system confronting bureaucrats so as to economize the use of scarce resources (e.g., by offering bonuses for efficient behavior), encourage privatization of the bureaucrat's output where possible, and establish more competent and rigorous legislative oversight of government agencies.

IMPLICATIONS FOR THE GROWTH OF GOVERNMENT

Given the weak incentives for voters to acquire all relevant information and the ever-present incentives for politicians to look to short-term strategies or policies to enhance their reelection possibilities, many political/legislative outcomes—a significant segment of the "Law" in "Law and Economics"—are likely to be inefficient. Buchanan (1977, p. 13) argues that the effects are far from benign:

> If the behavior of politicians in seeking and securing "political income" while holding elective office does nothing but create some slack between the working of practical government and an idealized drawing-board model, there would be no cause for concern here. But if this behavior of politicians biases results consistently in the direction of larger governments, it becomes relevant for our purpose. The presence of such bias seems clearly established.

That is, these short-term, inefficient policies and strategies are pursued due to their political attractiveness and are considered detrimental to social welfare in the long run. The problem here—and this is at the heart of public choice analysis—is the continuing conflict between the so-called *good politics* and *sound economics* (Gwartney and Wagner 1988, pp. 7–14).

Large government provides a setting conducive to those in political office engaging in all sorts of illegal operations, including corruption and graft:

The prospect for profitable bribes, kickbacks, or by-product deals is directly related to the size and complexity of total government budgets, and, more generally, of the total government operation in the economy. With minimal governmental intrusion into the economy, with minimal and quasi-permanent spending components, the grasping politician may have little or no opportunities for graft. However, with a complex public sector, and one that involves new and expanding spending programs, there may be numerous opportunities. (Buchanan 1977, p. 158)

This, of course, means that the growth of government feeds on itself; that is, government growth increases the potential for graft and corruption, which leads to the passage of legislation that further increases the size of government, which in turn further increases the potential for graft and corruption, and so on. As we noted earlier, to the extent that public choice theory is an accurate description of the machinations and outcomes of the political process, it is something less than a pretty picture.

Interest Group Theory

The demand and supply sides of the political process actually come together in one of the more significant sets of models to emerge from the early stages of public choice analysis. The theory of interest group behavior actually evolved out of the Chicago economics tradition in the guise of the "capture theory of regulation," pioneered by George Stigler (1971), Sam Peltzman (1976), and Richard Posner (1974).[50] This line of analysis was further broadened by Gary Becker (1983, 1985) and Donald Wittman (1995) on the Chicago side, and by McCormick and Tollison (1981) from the Virginia school.[51] This positive strand of interest group theory is complemented by a normative strand that builds on Gordon Tullock's (1967) pioneering work on rent-seeking behavior and is dealt with in the "Public Choice at Work" section later in this chapter.

The positive analysis of interest groups combines supply and demand in models of the interest group behavior that ask the question, "Why do special interests groups have the power to exercise such a seemingly disproportionate influence within the political process?" The idea behind much of interest group theory is that concentrated interest groups can often benefit at the expense of more widely scattered groups, even if the diffuse group has much more at stake in the aggregate. One of the early insights of Olson was to observe

[50] See Ekelund and Tollison (2003).
[51] See Mitchell (2001).

that the free-rider problem[52] makes it almost impossible to organize large groups of individuals to provide public goods whose benefits are broadly dispersed. This being the case, Olson argued that political activity should be dominated by smaller, well-organized, and readily identifiable groups seeking public projects that benefit themselves but are financed by the public at large. The reason for this lies in basic incentive effects—in particular, as we have shown, the fact that a self-interested voter is unlikely to take the time to inform himself and to vote intelligently, given the extremely low probability that his vote will affect the outcome of an election. As a consequence, ordinary voters simply do not have an incentive to acquire the necessary information or, for that matter, to bother to vote. By contrast, because the members of a concentrated interest group, individually, have more at stake with respect to the issues that concern them, they tend both to inform themselves and to participate actively in the political process. This, in turn, channels political outcomes in the direction favored by interest groups.

Public interest theories are based on a straightforward model of supply and demand, one that, in effect, describes a market for political outcomes that ultimately determine public policy. The central underlying notion on the demand side is that interest groups take form when the costs of organizing are low relative to the expected benefits. As described by Shughart and Tollison (1998, pp. 953–954),

> Recognizing that government can intervene selectively to help or hurt them in myriad ways, individuals have incentives to band together for the purpose of influencing policy outcomes in their own favor. The logic of collective action suggests that some of these groups will be more successful than others in mustering political influence. This differential effectiveness in securing gains and in avoiding losses creates the conditions necessary for the emergence of a market in which an ordinary supply and demand process endogenously determines public policy. . . . In the interest-group theory of government, well-organized pressure groups demand politically mediated wealth transfers, while less organized groups "supply" them by having their wealth lowered directly or indirectly. Politicians broker these transfers, pairing suppliers with demanders to establish political market equilibrium.

Thus, in the political arena we find elected suppliers who have to resolve conflicting demands placed on them by the electorate.

The first well-developed theory of interest group activity is the theory of regulation developed by Stigler and then extended by Peltzman and Becker. It

---

[52] With respect to public goods, the free rider problem rears its head when individuals or groups seek to enjoy the benefits of a public good (for example, national defense) that is apt to be provided and from which they can not typically be excluded, but without contributing revenues to help cover the cost.

was Stigler's contention that "regulation is acquired by the industry and is designed and operated primarily for its benefit" (1971, p. 3). He hypothesized that firms have a clear advantage over consumers since firms are fewer in number, making it both less costly to coordinate interest group organizations giving greater potential for higher, more concentrated, per capita gains. In addition, it is usually less costly for firms to organize, especially in those sectors where trade associations are present. Stigler identified two possible mechanisms to make effective use of the state. The first is to rely on subsidies; the second is to get the government to limit entry into the industry or, in affect, limit output. As he said, "every industry or occupation that has enough political power to utilize the state will seek to control entry" (Stigler 1971, p. 5). In his model, parties of interest, in an attempt to block or substantially increase the cost of entry, would lobby for protective tariffs, occupational licensing, or limits on the creation of new firms. In Stigler's view, elected political suppliers remain ever-ready to fulfill the demands of those who surface in the strongest position with a coherent request, particularly if it means future political support, campaign contributions, future government contracts, or even, for some, bribes. What happens, in effect, is that the regulated party essentially "captures" the regulator and is able to massage regulatory policy to promote its own interests. The effect, as Peltzman (1976, p. 212) observed, is that "between the two main contending interests in regulatory processes, the producer interest tends to prevail over the consumer interest."

While Stigler explained some of what was transpiring in the real world, producers (firms and industry associations) were not, in fact, winning all of the political-economic battles. For example, if firms and industry associations had the upper hand, one would not have expected the issuance of the many regulations set forth under the Occupational Safety and Health Administration, nor the broad-scale business deregulation in trucking, airlines, securities brokerage houses, the natural gas industry, etc. That is, Stigler's model, with its implication that producer interests end up trumping consumer interests, did not seem to explain political outcomes fully. It was against this background that Peltzman extended Stigler's demand-oriented model of firm and industry association behavior by adding a more detailed focus on the supply side. Peltzman argued that it might well be in the interest of the elected political supplier to restrict or enhance barriers to entry, as suggested by Stigler, if he thought that the gains to producers would be sufficiently large and if the consumers, who would bear the brunt of the associated costs, were unlikely to retaliate at the next election. Peltzman however, goes on to suggest that if these conditions are not met, the elected political supplier may, in fact, not restrict entry. The conclusion is a straightforward benefit-cost story: the regulator has an incentive to restrict entry to the point where the votes gained from the last one-dollar price increase resulting from the regulation is exactly equal to the number of consumer votes that are lost as a consequence. This led him to conclude

that elected political suppliers will not always serve the interests of firms and industry associations. Instead, depending upon a variety of variables related to the degree and intensity of support and opposition (what he terms the "support and opposition functions"), the political equilibrium could come to rest on either side.

Becker took the analysis one step further by focusing not on the conflict between producers and consumers, but on what he termed "pressure groups" and suggesting that most regulations come down to either granting an indirect subsidy to someone or imposing an indirect tax on someone. As described by Joe B. Stevens (1993, p. 224), the Becker model is "a model on competition for political influence—who gets the subsidies and how much, and who will bear the tax." Pressure groups exert their influence through lobbying, campaign contributions, and other expenditures, in terms of both time and money. They will also expend resources to limit free riding within their pressure group. Becker's model is predicated on the idea that when elected political suppliers are persuaded to take an action that will transfer income, it will be in their interest to do so, and to do so in an efficient manner.

This last point—that the result is efficient—is of particular import, as it differentiates this variant of interest group theory from the work of Stigler and Peltzman, and of McCormick and Tollison (1981), and from most of the rest of public choice analysis generally. Becker argued that, just as competition among firms yields efficient market outcomes, so too does competition among a variety of political pressure groups. Hence, the political equilibrium will tend to be efficient because "higher subsidies and taxes tend to raise the countervailing political power of taxpayers" (Becker 1985, p. 334), and so it is the pressure-group competition for political outcomes that will see to it that the government will select that combination of taxes and subsidies that tend to be more efficient (in the Kaldor-Hicks sense) rather than less efficient.

The efficiency model has been further refined by Donald A. Wittman (1989, 1995), who examines the market for political action in the context of demanding interest groups and entrepreneurial suppliers, where agents have relatively full information and markets operate in fairly costless fashion. Inefficient policies imply gains that remain to be exploited, and, in a competitive environment, entrepreneurs will enter the market to exploit those gains—to move parties from positions off contract curves to positions on them. Competition disciplines the legislators supplying services in another way: the failure to operate efficiently on an ongoing basis forces exit from the market, just as in the market for goods and services. Competition also forces "production" according to the dictates of comparative advantage. In a political context, then, government will choose to engage only in those activities in which it has such an advantage. Thus, government seems to have a comparative advantage in designing restrictions on pollution—but how should pollution be restricted? One option is taxes; another is regulations. As Wittman points out, an effective pollution tax scheme requires the government to have a great deal of information

about the marginal benefits and costs of pollution and of pollution abatement in order to specify a tax that will lead to the desired level of pollution reduction. Given that acquiring this information is very costly, regulations would seem to be the preferred option—and that indeed is what we observe.

This is not to say that the Becker-Wittman approach concludes that all government operations are efficient, or that there is no waste associated with government activity. What does emerge, however, is the conclusion that, at minimum, the policies in place tend to be more efficient than the alternatives and government failure is not necessarily any worse a problem than market failure.

CONSTITUTIONAL CHOICES: CONTRACTARIAN PUBLIC CHOICE THEORY

It should be clear by this point that political outcomes are a function of the rules governing voting, legislative action, and bureaucratic behavior. While we have only scratched the surface of possibilities here, it should also be evident that different rules formed through the political process can give rise to widely diverging outcomes, which, in turn, result in vastly different allocations of resources and distributions of gains and losses. For example, we could see this quite plainly in our discussion of unanimity and majority voting rules. The fact that there are a multitude of possible rules to govern political decision-making, and that these rules have very different implications for the end result of the political decision-making process, raises two fundamental issues: what determines the rules in place at any given point in time, and what should those rules be?[53]

[53] An important related question is whether there is any ethically acceptable scheme (i.e., voting method) for translating individual preferences into collective preferences. Arrow's impossibility theorem suggests that there is not. Arrow suggested that, in a democratic society, a collective decision-making rule should satisfy the following ethical criteria:

1. It can produce a decision whatever the configuration of voters' preferences; thus, for example, the procedure must not fall apart if some people have multi-peaked preferences.

2. It must be able to rank all possible outcomes.

3. It must be responsive to individuals' preferences. Specifically, if every individual prefers A to B, then society's ranking must prefer A to B.

4. It must be consistent in the sense that if A is preferred to B and B is preferred to C, then A is preferred to C.

5. Society's ranking of A and B depends only on individuals' rankings of A and B. Thus, the collective ranking of defense expenditures and foreign aid, for example, does not depend on how individuals rank either of them relative to research on a cure for AIDS. This assumption is sometimes called independence of irrelevant alternatives.

6. Dictatorship is ruled out. Social preferences must not reflect the preferences of only a single individual (Rosen 1995, p. 130; emphases omitted) Arrow's impossibility theorem shows that there is no collective decision-making scheme that can satisfy these six reasonable ethical properties: If anyone of these properties is dropped, however, it is possible to construct a decision rule that satisfies the remaining five.

These questions take us into the realm of constitutional political economy, where by "constitution" we mean the social contract or the document that "creates the institutions and establishes the rules under which the political process subsequently plays out" (Shughart and Razzolini 2001, p. xxx). This includes the specification of "all those rules, constraints, laws conventions, customs and institutional arrangements that jointly constitute the social order" (Brennan and Hamlin 2001, p. 117). The constitutional choice process specifies what aspects of social interaction will be governed by collective choice processes, together with the specific decision-making rules that will be applied to particular classes of decisions. In doing so, it defines the structure and boundaries of the institutions of government—executive, legislative, the administrative, and judicial institutions—as well as the relative power of each. In addition, it specifies the procedures for changing the rules once the original constitution is in place. The constitutional stage, then, is the a priori stage of choice that determines the rules and processes that will govern subsequent in-period decision-making.[54]

The attraction of constitutional political economy to its proponents is that it is rooted in a catallactic process that generates mutual gains from bargains over constitutional rules. The underlying theory here derives from the Edgeworth box model of the exchange process, as detailed in appendix B of chapter 1. There, we laid out a model of two self-interested individuals engaged in an exchange process in a two-good world, an interaction among individuals that are availing themselves of the "natural" tendencies to engage "spontaneously" in those trades that enhance their welfare—resulting in the now-familiar gains from trade. Applying this catallactic process at the constitutional level, the rules of the game are described as the outcome of a process of trade, or exchange, among members of society, and this outcome maximizes value to those doing the trading. While focusing on the formation of rules rather than what happens once the rules are in place, constitutional economics shares certain methodological features with much of conventional public choice. Brennan and Hamlin (2001, p. 119) point up the similarities when they note that, "in deriving the properties of alternative institutional arrangements, constitutional economics is characterized by its predilection for methodological individualism, a focus on the role of relative prices (or incentive effects), a tendency to equilibrium analysis, the assumption that agents are rational in pursuit of the goals, and further the assumption that wealth maximization is significant (perhaps predominant) among such goals." Where constitutional economics differs from conventional public choice is in its more extensive reliance on the catallactic approach and its more overtly normative emphasis.[55]

---

[54] "In-period" decision making refers to decisions made by voters, legislators, and bureaucrats under the rules previously established at the constitutional stage of choice.

[55] A representative statement here is van Aakan's: "Constitutional economics focuses on normative questions" leaving the economic analysis of the legislature and bureaucracy to those engaged in positive public choice (2003, p. 4 at note 5).

Constitutional political economy sees political choice as a two-stage process. In the first stage, the rules of the game are determined and approved unanimously by the members of society. At the second, in-period stage of choice, political decisions—direct democratic, legislative, and bureaucratic—are made in the shadow of the first-stage rules. While the rules themselves are approved by unanimous consent at the constitutional stage, they may well specify something less than unanimity at the institutional/political stage, for reasons discussed earlier in our examination of voting rules. The rationale for unanimity at the constitutional stage is straightforward. The contractarian base on which constitutional political economy is built views the individual as not only the basic unit of analysis but also the "location of value." Moreover, there is no a priori reason why discrimination should be allowed, nor any rationale for allowing the views of some to count for more than those of others or to be imposed upon others (Brennan and Buchanan 1985, pp. 21–22). Given this, "The rules of political order, including the definition of the rights of persons, can be legitimately derived only from the agreement among individuals as members of the polity" (p. 26). It seems reasonable to expect, then, that within such a context, "Individuals will be led, by their own evaluation of alternative prospects, to establish by unanimous agreement a collectivity, or polity, charged with the performance of specific functions, including, first, the provision of the services of the protective or minimal state and, second, the possible provision of genuinely collective consumption services" (p. 22).

While individuals are assumed to be utility maximizers at the constitutional stage of choice, the constitutional stage is thought to better channel self-interested action to the larger social benefit than does the in-period political choice process. By virtue of its ex ante position, agents at the constitutional stage are essentially making choices "behind the veil." As such, "[t]he move to the constitutional level reduces the agent's information about her own particular circumstances, or about the impact of the proposed constitutional rule on her own life, and thereby induces her to opt for the set of rules that offers the best outcome *whatever* the particular circumstance she may find herself in at the level of in-period choice" (Brennan and Hamlin 2001, p. 120). The choice of *rules* rather than *outcomes* makes maximization just that much more uncertain. When participants in the constitutional choice process make choices knowing full well that any outcomes will apply equally to all of them, "they have much less incentive to try to hold out for purely distributional gains" than one would observe in many other strategic situations (Brennan and Buchanan 1985, p. 28).

This uncertainty as to what a person's end position will be following the adoption of the constitution has a moderating effect that suggests that people "will tend to agree on arrangements that might be called 'fair' in the sense that the pattern of outcomes generated under such arrangements will be broadly acceptable, regardless of where the participant might be located in such outcomes" (Brennan and Buchanan 1985, p. 30). For example, while someone

who *knows* they will be (or are) a "have" might well vote for rules that make it difficult to transfer wealth from rich to poor and someone who *knows* that they will be (or are) a "have not" might tend to vote for rules that facilitate redistribution, people operating behind the veil, who do not know in what position they will ultimately end up, will be likely to choose a middle ground.

The normative thrust of constitutional political economy comes in because, as Shughart and Razzolini (2001, pp. xxx–xxxi) point out, "If voters are not well informed, if incumbency confers substantial benefits on the politicians currently in office, and if special interests dominate political processes at the expense of majoritarian interests, then the constitution imposes the only operative check on 'in-period' politics." And we have seen over and over in our discussion of conventional public choice theory the inefficiency problems associated with much of that political activity. Indeed, as Johnson (1991, p. 345) has observed, contractarian public choice "has centered on analyzing rules limiting the power of governments," suggesting that government, as presently constituted, "is *the* source of much uncertainty about the future application of rules and *the* source of inefficient rules in both the private and political markets." The question then becomes that of determining the appropriate rules to govern collective decision-making in light of these and other concerns.

The reader might well be wondering why this is an issue at all, given that the United States and other countries of the Western world already have constitutions in place.[56] One reason is that constitutional political economy is both backward-looking and forward-looking. As regards its backward-looking nature, the contractarian construction, as Brennan and Buchanan (1985, p. 19) note, is itself "used retrospectively in a metaphorically legitimizing . . . sense." The point is not that states were formed under such constitutional processes, but whether existing states—their rules—can be legitimized in the sense that they could be construed "as if" having emerged from such a process. Brennan and Buchanan (1985, p. 22) contend that "If . . . within broad limits, the state can be legitimized 'as if' it emerged contractually, the way is left open for constructive constitutional reform. Existing rules can be changed contractually even if they did not so emerge."

As to the constitutional political economy being forward-looking, the rules of the game are not given once and for all, but are subject to revision. The fact that the political processes generate winners and losers on an on-going basis means that it is to be expected that there are those who will attempt to revise the rules to further their own interests. The rules may be altered as a result of the direct political activities of individuals, segments of the community, or the community at large, and the goal behind attempts to change the rules is to in some way broaden or narrow the range of discretion, and the extent of the

---

[56] Obviously, there are any number of countries in which new constitutions have been written over the past two decades with the fall of communism and with the moves toward or away from democracy in various third-world countries.

constraints facing the legislature or the bureaucracy. These activities are often directed at the legislature as opposed to bureaucracies, although bureaucratic rules are sometimes altered through political activities of specific interest groups (e.g., farm, labor, or education lobbies) as well as through the efforts of politicians and the bureaucrats themselves.

In terms of our fundamental questions, the issue then becomes, In what direction shall we change the law governing the political decision-making process? That is, what reforms are needed? For example, which voting rules or procedures will provide voters with an incentive to cast informed votes on political candidates or on the relevant public issues such as which public goods to provide, how much of the public good in question should be provided, and the amount to authorize for expenditure, so as to enhance the prospect of realizing a political outcome that provides for an efficient allocation of society's scarce resources? It is here that we see the link between conventional public choice and constitutional economics. Answers to these questions require something more than a nodding acquaintance with the insights of conventional public choice theory, which provide us with an enhanced understanding of the nexus between the institutional rules—political and bureaucratic—and the subsequent performance we can reasonably expect in making changes.

In sum, the road to an efficient constitution runs through the analysis of voting rules, political behavior, legislative action, and bureaucratic decision-making outlined earlier in this chapter. What is clear is the implication that "reform or improvement in political outcomes or results is to be sought through possible changes in the rules, in the set of constraints within which political decisions are made, in the *Constitution*, and not in changes in day-to-day policy that temporary politicians may be somehow persuaded to follow" (Buchanan 1984b, p. 442).

This is where the proponents of catallaxy locate the place of economists in the public policy-making process. Simply put, within the context of politics and political decision-making, the role of the economist is to search out, invent, and broker social (re)arrangements that will embody Pareto-superior moves (Buchanan 1975b, p. 227).[57] To this end, public choice theory focuses on the potential for complex exchange in the political arena under the rules of unanimous consent (to ensure Pareto-superior results), and the compensation requirement.[58] That is, the normative thrust of public choice theory is to structure a political process where values are revealed through the political actions of individuals, and consensus among the individuals of the choosing group becomes the sole affirmation of social value. Like the market, political institutions are to

---

[57] Buchanan (1986, p. 65) "interprets the political process as a *generalization of the market*" (emphasis in original).

[58] As described by Buchanan (1959, p. 129), the requirement for (Kaldor-Hicks) compensation is essential, "not in order to maintain any initial distribution on ethical grounds, but in order to decide which one from among the many possible social policy changes does, in fact, satisfy the genuine Pareto rule. Compensation is the only device available to the political economist for this purpose."

be structured around the common unifying principle of gains-from-trade with a prescriptive focus on cost-minimizing rights structures together with conflict resolution by contracted agreements, vote trading, vote selling, package deals, compensation, and compromise (Reisman 1990, p. 116).

The catallactic approach to public choice envisions the economist as proffering a social policy solution as "presumptively efficient" (that is, as a tentative hypothesis that a proposed solution is efficient) and then observing whether the solution finds support through the consensus of the individuals in the society. To the extent that a presumptively efficient policy (structured around inclusive, complex trading, and exchange agreements) can garner unanimous agreement, the proponents of the catallactic approach can unambiguously recommend that particular policy. That is, not only does unanimity agreement legitimate outcomes, it also ensures efficiency:

> The economist, who conceptually observes the trading process and who sees no violation of the basic rules, can assign an "efficient," or "maximum value," label to the equilibrium result. In so doing, he is not evaluating the result against any scale external to the participants in the trade, nor is he introducing some value scale of his own. Within the rules, as defined, the trading outcome must always be "efficient," and there is no way the economist can define an "efficient" allocation independent of trade itself. (Brennan and Buchanan 1985, pp. 24–25)

In the constitutional context, then, "there is no resort to any source of value external to the expressed preferences of the individuals who join together in political community. . . . "Social welfare" cannot be defined independently, since, as such, it cannot exist" (Brennan and Buchanan 1985, p. 22).

It is here that we see major points of distinction from the Chicago school branch of public choice theory. The Chicago approach embodies the maximization-scarcity-allocation-efficiency paradigm with its emphasis on the efficient outcome—"a presumably objectifiable allocative norm that remains conceptually independent of individual choices" (Buchanan 1986, p. 25). The essential points made by the Virginia proponents of catallaxy are, first, that there is no external standard or scale (e.g., efficiency) through which end states can be valued, and, second, that the appropriateness or correctness of a public policy (or legal change) is *not* the improvement in an independent, observable assessment of allocative efficiency, but is instead agreement—consensus among the group. In a sense, a policy is fair because the individuals in the society unanimously adopted it; they did not adopt it because it was a priori "fair."[59]

---

[59] As Buchanan has stated, "In the subjectivist-contractarian perspective, 'efficiency' cannot be said to exist except as determined by the process through which results are generated, and criteria for evaluating patterns of results must be applied only to processes" (1986, p. 102); and "There is no way an economist can define an efficient allocation independently of the trade itself" (Brennan and Buchanan 1985, p. 25).

In answer to the question, "In what direction shall we change the law?" Buchanan offers the catallactic criterion as an evaluation mechanism: "That which emerges from the trading or exchange process, conceived in its narrowest or its broadest terms, is not the solution to a maximizing problem, despite the presence of scarce resources and the conflict among ends. That which emerges is that which emerges and that is that" (Buchanan 1975b, p. 226).

PUBLIC CHOICE AT WORK

Rent Seeking

We have seen in our discussion of interest group behavior that these groups work to effect transfers to themselves from the larger population and noted the conflicting views as to whether these transfers were efficiency-enhancing or diminishing. There is, however, one efficiency angle that was not pursued in that discussion, and it relates to the idea of "rent seeking," the underlying theory behind which was first articulated in Gordon Tullock's (1967) classic article on the subject.

Rents are simply returns above the norm—an extra return to a valuable resource that is in extremely limited supply, whether that be athletic talent, a highly demanded product whose production is protected by patents, or a more overt monopoly position. The pursuit of these rents is a normal part of life in a market economy.[60] Entrepreneurs pursue rents by enhancing the demand for their product through product development, inventing new products, acquiring a better technology to produce their product, and finding ways to reduce the costs of their factors of production that go into making the product—all of which serves to provide an entrepreneur with short-term profits. Neoclassical price theory predicts that profits tend to be equalized by the flow of investments across a wide variety of opportunities. So, if an opportunity for substantially higher profits emerges, we can expect that it will attract investment until the returns are driven down to a level equal to those generally available throughout the rest of the economy. As long as the market economy is sufficiently competitive, these profits (temporary rents) will be dissipated in the long run and consumers will have an efficiently produced bundle of goods and services from which to select at competitive prices.

---

[60] In economics, the term "rent" has been variously used sometimes as (i) the price paid for one of the factors of production, namely land; (ii) the price paid for those resources fixed in supply (which eliminates any incentive function as the supply of the resource does not respond to a change in price); (iii) the price paid for nonreproducible assets (for example the payments made for the works of expired artists or payments for unique skills in sports); and (iv) the return to monopolists—monopoly rents, which while resulting in wealth transfers, do not serve any productive purposes.

This is not the case, however, for those goods and services whose quantities cannot expand to meet demand, including in those cases where the available quantity is held in check by the government: the competitive process cannot dissipate the rents. These rents have become a major concerns of public choice theorists[61] largely because, as Mueller observed, they are "omnipresent." Specifically, they "exist wherever information and mobility asymmetries impede the flow of resources. They exist in private good markets, factor markets, asset markets, and political markets. When rents exist, rent seeking can be expected to exist" (Mueller 1989, p. 245). Within the political arena, they take the form of special privileges, monopoly positions, and other forms of transfers granted to certain individuals or groups through government action. The focus of the analysis in the rent-seeking literature is not on the rents themselves, or even on the resource misallocations associated with the rent-generating positions. Rather, it is on the use of resources expended to acquire or maintain these privileged positions—costly lobbyists, lawyers, accountants, press agents, and economists—resources that could have instead been used in economically productive activities are used by parties attempting to get a piece of those scarcity-induced rents. This may take the form of attempting to acquire an exclusive franchise that the government has created or trying to persuade those in the political arena to change the law so as to block entry and thereby create rents (i.e., new profit opportunities). Thus, the theory goes, for those goods and services that cannot be expanded (or can be purposely held in political check), we should anticipate rent-seeking investments.[62]

So, for example, if the capitalized value of an exclusive franchise to provide vending at the city's sports stadiums generates an expected (capitalized) profit of five million dollars over three years, prospective monopolists would be willing to spend substantial sums to secure that franchise. Some have argued that, in the limit, competition will almost fully dissipate these rents. If other opportunities yield an expected profit of 1 million dollars over the same period, firms will be willing to spend up to four million dollars to acquire the franchise and the rents it brings with it. If there were, say, five firms competing for this franchise, one could easily expect to see ten million dollars spent on lobbying and related rent-seeking activities. The costs associated with rent seeking are not limited to the demand side, either. It also includes the efforts and the resources used up by the government officials who, in various ways, respond to the rent seekers actions or compete to become the recipients of

---

[61] For critiques of this literature see Samuels and Mercuro (1984) and Medema (1991).

[62] Another interesting analysis of rent seeking can be found in Rubin (2005b). He takes on the efficiency of the common law literature described in chapter 2. Rubin contends that, notwithstanding the belief that the structure of common law would not allow rent seeking, in fact, the rise in the scope of tort law (also described in chapter 2) is partly a product of the organized lobbying and litigating rent-seeking activities of attorneys, businesses, and doctors.

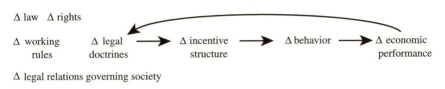

Δ law   Δ rights

Δ working   Δ legal   ⟶   Δ incentive   ⟶   Δ behavior   ⟶   Δ economic
    rules   doctrines   structure   performance

Δ legal relations governing society

FIGURE 3-6. Rent-Seeking Behavior

their rent-seeking largesse, as well as the third-party distortions resulting from the actions of either the rent-seeking parties or the government.

This rent-seeking activity is one facet of the spectrum of activities associated with the reverse link of actions going from right to left in the arc depicted in figure 3-6.[63] As we described in chapter 1, in a dynamic economy, where economic circumstances and opportunities are constantly changing as consumer demands shift, technologies change, new resources are discovered, or old ones move toward depletion, and competition increases or decreases, individuals and groups will look for economic advantage *both* through the economy per se and through the aegis of the state. With respect to the latter, new economic circumstances will invite new calls for changes in law—that is, will give rise to rent seeking. Good, bad, or indifferent, it is simply a fact of political life.

That the analysis of rent-seeking behavior is normatively charged is reflected in the definition of rent seeking as "the resource-wasting activities of individuals in seeking transfers of wealth through the aegis of the state" (Buchanan, Tollison, and Tullock 1980, p. ix).[64] The impact of these rent-seeking activities is wasteful in that "[t]he nation's resources are withdrawn from productive activity and put to rent-seeking activity by the monopolist because he is willing to pay a higher price. The monopolist gains a monopoly right, but citizens lose because the resources which could have been producing real goods and services, are used to chase rents" (Johnson 1991, pp. 329–30). To make matters worse, successful rent seeking has incentive effects that generate increasing levels of rent-seeking activity:

> Rent seeking analysis can be applied to many activities of the modern state, including the making of money transfers to specified classes of recipients. If mothers with dependent children are granted payments for being mothers, we can predict that we shall soon have more such mothers. If the unemployed are offered higher payments, we predict that the number of unemployed will increase. Or, if

[63] This is the same legal centralist diagram that we saw in chapter 1, figure 1-5.

[64] While the concept is said to have been first articulated by Tullock (1967), the term "rent seeking" was originally coined by Krueger (1974). Extensive discussions of rent seeking can be found in Buchanan, Tollison, and Tullock (1980), Mueller (2003, ch. 15), and Tullock (1993).

access to membership in recipient classes is arbitrarily restricted [e.g., when the state licenses an occupation or allocates TV spectra etc.], . . . we must expect that the utility-maximizing behavior of individuals will lead them to waste more resources in trying to secure the "rents" or "profits" promised by government. (Buchanan 1988, p. 8)

To complicate matters further, public choice recognizes that the wastes associated with rent seeking may be the product of political investments that are consistent with rational behavior on the part of all participants (Buchanan 1980, p. 9). Rational behavior notwithstanding, this waste must be minimized, and the remedies prescribed by the public choice approach to avoid waste include (i) attenuating the role of government regulation, (ii) avoiding the establishment of rent-creating government institutions, and (iii) adopting constitutional reforms that require supra-majorities (two-thirds or three-fourths majorities) to pass rent-creating legislation. For the advocates of public choice, the key is to design institutions that facilitate competition for those rents that accompany newly created surpluses or new wealth creation and that discourage the wasteful competition for existing rents.[65]

Public Choice and Judicial Activism

In chapter 1, we explored the myth that judges interpret rather than make law. The extent to which people embrace this myth is often highly correlated with their propensity to castigate so-called judicial activism. One of the earliest indications within Law and Economics of a visible divide over the issue of judicial activism manifested itself between the Chicago approach to law and economics and public choice theory. The Chicago school's advocacy of an engaged judiciary and of reliance on common law over statutes in the law-making process derives from the types of insights regarding the ineffciencies associated with political behavior that have come out of conventional public choice analysis. Judges, in contrast, are not thought to be subject to the same forces for inefficiency as are politicians. The effect is that the common law tends *toward efficiency*, whereas the machinations of the political process (outside of the Becker-Wittman model, at least) suggest that the tendency of statute law is *toward inefficiency*.

That there is a rift here was evident in Buchanan's (1974) review of the first edition of Richard Posner's *Economic Analysis of Law*. Buchanan describes the underlying premises and implications of Posner's interpretation of legal history, particularly where Posner argues that much of the development of the common law can be, in part, attributed to the belief that judges were, or

---

[65] See Johnson (1991, pp. 330–32, 334–35) and Mueller (1989, pp. 244–46).

behaved "as if" they were, guided by the efficiency criterion in deciding cases. Buchanan maintains a two-part critique of Posner's position. The first element of his critique stems from his own position that the market economy's socio-political function is that of "minimizing the necessity of resorting to internal ethical constraints on human behavior and/or external legal-governmental-political restrictions" (Buchanan 1974, p.486). The second element focuses on the implication of Posner's position that "judge-made common law is superior to legislation that emanates from the legislature" (Buchanan 1974, p. 488).

It is uncontroversial that once the "rules of the game" are set in place, they need to be enforced. Thus arises the need for what Buchanan terms the "protective state," or what is sometimes referred to as the "judicial state." In contractarian public choice, the role of the judiciary is characterized as that of the referee, as a neutral enforcer of the rules that have been established in forming the initial social contract at the constitutional stage of choice. The idea is to have courts mechanically apply preexisting rules and thereby avoid having the judge make the law. That is, at the constitutional stage of choice, "the participants agree on the structure of individual rights or claims to be enforced, and violation requires only the findings of fact and the automatic administration of sanctions" (Buchanan 1975a, p. 69). In other words, "Properly interpreted, 'the law' which is enforced is that which is specified to be enforced in the initial contract whatever this might be." This leads Buchanan to conclude that the judge or the court "makes no choices in the strict meaning of this term (p. 69)." This perspective on the role of the courts and judges puts public choice at odds with the role of the courts and judges as envisioned by most proponents of the Chicago approach to law and economics. Within public choice analysis we witness a preference for a much reduced role for the courts.

This also has implications for legal education, in Buchanan's view. Even with all of the significant issues of legal-economic policy facing society, Buchanan questions the whole idea of introducing economic theory into the curriculum of law schools, particularly if such teaching were "to train potential jurists [to be] void of any qualms about legislating for all of us" (Buchanan 1974, p. 491). He strongly urges that "the judge should not change the basic law," even if guided by the efficiency criterion in doing so, "because, in such behavior, he would be explicitly abandoning his role of jurist for that of legislator. He would be 'making law' " (Buchanan 1974, p. 490). Buchanan then closes his discussion by worrying openly about "the potential excesses of a Posner court guided by the extra-legal criterion of "maximum value"—that is, efficiency (Buchanan 1974, pp. 491–92).

Years later, Posner (1987c), by then a federal judge and the leading proponent of the Chicago approach to law and economics, spoke to the issue of the courts and judge-made law. The title of his article, *What Am I? A Potted Plant?* gives away the message. In the article, Judge Posner takes on the strict

constructionists (i.e., the legal formalists) who continue to propagate the myth that "modern American courts are too aggressive, too 'activist,' too prone to substitute their own policy preferences for those of the elected branches of government" (Posner 1987c, p. 23). He notes that the strict constructionists continue to assert that the "legislators make the law; judges find and apply it" (1987c, p. 23). As Posner points out, there has never been a time when the courts of the United States, state or federal, behaved in this manner. Morever, the strict constructionists paint an unrealistic picture of "a populist that acts only with the consent of the governed," thereby ignoring the effectiveness of interest groups. Nowhere in the Constitution, he says, is there a mandate that states either "Read me broadly!" or "Read me narrowly." As Posner observes, "[T]hat decision is a matter of political theory." In fact, he points out that "judges have been entrusted with making policy from the start" (pp. 23–25). As to imprudent decisions or outcomes of liberal judicial activists, however imprudent these may be to some, Posner asserts that "there is no use in strict constructionists pretending that it is not law but politics because it involves an exercise in discretion. . . . It is not bad law or no law just because it violates the tenets of strict construction" (p. 25).

CONCLUSION

Public choice theory operates on the premise that while "some" politicians, bureaucrats, and regulators may, for a time, make choices based on what they believe will advance the public interest, the evidence suggests that, over time, these are *not* motives upon which we can depend in trying to design future political institutions, bureaucracies, or regulatory agencies that perform efficiently. This being the case, as distinct from the more judicially focused, common-law-oriented nature of Chicago law and economics, conventional public choice theory endeavors to describe the creation and implementation of law as it pertains to the political process—the demand for law and the supply of law—in an effort to assess the impact of alternative laws and rules governing the political process. Notwithstanding the subtle differences in approach between the homo economicus branch and the catallaxy branch, together they comprise what can be conceived of as an inclusive theory of public choice. These approaches are in many ways complementary, and public choice theory has developed by blending these two branches of theory into a rich literature that reflects the combination of their central elements. Looking back on the paths these two branches took from 1960, Buchanan (1986, p. 26) characterized their development as follows:

> In the 1960s, 1970s, and early in the 1980s varying contributions have represented differing weighted combinations of the two central elements in the inclusive public choice perspective. Works on the theory of bureaucracy and bureaucratic

behavior and on the theory of regulation have been weighted toward the *homo economicus* element, whereas works on constitutional analysis have been more derivative from the politics-as-exchange paradigm.

As such, public choice theory offers its own distinct perspective on our three fundamental questions about the law.

Institutional Law and Economics

> We are interested here in what governs institutional
> and systemic performance and how we may,
> objectively and nonpresumptively, analyze and
> understand the variables governing performance. The
> underlying motivation is twofold: First, to enable us
> to better know what is going on in the economy and
> the polity; and second, to enable us to better choose
> and effectuate meaningful and consequential
> institutional changes. The focus is on human
> interdependence and how alternative property rights
> affect its outcome.
> *(A. Allan Schmid 1987, p. xi)*

INTRODUCTION

THE INSTITUTIONAL approach to law and economics has its roots in the work of economists such as Henry Carter Adams (1954) on economics and jurisprudence, Richard T. Ely (1914) on the relation of property and contract to the distribution of wealth, John R. Commons (1924, 1925) on the legal foundations of the economic system, and Wesley C. Mitchell (1927) on the role of the price system and its place in the modern economy. Important elements of the Institutional approach can also be found in the work of one of the founding fathers of Institutional economics, Thorstein Veblen (1899, 1904), of lawyer-economists such as Walton H. Hamilton (1932) and Robert Lee Hale (1952), and of legal scholars such as Karl Llewellyn (1925), Jerome Frank (1930), and Roscoe Pound (1911a,b, 1912). Institutional economics—a label said to have been coined by Walton H. Hamilton in 1919—is essentially an American contribution to economic thought that, like Legal Realism, is said to have "had its heyday in the 1920s and early 1930s" (Bell, 1967). Nonetheless, it continues to have a relatively strong presence today in the United States and, to a lesser extent, in Europe. So that the reader can better understand the foundations upon which present-day Institutional law and economics rests, we will begin our discussion with a brief overview of Institutional economics.[1]

---

[1] This synoptic review of institutional economics draws on Bell (1967), Gordon (1964), Srivastava (1965), and Whalen (1996). For extensive overviews of institutional economics, see also Hodgson, Samuels, and Tool (1994), Samuels (1988), Tool (1988, 1993), and Rutherford (1998).

THE EVOLUTION OF THE INSTITUTIONALIST APPROACH

Early Institutional Economics: People and Ideas

Institutional economics developed as an approach to the study of economic society in an age when economics was a very pluralistic discipline.[2] As its name implies, Institutional economics places at the center of analysis the study of the institutions of the economic system. Institutions are variously and broadly defined within Institutional economics. John R. Commons (1934) defined an institution as "collective action in restraint, liberation, and expansion of individual action," thereby emphasizing the social bases of the individual, which orthodox economists took as given and self-subsistent. Thorstein Veblen (1899) defined institutions as "widely followed habits of thought and the practices which prevail in any given period," thereby emphasizing their problematic and belief-oriented nature. Herbert J. Davenport essentially combined the two definitions in his description of an institution as "a working consensus of human thought or habits—a generally-established attitude of mind and a generally-adopted custom of action as, for example, private property, inheritance, government, taxation, competition, and credit" (cited in Srivastava 1965, p. 470).

Institutional economics has often been described as part of "a revolt against formalism" (Spiegel 1971, p. 629), a revolt that took place in law, in history, and in economics at about the same time. Institutional economics, as part of that revolt, was led by a group of young American scholars who, after World War I, engaged in a critique of certain of the formalistic doctrines central to the economics of the day. In economics, formalism was taken to be the *abstract deductive* reasoning of orthodox economic analysis that enthroned universally valid reason; assumed passive, rational, utility-maximizing behavior; and demonstrated an inordinate concern over the equilibria of comparative statics—in particular, utility analysis of consumer behavior and the marginal productivity theory of distribution.

Instead, Institutionalists focused their efforts on *inductive* analyses of specific institutional aspects of the American economy. While their principal emphasis was on using the inductive method to describe the constituent elements of the economy, the Institutionalists never employed the inductive method to extremes and thereby were still able to make substantive theoretical generalizations. As noted by Walter S. Buckingham (1958, pp. 107–8), "[T]he development of generalizations gave institutional economics more of a theoretical content than the largely descriptive [German] historical school was ever able to attain. Institutional theory is by no means as refined and exact as orthodox theory, but is not so abstract and lacking in empirical content either."

Charles J. Whalen (1996) describes three distinct influences that contributed to the emergence of the Institutionalist school of thought. One was the

---

[2] See Morgan and Rutherford (1998).

German historical school, which influenced such early Institutionalist thinkers as Richard T. Ely.[3] The German historical school, founded by Wilhelm Roscher (1817–94) and later dominated by Gustav von Schmoller (1838–1917), emerged, at least in part, as a reaction against classical economic thinking in the mid-nineteenth century. The Historical school emphasized the dynamics of economic development, the need to use empirical data (rather than abstract ideas) to ground economic theories, and the necessity of paying particular attention to human institutions. This emphasis on gathering facts and studying them in relation to their historical significance rather than as isolated, objective data in static, timeless models, had a direct bearing on the methodology of emerging Institutionalist economics.

The second influence was from American pragmatic philosophy as set forth by, among others, Charles Sanders Peirce, William James, and John Dewey. Proponents of American pragmatic philosophy recognized an uncertainty inherent in understanding and looked for philosophical methods for establishing the meaning of concepts and beliefs. The analysis of social phenomena had to be conducted within systems of relationships among individuals in their empirical settings. The pragmatic approach largely replaced a priori abstract reasoning with empirical studies. Contrary to the narrow, uniform "rational behavior" assumption in orthodox microeconomics, choices were pragmatically perceived to be made in a world of ever-changing empirical objects and emerging economic, political, and social institutions. "True" ideas are those to which responsible investigators would assent after thorough examination, that is, after considering what conceivable effects of a practical kind a theory or object holds. Thus, only those hypotheses that contributed to organizing data garnered through sense perceptions related to the real world (i.e., those that held practical significance), and did so in a progressive and unifying manner, were taken to be legitimate. In short, an idea was right if it had "fruitful" consequences. The pragmatist emphasis on the uncertainty inherent in understanding served to provide an epistemological foundation and a social philosophy upon which to erect the basic tenets of Institutional economic thought.

The third influence came through Thornstein Veblen's turn-of-the-century writings focusing on the evolutionary facet of economic development, within which one can trace many of the origins of and early insights into Institutional economic thought. Veblen studied political economy and philosophy, spoke some twenty-six languages, and is considered by many the founder of Institutionalism. In his studies he was most influenced by John Bates Clark, professor of political economy at Carleton College; he subsequently received his doctorate from Yale. In 1892 he was brought to the newly founded University of Chicago by J. Laurence Laughlin, then head of the Department of Economics, and during his tenure there, he edited the *Journal of Political Economy* for

---

[3] On the German historical school's roots of Institutional economics, see Richter (1996).

over a decade. Thereafter he moved around through several different academic positions over the course of a somewhat eccentric and controversial career.[4]

A strong critic of orthodox economic thinking, Veblen rejected the mechanistic view of economic society reflected in static equilibrium analysis and instead focused on what he termed an evolutionary method of economic analysis. He believed that the material environment, technology, and propensities of human nature condition the emergence and growth of institutions, and he insisted on a critical examination of capitalistic institutions—especially what he termed industry and business, along with the economic power they were able to exercise—to understand economic society. Toward that end, he emphasized the necessity of understanding both group habits and institutions, and not merely how these institutions worked, but how they evolved. In his most renowned book, *The Theory of the Leisure Class* (1899), Veblen provided a critique of the pecuniary behavior of people in the context of their cultural background and inherited traits, arguing that the orthodox hedonistic conception of man as a lightning calculator of pleasure and pain was overly narrow and outmoded. He described the idea of a two-class society: the productive class, which was made up of those who produced socially, and the leisure class, who depended upon the wasteful effort of acquisition. From this, Veblen developed a theory of consumption based on broad cultural factors that influence human personality, avoiding what he considered to be the narrow, individualistic thrust of orthodox economics. Veblen's (e.g., 1904, 1923) analysis of industrial capitalism was couched in terms of a dichotomy between business and industrial interests, the former negative and the latter positive. Business, he said, is about the making of money and the acquisition of economic power. Industry, in contrast, is the amalgam of tools and skills in the production of goods and services. There is, according to Veblen, a conflict between these interests, in that the tendency of industry is toward greater productivity, which would result in lower profits, a factor that worked against business interests. This, he argued, leads businessmen to attempt to retard industrial progress that would benefit consumers. In doing so, Veblen attempted to demonstrate what he considered to be the managerial and administered character of the modern capitalist economic system, as against the individualist and competitive nature attributed to it in public discourse and within orthodox economic theory.[5]

Certain of Veblen's ideas were given further development by Clarence E. Ayres, who received his doctorate from the University of Chicago in 1917 and

---

[4] His career is concisely described in Heilbroner (1999, ch. 8).

[5] It should be noted that Veblen placed substantial emphasis on the role of the state in giving effect to the power that he saw these business interests exerting and the manner in which this was done. Thus, although Institutional law and economics has taken its cue primarily from Commons, there are certain aspects of Veblen's work that dovetail nicely with this tradition. See, for example, Duxbury (1995, pp. 108–116) and Samuels (1995).

became interested in Institutional thought during the course of his studies of philosophy (under Dewey) and economics (under Veblen). Upon taking up a position at Amherst, he came under the influence of Walton Hamilton, a severe critic of orthodox economic thinking. It was during his tenure at Amherst that Ayres came to reject that keystone of neoclassical economic thought—marginal analysis. Thereafter, he was to spend the remainder of his career in search of a new economic framework that could better explain the economic forces shaping modern economies. Indeed, it was Ayres who became the chief exemplar of Institutionalist economic thought in the post–World War II period, when from his base at the University of Texas-Austin he and his students developed the Veblenian-Ayresian perspective within Institutionalism (Breit 1973, pp. 244–45).

Ayres's perspective is perhaps best reflected in his treatise *The Theory of Economic Progress* (1944), in which he undertook both to explain and apply Institutional economic thought with respect to the field of economic development. *The Theory of Economic Progress* is a theoretical work that attempts to explain the forces that have shaped the economy, focusing those factors that accelerated the development as well as those that have impeded it.[6] Ayres saw human activity as reflective of two basic and ever-present forces: "technological behavior," a productive and progressive force, and "ceremonial behavior" (as manifested in, for example, hierarchies, mores, culture, and ideology), which is counterproductive and inhibits change, acting as a curb on technological progress. The central theme of this work is that exponentially expanding and advancing "technology," defined broadly as all human activities involving the use of tools, and thus including both human and physical capital, is responsible for the enormous changes in the welfare of society. The focus is not so much on the individuals, but on the technological progress as related to the advancement of the tools (i.e., the objective instruments capable of being variously combined) and the role of this in enhancing economic progress. Since the ceremonial institutions resist change, he argued, progress is a function of the relative strength of these progressive and inhibiting forces, the variance of which relative strength helps to explain the differential rates of development across societies and cultures. Thus, for Ayres, the challenge confronting economics is to "devise new organizational forms, to pragmatically develop organizational arts to match, rather than contradict, our science and technology" (Breit 1973, pp. 255–56).

Another contributor to Institutional economic thought was Robert Lee Hale who received his L.L.B. from Harvard University in 1909 and his Ph.D. in economics from Columbia University in 1918.[7] He subsequently held a joint

---

[6] See Breit (1973).

[7] The following discussion of Hale draws on Dorfman (1959), Samuels (1973), Duxbury (1990, 1995), and Mercuro, Medema, and Samuels (2005); see also Fried (1998).

appointment in the economics department and the law school at Columbia and moved to the law school on a full-time basis in 1928. His emphasis on the integration of economics and law was reflected both in his teaching, particularly his course on "Legal Factors in Economic Society," and in his writing, much of which dealt with the regulation of railroads and public utilities—fields in which an understanding of the interface between economics and law has always been fundamental.[8] Hale wrote extensively on the legal and economic theory of rate-base valuation, as well as on the regulation of rate structure and level, and his writings were instrumental in the adoption by the courts of the "prudent investment" doctrine of valuation for public utilities (Dorfman 1959, p. 161).

Hale can perhaps best be described as a Legal Realist who drew upon the emerging tradition of Institutionalism (Duxbury 1995, pp. 107–8). Consistent with the Realist ideas being debated at the time, Hale's work was very much a challenge to and critique of the dominant tradition of laissez-faire capitalism. Like John R. Commons, whose contributions will be discussed later, Hale was influenced by Wesley H. Hohfeld's articulation of "fundamental legal conceptions," which, in Hohfeld's mind, were the "lowest common denominators of law" (Cotterrell 1989, p. 88). As described by Samuels, Hale's paradigm was comprised of the concepts of voluntary freedom, volitional freedom, coercion, power, and government. Legal and economic processes were viewed as inseparable. Hale described the economy as a structure of coercive power arrangements and relationships that necessitated an understanding of the formation and structure of the underlying distribution of economic power. As such, the economy was seen as a system of power operating through a system of coercion, and thus the economic freedom expressed by the courts of the day was merely freedom to engage in economic coercion. Hale's brand of legal economics, as reflected in both his writing and his teaching, gradually evolved into a "theory of the economy as a system of mutual coercion and the legal basis thereof" (Samuels 1973, p. 25), and his perspective was most fully spelled out in his classic book, *Freedom Through Law* (1952).

Hale did not view this coercion as something to be condemned, but, rather, as a basic fact of economic life. As such, he argued, if, for example, income is in fact the fruit of coercion, abetted actively or passively by government, then it cannot be said that overt coercive redistributions of income by government are themselves wrong (Dorfman 1959, pp. 162–163). Hale's Hohfeldian perspective on rights led him to view nearly every statute with economic implications as impacting negatively upon someone's liberty or property. Given this, he believed that it was essential for the courts to undertake an intelligent balancing of the gains and losses brought about by the particular statutes brought

---

[8] As noted later, the work of Harry Trebing (1976, 1989) is exemplary of the contemporary Institutionalist analysis of public utility regulation.

before them—a process which, he said, requires "a realistic understanding of the economic effect of the legislation" (quoted in Dorfman 1959, p. 163). Although Hale believed that ethical judgments must ultimately be the basis upon which the court's decisions are made, he felt that the judicial application of economic principles was necessary to ascertain the economic consequences—allocative and distributive—of the legislation whose constitutionality the court was asked to evaluate (Hale 1924, 1927).[9]

Finally, the work of John R. Commons is of particular importance to Institutional law and economics. Like Veblen, Commons was a student of Ely, who instilled in his students the inductive method of study and emphasized both the historical facets of and legal issues within the study of economics. Early on, while they were at Johns Hopkins University, Ely interested Commons in the field of labor economics. Later, following short and somewhat turbulent stints at Indiana and Syracuse Universities, Ely was instrumental in helping to place Commons at the University of Wisconsin, where Commons spent most of his academic life. Commons's intellectual interests ranged across industrial relations, labor reform legislation, public utility regulation, and price stabilization. Besides teaching and writing at the University of Wisconsin, he was also very involved in public life and served on an array of state and federal commissions. It was while at Wisconsin in 1934 that Commons published *Institutional Economics: Its Place in Political Economy.* For Commons, Institutional economics was an economics of rights, duties, liberties, and exposures. Commons rejected the exclusive emphasis on methodological individualism reflected in orthodox theory; instead he gave collective and corporate action its due place in economic analysis. Likewise, Commons rejected the economics of a harmony of interests and instead centered his analysis on the nature of the disputes and conflicts of interest inherent in a modern economy. Commons optimistically believed that the primary economic institutions could be formed and reshaped (as needed) to conform to the social changes inherent within a society, a belief that led him to probe extensively the impact of institutions, such as the law, on economic structure and performance, and to become actively involved in various reform activities.

Based on the writings of these early contributors and the many who followed in their footsteps, what emerged as Institutionalist economics is a rather heterodox approach to analyzing economic society. In its more modern form, as a school of thought, Institutional economics suggests a series of propositions, which, when taken together, provide an alternative approach within economic analysis. As will become evident, these propositions, together with the

---

[9] Although Posner (1995, p. 3) contends that the Legal Realists had little influence on the Chicago approach to law and economics, he does allow that Hale "anticipated some of the discoveries . . . of law and economics" as we know it today.

focus contributed by Commons, provide the foundation upon which Institutional law and economics rests:[10]

- Economic behavior is strongly conditioned by the institutional environment within which economic activity takes place, and, simultaneously, economic behavior affects the structure of the institutional environment.
- The mutual interaction between the institutions and the behavior of economic actors is an evolutionary process, hence the need for an "evolutionary approach" to economics.[11]
- In analyzing the evolutionary processes contained therein, emphasis is directed to the role played by the conditions imposed by modern technology and the monetary institutions of modern, mixed-market capitalism.
- Emphasis is centered upon conflict within the economic sphere of society as opposed to harmonious order inherent within the cooperative, spontaneous, and unconscious free play of economic actors within the market.
- There is a clear and present need to channel the conflict inherent in economic relationships by structuring institutions to establish a system of social control over economic activity.
- Institutionalism requires an interdisciplinary approach calling on psychology, sociology, anthropology, and law to help understand the behavior of economic actors and thereby generate more accurate assumptions in describing their behavior.

It should be clear that these propositions offer a partial rejection of the positivist, price-theoretic approach maintained by the more orthodox neoclassical microeconomics. They are also manifestations of the Institutionalist position that the framework of orthodox economic analysis does not allow it to address certain fundamentally important features of economic activity. On the other hand, Institutional economics is presented by its proponents as an evolutionary theory that is based on more "realistic" behavioral assumptions derived from a broad array of social science knowledge and a fuller appreciation for and understanding of the institutions driving a mixed-market economy.[12] Both Veblen and Commons incorporated the research findings of the behavioral

---

[10] The following propositions were set forth by Gordon (1964, pp. 124–25).

[11] This evolutionary facet of Institutional economics underlies the name of the Association for Evolutionary Economics, which has maintained some intellectual continuity and focus among this group of economists. The association publishes its own journal, the *Journal of Economic Issues*. The recently founded *Journal of Institutional Economics* also publishes a great deal of work with an Institutionalist perspective, but with a somewhat more European flavor.

[12] The drive for realistic assumptions led the early Institutionalists in particular to extensive data-collection efforts. A pioneer in this regard was Wesley C. Mitchell, who is best known for his extensive studies of business cycles, and who also founded the National Bureau of Economic Research, which has become a major center for empirical work in economics.

sciences into economics. Following that tradition, contemporary Institutionalists reject the assumption of fixed preferences and explore the hypothesis that
law systematically influences the formation and re-formation of preferences
(Schmid 1987, ch. 10; 2004).

John R. Commons and the Wisconsin Law
and Economics Tradition . . . Continued

Although each of the aforementioned scholars played an important role in the
development of the Institutional approach to economics, and therefore ultimately of Institutional law and economics, it is Commons who, through the
Wisconsin tradition, stands as the central figure within the development of this
approach. Commons's central concern was with uncovering the development,
evolution, and workings of the institutions that ultimately impact the performance of the economic system. A major part of this work involved an examination of the legal foundations of the capitalist economic system, particularly
in his classic treatise *Legal Foundations of Capitalism* (1924). This book was
a theoretical work unlike anything that had come before and benefited from
Commons's close contact with law through his involvement with the courts,
his serving on government commissions, and his drafting of legislation. The
emphasis of the book is on describing the role of law and the courts and how
they determine the elements of an economic system. Like his predecessors,
Commons believed all economic institutions are subject to evolution. Whether
describing the institution of capitalism, private property, or the state itself,
each was shown to receive its sanction from the authorities—the church, the
state, the courts—through an evolutionary process. Commons undertook an
analysis of a wide variety of cases, working rules, and statutes to probe their
impacts on the development of the modern capitalist system, and thereby to illuminate the interrelations between legal and economic processes. Through
this analysis, Commons showed how, on the one hand, economy influences
law as the economic system brings to bear pressures on political and legal systems for legal change that facilitates a particular direction of evolution, and,
on the other hand, how law influences economy—that is, how legal change facilitates the development of economic activity in a particular direction.

Commons's primary interest in *Legal Foundations* was to uncover the values underlying the working rules that govern social-economic relations, and
he found this in the courts' use of the term "reasonable value." He argued that
legal history showed certain well-defined tendencies on the part of the courts
to eliminate the destructive practices of capitalistic institutions, while at the
same time ascertaining the "reasonable" policies that should be followed in a
competitive system. Thus, "reasonable values" could be used to ground policies that would bring about compromises in arenas of economic conflict,

namely, labor disputes, public-utility rate making, tax policy, pricing, and so on (Bell 1967, pp. 556–57). Specifically, as the definition of what types of activities were considered reasonable evolved over time, so too did the legal rules governing social-economic relations. Thus in the West there arose a movement from a feudal and agrarian society to a capitalist system, with economic change driving legal change, which in turn facilitated the economic transformations.[13]

Much of Commons's analysis consisted of tracing this unfolding legal-economic evolution to illustrate the pervasiveness of this legal-economic nexus, for example, the effects of the transformation of the legal definition of property and its impact on business, and the effects of law on the employment relation within the firm, on the market mechanism, and on the wage bargain. Commons, however, also lays out in great detail the mechanisms through which law and economy influence one another. Of particular import here is his analysis of the role played by rights and working rules within the economic system. Here he presents a systematic discussion of why rights matter—and thus why law matters—within the economic system, and why the development of economic theory should proceed with attention to the role of law and legal change in structuring economic activity and performance. Moreover, through his work on proportional representation, Commons (1907) explored the manner in which rules influence whose preferences will count within the political process, and through this he laid the foundation for an Institutionalist approach to the study of constitutional choices.

Unlike Chicago law and economics and public choice, Institutional law and economics really has no identifiable launch date. As we have noted, Institutional economics, from its inception, was inherently interested in the interaction between legal and economic institutions and in legal-economic questions. Institutional "law and economics" gradually emerged over time as those beyond the University of Wisconsin took a deep and abiding interest in the interrelationships between law and the economy. Today the major contributions come from Michigan State University, through the work of Warren J. Samuels and A. Allan Schmid.[14] Others at Michigan State University who continue to contribute to this tradition include Harry Trebing,[15] who has made substantial and influential contributions to the analysis of regulation and public utilities, and Robert A. Solo,[16] much of whose work focuses on monopoly regulation and institutional change. The focus of the Institutional approach is

[13] As we have seen in chapter 2, the Chicago school argues along a similar line regarding the history of the common law, but makes "efficiency" rather than "reasonable value" the explanatory concept.

[14] For a comprehensive overview of the various contributors from Michigan State University, see Schmid (2002).

[15] See, for example, Trebing (1976, 1989) and Trebing and Estabrooks (1993).

[16] See, for example, Solo (1967, 1974, 1982).

on the relations between legal (or governmental) and economic processes, rather than on the application of microeconomic theory to the law.

Although most economists identify the beginning of Law and Economics with the Chicago school, its roots, as pointed out in chapter 1, actually lie in part within the Institutionalist tradition several decades earlier (Samuels 1993). Whereas certain aspects of the Institutional law and economics' literature have been quite critical of the Chicago approach, Samuels (1981, pp. 148–49), for one, has praised Posner for his role in once again bringing to the attention of economists and legal scholars alike how economic conditions affect the law, and conversely.

In contrast to the other approaches examined in this book, the Institutional approach draws no distinction among jurisprudential, legislative, bureaucratic, or regulatory treatments, seeing them all as particular manifestations of the interrelation of government and the economy, or legal and economic processes. Underlying the major thrust of the Institutional approach to law and economics are two complementary modes of analysis, one focusing on legal structure and the other on legal-economic behavior. From the perspective of the legal-centralist approach of Law and Economics, described in chapter 1 (and, for the moment, ignoring the reverse link), we have seen that changing law has a direct impact on economic performance:

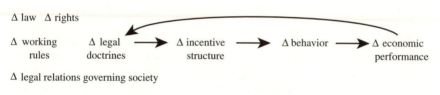

FIGURE 4-1. Mutual Interaction

Institutional law and economics, however, emphasizes the interrelations and *mutual* interaction between government and the economy, with the effect that its perspective reflects important feedback effects (see reverse link in figure 4-1) from economic performance back to law. That economic factors give rise to pressures for legal change may seem reminiscent of the analysis of rent seeking in public choice theory described in chapter 3. From the vantage point of the Institutional approach to law and economics, however, it merely is an attempt to describe, non-presumptively, what actually takes place in the legal-economic-political arena.

Much, though not all, of the work of Schmid has tended to concentrate on the "structure → performance" linkage, with an emphasis on empirical work that explores the economic impact of alternative legal structures.[17] Schmid brings to

---

[17] A concise statement of Schmid's approach to Institutional law and economics is contained in his book *Property, Power, and Public Choice: An Inquiry Into Law and Economics*, 2d ed.

the forefront the many varieties of human interdependence, focusing on both (i) the various types of transactions—bargained, administrative, and status and grant transactions—and (ii) the varied interdependencies that emerge—technological, pecuniary, and political externalities arising from incompatible use, exclusion costs, information costs, and economies of scale. In Schmid's view, the Institutional approach to law and economics must ask, "How do the rules of property structure human relationships and affect participation in decisions when interests conflict or when shared objectives are to be implemented? How do the results affect performance of the economy?" (Schmid 1987, p. 188).

The work of Samuels, in contrast, has tended to concentrate on describing the conduct or behavior of individuals and groups in the legal-economic arena on the "conduct → performance" linkage, with particular attention paid to the ubiquitous role of government (in all of its manifestations) in the remaking of law for economic and other reasons. For Samuels, the organizing concept is that of the *legal-economic nexus*, wherein, as he (Samuels 1989a, p. 1567) describes it, "[T]he law is a function of the economy, and the economy (especially its structure), is a function of law. . . . [Law and economy] are jointly produced, *not* independently given and *not* merely interacting." Through the legal-economic nexus is worked out the structure of the law and the economic system, where each serves as both an dependent and an independent variable in the construction of legal-economic reality. Legal rules govern "the terms of access to and participation in the economy by potential economic actors," and "property and other rights. . . . govern whose preferences will be given effect through the market" (Samuels 1975, p. 66). The focus of the Institutional approach is thus on delving into the workings of the legal-economic nexus to understand its processes and thereby conduct an in-depth analysis of the consequences of choice. Resource allocation and the distribution of income and wealth are explained "in terms of a complex causal chain involving both allocation and distribution as functions of market forces that depend in turn on power, rights, and the use of government" (Samuels and Schmid 1981, p. 4).

Both branches of the Institutional approach are avowedly positive; neither has a normative component comparable to that of the Chicago school or the constitutional political economy literature within public choice analysis. As Samuels and Schmid (1981, p. 1) describe it in the introduction to their book on Institutional law and economics, "Our principal goal is quite simply to understand what is going on—to identify the instrumental variables and fundamental issues and processes—in the operation of legal institutions of economic significance," and to promote "the development of skills with which to analyze and predict the performance consequences of alternative institutional

---

(1987), especially "Chapter 1: A General Paradigm of Institutions and Performance" (pp. 3–24); "Chapter 2: Property in a Social Context" (pp. 25–35); and "Chapter 3: Restatement of Paradigm" (pp. 181–96). For examples of empirical studies undertaken by Schmid, see Schmid (1987, pp. 257–91).

designs."[18] The Institutional approach to law and economics is best understood as embodying two complementary branches that differ only with respect to the relative emphasis given to "structure" and "conduct," as outlined earlier. In total, the Institutional approach emphasizes the need to explain and analyze the available alternatives and the consequences of choice at the constitutional, institutional, and economic impact stages.[19] As such, the analysis focuses on assessing the varied impacts—allocational, distributional, monetary, and otherwise—of changing constitutional rules, working rules, legal doctrines, and property rights.

CENTRAL THEMES OF INSTITUTIONAL LAW AND ECONOMICS

Several themes emerge in the Institutional law and economics literature, and these themes are clearly related to fundamental elements of Institutional economics in general. As we previously pointed out, Institutional economics represents a system of thought that originated in America in the first quarter of the century, and its central premise is that economic institutions motivate all economic activities. Within Institutionalism, habits, customs, social patterns, and legal and economic arrangements are seen to be the primary factors and forces governing economic life. Economic institutions are considered to be the combined product of evolution, power, and technology. With this as a predicate, it is no surprise that much of the work within Institutional law and economics has concentrated on describing and analyzing economic life in the context of the full array of surrounding social institutions.

The Evolution of Law and Economy

One of the factors emphasized by Commons in his discussion of the legal foundations of the capitalist economic system is the evolutionary nature of the economic system, and, most importantly for the present discussion, the role of the evolution of law in structuring the evolution of the economic system. One prominent example of this is his discussion of the evolution of the law of property.

Prior to the late nineteenth century, the U.S. courts held to a physical conception of property, a view that defined property as value in use rather than value in exchange (Commons 1924, p. 12). One of the implications of this

---

[18] In addition to the essays found in Samuels and Schmid and the references cited herein, examples of the Institutional approach to law and economics can be found in Schmid (1989, 1994), Mercuro and Ryan (1984), Liebhafsky (1987), Samuels (1992), Bromley (1989), Seidman (1973), Ostrom (1986a,b), Parsons (1974), Kanal (1985), and Carter (1985).

[19] See the discussion of the three stages of choice in chapter 1.

definition of property was that governmental deprivations of exchange value did not require compensation under the Fifth and Fourteenth Amendments. As Commons points out, it was only in the 1870s that the idea of property as value in exchange first began to creep into dissenting opinions of the U.S. Supreme Court, and it was not until the 1890s that the court finally made the transition from a definition of property as a thing having only use value to a definition that conceived of property as the exchange value of anything (Commons 1924, pp. 12–14). In making this transition, the court was saying not only that physical things are property, but that "the *expected earning power* of those things is property," and thus "[t]o deprive the owners of the *exchange value* of their property is equivalent to depriving them of their property" (Commons 1924, p. 16; emphasis in original). Thus, no longer were physical seizures of property the only "takings" requiring compensation; it now became the case that activities (including government regulations) that reduced the exchange value of things could give rise to claims for compensation. In the 1897 Allegeyer case (*Allegeyer v. Louisiana*, 165 U.S. 578 (1897)), this was further expanded to include liberty of access to markets, an important component in the determination of exchange values (Commons 1924, p. 17). The definition of property as corporeal property had been expanded to include both incorporeal property—e.g., debt instruments or promises to pay—and intangible property—"anything that enables one to obtain from others an income in the process of buying and selling, borrowing and lending, hiring and hiring out, renting and leasing, in any of the transactions of the modern business" (Commons 1924, p. 19). The import of this for the development of the capitalist system is set forth by Commons in the context of farming:

> The isolated, colonial, or frontier farmer might produce and consume things, attentive only to their use-value, but the modern farmer lives by producing "social-use values" and buying other social-use-values produced and sold by other business men. In this way he also "produces" exchange-value, that is, assets. He farms for sale, not for use, and while he has the doubtful alternative of falling back on his own natural resources if he cannot sell his products, yet his farm and crops are valuable because they are business assets, that is, exchange-values, while his liabilities are his debts and his taxes, all of them measured by his expectations and realizations on the commodity markets and money markets, in terms of exchange-value or price. (Commons 1924, p. 21)

That is, what distinguishes capitalism from the colonial and feudal systems it replaced is the transition from production for one's own use to "production for the use of others and acquisition for the use of self" (Commons 1924, p. 21), and it was in part the adoption of this more expansive definition of property that helped to facilitate this economic transition.

Following on the work of Institutionalists such as Commons, the Institutional approach to law and economics is evolutionary, emphasizing the importance of

the historical process and the evolutionary change of law through time. As described by Samuels (1989a, p.1578), the legal-economic nexus "is a continuing, explorative, and emergent process through which are worked out ongoing solutions to legal problems." As captured by the reverse link in figure 4-1, the structure of legal-economic institutions—the state (whether in the context of the legislature, the bureaucracy, or the judiciary), the firm/corporation, or the market—channels legal-economic decision-making, and this structure is seen as the outcome of an evolutionary process of legal-economic change rather than as movement to a steady-state equilibrium (Schmid 1989, p. 66). Legal change, although gradual, has been continuous and "has led to major transformations of the legal system and of the pattern of rights and, thereby, of the system of economic organization and control" (Samuels and Mercuro 1979, p. 167). The pervasiveness of legal change and the ongoing process of legal-economic reconstruction through the nexus process thus makes necessary an evolutionary-historical approach that accounts for the array of factors and forces promoting both continuity and change over time.[20]

Continuity versus Change

Another of the fundamental ideas explored within the Institutionalist approach to law and economics is the ever-present tension between continuity and change. The evolutionary path of the legal-economic system is derivative of the legal-economic policy choices that are made over time. From within the policy-making processes, be they legislative, bureaucratic, or judicial, arise forces that, through acts of commission or omission, serve to maintain the status quo structure of legal-economic institutions and relations—that is, that provide for continuity. On the other hand, there are always forces within a mixed-market economy that promote an alteration in these institutions and relations—that is, that opt for change. The ongoing choice process within the legal-economic arena will thus determine both the institutional structures that obtain at any given point in time and whether the status quo institutional structures, or some other, will prevail in the future. In other words, this choice process determines whether there will be change, and if so, how much. It must be recognized, say the Institutionalists, that the formation of legal-economic policy takes place in an arena within which there is the ever-present tension between continuity and change. Each is the outcome of the policy-making process, and, more specifically, of the interaction between the groups supporting the respective forces of continuity and change and the power that each can bring to bear on this process (Samuels 1966, pp. 267–73).

---

[20] See, for example, Field (1979, 1981) and Bromley (1989, ch. 2).

Mutual Interdependence, Conflict, and the Problem of Order

The Institutionalists view the legal-economic system as a system of mutual interdependence rather than atomistic independence. The economy, says Schmid (1989, p. 59), is "a universe of human relations," not merely "a universe of commodities," and within this world each individual has scarcity relationships with others. Thus, from the vantage point of Institutional law and economics, the firm is seen as something more than a nexus of contracts.[21] Although it may be that part of life deals with movements from positions off of contract curves to positions on contract curves in the process of exhausting gains from trade, the Institutionalist approach places strong emphasis on (i) who gets to play, (ii) where one starts in the game, and (iii) the strategic behavior (i.e., the conscious, calculated choices) of participants that frame the position, role, and status of each individual.

Given the importance of human interdependence and the emphasis on who plays and what are the starting points, the view of the world evidenced within the Institutionalist approach is one of conflict rather than harmony. Because of this, "[t]he role of the legal system, including both common and constitutional law, is to provide a framework or a process for conflict resolution and the development of legal rights" (Samuels and Mercuro 1979, p. 166). The fundamental problem here is that of order, which Samuels (1972a, p. 584) defines as "the reconciling of freedom and control, or autonomy and coordination including hierarchy and equality, with continuity and change." "The ultimate meaning of the legal and economic processes," says Samuels (1971, p. 449), "is in terms of their functioning toward resolving the problem(s) of order." The existence of conflicting interests necessitates both a process (or processes) for deciding between these competing interests and a method (or methods) for determining how these conflicts are to be resolved.

Thus, society is recognized, at least in part, as a cooperative venture for mutual advantage where there is both an identity and a conflict of interests in ongoing human relations. Within this system of mutual interdependence, societal institutions, including the legal system, both enhance the scope of cooperative endeavors and channel political-legal-economic conflict toward resolution (Mercuro 1989, p. 2). The resolution of these conflicts, of whose interests government will give effect through law and otherwise, is the resolution of the problem of order in society—a working out of a societal structure that promotes coherence, security, and orderliness in human relations. Indeed, the manner by which a society comes to channel conflict says much about its ultimate character.

---

[21] In this regard it has been described as a community designed in part to suspend narrow, individualistic calculations of advantage and facilitate the learning of shared objectives. See, for example, Hodgson (1988), Eisenberg (1990), and Leibenstein (1987).

Rights, Power, and Government

From the Institutional perspective, law is fundamentally a matter of rights creation and re-creation. Consistent with the positive, descriptive nature of this approach, Institutionalists are concerned with the rights (re)creation process and the impact of this process on legal-economic decision-making and activity. To understand the importance of rights from the Institutional perspective, it is first necessary to understand the Institutionalist conception of the determination of the individual choice process and the activities open to individuals.

Individual decision-making is a function of one's opportunity set, which "consists of the available alternatives for action or choice, each with a relative opportunity cost, which are open to the individual" (Samuels 1974, p. 120). These opportunity sets, however, are not without limit in their scope; rather, reflecting human interdependence and scarcity, each individual's opportunity set is constrained, and indeed shaped, by the opportunity sets of others in society. Each individual desires to make choices from a set that is as unconstrained as possible, which, in turn, means that individuals will wish to control the choices, and hence opportunity sets, of others who may constrain their choice. The extent of each individual's ability to determine his or her own choices and to influence the opportunity sets, and hence choices, of others is the outcome of a process of *mutual coercion*, where the ability to coerce is simply the ability of A to impact B's opportunity set without B's consent. An individual's capacity to exercise coercion is, in turn, a function of that individual's *power*, defined as "the means or capacity with which to exercise choice" (Samuels 1972b, p. 65), and this power is relative to the power of others. Thus, "[t]he opportunity set of the individual, within which he attempts a constrained maximizing equilibrium, is a function of the total structure of mutual coercion, grounded upon relative power" (Samuels 1972b, p. 65). Moreover, power is also a dependent variable in this process, being a function of the choices made from opportunity sets that exist and evolve through time (Samuels 1972b, p. 66).

The ongoing delineation and redefinition of opportunity sets, through the machinations of power and mutual coercion in the face of conflicts, gives rise to disputes that necessitate resolution. For example, the upstream polluting factory's choice of production technology impacts and conflicts with the choice of activities of the downstream water user, and conversely. The upstream user cannot exercise choice without impacting the choice of downstream users, and conversely. The resolution of such conflicts comes through the creation and assignment (or reassignment) of legal rights, which define the scope of choices open to each individual and the degree to which each is exposed to the choices of others. Thus, power, and hence coercion and the resulting opportunity sets and choices, are a function of rights.

The origin of rights in the resolution of conflicts of interest brings to the fore

the point that rights have a dual nature—"the opportunity set enhancement of those who have rights and the opportunity set restriction of those who are exposed to them" (Samuels 1974, p. 122). Virtually every legal change imposes both benefits and costs, the enhancement of some opportunity sets and the simultaneous restriction of others. Externalities are thus ubiquitous and reciprocal: any (re)definition, (re)allocation, or change in the degree of enforcement of rights benefits some interests and harms others; the externality remains—its effects are merely shifted. In Institutional law and economics, systems of property, tort, and contract law, then, do not provide *solutions* to situations of externality, but rather only *resolutions,* inasmuch as externalities, and hence the associated stream of benefits and harms, are channeled in a particular direction through the legal delimitation of rights.

Government is seen to play a central and inevitable role within this process, for rights are not rights because they are preexisting, but rather because they are protected by government.[22] Rights are thus relative to and contingent upon "the legal limitations inherent in their identification and interpretation, the exercise by others of their rights, and legal and nonlegal change" (Samuels 1974, p. 118). Each of these factors is a function of the rights creation (and recreation) process, and hence of the ability of individuals to secure rights, or a change therein, through the use and control of government. Government thus becomes an object of control for those seeking private legal-economic gain or advantage, "a mode through which relative rights and therefore relative market (income securing) status is given effect" (Samuels 1971, pp. 441–42). The question is not, then, one of more versus less government, but rather of whose interests government gives effect through law—more specifically, through the process of rights creation and re-creation. The Institutionalists thus see terms such as regulation, deregulation, and government intervention as misleading, in that government is omnipresent (Lang 1980; Breimyer 1991). For example, although it is often said that the adoption of workplace safety regulations constitutes an intervention of government into the market, the Institutionalists claim that such activity represents merely a change in rights, or in the interests to which government gives effect—a movement that expands the rights/opportunity sets of workers and reduces the rights/opportunity sets of employers. The issue as to who will have rights thus turns on whose interests government allows to be realized and who is able to use government for what ends. The critical matter, says Samuels, is who is able to control and use the legal-economic nexus to control legal-economic continuity or change (Samuels 1971, p. 440).[23]

The reciprocal nature of externalities has the effect that the decision as

---

[22] "Rights are whatever interests government protects vis-à-vis other interests when there is a conflict" (Samuels 1974, p. 127). See also Samuels (1974, pp. 118–19).

[23] See also Samuels (1989a, p. 1578).

to whose interests are protected as rights is necessarily a function of a choice process, where that choice will determine who will have rights and who will be exposed to the exercise of those rights, and who will be able to inflict gains and losses on others, and to what extent (Samuels and Mercuro 1979, pp. 172–174). This inevitable necessity of choice reveals that law is not something that is given or to be discovered, but is instead a human artifact marked by deliberative and nondeliberative human choice (Samuels 1981, p. 168). This human choice process necessitates the introduction of value judgments in choosing between competing interests, and legal-economic outcomes are thus "an expression of the values of those who have participated and prevailed at each stage of choice in the political-legal-economic arena"—that is, those who are able to use government most effectively to further their own ends (Mercuro 1989, p. 10).

Recognition of the necessity of choice reveals the tentative, selective, and partial nature of the application of specific legal rules, which are themselves both subject and outcome of the choice process. The use of tests, rules, and the like "is essentially selective and arbitrary. Their use in any particular case is a matter of decision, of ultimate pure choice. . . . There is no automatic litmus test by which the tests themselves can be selected for applicability. They are categories (empty boxes) with variable selective contents whose adoption is almost if not wholly subjective" (Samuels and Mercuro 1979, p. 177). The rights generated through the use of tests, rules, and so on reflect selective perception both with respect to the test or rule actually applied and with respect to facts, gains, and losses as applied. Justice, then, reflects not some given set of high foundational principles, but rather a normative valuational process that determines the laws, norms, and values that are to govern living (Samuels 1971, p. 444).[24] The legal-economic nexus is that sphere of decision-making that reflects the working out of whose interests are to count as rights, whose values are to dominate, and who is to make these decisions. The resolution of these issues determines not just rights but also the allocation and distribution of resources in society, and hence power, income, and wealth.

The Problematic Nature of Efficiency

One of the hallmarks of the Institutional approach is the rejection of the Chicago emphasis on the determination of *the* efficient resolution of legal disputes or as a singular guide in changing law. The Institutionalists do not reject efficiency as an important variable in legal-economic analysis, but rather maintain that efficiency is not unique and therefore cannot determine the assignment of rights (Samuels 1989a, p. 1563). It is not merely a question of adding something to the concept of efficiency, but, rather, of what is subsumed or included within the concept. Concerns about the problematic nature of

---

[24] See also Samuels and Mercuro (1979, pp. 160–63).

efficiency can be traced back to the work of the early Institutionalists, especially J. M. Clark, who cautioned policymakers not to try to base policy decisions on the anticipated "optimal" results that might come about using efficiency analysis. In doing so, Clark (1939, p. 493) wrote,

> We must be on guard . . . against the tendency of the reformer to compare the imperfections of existing conditions with the anticipated results of his reform measures, conceived as working perfectly. They will not work perfectly, and this had better be expected from the start. We should learn to compare existing imperfect conditions with the other imperfections which experience teaches us are sure to result from attempts at control.

The starting point here is the recognition that economic activity—prices, costs, outputs, risk, income, wealth, and so on—is not some sort of natural phenomenon, but rather is determined by the structure of rights that exists in society, with the levels of and changes in each of these variables being in part a function of rights, and hence of the legal structure and legal change over time.[25] Each particular rights structure will give rise to a particular set of prices, costs, outputs, and the like, and thus to a particular efficient allocation of resources. Hence, there is no unique efficient result. For the Institutionalists, the purportedly positivist Chicago school rhetoric of "atomistic industries" or "contestable markets" and the associated concept of "price-taking behavior" is exposed as nothing more than deeply normative "rights-taking behavior" (Samuels and Mercuro 1984). The Institutionalists maintain that inasmuch as rights underlie product prices and thus costs, to talk of "price-takers" bypasses virtually all that is important in Law and Economics.

Because efficiency is a function of rights, and not the other way around, it is circular to maintain that efficiency alone can determine rights. Since costs, prices, outputs, wealth, and so on are derivative of a particular rights structure, so too are cost minimization, value-of-output maximization, and wealth maximization. Different specifications of rights will lead to different, and economically noncomparable, minimizing or maximizing valuations. The result is that an outcome that is claimed to be efficient is efficient only with regard to the assumed initial structure of rights (Schmid 1989, pp. 68–69). Thus, as Samuels (1981, p. 154) asserts, "To argue that wealth maximization [or any other efficiency criterion] can determine rights serves only to mask a choice of which interests to protect as rights. Legal decisions or changes can be said to be efficient only from the point of view of the party whose interests are given effect through the identification and assignment of rights."[26]

---

[25] See Samuels (1971, p. 440), Samuels (1989a, p. 1565), and Schmid (1989, p. 67).

[26] Posner (2001b, ch. 3) now recognizes that there are issues of the relationship between efficiency and the distribution of wealth that make the wealth-maximization criterion problematic on ethical grounds, but he continues to defend it on pragmatic grounds.

Moreover, the invocation of valuation criteria to measure efficiency requires an antecedent normative specification as to which is the appropriate one to be used. Social output (the aggregate well-being of society), consumptive output (the value of goods from the consumer point of view), and productive output (the value of goods from the producer point of view, i.e., profits) are three examples of the alternatives that are available. The choice of a particular definition of valuation criteria, which, in effect, is the choice of a particular social welfare function where many are possible, will drive the decision as to what constitutes the efficient allocation (Samuels 1978, pp. 102–4).

Beyond the issue as to which valuation criteria are to be used in determining efficiency is the question as to the specification of the objects of the maximization process. In a mixed-market economy the market does not allocate resources apart and distinct from government. Indeed, the allocation and distribution of goods and resources is accomplished through markets, which, in turn, are a function of government institutions and power structures that form and operate through them. In this regard, the definition of "output" or of a "resource"—of what it is that one is to be efficient about—requires an antecedent normative specification as to what constitutes a particular good or a particular factor of production.[27] Two simple examples illustrate the point. First, in the market for automobiles, what constitutes an automobile includes, among other things, the rights governing: (i) the very definition of an automobile (now including air bags and a catalytic converter together with severe legal sanctions for disconnecting either), (ii) the government mandated standards and tests that govern automobile production, and (iii) the terms, conditions, and the enforcement of warranties. It is the government-structured definition, assignment, and enforcement of rights that shape the market for automobiles—it is not a question of an automobile market with government or without government. In a like manner, on the input side, what constitutes labor includes, among other things, (i) the rights governing child labor laws, (ii) occupational health and safety laws, and (iii) minimum wage laws. Again, it is not a question of a labor market with government or without government. The market for automobiles, for labor, indeed markets for all goods and services, are a function of government institutionalized markets complemented by government.

Thus, in Institutional law and economics, there is a recognition of the multiplicity of efficient solutions and the contingency of any given efficient solution on the presumed structure of rights and the definition of inputs and outputs, all this revealing the inherent normative element that is present in efficiency-based decision-making. Each possible legal solution points to a different efficient outcome; further, "[t]here is no independent test by which the law's solutions can

---

[27] For a discussion of the impacts associated with redefining products and factors of production, see Lang (1980).

be said to be *the* efficient solution" (Samuels 1981, p. 155). The determination of a particular efficient solution involves a normative and selective choice as to whose interests will be accommodated, who will realize gains, and who will realize losses.

INSTITUTIONALIST INTERPRETATIONS
OF LEGAL-ECONOMIC CONCEPTS

Distribution

Institutionalists see questions of efficiency as inevitably bound up with issues of distribution. As Samuels and Schmid (1981, p. 2) describe it, "[T]he concept of efficiency as separate from distribution is false." Rights determination is a normative activity with both efficiency and distributional consequences, determining which efficient allocation and which distribution of benefits and costs will carry the day. Rights determine the distribution of income and wealth, which in turn determines the efficient solution that is reached—but at the same time, the specification of rights, and the resulting efficient outcome, structure the future distribution of income and wealth in society. The choice of rights, then, is ultimately a distributional issue: "With no unique optimal use of resources and opportunities independent of rights identification and assignment, the legal system must select the [distributional] result to be pursued: *the definition of the efficient solution is both the object and the subject of the legal system*" (Samuels 1978, p. 106; emphasis in original). Thus, as described by Schmid (1989, p. 69), "[T]he whole point is that global welfare maximization is meaningless," and "[t]o recommend one right over another, analysts must take their stand as naked normativists without the comfort of the Pareto-better cloak or any other formalism." In part because of this, then, the Institutionalists maintain that "[t]he distribution problem, viz., of power, income, wealth, opportunity, exposure, and sacrifice, is critical to legal-economic research and policy" (Samuels 1975, p. 70).

Efficiency of the Common Law

This line of reasoning also leads Institutionalists to reject the Chicago efficiency theory of the common law. Any given rights structure will produce an efficient or wealth-maximizing outcome, and thus "[t]he so-called efficiency of the common law is an 'empirical regularity' only in the sense that every common law specification of rights can produce a unique, wealth-maximizing outcome" (Samuels 1981, p. 162). If different interests had been protected as rights, different efficient outcomes would have occurred. The choice of certain

rights structures reflects a normative choice for a particular efficient pattern of law and economic development over time, where different decisions would have led to different patterns of efficient development. Thus, says Samuels (1981, p. 162), the literature purporting to explain the efficient development of the common law " 'explains' everything and nothing." "Wealth maximization," he says, "cannot . . . explain the evolution of the common law: any developmental logic concerning rights in a market economy would have led the common law to some wealth-maximizing result" (Samuels 1981, p. 154).

Rent Seeking

Proponents of Institutionalist law and economics also reject the public choice school's efficiency-based approach to the analysis of rent-seeking behavior.[28] Here, rent-seeking activities are defined as "resource-wasting activities of individuals in seeking transfers of wealth through the aegis of the state" (Buchanan, Tollison, and Tullock 1980, p. ix). In this view, if scarce resources are expended by agents in an attempt to garner a privileged position (e.g., an exclusive monopoly franchise) from the state, or, if the state is used (e.g., through legislative activities or lobbying) to alter product and/or factor prices to enhance profits without a concomitant increase in output, such activities are termed rent seeking and deemed wasteful. The normative thrust of this theory thus becomes one of promoting policies designed to avoid wasteful, rent-seeking activities, which often involves a greater, more exclusive reliance on markets and a scaling back of government.

The Institutionalist discussion of rent seeking does not deny the pervasive nature of individuals seeking transfers of wealth through the political process; here, it stands foursquare with positive public choice theory. The problem, for the Institutionalists, comes with the attribution of "waste" to the resources expended in the process. The intellectual construct employed by proponents of the rent-seeking literature is that of the competitive market economy and the legitimized product and factor prices and thus profits that obtain therefrom. Prices and profits that occur consequent to standard marketplace phenomena—such as the entering and exiting of firms into and from industries, adopting new technologies, altering the scale of plant, and so on—are all legitimate. When prices and profits are altered by and/or through the aegis of the state, however, this is said to result in waste.

From the standpoint of Institutional law and economics, this characterization of rent seeking is an exercise in selective perception and market legitimation (Samuels and Mercuro 1984, pp. 55–70). As the Institutionalists have pointed out, to use today's market prices and profits as a basis to determine

---

[28] See section on rent seeking in chapter 3.

rents and wastes is to give propriety to extant laws governing the production of goods while at the same time selectively culling out one subset of rights to make claims of rent-seeking, wasteful activity. It is the proponents' reliance on the model of competition that gives effect to this selective perception. As is made clear in Institutionalist law and economics, positive models of the economy predicated on price-taking behavior are in reality normative models of rights-taking behavior. Market prices are not absolute, predetermined, and independent of law, but, rather, are a partial function of rights—the latter related directly to the government's ubiquitous role in creating, defining, assigning, enforcing, and altering rights. Moreover, it is emphasized that today's prevailing market prices of products and factors of production are all predicated upon the past use of the state and past rent-seeking activities. Market-generated product and factor prices that make up a firm's revenue-cost calculation are property-rights specific; as a consequence, so too is its net revenue calculation a function of rights. The government's role in the economy remains ubiquitous, and, accordingly, a theory that purports to identify rent-seeking behavior and the economic wastes therefrom begs the question. There are no *correct* rights, prices, profits, or correct structure of rents. Thus, rent-seeking theory is characterized as an artificial, misguided normative theory that will "mislead positive analysis and generate artificial distinctions and thereby provide no real basis for distinguishing between permissible and impermissible activities" (Samuels and Mercuro 1984, p. 67).[29]

A COMPARATIVE INSTITUTIONAL
APPROACH TO LAW AND ECONOMICS

The foundation for an Institutionalist law and economics is thus a coming to grips with the interrelations between legal (broadly conceived) and economic processes. Samuels (1975, p. 72) identifies three efforts that are central to this process: (i) "models of legal-political and economic interaction" must be developed; (ii) "objective, positive, empirical studies of government as both a dependent and independent variable, and of economic activity as both an input and an output of political-legal processes" must be undertaken; and (iii) efforts must be made "to wed both theoretical and empirical analyses toward a self-consciously objective, positive comprehension of law and economics." According to Samuels (1975, p. 72), such analysis will serve the twin purposes of deepening the understanding of legal and economic processes and their interrelations, and provide "a more realistic and knowledgeable basis on which to predict the probable performance consequences of both political and economic change or reform."

[29] On this topic, see also Medema (1991).

The import of this becomes clear in the Institutionalist assertion that the essential normative element in political-legal-economic decision-making means that a choice must be made between alternative efficiency-distributional results and hence between alternative political-legal-economic institutional structures. This, in turn, necessitates a comparative institutional approach to legal-economic analysis.[30] The institutional structure cannot, in this view, merely be assumed away or taken as given. Rather, it must be the subject of study and, more specifically, the legal-economic decision-making process must involve a comparison of the effects of institutional alternatives on social well-being.

The comparative institutional approach is general rather than partial (Samuels 1972a, pp. 582, 585), and its scope consists in describing and analyzing "the systematic relationship between 1) the structure of political-legal economic institutions, focusing on the rights and rules by which they operate; 2) the conduct or observed behavior in light of the incentives (penalties and rewards) created by the structure of institutions; 3) the consequent economic performance, i.e., the allocation *and* distribution of resources that determine the character of economic life under these institutions" (Mercuro 1989, p. 11; emphasis in original). Specifically, a comparative institutional approach to law and economics emphasizes the need to explain and analyze the available alternatives and the consequences of public policy choices at the constitutional, institutional, and economic impact stages of choice. The underlying logic inherent in such an approach is that public policy involves altering the *law*—that is, (i) changing the constitution, (ii) altering working rules or legal doctrines, or (iii) refashioning the various legal relations governing society and thereby deciding which resources will come under which system of social control: the market sector using private property rights, the public sector using status rights, the communal sector using communal property, or just leaving resources as open-access resources. The belief is that the goals of public policy being sought will not come about by changing law willy-nilly or in an ad hoc manner, but by structuring and adopting those laws, rights, rules, and doctrines for which there is a known nexus between the said change in law and the consequent outcome.[31]

---

[30] The need for a comparative institutional approach has long been recognized. Other proponents of a comparative institutional approach (not necessarily coming from a perspective identical to that of the Institutionalists) include Demsetz (1969), Komesar (1981, 1994), Stewart (1987), Shepsle and Weingast (1984), and some of those working under the banner of the New Institutional Economics (see ch. 5 in this book). Also, using game theory, Aoki (2001) provides a conceptual and analytical framework for understanding the evolution and impact of alternative institutions.

[31] Vincent Ostrom (1976, p. 852) described the need as follows:

> The consideration of alternative solutions . . . requires a consideration of the probable consequences which will be evoked by each of the different alternative possibilities. A warrantable knowledge about the effects of alternative structural arrangements is necessary before policy makers can formulate policy instruments that are capable of avoiding a pathological state of affairs and realizing some more productive potential. In this sense, the intellectual foundations of institutional analysis can contribute to institutional design.

The purpose of such an approach is to explain and compare the outcomes that will occur under real, discrete, alternative institutional structures, and to do so not just in terms of efficiency, but also in terms of the distribution of income and wealth, employment rates, and any other factors that may affect the quality of life or the productive capacity of firms.[32] With regard to focusing on efficiency as the dominant performance indicator, Samuels suggests that "[f]or law to be preoccupied solely with economic maximization would rob law of life and of much of what makes for human meaning and significance" (Samuels 1981, p. 165). Contrary to the Chicago school's normative prescriptions or public choice catallatics, the goal here is not normative judgment but description: "A viable approach to the study of the interrelations between law and economics should be content with describing the full array of economic impacts . . . of alternative institutions and legal arrangements together with an articulation of whose interests will be served and at whose expense" (Mercuro 1989, p. 12). Such analysis will not privilege one set of interests over others, but it will better enable those who study and participate in the processes of the legal-economic nexus to understand these processes and their resulting effects on law and economy (Samuels 1989a, p. 1578).[33]

Of course, normative judgments must be made in the process of reaching legal decisions. Recognizing this, the Institutional approach emphasizes the need for openness and values clarification in the political-legal-economic decision-making process, a legacy of the Legal Realist movement within the law (Samuels 1989a, p. 1573). For example, in calling for a more inclusive list of performance indicators, the suggestion is not just to extend the list of indicators—more is involved. A comparative institutional approach asks for a deeper appreciation and articulation of the antecedent normative premises that are used in the selective identification and definition of each and every performance indicator (Mercuro 2001). Economists, legal scholars, policymakers, and judges should strive to make the value premises underlying their conclusions as explicit as possible, so that the choice process can be effectuated "carefully and overtly" rather than "carelessly and covertly" (Samuels 1978, p. 113).[34] This call for openness is clearly tied to the comparative Institutional method:

> Not only should normative premises be made explicit, but an array of studies should
> be conducted on the basis of *alternative* normative (and factual) assumptions. To do

---

[32] See Mercuro (2001) for a discussion of seven performance indicators that goes beyond the familiar discussions of (i) efficiency and (ii) distribution, and includes (iii) legal order/continuity, (iv) freedom to/freedom from, (v) macroeconomic indicators, (vi) definitions of inputs/outputs, and (vii) ecological integrity.

[33] A sample of Institutionalist-oriented case studies include Seidman (1973), Croyle (1979), Carter (1985), Schmid (1985), Wandschneider (1986), Rutherford (1994), and Hodgson (1998). In addition, a law review article by Skeeters (1999) titled *"Man O War Restaurants, Inc. v. Martin*: Law Altering Economic Performance" (which analyzes the rules governing stock repurchase agreements) utilizes the comparative institutional approach previously described.

[34] See also Samuels (1989b).

only one study is to give effect to only one perception and specification of outputs, costs, benefits, and rights. Alternative studies call attention to the subtle intrusion of ideology and partisanship, emphasize the necessary and inevitable critical choice of underlying values, highlight the fundamental distributional consequences that depend on the political determination of output definitions, and so forth. (Samuels 1978, p. 112; emphasis in original)

The obfuscation of values and underlying normative premises within so much of the Chicago approach to law and economics and public choice theory is the bane of the comparative institutional approach. Relying solely on the Pareto-efficiency criterion serves to obfuscate and impede the normative choice process that is necessarily at work in the legal-economic nexus.[35]

INSTITUTIONAL LAW AND ECONOMICS AT WORK

The Structure-Performance Relation

The Institutionalists' previously mentioned qualms about the overuse of efficiency analysis translate into an approach that is concerned not with making assessments based on abstract ideals, such as attaching labels of "efficient" or "inefficient" to particular legal rules or institutional structures, but with describing and making comparisons among the real alternatives that are open to society. As evidenced, for example, in Schmid (1987), such analysis takes place under a situation-specific structure-conduct-performance paradigm, in which alternative institutional structures, such as different definitions and assignments of property rights, and inherent sources of interdependency are identified. These, in turn, are linked to the (dis)incentives created and the consequences for individual, firm, and government behavior, and, in general, for economic performance and quality of life. As such, it reflects a "total" approach to policy analysis (Schmid 1987, pp. 257–58), one that emphasizes the link between structure and performance.

To see how the Institutional approach to these issues works, and how it contrasts with the more neoclassical approaches to law and economics, let us consider Schmid's example of water pollution and the choice between regulatory standards and charges (or user fees).[36] The conventional economic approach to this issue is to recommend charges (pollution taxes) over standards on the grounds that they are more efficient: they accomplish the same reduction in pollution at a lower cost.[37] The reasoning behind this is as follows: Regulatory

---

[35] See, for example, Bromley (1989), Calabresi (1985, 1991), Griffin (1991, 1995), Lang (1980), and Mishan (1972).

[36] This example is drawn from Schmid (1987, pp. 263–66).

[37] See, for example, Baumol and Oates (1988), Stewart (1988), Ackerman and Stewart (1988), and Ballard and Medema (1993).

standards mandate that, to accomplish an aggregate reduction of x percent in pollution, each producer must reduce its discharge by this same x percent. This across-the-board approach does not take into account the fact that the costliness of pollution abatement may vary widely across firms. Efficiency considerations would suggest that those who can reduce pollution at a lower cost be forced to bear a larger share of this burden, to accomplish this aggregate reduction in pollution at the minimum cost to society. The charges approach, in contrast, sets a fee to be charged for each unit of pollution emitted. Under such a scheme, each polluter will compare the cost of abating an additional unit of pollution with the cost of the charge. Those firms that can abate pollution more cheaply will find it profitable to undertake relatively more abatement (and thus less polluting) as compared to those firms with higher costs of abatement. Thus, a tax that is set at a level sufficient to achieve an x percent reduction in aggregate pollution will have the effect of placing a larger share of the burden of this pollution reduction onto the firms with lower costs of abatement and will, in the process, achieve the x percent reduction in total pollution at a lower total cost than would obtain under the use of a regulatory standard; that is, a system of charges is more efficient than the employment of a regulatory standard. Moreover, by raising revenue for the government, these taxes allow for the reduction of other, distortionary, taxes.

Schmid (1987, pp. 264–65) maintains that such analysis is incomplete, in that it focuses exclusively on cost levels, ignoring their distribution and thus the differential effects of these policies across firms (see also Samuels and Schmid 1976). The comparative Institutional approach to law and economics that he advocates entails not only an examination of these differential costs, but also of looking beyond them to the underlying property rights and opportunity sets and their distributional implications. Schmid maintains that a regulatory standard implies that each firm has a right to discharge a certain quantity of waste,[38] whereas "third-party environmentalists" are given a de facto ownership claim over the remaining share of the water. The use of regulatory standards, which require each firm to reduce its discharge by the same percentage, holds the relative property rights of each firm constant at their pre-regulatory levels.[39]

A charge on emissions alters the property rights and opportunity sets relationship, in that it implies that rights over the resource are owned by the government and that firms can, in a sense, purchase a portion of these rights by paying the specified charge. Under this system, the firms with higher abatement costs are allowed to substitute the lower tax cum discharge costs for the

---

[38] As such, says Schmid, regulatory standards are not unlike the employment of the doctrine of reasonable use.

[39] Taking this logic a step further, increases in the regulatory standard hold constant the relative ownership shares of the firms, but reduce the firms's ownership shares relative to those of the third-party environmentalists.

higher-cost abatement and thus receive a greater right to the use of the stream than would obtain under the system of regulatory standards. As compared to the standards scheme, we see, in effect, a transfer of rights to the use of the stream from low-cost to high-cost abaters. Because the payments for these rights to use the stream go to the government, rather than to the low-cost abaters whose rights to the stream have been reduced, we also see a redistribution of income among the firms. Thus, the decision as to which abatement-inducing scheme to adopt impacts the relative well-being of the firms involved. One might expect that low-cost abaters will prefer a regulatory scheme, whereas high-cost abaters will prefer a system of charges. This, and the size of each group, in turn will affect the relative pressures brought to bear upon government for one system versus the other.

As Schmid (1987, pp. 265–66) points out, the comparative institutional approach reveals that "[w]hen the rights of third-party environmentalists are expanded, a conflict arises between . . . industrial firms in the sharing of the costs of redistribution. Thus, there is a conflict between achieving equal treatment between two firms and achieving the lowest cost of attaining a given stream quality." The decision, then, is not simply about costs, but about the distribution of these costs among affected parties. Of course, the same analysis applies to the decision one step previous to that considered here—that is, the decision to adopt a policy to reduce pollution or to maintain the status quo. This decision influences the distribution of rights, and thus costs and incomes, between firms and third-party environmentalists. Decision-making at either of these levels does not, under the comparative institutional approach, admit to an easy answer. The goal is an evaluation of the substantive effects of alternative policy mechanisms (institutional structures) on affected parties. Beyond this, the decision as to which institutional structure to adopt becomes fundamentally a choice as to whose interests are to count.

The Legal-Economic Nexus

A useful application of the conduct-oriented approach advocated by Samuels is found in his discussion of *Miller v. Schoene*.[40] This case revolved around a 1914 statute passed by the Virginia State legislature which gave the state entomologist the power to investigate, condemn, and destroy, without compensation, red cedar trees within a two-mile radius of an apple orchard if it could be shown that the red cedar trees constituted a menace to the health of the apple orchards. Red cedar rust, a fungus harmless to red cedar trees, is harmful to the leaves and fruit of apple trees and is known to migrate from the former to

---

[40] *Miller v. Schoene* 276 U.S. 272 (1928); for various legal-economic analyses of this case, see Buchanan (1972b), Mercuro and Ryan (1980), and Fischel (2004).

the latter, causing an economic loss to apple orchard owners. The plaintiffs, the red cedar owners, argued that this statute unconstitutionally deprived them of their property without just compensation. The case made its way to the U.S. Supreme Court, where the court denied the challenge to the statute. Speaking for the Court, Mr. Justice Stone wrote,

> On the evidence we may accept the conclusion of the Supreme Court of Appeals that the state was under the necessity of making a choice between the preservation of one class of property and that of the other wherever both existed in dangerous proximity. It would have been nonetheless a choice if, instead of enacting the present statute, the state, by doing nothing, had permitted serious injury to the apple orchards within its borders to go on unchecked. When forced to such a choice the state does not exceed its constitutional powers by deciding upon the destruction of one class of property in order to save another which, in the judgment of the legislature, is of greater value to the public. (*Miller v. Schoene*, at 279–280, quoted in Samuels 1971, pp. 437–38)

Commenting on this decision, Samuels (1971, pp. 438–39) points out the manner in which Justice Stone's opinion brings to the fore the inevitable necessity of choice in resolving questions of rights, and does so in a manner that is clearly tied to the themes of the Institutional approach to law and economics, set forth earlier, while eschewing the search for any globally efficient solution:

> The state had to make a choice as to which property owner was to be made not only formally secure but practically viable in his legal rights. The Court, as part of the state, had to make a judgment as to which owner would be visited with injury and which protected. The state, ultimately the Court, had to decide which party would have what capacity to coerce the other, meaning by coercion the impact of one party [on] the actions of the other. There was a direct conflict between two private interests (between two private rights claimants) which required choice, and choice on the basis of some (rational) criterion, in the instant case involving the criterion(ia) which the legislature and the courts embodied or read into the concept of public interest, public value, or the public welfare, ultimately through the vehicle of the police power. (Samuels 1971, pp. 438–39)

Samuels argues that, in the absence of the cedar rust statute, the structure of rights puts the apple orchard owners at a disadvantage in that the law gives the cedar tree owners the freedom to visit injury upon them, They are also, moreover, at a coercive disadvantage in that the burden of coming to an agreement that mitigates the damage lies with them and the flow of attendant payments runs from them to the red cedar owners. Under the cedar rust statute, just the opposite conditions obtain. The orchard owners are protected from harm, injury is visited upon the red cedar owners, and the coercive advantage instead rests with the orchard owners. As a result, the burden of coming to an agreement that mitigates injury to the red cedar owners lies with the red cedar owners,

meaning that the flow of payment for mitigation of injury runs from the red cedar owners to the orchard owners (p. 439). Thus, as Samuels notes, "[R]elative rights, . . . the pattern of mutual coercion, . . . the distribution of relative risk, business costs, . . . resource allocation, income distribution and the general level of income are a partial function of law" (p. 440).

As Samuels (1971, pp. 441–42) goes on to point out, this case is also illustrative of the role of positive description in Institutional law and economics and, thus, in describing the inevitable governmental presence within the legal-economic process. In the absence of the cedar rust statute, the government is, through the status quo rights structure, giving effect to the interests of the red cedar owners, to whose advantage the status quo works. Under the statute, of course, the government is giving effect to the interests of the apple orchard owners. The point to be made, according to Samuels, is that the government is equally present in either case: "government had to choose between the effective promotion of one group or the other: government is in both cases a participant in the economic decision-making process." When the cedar rust statute was enacted, it did not accomplish "an intrusion of government into a situation in which it had hitherto been absent, but rather a change of the interests to which effective legal support would be given" (p. 441).

This case is also suggestive of the issue of individuals and organizations using government (in a nonpejorative sense) for their own ends and thus, more generally, of the idea of using government to direct the allocation and distribution of resources within the economic system. The point here is that economic performance and conditions are a partial function of who is able to use government for what ends. In the present case, we see two groups competing to influence or use government: the owners of the red cedar trees, which, as Samuels (1971, p. 443) notes, "are of primarily ornamental use, with some use and value as timber," and apple orchard owners, who make up a major industry in Virginia. As Samuels points out, the apple orchard owners were a well-organized and influential group, whereas the red cedar owners were not, and the legislature was sensitive to the relative strength, economic and political, of these two concerns. Perhaps not surprisingly, then, it responded by protecting the interests of the more economically important and politically influential group. This is not to normatively advocate for one position or the other, but simply to make clear that competing interests will attempt to influence (or use) government to promote their own ends in a world of scarcity and choice. This is, according to Samuels (1971, pp. 444, 445), yet another illustration of the idea that "the issue is not government or no government but which interests, that is, whose interests the state is used to effectuate," and, at a deeper level, of the ultimate necessity and specificity of choice "which no reference to general or neutral principles will avoid." As such, an understanding of the legal-economic process, and of the determinants of the outcomes generated within the economic system, cannot be obtained apart from the recognition that government is a player in the

resolution of scarcity-based conflicts and that such resolutions are a function of the relative pressures brought to bear upon government and of who is able to secure the promotion of their interests through government.

A further issue raised by this case is that of compensation for harm and its relation to rights, allocation, and distribution. The cedar rust statute did not provide for compensation to owners for the value lost in the destruction of the red cedar trees. Samuels maintains that the larger question is not really compensation versus no compensation, since to compensate for all injuries visited by the law of property, or even changes therein, would impose a nearly impossible financial burden on society. Rather, the question really becomes "*when* should compensation be paid?" (Samuels 1971, p. 446; emphasis in original).[41] The issue of compensation is part of the question of who visits injury upon whom, and thus of one pattern of cost and income distribution versus another. In this situation, one is speaking not so much of (to take the present example) red cedar owners versus apple orchard owners, but of one party (the party who, in the absence of compensation, would be injured) versus society as a whole, which is forced to bear the burden of the compensation payments. That is, the law of property determines not only the allocation and distribution of resources and income across claimants to a particular dispute, but also, through the compensation principle, across society as a whole. Thus, the question of the extent of the ability of government to impact the use of private property without compensation (the use and extent of the police power) has implications beyond the parties to specific disputes.

Thus, this case, says Samuels, brings to the fore a number of important aspects of the interrelations between legal and economic processes:

> There is, first of all, an existential necessity of choice over relative rights, relative capacity to visit injury or costs, and mutual coercive power (or claims to income). The economy, in which the legal process is so obviously involved, is a system of relative rights, of exposure to costs shifted by others, and of the coercive impact of others. In choosing between conflicting rights' claimants, furthermore, the choice is between one interest or another. The choice is over capacities to participate in the economic decision-making process. . . . These choices are a function of rights which are a function of law; so that, *inter alia*, income distribution through relative claims to income is a partial function of law. It is ineluctable, then, that government is involved in the fundamental character, structure, and results of the private sector. Policy issues thus become which or whose rights will government operate to effectively secure, which rights will government no longer operate to effectively secure and which new rights, that is, the use of government to change the effective pattern of rights or realization of interests. (1971, p. 442)

---

[41] For other treatments of the Institutionalist approach to the compensation issue, see Samuels (1974) and Samuels and Mercuro (1979, 1980).

CONCLUSION

The overtly positive and even agnostic approach of Institutional law and economics is not comforting to those who would seek refuge in determinate solutions to the questions of legal-economic policy, and some may well be inclined to dismiss it on this ground, Against this, Schmid responds, "If [Institutional law and economics] has no dispositive answer to resolve policy arguments, what is it good for? It can identify many less than obvious sources of power in an economy so that people can know where their welfare comes from. It can raise the level of normative debate so that issues can be joined and people can live with tragic choices rather than ignoring and dismissing them" (1994, pp. 36–37). Whereas singular solutions to legal-economic issues reflect only one particular set of value premises and one particular conception of the facts, benefits, and costs at issue, the Institutional law and economics, by recognizing the multiplicity of potential solutions and underlying value premises, attempts to flesh out the alternative possibilities that are open to society in the ongoing social construction and reconstruction of legal-economic reality.

CHAPTER 5

The New Institutional Economics

> [T]he state is a two-edged sword: "The existence of a
> state is essential for economic growth; the state,
> however, is the source of man-made decline."
> *(Eggertsson 1990, p. 317, quoting North, 1981, p. 20)*

> In the language of the new institutional economics,
> providing a secure and predictable political
> foundation for the markets requires a form of
> governance structure [with a clear focus on] the
> design of political institutions that *credibly commit*
> the state to preserving markets.
> *(Barry Weingast 1995, p. 2)*

INTRODUCTION

THE New Institutional Economics (NIE), like Institutional economics, begins with the fundamental premise that institutions are important factors in the determination of economic structure, and hence performance. More specifically, NIE asserts that (1) institutions do matter, (2) the determinants of institutions can be explained and understood using the tools of economic theory, and (3) the structure of institutions affects economic performance in systematic and predictable ways.[1] One component of this institutional structure is the legal framework of a society—in modern parlance, the body of constitutional, statute, and common law, along with governmental agency rules and regulations that help order economic relations within a society. While broadly concerned with the legal-governmental institutions, NIE emphasizes the interplay between the evolution of legal institutions and market forces. With this basic insight as a starting point, NIE draws on several traditions within economics (mostly of neoclassical orientation), each of which makes its own contribution to NIE's effort to describe and explain those institutions that have the greatest impact on economic performance. Nonetheless, as Furubotn and Richter (1998, p. 465) correctly point out, when a transition is made from neoclassical economics to NIE, the economic problem is radically changed, in that the individual decision-makers find themselves in a world quite different from that

---

[1] See Matthews (1986).

envisioned in the neoclassical conception. The evolution of NIE has been nicely characterized by one of its leading exponents, Oliver E. Williamson (1999, p. 9), who said,

> NIE has progressed not by advancing an overarching theory but by uncovering and explicating the microanalytic features [of institutions] . . . and by piling block upon block until the cumulative value added can not be denied.

The moniker *New* Institutional Economics is used by its advocates in part for the expressed purpose of distancing themselves from the theories and concepts of Institutional economics (briefly described in chapter 4). Many proponents of NIE dismiss Institutional economics as an atheoretical, purely descriptive, inductive undertaking, whereas NIE is said to be analytical in that it relies more on deductive theorizing.[2] Many of the most significant contributions to this approach to Law and Economics are found in the *Journal of Law, Economics, and Organization* and the *Journal of Institutional and Theoretical Economics*.[3] Evidence of the continuing development of the field includes the establishment of the International Society for New Institutional Economics (in 1997 with its associated *ISNIE Newsletter*),[4] the European School on New Institutional Economics (founded in 2002 and now meeting each summer on the French island of Corsica),[5] and the Ronald Coase Institute, which provides workshops in the NIE for young scholars around the globe.

This chapter attempts to describe the foundational elements of NIE, beginning with a brief review of the early contributions from property rights economists and from a group of economic historians who have attempted to explain the development and significance of property rights throughout history. Thereafter, we will present the core theory of the NIE, including applications of the theory at work.[6]

---

[2] The attempt by NIE to distance itself from Institutional economics is found throughout the literature; for example see Voight and Engerer (2002, p. 128) and Drobak and Nye (1997, p. xv). For an excellent discussion comparing the two schools of thought, see Hutchinson (1984).

[3] In 1984, a symposium edition titled "The New Institutional Economics" was published in the *Journal of Institutional and Theoretical Economics* 140 (1984).

[4] ISNIE was founded in 1997 across some forty-eight nations; see their Mission Statement on their website at www.isnie.org.

[5] The European Summer School on New Institutional Economics (ESNIE) is largely a French initiative organized under the leadership of Eric Brousseau, Bruno Deffains, and Claude Ménard; the first classes of the ESNIE were held in the summer of 2002. The goal of the ESNIE is to develop knowledge and research in New Institutional Economics in Europe; see their website, www.esnie.org.

[6] It must be underscored that, given the lack of an overarching theory, these several sections bleed over into each other. Thus, the reader is forewarned not to expect clear lines of demarcation (our headings notwithstanding). More comprehensive overviews of NIE include Eggertsson (1990), Furubotn and Richter (1991a, 1998), Coase (1984, 1992a, 1992b), Werin and Wijkander (1992), Pejovich (1995), and Drobak and Nye (1997); see especially Ménard (2004) and Ménard and Shirley (2005).

EARLY CONTRIBUTIONS: PROPERTY RIGHTS ECONOMICS
AND THE NEW ECONOMIC HISTORY

One of the building blocks of NIE flows out of the Chicago tradition and is evidenced in the work on the economics of property rights by Armen A. Alchian (1959, 1961), Ronald H. Coase (1960), Harold Demsetz (1964, 1967), Steven Cheung (1969, 1970), Eirik Furubotn and Svetozar Pejovich (1972, 1974), and Svetozar Pejovich (1972). The property rights approach emerged as economists began to appreciate that the various types of legal-institutional arrangements that constrain the behavior of individuals and firms might have a significant impact on the allocation of society's scarce resources.[7] The main postulate of the economics of property rights is that the nature and form of these rights fundamentally influence the allocation of resources and the distribution of income in the economy (Veljanovski 1982, pp. 68–70). The emphasis on the nexus between politics (especially the political structure) and market performance within NIE thinking is ubiquitous. As Barry Weingast (1995, p. 2) observed, "In the language of the new institutional economics, providing a secure and predictable political foundation for the markets requires a form of governance structure" with a clear focus on "the design of political institutions that *credibly commit* the state to preserving markets" (emphasis in the original). Consequently, the proponents of the study of alternative property rights regimes believed that empirical studies regarding the development of property rights can provide significant insights into the performance of the private market economy, often relying on theories that operated on "the unsubstantiated proposition that the way to make markets work is to introduce more private property" (Alchian 1974, p. xiv). Although owing its origins to the work of many Chicago-oriented economists, the property rights approach now serves as one of the fundamental intellectual underpinnings for the New Institutional Economics and has moved well beyond orthodox Chicago thinking. Nonetheless, in many respects, core elements of the property rights approach remain consistent with the core elements of the Chicago approach to law and economics.[8]

The field of economic history has produced a second stream of literature that influences the work of NIE. As John Drobak and John V. C. Nye (1997,

---

[7] Useful surveys of the economics of property rights literature are found in Furubotn and Pejovich (1972), De Alessi (1980), Eggertsson (1990), and Colombatto (2004).

[8] Posner (1995, ch. 21) provides a critique of the NIE from the Chicago law and economics perspective. We should also note at this point that the nexus between neoclassical economics and NIE remains unclear, a fact observed by Stephan Voight and Hella Engerer (2002, p. 129): "[I]t remains an open question whether the NIE basically remains within the neoclassical paradigm and simply deals with a number of questions hitherto neglected by mainstream theory or if the NIE is indeed an entirely new paradigm that is incomparable with neoclassical economics." Many of the harshest critics of neoclassical economics contend that the NIE is characterized by the same basic flaws that they find in the neoclassical approach.

p. xvii) point out, "Anyone forced to consider economic growth in the medium and long run finds it hard to take rules and institutions as fixed." Unlike the earlier economic historians who were interested in describing the sources of economic growth (focusing on macroeconomic variables and national income accounts), the "new economic historians" (sometimes referred to as "cliometricians") were more geared to price-theoretic and comparative analysis.[9]

The focus of this group of economic historians is on trying to identify the key transmission mechanisms between evolving legal institutions and the emerging economy. From this literature flows the idea that there was some inherent process that resulted in either efficient institutions generally, or an efficient structure of property rights for some particular segment of the economy.[10] It should be clear that, intellectually, there is an obvious nexus between the work of the property rights economists and the efforts of the new economic historians, as exemplified by the work of Douglass North and L. E. Davis (1971), Douglass C. North and Robert Thomas (1973), as well as Harold Demsetz (1967), John R. Umbeck (1981), and Gary Libecap (1989a). Each of these studies departed somewhat from the standard assumptions of neoclassical economics, and instead went on to search for a more dynamic theory that could explain the evolution of economies through time, often focusing on the proposition that the efficiency of a market is directly shaped by the surrounding institutional framework.

THE CORE STRUCTURE OF NIE THEORY

While NIE has its roots in the economics of property rights and the work of the new economic historians, NIE remains rather heterogeneous within itself. It is, as Williamson stated, "building block by block." Two foundational principles, underlie much of the work in this area. The first is that individuals are assumed to pursue their self-interest rationally, subject to constraint. These constraints, however, are more numerous and severe than those assumed in neoclassical economic theory. They include the existence and definition of property rights and transaction costs, as well as a recognition of the limited computational capacity of the human mind. The latter idea is reflected in Herbert

---

[9] North (1997, p. 5) recounts that in the 1960s and 1970s, "economics departments very quickly became interested in having new economic historians, or, as we came to call ourselves, cliometricians (Clio being the muse of history)."

[10] On this general topic, see also Libecap (1986). More recently, Merrill (2002, p. S331) has observed, "Given the assumption of fixed property that otherwise prevails in economic literature [as in conventional price theory], explaining the evolution of property rights is one of the great challenges for the economic analysis of law."

Simon's (1961, p. xxiv) concept of "bounded rationality" wherein human be-havior is said to be *"intendedly* rational, but only *limitedly* so." That is, Si-mon maintained that if both the knowledge and the computational power of the decision-maker are severely limited, then, to understand and explain the outcomes of the choice process, we must theorize about the reasoning pro-cesses that actually generate choices in the real world. As a consequence, many within NIE argue against models that assume formal rational behavior, and instead advocate the use of models based on the concept of bounded ra-tionality.[11]

There is also some degree of overlap between the NIE and the literature on experimental—behavioral law and economics. For example, North (1997, p. 11) sees the cognitive science–institutional literature as an extension of work com-ing under the heading of NIE. They are linked in the following way. In trying to understand why people make certain choices, many New Institutional econ-omists questioned the rationality postulate and, as a consequence, incorpo-rated the concept of bounded rationality, as noted earlier. More recently, some of those working in NIE and in experimental-behavioral law and economics have moved beyond bounded rationality and are delving into the field of cog-nitive science, where the neural sciences are integrated with philosophy and psychology. In doing so, they advance the notion that learning is impacted by the cumulative experiences of past generations and focus on how individuals explain and interpret the world around them. Simply put, the effort is to ex-plore "how the mind works, that is, how human learning occurs" (North 1997, p. 11). In all this, the hope is to come to a deeper understanding (well beyond simple rationality and even beyond bounded rationality) of just how and why institutional-economic choices have been made and how they impact the per-formance of the economy.

The second foundational principle of NIE, at least within many quarters, is the idea of wealth maximization—the search for institutional structures that enhance society's wealth-producing capacity. Here it is argued that the value of resources is tied directly to the bundles of rights running with the resources. In short, the more complete and definite the specification of property rights (that is, the less attenuated the rights structure), the more uncertainty is dimin-ished, which, in turn, tends to promote a more efficient allocation of resources. Given these two foundational principles, NIE has largely been dominated by positive theorizing and empirical work that analyzes the role of different insti-tutional structures and how these structures systematically affect economic performance across time.

---

[11] Furubotn and Richter (1998, p. 447) have identified a consensus definition of bounded ra-tionality: "purposive behavior conditioned by the cognitive limits of decision makers" noting, nonetheless, that "understandings of the concept differ."

Definitions and Central Concepts in NIE

North (1990b, p. 3) defines institutions as "the rules of the game in a society or, more formally, . . . the humanly devised constraints that shape human interaction." As such, he says, these institutions "structure incentives in human exchange, whether political, social, or economic." These institutions include both formal rules, such as the law, and informal mechanisms, such as customs, conventions, codes of conduct, and social norms. Our discussion here will focus on formal legal mechanisms.[12] The NIE analysis of institutions focuses on three central concepts: property rights, contracting, and transaction costs, and the interrelationships among all three. *Property rights*, says Gary Libecap (1989a, p. 1), "are the social institutions that define or delimit the range of privileges granted to individuals to specific assets," and as such function in the determination of the value of an asset by setting the range of its productivity or exchangability. *Contracting* is the process through which property rights are established, assigned, or modified (Libecap 1989a, p. 4; Eggertsson 1990, p. 45). This contracting process, wherein the legal rights to these assets are transferred, underlies the process of exchange—the physical transfer of assets.[13] Neoclassical economic theory, in contrast, focuses on the exchange process alone, which is sometimes simultaneous with and sometimes subsequent to the actual transaction over rights. Moreover, in NIE, the possibilities and limitations of exchange are a function of the transactional or contracting framework—that is, the legal structure, the discussion of which is virtually absent from neoclassical theory. Within NIE, contracting is seen to proceed both at a micro-level, wherein private individuals or groups bargain over rights, and at a macro-level, wherein some combination of private individuals or groups, politicians, bureaucrats, and judges bargain over the basic legal framework that establishes the social, legal, and economic structure (Libecap 1989a, p. 4). *Transaction costs*, like contracting, are relevant at both the micro- and macro-levels and can be conceptualized, in a general sense, as the costs associated with the creation, maintenance, or modification of institutions, such as property rights.[14] Thus, at the micro-level, transaction costs consist of those costs associated with contracting between private parties, whereas, at the macro-level, transaction costs may be said to consist of the costs involved in the bargaining process through which the institutional framework of society is established or modified (Furubotn and Richter 1991b, p. 8; Eggertsson 1990, pp. 14–15).

[12] We explore the literature on the relationship between social norms and Law and Economics in chapter 7.

[13] Williamson (1975, p. 3) acknowledges the influence of the institutional economist John R. Commons on the NIE view of the centrality of transactions in economic activity.

[14] Arrow (1969, p. 48) calls transaction costs the "costs of running the economic system"; Williamson (1985, p. 19) says that transaction costs are "the economic equivalent of friction in physical systems."

Institutional Environment and Institutional Arrangements (or Governance)

As our discussion suggests, NIE analysis proceeds at two different levels: the more macro-oriented *institutional environment*, and the other, more micro-oriented *institutional arrangements* or *governance*.[15] In fact, however, the institutional environment and institutional arrangements/governance structures are interactive: the institutional environment sets the general framework within which institutional arrangements take place, and institutional arrangements, their effects, or the difficulties in devising them, may effect pressures for changes in the institutional environment. As the legal-economic analysis of NIE proceeds at each of these two levels, our discussion will treat them in turn.[16]

INSTITUTIONAL ENVIRONMENT

The first level—the *institutional environment*—constitutes the framework within which human interaction takes place. It provides the so-called "rules of the game," which, in effect, are the institutional background constraints under which individuals in society make choices. They constitute the set of fundamental political, legal, and social ground rules that, by guiding individual behavior, establish the basis for macro-level production, exchange, and distribution. At this first level, the focus is on the effects that various institutional environments have on economic development and performance in a macroeconomic context, as well as explaining how various institutional environments evolved.

In NIE, the evolution of the institutional environment—the ongoing creation and revision of background rules and constraints—is most often explained using theories and rationales that emphasize the spontaneous nature of

---

[15] These two levels of analysis are described by North and Davis (1971, pp. 6–7; quoted in Williamson 1993a, p. 53) and also described by Klein (1999, p. 458). Williamson (1999, pp. 9–12) describes four levels of analysis: (i) the level of social embeddedness (social theory including the study of norms, customs, mores, and traditions); (ii) the institutional environment (economics of property rights and positive political theory); (iii) institutions of governance (transactions costs, contractual relations, ex ante incentives, and ex post stage of contracts); and (iv) neoclassical economic analysis. He then goes on to assert that NIE has mainly concentrated on levels (ii) and (iii). These same two levels are also set forth in Furubotn and Richter (1998, pp. 264–65). Indeed, Furubotn and Richter (1998) provide an extensive review of the NIE literature in four chapters of their book: chapter 6—"The New Institutional Economics Applied to Markets, Firms, and the State," chapter 7—"The New Institutional Economics of the Market," chapter 8—"The New Institutional Economics of the Firm," and chapter 9—"The New Institutional Economics of the State."

[16] As Klein (1999) and Voight and Engerer (2002) have observed, the study of governance—in particular, the theory of the firm—is arguably more developed than the study of the institutional environment.

that evolution and eschewing explanations that concentrate on the deliberate actions of the collective or government. They primary focus is on two categories of background rules and constraints—the formal legal environment and the informal social norms.[17] The legal environment is comprised of the formal, explicit rules manifested in the constitution, statutes, common law doctrine, and rights and rules. Rules governing elections, property rights regimes, and the right of contract are all examples of what constitutes the formal legal environment. NIE scholarship that analyzes the formal legal environment has focused on two particular areas of law—property law and contract law—and consequently devotes its attention to the formation and structure of property rights regimes and the many nuances of contracting. Unlike the treatment of disputes in property and contract law within the Chicago approach to law and economics, where these disputes are seen to be resolved by the courts (agents of the state), in NIE—and this is one of the recurring themes throughout all of NIE—the focus is on private solutions: "[I]n many instances the participants can devise more satisfactory solutions to their disputes than can professionals constrained to apply general rules on the basis of limited knowledge of the dispute" (Klein 2000, p. 459, quoting Galanter 1981, p. 4). In particular, the concern is with explaining how parties devise these mechanisms to order disputes privately and how these mechanisms function to do so.

Legal-Economic Analysis of Institutional Environments

The formal rules of the legal environment analyzed by NIE make up an important part of a society's institutional environment. North (1990b, p. 47) distinguishes among three types of formal rules that govern relations within a society—political rules, economic rules, and contracts.[18] First, the *political rules* of a society "broadly define the hierarchical structure of the polity, its basic decision structure, and the explicit characteristics of agenda control." Second, the *economic rules* "define property rights, that is, the bundle of rights over the use and income to be derived from property and the ability to alienate an asset or resource." Finally, *contracts* "contain the provisions specific to a particular agreement in exchange." Taken together, these three types of formal rules, by defining opportunity sets, facilitate political and economic exchange within the existing institutional structure. These rules are also used to change the institutional structure in an attempt to garner additional gains from trade and thus the accompanying increases in wealth. It must also be understood that these rules are interdependent, and the causation is multidirectional. That is, although a given set of political rules will give rise to a particular set of economic rules that in turn structures contracts, it is also the case that pressure

---

[17] Again, the latter are more fully explored in chapter 7.

[18] See also North (1989, 1993b).

for new forms of contractual structure can lead to changes in economic and political rules (North 1989, p. 662).

To appreciate better the "building blocks" of NIE that make up the institutional environment, the next four subsections will focus on interrelations among three of NIE's fundamental components—property rights, contracting, and transaction costs—including a brief discussion of the political arena that looms so large in any discussion of the institutional environment.

Property Rights and Transaction Costs

The importance of property rights in economic analysis and in determining economic performance rests on two facets of their operation.[19] First, property rights determine ownership and thus the streams of benefits and costs of resource use and the allocation thereof across individuals; in short, property rights structure the incentives that determine economic behavior and performance. Second, property rights define the set of actors within an economic system by "assigning to specific individuals the authority to decide how specific resources may be used" (De Alessi and Staaf 1989, p. 179). In this dual capacity, property rights significantly influence the distribution of wealth and power within an economic system. Different property rights structures thus give rise to differential opportunity sets and thus, different allocations of benefits and costs among economic agents, and thereby affect economic choices through their respective structures of incentives and constraints.

NIE recognizes, following Gary Becker (1965) and Kelvin Lancaster (1966), that individuals derive utility, not from goods and services per se, but from the various attributes of a good or the various separate activities that go into the performance of a service. Thus, for example, on the product side, the automobile is a bundle of attributes that includes power, fuel economy, comfort, quality, and even image, and these attributes and their extent function prominently in determining its value. In a like manner, no factor of production is unidimensional; each one has various attributes that find value in the resources markets. For example, on the factor side, a plot of land is not just a plot of land per se, but a bundle of attributes including the extent of its agricultural productivity, aesthetic qualities, or potential for commercial development of various kinds. As such, a product or factor of production is defined not only by its technical/physical properties, but also by both the bundle of rights that attach to it and the associated attributes. The result is that exchange in product and factor markets is not merely the transference of goods and services or a factor of production, but an exchange of the diverse attributes and activities as well as the bundle or rights related to both. Further, these valuable attributes and rights must be defined, measured, and enforced to be transferable in exchange.

[19] See Libecap (1989a, pp. 2, 10) and De Alessi and Staaf (1989, p. 179).

Given the presence of imperfect information over attributes and rights structure, individuals must incur measurement costs—which are a form of transaction cost—in attempting to determine the nature of these valuable attributes and the rights. As the number and variety of attributes and possible rights structure increases, so too do the costs of measurement and thus the complexity of exchange (North 1990b, p. 29). Other factors, such as the degree of observability of a resource or the extent to which a resource is migratory, will also influence measurement costs (Libecap 1989a, p. 26). Given that these attributes and the associated structure of rights have value, measurement problems will contribute to the costliness of exchange by causing the parties to a potential exchange to expend resources in the attempt to determine the attributes and rights and their values. Because measurement costs are positive, rights will never be fully specified over all attributes, as the expected benefits of more fully specified rights will at some point be outweighed by the expected costs of measurement (North 1990a, pp. 191–92; Barzel 1989, pp. 64–65). Thus, the greater the costs of measurement of attributes/rights associated with a given product or factor of production, the less well-defined the property rights associated with it, and thus the greater will be the extent to which the development or exchange of that product/resource is inhibited.[20]

Because of the problematic nature of measuring certain attributes, and because of the incentives for individuals to engage in opportunistic behavior (such as attempting to increase one's benefits from an exchange agreement by, for example, shirking or concealing information), the problem of enforcement also comes into play in the exchange process. Instantaneous transactions over unidimensional goods and factors of production are typically easy to enforce. Exchange relationships involving multidimensional goods and resources, and particularly those that occur over time and space, however, enhance the risk that self-interest-seeking individuals will fail to live up to the agreement, failing to make good on contractual promises made in the past. Thus, some enforcement mechanism is necessary to induce individuals to form such exchange relationships (North 1990b, p. 33; 1993b, p. 247). The difficulty, of course, is that enforcement, like measurement, although having the benefit of reducing uncertainty in the exchange environment, is also costly.[21] Beyond the costs of establishing an enforcement mechanism, additional enforcement costs arise from attempts to detect and measure violations and impose penalties on the violators (North 1990b, p. 58). This means that certain rights will be left unspecified (perhaps left in open access), and that enforcement of some specified property rights will be less than perfect. Individuals may thus have an incentive

---

[20] The rationale for the reduced incentives to develop and exchange resources when property rights are *less well defined* follows the line of argument developed later in this subsection with respect to common-pool or open-access resources.

[21] Enforcement costs being another class of transaction costs.

to expend resources in the attempt to capture the value associated with these attributes or rights, as well as to defend against its capture by others. Because of the potential conflicts brought on by the ever-present problems associated with measurement and enforcement, individuals have an incentive to structure contracts in such a way that these adverse incentive effects are minimized.

To understand more clearly the role played by property rights within an economic system, we must begin by conceptualizing a situation in which (private) property rights are absent—that is, where individuals "lack exclusive, transferable rights to the use of [a] resource" (De Alessi 1980, p. 5). Resources here would be termed "common pool" or "open access." Early analyses by H. Scott Gordon (1954), Harold Demsetz (1967), Garrett Hardin (1968), and Steven Cheung (1970) of such common-pool situations reveal that, except where supply exceeds demand at a zero price, the absence of property rights generates losses owing to overexploitation of the open-access resource, as the absence of private rights reduces the incentives of individuals to consider the full social costs of their actions. Consider, for example, the case of a parcel of land that is suitable for agricultural use, but over which no private property rights are assigned. Assume that the parcel lies between the farms of Farmer A and Farmer B. If Farmer A were to allow the land that he typically cultivates to lie fallow for a year so as to let the soil regenerate, then, because it is an open-access resource, Farmer B would likely step in and cultivate that land himself, thus frustrating A's purpose. Consequently, Farmer A has no incentive to let the land lie fallow, and the productivity of the land will eventually be reduced, to the detriment of society. Indeed, Anthony Bottomly's (1963) analysis of land use in Tripolitania suggests that lands held as open-access resources had lower crop yields on average than privately held lands. Similarly, Richard Agnello and Lawrence Donnelley (1975) show that oyster harvests are substantially higher when held as open-access resources than under private property rights structures, an effect that will, in the long run, lead to lower yields in the common-pool beds.[22] There are other problems that directly contribute to the losses associated with open-access resources as well (Libecap 1989a, pp. 12–13). One is the reduced incentive to invest in the development of open-access resources due to the inability of the investors to capture sufficient returns from their investments in such common-pool situations. A second is the difficulty, if not impossibility, of attempting to transfer such resources to higher-valued uses. Third, there are the excessive expenditures on exclusionary, loss-preventing activities, such as trying to prevent others from appropriating your crops, which are not protected by private property rights. All of these have the effect of contributing to the losses associated with the existence of open-access resources.

---

[22] Much of this literature has served as the basis upon which to establish and use markets for resources such as air, water, wetlands, fisheries and so on; see Tietenberg (2002) and Cole (2002).

De Alessi's (1990, p. 8) characterization of the bundle of rights that attends a resource also helps in understanding how property rights affect the use of, income streams from, and transferability of resources: "The bundle of rights associated with a particular resource typically is partitioned"; some of these rights may be "non-exclusive and non-transferable," some may be "exclusive but non-transferable," and still others may be both "exclusive and transferable." By defining the constraints facing the owner, the property rights bundle affects the individual choice process and the uses to which resources are ultimately put.[23] As one moves across the spectrum from private property at one extreme to open-access resources on the other, the incentives to economize on resource use in socially optimal ways become weaker, and thus the associated welfare losses tend to rise (De Alessi 1980, p. 40). Given individual and group preferences (which govern perceived benefits), NIE has devoted time and attention to the analysis of property rights formation and transformation. In this, they have explored the economic and social factors that create opportunities and incentives for establishing or altering property rights, and how those factors contribute to the costs of establishing and enforcing a particular property rights regime.

One immediate question that emerges is, "Why do we observe common-pool situations in the first place, or, why we do not observe well-defined, fully specified property rights over all of society's resources?" Part of the answer was provided by Coase's (1937, 1960) examination of the costs of economic organization. As he demonstrated, when transaction costs are positive, institutions matter and shape the resultant market structure, conduct, and hence performance. Recognition of this gives some credence to the explanation as to why seemingly inefficient rights, rules, and institutions exist and are perpetuated.[24] NIE has incorporated this aspect of Coase's insight into its formal analysis, arguing that since there are costs to establishing and enforcing property rights, individuals or groups will devote resources to securing the establishment of or a change in property rights only when they perceive that the benefits from such a change will outweigh the costs. Thus, although open-access resources result in common-pool losses, they do save society the costs of specifying and enforcing private property rights. Alternatively stated, although private property rights minimize common-pool losses, they involve costs of specification and enforcement that may be sufficiently large so that a society is either unable or unwilling to incur them to bring private property rights into existence (Cheung 1992, p. 59). The point to be made here is that

---

[23] For a discussion of common versus usufruct (the right to enjoy use without ownership) versus private property rights, see De Alessi (1980).

[24] North (1981) attempted to lay out a rationale for this behavior and concluded that the two primary sources of inefficient rules were what he termed a "competitive constraint" and a "transaction cost constraint."

high transaction costs may serve to preclude the realization of the gains that accompany the establishment of private property rights over a resource that was heretofore left in open access.

The Establishment of Property Rights

It should be evident, given the important role of property rights within NIE, that those interested in the field would feel compelled to investigate "the general mechanism through which changes in cost-benefit calculations are translated into the development of property rights" (Furubotn and Richter 1991b, p. 16). Much of the legal-economic analysis of institutional environments has been carried out in the tradition of, and constitutes a marked extension of, the property rights approach as exemplified in the work of North (1981, 1984, 1990b), Yoram Barzel (1989), and Libecap (1989a,b).

We have seen in the foregoing discussion that the establishment of property rights can promote wealth-enhancing exchanges. How, then, are property rights established or changed? Furubotn and Richter (1991b, p. 16) provide a succinct answer to this question: new property rights and changes in property rights come about "because certain individuals or groups within an economy believe it profitable to restructure the system and are willing to bear the costs of bringing about such change."[25] Such initiatives may occur due to changes in relative prices, production or enforcement technology, individual preferences, or certain political parameters (Libecap 1989a, p. 16). That is, the current property rights structure and/or associated informal constraints (e.g., social norms and customs) may be incapable of supporting newly developed opportunities for wealth-creating exchanges, leading to a demand for new or revised rights.

More specifically, economic historians working from a New Institutional perspective have tried to spell out the manner by which new property rights evolve, arguing that if well-structured private property rights are expected to release net aggregate gains, then the potential beneficiaries will seek the enactment of such rights structures. Theirs is an economic model where the demand for efficient property rights reflects the needs of market agents, and where it is recognized that institutions, together with technology, affect economic performance by determining the costs of production. Hence, on the one hand, the key element for economic performance is found in the formation of secure and productive property rights, and, on the other hand, it is argued that market forces will provide the evolutionary push needed to produce efficient institutions and/or an efficient structure of property rights. Simply put, an efficient structure of private property rights will emerge as a result of market forces. Their empirical research suggests that the standard theory of production and exchange is capable of explaining the emergence of the institution of property

---

[25] An empirical illustration of this line of reasoning is provided in Hayami and Ruttan (1984).

rights over scarce resources, and that the emergence and development of new property rights can be explained as a consequence of value-seeking behavior brought on by new technologies and market opportunities in the face of a variety of transaction costs.

A few examples of empirical studies will provide the reader with a sense for this literature. Demsetz (1967) describes the activities of the local Montagnais Indians in conjunction with the increased value of fur-bearing animals in the Labrador Peninsula in the seventeenth century. He argues that consequent to the increase in these values, the Indians established rights to beaver habitats where no rights had previously existed. That is, Demsetz shows that, prior to the arrival of the Europeans, the value of beaver pelts was quite low and beaver habitats were typically held as an open-access resource. Once the European market for beaver pelts began to take hold, however, and the value of their fur increased, it became cost-effective to establish institutions (converting some habitats into private property) that would thereby encourage husbandry of beaver and reduce competition over hunting.[26]

In a similar vein, Umbeck (1981) examined the land and mineral property rights regimes during the California Gold Rush in the mid-1800s.[27] When gold was discovered in 1848, the land was occupied by the U.S. military. Shortly thereafter, with the signing of a treaty with Mexico to acquire the land, the U.S. government, while abolishing the Mexican law covering the land and mineral rights, neglected to replace the law until 1866. Thus, for this period of time, property rights to land and mineral resources were nonexistent. Nonetheless, with the onset of successful mining operations, property rights to the gold and gold-bearing river beds were effectively defined and protected by the gold seekers, thereby encouraging investments in gold mining and preventing the wasteful protective-defensive resource diversions that would be necessary to protect ongoing individual gold mining operations.

Similarly, Anderson and Hill (1975) examined how the development of economical means of fencing off lands—largely with barbed-wire fencing—made the enforcement of private rights more economical and thus helped to stimulate the development of private land rights in the western United States. Prior to the invention of barbed wire fencing, cowboys, via patrols and encampments, essentially functioned as human fences to prevent rustling and straying. The advent of barbed wire fencing in the 1860s allowed ranchers to substitute a low-cost capital fencing for high-cost labor fencing. The extent of the associated reduction in property rights definition and enforcement costs is illus-

---

[26] In April 2001, a conference on "The Evolution of Property Rights" was held at Northwestern University School of Law. The purpose of the conference was to reexamine the Demsetz thesis that property rights emerge when the social benefits of establishing such rights exceed their social costs. Thereafter, the *Journal of Legal Studies* published a symposium edition (volume 31, June 2002) comprising papers inspired by that conference.

[27] See also Umbeck (1977a,b).

trated by the fact that more than 80 million pounds of barbed wire were sold within the next twenty years.[28]

With this understanding of the NIE explanation of the nexus between property rights and transaction costs, we can turn to their explanation of how contracting fits into the analysis of the institutional environment.

Contracting and Transaction Costs

The extent to which complex exchange can proceed within a society is a function of the ability of agents to transact within a contractual framework that minimizes the degree of uncertainty about contractual performance (North 1990b, p. 34). Those who transact do not consider all the costs involved, and information costs prevent the state from knowing the efficient amount of state enforcement. As a result, the net gains from exchange are the standard gains of neoclassical economic theory, less the costs of measurement, enforcement, as well as those costs that arise because measurement and enforcement are imperfect (North 1990b, p. 31). To have complex exchange (i.e., for the benefits of such exchange to outweigh the costs), it is necessary to set in place institutional mechanisms that will induce potential parties to exchange to incur the relevant transaction costs, or agree to exchange in the presence of imperfectly delineated property rights. Because of the difficulty of designing self-enforcing contracts for complex exchanges, it is in the interests of the parties and/or society to develop enforcement institutions.[29] One sees this evidenced among private parties through mechanisms such as private third-party mediation or arbitration.

Private initiatives notwithstanding, NIE recognizes that much of the burden of reducing the costs of enforcement that thereby encourages exchange, falls on the state. Historical evidence suggests that a well-organized system of complex exchange within a society cannot proceed without a political order (North 1990b, pp. 34–35, 54; Libecap 1989a). Eggertsson (1990, p. 317) expresses this point forcefully: "Without the state, its institutions, and the supportive framework of property rights, high transaction costs will paralyze complex production systems, and specific investments in long-term exchange relationships will not be forthcoming." Even more to the point is North's (1993b, p. 245) statement that the effectiveness with which agreements are enforced "is the single most crucial determinant of economic performance." The state, says North (1981, p. 27; quoted in Eggertsson 1990, p. 320), seems to have a comparative advantage in the sort of enforcement institutions that facilitate exchange: "The economies of scale associated with devising a system of law, justice, and defense are the underlying source of civilization." The formal rules of the state work with (or in place of) informal constraints, such as

---

[28] See also the discussion by Anderson and Hill (2004).

[29] Issues related to the design of self-enforcing contracts will be discussed below.

custom, reputation, and social norms. By lowering the various transaction costs associated with exchange, they promote the formation of more complex exchange agreements that enhance economic development. NIE incorporates Coase's recognition of the importance of positive transaction costs to explain why it is possible for "economies [to] become 'stuck' at very inefficient levels if the institutions are not in place to lower transaction costs. The invisible hand result of efficient free market economies occurs only under a strict institutional framework that eliminates transaction costs" (Yeager 1997, p. 5),[30] and so North (1991, p. 98) can conclude,

> Economic development, then, is institutional development. The central issue of economic history and of economic development is to account for the evolution of political and economic institutions that create an economic environment that induces increasing productivity.

Based on the foregoing, then, we can say that transaction costs arise primarily due to information costs, which consist of the costs "of contracting and negotiating, . . . of measuring and policing property rights, of engaging in politics for power, of monitoring performances, and of organizing activities" (Cheung 1992, p. 51). A study by John Wallis and North (1986) shows that transaction costs made up 45 percent of gross national product in the United States in 1970. Because of the magnitude of these costs, the proponents of the NIE approach argue that many otherwise wealth-creating transactions will simply not take place in the absence of a carefully structured institutional environment.

In sum, the legal-economic system plays an important role in determining the allocation of resources in society, in part through its impact on the cost of transacting. Specifically, new legal arrangements can affect production and exchange by reducing transaction costs, thereby allowing resources to flow to higher-valued uses (North 1990b, p. 31). This then becomes the normative thrust of NIE: to find and structure an institutional environment—a precise structure of formal legal institutions—that will lower transaction costs and thereby facilitate trade through efficient contracts. It should be evident that, within NIE, this particular observation provides a clear role for a "more" activist government, certainly more than many advocates of public choice theory would be comfortable with. That is, since the structure of institutions does matter for the attainment of an efficient allocation and distribution of society's scarce resources, it is the role of government to get those institutions "correctly" structured. It is here, as North (1997, p. 8) observed, that the NIE meets public choice theory and, in doing so, raises a question that still remains a matter of debate: "Was the polity simply a leviathan to be contained as Buchanan and the Virginia school of public choice suggested? That made the

---

[30] A brief outline of North's theory on the impact of alternative institutional structures on economic performance is provided in the section "The NIE at Work."

state little more than a giant theft machine." Or were the property rights theorists correct in arguing that "the political creation of secure and productive property rights [was] the key to economic growth"? Both public choice theory and NIE continue to struggle with this fundamental dilemma.[31]

What emerges from the foregoing analysis of the institutional environment are two of the fundamental implications of NIE theory: (i) that market forces would provide the evolutionary push needed to produce efficient institutions and/or an efficient structure of property rights, and (ii) that economic development is contingent upon the evolution of institutions that support efficient commercial contractual relationships. In each of these, it should be evident that the political arena is inherently important in coming to an understanding of the institutional environment—the issue to which we now turn.

The Political Arena, Contracting, and Property Rights

At the level of the institutional environment, the establishment or change of property rights structures and institutions is conceived of as a contracting process that takes place within the political arena, and thus reflects the preferences of and constraints upon those operating therein. While NIE sees that there are clear economic benefits associated with moving toward private property rights structures, they do not come without cost. Aside from the costs of enforcing rights, efforts to move toward private property also include the bargaining costs associated with seeking such changes through the political process, broadly defined to encompass the efforts to reach bargains over rights structures within a community. Thus, as long as expected benefits are sufficiently large, it will often pay to devote resources to lobbying efforts, including the establishment of formal lobbying organizations, in the attempt to effect legal change through the political process.

Pressures supporting and opposing new or changed rights structures will be brought to bear by those who stand to gain or lose under the proposed system, and the greater the share of society's resources impacted by the proposed change, the greater will be the expenditure on offensive and defensive efforts

---

[31] It is interesting to observe that at about the same time that NIE came forward with its economic analysis of the mechanism by which society spontaneously transfers resources from a state of open-access property to some form of private property, others, namely the "interest group theorists" came up with an alternative explanation (these were reviewed in chapter 3). Against the NIE proponents who argued that the mechanism to move to private property is due to (i) wealth-maximizing behavior (in a low transaction cost environment) and/or (ii) the superior entrepreneurial talents and efforts of some individuals, the interest group theory advocates suggest that the driving force toward privatization can be better explained as rent-seeking activity undertaken by parties of interest that expect to benefit from the move. The state of the debate was best summed up by Levmore (2002, p. S433) who, in commenting on the explanatory potential of the wealth-maximizing (Demsetz-like) theories or descriptions of this mechanism, observed that "for every transaction-cost story about changed access or other property rights, there is a suspicious—even pessimistic—interest group explanation."

by affected parties (North 1990b, p. 87). The result is a bargaining process wherein each group seeks as large a share of the potential gains as it can get; where each group will give its approval only if it expects that, under the attendant outcome, it will be at least as well off as under the status quo. Given a situation in which institutional change will result in net gains to society, the question becomes one of devising a method (which may include compensating losers) to allocate these gains in a way that will result in the adoption of the change, while still maintaining, to the greatest extent possible, the productive (wealth-enhancing) advantages of the change. The problem, from a wealth-maximization perspective, is that the costly bargaining process may use up some of society's scarce resources, and different distributions alter the nature of property rights and thus the size of the potential gain from their establishment or change (Libecap 1989b, pp. 215–16). Moreover, there is always a danger that, to secure agreement, those who gain would be forced to compensate some of those who lose from the proposed change to such an extent that the resulting net gains to the winners are reduced sufficiently to cause them to withdraw their support for the endeavor. The result, then, is that a wealth-enhancing change is not accomplished.

The ability to reach such an agreement through the political process is a function of (1) the size of the expected gain (larger expected gains increases the likelihood of being able to reach agreements), (2) the number of bargaining parties (the fewer the parties of interest, the greater the likelihood of an agreement), (3) the extent to which their interests converge (more convergent interests increase the likelihood of agreement), (4) the extent to which information is imperfect—the impact here is twofold: (i) imperfect information affects the ability to ascertain gains and losses accurately and thus structure the appropriate side payments to compensate powerful "losing" interests for supporting the change, and (ii) it also affects the potential for deception among the various bargaining parties; and (5) whether the distribution of the gains are broadly or more narrowly concentrated (with more narrow concentrations reducing the likelihood of reaching an agreement because too many interests will be harmed) (Libecap 1989a, pp. 21–26).

Within NIE, the political process is seen to exist, at least in part, to facilitate exchange between various interest groups. As such, this political bargaining process reflects the pressures brought to bear by interest groups supporting the maintenance of the status quo or various changes in the status quo. Legislators, who wish to maximize their reelection potential, will endeavor to respond to the interests of those groups who can most greatly impact their reelection possibilities. Because of the divergence of interests that often occurs within society, a clear majority for or against a proposal may not emerge, forcing legislators who strongly favor certain causes to attempt to strike deals with other legislators who have different favorite causes. A legislator will attempt to

strike bargains that induce others to vote for projects that provide relatively large benefits for his constituents, while offering in exchange to vote for things that impose low costs on his constituents. The end result is that, if the exchange is consummated, he will have provided a net gain (hopefully substantial) to his constituents.

This may sound similar to the logrolling process of public choice theory, but the NIE approach is in fact different. As we noted in chapter 3, the public choice theory of logrolling assumes that legislative bargains are fully executed by the parties to the bargain—that when legislators agree to trade votes, they follow through on their promises. The NIE view, in contrast, emphasizes the potential consequences of the fact that these bargains, which are made at a given point in time, are in fact carried out—but *over time*; that is, one action is given today with a promise, or commitment, for a reciprocal action in the future. This time element raises the potential for opportunistic behavior by legislators, such as refusing to vote as promised or attempting to reverse legislation voted for as part of a promise. It also allows for altered performance by legislators as an honest response to altered circumstances—for example, changes in voter preferences or certain political circumstances—rather than opportunistic behavior.[32]

Given the potential for opportunistic behavior here, the existence of imperfect information raises the question, "How does credible commitment evolve to enable agreements to be reached when the payoffs are in the future and on completely different issues?" (North 1990b, p. 51). Although both self-enforcement and reputation effects play a role here, North suggests that they are of limited effectiveness because of the costs of measurement and enforcement. More generally, Eggertsson (1990, p. 71) suggests that "[i]n exchanges between politicians, transaction costs tend to be high because there is no powerful third party that helps to enforce contracts in these areas, unlike the situation in the marketplace." The result is the development of political institutions that resolve these enforcement problems, or, as Eggertsson (1990, p. 72) puts it, which serve as "capital structures designed to produce a flow of stable policy outcomes." North (1990b, p. 50) says that we see "political institutions [that] constitute ex ante agreements among politicians. They reduce uncertainty by creating a stable structure of exchange. The result is a complicated system of committee structure, consisting of both formal rules and informal methods of organization." The organizational structures of political bodies are adopted in an effort to reduce transaction costs that may impede consummation of political changes. Although not eliminating transaction costs, the agenda rules and committee structures of legislatures assign defined committee jurisdictions (in effect, property rights) over certain types of legislation,

---

[32] See Eggertsson (1990, p. 356) and Weingast and Marshall (1988).

making outcomes less subject to the vagaries of majoritarian processes (Weingast and Marshall 1988).[33]

The import of this legal-economic analysis goes beyond explaining the political process per se. The property rights structure that exists at any given point in time, or that develops through the political bargaining process, will be determined by these political bargaining issues and their resolution, along with the technological issues surrounding the ability to define, measure, and enforce property rights claims (Libecap 1989a, p. 12). Because of heterogeneity among competing interest groups and the often-sizable stakes of the game, it is likely that there will be regular and substantial conflict over changes in property rights, and, as a result, "institutional change is likely to be an incremental process with modest adjustments from status quo conditions" (Libecap 1989b, p. 220). Moreover, although exchange leads to efficiency in the frictionless (zero transaction costs) world of neoclassical economic theory, and although the foregoing discussion suggests that property rights will be created or altered when it is efficient to do so (i.e., when the benefits exceed the costs), we do, in fact, still see inefficient property rights arrangements in the real world. In fact, although the political rules are designed to facilitate exchange by lowering transaction costs, we frequently see inefficient outcomes, which is to say, there is no guarantee that the outcome of political exchange will be efficient. North (1990b, pp. 51–52) contends that they are a manifestation of inefficiencies within the political exchange process, resulting from, for example, agency problems[34] between legislator and constituent or between legislator and bureaucrat; rational ignorance on the part of constituents; legislators' desire not to offend powerful interests by enacting rules that, although efficient, go against their interests; or a preference by politicians for an inefficient rights structure because it generates more tax revenue. Thus, although low transaction costs and accurate information will result in the adoption of efficient property rights structures, the frequent lack of such conditions makes inefficient rights structures a condition of economic life. As Eggertsson (1990, p. 317, quoting North 1981, p. 20) suggests, "the state is a two-edged sword: 'The existence of a state is essential for economic growth; the state, however, is the source of man-made decline.' "

INSTITUTIONAL ARRANGEMENTS—GOVERNANCE

The second level of analysis within the NIE, *institutional arrangements*, focuses on what Williamson (1993a, p. 53) calls the "institutions of governance"

---

[33] This discussion of the political contracting process is an illustration of the extension of these contracting ideas into the political arena. The fact that the political contracting process influences the development of social institutions exemplifies the multidirectional interrelations between institutional environments and institutional arrangements.

[34] Agency issues will be discussed later in the section on governance.

that exist within a given first-level institutional environment. This second level is devoted to a microeconomic analysis of the choice of governance structures of private actors. An institutional arrangement is a specific arrangement between economic units that governs the ways in which these units can cooperate or compete. The governance structures are often designed by the trading parties themselves to mediate particular economic relationships, and, as described by Williamson (1999, p. 12) "governance is an effort to craft order, thereby to mitigate conflict and realize mutual gains." It can "provide a structure within which its members can cooperate . . . or provide a mechanism that can effect a change in laws or property rights" (Williamson 1993a, p. 53).[35] Thus, at the institutional arrangement level, NIE has an ongoing interest in issues such as the structure of corporate governance, vertical integration of firms, the organizational rules of public bureaucracies and nonprofit organizations, and long-term contracts (Klein 2000, p. 458). As Stefan Voight and Hella Engerer (2002, pp. 128–29) observe, at the governance level, NIE explores "under what conditions exchange will be secured at least cost via the market and under what conditions it will be secured within organizations, i.e. firms." They go on to point out that, in the more recent literature, "the concept of the firm has now been extended to a variety of hybrids to reflect a continuum of governance structures."

Legal-Economic Analysis of Institutional Arrangements: Governance

While the institutional environment provides a set of rules or a framework within which production, exchange, and distribution take place, institutional arrangements—of governance structures—determine the specific set of functional relations among parties. The basic rules of contracting at the first level help determine the contractual environment, but specific contractual agreements constitute the institutional arrangements or governance structures that actually determine the ongoing production, exchange, and distribution process, and thereby directly affect economic performance. We have seen from the foregoing discussion that formal political and economic rules, as well as measurement and enforcement mechanisms generally, are costly to establish and maintain, and, in many cases, the costs of adding to or altering formal mechanisms may exceed the gains. This means that, even in the presence of the state, measurement and, thus, enforcement will be less than perfect. Because first-level formal and informal rules and constraints will not be sufficient to ensure contractual performance, the only way to do so—and thus

---

[35] Furubotn and Richter (1998, p. 265) have characterized the fundamental challenge for NIE as one of trying to determine the solution to the problem of coordinating economic transactions between individuals by mutual agreement, where relational contracts are the focus of concern and are used to explain cooperation among individuals in a world with unforeseeable events. According to Furubotn and Richter, with markets and hierarchies as the two extremes, the goal of NIE is to determine which institutional arrangement is economically preferable and in which circumstances.

provide the greatest possible incentive to engage in wealth-enhancing exchange relationships—is to make it in each party's interest to live up to the agreement. The NIE therefore asserts that the institutional environment can only do so much; institutional arrangements—the realm of governance—become more important to ensure performance in actual situations and in specific cases. Within NIE, two separate though related initiatives, the property rights–agency approach and the transaction cost approach, are directly concerned with contractual performance.

Over the past decade, the most extensive research within the evolving literature on institutional arrangements has gone into analyzing the governance processes of production—that is, relationships within the firm—and thus the major emphasis of the discussion here will be on the contracting processes of firms.[36] NIE's exploration into the workings of the firm is in marked contrast to the neoclassical theory of the firm—the so-called production function approach—which, for all intents and purposes, describes the firm as a "black box" that transforms inputs into outputs given the firm's technology. Whereas neoclassical economics assumes that contracts are fully defined, instantaneously consummated, and perfectly enforced by the courts—which makes the identity of the contracting parties essentially irrelevant—both the property rights–agency approach and the transaction cost approach recognize that these assumptions are often not reflective of real-world contracting processes. NIE thus attempts to deal with the fact that observed contracts are often incomplete and are carried out over time, and that judicial enforcement is both imperfect and, in many instances, bypassed by the contracting parties in favor of alternative dispute resolution mechanisms. In addition, both the property rights–agency approach and the transaction cost approach posit that the goal of the agents involved in the contracting process is to select or devise contractual forms (within the limits allowed and enforceable by law) that minimize transaction costs. Each of these two approaches casts the analysis of the contracting process in a somewhat different light, and we will examine them in turn.

Property Rights, the Contracting Process, and Agency

While much of the literature within the property rights approach focuses on the analysis of institutional environments (as described earlier), property rights have also been brought into and fruitfully applied to the analysis of institutional arrangements and, specifically, the contracting process. Indeed, given that contracts function as mechanisms to transfer property rights between economic agents, it should not be surprising then, to find that the explanation and analysis of the firm by NIE necessarily involves analyzing the nexus between property rights and contracting. Cheung (1970, p. 50) describes

---

[36] See, however, the earlier discussion of contracting in the political process.

this in a way that clearly links the issue of contracting to the importance of property rights:

> Combining resources of several owners for production involves partial or outright transfers of property rights through a contract. A contract for the partial transfer of rights, such as leasing or hiring, embodies a *structure*. The stipulations, or terms, which constitute the structure of the contract are, as a rule, designed to specify (a) the distribution of income among the participants, and (b) the conditions of resource use.

Elsewhere, Cheung (1992, p. 56) signals the importance of institutional contracting arrangements, observing that "[a]lmost every individual in our society is a contractor, or a subcontractor, or a sub subcontractor, and we all compete. Subject to enforcement costs, the written and unwritten terms of contracts dictate how production and exchange activities are organized and conducted. It is the observed contractual or institutional arrangements that require explanation." Contracts are the vehicles that facilitate exchange, which can run the gamut from simple market exchange to the internal exchange of the vertically integrated firm; in addition, different exchange mechanisms require different forms of contractual arrangement. The choice of contractual arrangements is a function of several factors, including transaction costs, risk, legal-political arrangements, social customs, and the technical attributes of the assets involved in the contracting process. Thus, one of the central concerns of positive analysis within NIE is to describe the various contractual arrangements that are observed in the real world, and to explore why particular types of contractual arrangements dominate others in particular circumstances.[37]

As Cheung goes on to point out, prices are often only one of many terms specified within the contract. Other terms may deal with the timing of deliveries, quality assurance, and mechanisms to deal with the risks of nonperformance. Moreover, as North (1990b, p. 52) suggests, the institutional environment, of which property rights are a central component, plays a fundamental role in setting the parameters for the contracting process by establishing the incentives and constraints that individuals face. The contracts that we observe— as institutional arrangements—reflect the opportunity sets and incentives embedded in the existing property rights structure.

From the vantage point of NIE, the vast majority of contracting in modern capitalist economies is effectuated with firms as buyers and/or sellers, and often within the firm itself. The NIE view of the firm posits the firm as a nexus of contractual relationships. The firm's contracting relationships exist with the suppliers of various input goods and services to the firm, including the employment relation and production relationships internal to the firm, and those

---

[37] This topic will be given extensive treatment later in the chapter.

to whom the firm sells the goods and services that it produces. Given the extent and diversity of potential contracting relations, the law of contracts and the form of contractual relationships play a crucial role in determining the organizational structure of the firm. Specifically, the NIE hypothesis is that "business firms exist to reduce postcontractual opportunistic behavior by lowering the cost of monitoring exchange (including effort) and directing the allocation of joint cooperating units" (De Alessi and Staaf 1989, pp. 180–81). It is within this context that agency issues come into play.

Agency. An important problem that arises within the transacting (or contracting) process is that of agency: "An agency relationship is established when a principal delegates some rights—for example, user rights over a resource—to an agent who is bounded by a (formal or informal) contract to represent the principal's interests in return for payment of some kind" (Eggertsson 1990, pp. 40–41). Agency relationships exist in many forms, including owner-manager, manager-worker, voter-legislator, and legislator-bureaucrat. The central problem of agency is that the goals of the agent may not correspond exactly to those of the principal, which necessitates some sort of monitoring to ensure that the agent's behavior reflects the principal's interests. Because monitoring is costly, however, it is usually unfeasible or impossible for principals to perfectly monitor agent performance, thus giving rise to the possibility of opportunistic behavior (such as shirking) on the part of the agent when his and the principal's interests diverge. This opportunistic behavior imposes two types of costs on the principal: the direct agency cost that arises due to opportunistic behavior on the part of the agent (e.g., inefficiencies in production that arise from employee shirking), and the monitoring cost that accompanies attempts by the principal to monitor agent performance. Because monitoring is costly, the principal will incur additional monitoring costs only as long as the reduction in direct agency cost is greater than the additional monitoring cost. The result that obtains will almost certainly include some (often substantial) amount of direct agency cost.

For example, whereas the utility of a firm's owner (the principal) is a direct function of the firm's profits, the employee's (agent's) utility, which is a function of, among other things, income and leisure, may be maximized through behavior on the job that does not serve to maximize the firm's profits. That is, the worker may have an incentive to shirk because the reduction in work effort (which lowers the firm's profits) does not result in a corresponding reduction in the worker's income. Thus, the owner will wish to monitor the employee in an attempt to ensure that the employee's behavior furthers the owner's interests (that is, maximizes the firm's profits). The inability of the owner to fully monitor employee performance, however, leads to a scenario in which the worker acts on the incentive to shirk. These monitoring and incentive issues

are especially important where production is organized on a team basis.[38] If the contribution to team output generated by each member of the team is difficult to measure, each member has an incentive to shirk. Moreover, if the monitor (or manager) is unable to capture the full returns to monitoring, the monitor too has an incentive to shirk.[39] Given this, and the costliness of monitoring, the issue becomes one of establishing and institutionalizing an incentive system whereby shirking is discouraged, and thus minimized.

It will sometimes be the case that the forces of competition are sufficient to vitiate these types of monitoring problems. For example, competition among teams or for "membership" on teams may be sufficiently powerful to induce forthright anti-shirking efforts on the part of teams or team members. Similarly, competition in the market for monitors/managers may be sufficient to largely eliminate shirking among them. In many instances, however, an absence of sufficient competition or information about performance may make such solutions problematic.[40]

In the absence of efficacious competition or low-cost information that facilitates effective control of agent performance, principals can attempt to reduce agency costs through appropriately structured contracts—that is, contracts that attempt to align the agent's interests with those of the principal. One prominent manifestation of such incentive-alignment schemes in modern employer-employee contracts is the profit-sharing arrangement. Here the employer offers the employee a share of the firm's profits as a performance bonus. The employee's income, then, is tied not just to the wage, but also to overall firm performance, to which the worker contributes through his or her work effort. The effect is that the incentives of the employee are aligned more closely to the employer's interests, thereby inducing the employee to perform in a manner that corresponds more closely to the employer's interests.

Consider another agency example where an owner-manager decides to sell a portion of his equity in the firm.[41] Because he now owns less than the full equity value of the firm, the cost to him of expending firm resources on various perquisites, as well as the benefits to him from seeking out new, profit-enhancing activities for the firm, are correspondingly reduced. The ability of prospective shareholders in the firm to anticipate these incentives, however, leads them to recognize that resources will have to be expended to monitor

---

[38] Production is organized in teams when the productive abilities of individuals working together in a team relationship exceed the sum of the outputs that could be produced with each individual working separately. See, for example, Alchian and Demsetz (1972) and Eggertsson (1990, ch. 6).

[39] That is, who monitors the monitor? See Jensen and Meckling (1976) and the discussion that follows.

[40] See Eggertsson (1990, pp. 134–35) and De Alessi and Staaf (1989, pp. 180–82).

[41] This example is adapted from Jensen and Meckling (1976, pp. 312–13).

this individual's performance. The shareholders, in turn, will reduce the price that they are willing to pay for ownership shares, thereby increasing the cost to the owner-manager of raising capital in equity markets. The lower the share of this owner-manager's equity in the firm, the greater his incentive is to indulge in perquisites and the lower his incentive is to increase the firm's profits, hence the greater the associated monitoring cost and the lower the willingness of potential investors to pay for a given equity share.

One method by which agents may attempt to guarantee their performance is through bonding, a situation where, within the contracting process, the agent offers the principal some collateral as security against the agent's opportunistic behavior (Eggertsson 1990, p. 42). Within the previous shareholder-manager example, this bonding may take the form of "contractual guarantees to have the financial accounts audited by a public accountant, explicit bonding against malfeasance on the part of the manager, and contractual limitations on the manager's decision-making power" (Jensen and Meckling 1976, p. 325). Bonding activities, however, impose additional costs on the firm by increasing the cost of contracting and/or by imposing direct costs on the firm through, for example, the hiring of auditors or through the foregone profit opportunities that arise because, owing to the restrictions on his behavior, the manager cannot always take full advantage of new profit opportunities that present themselves.

Agency problems may also arise in contracts between firms, such as where one firm contracts to supply inputs to another firm. Here we have, in essence, a reciprocal principal-agent problem wherein neither party can be absolutely certain that the other party will perform as agreed in the contract. For example, the buyer may have concerns about on-time delivery, whereas the seller may have concerns about potential modification or cancellation of the order by the buyer. When at least one party has a strong interest in performance that accords with the specific contractual terms, it may be in the interest of the parties to insert, say, penalty clauses into the contract for failure to perform in accordance with the agreement. Although the insertion of such clauses entails additional bargaining costs, the parties will be willing to bargain over these clauses if the expected incentive-alignment benefits outweigh the associated bargaining costs.

The general theme that emerges from the agency literature, then, is that, because of imperfect measurement and enforcement, one party may be able to affect adversely the value of certain attributes of the product or the resource in question. The solution is to structure the contract so as to make this party a residual claimant over the returns associated with those attributes, thus giving this party an incentive to maximize its value. More specifically, the greater the extent to which an individual can influence the value of an asset, the greater should be the extent of his claim over the value of, or the income from, that asset (Barzel 1989, p. 41; North 1990a, pp. 187–88). For example, by structuring the monitor's contract so as to give him some residual claim over the returns to the monitoring function, one reduces the monitor's incentive to

shirk.[42] In the realm of quality assurance in goods markets, since manufacturers have relatively more control over the short-term quality or durability of an asset, the warranty or guarantee places on them the responsibility for making good on defects that occur over short-time horizons and thus gives the manufacturer an incentive to take cost-justified quality-assurance steps. In the longer term, however, the buyer's use of the asset has an important effect on its continued quality or durability. The fact that some or all of the warranty terms expire after a comparatively short period gives the buyer relatively more responsibility for those factors that he can affect and frees the producer from being victimized by opportunistic behavior on the part of the buyer.

These same issues also influence the organizational structure of the firm—that is, the decision to contract with an outside supplier or organize a set of transactions internally.[43] When a contract is incomplete, the right to determine outcomes regarding the missing elements of the contract lies with the agent who has property rights over the nonhuman assets in question (that is, residual rights of control). For example, suppose that A contracted with B for B to deliver 100 units of a good to A. Suppose B controls the manufacture of the good. Then A later determines that it instead needs 110 units of the good—however, B (because he controls the manufacture of the good) has the residual rights of control and will sell these additional units to A only if A meets its price (or not at all if B has more pressing matters). The situation is very different if A owns B. In that case, A has the residual rights of control and can compel B to sell to A at A's desired price. If A owns B and B's managers do not want to sell to A, then A can fire B's managers and hire new ones who will sell to A, provided the production of the good is dependent on nonhuman as opposed to human capital (that is, specific knowledge that only B's managers possess). The benefit of A owning B is that A can compel performance and hence purchase the good at a lower cost than if B was independent. Furthermore, A will have a greater incentive to invest in the relationship because of the reduced threat of B expropriating A's return. B's workers are also likely to be more attuned to A's interests when A owns B because it is in the workers' self-interest—they will not see some of their return to increased productivity siphoned off by the owners of B. On the cost side, B's mangers may have a reduced incentive to come up with innovations if B is owned by A, since they are unlikely to be able to extract as much of the surplus from these innovations as they would if B were independent. Since B has no residual rights of control, bargaining power is greatly reduced (Hart 1990, pp. 162–63).

The solution here, according to Oliver Hart, is to have unified common ownership—that is, a "firm" relationship—rather than one company owning the other. If agents have access to both sets of assets, then they are able to

---

[42] See, for example, Barzel (1985, 1987) and Eggertsson (1990, ch. 6).

[43] The following discussion draws on Grossman and Hart (1986) and Hart (1990).

benefit from increases in their marginal productivities (Hart 1990, p. 163). The extent to which one set of agents' actions is linked to another will then determine the extent of integration versus the use of long-term contractual arrangements. For example, if the unified A and B (A-B) transacts with C, but this relation constitutes only a small portion of the total business of both A-B and C, then long-term contracting is preferred to vertical integration. The reasoning here is that integration increases hold-up problems (as A-B expropriates the surplus of C, much of which is not related to C's dealings with A-B),[44] thereby reducing the incentives of the workers and managers of C.

Within the firm, one might expect that as firm size increases (or, more generally, with the emergence of the large modern corporation), both the expected direct agency costs and the costs of monitoring will increase, leading the firm's owners to attempt to devise incentive-alignment schemes that can be incorporated into contractual agreements. The contracts (and hence firms and their structures) that have emerged over time "are the products of a historical process in which there were strong incentives for individuals to minimize agency costs" (Jensen and Meckling 1976, p. 357). As we have seen in our discussion of the institutional environment, however, increasing contractual complexity is costly, with the result that the optimal contract, like optimal monitoring, will result in some positive optimal direct agency cost. The extent to which these types of incentive-alignment mechanisms are incorporated into contracts is a function of the size of the relevant transaction costs—the costs of including such terms in the contract (mainly bargaining costs) as compared to the costs of additional monitoring of agent performance, and both of these as compared to the direct agency costs anticipated by the principal.

Transaction Cost Economics

Transaction cost economics (TCE) is part of the NIE tradition and draws on the literatures of law, economics, and organization to study governance institutions within the economic system.[45] TCE begins with the insight—which, as Williamson acknowledges, owes to John R. Commons (1934)—that the transaction is the basic unit of economic analysis. Using this insight, along with Coase's (1937, 1960) analyses of transaction costs, Chester Barnard's (1938) work on organization theory, and the law of contracts, the transaction cost approach analyzes the emergence of governance structures within the economic system and does so largely from the perspective of economizing on transaction costs. Coase (1999, p. 4) described it as follows:

---

[44] The issue of hold-up problems is later addressed in detail.

[45] A note on terminology is in order here. The particular vein of NIE research discussed in this section goes by the name of "transaction cost economics," following the lead of Oliver Williamson. As should be apparent from the foregoing discussion, however, the use of transaction cost analysis is pervasive within NIE, and thus the ideas discussed in this section are but just one manifestation of transaction cost analysis, in spite of the label attached to them. See also Williamson (1993b).

The costs of exchange [i.e., transaction costs] depend on the institutions of a country—the legal system (including property rights and their enforcement), the political system, the educational system, the culture. These institutions in effect govern the performance of the economic system.

Within this general approach, the law of contracts and the contracting process are seen to play an important role in determining the form of economic organization. Simply put, TCE is "the study of alternative institutions of governance," and it "tries to explain how trading partners choose from the set of feasible institutional alternatives, the arrangement that protects their relationship-specific investments at least cost" (Klein 2000, p. 468). The correct (read "least-cost") governance structure comes about because the background market forces—the ongoing exchange relationships—work to cause an efficient sorting among the possible alternatives by adhering to behavior consistent with transaction cost economizing. From this perspective, "Market failures may be seen as failures only in the limited sense that they involve transaction costs that can be attenuated by substituting internal organization [e.g., vertical integration] for market exchange" (Furubotn and Richter 1998, p. 64).

Recall that neoclassical economic theory assumes that contracts are complete—fully defined, instantaneously consummated, and perfectly enforced by courts. As such, future contingencies are assumed to be considered in the ex ante stage of contracting and the identity of the contracting parties is thus essentially irrelevant. The TCE approach, however, recognizes that, although these assumptions may apply in certain circumstances, it is more often the case that contracts are unavoidably incomplete, that contractual performance is carried out over time, and that court enforcement is imperfect and is indeed bypassed in many instances in favor of private dispute-resolution mechanisms. Because of these phenomena, the identity of the contracting parties does matter. Given this, TCE focuses on the execution stage of contract and emphasizes ex post arrangements and the design of extrajudicial mechanisms (often set up by the parties within the contract) to resolve disputes among contracting parties.

The three pillars of TCE are (1) the bounded rationality of economic agents—behavior that is, according to Herbert Simon (1961, p. xxiv), "*intendedly* rational, but only *limitedly* so"; (2) opportunistic behavior, which Williamson (1985, p. 30) defines as "self-interest seeking with guile"—in essence taking advantage, perhaps due to having a temporary monopoly or superior information; and (3) asset specificity—the fact that there are investments in certain transaction-specific assets due to specialized human and/or physical capital requirements, in which case relationship-specific investments may well accompany the contracting or transacting process. These three features of the transacting process serve to differentiate the perspective on contracts within TCE from the perspectives of mainstream economic theory and

the property rights–agency approach. Specifically, when bounded rationality, opportunism, and asset specificity exist simultaneously, we have an environment wherein "[p]lanning is necessarily incomplete (because of bounded rationality), promise predictably breaks down (because of opportunism), and the precise identity of the parties now matters (because of asset specificity). This is the world of governance. Since the efficacy of court ordering is problematic, contract execution falls heavily on the institutions of private ordering. This is the world with which transaction cost economics is concerned" (Williamson 1985, p. 32). The role of these governance structures (i.e., "the institutions of private ordering") in TCE is twofold: (1) to resolve conflicts that arise over the course of the contractual relationship, and, more importantly, (2) to head off or attenuate potential disputes (Williamson 1984, p. 55; 1985, p. 29).

Market, hybrid, and hierarchical governance structures. As TCE has evolved over time, one constant has been its recognition that, in all but the simplest of contracts, a governance structure is needed to protect the transacting parties from the many "hazards" that arise in complex exchanges. As a consequence, the range of the possible governance structures has grown to handle the myriad of problems that may arise. While there are two polar extremes of governance structures—at one extreme, the market (the idea of the spot market), and at the other, hierarchy (the fully integrated firm)—between these two lie a variety of hybrid structures to help remedy the hazards that tend to arise in complex exchanges. Furubotn and Richter (1998, p. 265) suggest that "depending on circumstances, relational contracts are 'administered,' 'organized,' or 'governed' by different 'governance structures,' 'orders,' or 'constitutions' which are explicitly or implicitly developed through the activities of cooperating individuals . . . [where] markets and hierarchies are the two extremes." As Klein (2000, pp. 468–69) describes the continuum, "[T]he movement from market to hierarchy . . . entails a tradeoff between the high-powered incentives and adaptive properties of the market and the safeguards and central coordinating properties of the [vertically integrated] firm." Moreover, these different types of governance structures are associated with and supported by different types of contract law or contractual environments.

Contractual environments. Drawing, in part, on the work of Ian Macneil (1974, 1978, 1981), Williamson (1991) suggests that three basic forms of contract law—classical, neoclassical, and forbearance—each works to determine the organizational structure of the firm's transactional activities. Specifically, classical contract law supports market contracting, neoclassical contract law supports hybrid modes of contracting, and forbearance law supports hierarchical modes of contracting.

1. *Classical contract law.* As described earlier, the view of contract in mainstream economic theory is one where discrete, autonomous market exchange is instantaneously consummated under the aegis of fully specified contracts, with monetized commodities being exchanged for money payments,

and where contracts are perfectly enforced by courts. Here, relational considerations are absent and the identity of the contracting parties is irrelevant. Even where contractual performance is not instantaneous, future considerations are dealt with in the present (e.g., through specific contingency clauses specified in the contract) so that relational considerations are absent. Such contracts are not merely theoretical fictions, but are, in fact, observed in the real world, particularly in "thick" market situations where, for example, a firm has many alternative sources of supply for a given input, among which it can switch at negligible cost. In such a market, the firm can acquire that input through a series of short-term contracts executed over time with the supplier offering the lowest price on that input at that point in time. The combination of short-term contracts and the multiplicity of alternative suppliers secures the firm from the hazards of opportunistic behavior on the part of its trading partners.

These discrete market transactions are facilitated and supported within a framework of classical contract law in several ways having to do with the characteristics of classical contract law. Classical contract law (i) treats the identity of the contracting parties as irrelevant, (ii) emphasizes clearly spelled-out contractual terms and provides rigorous court enforcement of these terms (as well as giving precedence to terms that are written down over those that are communicated orally) and emphasizes that offer and acceptance commit one to a contractual relation and the attendant risks, (iii) limits the scope of remedies primarily to specific performance or expectation damages, which makes the end-value of the contract predictable, (iv) discourages the introduction of third parties (including arbitrators or mediators) into the relation, and (v) provides a well-defined body of law to deal with matters not specifically covered in the contract (Macneil 1978, pp. 862–65). As such, classical contract law functions to preclude the types of relational problems discussed previously and facilitates contractual situations where specification of the relevant contractual terms and the performance of the contract are nonproblematic; in short, it facilitates market organization.[46]

Although discrete market organization and contracting play an important role within the modern capitalist economic system, increasing situational complexity and the pervasiveness of uncertainty will often require that, for reasons of transaction cost economies, contracts be made over long time periods and be less than fully specified. As we have seen, this will manifest itself in intentional contractual gaps and/or the establishment of formulas or governance mechanisms through which parties can adapt their relations to changing circumstances or fill contractual gaps. These factors become more important the longer the time horizon of the contract and the greater the extent to which the parties invest specific assets in the relationship. The relationship itself,

---

[46] See, more generally, Macneil (1974, 1978, 1981) and Williamson (1985, 1991).

then, takes on value, and continuity (and thus party identity) assumes a substantial degree of importance. It should be clear from the foregoing discussion that classical contract law is not well suited to this sort of relational contracting because of its emphasis on specific terms, its discouragement of third-party resolution mechanisms, and its limited range of dispute-resolution options. The forces of contractual gaps, time, uncertainty, and specific investments can raise the specter of opportunistic behavior and thus contractual disputes. Classical contract law does not allow for the possibility that these disputes may be more efficiently dealt with through extrajudicial mechanisms such as arbitration or mediation because of both the relatively lower costs of these mechanisms and the greater latitude that an arbitrator or mediator has in attempting to come to grips with the facts at issue in a dispute. As a result, contracts may set up these types of hybrid (Williamson's term) or relational (Goldberg's term) governance structures as a first resort in the dispute or gap filling process.

2. *Neoclassical contract law.* Neoclassical contract law offers a much more fertile framework for these hybrid forms of organization because, although built on the basic framework of classical contract law, it diverges from the classical framework by virtue of its enhanced flexibility.[47] At the most basic level, neoclassical contract law recognizes the fact that contractual incompleteness is often an optimal response to uncertainty, and as such allows that gaps and adjustment mechanisms put into place by the contracting parties should be recognized as contractual terms within certain limits. Whereas, under classical contract law, dispute resolution is effected through the judicial system, neoclassical contract law gives a great deal of credence to the governance structures that attend hybrid forms of organization. Karl Llewellyn (1931, p. 737; quoted in Williamson 1991, p. 272) describes this contractual framework as "a framework highly adjustable, a framework which almost never accurately indicates the real working relations, but which affords a rough indication around which such relations vary, an occasional guide in cases of doubt, and a norm of ultimate appeal when the relations cease in fact to work." In addition, neoclassical contract law embodies a set of excuse doctrines—including impossibility of performance, frustration of purpose, mistake, and unconscionability—which allow contracting parties to avoid excessively costly adaptations. The flexibility of the courts to excuse contractual performance functions as a curb on opportunistic behavior and promotes adaptive efforts on the part of the contracting parties (Williamson 1991, p. 273).

As evidence of the elasticity of neoclassical contracts, Williamson (1991, p. 272) offers the following example, taken from a thirty-two-year coal supply agreement between the Nevada Power Company and the Northwest Trading Company:

---

[47] See Macneil (1978, pp. 870–80) from which the following discussion is drawn.

In the event an inequitable condition occurs which adversely affects one Party, it shall then be the joint and equal responsibility of both Parties to act promptly and in good faith to determine the action required to cure or adjust for the inequity and effectively to implement such action. Upon written claim of inequity served by one Party upon the other, the Parties shall act jointly to reach an agreement concerning the claimed inequity within sixty (60) days of the date of such written claim. An adjusted base coal price that differs from the market price by more than ten percent (10%) shall constitute a hardship. The Party claiming inequity shall include in its claim such information and data as may be reasonably necessary to substantiate the claim and shall freely and without delay furnish such other information and data as the other Party reasonably may deem relevant and necessary. If the Parties cannot reach agreement within sixty (60) days the matter shall be submitted to arbitration.

Williamson goes on to note that this contract is distinguished from a classical contract in that it "1) contemplates unanticipated disturbances for which adaptation is needed, 2) provides a zone of tolerance (of +/− 10%) within which misalignments will be absorbed, 3) requires information disclosure and substantiation if adaptation is proposed, and 4) provides for arbitration in the event voluntary agreement fails" (1991, p. 272).

In spite of the increased flexibility of hybrid organizational forms and neoclassical contract law, they still may not be sufficiently elastic to promote continuity and adaptation in the face of extreme deviations between actual and expected circumstances. The self-interested bargaining that occurs to fill gaps or resolve disputes may involve significant costs. For example, when circumstances become such that the contract is maladapted to existing conditions, the costs that result from this maladaption and attempts to resolve it through the extrajudicial mechanisms of hybrid organization may be severe (Williamson 1991, pp. 278–79). That is, the costs of the mechanisms necessary to maintain the relation may be prohibitive, or the mechanisms may simply be insufficient to preclude wholesale defections from contractual agreements, and thus even more flexible organizational/contractual arrangements are necessary. Such arrangements are to be found in hierarchy, or internal organization, which, according to Williamson (1991, p. 279), functions as the organizational form "of last resort" when market or hybrid modes fail or are expected to fail.

Hierarchical organization substitutes administrative control for the formulas or third-party governance mechanisms of hybrid organization. As such, hierarchy economizes on transaction costs in several ways, ways which are driven by the ability to resolve disputes by fiat rather than through arbitration or the courts. These include the ideas that, within hierarchy, information is more easily acquired, less formal documentation is necessary, direct costs of using more formal mechanisms (e.g., lawyer, court, or arbitration costs) can be avoided, disputes can be resolved in a more timely fashion, and the potential

for defection within a hierarchical relationship is reduced (Williamson 1991, p. 280). At the same time, however, hierarchical organization can impose substantial bureaucracy-related costs on the firm, costs that will not be worth incurring if one does not anticipate that adaptation problems will become severe (and costly).

3. *Forbearance law.* Williamson (1991, pp. 274–76) suggests that hierarchical organization is supported by forbearance law, which facilitates the use of administrative fiat as a dispute resolution mechanism. Williamson (1991, p. 274) describes this as follows.

> [W]hereas courts routinely grant standing to firms should there be disputes over prices, the damages to be ascribed to delays, failures of quality, and the like, courts will refuse to hear disputes between one internal division and another over technical issues. Access to the courts being denied, the parties must resolve their differences internally. Accordingly, hierarchy is its own court of ultimate appeal.

Were the courts to grant standing to the parties to such internal disputes, or were the law to mandate third-party arbitration, the working of the hierarchical system would be undermined, robbing it of much of its useful function. By recognizing hierarchy as an individual authoritative relation, forbearance law has the effect that parties to an internal dispute must resolve the dispute among themselves or, upon failure to do so, appeal to higher authorities within the hierarchy for final dispute resolution. By granting hierarchies fiat power, then, forbearance law allows for adaptive mechanisms that are not allowed under classical and neoclassical contract law and thus are not present within market or hybrid forms of organization.

4. *Summary.* In TCE, changes in contract law—whether of the classical, neoclassical, or forbearance variety—affect the relative costs of the supporting modes of contracting, that is, the alternative contractual/governance arrangements.[48] For example, the broadening or narrowing of the excuse doctrine in neoclassical contract law will, respectively, increase or decrease the opportunities for agents to defect from contractual relationships, and thus impact the costs of hybrid modes of organization. If excuse doctrine is drawn too broadly, parties may be reluctant to make specific investments in a contractual relationship because of the relative ease with which the other party may be able to defect from the contract. Similarly, if excuse doctrine is drawn too strictly, parties may be reluctant to make specific investments because of the high costs that may result if the other party insists on performance in accordance with the terms of the contract in the face of adverse conditions that would render such performance excessively costly for the former party. In TCE, the evaluation of a given structure of excuse doctrine, or of changes therein, should thus proceed on the basis of its effects on the costs of hybrid modes of contracting. In

---

[48] This discussion is based on Williamson (1991, p. 290).

like manner, changes in forbearance doctrine affect the relative costs of hierarchical modes of organization. For example, should courts resolve to grant standing to intra-firm disputes, the costs of hierarchy would increase. TCE would argue that the evaluation of changes in forbearance doctrine should proceed on the basis of their effects on the costs of hierarchical modes of organization.

It should be noted that this focus of TCE is consistent with some of the early writings on coordination by F. A. Hayek (1945) and Chester Barnard (1938), who emphasized that adaptation to changing circumstances is a central problem of economic coordination. Yet, whereas Hayek finds the mechanism for adaptation in the market, Barnard finds it in internal organization, or hierarchy. The seeming incongruence between these two views is essentially resolved in the foregoing discussion. Although markets serve as efficacious adaptation mechanisms for certain types of contractual relations, the increasing severity of adaptation problems requires more expansive modes of coordination—perhaps hybrids, perhaps hierarchy. Because classical contract law, which sets up an environment that is well suited for market organization, is ill suited to hybrid and hierarchical organization, other forms of contract law—neoclassical and forbearance—have developed to facilitate these other forms of organization.[49]

We have seen, then, that three different types of contract law, or contractual environment—classical, neoclassical, and forbearance—support, respectively, three different types of governance structures: market, hybrid, and hierarchy. There will be a single type of governance structure that economizes on the cost of organizing a particular transaction. The prescription for organization that emerges from this analysis is to "align transactions (which differ in their attributes) with governance structures (the costs and competencies of which differ) in a discriminating (mainly, transaction cost economizing) way" (Williamson 1988, p. 73), or, stated slightly differently, to "*[o]rganize transactions so as to economize on bounded rationality while simultaneously safeguarding them against the hazards of opportunism*" (Williamson 1985, p. 32, emphasis in original).

These processes are illustrated very nicely by the *make* versus *buy* decisions faced by firms in securing production inputs. The firm can choose to produce the input itself (*make*) through hierarchical organization, or it may choose to purchase the input (*buy*) through a series of spot-market transactions (market organization) or by establishing a more complex long-term contractual relationship with a single supplier (hybrid organization). The choice of contractual/organizational arrangements will be a function of the transaction cost-related factors discussed earlier. The interplay of the organizational structures and the characteristics of the type of transaction under consideration will work

[49] See Williamson (1991, pp. 277–79; 1985, 1990).

together to determine the matching of transactions and governance structures. Because different types of transactions have different characteristics, we observe that complex firms do not use solely market, hybrid, or hierarchical organization, but rather a mixture of them as fits the needs of the firm.

NIE AT WORK

Institutional Environment: Institutions and Economic Growth

Neoclassical economic growth theory, pioneered by Robert Solow, posits economies that converge to similar rates of growth. That is, developing economies, it is suggested, will take advantage of productivity and technological advances available to them and catch up to the point where they can match the performance of developed nations. In reality, however, such convergence is often absent, as some countries grow rapidly (on average), while others are plagued by consistently poor economic performance—even in the face of large amounts of foreign assistance given with the goal of stimulating development.

New Institutionalists such as North and Libecap have argued that these differential rates of economic performance have their roots in institutional structures that differ across countries or regions.[50] In countries with poorly performing economies, institutions such as educational systems that promote innovation and a productive work force, patent laws and other forms of property rights that protect innovation, capital markets that allow for investment in performance-enhancing plants and equipment, and a competitive process that pushes firms toward greater efficiency are often absent, poorly structured, or ill defined. That is, institutions in some nations are structured in such a way that productivity and technological advancement are promoted, while institutional structures in other nations retard productivity and technological advances. Profit-seeking behavior in the former situation entails productivity-enhancing behavior, whereas in the latter case it tends to entail rent-seeking activities on the part of firms. The latter nations, then, are left consistently behind the curve in terms of economic performance and are institutionally stuck in a rut from which they are unable to extricate themselves.

If inefficient institutions breed stagnation and efficient ones give rise to growth, how is it that inefficient institutions persist? Growth increases the size of the pie, after all. In an environment where transaction costs are zero, we would expect that the prevailing institutions would be those that promoted efficient resource use and a solid rate of economic growth. Moreover, we would also expect, consistent with neoclassical growth theory, that institutions would immediately adjust—efficiently adapt—to meet changing circumstances. Any

---

[50] See, for example, North (1979, 1981) and Libecap (1989a); see also Eggertsson (1990).

given institutional structure gives rise to vested interests, however, and these interests are likely to be harmed by institutional change. Again, if transaction costs were zero, those suffering losses could be compensated for change-induced losses, as suggested by the Coase theorem; the same would be true if transaction costs were positive, but sufficiently low to facilitate a bargained solution. When transaction costs are positive, however, and the vested interests are sufficient to preclude private, efficiency-enhancing bargains, a rationale arises for the existence of government, along with its power of compulsion. In such instances, the role of government will be to structure or revise institutions in an effort to lower transaction costs, facilitate bargained solutions, and thereby grow the economy.

In addition, the existence of groups who will lose from institutional change make political bargains that much more difficult to consummate. Those who expect to gain from the change will exert pressure toward that end, while potential losers will exert pressure in the opposite direction. How this is all worked out is a function of the magnitude of the available gains relative to the losses and, perhaps, the ability to work out compensation for the losers, as well as the political structure in place and its ability to foster performance-enhancing institutional change in a timely and efficient manner. As Libecap (1989a, pp. 7–8) has pointed out, "[T]he heart of the contracting problem is devising politically acceptable allocation mechanisms to assign the gains from institutional change, while maintaining its production advantages. By compensating those potentially harmed in the proposed definition of rights and by increasing the shares of influential parties, a political consensus for institutional change can emerge." However, he continues, these things alter the size of the available gains and if, in doing so, the "influential parties" cannot be compensated in an amount sufficient to get them to favor the change, that performance-enhancing change may not occur.

North (1979, 1981) has developed a useful framework for analyzing the relationship between economic growth and institutional structures. Knowledge and resource endowments determine the technical limits to growth; property rights and related institutional structures, however, determine the structural limits to growth. For growth to occur at a rate consistent with technological possibilities, then, the institutional structure of the economy must facilitate the maximum possible exploitation of these possibilities. Otherwise, the improperly-specified pattern of property rights, for example, will preclude the economy from growing commensurate with its technological capacity. Given that political outcomes determine these rights structures, the question is to what extent the political process aligns the technical and structural aspects. As Eggertsson (1990, pp. 319–20) points out,

Modern technology creates the potential for very high levels of productivity. These high levels of output cannot be reached without elaborate specialization in

production and complex webs of exchange among unrelated individuals, extending across both time and space. In general, we can say that the more advanced the technology, the more complex the transactions, and the higher the transaction costs of utilizing the technology.

Given this, transaction-cost-reducing property rights structures must be put into place to facilitate the use of advanced technology. As government tends to have a comparative advantage in supplying these types of institutional structures, we have here a piece of the rationale for the existence of the state as well.

Economic growth is a function of "the willingness of individual owners to supply specific appropriable assets" that, in turn, allow society to take advantages of technological possibilities to the greatest extent possible. This investment, however, will occur only if there exists a property rights structure (with attendant dispute resolution process and enforcement mechanisms) that makes such investment worthwhile (Eggertsson 1990, p. 320). North and Thomas (1973, p. 8) make a similar point and in even greater detail:

> Economic growth will occur if property rights make it worthwhile to undertake socially productive activity. The creating, specifying and enacting of such property rights are costly. . . . As the potential grows for private gains to exceed transaction costs, efforts will be made to establish such property rights. Governments take over the protection and enforcement of property rights because they can do it at a lower cost than private volunteer groups.

They point out, however, that this does not guarantee that the optimal institutional structure will be put into place. Rather, "the fiscal needs of government may induce the protection of certain property rights which hinder rather than promote growth." In fact, North (1981) offers a great deal of historical evidence indicating that the institutional structures put into place by governments often keep the economy from growing at a rate anywhere near to that which would be technologically possible under the optimal rights structure. The lack of development and growth, then, can often be attributed to institutional failure.

Governance: The Holdup Problem

Because of the transaction costs that accompany the contracting process, most importantly the costs of attempting to anticipate future events and haggling over related contractual contingencies that may or may not come into play over the life of the contract, parties will often elect to leave gaps in the contractual arrangement. These gaps can then be dealt with as circumstances evolve over the course of the contract through processes that entail lower expected costs than would obtain if the parties attempted to specify terms explicitly within the

contract itself dealing with all relevant contingencies. In addition, since courts are likely to enforce clearly spelled-out contractual terms, parties have an additional incentive to leave certain terms out of the contracts to avoid committing themselves to potential future courses of action that may impose substantial costs. Thus, in a situation where events arise such that efficiency and profit maximization would dictate that Party A opt out of some or all of its contract with Party B, Party B may have an incentive to engage in activities that make breach extremely expensive for A, as B recognizes that the threat that the court will order specific performance means that it can extort substantial rents from A in return for allowing A to opt out of the contract.

While not denying the importance of the ex ante incentive alignment issues raised by the agency and property rights approaches, TCE has focused much of its efforts on resolving a variety of contractual hazards in an ex post context. Klein (2000, pp. 467–68) enumerates several such hazards: (i) bilateral dependence, (ii) weak property rights, (iii) measurement difficulties or oversearching, (iv) intertemporal issues, (v) weakness in the institutional environment, and, our concern here, (vi) the "holdup problem."[51] The holdup problem is probably the best known of the contractual hazards dealt with in the TCE literature, and it arises over the course of the contractual relationship due to ex post opportunistic behavior by one of the contracting parties. That is, risk of "hold-up" arises because of "the probability that transactors may violate the intent of their contractual understanding by expropriating quasi-rents from the specific reliance investments that have been made by the contracting parties" (Klein 1992, p. 150),[52] where the quasi-rents are defined as the difference between an asset's value in its current use and the value of that asset in its next best use. The potential for hold-ups is made possible by the long-term nature of a contract and by the presence of specific investments in the contractual relationship. These investments cannot be recouped if there is a defection from the contractual agreement. This may give one of the parties an incentive to attempt to capture some of the other party's surplus from the contract, knowing that the other party's incentive to defect from the contract will be minimized by its nonrecoverable specific investment in the relationship. Simply put, depending upon the level of specific investments made by the contracting parties, one of the parties to the contract can get "locked in," with the extent of the "lock in" varying with the size of its nonrecoverable investment. This raises the possibility of a "holdup" in which one party expropriates the quasi-rent of the other, "locked-in" party.

Excessive concern about potential hold-ups, however, will weaken the incentive for parties to invest in long-term contractual relations that require

---

[51] See Klein (2000, pp. 467–68) for a further elaboration of the other hazards.

[52] For a discussion of holdup problems and quasi-rents, see Klein, Crawford, and Alchian (1978).

specific investments, causing the parties to substitute less efficient, short-term contracts for more efficient, long-term ones. In the light of this dilemma, the focus of TCE becomes one of devising contractual arrangements that attempt to minimize holdup risks in a long-term cooperative relation characterized by reliance investments by one or both parties that are specific to the venture at issue, in order that parties can form mutually beneficial exchange relationships in which both parties have confidence.

TCE has explored three different mechanisms to help safeguard against the holdup problem.[53] One remedy is vertical integration. Heretofore, the conventional wisdom in neoclassical economics was that the primary motivation of firms to engage in vertical integration is to gain control of the factor markets and distribution channels and thereby acquire the related monopoly rents. Empirical studies within the TCE tradition, however, have suggested that, in fact, firms engage in such activities to realize the transaction-cost-minimizing benefits that are possible under vertical integration.[54] In summarizing the empirical evidence, Klein (2000, p. 473) was able to conclude that "the cumulative evidence from different studies and industries is quite consistent with the basic theory" of TCE. A second remedy employed by firms to protect themselves from expropriation of specialized investments is the so-called hybrid remedy. This can take several forms, including the use of long-term contracts, partial ownership agreements (termed "equity linkages"), or private franchise contracts. A third remedy, consistent with one of the recurring themes of TCE, is to rely on private solutions between the parties to the dispute. That is, TCE has studied an array of informal trade agreements entered into by parties—agreements to offset relationship-specific investments—that enhance the efficiency of the transaction.

Although much of this discussion deals with specific investments in terms of the resulting threat, or holdup, potential, these specific investments can also be used to secure contractual commitment.[55] Specifically, specific investments can function to make contractual agreements self-enforcing.[56] This process works as follows. In the presence of specific investments, the parties can leave certain contractual terms unspecified and handle holdup threats by recourse to various private enforcement mechanisms, one of which is the attempt to

[53] This paragraph is a very brief summary of an excellent review of the empirical literature provided by Klein (2000, pp. 467, 472–77).

[54] Some of the early empirical studies exploring this issue include the works of Monteverde and Teece (1982), Globerman (1980), and Walker and Weber (1984, 1987).

[55] Williamson (1983, p. 519) draws the following distinction between credible commitments and credible threats: "The former involve reciprocal acts designed to safeguard a relationship, while the latter are unilateral efforts to preempt an advantage." See also Williamson (1985, chs. 7, 8), North (1993a), and Eggertsson (1993).

[56] Telser defines a self-enforcing agreement as one in which, if "one party violates the terms the only recourse of the other [party] is to terminate the agreement" (Telser 1981, p. 27; quoted in Williamson 1985, p. 168).

secure credible commitments. The party contemplating engaging in holdup behavior will recognize that the threat of termination of the contractual agreement by the other party, made easier by the contractual gaps, raises the possibility of the loss of specific investments and, in addition, reputation (the latter raising others' expected costs of doing business with this party, which will cause them to demand more favorable contractual terms in their dealings with this party to account for holdup risks). The holdup decision, then, becomes one of weighing expected benefits against expected costs, and if the expected costs are sufficiently high, there is a range of conditions over which the contractual arrangement will be self-enforcing (Klein 1992, pp. 153–57).

From this perspective, the presence of specific investments made in reliance on (or in support of) the contract functions to establish "hostages" (Williamson's [1983, 1985] term) or "private enforcement capital" (Klein's [1992] term) that aids in making contracts self-enforcing. These investments serve to bond one to the contractual relation by raising the costs of defections and signaling to the other party one's commitment to the contractual relationship. By offering to invest specific assets in the exchange relation (perhaps in return for reciprocal investments by the other party), one can signal one's commitment to the continuance of the relationship and mitigate, in the eyes of the other party, the potential that one might engage in holdup activity. This private enforcement capital functions as both substitute for and complement to explicit contractual terms. That is, private enforcement capital can be substituted for explicit contractual terms as a mechanism to increase the probability of performance when using it is cheaper than the expected costs of including additional explicit terms in the contract. In addition, the private enforcement capital works along with the court-enforceable specific terms to define the self-enforcing range of the contract ex post. The distribution of this private enforcement capital among the contracting parties is also important in that it affects the holdup incentives of each party and thus the range of conditions over which the contract is self-enforcing (Klein 1992, pp. 159, 161–62). As Williamson (1985, p. 30) notes, these arrangements, by effecting adaptability and promoting continuity, create economic value. Of course, it will happen that, in certain cases, the actual conditions that emerge will diverge from expected conditions to such an extent that hold-ups become worthwhile.[57]

The use of hostages is only one mechanism through which parties may deal with the uncertainty that attends long-term contractual relationships. Because the time element introduces uncertainty into the picture, parties will often choose to forego costly efforts to make contracts more explicit in favor of a

---

[57] This discussion illustrates that the property rights/agency and TCE approaches to contracting are not mutually exclusive. In a sense, the hostages function as an incentive-alignment mechanisms among the contracting parties. Where the hostages are offered within the confines of the contract, these approaches converge. The TCE approach recognizes, however, that hostage offers may also exist outside of the confines of the contract (Klein 1992, p. 159). See also Klein (1985).

situation where the contract sets up some formula or governance structure through which contractual terms can be adjusted over time.[58] As Victor Goldberg has pointed out, the longer that parties expect their relationship to continue, and the greater the complexity and uncertainty of the environment in which they are dealing, the smaller will be the emphasis on the use of explicit contractual terms of exchange. Rather, "[t]he emphasis will instead be on establishing rules to govern the relationship: rules determining the appropriate length of the relationship; rules determining the process of adjustment to unexpected factors that arise in the course of the relationship; and rules concerning the termination of that relationship" (Goldberg 1976b, p. 432). For example, many long-term contracts do not specify the price at which goods will be purchased over time, but rather a pricing rule (e.g., cost-plus pricing). Such a pricing rule serves to minimize the occurrence of disputes when the supplier wishes to alter the price being charged because its input costs have risen. Alternatively (or complementary to this), the parties may set up contractual mechanisms, such as recourse to mediation or binding arbitration, which will be used to resolve disputes that the parties are unable to settle among themselves. These arrangements may function in place of or along with the use of hostages in the contracting process.[59]

Thus, whereas the ex ante transaction costs of the property rights/agency approach consist of those costs associated with drafting, negotiating, and devising safeguards for contracts, the ex post transaction costs emphasized within TCE include maladaption costs (those costs that arise when disturbances expose gaps in long-term contracts that necessitate gap-filling and realignment of the contractual relation, during which time the transaction will likely be maladapted to the environment), certain haggling costs, setup costs for governance structures to effect dispute resolution, and bonding costs that may be necessary to secure credible commitments. Although ex post transaction costs draw attention to the different aspects of the contracting process than do those costs incurred ex ante, it bears keeping in mind that ex ante and ex post transaction costs are interdependent (Williamson 1985, p. 21).

CONCLUSION

Some have suggested that the NIE has skyrocketed in scope and influence over the past three decades and represents one of the most exciting projects

[58] See Goldberg (1976a,b), Macneil (1974), and Williamson (e.g., 1984, 1985, 1991).

[59] This discussion is indicative of another major point of divergence between the property rights/agency and TCE approaches: the property rights/agency literature implicitly or explicitly relies on the ability of courts to resolve any disputes that may arise, whereas TCE emphasizes that parties may choose to establish extrajudicial dispute resolution mechanisms to forestall recourse to litigation. See Klein (1992, p. 159) and Williamson (1985, pp. 26–32).

within law and economics today. Others, such as Richard Posner (1993c), seem to think that the NIE has contributed relatively little on the theoretical front. If Posner is correct, then, as Furubotn and Richter (1998, p. 440) have pointed out, the NIE can hardly represent the sort of paradigm shift that its proponents claim. The resolution of this debate, and of the nature of the NIE's long-term contribution remains to be seen. What is clear, however, is that the Nobel Prizes awarded to Ronald Coase and Douglass North have given this work a degree of validation that has served only to stimulate the expansion of work being done under the banner of the NIE.

CHAPTER 6

Branching Out: New Haven, Modern Civic Republican, and Austrian Approaches

THE FOREGOING discussions of the Chicago school, public choice, Institutional, and New Institutional approaches to law and economics have, we hope, given the reader a good sense for the evolution and current status of thinking about legal-economic issues. In spite of the major contributions that these various movements have made to our understanding of these issues over the better part of the past century, they by no means exhaust the broad tent that is Law and Economics. In this chapter, we present sketches of three additional approaches to Law and Economics that are at once current in the literature and have important commonalities with one or more of the approaches discussed in the previous chapters. These are the New Haven school, Modern Civic Republicanism, and Austrian law and economics. It would not be unfair to say that each of these approaches evidences a healthy respect for what economic thinking has to offer the analysis of legal-economic policy issues but at the same time reflects a "there is more to life than economics" perspective.

THE NEW HAVEN SCHOOL OF LAW AND ECONOMICS

> Both Chicagoans and [New Haven scholars] are
> concerned with the economist's core interest in
> Pareto efficiency and the operation of economic
> incentives, but in combination they provide a more
> balanced view of modern work in political economy
> that bears on the evaluation and reform of legal
> doctrines and institutions.
> *(Susan Rose-Ackerman 1989, p. 251)*

The New Haven school takes as its field of study the entire modern regulatory welfare state and bases its approach on the twin intellectual foundations of public policy analysis and social choice theory.[1] As a consequence, the New Haven view of the task of law and economics is (1) "to define the economic

---

[1] Some contributors to this area of Law and Economics have labeled it "the Legal Reformist school," others call it "the Progressive school," and still others are content with the "New Haven" label. As many of the contributors have (or have had) some affiliation with the Yale law school, we follow Ackerman (1986, pp. 929–30) and Fiss (1986, pp. 7, 15) and opt for the "New Haven

justification for public action," (2) "to analyze political and bureaucratic institutions realistically," and (3) "to define useful roles for the courts within this modern policy-making system" (Rose-Ackerman 1992, p. 3). Proponents of the New Haven view suggest that this approach to law and economics is necessitated by the increasingly prominent role played by the regulatory process and administrative law within the modem welfare state. This legal transformation, they point out, has "forced both judges and legal scholars to reexamine the roles of Congress, the agencies, and the courts" (Rose-Ackerman 1992, p. 8).

The New Haven approach has in common with the Chicago and public choice perspectives a recognition of the important role played by the problem of scarcity in legal-economic problems, as well as of the virtues of the market for allocating resources. At the same time, however, the New Haven school emphasizes the presence of multiple sources of market failure, and that these market failures necessitate some form of government intervention. In maintaining that government intervention can be justified based on existing market failures, they argue that legal-economic policy should work toward the correction of these failures, but with a recognized concern for *both allocative and distributional impacts* (Rose-Ackerman 1992, pp. 6–7, 9). That is, along with efficiency analysis should come a continuing concern for distribution and with that, a concern for *justice and fairness*. Moreover, the market-failure-correcting policies should be set in place based on cost-benefit analysis whenever possible, and this process should include the evaluation of *all* benefits and costs (e.g., lives saved, acres of wilderness preserved, and so on), not just those benefits and costs that can be measured in explicit dollar terms (Rose-Ackerman 1992, pp. 16–17).

The origins of the New Haven school can be traced back to the seminal contributions of Guido Calabresi. Two of his early articles—"Some Thoughts on Risk Distribution and the Law of Torts" (1961) and, with A. Douglas Melamed, "Property Rules, Liability Rules, and Inalienability: One View of the Cathedral" (1972)—are classics in the economic analysis of law. The former article attempts to provide a detailed economic analysis of tort law, focusing on the relationship between rules of liability and the spreading of loss. In 1970 Calabresi followed up this article with his now classic book, *The Cost of Accidents: A Legal and Economic Analysis*, which further developed his 1961 analysis. Here, Calabresi provided an economic analysis of the goals and functions of liability rules and laid the foundation for further explorations into the economics of tort law.[2] In this book, Calabresi argues that the principal aim of rules of liablity for accidents is the reduction of accident costs. Specifically, he contends that this

---

school" label. Some of the works that underline the ideas contained in the New Haven approach to law and economics include Rose-Ackerman (1989, 1992), Ackerman (1984), Ackerman and Stewart (1988), and Sunstein (1990).

[2] The contribution of Shavell (1987) marks a major extension of Calabresi's path-breaking work. Evidence of Calabresi's impact on the theory of tort law is explored in Komesar (1990). See also Hylton (2004).

goal of accident-cost reduction includes (1) the reduction in the number and severity of accidents (which he terms primary accident-cost reduction), (2) reduction in the social costs of accidents (secondary accident-cost reduction), and (3) reduction in the administrative costs associated with accidents (the tertiary or efficiency accident-cost reduction) (Calabresi 1970, pp. 24–31).

The following example will illustrate Calabresi's approach to liability formulation. Let us suppose that legal policymakers have come up with five different liability rules that can help diminish accidents. These liability rules, and their respective impacts, are shown in table 6-1. Each of the five liability rules generates a particular damage award to the victim, with Rule #1 resulting in the lowest damage award and Rule #5 the highest damage award. As a consequence, each of these liability rules induces a different level of precaution on the part of potential injurers.[3] As we move from Rule #1 to Rule #5, the induced level of precaution increases, thereby reducing both the probability of accidents and the expected accident losses.

It should be clear from this example that, either through statutory enactment or the wisdom of efficiency-oriented common law judges, the law of torts ought to embody Rule #3, which is the most efficient (least-cost) rule. Here, total accident costs are minimized at $16. The other liability rules, because of their respective impacts on precaution costs vis-à-vis expected accident losses, generate higher total costs to society than does Rule #3. For example, a move from Rule #3 to Rule #4 will induce potential injurers to spend an additional $4 on precaution while reducing the expected damages by only $3, which is not cost justified. In addition, the adoption and application of Rule #3 in present cases serves as a signal to the rest of society that, in the future, they will be held liable for failure to take the appropriate, cost-justified level of precaution. This signal provides the necessary incentives to induce efficient behavior.

Both here and in a later extension of his argument (Calabresi and Hirschoff 1972, p. 19), Calabresi argues that liability should be placed on the least-cost avoider—that is, on the person who is in the best position to undertake cost-benefit analysis as between accident costs and accident-avoidance costs and act on this information once the relative costs have been determined. That having been said, in both *The Cost of Accidents* and in a subsequent article analyzing four alternative rules of liability (Calabresi and Klevorick 1985), Calabresi concludes that specific remedies can be proffered only after extensive empirical research. The problem, he says, is that the data necessary to make these empirical judgments is very difficult to obtain (Calabresi 1970, p. 14).[4]

---

[3] We are assuming, for simplicity, that the potential victim cannot take precaution here. The example, however, easily generalizes to a situation in which both potential injurer and potential victim can take precaution. See Cooter and Ulen (2004, chs. 8, 9), Posner (1992, ch. 6), and Shavell (2004, chs. 8–12). See also page 130, above.

[4] As Calabresi and Klevorick (1985, p. 626) conclude, "Ultimately, the choice among . . . the [tests/rules] . . . is, as we have repeatedly said, profoundly empirical."

TABLE 6-1

Liability Rules	Individual's Level of Precaution	Cost of Precaution	Accident Probability	Expected Accident Losses	Total Accident Costs
#1	none	$ 0	15%	$20	$20
#2	low	$ 2	11%	$16	$18
#3	moderate	$ 5	7%	$11	$16
#4	high	$ 9	4%	$ 8	$17
#5	extreme	$14	1%	$ 5	$19

This indeterminacy led Izhak Englard (1993, p. 32), for one, to conclude that "Calabresi's economic analysis, for all its sophistication and subtlety, can do no more than demonstrate the relevant considerations . . . concrete solutions still require policy decisions."

Calabresi and Melamed's article on property rules and liability rules actually takes off from Coase's analysis in "The Problem of Social Cost" (1960) to analyze the choice of remedies for resolving disputes over incompatible property uses. In a situation where one party has illegitimately interfered with another party's property (the typical instance of a negative externality) and the assignment of rights, or entitlements, has been determined, the court may choose to protect this entitlement in one of two ways: through an injunction or by mandating the payment of compensatory damages. Calabresi and Melamed argue that, in making the choice between these alternative remedies, the court should base its decision on the ability of the parties to cooperate to resolve the dispute. If there are significant obstacles to bargaining, compensatory damages should be mandated. Alternatively, if transaction costs are perceived to be low and thus there are few obstacles to cooperation, the injunctive remedy is preferable because the parties themselves can (and will) then bargain to the efficient result if the injunctive remedy itself does not directly generate an efficient allocation of resources.[5]

While clearly concerned with the cost-related aspects of tort law, Calabresi's writings have not focused exclusively on efficiency, but, rather, have evidenced a continuing concern for justice and fairness—one of the hallmarks of the New Haven approach. As Calabresi (1970, p. 24) has emphasized, any system of accident law has two principal goals: "First, it must be just or fair; and second, it must reduce the costs of accidents." Calabresi then went on to state that "[n]o system of accident law can operate unless it takes into account which acts are deemed good, which deemed evil, and which deemed neutral. Any system of

---

[5] This insight has been modified, qualified, and extended in more recent work by Polinsky (1979, 1980), Ayres and Talley (1995), and Kaplow and Shavell (1995a,b).

accident law that encourages evil acts will seem unjust to critic and community even if economically it is very efficient indeed" (Calabresi 1970, p. 294). Far from considering distribution outside of the purview of economics, Calabresi has argued forcefully that "lawyer-economists can have a great deal to say, as scholars, about what is distributively desirable." Specifically, he believes that we "can develop scholarly definitions of just distributions, both theoretical definitions and definitions based on empirical studies" (Calabresi 1991, p. 1228). Thus, while Calabresi's analysis certainly impacted the development of Chicago law and economics and its efficiency-oriented approach, the New Haven school's continuing concern for efficiency and distribution, as well as justice and fairness, too, has its origins in the seminal works of Guido Calabresi.

This twin focus on efficiency and justice is worked out within the context of a system that establishes a presumption in favor of individual choice and the use of mechanisms that promote such choices, including the market and the democratic political process. Given this, the New Haven school prefers policy mechanisms that create incentives to influence individual choice. Consequently, they place less emphasis on the use of the common law remedies relied upon so heavily within the Chicago approach to law and economics. They seek a deeper understanding of the interaction between law and potential market incentives. Within the New Haven school, government has a much wider role, including the use of statutes and regulations, and a greater reliance on well-structured government institutions (i.e., an efficient bureaucracy), and on taxes and subsidies along with government-established markets to help remedy pockets of market failure in society.[6] They work to fashion policies that better use the market to achieve regulatory ends with the principal aim of substituting incentive-based regulation for command and control regulation.[7] One particular focus has been to work to create markets in pollution rights and other resources not normally associated with market allocations. For example, the centerpiece of Title IV of the 1990 amendments to the Clean Air Act was the pollution rights trading program for sulfur-dioxide (SO_2) emissions.[8] Also, in the arid and semi-arid West, where most of the senior water rights are held by farmers and irrigation districts, there is a growing trend toward moving these rights from lower- to higher-valued uses by employing water banks—essentially clearinghouses to facilitate water transfers. This can occur via temporary, short-term leases, options to purchase during dry periods, or one-time purchases through the water banks.[9] We

---

[6] Hanson and Logue (1998), in engaging the debates over smoking policy, have proposed an ex post incentive-based regime to regulate smoking—a system of enterprise liability that holds manufacturers liable for all the harms caused by their products.

[7] Generally see Tietenberg (2003) and Sterner (2003, ch. 8); also see Rose-Ackerman (1992); Ayres and Braithwaite (1992). On the distinction between economic and incentives versus command and control, see Harrington and Morgenstern (2004).

[8] See Burtraw (1996).

[9] See Frederick (1998).

have also witnessed widespread wetland mitigation banking that serves to make possible the off-site wetland creation, enhancement, and restoration for the expressed purpose of mitigating unavoidable adverse wetland losses in advance of development. This is accomplished through the sale of mitigation credits to permit applicants who are seeking off-site mitigation to offset on-site development activities.[10] Finally we have seen the emergence of rights-based fishing with the assignment of individual, transferable quotas to fish particular stocks of fish.[11]

The market, here, becomes a vehicle for the implementation of policies that efficiently achieve certain regulatory aims that serve to increase social welfare, broadly defined. Because of this, they emphasize the importance of studying the operations of governmental institutions and the use of the tools of public policy analysis and social choice analysis—always with an eye on both allocative and distributional impacts—in the search for solutions to legal-economic problems (Rose-Ackerman 1992, p. 6).

From a normative perspective, New Haven scholars take the position that once one truly understands the *functional* role of government, the modern regulatory system is revealed as superior not only to more highly collectivist alternatives, but also to its common law predecessor. In fact, it is argued that in many contexts "the problem is one of too little rather than too much regulation" (Sunstein 1990, pp. 227–33). The goal, then, from the New Haven perspective, "is a reformed administrative law that will incorporate a richer range of both empirical and theoretical concerns and will respond more effectively to the needs of public officials, politicians, and private citizens" (Rose-Ackerman 1992, p. 8).

The New Haven school's emphasis on the study of all aspects of the governmental policy process necessitates a model of governmental behavior, and the model used here is that of the rational actor. This rational actor model has certain commonalities with the various other schools of thought explored in this book, and New Haven is strongly committed to the view that, in a positive sense, there is much to learn from Chicago and from public choice. What is absent from the New Haven approach, however, is the normative presumption favoring the status quo distribution of wealth and property and the conservative ideological element often attributed to the public choice and Chicago approaches to law and economics. Rather, the proponents of the New Haven approach "recognize that the existing distribution of property rights [and hence wealth] is highly contingent and lacks strong normative justification" (Rose-Ackerman 1992, p. 6). They argue that policy analysts should endeavor to determine the various available policy options in dealing with situations of market failure, and that they should do so without privileging the status quo, as in the case of public choice, and without a presumption in favor

---

[10] See Dennison and Schmid (1997).
[11] See De Alessi (1998).

of common law resolutions, as in the case of the Chicago school (Rose-Ackerman 1992, pp. 3, 16).[12]

The New Haven School at Work

The dichotomy between the Chicago emphasis on the efficacy and efficiency of the common law and the New Haven emphasis on a more broadly based policy-making approach to law and economics is nicely illustrated within the realm of torts. Whereas the Chicago school promotes the design of least-cost-avoider rules to promote efficient common law remedies for dealing with situations of harmful effects, the New Haven approach emphasizes a much greater reliance on statutes to address these situations. Under the New Haven approach, the role of the common law should be narrowly defined and channeled to "augment regulatory enforcement" and to deal with "situations that would be poorly resolved by broad-based regulations" (Rose-Ackerman 1992, p. 131).

As evidence for this point, Steven Shavell (1987, pp. 277–90) suggests several advantages that attend a statute-based system: (i) statutes are preferable when harms are diffused through the population, creating reduced incentives for individuals to sue and high costs of organizing for group lawsuits; (ii) statutes can provide deterrence in situations where those causing the harm lack sufficient resources to pay for the harm caused and who will thus not be strongly deterred by ex post common law compensation systems; (iii) ex ante statutes get around the problem of demonstrating causation that often affects tort cases; (iv) when various injury situations have similar benefit-cost effects, statutes can impose uniform rules on similarly situated injurers, thereby avoiding the need to adjudicate many individual cases; (v) there are many situations where the costs of administering a statutory system are lower than the costs of administering a tort system.[13] Expanding on this theme, Susan Rose-Ackerman (1992, p. 121) suggests that toxic torts, products liability, and medical malpractice are especially suited for statutory control. Such statutes, it is argued, should take the form of ex ante incentive schemes, whereby firms respond to the cost of damages set forth in the statute. In such situations, the law of tort should submit to the greater authority of the statute and courts should be content with (i) adjudicating disputes over gaps in statutes and (ii) resolving situations where statutes have not yet been enacted or are not feasible given the idiosyncratic nature of tortuous acts (Rose-Ackerman 1992, pp. 128–313).

---

[12] Rose-Ackerman (1992, p. 20) calls the Chicago approach to law and economics "deeply flawed" as "a comprehensive view of the relationship of law to economic analysis." More generally, see Rose-Ackerman (1992, chapter 2).

[13] See also Rose-Ackerman (1992, pp. 120–21).

MODERN CIVIC REPUBLICANISM

[Advocates of modern civic republicanism] argue
that the constitution provides the framework for
an organic community composed of socially
constructed individuals, who join together in
government to identify and pursue civic virtue.
(Gey 1993, p. 806)

Many public choice scholars contend that their analysis is not at all driven by
cynicism, but merely by the desire to describe dispassionately the operation of
the political process, to present a coherent theory of government failure to parallel the more prevalent theory of market failure, and to provide an economic
analysis of the mechanisms of government for combining private preferences
into social decisions.[14] Daniel A. Farber and Philip P. Frickey, in contrast, argue
that the core of the economic models of public choice maintain a rather jaundiced view of the motivation of legislators and bureaucrats (1991, pp. 2, 22).
The antithesis of the public choice portrayal of government is provided by what
has come to be known as "modern civic republicanism."[15] Civic republicanism,
as Kathryn Abrams (1988, p. 1591) recounts, was a collectivist strain of American politics and was a major focus of concern for historians in the 1960s.
Later, in the early 1980s, it became an alternative to Rawlsian liberalism. Then,
in the mid-1980s, legal scholars appropriated the core ideas culminating in
what today is known as the modern civic republicanism. Simply stated, it is a
philosophy of government and politics that places great value on communal political life and a collective, deliberative dialogue that articulates and forms
shared values.[16] As should become evident, in many respects, proponents of
civic republicanism are more closely aligned with the work of the New Haven
school of law and economics and, accordingly, are at odds with many of the
core ideas of the Virginia and Chicago strands of public choice theory.

---

[14] This characterization is set forth in the various contributions to the "Symposium on the Theory of Public Choice," *Virginia Law Review* (March 1988). For example, see the contributions by
Geoffrey Brennan and James M. Buchanan, Dwight R. Lee, and, especially, the critical analysis of
public choice theory by Mark Kelman.

[15] This synoptic review of modern civic republicanism borrows heavily from Farber and Frickey
(1991, pp. 42–47) and the several contributions to the "Symposium: The Republican Civic Tradition," *Yale Law Journal* (July 1988); see especially the contributions by Michelman (1988) and
Sunstein (1988). Elsewhere, see also Fallon (1989), Michelman (1986), and Sunstein (1990).

[16] Epstein (1988, pp. 1634–35) points out that theories within the republican tradition, in all of
their early forms, "shared the common premise that governance was the collective responsibility
of the people who were governed [either directly or through their representatives]" and "stood in
opposition to other forms of democratic and constitutional theory, such as Lockean natural rights
and social contract theory." As Gey (1993, p. 805) reminds us, however, "Modern civic republicans disagree among themselves about basic issues, such as the identity of their historical predecessors and the relationship of civic republicanism to traditional liberalism."

Modern civic republicanism provides an alternative normative scheme to modern liberalism, interest group pluralism, and the rational maximizing models of the Chicago approach to law and economics and public choice theory. It is an alternative vision of public decision-making—a version of democratic self-governance, combined with an aspiration for collective decision-making—that goes beyond the mere aggregation of individuals' preferences into some vector of public decision-making (Mashaw 1988, p. 1685). Its focus is on the nature and the character of the collective political process in the context of representative government and is best viewed as "a constellation of beliefs centering around (i) the existence and legitimacy of public values and the common good, (ii) the use of citizen deliberation as the principal democratic decision-making tool, and (iii) the state's legitimate role in fostering civic virtue among its citizens" (Poisner 1996, p. 56). From the vantage point of Law and Economics, modern civic republicanism represents yet another perspective on the role of the state in determining the allocation of society's scarce resources—one with clear and direct economic implications. If it were to be adopted as the preferred public-choice method for answering the question, "In what direction shall we change the law?" it would result in an allocation of resources that would likely be substantially different from the allocative and distributional outcomes resulting from public choice catallatics or any of the other means of social control discussed in this book.

The underpinnings of modern civic republicanism lie in the corpus of ideas popularized by James Madison in his revision of classical republican thought.[17] The American Revolution, ultimately, was a struggle against centralized government authority, and the antifederalists stood fast in their support of the classical republican position. In particular, they argued for small political units in which citizens would participate actively in government decision-making, which they viewed as a continuous process of collective self-definition and direct self-governance. The antifederalists argued against a national system of government with remote national representatives, believing that such a structure of government would undermine the very principles fought for in the Revolution. Madison's revision of classical republican thought was based on the evidence that in a large country, the classical republican belief in small-scale democracy—a system of direct, active citizen participation—was unworkable and unrealistic. His primary concern with the classical republican thought was that, in practice, it gave rise to opportunistic behavior and promoted factional warfare over a wide variety of public policies. As a consequence, Madison's version of republicanism included the idea of a large republic with comparatively well-insulated representatives in the belief that, with a large enough republic, political factions would be so numerous

---

[17] This brief historical account of Madison's revisions to classical republican thought is from Sunstein (1990, pp. 12–18). For a more detailed account see Appleby (1978) and Wood (1972).

that they would tend to hold each other in check. That is, in the view of Madison, the well-insulated representatives would be able to escape the pressures of powerful political factions and, instead, concentrate on the deliberative tasks of politics and thereby promote the common good.

Of course, as a backdrop to this debate, the advocates of liberalism were ever present and, in many respects, stood in direct opposition against those who advocated for either form of republicanism. The basic tenets of the liberals' position included such things as protection from the government, taking the existing preferences and prevailing entitlements as exogenous to politics, having little regard for political and economic equality, and protecting individual self-interest. As recounted by Epstein (1988, p. 1566), while the republican principles had dominated in the period of time leading up to the framing of the U.S. Constitution, during the framing period, a conflict emerged between liberalism and republicanism, and, as history has recorded, liberalism won out.[18] This was largely manifested in the original Constitution leading Sunstein (1990, p. 17) to observe, "In these respects, the original constitutional rights were 'negative' in character—rights to be free from governmental intrusion, rather than rights to affirmative governmental assistance."

Modern civic republicanism tries to distinguish itself from liberalism (for historical reasons) as well as from the modern conception of interest group pluralism (and hence from the public choice theory of government). Within interest group pluralism, individuals—cognizant of their original endowments, the costs of transacting, and the costs of political defeat as well as the benefits of political victory—are seen to bring their own set of arbitrary, external, and (relatively) unalterable preferences to the political marketplace and to engage in those "deals" that leave them better off (Epstein 1988, p. 1637). For the pluralists, "The common good amounts to an aggregation of individual preferences" (Sunstein 1985, p. 32–33). From the vantage point of modern civic republicanism, however, the pluralists' conception of the common good is inadequate. It is a view of the political, choice-making process that generates a political outcome that is nothing more than one of many possible transitory political outcomes or choices, each reflecting individual preferences and the current conditions and power relationships within society. Thus, they believe pluralism is inherently flawed by virtue of its tendency to equate the "public interest" with the arbitrary outcome dictated by self-interested aggregated preferences, where the pre-political wealth endowments, initial entitlements, and preference formation are ignored but nonetheless controlling. For advocates of modern civic republicanism, it is (i) the pre-choice environment, (ii) the methods by which consensus is articulated and reached, and (iii) the

---

[18] West (1990, p. 60–61) writes, "Modern civic republicanism rests on a synthesis of aspects of the classical republicanism partly embraced but largely rejected by the drafters of the Constitution with some of the pluralistic values and traditions of modern liberalism."

nature of the final outcome that are all of great significance in the making of public choices—factors largely ignored by the pluralists. With these underpinnings, modern civic republicanism places much faith in a normative approach to public decision-making that appeals to norms broader than individual private interests; its emphasis is on the belief of shared values together with the possibility of identifying a common good.[19] As such, it envisions a public arena in which decisions are made in the legislature through principled deliberation and reasoned dialogue by individuals who think rationally and who are capable of abstracting from their private position and experiences.[20]

In Sunstein's formulation, modern civic republicanism is characterized by commitments to four central principles all of which channel into civic virtue.[21] Civic virtue is the centerpiece of the republican conception of government; it is its animating principle. In this context, virtue is defined by the political process of dialogue and ultimate agreement over fundamental collective goals and aspirations (Gey 1993, p. 807). As a consequence, one of the primary functions of government is to help order values and to define virtue, and thereby educate its citizenry to be virtuous (Sherry 1986, p 552). The four central principles are

- *Deliberation* in politics is made possible by civic virtue. Within deliberation, private interests, although relevant inputs into politics, are neither pre-political nor exogenous to the decision-making process; they are the object of critical scrutiny. Whatever concept of virtue a citizen develops outside his or her political involvement, it should be left at the door when that citizen enters the government's chambers of deliberation. That is, "prepolitical differences are an inadmissible basis for resolution of political controversy; and so modern civic republicanism depend[s] on an expectation that citizens should entirely abandon their private identities when they come to politics" (Sunstein 1988, p. 1564). It is the subsequent republican dialogue among citizens that will channel the thoughts, attitudes, and behavior of every individual within society; ultimately produce a set of definitive principles for society; and thereby guide every other subsequent decision to be made by the collective political body. The approach "require[s] public regarding justifications offered after multiple points of view have been consulted and (to the extent possible) genuinely understood" (Sunstein 1988, p. 1575). Given a measure of distance from prevailing issues and practices, the preferences of political actors are revisable in light of the collec-

---

[19] As Epstein (1988, p. 1637) points out, modern civic republicanism has a difficult time claiming to be a positive, descriptive undertaking: "As a descriptive matter, there is abundant evidence that all too often politics is just the way the pluralists describe it: ceaseless compromises between competing factions none of which would pay a nickel to advance the common good, even if they could identify it."

[20] This point is made by both Fitts (1988, p. 1651) and Bell and Bansal (1988, p. 1610).

[21] These four principles are fully defined in Sunstein (1988, pp. 1541–42, 1547–58).

tive discussion and debate. In short, the deliberative process has a transformative dimension. The requirement of deliberation is designed to ensure that political outcomes will be supported by reference to consensus among political equals. In other words, the political dialogue will produce—and then encourage and cultivate—civic virtue (Gey 1993, p. 808).

- Modern civic republicanism includes an *equality* among political actors together with a commitment to eliminate disparities in political participation and to reduce asymmetrical influence among individuals or social groups. In addition, for many advocates of the modern civic republican tradition, there is a clear nexus between economic equality and republicanism, where the former is a necessary condition for the latter. The essential point here is that if people are to come together in the deliberative process (as described earlier) with a sense of civic virtue, then, to the extent possible, they should come as equals with respect to access, influence, and distribution of wealth and property.

- Modern civic republicanism also includes *universalism,* which embodies the belief in the possibility of mediating different approaches to politics or different conceptions of the public good through deliberation, dialogue, and discussion. As such, universalism is a regulative ideal—not so much to provide a voice for non-elites, but to maximize the impersonality of government. Under the principle of universalism, political outcomes are not limited to Pareto-better improvements based on exogenous preferences and practices but are instead the outcome of mediation based on practical reasoning that yields outcomes that are substantively correct and reflect the common good. Thus, decisions that advance the common good or the public interest are the product of a deliberative process; solutions do not exist independently waiting to be discovered by the process. Further, they gain their legitimacy as expressions of the common good in the sense that they are grounded in values that people pursue, not individually, but as a community.

- Finally, modern civic republicanism includes *citizenship*—the mechanism to institutionalize citizen control over its political institutions with a commitment to decentralization. The element of citizenship also constitutes the vehicle for citizens to inculcate in other members a sense of community, a sense of empathy, and a commitment to virtue. With these components of citizenship established as foundational beliefs, the subsequent deliberative process is both functional and instrumental. That is, citizenship includes the broad guarantee of rights of participation, a participation that is both functional (e.g., monitors the behavior of representatives and their decisions) and instrumental (e.g., a vehicle for inculcating empathy, virtue, and other feelings of community and citizenship). It seeks to have citizen control over national institutions and promotes local control through decentralization and self-determination.

Taken together, these four principles reflect the basic philosophy of modern civic republicanism for promoting a public-regarding dialogue among political

actors and the common good derived therefrom. In the context of Law and Economics and in response to questions as to the direction in which we should change the law, modern civic republicanism suggests that the law should be changed when such change is supported by argument and reason—where argument and reason operate under the banner of civic virtue and with an eye on the common good, rather than being the exclusive outcome of the sort of self-interested dealing reflected in the public choice approach (Sunstein 1988, p. 1544).

In modern civic republicanism, political participants are seen to subordinate their private interests to the public and common good in *and* through the ongoing process of collective self-determination. Because the collective social environment inevitably shapes the individuals residing within it, social interactions of every sort mold individuals. Furthermore, if the social shaping of the individual is inevitable, the political deliberative process should be designed in such a way to ensure that the shaping is done correctly. Republicanism views politics as a distinct—and in many respects a superior—sphere as compared with the private sector ordering of life. For modern civic republicanism, political life goes well beyond the use of government to further the ends of private life (an underlying tenet of liberalism); a citizen's participation in political life enables him to work to further a common enterprise and thereby rise above the mere private concerns of the private sector.

In modern civic republicanism, the role of government is, in part, to serve as a creative force; it is both a moral teacher and a reflection of public opinion. Government is the arena in which individual preferences (those held so sacrosanct in public choice theory) are formed and reformed in the ongoing public-spirited debate and dialogue that goes toward determining which public policies fall within the domain of the common good. Existing desires are revisable in light of collective discussion and debate over relevant information and alternative perspectives. Republicanism does not require a romantic dissolution of political differences and disagreements. Indeed, political differences and disagreements form the very basis of the political dialogue, and hence constitute a creative and educational force. Frank I. Michelman (1979, p. 509) concurs, observing that "[p]olitics must be a joint and mutual search for good or right answers to the question of directions for our evolving selves." As the informed debate moves forward, preferences take shape, and individuals, now armed with an understanding of the greater good that is being sought, subordinate their own private interests and accordingly discipline their own private pursuits so as to realize the greater common good. As Epstein (1988, p. 1637) puts it, in modern civic republicanism, "politics offers a calling in which we can find the highest expression of individual self worth and respect. Politics becomes a noble undertaking."

Modern Civic Republicanism at Work

Sunstein's application of civic republican thinking to the *Lochner* era serves as a useful illustration of the modern civic republican approach.[22] The *Lochner* era was a period in time from 1905 through the early 1930s when the judiciary relied heavily upon the due process clause of the Constitution to invalidate what were held to be unduly restrictive (and hence arbitrary and capricious) economic regulations. In *Lochner* v. *New York,* the U.S. Supreme Court struck down a New York State statute that set a maximum number of working hours for confectionery and bakery workers at ten hours per day or sixty hours per week. The Supreme Court held that the statute violated the due process clause of the Fourteenth Amendment and stated, "The [legislative] act must have a . . . direct relation, as a means to an end, and the end itself must be appropriate and legitimate, before an act can be held to be valid which interferes with the general right of an individual to be free in his person and in his power to contract in relation to his own labor" *(Lochner* v. *New York,* at 57–58).

In reviewing the *Lochner* era from the vantage point of modern civic republicanism, Sunstein argues that the court's positing of the existence of a natural and pre-political private sphere served as a brake on economic legislation.[23] Modern civic republicanism is skeptical of judicial approaches to law and politics that rely on rights that are said to antedate legal and political deliberation. Thus, the underlying problem with the decision by the *Lochner* court was that it relied on self-described, status quo, common law baselines. Sunstein argues that the values supporting such classifications are the product of social power; they must be subject to political and legal scrutiny and review. Accordingly, the court in adopting its position in *Lochner* ignores the constitutive functions of law and therefore the ways in which existing practices are dependent on past and present choices of the legal system.

In Law and Economics, both the development of law and the underlying principles from which that law emerges remain at issue. The deliberative nature of modern civic republicanism remains an alternative to the interest group pluralism inherent in the Chicago and Virginia variants of public choice theory. It should be evident by now that governance under modern civic republicanism would be substantially different than under public choice theory (in any of its variations); these are two very different systems of social control in direct conflict with one another, and this conflict is well illustrated in the comparison made between the two approaches by Farber and Frickey:

[22] A era of time associated with the case *Lochner* v. *New York,* 198 U.S. 45 (1905).

[23] As a case study, this section borrows heavily directly from Sunstein's (1988, pp. 1579–80) discussion of the *Lochner* era.

[W]here public choice theory risks cynicism, republicanism can verge danger-
ously close on romanticism. . . . Where public choice theorists find voter turnout
inexplicable, republicans find it a paradigm case of civic virtue. Where public
choice theorists see self-interest behind every statute, republicans hope to find a
quest for the public good. And where public choice theorists see haphazard cycling and strategic behavior, republicans discern the possibility of genuine political dialogue. (Farber and Frickey 1991, p. 45)

It remains to be seen whether the future will bring a theory that integrates the
best that each of these approaches has to offer.

THE AUSTRIAN APPROACH TO LAW AND ECONOMICS

[The] Austrian framework for understanding and
evaluating the legal process . . . could be applied to
explain social behavior in a number of contexts
at least as well as does the neoclassical paradigm
and, in addition, may help to identify and trace the
effects of significant factors that the neoclassical
framework is unable to recognize.
(Gregory Scott Crespi 1998, pp. 373–74)

The Austrian approach to law and economics, as its name suggests, derives
from the work of the Austrian school of economics. The Austrian school's
genesis is in the work of Carl Menger, one of the principals in the marginal
revolution that, in time, gave rise to neoclassical economics.[24] Menger's analysis received further development at the hands of his two most prominent disciples, Eugen von Böhm-Bawerk and Friedrich von Weiser. The 1920s and
1930s saw a new generation of scholars move to the forefront, including Ludwig von Mises, Friedrich von Hayek (he received the Nobel Prize in economics in 1974), Hans Mayer, Fritz Machlup, and Gottfried Haberler. Based on
their contributions, the idea of a distinctive "Austrian approach" was solidified,
and its scope extended across the field of economics. The Keynesian revolution
in the middle third of the twentieth century, however, pushed the Austrian approach into the background. The Cambridge school's focus on economic management, of which Keynesian macroeconomics was a centerpiece, and the attractiveness of aggregate demand management tools for policymakers were all
but irresistible.

The stagflation of the 1970s presented a set of problems that Keynesian
economics could not explain or resolve, and the resulting discredit opened the

---

[24] See, for example, Menger's *Grundsatze der Volkswirtschaftslehre* (1871), translated into English as *Principles of Economics* (1976, reprinted in 1981).

door for both new approaches and a reexamination of the old. Austrian economics reemerged as something of a force, particularly in the hands of its most prominent exponents, Israel Kirzner and Murray Rothbard. New York University and George Mason University, along with the Ludwig von Mises Institute at Auburn University, became centers of Austrian scholarship and discourse, and a publishing program of journals and book series provided both an outlet for this scholarship and a vehicle for publicizing the Austrian approach.[25]

The Austrian approach has features in common with the Chicago school, public choice, Institutionalism, and the New Institutional Economics.[26] Austrian economics, like its neoclassical cousin, employs simplified theoretical models that abstract from significant features of real-world social phenomena for the sake of analytical tractability. Each tends to ground its models in methodological individualism, taking the individual, rather than the collective, as the basic unit of analysis and viewing collectives as more or less the summation of individual actors. These individual agents are viewed as responding rationally to the presence of scarcity, using their knowledge and the information that becomes available to make choices that they believe will best facilitate their goals. This choice activity takes place within the context of a system in which relative prices continuously adjust so as to coordinate economic activity.

There are also, however, important differences between the Austrian and neoclassical approaches, and here the Austrians find some common ground with the various other approaches to Law and Economics surveyed in this volume. From the standpoint of individual behavior, the Austrians see preferences as endogenous and malleable, as against the traditional neoclassical assumption that preferences are fixed and exogenously given. Second, Austrians have long emphasized the pervasiveness of uncertainty and imperfect information, and the associated inevitable limits on human knowledge. Disequilibrium is an ignorance-driven phenomena, but this ignorance gives rise to opportunities for gain that can be exploited by entrepreneurial agents. This entrepreneurial activity, in turn, generates knowledge, technology, and products that push the market in new directions. This has important implications both for the predictability of individual choices (and thus econometric estimation) and for policy analysis and efficiency-related judgments—about which more later. Third, the Austrian approach emphasizes the importance of social and legal institutions—from habits and social norms to legal rules—in structuring the market process. In contrast to the a-institutional nature of neoclassical economics, the Austrians emphasize both the contingency of outcomes on the

---

[25] The journals in the field include the *Review of Austrian Economics, Quarterly Journal of Austrian Economics*, and *Advances in Austrian Economics*.

[26] See, for example, Teijl and Holzhauer (1995).

institutional setting and the unsettled, evolving nature of the institutional framework.

While both Austrian and neoclassical models abstract from significant elements of economic reality, "realism" receives more attention within the Austrian tradition than it does in neoclassical economics, where analytical tractability and the ability to derive policy "predictions" (in a theoretical sense) have a much more prominent methodological place. The Austrian approach thus tends to evidence greater realism in assumptions and more complex theoretical constructs. This makes the Austrian approach less reductionistic than the neoclassical, as a result of which the Austrians end up (almost of necessity in many instances) eschewing mathematical techniques and approaches.

Austrian economics sees the individual choice process as occurring in a dynamic, intertemporal setting in which events can change preferences or relative desires arising from preferences. As such, the passage of time makes the choice process something of an evolving and less-than-stable phenomenon—giving rise to, among other things, the preference endogeneity and uncertainty problems mentioned previously. This, in turn, makes the concept of a stable and determinate equilibria of neoclassical economics a pipe dream from an Austrian perspective. Indeed, the debate on this score among the Austrians is over whether equilibrium, as a conceptual construct, is in any way useful. The focus, then, is on the processes engendered by the operation of the market, rather than the set of prices and quantities associated with an equilibrium outcome.

The issue of the passage of time bears heavily on the Austrian approach to social institutions, such as law, habits, and the market, which focuses not just on their influence but also on the processes associated with their emergence and evolution. Central here is the concept of *spontaneous order,* which, in a nutshell, says that institutions evolve through, and can only be explained in terms of, individual human action, rather than any sort of collective process of organization, design, or planning.[27] Some of these consequences are completely unintended, others only partially so. In the case of the market, "[t]he spontaneous order results from individuals adapting themselves to circumstances they perceive in the market. Prices send signals to producers and consumers, who in turn interpret this information and use it to guide their actions. It is unnecessary and impossible for any person to know or understand the full complexity of the extended order" (Schwartzstein 1992, p. 1128).

Legal rules, too, are said to evolve in a spontaneous manner rather than from the conscious planning of governmental entities, such as legislatures, bu-

---

[27] Ebeling (1991, p. 33) goes so far as to say that "it is only through the emergence and existence of such unplanned or 'spontaneous' institutions that a society of great economic and cultural complexity can be maintained, because only such institutions are able to integrate and use more knowledge than any social engineer could ever hope to either master . . . or successfully apply."

reaucrats, and courts. Often, this involves the evolution of legal rules out of customs and practices commonplace in society. This is not to say that judges and legislators have no law-making role to play; in fact, the evolution of social-economic activity exposes gaps in existing rules, and judges and legislators must sometimes act to fill these gaps. Hayek argues, however, that "the judge [is not] free to pronounce any rule he likes"; rather, "[t]he rules which he pronounces will have to fill a definite gap in the body of already recognized rules in a manner that will serve to maintain and improve that order of actions which the already existing rules make possible (Hayek 1973, vol. 1, p. 100).

These institutions, be they habits, customs, or legal rules, are all aspects of the response of agents to the pervasive nature of uncertainty and need for means to deal with it in the social sphere. For example, Linda Schwartzstein points out that in this sense the Austrian approach to law and economics resonates particularly well with the law of contracts, where the legal process revolves around the "attempt to determine what the intentions of the parties were, to provide legal rules which approximate these intentions, and provide remedies to respond to situations where unanticipated events or unintended consequences frustrate the purposeful action of the parties to the contract" (Schwartzstein 1992, p. 1130). More generally, *all* of these institutional structures assist in the coordination of activity among agents and do so in a way that substitutes regularity for uncertainty—but only to a limited extent. Because of this, says Schwartzstein (1992, p. 1131),

> The Austrian view of legal institutions takes into account the richness and complexity of society. Law is seen as a dynamic institution, and legal rules can be seen in that context. . . . Austrians recognize that preferences are being formed and reformed constantly. People often have inconsistent preferences that are competing with one another and which have to find a resolution. Economics and law are part of a creative, ongoing process, in which new discoveries are always being made.

Like the Institutionalists, the Austrians view the neoclassical emphasis on efficiency as both misguided and unworkable. Given that preferences and institutions are endogenous, changes in law can alter them. As such, "It is meaningless . . . to attempt to assess the consequences of a policy alteration with any yardsticks of 'efficiency' that are based upon the original institutional structure" (Crespi 1998, p. 331). That the Austrians consider costs to be purely subjective only adds to the problem of tallying up benefits and costs to make efficiency-based judgments. Beyond this, the pervasiveness of information problems in the economy make it impossible for government to make informed policy judgments. These information problems were at the heart of the Austrian critique of socialism during the great "socialist calculation debate" in economics in the 1930s, but they are said by the Austrians to apply every bit as much to "fine tuning" on the policy front as to wholesale planning. Within the

Austrian system, prices are considered the primary mechanism for the dispersal of knowledge, and it is these prices that provide the information regarding entrepreneurial opportunities that drive economic growth.

An example of the effects of these problems of information and knowledge can be found in the analysis of externalities within the Austrian tradition. Gregory Scott Crespi (1998, p. 351), drawing on the work of Roy Cordato, sketches the problem in a way that clearly indicates the distinctions between the Austrian approach and its neoclassical counterpart:

> [T]he existence of negative externalities is a non-problem if property rights are well defined. Those persons adversely affected by an individual's exercise of his property rights are free to contract with him in the market to have him cease or alter his behavior. If they choose not to do so, then they have simply foregone one of their market options. The fact that their failure to do so may be because of high transaction costs rather than costs of another sort is of no particular significance, and does not justify government intervention, even if the government has access to accurate information concerning the size and distribution of these transaction costs, which is most unlikely to be the case.[28]

Crespi describes Cordato's rationale for this as follows:

> [F]rom an Austrian perspective, one simply cannot infer from a person's failure to participate in a market transaction the basis for that refusal. Since it can never be determined that a contractual arrangement that would have internalized external [costs] would have occurred, but for transaction costs, Cordato concludes that it is improper for the government to act on that unfounded assumption. (p. 352)[29]

These same concerns lead many Austrians to take issue with the Coasian/ Chicago approach to property rights. It should be obvious by now that, from an Austrian perspective, the wealth-maximization approach to rights determination is rendered impossible because of information problems. But there is more to it than this. From an Austrian perspective, the issue is who had the rights in the first place—that is, before the dispute arose. The holder of this prior right, it is argued, should prevail in a property dispute. This jives nicely with the Austrian emphasis on stability in rights structures to facilitate planning, but it is also imbued by the Austrians with a degree of moral authority that is absent from the Chicago method.[30]

A good example of the problematics of efficiency and its implications in Austrian law and economics can be found in Mario Rizzo's discussion of tort law.[31]

---

[28] See Cordato (1992, pp. 16–23).

[29] Cordato uses this argument to argue against the transaction-costs case for government provision of public goods as well (1992, pp. 23–27).

[30] See Cordato (1992, pp. 92–110).

[31] See, for example, Rizzo (1980a,b, 1982).

Consider the Hand formula for determining negligence, discussed in chapter 2, which says that cost-justified precautions are those for which the cost of undertaking precaution is less than the expected damages—given by the damages expected to result from an accident, weighted by probability of an accident occurring if no precaution is taken. From an Austrian perspective, this presents a host of problems—in particular, regarding the abilities of the individuals who could take precaution to estimate costs and probabilities to make a judgment as to its appropriateness of precaution, and the ability of judges to do likewise in adjudicating cases. Because of these information-related problems, Rizzo argues that the standard of liability tort should be strict liability, rather than negligence. The virtue of strict liability here is that, by making the person who could have prevented the accident strictly liable for all harm caused, problems related to information and calculation are removed from the problem. This enhances the ability of agents to plan for the potential consequences of their conduct and thereby eases the burden of the tort system on individuals and the courts. The reader will note that this is consistent with Cordato's description of social efficiency and its implications—as Cordato himself notes (1989, pp. 241–242).

But if not efficiency, then what? The Austrian benchmark for normative analysis is the facilitation of the market process. In particular, the concern is with the impact of governmental policy actions on the individual's ability to recognize and freedom to act upon entrepreneurial opportunities or otherwise facilitate the satisfaction of preferences under the aegis of a social process— the market—that Austrians believe is best suited for these actions. Cordato uses the terms "social efficiency" and "catallactic efficiency" to describe the goal of legal economic policy.[32] As he has put it, "[T]he efficiency of the economic system is judged by the extent to which it encourages individuals to pursue their own goals efficiently" (1989, p. 239).[33] The legal system, in turn, can facilitate this via "legal institutions that minimize conflicts in the use of resources and allow the economic system to maximize the dissemination of knowledge" (Cordato 1989, p. 239). From a normative perspective, Cordato argues that this is best accomplished via fully specified property rights and free markets. Taken together, they facilitate the dissemination of information in the broadest possible fashion and provide the sort of certainty and stability that facilitate planning by economic agents (Cordato 1989, pp. 239–41). By minimizing the conflicts associated with resource acquisition and use, they also facilitate individuals gathering the necessary physical resources to pursue their activities.

---

[32] Cordato supplanted the second term with the first in his *Welfare Economics and Externalities in an Open-Ended Universe: A Modern Austrian Perspective* (1992).

[33] Schwartzstein says that the normative standard should be reducing uncertainty while accommodating change (1994, p. 1068).

Austrian Law and Economics at Work

The endogeneity of the legal system becomes quite obvious in examining the link between entrepreneurialism and the law: the law defines the possibilities and limits of individual actions; changing circumstances give rise to new opportunities that at times can be realized only through an alteration of relative rights; entrepreneurs then attempt to use the legal system to accomplish such changes to facilitate their larger aims. Given the process-oriented view of the market held by the Austrians, market activity will regularly give rise to these opportunities, which, in turn makes law a very fluid and dynamic institution. Given that evolution of legal rules can feed back into preference formation and alteration, the end result is a highly complex, interactive, and unpredictable dance among components of the social system.[34]

Schwartzstein (1994) offers a model that seemingly combines elements of our earlier discussions of the efficiency of the common law and rent seeking. She posits lawyers as entrepreneurs who operate in markets—courts—in which judges are the audience or customers for their products. These products consist of novel arguments or interpretations of legal rules that further the interests of their clients, and the entrepreneurial activity thus consists both of devising these arguments and interpretations and convincing judges to adopt them as law. The lawyers, then, can win fame and fortune through the reputation effects so created, via the first-mover advantage that this confers over rival attorneys. The attempts by rivals to copy these strategies and employ them in their own cases facilitates the spread of these new legal rules, potentially triggers further innovations by the new entrants, and eventually dissipates the entrepreneurial advantage of the first-mover.

Judges, here, are not simply passive receivers of these novel legal arguments made by lawyer-entrepreneurs. Rather, the judges, too play an entrepreneurial role in that, by creating new law via the acceptance and application of the novel arguments made by the lawyer-entrepreneurs, the judges increase their own position within the legal community, so long, at least, as they are not seen as making outrageous decisions simply for the sake of novelty. In this latter sense, then, the judges are somewhat more restricted than attorneys in their ability to carry on in entrepreneurial fashion: they need to pay some attention to precedent while, at the same time, remaining open to novel arguments. The lawyer-entrepreneurs, then, are the force for change within the legal system, while the courts apply the discipline of the market to the lawyer-entrepreneurs by rejecting many of the novel arguments that the lawyers offer at trial and, in the process. This at once tempers what one might call frivolous entrepreneurial activity to some extent and facilitates a degree of stability and certainty within the legal process.

[34] See, for example, Crespi (1998, pp. 337–38).

The reader might recognize in this shades of the efficiency theory of the common law—in particular, that approach to it that says inefficient rules will be litigated more extensively than efficient rules and, via that litigation, will eventually evolve in an efficient direction. The Austrians, however, reject the efficiency of the common law thesis out of hand. While individuals litigate in the attempt to exploit opportunities for gain, judges do not have sufficient information to guide common law rules in the direction of efficiency, nor do economists and lawyers have the information necessary to make ex post (or ex ante) judgments as to the efficiency of legal outcomes. In this sense, the traditional economic approach to these issues overestimates the informational and computational capacities of the legal decision-makers (Krecke 2003).

CHAPTER 7

Social Norms and Law and Economics

> Where norms govern individual behavior, one cannot
> correctly assess the effect of formal, state-enforced
> rules [read "law," "rights," "working rules," "legal
> doctrines," etc.] without understanding the informal
> rules also at work. . . . [F]ormal and informal rules
> form a complex web of incentives that influence
> behavior; a new economics literature has begun to
> view norms as central to the study of law.
> *(McAdams 1997, pp. 346, 350)*

INTRODUCTION

THE ANALYSIS of social norms has become an important—many would say the hottest—movement in contemporary Law and Economics (Ellickson 1998, p. 543). While traditional legal theory was built on the notion of reasonable individuals who are "socialized into the norms and conventions of a community" (Cooter and Ulen 1988, p. 11) and behave according to those dictates, most approaches to Law and Economics have relied almost exclusively on the rational choice model of human behavior—an approach that has largely ignored the role of forces such as social norms on individual behavior. The genesis of social norms analysis in the Law and Economics' literature is often attributed to Robert Ellickson's path-breaking book, *Order without Law*, which was published in 1991. In the ensuing years, the scholarship in this area has grown exponentially and reflects several different perspectives on the role and analysis of norms.[1] Lawrence E. Mitchell (1999, p. 179) notes that this work began to take hold as legal-economic scholars sought to "understand the role that norms play in ordering society and social groups outside the sphere of norms promulgated by the state, and the ways in which these social norms interact with the norms we call law." This line of inquiry, he said, offered "enormous potential to enrich our understanding of the ways in which we . . . cooperate with one another to achieve both individual and common goals."

---

[1] Four law review symposia have been devoted to the topic: "Law, Economics, and Norms," *University of Pennsylvania Law Review* 144 (1996); "Law and Society & Law and Economics," *Wisconsin Law Review* 1997 (1997); "The Nature and Sources, Formal and Informal, of Law," *Cornell Law Review* 82 (1997); and "The Informal Economy," *Yale Law Journal* 103 (1994). See also Koford and Miller (1991a), Eric Posner (2000), and Hechter and Opp (2001).

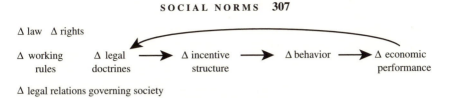

FIGURE 7-1. Legal Centralism

Specifically, proponents of the social norms' approaches argue that the inclusion of social norms into Law and Economics' models makes for robust explanations of behavior and more accurate predictions of the effects of legal change. In the remainder of this chapter we will outline some of the work in this area as well as highlight issues and questions that confront those trying to incorporate social norms into the field of Law and Economics.

We have emphasized throughout this book that much of Law and Economics hinges on the recognition that changed law alters incentives and thereby channels the behavior of individuals in society through the threat of legal sanctions. This legal centralist or consequentialist account of law employs a rational choice or behavioralist approach to describing and evaluating outcomes brought on by legal change. The legal centralist approach was depicted graphically in figure 1-1, which is reproduced in figure 7-1. Here, we can see the path via which a change in law will systematically alter incentives, which alters behavior and, ultimately, economic performance.

From this vantage point, a legal change, for example, the prospect of having to pay higher civil fines or serve longer criminal jail sentences, raises the price of conduct that violates the prevailing laws. This higher price alters the relative magnitude of the benefits and costs associated with those forms of conduct and thus will reduce their frequency. For example, raising the fine for speeding causes fewer people to exceed the speed limit, more severe penalties for cheating on one's taxes results in greater compliance with tax laws, and higher penalties for polluting reduce the amount of pollution emitted into the environment. For the legal centralists, then, the way to change behavior is to change incentives through changes in law. This approach gains legitimacy to the extent that it can be shown that there is a known and reliable nexus between the said change in law and the consequent outcome.

While the legal-centralist argument still constitutes the core thinking in much of Law and Economics, the social norms' literature emphasizes that values infused into the habits, customs, mores, and social norms also influence or regulate conduct. That is, certain patterns of behavior may also be induced, not only by changing law, but also by altering habits, customs, mores, and social norms. The argument here is that there is something fundamental about the nature of human interaction that is not adequately explained by the extant models of human behavior found in the various schools of thought in Law and Economics—particularly the rational-choice based approach used by both the

Chicago approach to law and economics and public choice theory, described, respectively, in chapters 2 and 3.

DEFINING TERMS

At this point, we need to define some terminology. By "habit" we mean individualized repetitive behavior that is undertaken without forethought; one behaves a certain way without reflecting on how it might be done differently or the impact if it were done differently. "Custom" includes the surrounding social structure and suggests that individuals in the social group will behave in a similar manner when confronted with the identical circumstances. "Mores" are folk ways so basic as to develop the force of law.[2] Thus, habits, customs, and mores tend to channel human behavior in particular directions. The legal-economic consequences of their role becomes important because when an individual's behavior is systematically influenced by habits, customs, and mores in ways that, for example, rational choice theory would not predict, those predictions coming out of a legal-centralist approach may overstate or understate the behavioral response to a proposed change in law.

Moving on to social norms, we will use Richard A. Posner's (1997, p. 365) definition of a norm as "a rule that is neither promulgated by an official source, such as a court or a legislature, nor is enforced by the threat of legal sanctions, yet is regularly complied with." Robert S. Goldfarb and William B. Griffith (1991, p. 60) described norms as "rules of behavior that constrain the individual's interactions with others," noting in particular that they "often operate to constrain the full-blown pursuit of 'narrow self-interest.' "[3] Social norms are typically not thought to spell out a precise set of behaviors to follow, but instead, like habits, customs, and mores, tend to rule out a range of actions or behaviors.[4]

Contributors to the social norms' literature come from the disciplines of economics, law, political science, sociology, and philosophy, and each in their own way attempts to explain the origin, function, and impact of social norms. They share the view that the social-norm producing process—broadly conceived as the complex arena of learning and socialization through education, religion, peer behavior, family, and surrounding culture—may also explain why some people do not speed on the highway, do not avoid their tax obligations, and do

---

[2] These definitions are taken from Koford and Miller (1991b, pp. 22–26).

[3] More generally Brennen (1991, p. 85) writes that norms are "behavior-guiding moral principles." The fact that the definition of a social norm varies so much among contributors has led Basu (1998, p. 476) to conclude that "Like cows, social norms are easier to recognize than to define."

[4] All of these definitions notwithstanding, to avoid the tedious need for duplicative listings, we will follow the lead of many contributors to the literature and, for the most part, from here on conflate all of these terms—"habits," "customs," "mores," and "norms" into the inclusive term "social norms."

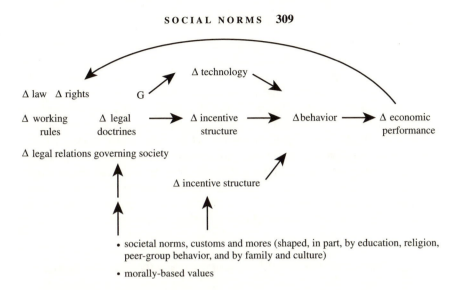

FIGURE 7-2. Social Norms, Technology, and Economic Performance

not pollute the environment, even when the cost of doing so is low relative to the perceived benefit, in a traditional economic sense. As Richard H. McAdams (1997, p. 346) puts it, "Where norms govern individual behavior, one cannot correctly assess the effect of formal, state-enforced rules without understanding the informal rules [e.g., social norms] also at work."[5] Hence, it is not enough to say (as we have described in chapter 1) that legal change affects incentives, behavior, and ultimately economic performance; there is more to it (see figure 7-2).

First, law is, in part, the outcome of a complex process whose evolution is inspired by morally based values and social norms—themselves embedded in a long tradition of political and legal thought. This relation is depicted in figure 7-2 by the vertical arrows going from social norms and morally based values up to the law.[6] Beyond the incentives created by the legal structure, behavior is also a function of both (1) the content of societal norms, customs, and mores that create yet an additional set of incentives and thereby also induce certain patterns of preference formation that impact economic performance,[7] and (2) the morally

---

[5] Lessig (1998, p. 662) uses the term "regulation" to describe the combined relationships between (1) law and performance on the one hand, and (2) social norms and performance on the other. By this, Lessig means that both social norms and the law "regulate" behavior or conduct, and thus performance.

[6] The fact that the law (as well as behavior) is norm based is emphasized throughout this literature. Thus one reads that "[l]egal centralists believe both that the state is the fundamental basis of political organization and that law constitutes a unified hierarchical system of norms" (Yngvesson 1993, p. 1788). See also Cooter (1995).

[7] "In sum, formal and informal rules form a complex web of incentives that influence behavior" (McAdams 1997, p. 350).

based values that influence or regulate conduct, either working independently of social norms, working together with social norms, or working in opposition to the prevailing social norms. Furthermore, behavior is also affected by technology, which expands the choice set for production and consumption.[8]

From the vantage point of figure 7-2, not only are social norms and technology incorporated into the analysis, but so too is the recognition that as economic performance unfolds, as consumer demand shifts, as technologies change, as new resources are discovered and old ones move toward depletion, as new opportunities arise while past successes dwindle, and as competition ensues, the economy changes over time. In a dynamic economy there is a reverse link going from economic performance back to the law; that is, new economic circumstances will invite new calls for additional changes in law or new policy initiatives.

GOVERNMENT, TECHNOLOGY, AND ECONOMIC PERFORMANCE

Before delving into a discussion of the role of social norms and their impact, we will briefly explore the impact of government and technology on economic performance.[9] Technology expands the choice set in both production and consumption. As a consequence, new technologies affect individual and group behavior and ultimately economic performance. While technologies may come about through private initiatives, oftentimes the government is involved in driving certain technologies—sometimes directly, other times indirectly—by committing resources to them (see G ↗ in figure 7-2). The impact of government driven technologies on the economic sector manifests itself in different ways, four of which are touched on here.

First, the government can simply allocate resources to drive certain technologies to the direct benefit of particular industries. The fields of energy, transportation, agriculture, and medicine and pharmaceuticals and, of course, the military are sectors of the economy where government departments allocate their scarce resources to support selected technological initiatives (and, due to scarcity, not others).

Second, in other instances, the government's commitment of resources to certain fields (for example, the military) results in technological innovations that spill over into the nonmilitary sector. Nowhere is this more evident than in the case of the Defense Advanced Research Projects Agency (DARPA), the central research and development organization for the U.S. Department of Defense. This is an agency that brings together the academic, industrial, and mili-

---

[8] Government's impact on technology will be explored in the next section.

[9] This section on government, technology, and economic performance borrows from Mercuro (2004). It is intended to complete the discussion of the combined impact of changing law, social norms, and technology on the economy and should not be thought of as part of the social norms literature.

tary communities in an effort to invest in basic and innovative technologies and to explore revolutionary ideas dedicated to fostering and advancing technologies and systems that create significant advantages for the U.S. military.[10] While its focus is on military technologies, it also develops generic technologies—most notably those related to microelectronics, computing, networking, and other information technologies. The technologies that they have developed and are developing have nonmilitary applications and consequently those in the market sector have and will continue to adapt to bring their many innovations into the marketplace. As for technological developments outside of the military, DARPA's most significant accomplishment was in its work on ARPANET, a telecommunications network that was the precursor to the Internet.

Third, government also impacts economic performance by forcing certain technologies onto society, and, as expected, the market sector responds accordingly. Nowhere is this more evident than in the fields of environmental protection and homeland security. For the past forty years, the U.S. Environmental Protection Agency has largely relied on a command and control approach that has forced certain technologies (BAT—best available technologies) on select industries. The consequence is that individuals in the market sector are acutely attuned to the government-proscribed requirements, and have stepped in and supplied the required air-emissions and water-effluent abatement equipment. Precisely the same phenomenon is currently taking place as the Department of Homeland Security begins to require the government (at all levels) and private industries to adopt certain technologies and systems in its effort to defend the homeland. Again, just as with the case of environmental protection, we see firms in the market sector closely monitoring developments within the Department of Homeland Security and situating themselves in the marketplace ready to provide a market-sector response to government's technology-forcing directives.

The last example of the government's impact on technology and economics has to do with the online federal government information and services center run by the U.S. Small Business Administration.[11] This branch of the SBA views itself as the vehicle by which U.S. businesses can connect with federal agencies, providing firms with specific business tools and resources to grow their businesses and create jobs. It has tried to become an established nexus between government and all facets of business development, including information technology, resources for capital and credit, laws and regulations, and international trade information (for export promotion and financing international

---

[10] To get a sense of the many new technology initiatives and programs being undertaken under the auspicious of DARPA, see the lists provided by DARPA's Advanced Technology Office and the Defense Sciences Office at http://www.darpa.mil/body/off_programs.html.

[11] There are also several other units of the federal government that are in the technology information-provision business.

trade). It also has specific programs, such as Tech-Net, which describes itself as the electronic gateway of technology information and resources for and about small high-tech businesses. Essentially, Tech-Net is an Internet-based database of information concerning small business innovation research, technology transfer, and advanced technology programs.[12]

The point here is that many technologies result from the government's direct and indirect role in advancing certain technologies by committing resources to technological innovation and development and by providing information about new technologies—all of which impacts economic performance across the economy.[13]

AN ASIDE ON SOCIAL NORMS AND ECONOMICS IMPERIALISM

Before delving into a discussion of social norms and law and economics, it is important to take a moment to distinguish between economics imperialism on the one hand, and the social norms literature on the other. In a nutshell, there is a distinction to be made between using economics to address behavior that is morally based, and incorporating social norms into a larger behavior theory to inform economic thinking. Gary Becker, one of the founders of the Chicago school of law and economics and the individual most responsible for advancing economics imperialism,[14] has pioneered the economic analysis of moral behaviors such as charity, altruism, and honesty. Elements of these moral behaviors are said to provide utility—perhaps more for some people than for others, given people's differing preference structures—and enter the individual's utility function just as do other goods. Just as more books to read or more movies to watch enhance the individual's utility, so too can one's utility be enhanced by being the provider of charity or by engaging in altruistic or honest behavior. That is, people do not engage in these moral behaviors because it is "the right thing to do" in some philosophical or religious sense, but because (and to the extent that) they are better off in doing them than in not doing them.

The economics imperialism models accept the individual's preference set as a given and thus do not require a theory of preference formation; one need not ask why an individual's utility is enhanced by reading another book or watching another movie, or acting altruistically. Robert Cooter (1998, p. 597), a major contributor to the social norms literature, has criticized this type of economic analysis of moral behavior on the grounds that it "trivializes moral commitment by treating is as an exogenous taste." Those who support the

---

[12] See http://tech-net.sba.gov/index2.html.

[13] Our purpose here is merely to describe what is transpiring; there is no intention to advocate for or against this role of government.

[14] Gordon Tullock, too, played an extremely prominent role here.

extension of the economic approach to human behavior beyond those activities traditionally considered "economic" do offer a defense against critics who argue the narrowness, inaccuracy, or even the tautological nature of the rational choice model. For example, Charles Plott (1987, pp. 140–41) maintains, "The fact that preferences might include or reflect moral considerations [perhaps activities with a moral component] does not, on the surface, contradict a theory of rational choice or maximizing behavior." In what they consider the absence of a better or sufficiently operationalized alternative theory, the rational choice theorists remain content with the ex post rationale or explanation as to why we observe individuals engaging in behavior described as charitable or altruistic: it is because it enhances their welfare. As will be seen in the next sections, the social norms literature suggests that the process is somewhat more complex.

ISSUES IN COMPLIANCE AND ENFORCEMENT

Law and social norms both work to regulate behavior and, in particular, to induce patterns of behavior consistent with larger social goals. Our discussion of Chicago law and economics suggests that people comply with legal rules because of their unwillingness to bear the costs associated with noncompliance—usually fines or jail time. But what about social norms? What is it that causes people to comply with norms absent the forms of legal punishment that we witness in the legal arena? Two aspects of this question will be addressed. The first is the nature of the subject's compliance with respect to law as compared to compliance with social norms. The second deals with whether social norms are adhered to because they have been internalized or because of fear of external nonlegal sanctions. That is, with respect to the latter, the literature identifies and delineates norms as informal social regularities that individuals sometimes feel a compulsion to follow because of an internalized sense of duty or obligation,[15] or because of a fear of external nonlegal sanctions, or both (McAdams 1997, p. 340). Each of these will be explored.

Steven Shavell (2002) suggests that behavior can be regulated in three ways: (i) exclusively by law—for example, the entire spectrum of technical, administrative legal–compliance rules; (ii) exclusively by social norms—for example, keeping appointments and engaging in those many activities that come under the rubric of "good manners" and being a "good citizen"; or (iii) by both law and social norms—as illustrated by the common belief that most crimes and torts are thought to be both legally sanctionable and outside of

---

[15] As Koford and Miller (1991b, pp. 24) observed, "There is a large overlap between internalized norms and customs. Once learned, these norms become part of customary practice and individuals rarely reflect on them when they act." See also Etzioni (2000).

socially accepted norms.[16] Both social norms and the law rely on mechanisms beyond the self for enforcement and inducing the subjects' compliance, but these mechanisms differ in form and implications.[17] In the case of law, subjects comply under the will or sanction of the sovereign; in the case of norms, subjects comply under the will or sanction of the community. This distinction deserves some elaboration.

Law and legal change are expected to change individual behavior. We expect people to comply with laws because the sovereign has told us to do so and will punish us if we do not. Here we see a negative component to violating the law: we comply to avoid the negative impact of having to pay the raised fine for speeding, the more severe penalties for cheating on our taxes, or the higher penalties for polluting. On the other hand, individuals comply with social norms because the community has told them to do so. In this case, we have both negative and positive components. On the negative side, the community will punish us if we do not comply, by inflicting some form of disapproval and admonition, whether via psychic cost in suffering guilt through a sense of "letting down the community" or perhaps even physical ostracism such as being cut off from some or all of the benefits of participation in the community. On the positive side, if we do comply, the community rewards us for conforming to the social norms by expressing itself in ways that allow us to experience feelings of virtue, feel that we have lived up to our duty or obligation, enjoy the praise of the community, and experience an enhanced sense of esteem, or perhaps by allowing us to secure the larger resource benefits associated with community membership.

Both internally enforced social norms and externally enforced social norms provide signals as to what we should or should not do under a given set of circumstances and are therefore obligatory upon those individuals who wish to participate in the society that is at least partly constituted by such social norms. What the literature on internally enforced social norms emphasizes is the fact that the socialization process—through education, religion,

---

[16] Shavell (2002, p. 229 at n. 2) observed that a "sustained analysis of the optimal domains of law and of morality from an instrumental, economic perspective does not seem to have been undertaken."

[17] It should be noted here that the law and economics social norms literature has not reached any consensus as to how to treat organizational rules—what have been termed "working rules" in this book. There are no definitive categories lying between centralized formal law on the one hand and decentralized social norms on the other. Organizational rules fall between the two, raising the question, "Should we treat them as law or norms?" McAdams (1997, p. 351) described this quandary: "The distinction is important because some theorists prefer to use the term 'norms' to refer only to decentralized rules and regard organizational rules as a set of obligations falling between centralized law and decentralized norms." McAdams (1997, at fn 59) went on to observe that this was Ellickson's approach where he described "three sources of third-party control: governments provide legal rules, organizations provide organizational rules, and 'social forces' provide norm-based rules. . . . [Thus,] in this taxonomy, organizational rules therefore are not 'norms.' "

peer behavior, family, and surrounding culture—brings about the internalization of social norms. Individuals internalize the normative component of the adopted norms and thereby set up a parallel structure of incentives that induces them to behave in accordance with these norms (see figure 7–2). The self-enforcement comes about through self-administered feelings of guilt and disapproval, pride and status, and so on. Individuals behave in a manner consistent with the incentives fashioned through their socialization and, in doing so, with the internally enforced social norms.

This concern with internally enforced social norms marks a departure from neoclassical economics, which treats individual tastes and preferences as exogenous. As Ellickson (1998, p. 540) points out, the legal-economic models—particularly those advanced in the Chicago school—constructed on a neoclassical framework feature "unsocialized individuals in their analysis of hypothetical legal problems." Ellickson goes on to argue that by suppressing the role of socialization, the Chicago approach to law and economics intentionally or unintentionally exaggerates the focus, and thus the importance, of legal centralism. As against the models of neoclassical economics, the social norms approach posits that aspects of individual and group behavior can be explained as people behaving in a manner that complies with those societal norms that are "internalized" and thereby impact preference formation, affect behavior, and ultimately, impact economic performance.[18] The point, then, is that some social norms impact economic performance simply because they are internally enforced by agents and without reference to any sort of external sanction.

Externally enforced social norms also have a direct bearing on an individual's behavior and thus on economic performance. From this external vantage point, social norms are part of the background milieu against which individuals make choices. Once these norms are in place and incentives are established, the machinations of private and public choice unfold. To the extent that these norms differ across communities, the outcomes of the choice process, too, will differ.[19] Unlike internally enforced norms, those that are externally enforced rely on the efforts of the norm-generating community. External enforcement of social norms is more likely to the extent that (i) there is homo-

---

[18] This is sometimes referred to as the "rationality-limiting norm," whereby "certain alternatives may be infeasible to an individual not just because they are technologically infeasible or budgetarily infeasible [both consistent with neoclassical economic analysis] but because they are ruled out by the person's norms" (Basu 1998, p. 477). Basu goes on to define two other types of norms: some are "preference-changing norms" (e.g., the religious norm not to eat meat manifests itself into a preference for vegetarian foods) and others simply help society select an equilibrium—so-called "equilibrium-selection norms" (e.g., the decision to drive either on the right side or the left side of the street).

[19] The Institutionalists and New Institutional Economists would call this part of the institutional framework within which choices are made—a framework that conditions, informs, and in various ways both facilitates and constrains choice.

geneity of the social group, and hence a common core of external expectations; (ii) members of the group are well informed and similarly endowed; and (iii) the interacting parties have a continuing relationship be it in the form of friends, acquaintances, bystanders, neighbors, or trading partners.[20] Compliance with these norms occurs for both positive reasons—for example, to attain greater esteem or be granted a position of higher social status—and for negative ones—for example, to avoid ostracism or negative gossip. Thus, in acknowledging the presence of certain societal norms, some facets of individual and group behavior can be explained in terms of people behaving in a manner that complies with the externally enforced social norms, and this behavior, in turn, can impact economic performance.

It would seem, then, that social norms matter in legal-economic analysis for a number of reasons. McAdams (1997, pp. 347–50) offers an instructive matrix of three possible impacts on performance. First, social norms can matter because they sometimes control individual behavior to the exclusion of law. This is the case, for example, with laws governing the Prohibition movement of the 1920s and 1930s and the property norms followed by ranchers in Shasta County irrespective of the formal law.[21] Second, norms and law may work independently to influence behavior in the same direction. We see this in cases such as those where the laws to obligate tax paying are reenforced by the social norm to pay taxes, and the anti-theft laws are reenforced by the social norm not to steal. Finally, law may intentionally or unintentionally influence social norms themselves. For example, legal restrictions on public smoking may have strengthened an anti-smoking norm; the passage of the Civil Rights Act of 1964 may have affected the prevailing social norms sanctioning racial discrimination; and the passage of Title IX in 1972 may have influenced the prevailing social norms related to women's participation in high school and college sports. This matrix of possible impacts on performance is important because it brings to the fore the point that the effects of legal change will depend on the nature of the proposed legal change and the community of social norms to be engaged. Therefore the effects of a proposed change in law will likely vary, depending on whether the legal change is running with, running against, or altering prevailing social norms.[22] In their attempts to alter economic performance through legal change, policymakers of a legal-centralist

[20] Richard Posner (1998b, p. 554) describes some of this behavior or this class of interaction as "signaling theory" whereby "people engage in behavior that they may not value in order to signal their loyalty to the group with which they may have their most valuable interactions or, more broadly, in order to establish a network."

[21] The latter example is more fully explored in the section titled: "Social Norms at Work."

[22] As is elaborated on later, the fact that law can influence social norms/behavior and ultimately performance, is of great interest to the law and economics school of norms in that it provides a rationale for state activism for the New Chicago school.

bent in particular, if not in tune with the interaction of norms and legal rules in the area impacted by a proposed legal change, may drastically mis-estimate the effects of alterations in law and thus be less than successful in accomplishing their aims. Thus, in retrospect, given the force of these various arguments, Ellickson may have been right in criticizing Law and Economics in the early 1990s for having largely ignored the inclusion of social norms—norms that are now recognized as the central informal means of social control impacting economic performance (Ellickson 1991, pp.137–55).

SOCIAL NORMS AND THE EVOLUTION
OF THE "NEW" CHICAGO SCHOOL

Lawrence Lessig (1998) provides us with a simplified and useful delineation of the evolving treatment of social norms within the "Chicago" approach to law and economics (broadly conceived), culminating in what he calls the New Chicago school. The "old" Chicago school, in its several manifestations, argued against the widespread use of the law and argued for the dominance of other systems of social control—with the market being their preferred alternative. In its attempt to elevate the market, old Chicago arguments often functioned to diminish the significance of law. As Lessig (1998, p. 665) describes this view, "[L]aw is, relative to these other constraints, a less effective constraint: Its regulations, crude; its response, slow; its interventions, clumsy; and its effect often self-defeating. Other regulators, the old school argues, regulate better than law. Hence law, the argument goes, would better let these [other] regulators regulate." That is, the old Chicago perspective asserts that "Law should understand its own insignificance . . . and should step out of the way," allowing for more incentive-based market approaches, rather than the command and control-type regulations that typically carry the day.

The first-generation of law and economics theorists to incorporate social norms into their analysis and scrutinize their influence, like old Chicago, considered law and social norms to be relatively autonomous phenomena. Some of those contributing to this first generation of social norms literature came from the *Law & Society* movement, while other contributors, like Janet Landa, Cooter, and Ellickson, came from those more closely tied to the Chicago approach to law and economics.[23] The lesson they transmitted to their generation of legal-economic scholars was that, like law, norms do indeed regulate behavior. Within this first generation of literature, however, social norms were considered independent of the law and appeared fixed, essentially unmovable, and unyielding to the influences of law. As a consequence, since it is the forces

[23] See, for example, Landa (1981), Cooter and Landa (1984), and Ellickson (1991).

outside law—namely the complex process of socialization—that have a significant impact on behavior, and may, in fact, regulate behavior better than law, these early social norm theorists—not unlike their old Chicago counterparts—concluded that the state would and should be much less active.

It was against this anti-activist backdrop of the old Chicago school and the first generation norm theorists that the New Chicago asserted itself.[24] The "new" Chicago school includes scholars such as Cass Sunstein, Dan Kahan, Lawrence Lessig, Kenneth Dau-Schmidt, and Richard Pildes, and the focus of their approach is on the interdependence between law, social norms, and other "regulators" of behavior. For New Chicago, social norms are malleable and the law is there to help change or reform them. In this view, "[L]aw not only regulates behavior directly [à la legal centralists], but law also regulates behavior indirectly by regulating these other modalities of regulation directly"— of particular importance here, social norms (Lessig 1998, p. 666). Sunstein (1996b) contends that since law can strengthen the norms it embodies and weaken those it conflicts with or condemns, the government is in the unique position of being able to advance desirable norms and undermine unwanted ones. This law-norm nexus is also clearly expressed by McAdams (1997, p. 354), who observed that "arguably, the most important relationship between law and norms is *the ability of law to shape norms*" (emphasis added). He goes on to say that "[i]f legal rules sometimes change or create norms, one can not adequately compare an existing legal rule with its alternatives without considering how a change in the legal rule may affect the relevant norms" (p. 349). For New Chicago, the significance of this can not be overstated: the fact that law can and does affect social norms (as implied by the arrow, G ↘, going from law to social norms in figure 7–3), far from diminishing the role of the government, offers an expanded opportunity for state activity or regulation—here, to alter social norms and ultimately economic performance, in ways that will enhance social welfare.

It is here that one finds the roots of the New Chicago school's skepticism regarding the anti-activist posture of both the old Chicago approach to law and economics and the first-generation norm theorists. Proponents of the New Chicago approach recognize that "just because law cannot directly or simply control norms, it does not follow that there is not an influence in both ways (norms influencing law and law influencing norms) or that one cannot be used to change the other" (Lessig 1998, p. 673). New Chicago is focused on enhancing our understanding of the mechanisms through which this recip-

---

[24] Lessig described his use of the moniker "new" as follows: "The sense of 'new' that I mean here is 'new' for a Chicago school. The idea is to mark, within each of these separate departments, second-generation work for projects begun long ago. The label is less about discovery and more about organizing work that otherwise proceeds separately" (1998, p. 672). See Ellickson (1998, p. 548), who also provides a brief characterization of New Chicago.

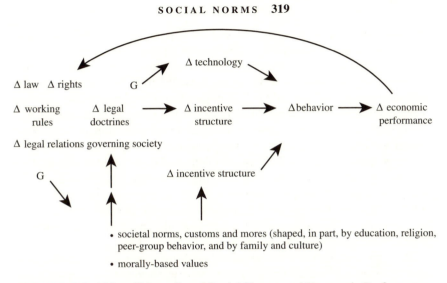

FIGURE 7-3. "New Chicago" and Social Norms and Economic Performance

rocal influence is effected, on the issues raised by these interactions, and, more importantly, on fashioning social norms as part of solutions to questions of public policy. In doing so, it "identifies alternatives as additional tools for a more effective activism. The moral of the old school is that the state should do less. The hope of the new is that the state can do more" (Lessig 1998, pp. 673, 661). In the same vein, Sunstein (1996b, pp. 907–8) refers to the use of law to influence norms as "norm management," a practice that he defends as "an important strategy for accomplishing the objectives of law, whatever those objectives may be." Given that "behavior is pervasively a function of norms" and that "norms account for many apparent oddities or anomalies in human behavior," the best way to improve social welfare may be via changes in norms. Government, he says, "deserves to have, and in any case inevitably does have, a large role in norm management."

Needless to say, this interest in and rationale for a more expansive role for government is not a development welcomed by many proponents of the Chicago approach to law and economics. Richard A. Posner, for one, has registered his objection. Posner does not believe that the government should be in the business of manipulating norms and preferences. He argues that "government has a role in encouraging people to be law-abiding," and that "one wants the government to be as neutral among contending social groups as possible." Things are different though, he says, "when it gets down to trying to get people to like each other, to change people's values and make them more tolerant— this whole notion of shaping people's preferences through government." Not

only does he not approve of this, he contends that, to "the extent that it is effective, it's likely to be totalitarian."[25] This dispute persists.

To this point, we have seen that the first-generation norm theorists have attempted to incorporate social norms formally into their legal-economic analysis (as depicted in figure 7–2), and that New Chicago not only includes social norms in its legal-economic analysis, but also takes the additional step of advocating the use government to change norms in an attempt to improve human well-being (as implied by the arrow, $G \searrow$, going from law to social norms in figure 7–3). The final aspect of the social norms literature that we want to explore here concerns the question of whether, and, if so, how Law and Economics scholarship should deal with the processes by which social norms evolve and change. That is, a pertinent question for analysis is where the Law and Economics research agenda should enter the nexus between norms, incentives, behavior, and performance.

This very question has been advanced by "sympathetic critics" of the "new norms jurisprudes"—the latter a moniker used to identify those who advance theories of social norms within the context of a behavioral approach that maintains a rational choice perspective, thus includes the old Chicago school, the first-generation norm theorists, and New Chicago.[26] That old Chicago and New Chicago adopt a rational choice perspective is not in dispute. As McAdams (1997, p. 339) points out, "In recent years, economists and rational choice theorists in philosophy and political science have started to use individual behavior to explain the origin and function of norms." As Lessig, himself a proponent of the New Chicago approach, notes, the New Chicago School has not completely jettisoned the underpinnings of Chicago law and economics; rather, the New Chicago "shares with the old an interest in alternative modalities of regulation . . . and adopts as well a rational choice perspective (Lessig 1998, p. 666; see also p. 665).

In his thoughtful critique of this movement, Mitchell (1999, p. 21) describes the work of the new norms jurisprudes as taking "an unrelenting behavioral approach to norms," one that "winds up narrowing instead of broadening their understanding, distorting instead of improving this explanation of norms." He goes on to say, that the new norms jurisprudes

> generally share the same basic goal, which is to establish a non-normative theory of norms. The methodological attitude is behavioural; the approach is entirely positivistic. They tend to share an underlying metanorm of efficient wealth or

---

[25] These quotes are taken from Rosen (1997, p. 176).

[26] The leading critic is Mitchell, and this section is drawn from his "friendly critique" of the "new norm jurisprudes" (1999). That it relies exclusively on rational choice is also consistent with Lessig's (1998, p. 665) observation of the old and New Chicago schools: "Chicago schools, as I mean the term, emphasize this multiplicity of constraint and understand it from the perspective of rational choice."

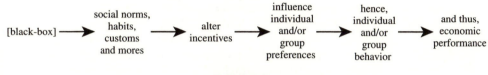

FIGURE 7-4.

welfare maximization, and all share the basic belief that people are motivated principally—if not solely—by self-interest. Most important, by limiting their inquiry to what they see, they are unable to explain, except at the most superficial level, how norms become normative—that is, how they come to tell us what we ought (or ought not) to do. (1999, pp. 208–9)[27]

The critique goes on the suggest that, by being bound to this behavioralist approach—which Mitchell has labeled a "black box" approach—new norms jurisprudes need only to study the impact of changing social norms on behavior. They need not get into underlying values and the evolving, nuanced obligations, duties, or compulsions that come about and bring about the evolution of social norms. This behavioralist approach seems content to start with extant social norms and then proceed to investigate the impact of changing social norms on incentives and behavior, and ultimately on performance. As Ellickson (1998, p. 550) has observed, "Although methodological individualism invites a theory of how actors manage to reform norms, many of us have ducked that challenge, in effect relegating norm change to a black box," as illustrated in figure 7–4.[28]

This group of critics contends that one cannot come to a true understanding of the role and impact of social norms via the rational choice accounts of behavior offered by the new norm jurisprudes. They base this contention on the their belief that accounts that focus merely on how people behave, and not why they act as they do, are insufficient. They contend that the new norms jurisprudes maintain a behavioralist posture consistent with their backgrounds in rational choice theory and law and economics, together with a myopic focus on norm efficiency and norm stability.[29] That analysis, they argue, focuses on descriptions of "behavioral characteristics that lead to and sustain norm creation," where social norms are depicted as "nothing more than preferences," with little attention paid to the processes of preference formation or to

[27] Elster (1991, p. 15) maintains a similar critique stating his belief that "social norms provide an important kind of motivation for action that is irreducible to rationality or indeed to any other form of optimizing mechanism."

[28] As Brennen (1991, p. 87) described this aversion, "[N]eoclassical economists have never aspired to predict, explain, or evaluate preferences themselves; their goal has been the prediction of behavior and the evaluation of policy and institutions based on those preferences."

[29] This characterization is fully developed in Mitchell (1999, pp.189–93).

the evaluation of the desirability of various alternative preference structures (Mitchell 1999, p. 190). As a result, Mitchell (1999, p.180) argues, "[The] relentlessly, behaviouralist accounts of norms provided by the new norms jurisprudes can barely begin to explain the emotionally, psychologically, intuitively, morally, and socially complex questions" underlying why individuals or groups adopt or conform to particular social norms.

These same critics argue that if legal-economic scholars focus on extant norms or state action dedicated to trying to change norms (in hopes of changing preference formation), without any real concern for how those social norms are formed and whether they are desirable, they have not gone far enough.[30] To understand anything meaningful about behavior, and ultimately performance, we need to explore how norms initially arise; that is, we need to understand the nature and source of the obligation that leads one to feel the need, the duty, or the compulsion to comply with social norms. As McAdams (1997, pp. 349, 354) has observed, while Law and Economics scholars may be deeply interested in how law can influence norms: "If we do not know how norms first arise, it would seem implausible to think we could predict how legal rules might change a particular norm." Proponents of this latter line of thinking argue that we need to understand both what goes into forming the social norms, habits, customs and mores, and the sense of obligation to comply with these social norms. That is, one needs to open the "black box" and focus attention on how underlying values lead to social norms creation and, from there, proceed to try to understand how the likes of the New Chicago norm managers would alter existing norms to better society.

These sympathetic critics are motivated by a belief that we need a richer understanding of norms—perhaps supplied by political scientists, philosophers, and others—at the heart of which should be a robust explanation of the formation, content, and stability of social norms. It is not enough, they argue, to assert that an obligation must be internalized to constitute a social norm and hence impact behavior. We must, they say, go beyond the standard response of new norms jurisprudence, that people conform to norms for merely instrumental reasons such as maximizing wealth or welfare, avoiding punishment, and seeking reward (Mitchell 1999, p. 191). The focus, instead, must be on understanding the process by which norms come into being and become internalized by members of society. A useful or complete law and economics of social norms model must answer the question, "What is it that leads us to feel the need to comply with social norms?" McAdams (1997, p. 352) makes this point directly:

> Despite the fact that norms govern behavior throughout society, the origin of norms is, for economists, something of a puzzle. Typically, the new literature

---

[30] For a concise review of some of the Law and Economics' explanations as to the origin and impact of social norms, see Eric Posner (1996, 1998a).

simply sets the issue aside. The decision to concentrate on the operation of extant norms is certainly defensible: we gain much by empirical studies of particular norms. Nonetheless, I believe it is fruitful for legal theory to focus on the more elemental question: How do norms initially arise?

MODELS OF SOCIAL NORMS

Before moving on to the next section, where we take a look directly at the law and economics of social norms "at work," we note that much of this literature is still in the relatively early stages of development.[31] Consequently, there are presently several different approaches and models that explore how one can incorporate social norms into legal-economic analysis. Here we present brief descriptions of five of them—by Robert Cooter, Lawrence Lessig, Richard H. McAdams, Cass Sunstein, and Eric Posner.

From Cooter's perspective, many economists engaged in the economic analysis of law practice a form of moral skepticism by exploring efficient institutional arrangements for rationally self-interested actors, largely to the exclusion of the role of social norms. He acknowledges the success of the various models built on this moral skepticism, but, not unlike the other models described in this section, Cooter points out that they often fail to explain significant activities of people (2000a, pp. 1578–79).

Cooter's model takes direct aim at the Becker approach, described earlier—an approach that models behavior by postulating "tastes" for anything (fairness, honesty, etc.) including morality. Indeed, he points out that economists "such as Gary Becker and George Stigler praised this reluctance [to explain tastes] as a methodological virtue linked to scientific rigor" (2000a, p.1592).[32] Cooter also argues that postulating a taste for morality [à al Stigler and Becker] raises the additional question, "What is the difference between an unselfish desire to treat others fairly and a selfish desire to satisfy a taste for treating others fairly?" (2000a, p. 1579). Cooter ends up advocating for (1) an economic theory that explores endogenous preferences, (2) an accepted method to investigate the internalization of values, and (3) a sustained inquiry into the question, "Where do tastes come from?" Cooter's overall aim is to get legal-economists to "describe the values internalized by people, predict the effects of internalized values on society, and explain why some people internalize values that others do not internalize" (2000a, p. 1579). In short, his is an

---

[31] In our effort to provide the reader with a very brief review of five different and highly nuanced models that attempt to incorporate social norms into legal-economic analysis, we distilled several rather lengthy articles down to three or four paragraphs each and, in doing so, have borrowed directly from those works, using their language so as to maintain and transmit their unique perspective on the role of social norms in Law and Economics.

[32] See Stigler and Becker (1977).

approach to Law and Economics that asks legal-economists to chart the distribution, effects, and causes of internalized values.

His definitions of law and social norms are consistent with many of the other models. On the one hand he recognizes the "imperative theory of law," where law is seen as an obligation backed by a state sanction.[33] On the other hand, a social norm can then be defined as an obligation backed by a nonlegal sanction, the latter of which may take the form of criticizing, blaming, refusing to deal with or shunning (insofar as the people who impose them are not state officials) (2000a, pp.1579–80). Cooter points out that one of the distinguishing characteristics between law and social norms is that legal systems, corporations, churches, and private organizations typically have rules (often within their by-laws) for making, amending, or extinguishing rules. More often than not, however, social norms lack rules for making rules; that is, no definite process exists to create, amend, or extinguish a rule of etiquette or a principle of morality.

In his descriptive model, a model that focuses on social norms that regulate civic acts, Cooter attempts to describe the interaction between actual norms and laws, and to lay out the distribution and effects of internalized values. He analogizes his model to the economic model of consumer theory. In consumer theory, the amount that a person is willing to pay for a good measures the strength of his preference for it. In a like manner, Cooter wants to measure the extent to which a person internalizes a social norm by the amount that he will pay to conform to it. In his analogy between norms and markets, final demand for a commodity corresponds to the intrinsic value (defined as "tastes" or "preferences") of obeying a social norm. Thus, a person who intrinsically values obeying a social norm will pay something to obey the norm for its own sake, independent of any resulting advantage or disadvantage. In addition, civic acts can also have instrumental value. The instrumental value of civic acts often depends on the advantage gained from having the reputation of being a good citizen. The cost of obeying a social norm is straightforward. Obedience often imposes direct costs in money, inconvenience, effort, risk, or lost opportunity. For example, complying with tax law costs money, cleaning up after a dog is unpleasant, and abstaining from smoking may require effort. A person who has internalized a norm is willing to sacrifice something to obey it (2000b, p. 6). He demonstrates how the interaction between willingness-to-pay and the actual cost of conforming to a social norm determines the equilibrium aggregate level of civic acts.

Normatively, Cooter argues that people change their preferences and internalize morality to improve their opportunities for cooperating with others. Within his model he distinguishes three effects of social norms on law, namely expression, deterrence, and internalization.[34] The state can influence choice by

[33] This is consistent with what has been termed here the "legal-centralist approach."

[34] Expression, deterrence, and internalization are fully developed in Cooter (2000b, pp. 10–20).

credible pronouncements of the law—utilizing its expressive power. When law aligns with social norms, the law can use state sanctions to supplement social sanctions to promote deterrence. Finally, to induce people to internalize values, the state must reward citizens for having civic virtue. For this purpose, state officials must bestow honors, awards, and praise, as well as their opposites (dishonor, punishments, and condemnations).

Since officials have remote relationships with citizens in modern states, the state has little power to induce people to make moral commitments. The primary influences on character are intimate relationships such as families, friends, and colleagues. Given these facts, the state itself will have limited success instilling civic virtue in citizens. Instead, the state should prompt family, friends, and colleagues to instill civic virtue in each other. When some citizens internalize respect for law, pronouncement of a new law can have an expressive effect that causes behavior to jump to a new equilibrium. Given appropriate internalization, legal expression can change behavior dramatically with little state expenditure on coercion. When norms fail on their own, the best system of social control often supplements them with law, that is, the state must align law with social norms. Social norms influence the response of citizens to law through expression, deterrence, and internalization and a better understanding of these effects, including the empirical estimation of their strength in practical situations, can improve social control in the modern state.

Lawrence Lessig's model aims at synthesizing economic and norm accounts of the regulation of behavior so as to better understand those structures of regulation that are outside law's direct effect. Changing laws, altering social norms, implementing different architecture, and raising/lowering prices, each in their own way, changes the constraint on a regulated entity, and changing each constraint changes the behavior of that entity being regulated. Specifically, behavior is regulated by four types of constraint, with law being just one of them. Lessig's conceptual model includes social norms as one of four "regulators"—the others being law, the market, and the prevailing architecture.[35] Specifically, he defines them as follows:

- Law . . . directs behavior in certain ways; it threatens sanctions ex post if those orders are not obeyed.
- Social norms regulate as well, however, they constrain an individual's behavior, but not through the centralized enforcement of a state. More typically, they constrain because of the enforcement of a community.
- Markets regulate through the device of price. The market constraint functions differently from law and norms, (even though the market rests on property and contract law). Given law, a set of social norms, and scarcity, the market presents a distinct set of constraints on individual and collective behavior.

---

[35] These four regulators are more fully described in Lessig (1998).

- Finally, there is the constraint of "architecture"—something akin to "nature" constituted of the surrounding spatial and temporal features in the world around us—whether made, or found. This architecture both restricts and enables in a way that directs or affects behavior. It is in this sense that architecture also regulates behavior.

"These four constraints, or modalities of regulation, operate together," says Lessig, "and, taken as a group, constitute a sum of forces that guide an individual to behave, or act, in a given way."

For our purposes, it is the role of social norms within the model that is of particular interest. For Lessig (1996, p. 2182) "[i]t is not enough to talk about social norms. We must also speak of social meaning." Here he tries to go beyond what he sees as the typical or usual social-norm "talk" and asserts that the price (or cost) of certain types of behavior "is a function of the action and the contextual understandings behind it. Norm talk focuses on the action and ignores the context" (Lessig 1996, p. 2183); hence he argues for "meaning talk."

One must be careful to recognize that Lessig is not concerned here with semantics; his focus is instead on pragmatics. The aim of meaning talk is to find a way "to speak of the frameworks of understanding within which individuals live; a way to describe what they take or understand various actions, or inactions, or statuses to be; and a way to understand how the understandings change" (1995, p. 952). Beyond this, Lessig is also concerned with how these social meanings can be used by social agents to advance individual or collective ends. In this, he also makes clear that the government has a role to play in that "governments, as well as others, act to construct the social structures, or social norms, or what I will call here, the social meanings that surround us" (Lessig 1995, p. 947).

Lessig argues for "meaning talk" that has both a descriptive dimension and, more importantly, a prescriptive component. As to the descriptive element, Lessig believes that meaning talk can "reveal something more about the contours to the costs of the different behaviors; it imports a language that can understand discontinuities in the valuation of similar behavior" (1996, p. 2185). It is the prescriptive facet of meaning talk, however, that has policy implications. As Lessig noted,

> Social structures are differentially plastic, and norms are part of social structures. But whether a norm is difficult to change depends upon more than mere inertia. . . . [I]t depends as well upon the cost or the price of continuing to engage that norm. To speak of these prices, however, requires meaning talk, and meaning talk might in turn cue us to better ways to regulate social norms. (1996, p. 2186)

Thus, for Lessig, constructing social meanings is a collective activity, and as with any collective activity, as with any public good, inducing individuals to

act to support or reconstruct a particular social meaning involves changing incentives, to induce them to change their behavior (1995, p. 1044).[36] To this end, Lessig emphasizes the interpretive dimension of social norms and underscores the need for the state to consider the social meaning of the behavior it seeks to regulate. He asserts that it is the social meaning of the norm that gives rise to its animating force; that is, what an act signals depends on the norms that define the act's social meaning. Once the interpretive dimension of the associated norm is known, one can fashion more workable legal policy—remedies and better predict the effect of legal change.

Richard McAdams has become a major advocate for incorporating social norms into economic analysis of law. His primary motivation in developing his model was to understand better and describe the connections between law and social norms and to overcome what he perceived as the many ambiguities that pervaded the social norms literature. He felt that much of what was there was unnecessarily ad hoc in nature and, to this end, offered his own theory of the origin and growth of social norms.

The predicates to the model (McAdams 1997, pp. 350–51) are three. First, norms are enforced by some means other than legal sanctions. Second, McAdams follows the line of literature that views norms as obligations. Third, while nonlegal obligations may be created and enforced in a centralized or decentralized manner, his model explicitly focuses on informal, decentralized obligations. Believing that social norms are a vitally useful tool for explaining behavior and predicting the effect of legal rules, his theory asserts that "the initial force behind the creation of social norms was the desire individuals have for *respect* or *prestige,* that is, for the relative *esteem* of others" (1997, p. 342; emphasis in original). Further, since individuals care about how they are evaluated in comparison to others, the preference for esteem is inherently relative. Thus, social norms arise because people seek the esteem of others—an individual's utility depends in part on the opinion which that individual perceives others to have of him/her.[37] The model also identifies several stages in the process of norm development, focusing on the dynamic forces that can cause weak desires for esteem to be transformed into powerful and controlling social norms.

---

[36] Lessig (1995, pp. 1008–15) goes on to identify four methods of self-conscious transformations or preservations of social meaning and suggests how each method acts as a potential solution to a collective action problem. There are two techniques of semiotics: (i) tying and (ii) ambiguation; and two techniques of behavior: (iii) inhibition and (iv) ritual. He argues that these are four common and sometimes successful methods for a government or for other social meaning architects to alter the balance of semiotic costs confronting someone engaging in, or not engaging in, a particular behavior.

[37] McAdams (1997, p. 356 at nn. 78, 79, 80) draws on such evidence as people paying for status goods to signal their wealth or "good taste"; that people incur material costs to cooperate in situations where their only reward is the respect and admiration of their peers; and that individuals conform their behavior or judgment to the unanimous view of those around them to avoid the disesteem accorded "deviants."

McAdams (1997, p. 358) lays out the conditions under which the desire for esteem produces a social norm. For some particular behavior X in a population of individuals, a norm may arise if (i) denying esteem is a costless means of punishing norm violators;[38] (ii) there is a consensus about the positive or negative esteem worthiness of engaging in X (that is, either most individuals in the relevant population grant, or most withhold, esteem from those who engage in X); (iii) there is some risk that others will detect whether one engages in X; and (iv) the existence of this consensus and risk of detection is well known within the relevant population. When these conditions exist, the desire for esteem necessarily creates either "costs of" or "benefits from" engaging in behavior X. That is, if the consensus in the community is that X deserves esteem, a norm will arise as long as the esteem benefits exceed, for most people, the costs of engaging in behavior X. Conversely, if the consensus in the community condemns behavior X, a norm will arise if, for most people, the esteem costs exceed the benefits of engaging in X. In addition, over time, competition for relative esteem may strengthen the norm, produce secondary enforcement norms—sometimes backed by material sanctions—and even cause the norm to be internalized. McAdams (1997, p. 364) describes the process as follows:

> If individuals desire esteem, and if these three conditions exist, it necessarily follows that one who violates a consensus incurs a cost. If the consensus is that behavior X is commendable and the absence of X is deplorable, and the consensus is well known, then A will deduce that others will think less of her if they detect her failure to do X. The esteem cost is the probability that a violation of the consensus will be detected multiplied by the value of the esteem that would then be lost. A norm arises when, for most individuals in the population, this esteem cost exceeds the cost of following the consensus. Thus, if most group members prefer bearing the cost of doing X to the esteem cost of failing to do X, most members will do X. Under these circumstances, we can say there is an esteem-based norm obligating individuals to do X.

In summary, McAdams believes that the esteem model provides an analytical clarity that resolves some of the troubling ambiguities in the literature over the meaning of social norms, provides a theory of social norm development, and offers a way to unite what may appear to be unrelated strands of the literature concerning internalized and non-internalized norms, broadly and narrowly defined norms, and group and societal norms.

Cass Sunstein's model is motivated in part by his belief that libertarians, some economic analysts of law, and many liberals give inadequate attention to the pervasive functions of social norms, social meanings, and social roles in society (1996a, p. 910). Like many of the other models, his has both a positive

---

[38] If it is not costless to enforce, then the free rider problem arises since if others enforce the norm, the individual can gain the norm's benefits without bearing enforcement costs.

and normative component. Descriptively, Sunstein seeks to understand the role that social norms play in determining choices, with a focus on their social or expressive meaning. He argues that behavior is pervasively a function of social norms and that norms account for many apparent oddities or anomalies in human behavior. Normatively, he defends the place of law in "norm management," arguing that an understanding of social norms will help illuminate effective regulatory policy and help guide legal change.

His is a rational choice model where norms are but part of the background against which benefits and costs are assessed. He takes issue with those who attempt to drive a wedge between so-called rational behavior and social-norm-induced behavior, asserting that those who allege a difference rely on obscure "state of nature" thinking that leads to wasted efforts to discern what people would like or prefer in some false world where social norms did not exist. This type of thinking, he believes, is doomed to failure; he argues instead that what is rational for an agent is a function of, and mediated by, social roles and associated social norms (1996a, pp. 909–10). In simple economic terms, people's choices are a function of social norms, which operate as "taxes" or "subsidies," and thus the costs and benefits of action, from the standpoint of individual agents, include the consequences of acting (in)consistently with social norms.

Sunstein also takes issue with the idea of "preferences"—and with the term itself—as typically used by economists to reveal choice, asserting that it is highly ambiguous and should be dispensed with altogether.[39] What lies behind choices, as he sees it, is an unruly amalgam of things—aspirations, tastes, physical states, responses to existing roles and norms, values, judgments, emotions, drives, beliefs, whims (1996a, p. 913). In his positive model, it is the interaction of these various elements that produce outcomes of a particular sort within a particular context. If one insists on using "preferences," it must be understood from the outset that these preferences are constructed, rather than elicited, by social situations, in the sense that they are very much a function of the setting and the prevailing social norms (1996a, p. 913). In dispensing with the concept of preferences, he contends that with respect to social norms, choice among options is channeled by an individual's benefit-cost calculation with respect to three factors: (1) intrinsic value, (2) reputational effects, and (3) effects on self-conception. He describes these as follows:

> **1.** The intrinsic value refers to whether [independent of reputational effects and the individual's self-conception] the option is fun, illuminating, pleasant, interesting, and so forth.

[39] Sunstein (1996a, pp. 909, 910) states, "The idea of 'preferences' elides morally important distinctions among the motivations and mental states of human agents," and that "when the idea of a 'preference' is unpacked, it becomes plain that the term is often too abstract and coarse-grained to be a reliable foundation for either normative or positive work."

2. Changes in social norms can alter the effects of reputational incentives (and, thereby have consequences for self-conception asserting that obedience of law is built in large part on the perceived reputational consequences of law violation, noting that those consequences might be favorable rather than unfavorable).

3. People's self-conceptions are very divergent, and each of our self-conceptions has many dimensions; for example, many of us may want not to be conformists, but also want not to diverge too much from what other people do and think. (Sunstein, 1996a, pp. 916 and 917)

Sunstein also stresses the point that social states can be far more fragile than is generally thought. Small shocks to publicly endorsed norms and roles decrease the cost of displaying deviant norms and rapidly bring about large-scale changes in publicly displayed judgments and desires. Hence, he focuses on what he terms "norm bandwagons" and "norm cascades." He suggests that "[n]orm bandwagons occur when the lowered cost of expressing new norms encourages an ever-increasing number of people to reject previously popular norms to a 'tipping point' where it is adherence to the old norms that produces social disapproval" (1996a, p. 912). He offers the following examples: "if smokers seem like pitiful dupes rather than exciting daredevils, the incidence of smoking will go down; or if people who fail to recycle are seen as oddballs, more people will recycle" (1996a, p. 911). On the other hand, norm cascades occur when societies experience rapid shifts toward new norms. He suggests that something of this kind happened with the attack on apartheid in South Africa, the rise of the feminist movement, and the assault on affirmative action (1996a, pp. 911–12).

Beyond his positive attempts to describe and better understand the role of social norms, Sunstein also believes, from a policy-regulatory perspective, that changes in social norms might be the best way to improve social well-being. Therefore the goal is to reconstruct existing social norms and to change the social meaning of action through a legal expression or statement about appropriate behavior. He recognizes that in the private sector so-called "norm entrepreneurs" attempt to change norms by identifying their bad/good consequences and trying to shift the bases of shame/pride, respectively. His main point, however, is that in many cases government deserves to have, and in any case inevitably does have, a large role in norm management. This enables Sunstein to conclude that "norm management is an important strategy for accomplishing the objectives of law, whatever those objectives may be" (1996a, p. 907).[40]

The unifying theme in his normative theory of social norms centers on the expressive function of law[41]—a term that he uses "to identify the function of

---

[40] "Laws designed to produce changes in norms will be my focus here" (Sunstein 1996b, p. 2026).

[41] By which he means "the function of law in expressing values with the particular goal of shifting social norms" (Sunstein 1996a, p. 910).

law in expressing social values and in encouraging social norms to move in particular directions" (1996a, p. 953). He makes it clear that he is speaking of "the function of law in 'making statements' as opposed to controlling behavior directly" (1996b, p. 2024). Elaborating on the expressive function of law, Sunstein points out that many people support a particular law because of the statements made by law, and disagreements about law are not so much about the consequences (for example, the flag burning amendment) as about the expressive content of law (1996b, p. 2024).[42] Rather than being concerned with laws that merely "speak," his focus is on defending laws that attempt to alter social norms (1996b, p. 2028), in that shifts in social norms are a low-cost method of achieving widely or universally held social goals. When social norms shift, the expressive content of acts shifts as well, thus producing changes in reputational incentives that alter behavior in new directions, eventually resulting in norm cascades. As Sunstein sees it, a good deal of governmental action is and must be self-consciously designed to change norms, meanings, or roles, and in that way to increase the individual benefits or decrease the individual costs associated with certain acts,[43] thus enabling him to conclude that "without understanding the expressive function of law, we will have a hard time getting an adequate handle on public views on such issues as civil rights, prostitution, the environment, endangered species, capital punishment, and abortion" (1996, p. 2029).

Eric Posner notes that the variety of types and forms of social norms requires that different models be used to understand and analyze the development and impact of these norms in different contexts.[44] Posner, for his part, explores the link among symbols, symbolic actions, and norms. In doing so, he advances a model of signaling activity to analyze the role played by symbols in individuals' behavior and beliefs, and how the legal system can influence and manipulate symbols. As Posner points out, symbols unquestionably exert influence on government policy, legal-economic and otherwise. Posner suggests that symbols matter because the attitudes that people take toward them reveal a great deal to others about those people's character and influence the willingness of others to form cooperative relationships with them. The link between symbols and norms comes in because, according to Posner, the power attached to the symbol means that "people's efforts to show respect for them

---

[42] He writes, "[T]he close attention American society pays to the [Supreme] Court's pronouncements is connected with the expressive or symbolic character of those pronouncements. When the Court makes a decision, it is often taken to be speaking on behalf of the nation's basic principles and commitments. . . . [P]erhaps the expressive effect of the Court's decisions, or their expressive function, better captures what is often at stake" (Sunstein 1996b, p. 2028).

[43] For example, he suggests that "government might try to inculcate or to remove shame, fear of which can be a powerful deterrent to behavior. The inculcation of shame operates as a kind of tax; the removal of shame might be seen as the elimination of a tax or even as a kind of subsidy" (Sunstein 1996a, p. 913).

[44] All references to "Posner" in the remainder of this section are to Eric Posner.

lead to significant forms of conformity that can be described as social norms" (1998b, p. 767).

Symbolic behavior is a normal and regularized part of life in society, and this symbolic behavior takes a wide variety of forms. For example, people "shake hands, applaud in theaters, salute the flag, wear stylish clothes, exchange wedding rings, bow, present gifts, observe diplomatic protocol, and show deference to superiors" (1998b, p. 767). Why, though, do people engage in these symbolic behaviors? Posner answers this question using a model of a "cooperation game," where cooperation refers to any kind of cooperative relationship that can be modeled as a repeated prisoner's dilemma, including business, family, and social relationships. The cooperation game approach suggests that people engage in symbolic behaviors because they want to induce others to cooperate with them, and they do so by sending signals. These signals show that they have a characteristic that they want the receiver(s) of the signal to believe that they have, but that the receiver is unable to observe directly.

The underlying motivation here is the presence of mutual gains from cooperation, accompanied by the problem that one can get burned if the other party cheats in a supposedly cooperative venture. Behavior is thus guided by the prospect of one's needing to deal with other members of society when future favorable transactions need to be executed, but under conditions of uncertainty. Posner's approach effectively posits norms as conventions that govern the behavior of individuals who are attempting to signal to the larger community that they are "good types" with whom to build productive long-term cooperative relationships. These signals are costly (sometimes more so, sometimes less so), but also give rise to associated benefits. Those who value the long-term gains from a cooperative relationship with others will invest in sending the signal, and the willingness to incur these costs will tend to provide evidence that one is a cooperative type.

In the resulting signaling equilibrium, several outcomes could obtain. The first and most obvious is a separating equilibrium, where "all the good types send the signal and match up with each other, and the bad types do not send the signal and either match up with each other or not at all" (Posner 2000, p. 19). That is, a separating equilibrium distinguishes the good types from the bad types. There may be times, however, when everyone sends the signal because the expected gains from doing so outweigh the costs for good types and bad types, giving rise to what is known as an active pooling equilibrium. In other cases, no one sends the signal because expected costs outweigh the gains for both good types and bad types—a passive pooling equilibrium.

In short, individuals comply and enforce certain social norms with a view toward developing long-run exchange relatioships. The norms here are endogenous: they describe the behavior that arises in equilibrium. As Posner (1998b, p. 797) points out, "It is not that X punishes Y for violating a social norm; rather, X (and many other people) avoids Y because Y's behavior

reveals to X that association with Y will not serve X's interests. Although in common speech we say that Y's behavior violates a social norm, the punishment is endogenous, not imposed by an external force." The effect is that "an important class of social norms arises from signaling games in which people choose actions that signal loyalty to states and communities" (1998b, p. 797). While people may engage in these behaviors because of certain intrinsic motivations, in many other cases they will engage in these behaviors only to show that they are loyal, giving it "the peculiarly empty quality of a symbol," where "people take little or no pleasure from the behavior, but engage in it for the sake of reputation" (1998b, p. 797).

Thus, the signaling model provides yet another perspective on the relationship between law and social norms. Laws and other forms of state action can affect signaling equilibria in multiple ways: (1) it can affect the cost of sending a signal; (2) it can affect the payoffs that senders and receivers receive from cooperation; (3) it can affect people's beliefs about the relative prevalence of good types and bad types in the population; and (4) it can affect the payoff to signal construction to the norm entrepreneur or even construct a signal itself (Posner 1998b, pp. 778, 789). The result is that a change in legal rules can give rise to a new signaling equilibrium, and the efficacy of the new law can be determined by comparing the new signaling equilibrium with the old one.[45]

Posner rejects the arguments of those who take the tack that social norms are almost certain to be efficient in certain contexts—such as small groups—arguing instead that efficiency is highly ambiguous a priori, and that efficiency judgments cannot move beyond the situation- and circumstance-specific. In fact, because norms tend to generate positive externalities, economic theory would suggest that they will be undersupplied. These two indicators of social norm inefficiency raise the question of government intervention to resolve the inefficiencies. As with efficiency questions, Posner contends that "one can make no presumptions" about whether intervention will make matters better rather than worse. This, too, depends on circumstances and on the agents and institutions doing the intervening (2000, pp. 176, 179).

The dependence of cooperation on the existence and form of symbols gives the government an incentive to intervene and create or otherwise regulate these symbols. He says, however, that there are good reasons to be wary of those pushing for state regulation of social meaning and of the very idea of the state engaging in such regulatory efforts:

> First, government officials do not stand outside the signaling game. They, like citizens, are prisoners of symbols when the symbols are sufficiently powerful. . . .

---

[45] If the law changes the equilibrium from separating to pooling, the signal, obviously, disappears. Regarding the ambiguity surrounding efficiency judgments as between signaling equilibria, see Posner (2000, ch. 10).

Second, the results of government efforts to change or sustain symbols, whether through legal devices or official exhortation, are inherently unpredictable. Thus, government efforts to change signals can backfire, leading to a strengthening of symbols that the government sought to change . . . or to reification of the desired symbol. (1998b, p. 798)

Posner goes on to point out that "when government efforts, whether deliberately or not, destroy or reify existing symbols, norm entrepreneurs will propose new symbols that may have worse effects than the old ones" (1998b, p. 798). Furthermore, rent-seekers may engage in wasteful competition in an attempt to use government as a means to convey their desired symbols (p. 796).

LAW, ECONOMICS, AND SOCIAL NORMS AT WORK

The Coase Theorem Meets Social Norms

In his book *Order without Law,* Robert Ellickson examines the empirical applicability of the Coase theorem by looking at actual cattle rancher and farmer disputes in Shasta County, California, a picturesque rural community in Northern California where cattlemen own and operate large family ranches. Also present there are retirees and other recent settlers who live on "ranchettes." These ranchette owners maintain properties that are generally smaller than those of the cattle ranchers, and, while they may keep a few farm animals on the property as a hobby, for the most part do not make significant income from agriculture. Ellickson describes the relations of cattle ranchers and the ranchette owners on several fronts, including incidents involving cattle which stray from the ranchers' property onto that of their neighbors or even onto the nearby highway, where cattle and drivers are often seriously injured and even killed in collisions.

Ellickson's narrative touches on the history of range law, including the pressures to close the range that grew through the nineteenth and early twentieth centuries. This culminated in the Estray Act of 1915, an act that made owners of livestock in most of the state strictly liable for trespass damage. Shasta County commissioners, however, have designated part of the land as "open range," meaning that the landowner whose property is trampled by trespassing cattle bears the cost of the damages, and other parts of the land as "closed range," meaning that it is the rancher who must pay for the damage caused by his wandering cattle. Against this legal backdrop, Ellickson explored three different types of legal disputes: (i) Who bears the cost of damage caused by trespassing cattle? (ii) How are costs allocated for fencing property boundaries? (iii) Who pays for the damage in auto accidents caused by cattle wandering onto the highway? According to California law, the county's designation of a

range as either "open" or "closed" is controlling only in the first scenario, that is, in the instances of cattle trespass. There is a separate California statute that governs the allocation of costs for boundary fences, and auto-cattle accidents are dealt with primarily through the standard rules of negligence regardless of whether the accident occurred in open- or closed-range territory.

After years of research, Ellickson concluded that the neighbors of Shasta County resolved their disputes without reference to the law, frequently in ignorance of the law, and sometimes in spite of the law. More specifically, he showed that the cattle ranchers and ranchette owners of Shasta County turned to informal norms rather than legal rules to resolve disputes. Ellickson demonstrated that resources were allocated in accordance with the established social norms of the community and, as such, controlled human interaction more directly than the prevailing law. It was the social norms, rather than the laws in place, that ultimately shaped their social order.

Of course, for our purposes here, what is important is the nature of those controlling social norms. Ellickson's explanation for the effectiveness of these norms turns on an argument that these ranchers and ranchette owners in Shasta County have a "continuing relationship" and thus constitute a "close-knit group" (Ellickson 1991, p. 178). Here, "neighborliness," and the "cooperation among neighbors" are important elements in the evolution, existence, and maintenance of social norms. This "close-knittedness" both arises from and gives effect to the dissemination of adequate information, reciprocal power, and ready sanctioning opportunities among parties to a potential conflict. That is, according to Ellickson (1991, pp. 177–78), "a close-knit group must be nonhierarchical; the informal power is broadly distributed among group members and the information pertinent to informal control must circulate easily among them." In addition, he argues that a close-knit group must also have "credible and reciprocal prospects for the application of power against one another and a good supply of information on past and present internal events" (1991, p. 181). Thus, close-knittedness is contingent on the existence of continuing relationships among members of the group (1991, pp. 65–66, 168).

For example, in a cattle trespass case, the victim of trespass telephones the cattle rancher to inform him that his cattle are loose and doing damage. The rancher typically would thank the caller, often apologize for the harm, and then go round up his straying cattle. In disputes over fencing, which can be very costly to resolve, Ellickson discovered that a rule of proportionality governed behavior: if there was a shared boundary between two ranchers, the neighboring ranchers would split the costs of installing a fence and divide up the responsibilities based upon the number of cattle each owned, rather than engage in cash transactions. When there was a common boundary between a rancher and a ranchette or other non-ranch property, the norm of proportionality,

then, required the rancher to pay for and build the fence.[46] In all of these cases, the problems were settled without reference to the law in place; indeed, changes in the law, which we would expect to affect who pays for the fence, had no impact at all on the distribution of costs.

In an extensive review of all facets of the interactions between ranchers and other residents of Shasta County, Ellickson came to the conclusion that "members of tight social groups will informally encourage each other to engage in cooperative behavior" (1991, p. 167). The norm that an owner of livestock is responsible for the acts of his animals thus exemplifies an "overarching norm of cooperation among neighbors" (p. 77). Such cooperation, he argues, maximizes the aggregate welfare of the members of a close-knit group (p. 167). In all, Ellickson maintains, farmers and ranchers achieve cooperative outcomes "by developing and enforcing adaptive norms of neighborliness that trump formal legal entitlements" (p. 4). These norms function as "nonhierarchical processes of coordination" (p. 5), processes that are central to his narrative of order—a basic legal function—the result of which is that neighborliness is shaped "beyond the reach of law" (p. 4).

Social Norms and the Diamond Industry Cartel

In an extensive analysis of the diamond industry, Lisa Bernstein (1992) explains how the economic performance of that industry is influenced by social norms that work in place of formal law.[47] She observed that the disputes among members of the diamond industry were not resolved through the courts nor by application of formal legal rules enunciated and enforced by the state. Instead, firms in the diamond industry had organized their own system of private governance to perform monitoring and punishment functions. This governance system employed a norm-based mechanism of contract enforcement to deter breach and resolve contractual disputes. Equally important, it endured.[48]

The DeBeers cartel distributes about 85 percent of the world's supply of diamonds to four brokers who, in turn, during the course of ten viewing sessions held in London each year, sell rough diamonds to some 150 to 200 dealers, known a sightholders. Most of the U.S. sightholders are members of the

[46] See Ellickson (1991, ch. 4). For a concise review of the facts of the fencing norms, see Walton (1999, pp. 160–161).

[47] This section simply draws on and presents an abbreviated restatement of the facts in accordance with Bernstein's 1992 article. We distilled a rather lengthy article down to the three-page review contained here and, in doing so, have borrowed directly from her article so as to maintain and transmit her excellent and detailed analysis of this industry.

[48] Janet Landa (1981, 1994, 1996) has undertaken a similar analysis of how social norms driven by a Confucian code of ethics govern contractual relationships among Chinese middleman traders.

New York Diamond Dealers Club (NYDDC), which comprises about 2000 sightholders, manufactures, wholesalers, and brokers. The cartel actively monitors all facets of the sale and distribution of the diamonds to the sightholders and controls the trade through a strict set of internal rules that are designed at once to facilitate trade and maintain the power of the cartel. For example, all diamonds must be paid for by the sightholders within seven days of acquisition. Because it takes roughly four months for a sightholder to turn a rough diamond into a cut and polished stone that can be offered for sale, the cartel provides financing for the sightholders' purchases but does so under its own set of rules and via its own set of approved banks—one of which is located in the same building as the club.

Smaller dealers and brokers do their business on the NYDDC trading floor. The larger, more important dealers conduct their business in private settings but do go regularly to the trading floor to get a sense of where the market prices are.[49] For the smaller dealers, the trading floor is the place where they can signal their trustworthiness, and it provides them with a secure place to make transactions. Much of the transacting process is structured by norms specific to the diamond trade. For example, when a buyer wants to make an offer to a seller, the diamond is placed into an envelop that is then folded and sealed in a precise manner. The date and the terms and conditions of the offer to buy are written on the envelop, and the buyer then signs the envelope across the seal. By convention, the offer is good until 1 p.m. the next day. If the seller wants to accept the offer, the deal is consummated with a handshake accompanied by the words *mazel u'brouch*. This creates a binding agreement. With this agreement in place, the parties then take the diamond(s) to be weighed and are issued an official weight slip listing the basic information on the nature of the agreement completed on the floor. A similar document is prepared when transactions are made in private offices rather than on the trading floor. These bills of sale are considered by the NYDDC to be definitive evidence of the transaction when disputes arise over the nature of the transaction, and place the matter firmly under the club's jurisdiction, thereby exposing the disputing parties to club sanctions if they take the matter court.

As Bernstein points out, these handshake contracts have many advantages over formal, legal ones, mostly via their effects in reducing transaction costs. For example, they tend to reduce costs both by reducing risk associated with the transaction and eliminating costly, time-consuming negotiations over payment terms. The major transaction-cost-reducing function, though, comes through the reduction of costs of acquiring reputation-related information about other parties. Information on reputations is crucial to contract formation in markets such as this one, where contract enforcement depends on damage to reputation and social ostracism. People will be unwilling to deal with those

---

[49] The NYDDC does not record the price or volume of daily transactions.

who do not deal honestly if they know about this dishonesty, which means that negative reputation effects can be disasterous for one's business. On the other hand, the secrecy norm with respect to those outside of the NYDDC is highly valued by club members. Because trade secrets may be revealed in civil courts, the parties to a dispute have a strong incentive to settle their dispute though club-level arbitration. In fact, as Bernstein notes, the preservation of the secrecy norm is one of the primary reasons why the industry has historically used extralegal agreements rather than relying on formal contract law.

All dealers agree, as a condition of membership, to take disputes between themselves and other club members to the club's binding arbitration system. That is, members may not seek any redress through the courts; doing so can result in a fine or expulsion from the NYDDC. Here, the club employs transaction-cost-reducing mechansims, including a mandatary prearbitration procedure where about 85 percent of all disputes are resolved. Those cases that are not settled through this prearbitration process are resolved in the more formal NYDDC dispute resolution bodies. If the club, for whatever reason, decides not to hear a case, the parties can seek remedies through formal law. Such is the extent of the extra-legal nature of this process that the NYDDC Board of Arbitrators does not even apply the New York state law of contract or its associated damage provisions. Instead, it resolves disputes based on the industry's norms and trade customs, some of which are codified in their by-laws, others of which simply exist as norms among group members. Typically, parties found to have breached a contract or engaged in unethical conduct can be ordered to pay a fine—which may have compensatory and punitive components—or to make a donation to charity. Refusal to pay the fine can lead to your membership being suspended or revoked.

One of the most important elements of the industry centers on the posting of reputation bonds and "psychic/social bonds." Reputation bonds are equal to the present value of the profit on future transactions that will not be realized if the promisor breaches. For transactions involving dealers who are not members of the club, the reputation bond is, effectively, the sole enforcement mechanism that avoids recourse to the courts. Moreover, while transactions among club members can be resolved through arbitration, the reputation bonds provide one avenue for the NYDDC arbitration panel to enforce its judgments among members. The less tangible "psychic/social cost bonds" are also effective enforcement mechanisms. When a so-called primary social cost bond is sacrificed, a breaching dealer's ability to communicate information about his reputation and his ability to obtain information about new business opportunities may well be diminished. When a so-called secondary social bond is sacrificed, the breaching dealer may experience guilt, loss of self-esteem, and questions about trustworthiness and competence, as well as losing out on opportunities for pleasurable associations.

Thus, as Bernstein makes clear, while some of the success of the diamond

industry is due to the manner by which trust and reputation are mechanisms that facilitate commercial transactions, the enduring success of the industry has at least as much to do with the fact that reputation effects and social bonds have been used to create a system of social norm-based private law—one that both reduces the costs of transacting and allows most transactions to be consummated and enforced apart from the formal legal system.

CONCLUSION: MARGINAL EVOLUTION OR PARADIGM SHIFT?

The foregoing discussion illustrates how the analysis of social norms in the context of law and economics can enhance our understanding of the interaction between the domains of law and social norms and how this can be applied to the analysis of legal-economic outcomes. The goal of this research is to promote an increased understanding of how formal law and social norms serve separately and jointly as regulators of individual behavior and the implications of this for the fashioning of both laws and social norms so as to best accomplish society's goals.

If one accepts the idea that the influence of social norms must be incorporated into Law and Economics, the question then arises as to the paradigmatic meaning of this for the field of Law and Economics. This raises the issue of whether the inclusion of social norms into a body of analysis so heavily dominated by rational choice theory constitutes a paradigm shift in the Kuhnian sense.[50] Ellickson argues the affirmative case:

> Kuhn's framework can be applied to the situation of classical law and economics—the paradigm developed by Ronald Coase, Guido Calabresi, and [Richard] Posner and others in the 1960s and 1970s. . . . Under the Kuhnian framework, the thesis that classical law and economics is in for significant change could be stated in either strong or weak form. The strong version is that the newly discovered phenomena are anomalies that ultimately cannot be reconciled with the classical paradigm and will lead to its demise. The weak version of the thesis asserts that normal science within law and economics can accommodate these phenomena.

Ellickson favors the weaker version, suggesting that "law and economics is in for a time of turbulent normal science, not extinction," and that the enormous surge in interest in social norms and related phenomena "promises to enrich" law and economics rather than signaling its demise (1998, pp. 539, 551, 537). Richard Posner (1998b, p. 565), on the other hand, disagrees with Ellickson, arguing that the inclusion of social norms into Law and Economics does not constitute a paradigm shift—strong or weak—but rather merely an extension of an ongoing progressive research program, "one that employs the same basic

---

[50] See Kuhn (1970).

paradigm, namely the theory of rational choice, of which both game theory and public choice can be viewed as extensions."

A more comprehensive approach to Law and Economics that includes an analysis of social norms still needs to be worked out. Laws and social norms are both key components of the social, political, and economic fabric against and within which economic activity takes place. Systematically ignoring either one of these can lead to faulty predictions of expected legal-economic performance followed by cries of frustration over "unintended consequences." There seems to be an emerging consensus—or at least a strong majority view—that (i) the structure of rights, rules, and legal doctrines; (ii) technology; and (iii) habits, customs, mores, and social norms all affect behavior and performance—in the case of habits, customs, mores and social norms, by inducing certain patterns of preference formation that directly affect behavior. In fact, it is fair to say that these concerns are now prominently reflected to some degree in all of the major schools of thought surveyed in this book.

EPILOGUE

Law, technology, and social norms are all important factors in driving economic performance. If the reader has taken anything at all from this book, we hope that it is a healthy appreciation for the complexity of these interrelations and the significant contributions that all of the various schools of thought surveyed here make to our understanding of them. Our discussion has highlighted certain of the fundamental disagreements that exist between schools—those over efficiency as a workable or ethical standard and over the usefulness of the rational-actor model being foremost among them. These differences across schools, however, and the "competing perspectives" aura that they bring to the discussion are vastly outweighed by their respective horses for courses utilities. Each school of thought—indeed, even each of the factions within each school of thought—trains a somewhat different lens on the questions that we posed early on in chapter 1, namely, "What is the law?" "Where does the law come from and how does the it acquire its legitimacy?" and, "In what direction shall we change the law?" As such, each emphasizes its own mode of reasoning and maintains its own stance on issues in legal-economic policy and, in doing so, brings out different facets of legal-economic problems and their potential resolutions.

From a more practical perspective, the influence of law, technology, and social norms is such that when policymakers are trying to attain a particular policy outcome, they must be careful not to fall victim to relying exclusively

on just one of these three major factors in proposing remedies. Each of these factors creates it own particular perspective on a problem and hence, its own particular agenda for dealing with that problem. For example, in policy debates, it is not all that unusual to witness proponents of "the technological fix" arguing for more science, technology, and resources to "build in" the remedy being sought. It is also not unusual to find proponents of the Chicago- and Virginia-based approaches to legal-economic policy advocating for market remedies (typically under the banner of "deregulation") as a singular basis for policy. And finally, once the door is open to changing social norms, one confronts more and more the social norm, NGO preachers calling for us to "do the 'right' thing."[51] As various legal-economic issues arise, it is clear that these factors are often in conflict and, even when they are not, most legal-economic issues are sufficiently complex so that it makes relying on any singular approach problematic. We believe that all singular solutions must be rejected whether with regard to technology, social norms, or among the schools of thought within Law and Economics. The quest must be to understand the role that social norms play in helping to order society (or social groups within the society) together with the role played by incentives promulgated by the state-sanctioned law, together with the impact brought on by changing technology, and the ways in which the triad of law, social norms, and technology interact to affect economic performance (broadly conceived). This, in turn, requires a broad-based, or eclectic, approach to Law and Economics.

We began this book by saying that we intended to provide an outline of the principle contours of the various approaches Law and Economics, and that we were not going to attempt to make judgments among them. This approach is perhaps less than comforting to those who want to be given "an approach" or "the best approach" to doing Law and Economics. The fact is that there isn't such a thing. Each of these schools of thought is far too narrow in scope to do justice to the breadth and totality of the interrelations between legal and economic processes. Taken together, however, they unlock the black box of legal-economic relationships that had so long been ignored in the development of economic and legal thinking. It may be true that, as many critics of Law and Economics have argued, law is far too important to be left to the economists. It is also however, far too important to be left to the lawyers, the ethicists, the political scientists, or the sociologists. Holmes was right: in the legal arena, the man of the future really has turned out to be "the man of statistics and the master of economics."[52] Both economics and the law are that much richer as a result.

---

[51] As Sunstein warns, however, once norms are introduced into the mix, "a reference to social norms will become a conclusory response to any apparently anomalous results" (1996b, p. 945) and of this, we must be careful. It has also been argued that this same sort of vacuous thinking has victimized policy-making with regard to the ubiquitous use of the concept of transaction costs.

[52] Holmes (1897, p. 469).

Abrams, Kathryn. "Law's Republicanism." *Yale Law Journal* 97 (July 1988): 1591–608.

Ackerman, Bruce A. "*Law and the Modern Mind* by Jerome Frank." *Daedalus* 103 (Winter 1974): 119–30.

———. *Reconstructing American Law*. Cambridge: Harvard University Press, 1984.

———. "Law, Economics, and the Problem of Legal Culture." *Duke Law Journal* 1986 (December 1986): 929–47.

Ackerman, Bruce A., and Richard B. Stewart. "Reforming Environmental Law: The Democratic Case for Market Incentives." *Columbia Journal of Environmental Law* 13, no. 2 (1988): 171–99.

Adams, Henry C. *Relation of the State to Industrial Action and Economics and Jurisprudence*. Edited by Joseph Dorfman. New York: Columbia University Press, 1954.

Agnello, Richard J., and Lawrence P. Donnelley. "Prices and Property Rights in the Fisheries." *Southern Economic Journal* 42 (October 1975): 253–62.

Alchian, Armen A. "Private Property and the Relative Cost of Tenure." Pp. 350–71 in *The Public Stake in Union Power*, edited by P. D. Bradley. Charlottesville: University of Virginia Press, 1959.

———. *Some Economics of Property*. Santa Monica, Calif.: Rand, 1961.

———. Foreword to *The Economics of Property* Rights, edited by Eirik G. Furubotn and Svetozar Pejovich. Cambridge, Mass.: Ballinger, 1974.

Alchian, Armen A., and Harold Demsetz. "Production, Information Costs, and Economic Organization." *American Economic Review* 62 (December 1972): 777–95.

Allen, Douglas W. "What Are Transaction Costs?" *Research in Law and Economics* 14 (1991): 1–18.

———. "Property Rights, Transaction Costs, and Coase: One More Time." Pp. 105–18 in *Coasean Economics: Law and Economics and the New Institutional Economics*, edited by Steven G. Medema. Boston: Kluwer, 1998.

Anderson, Terry L., and P. J. Hill. "The Evolution of Property Rights: A Study of the American West." *Journal of Law and Economics* 18 (April 1975): 163–79.

———. *The Not So Wild, Wild West: Property Rights on the Frontier*. Stanford: Stanford University Press, 2004.

Andrews, Neil, "Wormes in the Entrayles: The Corporate Citizen in Law?" *Murdoch University Electronic Journal of Law* 5 (June 1998), in electronic text at note 165.

Aoki, Masahiko. *Toward a Comparative Institutional Analysis*. Boston: MIT Press, 2001.

Appleby, Joyce. "The Social Origins of American Revolutionary Ideology." *Journal of American History* 64 (1978): 935–58.

Areeda Philip E. *Antitrust Law: An Analysis of Antitrust Principles and Their Application*. New York: Aspen Law and Business, 1978.

Arrow, Kenneth J. *Social Choice and Individual Values*. New York: Wiley, 1951.

————. "The Organization of Economic Activity: Issues Pertinent to the Choice of Market versus Nonmarket Allocation." Pp. 44–64 in *The Analysis and Evaluation of Public Expenditures: The PPB System.* Joint Economic Committee, 91st Cong.1st sess. Washington, D.C.: U.S. Government Printing Office, 1969.

Austin, John. *The Province of Jurisprudence Determined.* New York: B. Franklin, 1861.

————. *Lectures on Jurisprudence or The Philosophy of Positive Law.* London: J. Murray, 1885.

Ayres, Clarence E. *The Theory of Economic Progress.* Chapel Hill: University of North Carolina Press, 1944.

Ayres, Ian, and John Braithwaite. *Responsive Regulation: Transcending the Deregulation Debate.* New York: Oxford University Press, 1992.

Ayres, Ian, and Robert Gertner. "Filling Gaps in Incomplete Contracts: An Economic Theory of Default Rules." *Yale Law Journal* 99 (October 1989): 87–130.

Ayres, Ian, and Eric Talley. "Solomonic Bargaining: Dividing a Legal Entitlement to Facilitate Coasean Trade." *Yale Law Journal* 104 (March 1995): 1027–117.

Bain, Joe S. *Barriers to New Competition: Their Character and Consequences in Manufacturing Industries.* Cambridge: Harvard University Press, 1956.

Balkin, J. M. "Too Good to Be True: The Positive Economic Theory of Law." *Columbia Law Review* 87 (1987): 1447–89.

Ballard, Charles L., and Steven Medema. "The Marginal Efficiency Effects of Taxes and Subsidies in the Presence of Externalities: A Computational General Equilibrium Approach." *Journal of Public Economcs* 52 (September 1993): 199–216.

Ballard, Mark. "17-Front Tort War: One-third of States Have Bills Pending." *National Law Journal*, May 12, 2003, p. 1.

Barnard, Chester. *The Functions of the Executive.* Cambridge: Harvard University Press, 1938.

Barnes, David W., and Lynn A. Stout. *Cases and Materials on Law and Economics.* St. Paul: West, 1992.

Barone, E. "The Ministry of Production in the Collectivist State." Pp. 245–90 in *Collectivist Economic Planning*, edited by F. A. Hayek. London: Routledge, 1935.

Barzel, Yoram. "Transaction Costs: Are They Just Costs?" *Journal of Institutional and Theoretical Economics* 141, no. 1 (1985): 4–16.

————. "The Entrepreneur's Reward for Self-Policing." *Economic Inquiry* 25 (January 1987): 103–16.

————. *Economic Analysis of Property Rights.* Cambridge: Cambridge University Press, 1989.

Basu, Kaushik. "Social Norms and the Law." Pp. 476–81 in *The New Palgrave Dictionary of Economics and the Law*, edited by Peter Newman. London: Macmillan, 1998.

Bator, Francis M. "The Simple Analytics of Wealth Maximization." *American Economic Review* 47 (March 1957): 22–59.

Baumol, William J., and Wallace E. Oates. *The Theory of Environmental Policy.* 2d ed. Cambridge: Cambridge University Press, 1988.

Baxter, William F. "Antitrust in Transition: Crossing the Threshold of Change—Panel Discussion." Moderator: Richard A. Whiting; Panelists: Frederick M. Rowe,

William F. Baxter, Hon. Robert H. Bork, and Phillip Areeda. *Antitrust Law Journal* 54 (1985): 31–37.

Baye, Michael R. *Managerial Economics and Business Strategy.* 2d ed. Chicago: McGraw-Hill/Irwin, 1997.

Becker, Gary S. *The Economics of Discrimination.* Chicago: University of Chicago Press, 1957.

———. "A Theory of the Allocation of Time." *Economic Journal* 75 (September 1965): 493–517.

———. "Crime and Punishment: An Economic Approach." *Journal of Political Economy* 76 (1968): 169–217.

———. *The Economic Approach to Human Behavior.* Chicago: University of Chicago Press, 1976.

———. "A Theory of Competition Among Pressure Groups for Political Influence." *Quarterly Journal of Economics* 98 (1983): 371–400.

———. "Public Policies, Pressure Groups, and Dead Weight Costs." *Journal of Public Economics* 28, no.3 (December 1985): 329–47.

Becker, Gary S., and Robert J. Barro. "A Reformulation of the Economic Theory of Fertility." *Quarterly Journal of Economics* 103 (February 1988): 1–25.

Becker, Gary S., Michael Grossman, and Kevin M. Murphy. "Rational Addiction and the Effects of Price on Consumption." *American Economic Review* 81 (May 1991): 237–41.

Becker, Gary S., and Kevin M. Murphy. "The Family and the State." *Journal of Law and Economics* 31 (April 1988a): 1–18.

———. "A Theory of Rational Addiction." *Journal of Political Economy* 96 (August 1988b): 675–700.

Beecher-Monas, Erica. "Challenging Coase: Socioeconomic Explanations in the First-Year Contracts Course." Florida State University College of Law, Public Law and Legal Theory Working Paper No. 51 (2002). Available at http://ssrn.com/abstract_id=306565.

Bell, Derrick, and Preeta Bansal. "The Republican Revival and Racial Politics." *Yale Law Journal* 97 (July 1988): 1609–21.

Bell, John F. *A History of Economic Thought.* New York: Ronald, 1967.

Bergson, Abram. "A Reformulation of Certain Aspects of Welfare Economics." *Quarterly Journal of Economics* 52 (February 1938): 310–34.

Berolzheimer, Fritz. *The World's Legal Philosophies.* Boston: Boston Book Co., 1912. Reprint, South Hackensack, N.J.: Rothman Reprints, 1968.

Bernstein, Lisa. "Opting Out of the Legal System: Extralegal Contractual Relations in the Diamond Industry." *Journal of Legal Studies* 21 (1992): 115–57.

Black, Duncan. "On the Rationale of Group Decision Making." *Journal of Political Economy* 56 (1948a): 23–34.

———. "The Decisions of a Committee Using a Special Majority." *Econometrica* 16 (1948b): 245–61.

———. *The Theory of Committees and Elections.* Cambridge: Cambridge University Press, 1958.

Blaug, Mark. *Economic Theory in Retrospect.* 3d ed. Cambridge: Cambridge University Press, 1978.

Blumenthal, William. "Antitrust at the Millennium (Part I): Clear Agency Guidelines: Lessons from 1982." *Antitrust Law Journal* 68 (2000): 5–27.

Boadway, Robin W., and David E. Wildasin. *Public Sector Economics*. 2d ed. Boston: Little, Brown, 1984.

Bodenheimer, Edgar. *Jurisprudence: The Philosophy and Method of the Law*. Rev. ed. Cambridge: Harvard University Press, 1974.

Bork, Robert. *The Antitrust Paradox: A Policy at War with Itself*. 2d ed. New York: Basic Books, 1993.

Bottomly, Anthony. "The Effect of Common Ownership of Land Upon Resource Allocation in Tripolitania." *Land Economics* 39 (February 1963): 91–95.

Bouckaert, Boudewijn, and Gerrit De Geest, eds. *Encyclopedia of Law and Economics*. Northampton, Mass.: Edward Elgar, 2000.

Bowman, Ward S. *Patent and Antitrust Law: A Legal and Economic Appraisal*. Chicago: University of Chicago Press, 1973.

Breimyer, Harold. "Government Intervention: A Deceptive Label." *Choices* (2d qrt., 1991): 3.

Breit, William. "The Development of Clarence Ayres's Theoretical Institutionalism." *Social Science Quarterly* 54 (September 1973): 244–57.

Brennan, Geoffrey, and James M. Buchanan. *The Reason of Rules: Constitutional Political Economy*. Cambridge: Cambridge University Press, 1985.

Brennan, Geoffrey, and Alan Hamlin. "Constitutional Choice." Pp. 117–39 in *The Elgar Companion to Public Choice*, edited by William F. Shughart II and Laura Razzolini. Northampton, Mass.: Edward Elgar, 2001.

Brennen, Timothy J. "The Trouble with Norms." Pp. 85–94 in *Social Norms and Economic Institutions*, edited by Kenneth J. Koford and Jeffrey B. Miller. Ann Arbor: University of Michigan Press, 1991.

Brenner, Reuven. "Economics—An Imperialist Science?" *Journal of Legal Studies* 9 (January 1980): 179–88.

Bromley, Daniel W. *Economic Interests and Institutions*. New York: Basil Blackwell, 1989.

———. *Environment and the Economy: Property Rights and Public Policy*. Cambridge: Blackwell, 1991.

Bronfenbrenner, Martin. "Observations on the Chicago School(s)." *Journal of Political Economy* 60 (February 1962): 72–75.

Buchanan, James M. "Positive Economics, Welfare Economics, and Political Economy." *Journal of Law and Economics* 2 (October 1959): 124–38.

———. "La Scienza delle Finanze: The Italian Tradition in Fiscal Theory," Pp. 24–74 in *Fiscal Theory and Political Economy: Selected Essays*. Chapel Hill: University of North Carolina Press, 1960.

———. "Toward Analysis of Closed Behavioral Systems." Pp. 11–23 in *Theory of Public Choice*, edited by James M. Buchanan and Robert D. Tollison. Ann Arbor: University of Michigan Press, 1972a.

———. "Politics, Property, and the Law: An Alternative Interpretation of *Miller et al. v. Schoene*." *Journal of Law and Economics* 15 (October 1972b): 439–52.

———. "Good Economics—Bad Law." *Virginia Law Review* 60 (1974): 483–92.

———. *The Limits of Liberty*. Chicago: University of Chicago Press, 1975a.

————. "A Contractarian Paradigm for Applying Economic Theory." *American Economic Review* 65 (May 1975b): 225–30.

————. "Why Does Government Grow?" Pp. 3–18 in *Budgets and Bureaucrats: The Sources of Government Growth*, edited by Thomas Borcherding. Durham, N.C.: Duke University Press, 1977.

————. "Rent Seeking and Profit Seeking." Pp. 3–15 in *Toward a Theory of the Rent-Seeking Society*, edited by James M. Buchanan, Robert Tollison, and Gordon Tullock. College Station: Texas A&M University Press, 1980.

————. "Rights, Efficiency, and Exchange: The Irrelevance of Transaction Cost." Pp. 9–24 in *Ansprache, Eigentums und Verfagungsrechte*, edited by M. Neumann. Berlin: Duncker and Humbolt, 1983. Reprinted in *The Legacy of Ronald Coase in Economic Analysis, vol. II*, edited by Steven G. Medema, pp. 175–90. Northampton, Mass.: Edward Elgar, 1995.

————. "Politics without Romance: A Sketch of Positive Public Choice Theory and Its Normative Implications." Pp. 11–22 in *The Theory of Public Choice II*, edited by James M. Buchanan and Robert D. Tollison. Ann Arbor: University of Michigan Press, 1984a.

————. "Constitutional Restrictions on the Power of Government." Pp. 439–52 in *The Theory of Public Choice II*, edited by James M. Buchanan and Robert D. Tollison. Ann Arbor: University of Michigan Press, 1984b.

————. *Liberty, Market and State*. New York: New York University Press, 1986.

————. "An Individualistic Theory of the Political Process." Pp. 223–35 in *Economics: Between Predictive Science and Moral Philosophy*, compiled by Robert D. Tollison and Viktor J. Vanberg. College Station: Texas A&M University Press, 1987.

————. "The Economic Theory of Politics Reborn." *Challenge* 31 (March/April 1988): 4–10.

————. *Constitutional Economics*. Oxford: Basil Blackwell, 1991.

Buchanan, James M., and Robert D. Tollison, eds. *The Theory of Public Choice*. Ann Arbor: University of Michigan Press, 1972.

————, eds. *The Theory of Public Choice II*. Ann Arbor: University of Michigan Press, 1984.

Buchanan, James M., Robert D. Tollison, and Gordon Tullock. *Toward a Theory of the Rent-Seeking Society*. College Station: Texas A&M University Press, 1980.

Buchanan, James M., and Gordon Tullock. *The Calculus of Consent*. Ann Arbor: Universisity of Michigan Press, 1962.

Buckingham, Walter S. *Theoretical Economic Systems: A Comparative Analysis*. New York: Ronald, 1958.

Burger, Joanna, and Michael Gochfeld. "The Tragedy of the Commons—30 Years Later." *Environment* 40, no.10 (December 1998): 4–13, 26–27.

Burrows, Paul, and Cento G. Veljanovski. "Introduction: The Economic Approach to Law." Pp. 1–34 in *The Economic Approach to Law*, edited by Paul Burrows and Cento G. Veljanovski. London: Butterworths, 1981.

Burtraw, Dallas. "Trading Emissions to Clean the Air." *Resources (RFF)* (Winter 1996): 3–6.

Butler, David, and Austin Ranney, eds. *Referendums: A Comparative Study of Practice and Theory*. Washington, D.C.: American Institute for Public Policy Research, 1978.

————, eds. *Referendums Around the World: The Growing Use of Direct Democracy.* Washington, D.C.: AEI Press, 1994.

Calabresi, Guido. "Some Thoughts on Risk Distribution and the Law of Torts." *Yale Law Journal* 70 (March 1961): 499–553.

————. *The Cost of Accidents: A Legal and Economic Analysis.* New Haven: Yale University Press, 1970.

————. *Ideals, Beliefs, Attitudes, and the Law: Private Law Perspectives on a Public Law Problem.* Syracuse, NY: Syracuse University Press, 1985.

————. "The Pointlessness of Pareto: Carrying Coase Further." *Yale Law Journal* 100 (March 1991): 1211–37.

Calabresi, Guido, and Jon T. Hirschoff. "Towards a Test for Strict Liability in Torts." *Yale Law Journal* 81 (May 1972): 1055–85.

Calabresi, Guido, and Alvin K. Klevorick. "Four Tests for Liability in Torts." *Journal of Legal Studies* 14 (December 1985): 585–627.

Calabresi, Guido, and A. Douglas Melamed. "Property Rules, Liability Rules, and Inalienability: One View of the Cathedral." *Harvard Law Review* 85 (April 1972): 1089–128.

Carstensen, Peter C. "Antitrust Law and the Paradigm of Industrial Organization." *University of California Davis Law Review* 16 (1983): 487–525.

Carter, Michael R. "A Wisconsin Institutionalist Perspective on Microeconomic Theory of Institutions: The Insufficiency of Pareto Efficiency." *Journal of Economic Issues* 19 (September 1985): 797–813.

Cataldo, Bernard F., et al. *Introduction to Law and the Legal Process.* New York: Wiley, 1973.

Center for Legal Policy. *Trial Lawyers Inc.: A Report on the Lawsuit Industry in America 2003.* New York: Manhattan Institute, 2003.

Chase, Anthony. "The Birth of the Modern Law School." *American Journal of Legal History* 23 (1979): 329–48.

Cheung, Steven N. S. "Transaction Costs, Risk Aversion, and the Choice of Contractual Arrangements." *Journal of Law and Economics* 12 (April 1969): 23–42.

————. "The Structure of a Contract and the Theory of Non-exclusive Resource." *Journal of Law and Economics* 13 (April 1970): 49–70.

————. "The Myth of Social Cost." Cato Paper no. 16. San Francisco: Cato Institute, 1980.

————. "On the New Institutional Economics." Pp. 48–65 in *Contract Economics*, edited by Lars Werin and Hans Wijkander. Cambridge, Mass.: Basil Blackwell, 1992.

Clark, John Maurice. *Social Control of Business.* 2d ed. New York: McGraw Hill, 1939.

Coase, Ronald H. "The Nature of the Firm." *Economica*, 1, n.s. (November 1937): 386–405.

————. "The Problem of Social Cost." *Journal of Law and Economics* 3 (October 1960): 1–44.

————. "Discussion: The Regulated Industries." *American Economic Review* 54 (May 1964): 194–97.

————. "Economics and Contiguous Disciplines." *Journal of Legal Studies* 7 (1978): 201–11.

————. "The Coase Theorem and the Empty Core: A Comment." *Journal of Law and Economics* 24 (April 1981): 183–87.

————. "The New Institutional Economics." *Journal of Institutional and Theoretical Economics* 140 (March 1984): 229–31.

————. "Blackmail." *Virginia Law Review* 74 (May 1988): 655–76.

————. "The Institutional Structure of Production." *American Economic Review* 82 (September 1992a): 713–19.

————. "On the New Institutional Economics: Comments." Pp. 72–75 in *Contract Economics*, edited by Lars Werin and Hans Wijkander. Cambridge, Mass.: Basil Blackwell, 1992b.

————. "Law and Economics at Chicago." *Journal of Law and Economics* 36 (April 1993): 239–54.

————. "The Task of the Society." *ISNIE Newsletter* 2 (Fall 1999): 1–6.

Coats, A.W. "The Origins of the 'Chicago School(s)?'" *Journal of Political Economy* 61 (October 1963): 487–93.

Cole, Daniel H. *Pollution & Property*. Cambridge: Cambridge University Press, 2002.

Coleman, Jules. "Efficiency, Utility, and Wealth Maximization." *Hofstra Law Review* 8 (Spring 1980): 509–51.

————. *Markets, Morals and the Law*. Cambridge: Cambridge University Press, 1988.

Colombatto, Enrico. *The Elgar Companion to the Economics of Property Rights*, Northhampton, Mass: Edward Elgar, 2004.

————. "Crime, Kickers, and Transaction Structures." Pp. 313–28 in *Criminal Justice: Nomos XXVII*, edited by J. Roland Pennock and John W. Chapman. New York: New York University Press, 1985.

Commons, John R. *Proportional Representation*. 2nd ed. 1907. Reprint, New York: Augustus M. Kelley, 1967.

————. *Legal Foundations of Capitalism*. 1924. Reprint, Clifton, N.J.: Augustus M. Kelley, 1974.

————. "Law and Economics." *Yale Law Journal* 34 (February 1925): 371–82.

————. *Institutional Economics*. New York: Macmillan, 1934.

Cooter, Robert. "The Cost of Coase." *Journal of Legal Studies* 11 (January 1982a): 1–33.

————. "Law and the Imperialism of Economics: An Introduction to the Economic Analysis of Law and a Review of the Major Books." *UCLA Law Review* 29 (June–August 1982b): 1260–69.

————. "Unity in Tort, Contract and Property: The Model of Precaution." *California Law Review* 73 (January 1985): 1–45.

————. "Law and Unified Social Theory." *Journal of Law and Society* 22 (March 1995): 50–67.

————. "Expressive Law and Economics." *Journal of Legal Studies* 27 (1998): 585–608.

————. "Do Good Laws Make Good Citizens? An Economic Analysis of Internalized Norms." *Virginia Law Review* 86 (2000a): 1577–1601.

————. "Three Effects of Social Norms on Law: Expression, Deterrence, and Internalization." *Oregon Law Review* 79 (2000b): 1–22.

Cooter, Robert, and Lewis Kornhauser. "Can Litigation Improve the Law Without the Help of Judges?" *Journal of Legal Studies* 9 (1980): 139–63.

Cooter, Robert, and Janet T. Landa. "Personal Versus Impersonal Trade: The Size of Trading Groups and Contract Law." *International Review of Law and Economics* 4 (1984): 15–22.

Cooter, Robert, and Thomas Ulen. *Law and Economics.* Glenview, Ill.: Scott, Foresman, 1988.

———. *Law and Economics.* 4th ed. Boston: Pearson-Addisson-Wesley, 2004.

Cordato, Roy E. "Subjective Value, Time Passage, and the Economics of Harmful Effects." *Hamline Law Review* 12 (1989): 229–44.

———. *Welfare Economics and Externalities in an Open-Ended Universe: A Modern Austrian Perspective.* Boston: Kluwer, 1992.

Cotterrell, Roger. *The Politics of Jurisprudence.* London: Butterworths, 1989.

Coyle, Marcia. "In Washington, Old Fights Are New Again: Onlooker Recall 1990s Tort Reform Effort." *National Law Journal,* November 18, 2002, pp. 1, 18–19.

Craswell, Richard, and Alan Schwartz. *Foundations of Contract Law.* New York: Oxford University Press, 1994.

Crespi, Gregory Scott. "Exploring the Complicationist Gambit: An Austrian Approach to the Economic Analysis of Law." *Notre Dame Law Review* 73 (1998): 315–83.

Croyle, James. "An Impact Analysis of Judge-Made Products Liability Policies." *Law and Society* 13 (1979): 949–67.

Dahlman, Carl J. "The Problem of Externality." *Journal of Law and Economics* 22 (1979): 141–62.

Dales, John H. "Rights and Economics." Pp. 149–55 in *Perspectives of Property*, edited by Gene Wunderlich and W. L. Gibson, Jr. University Park: Institute for Research on Land and Water Resources, Pennsylvania State University, 1972.

De Alessi, Louis. "The Economics of Property Rights: A Review of the Evidence." *Research in Law and Economics* 2 (1980): 1–47.

———. "Form, Substance, and Welfare Comparisons in the Analysis of Institutions." *Journal of Institutional and Theoretical Economics* 146 (1990): 5–23.

De Alessi, Louis, and Robert J. Staaf. "Property Rights and Choice." Pp. 175–200 in *Law and Economics*, edited by Nicholas Mercuro. Boston: Kluwer, 1989.

De Alessi, Michael. *Fishing for Solutions.* Studies on the Environment, no. 11. London: Institute of Economic Affairs, 1998.

Demsetz, Harold. "The Exchange and Enforcement of Property Rights." *Journal of Law and Economics* 7 (October 1964): 11–26.

———. "Toward a Theory of Property Rights." *American Economic Review* 57 (May 1967): 347–59.

———. "Information and Efficiency: Another Viewpoint." *Journal of Law and Economics* 12 (April 1969): 1–22.

Dennison, Mark S., and James A. Schmid. *Wetland Mitigation: Mitigation Banking and Other Strategies for Development and Compliance.* Rockville, Md.: Government Institutes, 1997.

DeSerpa, Allan C. *Microeconomic Theory.* Boston: Allyn and Bacon, 1988.

Director, Aaron. *The Economics of Technocracy.* Public Policy Pamphlet No. 2. Chicago: University of Chicago Press, 1933.

Director, Aaron, and Edward H. Levi. "Law and the Future: Trade Regulation." *Northwestern Law Review* 51 (1951): 281–96.

Doherty, Michael, ed. *Jurisprudence: The Philosophy of Law*. 2d ed. London: Old Bailey Press, 2001.

Dorfman, Joseph. *The Economic Mind in American Civilization, Volumes IV and V: 1918–1933*. New York: Viking, 1959. Reissued, Clifton, N.J.: Augustus M. Kelley, 1969.

Downs, Anthony. *The Economic Theory of Democracy*. New York: Harper, 1957.

———. *Inside Bureaucracy*. Boston: Little, Brown, 1967.

Drobak, John, and John V. C. Nye, eds. *The Frontiers of the New Institutional Economics*. San Diego: Academic Press, 1997.

Duxbury, Neil. "Robert Hale and the Economy of Legal Force." *The Modern Law Review* 53 (July 1990): 421–44.

———. *Patterns of American Jurisprudence*. Oxford: Oxford University Press, 1995.

Dworkin, Ronald M. "Is Wealth a Value?" *Journal of Legal Studies* 9 (March 1980): 191–226.

———. *Law's Empire*. Cambridge, Mass.: Belknap, 1986.

Easterbrook, Frank H. "Ways of Criticizing the Court." *Harvard Law Review* 95 (February 1982): 802–32.

———. "The Limits of Antitrust." *Texas Law Review* 63 (1984a): 1–40.

———. "The Supreme Court, 1983 Term: Forward: The Court and the Economic System." *Harvard Law Review* 98 (1984b): 4–60.

———. "Workable Antitrust Policy." *Michigan Law Review* 84 (1986): 1696–713.

Ebeling, Richard M. "The Significance of Austrian Economics in Twentieth-Century Economic Thought." Pp. 1–40 in *Austrian Economics: Perspectives on the Past and Prospects for the Future*, vol. 17, edited by Richard M. Ebeling. Hillsdale, Mich.: Hillsdale College Press, 1991.

Eggertsson, Thráinn. *Economic Behavior and Institutions*. Cambridge: Cambridge University Press, 1990.

———. "Institutions and Credible Commitment: Comment." *Journal of Institutional and Theoretical Economics* 149 (March 1993): 24–28.

Eisenberg, Melvin A. "An Overview of Law and Economics." Working Paper No. 90–9, School of Law, University of California, Berkeley, 1990.

Ekelund, Robert B., Jr., and Robert D. Tollison. "The Interest Group Theory of Government." Pp. 357–78 in *The Elgar Companion to Public Choice*, edited by William F. Shughart II and Laura Razzolini. Northampton, Mass.: Edward Elgar, 2003.

Ellickson, Robert, *Order without Law: How Neighbors Settle Disputes*. Cambridge: Harvard University Press, 1991.

———. "Law and Economics Discovers Social Norms." *Journal of Legal Studies* 27 (June 1998): 537–52.

———. "The Evolution of Social Norms: A Perspective from the Legal Academy." Pp. 35–75 in *Social Norms*, edited by Michael Hechter and Karl-Deiter Opp. New York: Russell Sage Foundation, 2001.

Elster, Jon. *The Cement of Society: Studies in Rationality and Social Change*. Cambridge: Cambridge University Press, 1991.

Ely, Richard T. *Property and Contract in Their Relation to the Distribution of Wealth*, 2 vols. New York: Macmillan, 1914.

Emmett, Ross. *The Elgar Companion to Chicago School.* Northampton, Mass.: Edward Elgar, forthcoming.

Englard, Izhak. *The Philosophy of Tort Law.* Aldershot, England: Dartmouth, 1993.

Epstein, Richard A. "A Theory of Strict Liability." *Journal of Legal Studies* 2 (January 1973): 151–204.

———. "Modern Republicanism—Or the Flight from Substance." *Yale Law Journal* 97 (July 1988): 1633–50.

Etzioni, Amitai. "Social Norms: Internalization, Persuasion, and History." *Law & Society Review* 34 (2000): 157–78.

Faith, Roger L., and Robert D. Tollison. "Voter Search for Efficient Representation." *Research in Law and Economics* 5 (1983): 211–24.

Fallon, Richard A. "What Is Republicanism and Is It Worth Reviving?" *Harvard Law Review* 102 (May 1989): 1695–735.

Farber, Daniel A. "Parody Lost / Pragmatism Regained: The Ironic History of the Coase Theorem." *Virginia Law Review* 83 (1997): 397–428.

Farber, Daniel A., and Philip P. Frickey. *Law and Public Choice.* Chicago: University of Chicago Press, 1991.

Feldman, Allan M. *Welfare Economics and Social Choice Theory.* Boston: Martinus Nijhoff, 1980.

Ferejohn, John, and Barry Weingast. "Limitation of Statutes: Strategic Statutory Interpretation." *Georgetown Law Journal* 80 (February 1992): 565–82.

Field, Alexander J. "On the Explanation of Rules Using Rational Choice Models." *Journal of Economic Issues,* 13 (March) 1979: 49–72.

———. "The Problem with Neoclassical Institutional Economics." *Explorations in Economic History* 18 (April 1981): 174–98.

Fischel, William. "The Law and Economics of Cedar-Apple Rust: State Action and Just Compensation in *Miller v. Schoene.*" Dartmouth College Economics Department Working Paper (April 2004), pp. 1–70.

Fisher, William W., Morton J. Horwitz, and Thomas A. Reed. *American Legal Realism.* New York: Oxford University Press, 1993.

Fiss, Owen M. "The Death of Law?" *Cornell Law Review* 72 (November 1986): 1–16.

———. "The Law Regained." *Cornell Law Review* 74 (January 1989): 245–55.

Fitts, Michael A. "Look Before You Leap: Some Cautionary Notes on Civic Republicanism." *Yale Law Journal* 97 (July 1988): 1651–62.

Fox, Eleanor M. "The Modernization of Antitrust: A New Equilibrium, *Cornell Law Review* 66 (1981): 1140–91.

———. "The Battle for the Soul of Antitrust." *California Law Review* 75 (May 1987a): 917–24.

Fox, Eleanor M., and Lawrence A. Sullivan. "Antitrust—Retrospective and Prospective: Where Are We Coming From? Where Are We Going?" *New York University Law Review* 62 (1987b): 936–88.

Frank, Jerome. *Law and the Modern Mind.* New York: Brentano's, 1930.

Frederick, Kenneth D. "Marketing Water: The Obstacles and the Impetus." *Resources (RFF)* (Summer 1998): 7–10.

Fried, Barbara. *The Progressive Assault on Laissez Faire: Robert Hale and the First Law and Economics Movement.* Cambridge: Harvard University Press, 1998.

Friedman, David D. *Law's Order*. Princeton: Princeton University Press, 2000.

Friedman, Lawrence M. *A History of American Law*. New York: Simon and Schuster, 1973.

Fuller, Lon. *The Law in Quest of Itself*. Chicago: Foundation Press, 1940.

Fuller, Lon L. "The Case of the Speluncean Explorers." *Harvard Law Review* 62 (1949): 616–45.

Furubotn, Eirik G., and Svetozar Pejovich. "Property Rights and Economic Theory: A Survey of the Literature." *Journal of Economic Literature* 10 (December 1972): 1137–62.

———. *The Economics of Property Rights*. Cambridge, Mass.: Ballinger, 1974.

Furubotn, Eirik G., and Rudolf Richter, eds. *The New Institutional Economics*, College Station: Texas A&M University Press, 1991a.

———. "The New Institutional Economics: An Assessment." Pp. 1–32 in *The New Institutional Economics*, edited by Eirik G. Furubotn and Rudolf Richter. College Station: Texas A&M University Press, 1991b.

———. *Institutions and Economic Theory: The Contribution of the New Institutional Economics*. Ann Arbor: University of Michigan Press, 1998.

Galanter, Marc. "Justice in Many Rooms: Courts, Private Ordering, and Indigenous Law." *Journal of Legal Pluralism* 19 (1981): 1–47.

Gelhorn, Ernest, and Glen O. Robinson. "The Role of Economic Analysis in Legal Education." *Journal of Legal Education* 33 (June 1983): 247–73.

Gerhart, Peter M. "The Supreme Court and Antitrust Analysis: The (Near) Triumph of the Chicago School." *Supreme Court Review* 1982 (1982): 319–349.

Gey, Steven G. "The Unfortunate Revival of Civic Republicanism." *University of Pennsylvania Law Review* 141 (1993): 801–98.

Globerman, Steven. "Markets, Hierarchies and Innovation." *Journal of Economic Issues* 14 (1980): 977–98.

Goetz, Charles J., and Robert E. Scott. "Liquidated Damages, Penalties, and the Just Compensation Principle: Some Notes on an Enforcement Model and a Theory of Efficient Breach." *Columbia Law Review* 77 (May 1977): 554–94.

———. "The Mitigation Principle: Toward a General Theory of Contractual Obligation." *Virginia Law Review* 69 (September 1983): 967–1024.

Goldberg, Victor. "Toward an Expanded Economic Theory of Contract." *Journal of Economic Issues* 10 (March 1976a): 45–61.

———. "Regulation and Administered Contracts." *Bell Journal of Economics* 7 (Autumn 1976b): 426–48.

———, ed. *Readings in the Economics of Contract Law*. Cambridge: Cambridge University Press, 1989.

Goldfarb, Robert S., and William B. Griffith. "Amending the Economist's 'Rational Egoist' Model to Include Moral Values and Norms." Pp. 59–84 in *Social Norms and Economic Institutions*, edited by Kenneth J. Koford and Jeffrey B. Miller. Ann Arbor: University of Michigan Press, 1991.

Goodman, John C. "An Economic Theory of the Evolution of Common Law." *Journal of Legal Studies* 7 (June 1978): 393–406.

Gordon, H. Scott. "The Economic Theory of a Common-Property Resource: The Fishery." *Journal of Political Economy* 62 (April 1954): 124–42.

Gordon, Robert A. *Institutional Economics*. Berkeley: University of California Press, 1964.

Gordon, Robert W. "New Developments in Legal Theory." Pp. 413–25 in *The Politics of Law: A Progressive Critique*, edited by David Kairys. New York: Pantheon, 1990.

Gould, John P. "The Economics of Legal Conflicts." *Journal of Legal Studies* 2 (January 1973): 279–300.

Gould, J. P., and C. E. Ferguson. *Microeconomic Theory*. 5th ed. Homewood, Ill.: Richard D. Irwin, 1980.

Grembi, Veronica. "The Actual Role of Ronald Coase's and Guido Calabresi's Contributions to the New Law and Economics." Mimeo, University of Florence, 2003.

Grey, Thomas C. "Langdell's Orthodoxy." *University of Pittsburgh Law Review* 45 (Fall 1983): 1–53.

Griffin, Ronald. "The Welfare Analytics of Transaction Costs, Externalities and Institutional Choice." *American Journal of Agricultural Economics* 73 (August 1991): 601–14.

———. "On the Meaning of Economic Efficiency in Policy Analysis." *Land Economics* 71 (February 1995): 1–15.

Grossman, Sanford, and Oliver Hart. "The Costs and Benefits of Ownership: A Theory of Vertical and Lateral Integration." *Journal of Political Economy* 94 (August 1986): 691–719.

Groves, Harold Martin. *The Tax Philosophers*. Madison: University of Wisconsin Press, 1974.

Gunther, Gerald. *Learned Hand: The Man and the Judge*. Cambridge, Mass: Harvard University Press, 1994.

Gwartney, James D., and Richard Stroup. *Economics: Private and Public Choice*. New York: Harcourt Brace Jovanovich, 1980.

Gwartney, James D., and Richard E. Wagner. "Public Choice and the Conduct of Representative Government." Pp. 3–28 in *Public Choice and Constitutional Economics*, edited by James D. Gwartney and Richard E. Wagner. Greenwich, Conn.: JAI, 1988.

Hale, Robert Lee. "Economic Theory and the Statesman." Pp. 189–225 in *The Trend of Economics*, edited by Rexford G. Tugwell. New York: Knopf, 1924.

———. "Economics and the Law." Pp. 131–42 in *The Social Sciences and Their Interrelations*, edited by William F. Ogburn and Alexander A. Goldenweiser. Boston: Houghton Mifflin, 1927.

———. *Freedom Through Law*. New York: Columbia University Press, 1952.

Hall, Margaret E., ed. *Selected Writings of Benjamin Nathan Cardozo*. New York: Fallon, 1947.

Halper, Louise A. "Parables of Exchange: Foundations of Public Choice Theory and the Market Formalism of James Buchanan." *Cornell Journal of Law and Public Policy* 2 (Spring 1993): 230–78.

Hamilton, Walton H. "Property according to Locke." *Yale Law Journal* 41 (April 1932): 864–80.

Hampstead, Lord Lloyd of, and M.D.A. Freeman. *Lloyd's Introduction to Jurisprudence*. London: Stevens Carswell, 1985.

Hansmann, Henry. "The Current State of Law-and-Economics Scholarship." *Journal of Legal Education* 33 (1983): 217–36.

Hanson, Jon D., and Kyle D. Logue. "The Costs of Cigarettes: The Economic Case for Ex Post Incentive-Based Regulation." *Yale Law Journal* 10 (1998): 1163–361.

Hardin, Garrett. "Tragedy of the Commons." *Science*, vol. 162, December 13, 1968, pp. 1243–48.

Harrington, Winston, and Richard D. Morgenstern. "Economic Incentives versus Command and Control." *Resources (RFF)* (Fall/Winter 2004): 13–17.

Harris, Ron. "The Uses of History in Law and Economics." *Theoretical Inquiries in Law* 4 (July 2003): 659–96.

Hart, Henry M., and Albert M. Sacks. *The Legal Process: Basic Problems in the Making and Application of Law*. Cambridge, Mass.: tentative edition, 1958.

Hart, Oliver. "An Economist's Perspective on the Theory of the Firm." Pp. 154–71 in *Organization Theory: From Chester Barnard to the Present and Beyond*, edited by Oliver E. Williamson. New York: Oxford University Press, 1990.

Hayami, Yujiro, and Vernon W. Ruttan. "Toward a Theory of Induced Institutional Innovation." *Journal of Development Studies* 20 (July 1984): 203–23.

Hayek, Friedrich A. "The Use of Knowledge in Society." *American Economic Review* 35 (1945): 519–30.

———. *Law, Legislation and Liberty*. Chicago: University of Chicago Press, 1973.

Hayes, Michael T. *Lobbyists and Legislators: A Theory of Political Markets*. New Brunswick: Rutgers University Press, 1981.

Hayman, Robert L., Nancy Levit, and Richard Delgado. *Jurisprudence, Classical and Contemporary: From Natural Law to Postmodernism*. 2d ed. St. Paul, Minn.: West Group, 2002.

Hechter, Michael, and Karl-Deiter Opp, eds. *Social Norms*. New York: Russell Sage Foundation, 2001.

Heilbroner, Robert L. *The Worldly Philosophers*. 7th ed. New York: Simon and Schuster, 1999.

Herman, Samuel. "Economic Predilection and the Law." *American Political Science Review* 31 (October 1937): 821–41.

Hicks, J. R. "The Foundations of Welfare Economics." *Economic Journal* 49 (December 1939): 696–712.

Hirsch, Werner Z. *Law and Economics: An Introductory Analysis*. 2d ed. Boston: Academic Press, 1988. 3d ed., San Diego: Academic Press, 1999.

Hirshleifer, Jack, ed. *Evolutionary Models in Economics and Law, Volume 4—Research in Law and Economics*. Greenwich, Conn.: JAI Press, 1982.

Hodgson, Geoffrey M. *Economics and Institutions*. Philadelphia: University of Pennsylvania Press, 1988.

———. "The Approach of Institutional Economics." *Journal of Economic Literature* 36 (March 1998): 166–92.

Hodgson, Geoffrey M., Warren J. Samuels, and Mark R. Tool, eds. *The Elgar Companion to Institutional and Evolutionary Economics*. Northampton, Mass.: Edward Elgar, 1994.

Hoffman, Elizabeth, and Matthew L. Spitzer. "Willingness to Pay vs. Willingness to Accept: Legal and Economic Implications." *Washington University Law Quarterly* 71 (Spring 1993): 59–114.

Holdsworth, W. S. "A Neglected Aspect of the Relations Between Economic and Legal History." *Economic History Review* 1 (January 1927–28): 114–23.

Holmes, Oliver Wendell, Jr. "The Path of the Law." *Harvard Law Review* 10 (March 1897): 457–78.

———. *The Common Law*. Boston: Little Brown, 1923.

Horwitz, Morton. *The Transformation of American Law: 1780–1860*. Cambridge: Harvard University Press, 1977.

Hovenkamp, Herbert. "Antitrust Policy after Chicago." *Michigan Law Review* 84 (1985): 213–84.

———. "Chicago and its Alternatives." *Duke Law Journal* 1986 (December 1986): 1014–29.

———. "Law and Economics in the United States: A Brief Historical Survey." *Cambridge Journal of Economics* 19 (April 1995): 331–52.

Hunt, Alan. "The Critique of Law: What is 'Critical' about Critical Legal Studies?" *Journal of Law and Society* 14 (Spring 1987): 5–19.

Hutchinson, Terence W. "Institutionalist Economics Old and New." *Journal of Institutional and Theoretical Economics* 140 (1984): 20–29.

Hylton, Keith. "Calabresi and the Intellectual History of Law and Economics." *University of Maryland Law Review* (Symposium) 64 (2005): 85–107.

Jacobs, Michael S. "An Essay on the Normative Foundations of Antitrust Economics." *North Carolina Law Review* 74 (1995): 219–65.

Jensen, Michael C., and William H. Meckling. "Theory of the Firm: Managerial Behavior, Agency Costs and Ownership Structure." *Journal of Financial Economics* 3 (October 1976): 305–60.

Johnson, David B. *Public Choice: An Introduction to the New Political Economy*. Mountain View, Calif.: Bristlecone, 1991.

Johnston, Jason Scott. "Law, Economics, and Post-Realist Explanation." *Law & Society Review* 24 (1990): 1217–54.

Jost, Kenneth. "Too Many Lawsuits." *CQ Researcher* 2, no. 19 (May 22, 1992): 433–56.

Kahn, Peter L. "The Politics of Unregulation: Public Choice and Limits on Government." *Cornell Law Review* 75 (1990): 279–312.

Kahneman, Daniel, Jack L. Knetsch, and Richard Thaler. "Experimental Tests of the Endowment Effect and the Coase Theorem." *Journal of Political Economy* 98 (December 1990): 1325–48.

Kaldor, Nicholas. "Welfare Propositions in Economics." *Economic Journal* 49 (September 1939): 549–52.

Kanal, Don. "Institutional Economics: Perspectives on Economy and Society." *Journal of Economic Issues* 19 (September 1985): 815–28.

Kaplow, Louis, and Steven Shavell. "Do Liability Rules Facilitate Bargaining: A Reply to Ayres and Talley." *Yale Law Journal* 105 (April 1995a): 221–33.

———. "Property Rules Versus Liability Rules." Harvard Law School Discussion Paper No. 156 (March 1995b).

———. *Fairness Versus Welfare*. Cambridge: Harvard University Press, 2002.

Karp, David. "Tort Reform Isn't Enough." *Medical Economics* 80, no. 9 (May 2003): 101.

Katz, Avery Wiener. "Positivism and the Separation of Law and Economics." *Michigan Law Review* 94 (1996): 2229–69.

Katz, Wilbur. "A Four-Year Program for Legal Education." *University of Chicago Law Review* 4 (June 1937): 527–36.

Kaysen, Carl, and Donald Turner. *Antitrust Policy: An Economic and Legal Analysis.* Cambridge: Harvard University Press, 1959.

Kelsen, Hans. *General Theory of Law & State.* Cambridge: Harvard University Press, 1945.

———. *The Pure Theory of Law.* Translated from the second German edition of 1960 by Max Knight. Berkeley: University of California Press, 1967.

Kitch, Edmund W. "The Fire of Truth: A Remembrance of Law and Economics at Chicago, 1932–1970." *Journal of Law and Economics* 26 (April 1983a): 163–233.

———. "The Intellectual Foundations of 'Law and Economics.' " *Journal of Legal Education* 33 (June 1983b): 184–96.

Klein, Benjamin. "Self Enforcing Contracts." *Journal of Institutional and Theoretical Economics* 141 (December 1985): 594–600. Reprinted in *The New Institutional Economics*, edited by Eirik G. Furubotn and Rudolf Richter, pp. 89–95. College Station: Texas A&M University Press, 1991.

———. "Contracts and Incentives: The Role of Contracting Terms in Assuring Performance." Pp. 149–72 in *Contract Economics*, edited by Lars Werin and Hans Wijkander. Cambridge, Mass.: Basil Blackwell, 1992.

Klein, Benjamin, Robert Crawford, and Armen Alchian, "Vertical Integration, Appropriable Rents, and the Competitive Contracting Process," *Journal of Law and Economics* 21 (October 1978): 297–326.

Klein, Peter G. "New Institutional Economics." Pp. 456–89 in *Encyclopedia of Law and Economics*, edited by Boudewijn Bouckaert and Gerrit De Geest. Northampton, Mass.: Edward Elgar, 2000.

Koford, Kenneth J., and Jeffrey B. Miller, eds. *Social Norms and Economic Institutions.* Ann Arbor: University of Michigan Press, 1991a.

———. "Habit, Custom and Norms in Economics." Pp. 21–36 in *Social Norms and Economic Institutions*, edited by Kenneth J. Koford and Jeffrey B. Miller. Ann Arbor: University of Michigan Press, 1991b.

Kneese, Allen V. *Economics and the Environment.* New York: Penguin, 1977.

Komesar, Neil K. "In Search of a General Approach to Legal Analysis: A Comparative Institutional Alternative." *Michigan Law Review* 79 (June 1981): 1350–92.

———. "Injuries and Institutions: Tort Reform, Tort Theory, and Beyond." *New York University Law Review* 65 (April 1990): 23–77.

———. *Imperfect Alternatives: Choosing Institutions in Law, Economics, and Pubic Policy.* Chicago: University of Chicago Press, 1994.

Kornhauser, Lewis. "The Great Image of Authority." *Stanford Law Review* 36 (January 1984): 349–89.

———. "An Introduction to the Economic Analysis of Contract Remedies." *University of Chicago Law Review* 57 (Summer 1986): 683–725.

Kramer, Victor H. "Antitrust Today: The Baxterization of the Sherman & Clayton Acts." *Wisconsin Law Review* 1981 (1981): 1287–302.

Krecké, Elisabeth. "Economic Analysis and Legal Pragmatism." *International Review of Law and Economics* 23 (2003): 421–37.

Kreps, David M. *A Course in Microeconomic Theory.* Princeton: Princeton University Press, 1990.

Kronman, Anthony T. "Wealth Maximization as a Normative Principle." *Journal of Legal Studies* 9 (March 1980): 227–42.

Kronman, Anthony T., and Richard A. Posner, eds. *The Economics of Contract Law*. Boston: Little, Brown, 1979.

Krueger, Ann O. "The Political Economy of Rent Seeking." *American Economic Review* 64 (1974): 291–303.

Kuhn, Thomas S. *The Structure of Scientific Revolutions*. 2d ed. Chicago: University of Chicago Press, 1970.

Lancaster, Kelvin J. "A New Approach to Consumer Theory." *Journal of Political Economy*, 74 (April 1966): 132–57.

Landa, Janet T. "A Theory of the Ethnically Homogeneous Middleman Group: An Institutional Alternative to Contract Law." *Journal of Legal Studies* 10 (1981): 34–62.

———. *Trust, Ethnicity, and Identity: Beyond the New Institutional Economics of Ethnic Trading Networks, Contract Law, and Gift-exchange*. Ann Arbor: University of Michigan Press, 1994.

———. "Doing the Economics of Trust and Informal Institutions." Pp. 142–62 in *Foundations of Research in Economics: How Do Economists Do Economics?* edited by Steven G. Medema and Warren J. Samuels. Northampton, Mass.: Edward Elgar, 1996.

Lande, Robert H. "Commentary: Implications of Professor Scherer's Research for the Future of Antitrust." *Washburn Law Review* 29 (1990): 256–63.

Landes, William M. "An Economic Analysis of the Courts." *Journal of Law and Economics* 14 (April 1971): 61–107.

Landes, William M., and Richard A. Posner. "Causation in Tort Law: An Economic Approach." *Journal of Legal Studies* 12 (January 1983): 109–34.

———. *The Economic Structure of Tort Law*. Cambridge: Harvard University Press, 1987.

———. "The Influence of Economics on Law: A Quantitative Study." *Journal of Law and Economics* 36 (1993): 385–424.

———. "Symposium on the Trends in Legal Citations and Scholarship: Heavily Cited Articles in Law." *Chicago-Kent Law Review* 71 (1996): 825–38.

Lang, Mahlon G. "Economic Efficiency and Policy Comparisons." *American Journal of Agricultural Economics* 62 (November 1980): 772–77.

Langdell, Christopher C. *A Selection of Cases on the Law of Contracts*. Boston: Little, Brown, 1871.

Lazear, Edward. "Economic Imperialism." *Quarterly Journal of Economics* 115 (February 2000): 99–146.

Leibenstein, Harvey. *Inside the Firm*. Cambridge: Harvard University Press, 1987.

Lessig, Lawrence. "The Regulation of Social Meaning." *University of Chicago Law Review* 62 (1995): 943–1045.

———. "Social Meaning and Social Norms." *University of Pennsylvania Law Review* 144 (1996): 2181–89.

———. "The New Chicago School." *Journal of Legal Studies* 27 (1998): 661–91.

———. "The Prolific Iconoclast." *The American Lawyer* (December 1999): 105.

Levmore, Saul. "Two Stories about the Evolution of Property Rights." *Journal of Legal Studies* 32 (2002): S421–S451.

Libecap, Gary D. "Property Rights in Economic History: Implications for Research." *Explorations in Economic History* 23 (1986): 227–52.

———. *Contracting for Property Rights*. Cambridge: Cambridge University Press, 1989a.

————. "Distributional Issues in Contracting for Property Rights." *Journal of Institutional and Theoretical Economics* 145 (1989b): 6–24. Reprinted in *The New Institutional Economics*, edited by Eirik G. Furubotn and Rudolf Richter, pp. 214–32. College Station: Texas A&M University Press, 1991.

Liebhafsky, H. H. "Law and Economics from Different Perspectives." *Journal of Economic Issues* 21 (December 1987): 1809–36.

Lindahl, Eric. "Just Taxation—A Positive Solution." 1919. Reprinted in *Classics in the Theory of Public Finance*, edited by Richard A. Musgrave and Alan T. Peacock, pp. 168–76. New York: St. Martin's Press, 1967.

Litchman, Mark M. "Economics, the Basis of Law." *American Law Review* 61 (May–June 1927): 357–87.

Llewellyn, Karl N. "The Effect of Legal Institutions upon Economics." *American Economic Review* 15 (December 1925): 655–83.

————. "What Price Contract? An Essay in Perspective." *Yale Law Journal* 40 (March 1931): 704–51.

————. "The Constitution as an Institution." *Columbia Law Review* 34 (January 1934): 1–40.

Macneil, Ian R. "The Many Futures of Contracts." *Southern California Law Review* 47 (1974): 691–816.

————. "Contracts: Adjustment of Long-Term Economic Relations under Classical, Neoclassical, and Relational Contract Law." *Northwestern University Law Review* 72 (January–February 1978): 854–905.

————. "Economic Analysis of Contractual Relations." Pp. 61–92 in *The Economic Approach to Law*, edited by Paul Burrows and Cento G. Veljanovski. London: Butterworths, 1981.

Mashaw, Jerry. "As If Republican Interpretation." *Yale Law Journal* 97 (July 1988): 1685–723.

Mason, Edward S. "Monopoly in Law and Economics." *Yale Law Journal* 47 (1937): 34–49.

————. *Economic Concentration and the Monopoly Problem*. Cambridge: Harvard University Press, 1957.

Matthews, R.C.O. "The Economics of Institutions and the Sources of Economic Growth." *Economic Journal* 96 (1986): 903–18.

McAdams, Richard H. "The Origin, Development, and Regulation of Norms." *Michigan Law Review* 96 (1997): 338–427.

McCay, Bonnie J. "Common and Private Concerns." Pp. 111–26 in *Rights to Nature*, edited by S. Hanna, C. Folke, and K. G. Maler. Washington, D.C.: Island Press, 1996.

McChesney, Fred S., and William F. Shughart II, eds. *The Causes and Consequences of Antitrust: The Public-Choice Perspective*. Chicago: University of Chicago Press, 1995.

McCormick, Robert E. and Robert D. Tollison. *Politicians, Legislation, and the Economy: An Inquiry into the Interest-Group Theory of Government*. Boston: Martinus Nijhoff, 1981.

McCoubrey, Hilaire, and Nigel D. White. *Textbook on Jurisprudence*. 3d ed. London: Blackstone Press, 1999.

McKelvey, R., and N. Schofield. "Structural Instability of the Core." *Journal of Mathematical Economics* 15 (1986): 179–88.

McLean, Iain. *Public Choice: An Introduction*. Oxford: Basil Blackwell, 1987.

Medema, Steven G. "Another Look at the Problem of Rent Seeking." *Journal of Economic Issues* 25 (December 1991): 1049–65.

———. *Ronald H. Coase*. London: Macmillan, 1994.

———. *The Legacy of Ronald Coase in Economic Analysis*. 2 vols. Northampton, Mass.: Edward Elgar, 1995.

———. "Wandering the Road From Pluralism to Posner: The Transformation of Law and Economics, 1920s–1970s." In "The Transformation of American Economics: From Interwar Pluralism to Postwar Neoclassicism." *History of Political Economy (Annual Supplement)*, edited by Mary Morgan and Malcolm Rutherford, 30 (1998): 202–24.

———. " 'Related Disciplines': The Professionalization of Public Choice Analysis." In "The History of Applied Economics." *History of Political Economy (Annual Supplement)* 32 (2000): 289–323.

———. "The Economic Role of Government in the History of Economic Thought." Pp. 428–44 in *The Blackwell Companion to the History of Economic Thought*, edited by Jeff Biddle, John B. Davis, and Warren J. Samuels. Oxford: Blackwell, 2003.

———. " 'Marginalizing Government': From *La Scienza delle Finanze* to Wicksell." *History of Political Economy* 37 (spring 2005): 1–25.

———. "The Chicago School of Law and Economics." In *The Elgar Companion to the Chicago School*, edited by Ross Emmett. Northampton, Mass.: Edward Elgar, forthcoming 2007a.

———. "Richard A. Posner." In *The Elgar Companion to the Chicago School*, edited by Ross Emmett. Northampton, Mass.: Edward Elgar, forthcoming 2007b.

Medema, Steven G., and Richard O. Zerbe, Jr. "The Coase Theorem." Pp. 836–92 in *The Encyclopedia of Law and Economics*, edited by Boudewijn Bouckaert and Gerrit De Geest. Northampton, Mass.: Edward Elgar, 2000.

Ménard, Claude, ed. *The International Library of the New Institutional Economics*. 7 vols. Northhampton, Mass: Edward Elgar, 2004.

Ménard, Claude, and Mary M. Shirley, eds. *Handbook of New Institutional Economics* New York: Springer, 2005.

Menger, Carl. *Grundsätze der Volkswirthschaftslehre*. Vienna: Braumnalter, 1871. Translated as *Principles of Economics*, by J. Dingwall and B. F. Hoselitz. Glencoe, Ill.: Free Press, 1951. Reprinted in 1976 and 1981, New York: New York University Press.

Mensch, Elizabeth. "The History of Mainstream Legal Thought." Pp.13–37 in *The Politics of Law: A Progressive Critique*, edited by David Kairys. New York: Pantheon, 1990.

Mercuro, Nicholas. "Toward a Comparative Institutional Approach to the Study of Law and Economics." Pp. 1–26 in *Law and Economics*, edited by Nicholas Mercuro. Boston: Kluwer, 1989.

———, ed. *Ecology, Law and Economics*. Lanham, Md.: University Press of America, 1997.

———. "Relevant Output Categories for a Comparative Institutional Approach to Law and Economics." Pp. 217–57 in *Economics Broadly Considered*, edited by Jeff E. Biddle, John B. Davis, and Steven G. Medema. London: Routledge, 2001.

————. "The Market: What Lies Beneath?" *Journal des Economistes et des Etudes Humaines* 14 (December 2004): 21–34.

Mercuro, Nicholas, and Steven G. Medema. "Schools of Thought in Law and Economics: A Kuhnian Competition." Pp. 65–126 in *Law and Economics: New and Critical Perspectives*, edited by Robin Paul Malloy and Christopher K. Braun. New York: Peter Lang, 1995.

Mercuro, Nicholas, Steven G. Medema, and Warren J. Samuels. "Robert Lee Hale— Legal Economist." Pp. 531–44 in *The Elgar Companion to Law and Economics*, 2d ed., edited by Jürgen G. Backhaus. Northampton, Mass.: Edgar Elgar, 2005.

Mercuro, Nicholas, and Timothy P. Ryan. "Property Rights and Welfare Economics: *Miller et al. v. Schoene* Revisited." *Land Economics* 56 (May 1980): 202–12.

————. *Law, Economics and Public Policy.* Greenwich, Conn.: JAI Press, 1984.

Merrill, Thomas W. "Introduction: The Demsetz Thesis and the Evolution of Property Rights." *Journal of Legal Studies* 32 (2002): S331–S338.

Michelman, Frank I. "Norms and Normativity in the Economic Theory of Law." *Minnesota Law Review* 62 (July 1978): 1015–48.

————. "Politics and Values or What's Really Wrong with Rationality Review?" *Creighton Law Review* 13 (Winter 1979): 487–511.

————. "Traces of Self-Government." *Harvard Law Review* 100 (November 1986): 4–77.

————. "Law's Republic." *Yale Law Journal* 97 (July 1988): 1493–537.

————. "Thirteen Easy Pieces." *Michigan Law Review* 93 (1995): 1297–332.

Mikva, Abner J. "Foreword: Symposium on the Theory of Public Choice." *Virginia Law Review* 74 (March 1988): 167–77.

Miller, H. Laurence, Jr. "On the 'Chicago School of Economics.'" *Journal of Political Economy* 70 (February 1962): 64–69.

Minda, Gary. "The Lawyer-Economist at Chicago: Richard A. Posner and the *Economic Analysis of Law*." *Ohio State Law Journal* 39 (1978): 439–75.

————. *Postmodern Legal Movements.* New York: New York University Press, 1995.

Minow, Martha. "Law Turning Outward." *Telos* 73 (Fall 1987): 79–100.

Mishan, Ezra J. "Pareto Optimality and the Law." *Oxford Economic Papers* 19 (1967): 255–87.

————. "The Post-war Literature on Externalities: An Interpretative Essay." *Journal of Economic Literature* 9 (1971): 1–28.

————. "The Futility of Pareto-Efficiency in Policy Analysis." *American Economic Review* 62 (December 1972): 971–76.

Mitchell, Lawrence E. "Understanding Norms." *University of Toronto Law Journal* 49 (1999): 177–247.

Mitchell, Wesley C. *Business Cycles: The Problem and Its Setting.* New York: National Bureau of Economic Research, 1927.

Mitchell, William C. "Textbook Public Choice: A Review Essay." *Public Choice* 38 (1982): 97–112.

————. "Virginia, Rochester, and Bloomington: Twenty-Five Years of Public Choice and Political Science." *Public Choice* 56 (February 1988): 101–19.

————. "The Old and New Public Choice: Chicago versus Virginia." Pp. 3–32 in *The Elgar Companion to Public Choice*, edited by William F. Shughart II and Laura Razzolini. Northampton, Mass.: Edward Elgar, 2001.

Monahan, John, and Laurens Walker. *Social Science in Law: Cases and Materials*. 2d ed. Westbury, N.Y.: Foundation Press, 1990.

Monteverde, Kirk, and David J. Teece. "Supplier Switching Costs and Vertical Integration in the Automobile Industry." *Bell Journal of Economics* 13 (1982): 206–13.

Morgan, Mary, and Malcolm Rutherford. "The Transformation of American Economics: From Interwar Pluralism to Postwar Neoclassicism." *History of Political Economy (Annual Supplement)* 30 (1998).

Mueller, Dennis C. *Public Choice II*. Cambridge: Cambridge University Press, 1989.

———. *Public Choice III*. New York: Cambridge University Press, 2003.

Niskanen, William A. *Bureaucracy and Representative Government*. Chicago: Aldine, Atherton, 1971.

———. *Bureaucracy: Servant or Master?* Hobart Paperback No. 5. London: Institute of Economic Affairs, 1973.

———. *Bureaucracy and Public Economics*. Northampton, Mass.: Edward Elgar, 1994.

North, Douglass C. "A Framework for Analyzing the State in Economic History," *Explorations in Economic History* 16 (July 1979): 249–59.

———. *Structure and Change in Economic History*. New York: Norton, 1981.

———. "Transaction Costs, Institutions, and Economic History." *Journal of Institutional and Theoretical Economics* 140 (1984): 7–17. Reprinted in *The New Institutional Economics*, edited by Eirik G. Furubotn and Rudolf Richter, pp. 203–13. College Station: Texas A&M University Press, 1991.

———. "A Transaction Cost Approach to the Historical Development of Polities and Economies." *Journal of Institutional and Theoretical Economics* 145 (December 1989): 661–68. Reprinted in *The New Institutional Economics*, edited by Eirik G. Furubotn and Rudolf Richter, pp. 253–60. College Station: Texas A&M University Press, 1991.

———. "Institutions and a Transaction Cost Theory of Exchange." Pp. 182–94 in *Perspectives on Positive Political Economy*, edited by James E. Alt and Kenneth A. Shepsle. Cambridge: Cambridge University Press, 1990a.

———. *Institutions, Institutional Change, and Economic Performance*. Cambridge: Cambridge University Press, 1990b.

———. "Institutions." *Journal of Economic Perspectives* 5 (1991): 97–112.

———. "Institutions and Credible Commitment." *Journal of Institutional and Theoretical Economics* 149 (March 1993a): 11–23.

———. "Institutions and Economic Performance." Pp. 242–61 in *Rationality, Institutions and Economic Methodology*, edited by Uskali Maki, Bo Gustafsson, and Christian Knudsen. London: Routledge, 1993b.

———. "Prologue." Pp. 3–12 in *The Frontiers of the New Institutional Economics*, edited by John Drobak and John V. C. Nye. San Diego: Academic Press, 1997.

North, Douglas C., and Lance Davis (with the assistance of Calla Smorodin). *Institutional Change and American Economic Growth*. Cambridge: Cambridge University Press, 1971.

North, Douglas C., and Robert P. Thomas. *The Rise of the Western World: A New Economic History*. Cambridge: Cambridge University Press, 1973.

Note. "'Round and 'Round the Bramble Bush: From Legal Realism to Critical Legal Scholarship." *Harvard Law Review* 95 (May 1982): 1669–90.

Olson, Mancur. *The Logic of Collective Action*. Cambridge: Harvard University Press, 1965.

————. "The Proposed Interdisciplinary Committee on Nonmarket Decision-Making." Buchanan House Archives, George Mason University, 1966.

Ostrom, Elinor. "A Method of Institutional Analysis." Pp. 459–75 in *Guidance, Control and Evaluation in the Public Sector*, edited by Franz-Xarer Kaufman, Diandomenico Majone, and Vincent Ostrom. New York: Walter de Gruyter, 1986a.

————. "Multiorganizational Arrangements and Coordination: An Application of Institutional Analysis." Pp. 495–510 in *Guidance, Control and Evaluation in the Public Sector*, edited by F.-X. Kaufman, G. Majone, and V. Ostrom. Berlin: Walter de Gruyter, 1986b.

Ostrom, Elinor, Joanna Burger, C. B. Field, R. B. Norgaard, and D. Policansky. "Revisiting the Commons: Local Lessons, Global Challenges." *Science*, vol. 284, April 9, 1999, pp. 278–82.

Ostrom, Vincent. "John R. Commons's Foundation for Public Policy." *Journal of Economic Issues* 10 (1976): 839–57.

Packer, Herbert L., and Thomas Erlich. *New Directions in Legal Education*. New York: McGraw-Hill, 1973.

Parisi, Francesco. "Positive, Normative and Functional Schools in Law and Economics." Pp. 58–73 in *The Elgar Companion to Law and Economics*, 2d ed. edited by Jürgen Backhaus. Aldershot, England: Edward Elgar, 2005.

Parsons, Kenneth H. "The Institutional Basis for an Agricultural Market Economy." *Journal of Economic Issues* 8 (December 1974): 737–57.

Paton, G. W., and David P. Derham. *A Textbook of Jurisprudence*. 4th ed. Oxford: Oxford University Press, 1972.

Pejovich, Svetozar. "Towards an Economic Theory of the Creation and Specification of Property Rights." *Review of Social Economy* 30 (September 1972): 309–25.

————. *Economic Analysis of Institutions and Systems*. Dordrecht: Kluwer, 1995.

Peltzman, Sam. "Toward a More General Theory of Regulation." *Journal of Law and Economics* 19 (August 1976): 211–40.

————. "The Growth of Government." *Journal of Law and Economics* 23 (October 1980): 209–88.

Pigou, A. C. *The Economics of Welfare*. London: Macmillan, 1920; 4th ed., 1932.

Pindyck, Robert S., and Daniel L. Rubinfeld. *Microeconomics*. 2d ed. New York: Macmillan, 1992.

Pitt, Joseph C., Djavad Salehi-Isfahani, and Douglas W. Eckel. *The Production and Diffusion of Public Choice Political Economy: Reflections on the V.P.I. Center*. New York: Blackwell, 2004.

Plott, Charles. "Rational Choice in Experimental Markets" *Journal of Business* 59 (1986): S301–S327. Reprinted in *Rational Choice: The Contrast Between Economics and Psychology*, edited by Robin M. Hogarth and Melvin W. Reder, pp. 117–43. Chicago: University of Chicago Press, 1987.

Poincaré, Henri. *Science and Method*. New York: Dover, 1952; originally published in French in 1908.

Poisner, Jonathan. "A Civic Republican Perspective on the National Environmental Policy Act's Process for Citizen Participation." *Environmental Law* 26 (1996): 53–94.

Polinsky, A. Mitchell. "Controlling Externalities and Protecting Entitlements: Property Right, Liability, and Tax-Subsidy Approaches." *Journal of Legal Studies* 8 (January 1979): 1–48.

———. "Resolving Nuisance Disputes: The Simple Economics of Injunctive and Damage Remedies." *Stanford Law Review* 32 (July 1980): 1075–112.

———. *An Introduction to Law and Economics.* 2d ed. Boston: Little, Brown, 1989.

Posner, Eric. "The Regulation of Groups: The Influence of Legal and Nonlegal Sanctions on Collective Action." *University of Chicago Law Review* 63 (1996): 133–97.

———. "Efficient Norms." Pp. 19–24 in *The New Palgrave Dictionary of Economics and the Law,* vol. 2, edited by Peter Newman. New York: Stockton, 1998a.

———. "Symbols, Signals, and Social Norms in Politics and Law." *Journal of Legal Studies* 27 (1998b): 765–98.

———. *Law And Social Norms.* Cambridge: Harvard University Press, 2000.

———. "Economic Analysis of Contract Law after Three Decades: Success or Failure?" University of Chicago Law and Economics, Olin Working Paper No. 146, March 2002, pp. 1–44.

Posner, Richard A. "A Theory of Negligence." *Journal of Legal Studies* 1 (January 1972a): 29–96.

———. *Economic Analysis of Law.* 1st ed. Boston: Little, Brown, 1972b.

———. "Strict Liability: A Comment." *Journal of Legal Studies* 2 (January 1973): 205–21.

———. "Theories of Economic Regulation." *Bell Journal of Economics and Management Science* 5 (1974): 335–58.

———. "The Economic Approach to Law." *Texas Law Review* 53 (May 1975): 757–82.

———. "The Chicago School of Antitrust Analysis." *University of Pennsylvania Law Review* 127 (1978): 925–48.

———. "The Present Situation in Legal Scholarship." *Yale Law Journal* 90 (1981): 1113–30.

———. *The Economics of Justice.* Cambridge: Harvard University Press, 1983.

———. "The Decline of Law as an Autonomous Discipline: 1962–1987." *Harvard Law Review* 100 (February 1987a): 761–80.

———. "The Law and Economics Movement." *American Economic Review* 77 (May 1987b): 1–13.

———. "What Am I? A Potted Plant?" *New Republic* (September 28, 1987c): 23–25.

———. *The Problems of Jurisprudence.* Cambridge: Harvard University Press, 1990.

———. *Economic Analysis of Law.* 4th ed. Boston: Little, Brown, 1992.

———. "Gary Becker's Contributions to Law and Economics." *Journal of Legal Studies* 22 (June 1993a): 211–15.

———. "What Do Judges Maximize? (The Same Thing Everybody Else Does)." *Supreme Court Economic Review* 3 (1993b): 1–41.

———. "The New Institutional Economics Meets Law and Economics." *Journal of Institutional and Theoretical Economics*, 149: (1993c): 73–87.

———. *Overcoming Law.* Cambridge: Harvard University Press, 1995.

———. "Social Norms and the Law: An Economic Approach." *American Economic Review* 87 (1997): 365–69.

———. "Bentham's Influence on the Law and Economics Movement." *Current Legal Problems* 51 (1998a): 425–39.

———. "Social Norms, Social Meaning, and Economic Analysis of Law: A Comment." *Journal of Legal Studies* 27 (1998b): 553–65.

————. *The Problematics of Moral and Legal Theory*. Cambridge: Belknap Press, 1999.

————. *Antitrust Law: An Economic Perspective*. Chicago: University of Chicago Press, 2001a.

————. *Frontiers of Legal Theory*. Cambridge: Harvard University Press, 2001b.

————. *Economic Analysis of Law*. 6th ed. New York: Aspen, 2003.

————. "Guido Calabresi's *The Costs of Accidents*, a Reassessment." *University of Maryland Law Review* 64 (2005): 12–23.

Pound, Roscoe. "The Scope and Purpose of Sociological Jurisprudence, Part I." *Harvard Law Review* 24 (June 1911a): 591–619.

————. "The Scope and Purpose of Sociological Jurisprudence, Part II." *Harvard Law Review* 25 (December 1911b): 140–68.

————. "The Scope and Purpose of Sociological Jurisprudence, Part III." *Harvard Law Review* 25 (April 1912): 489–516.

————. *Introduction to the Philosophy of Law*. Rev. ed. New Haven: Yale University Press, 1954.

Price, Catherine M. *Welfare Economics in Theory and Practice*. London: Macmillan, 1977.

Priest, George. "The Common Law Process and the Selection of Efficient Legal Rules." *Journal of Legal Studies* 6 (January 1977): 65–82.

Purcell, Edward A., Jr. "American Jurisprudence Between the Wars: Legal Realism and the Crisis of Democratic Theory." Pp. 359–74 in *American Law and the Constitutional Order*, edited by Lawrence M. Friedman and Harry N. Scheiber. Cambridge: Harvard University Press, 1988.

Radnitzky, Gerard, and Peter Bernholz. *Economic Imperialism: The Economic Approach Applied Outside the Field of Economics*. New York: Paragon, 1987.

Rawls, John. *A Theory of Justice*. Cambridge: Harvard University Press, 1971.

Reder, Melvin W. "Chicago Economics: Permanence and Change." *Journal of Economic Literature* 20 (March 1982): 1–38.

Reisman, David. *The Political Economy of James Buchanan*. College Station: Texas A&M University Press, 1990.

Richter, Rudolf. "Bridging Old and New Institutional Economics: Gustov Schmoller, the Leader of the Younger German Historical School, Seen with Neoinstitutionalist's Eyes." *Journal of Institutional and Theoretical Economics* 152 (1996): 567–92.

Riker, William H. *The Theory of Political Coalitions*. New Haven: Yale University Press, 1962.

————. "Rhetorical Action in the Ratification Campaigns." Pp. 81–123 in *Agenda Formation*, edited by William H. Riker. Ann Arbor: University of Michigan Press, 1993.

Riker, William H., and Peter C. Ordeshook. *An Introduction to Positive Political Theory*. Englewood Cliffs, N.J.: Prentice-Hall, 1973.

Rizzo, Mario. "Law amid Flux: The Economics of Negligence and Strict Liability in Tort." *Journal of Legal Studies* 9 (March 1980a): 291–318.

————. "The Mirage of Efficiency." *Hofstra Law Review* 8 (1980b): 641–58.

————. "A Theory of Economic Loss in the Law of Torts." *Journal of Legal Studies* 11 (June 1982): 281–310.

Romer, Thomas, and Howard Rosenthal. "Median Voters or Budget Maximizers: Evidence from School Expenditure Referenda." *Economic Inquiry* 20 (October 1982): 556–78.

Rose-Ackerman, Susan. "Law and Economics: Paradigm, Politics, or Philosophy?" Pp. 233–58 in *Law and Economics*, edited by Nicholas Mercuro. Boston: Kluwer, 1989.

———. *Rethinking the Progressive Agenda: The Reform of the American Regulatory State*. New York: Free Press, 1992.

Rosen, Harvey S. *Public Finance*. 4th ed. Homewood, Ill.: Irwin, 1995.

Rosen, Jeffrey. "The Social Police." *New Yorker*, October 20 & 27, 1997, pp. 171–81.

Rowe, Frederick M. "Antitrust in Transition: Crossing the Threshold of Change— Panel Discussion." Moderator: Richard A. Whiting; Panelists: Frederick M. Rowe, William F. Baxter, Hon. Robert H. Bork, and Phillip Areeda. *Antitrust Law Journal* 54 (1985): 31–37.

Rowley, Charles K., and Alan T. Peacock. *Welfare Economics: A Liberal Restatement*. New York: Wiley, 1975.

Rubin, Edward L. "The New Legal Process, the Synthesis of Discourse, and the Micro-analysis of Institutions." *Harvard Law Review* 109 (April 1996): 1393–438.

Rubin, Paul H. "Why Is the Common Law Efficient?" *Journal of Legal Studies* 6 (January 1977): 51–63.

———. "Common Law and Statute Law." *Journal of Legal Studies* 11 (June 1982): 205–23.

———. "Micro and Macro Legal Efficiency: Supply and Demand." *Supreme Court Economic Review* 13 (2005a): 19–34.

———. "Public Choice and Tort Reform." *Public Choice* 124 (July 2005b): 223–36.

Rutherford, Malcolm. *Institutions in Economics: The Old and the New Institutionalism*. Cambridge: Cambridge University Press, 1994.

———, ed. *Classics in Institutional Economics: The Founders*. London: Pickering & Chatto, 1998.

———. "On the Economic Frontier: Walton Hamilton, Institutional Economics and Education." *History of Political Economy* 35 (Winter 2003): 611–53

———. "Institutional Economics at Columbia." *History of Political Economy* 36 (Spring 2004): 31–78.

Samuels, Warren J. *The Classical Theory of Economic Policy*. Cleveland: World, 1966.

———. "Interrelations Between Legal and Economic Processes." *Journal of Law and Economics* 14 (October 1971): 435–50.

———. "Ecosystem Policy and the Problem of Power." *Environmental Affairs* 2 (Winter 1972a): 580–96.

———. "Welfare Economics, Power, and Property." Pp. 61–127 in *Perspectives of Property*, edited by Gene Wunderlich and W. L. Gibson, Jr., University Park, Pa.: Institute for Research on Land and Water Resources, Pennsylvania State University, 1972b.

———. "The Economy as a System of Power and Its Legal Bases: The Legal Economics of Robert Lee Hale." *University of Miami Law Review* 27 (Spring/Summer 1973): 261–371.

———. "Commentary: An Economic Perspective on the Compensation Problem." *Wayne Law Review* 21 (November 1974): 113–34.

———. "Approaches to Legal-Economic Policy and Related Problems of Research." Pp. 65–73 in *Policy Studies and the Social Sciences*, edited by Stuart S. Nagel. Lexington, Mass.: Lexington, 1975.

————, ed. *The Chicago School of Political Economy*. East Lansing, Mich.: Graduate School of Business, Michigan State University, 1976.

————. "Normative Premises in Regulatory Theory." *Journal of Post Keynesian Economics* 1 (Fall 1978): 100–14.

————. "Maximization of Wealth as Justice: An Essay on Posnerian Law and Economics as Policy Analysis." *Texas Law Review* 60 (December 1981): 147–72.

————, ed. *Institutional Economics*. 3 Vols. Northampton, Mass.: Edward Elgar, 1988.

————. "The Legal-Economic Nexus." *George Washington Law Review* 57 (August 1989a): 1556–78.

————. "The Methodology of Economics and the Case for Policy Diffidence and Restraint." *Review of Social Economy* 42 (Summer 1989b): 113–33.

————. *Essays on the Economic Role of Government*. 2 vols. New York: New York University Press, 1992.

————. "Law and Economics: Some Early Journal Contributions." Pp. 217–85 in *Economic Thought and Discourse in the Twentieth Century*, edited by Warren J. Samuels, Jeff Biddle, and Thomas W. Patchak-Schuster. Northampton, Mass.: Edward Elgar, 1993.

————. "Reflections on the Intellectual Context and Significance of Thorstein Veblen." *Journal of Economic Issues* 29 (September 1995): 915–22.

Samuels, Warren J., and Nicholas Mercuro. "The Role and Resolution of the Compensation Principle in Society: Part One—The Role." *Research in Law and Economics* 1 (1979): 157–94.

————. "The Role and Resolution of the Compensation Principle in Society: Part Two—The Resolution." *Research in Law and Economics* 2 (1980): 103–28.

————. "A Critique of Rent-Seeking Theory." Pp. 55–70 in *Neoclassical Political Economy: The Analysis of Rent-Seeking and DUP Activities*, edited by David C. Colander. Cambridge, Mass.: Ballinger, 1984.

Samuels, Warren J., and A. Allan Schmid. "Polluters' Profit and Political Response: The Dynamics of Rights Creation." *Public Choice* 28 (Winter 1976): 99–105.

————. *Law and Economics: An Institutional Perspective*. Boston: Kluwer-Nijhoff, 1981.

Samuelson, Paul A. *Foundations of Economic Analysis*. Cambridge: Harvard University Press, 1947.

————. "Diagramatic Exposition of a Theory of Public Expenditure." *Review of Economics and Statistics* 37 (November 1955): 350–56.

————. "Social Indifference Curves." *Quarterly Journal of Economics* 70 (February 1956): 1–22.

Scherer, F. M. *Industrial Market Structure and Economic Performance*, Chicago: Rand McNally, 1970.

Schmid, A. Allan. "Biotechnology, Plant Variety Protection, and Changing Property Institutions in Agriculture." *North Central Journal of Agricultural Economics* 7 (July 1985): 129–38.

————. *Property, Power, and Public Choice: An Inquiry into Law and Economics*. 2d ed. New York: Praeger, 1987.

————. "Law and Economics: An Institutional Perspective." Pp. 57–85 in *Law and Economics*, edited by Nicholas Mercuro. Boston: Kluwer, 1989.

————. "Institutional Law and Economics." *European Journal of Law and Economics* 1 (March 1994): 33–51.

———. "The Spartan School of Institutional Economics at Michigan State University." Staff Paper 02-03, Department of Agricultural Economics, Michigan State University, February 1, 2002, pp. 1–25.

———. *Conflict and Cooperation: Institutional and Behavioral Economics.* Oxford: Blackwell Publishers, 2004.

Schön, Donald A. "Generative Metaphor: A Perspective on Problem-Setting in Social Policy." Pp. 254–83 in *Metaphor and Thought*, edited by Andrew Ortony. Cambridge: Cambridge University Press, 1979.

Schwartz, Alan. "The Case for Specific Performance." *Yale Law Journal* 2 (December 1979): 271–306.

Schwartzstein, Linda A. "Austrian Economics and the Current Debate Between Critical Legal Studies and Law and Economics." *Hofstra Law Review* 20 (Summer 1992): 1105–37.

———. "An Austrian Economic View of the Legal Process." *Ohio State Law Journal* 55 (1994): 1009–49.

Scitovsky, Tibor. "A Note on Welfare Propositions in Economics." *Review of Economic Studies* 9 (November 1941–42): 77–88.

Seidman, Robert. "Contract Law, the Free Market, and State Intervention: A Jurisprudential Perspective." *Journal of Economic Issues* 7 (December 1973): 553–76.

Seldon, Arthur. "Introduction." Pp. xii–xvi in *Constitutional Economics*, edited by James M. Buchanan. Oxford: Basil Blackwell, 1991.

Shavell, Steven. "Suit, Settlement, and Trial: A Theoretical Analysis under Alternative Methods for the Allocation of Legal Costs." *Journal of Legal Studies* 11 (January 1982): 55–82.

———. *Economic Analysis of Accident Law.* Cambridge: Harvard University Press, 1987.

———. "Law versus Morality as Regulators of Conduct." *American Law and Economics Review* 4 (2002): 227–57.

———. *Economic Analysis of Law.* Westbury: Foundation Press, 2004.

Shepsle, Kenneth A. "Prospects for Formal Models of Legislatures." *Legislative Studies Quarterly* 10 (February 1985): 5–19.

Shepsle, Kenneth A., and Barry Weingast. "Political Solutions to Market Problems." *American Political Science Review* 78 (June 1984): 417–34.

Sherry, Suzanna. "Civic Virtue and the Feminine Voice in Constitutional Adjudication." *Virginia Law Review* 72 (April 1986): 543–616.

Shughart, William F., II, and Laura Razzolini, eds. *The Elgar Companion to Public Choice.* Northampton, Mass.: Edward Elgar, 2001.

Shughart, William F., II, and Robert D. Tollison. "On the Growth of Government and the Political Economy of Legislation." *Research in Law and Economics* 9 (1986): 111–27.

———. "Interest Groups and the Courts." *George Mason Law Review* 6 (Summer 1998): 953–69.

Simon, Herbert A. *Administrative Behavior.* 2d ed. New York: Macmillan, 1961.

Simons, Henry C. *A Positive Program for Laissez Faire.* Public Policy Pamphlet No. 15. Chicago: University of Chicago Press, 1934.

———. *Personal Income Tax.* Chicago: University of Chicago Press, 1938.

————. *Economic Policy for a Free Society*. Chicago: University of Chicago Press, 1948.

————. *Federal Tax Reform*. Chicago: University of Chicago Press, 1950.

Skeel, David A., Jr. "Public Choice and the Future of Public-Choice Influenced Legal Scholarship." *Vanderbilt Law Review* 50 (1997): 647–76.

Skeeters, Jonathan M. "*Man O War Restaurants, Inc. v. Martin*: Law Altering Economic Performance." *Kentucky Law Review* 88 (1999): 135–59.

Smith, Adam. *An Inquiry into the Nature and Causes of the Wealth of Nations*. 1776. Reprint, New York: Modern Library, 1937.

————. *Lectures on Jurisprudence*. Oxford: Oxford University Press, 1978.

Solo Robert A. *Economic Organization and Social Systems*. New York: Bobbs-Merrill, 1967.

————. *The Political Authority and the Market System*. Cincinnati: South-Western, 1974.

————. *The Positive State*. Cincinnati: South-Western, 1982.

Sommerville, J. P. *Politics and Ideology in England 1603–1640*. London: Longmans, 1986.

Spiegel, Henry. *The Growth of Economic Thought*. Englewood Cliffs, N.J.: Prentice-Hall, 1971.

Srivastava, Sik. *History of Economic Thought*. Dehli: Atma Ram, 1965.

Staff Reporter. "Congress Dumbs Down Judges." *Wall Street Journal*, October 24, 2000, section A, p. 26.

Stearns, Maxwell. *Public Choice and Public Law: Readings and Commentary*. Ottawa: Anderson, 1997.

————. "Restoring Positive Law and Economics: Introduction to Public Choice Theme Issue." *George Mason Law Review* 6 (1998): 709–44.

Sterner, Thomas. *Policy Instruments for Environmental and Natural Resource Management*. Washington, D.C.: Resources for the Future, 2003.

Stevens, Joe B. *The Economics of Collective Choice*. Boulder, Colo.: Westview, 1993.

Stewart, Richard B. "Crisis in Tort Law? The Institutional Perspective." *University of Chicago Law Review* 54 (Winter 1987): 184–99.

————. "Controlling Environmental Risks Through Economic Incentives." *Columbia Journal of Environmental Law* 13 (1988): 153–69.

Stigler, George J. "The Economics of Information." *Journal of Political Economy* 69 (June 1961): 213–25.

————. "The Theory of Economic Regulation." *Bell Journal of Economics and Management Science* 2 (Spring 1971): 137–46.

————. "The Law and Economics of Public Policy: A Plea to the Scholars." *Journal of Legal Studies* 1 (1972): 1–12.

————. "The Sizes of Legislatures." *Journal of Legal Studies* 5 (January 1976): 17–34.

Stigler, George J., and Gary S. Becker. "De Gustibus Non Est Disputandum." *American Economic Review* 67 (March 1977): 76–90.

Stoll, Neal R., and Shepard Goldfein. "The Antitrust Millennium Awards." *New York Law Journal* (August 17, 1999): 3.

————. "Antitrust Trade and Practice: I Come to Bury Caesar, Not to Praise Him . . ." *New York Law Journal* 228 (August 20, 2002): 3.

Stone, Julius. *The Province and Function of Law.* Cambridge: Harvard University Press, 1950.

Summers, Robert S. "Pragmatic Instrumentalism in the Twentieth-Century American Legal Thought—A Synthesis and Critique of Our Dominant General Theory about Law and Its Use." *Cornell Law Review* 66 (June 1981): 861–948.

Sunstein, Cass R. "Interest Groups in American Public Law." *Stanford Law Review* 38 (1985): 29–87.

———. "Beyond the Republican Revival." *Yale Law Journal* 97 (July 1988): 1539–90.

———. *After the Rights Revolution: Reconceiving the Regulatory State.* Cambridge: Harvard University Press, 1990.

———. "Social Norms and Social Roles." *Columbia Law Review* 96 (1996a): 903–68.

———. "On the Expressive Function of Law." *University of Pennsylvania Law Review* 144 (1996b): 2021–53.

Teijl, Rob, and Rudi W. Holzhauer. "The Impact of the Austrian School on Law and Economics." Pp. 247–66 in *Essays in Law and Economics II: Contract Law, Regulation, and Reflections on Law and Economics*, edited by Boudewijn Bouckaert and Gerrit De Geest. Antwerpen: Maklu, 1995.

Telser, Lester. "A Theory of Self-Enforcing Agreements, *Journal of Business* 53 (February 1981): 27–44.

Tietenberg, Thomas. "The Tradable Permits Approach to Protecting the Commons: What Have We Learned?" Pp. 197–232 in *The Drama of the Commons*, edited by E. Ostrom et al., National Research Council, Committee on the Human Dimensions of Global Change. Washington, D.C.: National Academy Press, 2002.

———. *Environmental and Natural Resource Economics.* Boston: Addison Wesley, 2003.

Tool, Marc R. *Evolutionary Economics.* 2 vols. Armonk, N.Y.: M. E. Sharpe, 1988.

———, ed. *Institutional Economics: Theory, Method, Policy.* Boston: Kluwer, 1993.

Trebilcock, Michael J. "The Prospects of 'Law and Economics': A Canadian Perspective." *Journal of Legal Education* 33 (1983): 288–93.

Trebing, Harry M., ed. *New Dimensions in Public Utility Pricing.* East Lansing: Institute of Public Utilities, Michigan State University, 1976.

———. "Telecommunications Regulation—The Continuing Dilemma." Pp. 120–22 in *Public Utility Regulation*, edited by K. Nowotym, D. B. Smith, and H. M. Trebing. Boston: Kluwer, 1989.

Trebing, Harry M., and Maurice Estabrooks. "Telecommunications Policy in the Global Information Economy of the Nineties." Pp. 17–37 in *International Perspectives on Telecommunications Policy*, edited by Rodney Stevenson, T. H. Oum, and H. Oniki. Greenwich, Conn.: JAI Press, 1993.

Tullock, Gordon. *The Politics of Bureaucracy.* Washington, D.C.: Public Affairs Press, 1965.

———. "The Welfare Costs of Tarrifs, Monopolies and Theft." *Western Economic Journal* 5 (1967): 224–32.

———. *Rent Seeking.* Northampton, Mass.: Edward Elgar, 1993.

Tullock, Gordon, Arthur Seldon, and Gordon L. Brady. *Government Failure: A Primer in Public Choice.* Washington, D.C.: Cato Institute, 2002.

Ulen, Thomas S. "Law and Economics: Settled Issues and Open Questions." Pp. 201–31 in *Law and Economics*, edited by Nicholas Mercuro. Boston: Kluwer, 1989.

Umbeck, John. "The California Gold Rush: A Study of Emerging Property Rights." *Explorations in Economic History* 14 (1977a): 197–206.

———. "A Theory of Contract Choice and the California Gold Rush." *Journal of Law and Economics* 20 (October 1977b): 421–37.

———. "Might Makes Right: A Theory of the Formation and Initial Distribution of Property Rights." *Economic Inquiry* 19 (1981): 38–59.

van Aaken, Anne. "Deliberative Institutional Economics, or Does Homo Oeconomicus Argue? A Proposal for Combining New Institutional Economics with Discourse Theory." Pp. 3–32 in *Deliberation and Decision*, edited by Anne van Aaken, Christian List, and Christoph Luetge. Aldershot, England: Ashgate, 2004.

Varian, Hal R. *Microeconomic Analysis*. 3d ed. New York: Norton, 1992.

———. *Intermediate Microeconomics: A Modern Approach*. 3d ed. New York: Norton, 1993.

Veblen, Thorstein B. *Theory of the Leisure Class*. New York: Macmillan, 1889.

———. *The Theory of Business Enterprise*. New York: Scribner's, 1904.

———. *Absentee Ownership and Business Enterprise in Recent Times*. New York: B. W. Huebsch, 1923.

Veljanovski, Cento G. *The New Law-and-Economics*. Oxford: Centre for Socio-Legal Studies, 1982.

———. *The Economics of Law: An Introductory Text*. 2d impression. London: Institute of Economic Affairs, 1996.

Voight, Stephan, and Hella Engerer. "Institutions and Transition: Possible Policy Implications of the New Institutional Economics." Pp. 127–84 in *Frontiers in Economics*, edited by Klaus F. Zimmermann. Berlin: Springer-Verlag, 2002.

Walker, Gordon, and David Weber. "A Transaction Cost Approach to Make-or-Buy Decisions." *Administrative Science Quarterly* 29 (September 1984): 373–91.

———. "Supplier Competition, Uncertainty, and Make-or-Buy Decisions." *The Academy of Management Journal* 30 (September 1987): 589–96.

Walker, Mark Clarence. *The Strategic Use of Referendums: Power, Legitimacy, and Democracy*. New York: Palgrave Macmillan, 2003.

Wallis, John J., and Douglas C. North, "Measuring the Transaction Sector in the American Economy, 1870–1970." Pp. 95–161 in *Long-Term Factors in American Growth*, edited by Stanley L. Engerman and Robert E. Gallman. Chicago: University of Chicago Press, 1986.

Walton, R. Brent. "Ellickson's Paradox: It's Suicide to Maximize Welfare." *New York University Environmental Law Journal* 7 (1999): 153–200.

Wandschneider, Philip. "Neoclassical and Institutionalist Explanations of Changes in Northwest Water Institutions." *Journal of Economic Issues* 20 (March 1986): 87–107.

Weber, Max. *The Theory of Social and Economic Organization*. Edited by Talcott Parsons; (translated by A. M. Henderson and Talcott Parsons.) New York: Oxford University Press, 1947.

Wechsler, Herbert. "Toward Neutral Principles of Constitutional Law." *Harvard Law Review* 73 (1959): 1–35.

Weingast, Barry. "The Economic Role of Political Institution: Market-Preserving Federalism and Economic Development." *Journal of Law, Economics, and Organization* 11 (1995): 1–31.

Weingast, Barry R., and William J. Marshall. "The Industrial Organization of Congress; or Why Legislatures, Like Firms, Are Not Organized as Markets." *Journal of Political Economy* 96 (February 1988): 132–63.

Weingast, Barry R., Kenneth A. Shepsle, and Christopher Johnsen. "The Political Economy of Benefits and Costs: A Neoclassical Approach to Distributive Politics." *Journal of Political Economy* 89 (1981): 642–64.

Weinrib, Earnest J. *The Idea of Private Law*. Cambridge: Harvard University Press, 1995.

Werin, Lars, and Hans Wijkander. *Contract Economics*. Cambridge, Mass.: Blackwell, 1992.

West, Robin. "The Supreme Court, 1989 Term: Foreword: Taking Freedom Seriously." *Harvard Law Review* 104 (1990): 43–106.

Whalen, Charles J. "The Institutionalist Approach to Economics." Pp. 83–99 in *Beyond Neoclassical Economics: Heterodox Approaches to Economic Theory*, edited by Fred Foldvary. Northampton, Mass.: Edward Elgar, 1996.

White, Barbara Ann. "Countervailing Power—Different Rules for Different Markets? Conduct and Context in Antitrust Law and Economics." *Duke Law Journal* 41 (1992): 1045–94.

White, G. Edward. "From Sociological Jurisprudence to Realism: Jurisprudence and the Social Change in Early Twentieth-Century America." *Virginia Law Review* 58 (1972): 999–1028.

———. *Justice Oliver Wendell Holmes: Law and the Inner Self.* Oxford: Oxford University Press, 1993.

Wicksell, Knut. *Finanztheoretische Untersuchungen*. Jena: Gustav Fisher, 1896.

———. "A New Principle of Just Taxation." Pp. 72–118 in *Classics in the Theory of Public Finance*, edited by Richard A. Musgrave and Alan T. Peacock. New York: St. Martin's, 1967.

Wigdor, David. *Roscoe Pound: Philosopher of Law.* Westport, Conn.: Greenwood, 1974.

Williamson, Oliver E. *Markets and Hierarchies: Analysis and Antitrust Implications.* New York: The Free Press, 1975.

———. "Credible Commitments: Using Hostages to Support Exchange." *American Economic Review* 73 (September 1983): 519–40.

———. "The Economics of Governance: Framework and Implications." *Journal of Institutional and Theoretical Economics* 140 (March 1984): 195–223. Reprinted in *The New Institutional Economics*, edited by Eirik G. Furubotn and Rudolf Richter, 54–82. College Station: Texas A&M University Press, 1991.

———. *The Economic Institutions of Capitalism: Firms, Markets, Relational Contracting.* New York: The Free Press, 1985.

———. "The Logic of Economic Organization." *Journal of Law, Economics, and Organization* 4 (Spring 1988): 65–93.

———. "A Comparison of Alternative Approaches to Economic Organization." *Journal of Institutional and Theoretical Economics* 146 (1990): 61–71. Reprinted in *The New Institutional Economics*, edited by Eirik G. Furubotn and Rudolf Richter, pp. 104–14. College Station: Texas A&M University Press, 1991.

———. "Comparative Economic Organization: The Analysis of Discrete Structural Alternatives." *Administrative Science Quarterly* 36 (June 1991): 269–96.

———. "The Evolving Science of Organization." *Journal of Institutional and Theoretical Economics* 149 (March 1993a): 35–53.

———. "Transaction Cost Economics Meets Posnerian Law and Economics." *Journal of Institutional and Theoretical Economics* 149 (March 1993b): 99–118.

———. "The New Institutional Economics: Taking Stock/Looking Ahead." *ISNIE Newsletter* 2 (Fall 1999): 9–20.

Wittman, Donald. "Why Democracies Produce Efficient Results." *Journal of Political Economy* 97 (December 1989): 1395–424.

———. *The Myth of Democratic Failure: Why Political Institutions Are Efficient.* Chicago: University of Chicago Press, 1995.

Wright, Richard W. "Hand, Posner, and the Myth of the 'Hand Formula.'" *Theoretical Inquiries in Law* 4 (2003): 1–130. Available at http://ssrn.com/abstract=362800

Wonnacott, Paul, and Ronald Wonnacott. *An Introduction to Microeconomics.* New York: McGraw-Hill, 1979.

Wood, Gordon S. *The Creation of the American Republic 1776–1987.* New York: Norton, 1972.

Wood, Robert S. "History, Thought, and Images: The Development of International Law and Organization." *Virginia Journal of International Law* 12 (December 1971): 35–65.

Woodward, Calvin. "The Limits of Legal Realism: An Historical Perspective." *Virginia Law Review* 54 (May 1968): 689–739.

Yeager, Timothy J. "The New Institutional Economics and Its Relevance to Social Economics." *Forum for Social Economics* 27 (1997): 1–17.

Yngvesson, Barbara. "Beastly Neighbors: Continuing Relations in Cattle Country." *Yale Law Journal* 102 (1993): 1787–801.

Zerbe, Richard O., Jr. "The Problem of Social Cost in Retrospect." *Research in Law and Economics* 2 (1980): 83–102.

List of Cases

Abrams v. United States, 250 U.S. 616 (1919).

Allegeyer v. Louisiana, 165 U.S. 578 (1897).

Continental T. V., Inc. v. GTE Sylvania Inc., 433 U.S. 36 (1977).

Eyerman v. Mercantile Trust Co., 524 S.W.2d 210 (1975).

Lochner v. New York, 198 U.S. 45 (1905).

Matsushita Electronic Industrial Co., Ltd. v. Zenith Radio Corp., 475 U.S. 574 (1986).

Miller et al. v. Schoene, 276 U.S. 272 (1928).

Molitor v. Kaneland Community Unit District No. 302, 163 N.E.2d 89 (1959).

Northern Pacific Railway Co. v. United States, 356 U.S. 1 (1958).

Osborne v. Montgomery, 234 N.W.2d 372 (1931).

Penn Central Transportation Company v. City of New York, 438 U.S. 104 (1978).

Pennell v. City of San Jose, 485 U.S. 1 (1988).

Pierce v. Yakima Valley Memorial Hospital Ass'n, 260 P.2d 765 (1953).

Rosenberg v. Lipnick, 389 N.E.2d 385 (1979).

Sommer v. Kridel, 378 A.2d 767 (1973).

Southern Pacific Co. v. Jensen, 244 U.S. 205 (1917).
United States v. Aluminum Co. of America, 148 F.2d 416 (1945).
United States v. Carroll Towing Co., 159 F.2d 169 (1947).
United States v. Von's Grocery Co., 384 U.S. 270 (1966).
Wellington v. Rugg, 136 N.E. 831 (1922).

mente que es menester para la inteligencia de cosas tan altas; y si esto falta, nada sirve de lo demás.

Del Angélico Doctor Santo Tomás dice la Iglesia estas palabras: *In difficultatibus locorum Sacrae Scripturae ad orationem ieiunium adhibebat. Quin etiam sodali suo Fratri Reginaldo dicere solebat, quidquid sciret, non tam studio, aut labore suo peperisse, quam divinitus traditum accepisse* . Pues yo, tan distante de la virtud y las letras, ¿cómo había de tener ánimo para escribir? Y así, por tener algunos principios granjeados, estudiaba continuamente diversas cosas, sin tener para alguna particular inclinación, sino para todas en general; por lo cual, el haber estudiado en unas más que en otras no ha sido en mí elección, sino que el acaso de haber topado más a mano libros de aquellas facultades les ha dado, sin arbitrio mío, la preferencia. Y como no tenía interés que me moviese, ni límite de tiempo que me estrechase el continuado estudio de una cosa por la necesidad de los grados , casi a un tiempo estudiaba diversas cosas o dejaba unas por otras; bien que en eso observaba orden, porque a unas llamaba estudio y a otras diversión; y en éstas descansaba de las otras, de donde se sigue que he estudiado muchas cosas y nada sé, porque las unas han embarazado a las otras. Es verdad que esto digo de la parte práctica en las que la tienen, porque claro está que mientras se mueve la pluma descansa el compás, y mientras se toca el arpa sosiega el órgano, *et sic de caeteris* ; porque como es menester mucho uso corporal para adquirir hábito, nunca le puede tener perfecto quien se reparte en varios ejercicios; pero en lo formal y especulativo sucede al contrario, y quisiera yo persuadir a todos con mi experiencia a que no sólo no estorban, pero se ayudan dando luz y abriendo camino las unas para las otras, por variaciones y ocultos engarces—que para esta ca-

thor in such a way that they conform and are joined together with admirable unity and harmony. This is the very chain the ancients believed did issue from the mouth of Jupiter, from which were suspended all things linked one with another, As is demonstrated by the Reverend Father Athanasius Kircher in his curious book, *De Magnate*.[16] All things issue from God, Who is at once the center and the circumference from which and in which all lines begin and end.

I myself can affirm that what I have not understood in an author in one branch of knowledge I may understand in a second in a branch that seems remote from the first. And authors, in their elucidation, may suggest metaphorical examples in other arts: as when logicians say that to prove whether parts are equal, the means is to the extremes as a determined measure to two equidistant bodies; or in stating how the argument of the logician moves, in the manner of a straight line, along the shortest route, while that of the rhetorician moves as a curve, by the longest, but that both finally arrive at the same point.

And similarly, as it is when they say that the Exegetes are like an open hand, and the Scholastics like a closed fist. And thus it is no apology, nor do I offer it as such, to say that I have studied many subjects, seeing that each augments the other; but that I have not profited is the fault of my own ineptitude and the inadequacy of my intelligence, not the fault of the variety. But what may be offered as exoneration is that I undertook this great task without benefit of teacher, or fellow students with whom to confer and discuss, having for a master no other than a mute book, and for a colleague, an insentient inkwell; and in the stead of explication and exercise, many obstructions, not merely those of my religious obligations (for it is already known how useful and advantageous is the time employed in them), rather, all the attendant details of living in a community: how I might be reading, and those in the adjoining

dena universal les puso la sabiduría de su Autor—, de manera que parece se corresponden y están unidas con admirable trabazón y concierto. Es la cadena que fingieron los antiguos que salía de la boca de Júpiter, de donde pendían todas las cosas eslabonadas unas con otras. Así lo demuestra el R. P. Atanasio Quirquerio en su curioso libro *De Magnete* . Todas las cosas salen de Dios, que es el centro a un tiempo y la circunferencia de donde salen y donde paran todas las líneas criadas.

Yo de mí puedo asegurar que lo que no entiendo en un autor de una facultad lo suelo entender en otro de otra que parece muy distante; y esos propios, al explicarse, abren ejemplos metafóricos de otras artes, como cuando dicen los lógicos que el medio se ha con los términos como se ha una medida con dos cuerpos distantes, para conferir si son iguales o no; y que la oración del lógico anda como la línea recta, por el camino más breve, y la del retórico se mueve, como la corva, por el más largo, pero van a un mismo punto los dos; y cuando dicen que los expositores son como la mano abierta y los escolásticos como el puño cerrado. Y así no es disculpa, ni por tal la doy, el haber estudiado diversas cosas, pues éstas antes se ayudan, sino que el no haber aprovechado ha sido ineptitud mía y debilidad de mi entendimiento, no culpa de la variedad. Lo que sí pudiera ser descargo mío es el sumo trabajo no sólo en carecer de maestro, sino de condiscípulos con quienes conferir y ejercitar lo estudiado, teniendo sólo por maestro un libro mudo, por condiscípulo un tintero insensible; y en vez de explicación y ejercicio, muchos estorbos, no sólo los de mis religiosas obligaciones (que éstas ya se sabe cuán útil y provechosamente gastan el tiempo), sino de aquellas cosas accesorias de una comunidad: como estar yo leyendo y antojárseles en la

cell would wish to play their instruments, and sing; how I might be studying, and two servants who had quarreled would select me to judge their dispute; or how I might be writing, and a friend come to visit me, doing me no favor but with the best of will, at which time one must not only accept the inconvenience, but be grateful for the hurt. And such occurrences are the normal state of affairs, for as the times I set apart for study are those remaining after the ordinary duties of the community are fulfilled, they are the same moments available to my sisters, in which they may come to interrupt my labor; and only those who have experience of such a community will know how true this is, and how it is only the strength of my vocation that allows me happiness; that, and the great love existing between me and my beloved sisters, for as love is union, it knows no extremes of distance.

With this I confess how interminable has been my labor; and how I am unable to say what I have with envy heard others state — that they have not been plagued by the thirst for knowledge: blessed are they. For me, not the knowing (for still I do not know), merely the desiring to know, has been such torment that I can say, as has my Father Saint Jerome (although not with his accomplishment) . . . *my conscience is witness to what effort I have expended, what difficulties I have suffered, how many times I have despaired, how often I have ceased my labors and turned to them again, driven by the hunger for knowledge; my conscience is witness, and that of those who have lived beside me.*[17] With the exception of the companions and witnesses (for I have been denied even this consolation), I can attest to the truth of these words. And to the fact that even so, my dark inclination has been so great that it has conquered all else!

It has been my fortune that, among other benefices, I owe to God a most tender and affable nature, and because of it my sisters (who being good women do not take note of my faults) hold me in great affection, and take pleasure in

celda vecina tocar y cantar; estar yo estudiando y pelear dos criadas y venirme a constituir juez de su pendencia; estar yo escribiendo y venir una amiga a visitarme, haciéndome muy mala obra con muy buena voluntad, donde es preciso no sólo admitir el embarazo, pero quedar agradecida del perjuicio. Y esto es continuamente, porque como los ratos que destino a mi estudio son los que sobran de lo regular de la comunidad, esos mismos les sobran a las otras para venirme a estorbar; y sólo saben cuánta verdad es ésta los que tienen experiencia de vida común, donde sólo la fuerza de la vocación puede hacer que mi natural esté gustoso, y el mucho amor que hay entre mí y mis amadas hermanas, que como el amor es unión, no hay para él extremos distantes.

En esto sí confieso que ha sido inexplicable   mi trabajo; y así no puedo decir lo que con envidia oigo a otros: que no les ha costado afán el saber. ¡Dichosos ellos! A mí, no el saber (que aún no sé), sólo el desear saber me le ha costado tan grande que pudiera decir con mi Padre San Jerónimo (aunque no con su aprovechamiento): *Quid ibi laboris insumpserim, quid sustinuerim difficultatis, quoties desperaverim, quotiesque cessaverim et contentione discendi rursus inceperim; testis est conscientia, tam mea, qui passus sum, quam eorum qui mecum duxerunt vitam* . Menos los compañeros y testigos (que aun de ese alivio he carecido), lo demás bien puedo asegurar con verdad. ¡Y que haya sido tal esta mi negra inclinación que todo lo haya vencido!

Solía sucederme que, como entre otros beneficios, debo a Dios un natural tan blando y tan afable y las religiosas me aman mucho por él (sin reparar, como buenas, en mis faltas) y con esto gustan mucho de mi compañía; conociendo esto, y movida del grande amor que las tengo, con mayor motivo que ellas a mí, gusto

my company; and knowing this, and moved by the great love I hold for them — having greater reason than they — I enjoy even more *their* company. Thus I was wont in our rare idle moments to visit among them, offering them consolation and entertaining myself in their conversation. I could not help but note, however, that in these times I was neglecting my study, and I made a vow not to enter any cell unless obliged by obedience or charity; for without such a compelling constraint — the constraint of mere intention not being sufficient — my love would be more powerful than my will. I would (knowing well my frailty) make this vow for the period of a few weeks, or a month; and when that time had expired, I would allow myself a brief respite of a day or two before renewing it, using that time not so much for rest (for *not* studying has never been restful for me) as to assure that I not be deemed cold, remote, or ungrateful in the little-deserved affection of my dearest sisters.

In this practice one may recognize the strength of my inclination. I give thanks to God, Who willed that such an ungovernable force be turned toward letters and not to some other vice. From this it may also be inferred how obdurately against the current my poor studies have sailed (more accurately, have foundered). For still to be related is the most arduous of my difficulties — those mentioned until now, either compulsory or fortuitous, being merely tangential — and still unreported the more-directly aimed slings and arrows that have acted to impede and prevent the exercise of my study. Who would have doubted, having witnessed such general approbation, that I sailed before the wind across calm seas, amid the laurels of widespread acclaim. But our Lord God knows that it has not been so; He knows how from amongst the blossoms of this very acclaim emerged such a number of aroused vipers, hissing their emulation and their persecution, that one could not count them. But the most noxious, those who most deeply

más de la suya; así, me solía ir los ratos que a unas y a otras nos sobraban a consolarlas y recrearme con su conversación. Reparé que en este tiempo hacía falta a mi estudio , y hacía voto de no entrar en celda alguna si no me obligase a ello la obediencia o la caridad, porque sin este freno tan duro, al de sólo propósito le rompiera el amor; y este voto (conociendo mi fragilidad) le hacía por un mes o por quince días; y dando, cuando se cumplía, un día o dos de treguas, lo volvía a renovar, sirviendo este día no tanto a mi descanso (pues nunca lo ha sido para mí el no estudiar) cuanto a que no me tuviesen por áspera, retirada e ingrata al no merecido cariño de mis carísimas hermanas.

Bien se deja en esto conocer cuál es la fuerza de mi inclinación. Bendito sea Dios, que quiso fuese hacia las letras y no hacia otro vicio que fuera en mí casi insuperable; y bien se infiere también cuán contra la corriente han navegado (o, por mejor decir, han naufragado) mis pobres estudios. Pues aún falta por referir lo más arduo de las dificultades, que las de hasta aquí sólo han sido estorbos obligatorios y casuales, que indirectamente lo son, y faltan los positivos, que directamente han tirado a estorbar y prohibir el ejercicio. ¿Quién no creerá, viendo tan generales aplausos, que he navegado viento en popa y mar en leche sobre las palmas de las aclamaciones comunes? Pues Dios sabe que no ha sido muy así, porque entre las flores de esas mismas aclamaciones se han levantado y despertado tales áspides de emulaciones y persecuciones cuantas no podré contar, y los que más nocivos y sensibles para mí han sido no son aquellos que con declarado odio y malevolencia me han perseguido, sino los que amándome y deseando mi bien (y por ventura mereciendo mucho con Dios por la buena intención) me han mortificado y atormentado más que los otros con aquel: *No conviene a la santa ignorancia que deben, este estudio; se ha de*

wounded me, have not been those who persecuted me with open loathing and malice, but rather those who in loving me and desiring my well-being (and who are deserving of God's blessing for their good intent) have mortified and tormented me more than those others with their abhorrence. "Such studies are not in conformity with sacred innocence; surely she will be lost; surely she will, by cause of her very perspicacity and acuity, grow heady at such exalted heights." How was I to endure? An uncommon sort of martyrdom in which I was both martyr and executioner. And for my (in me, twice hapless) facility in making verses, even though they be sacred verses, what sorrows have I not suffered? What sorrows not ceased to suffer? Be assured, lady, it is often that I have meditated on how one who distinguishes himself — or one on whom God chooses to confer distinction, for it is only He who may do so — is received as a common enemy, because it seems to some that he usurps the applause they deserve, or that he dams up the admiration to which they aspired, and so they persecute that person.

That politically barbaric law of Athens by which any person who excelled by cause of his natural gifts and virtues was exiled from his Republic in order that he not threaten the public freedom still endures, is still observed in our day, although not for the reasons held by the Athenians. Those reasons have been replaced by another, no less efficient though not as well founded, seeming, rather, a maxim more appropriate to that impious Machiavelli — which is to abhor one who excels, because he deprives others of regard. And thus it happens, and thus it has always happened.

For if not, what was the cause of the rage and loathing the Pharisees directed against Christ, there being so many reasons to love Him? If we behold His presence, what is more to be loved than that Divine beauty? What more powerful to stir one's heart? For if ordinary human beauty

46

perder, se ha de desvanecer en tanta altura con su misma perspicacia y agudeza. ¿Qué me habrá costado resistir esto? ¡Rara especie de martirio, donde yo era el mártir y me era el verdugo!

Pues por la—en mí dos veces infeliz—habilidad de hacer versos, aunque fuesen sagrados, ¿qué pesadumbres no me han dado o cuáles no me han dejado de dar? Cierto, Señora mía, que algunas veces me pongo a considerar que el que se señala—o le señala Dios, que es quien sólo lo puede hacer—es recibido como enemigo común, porque parece a algunos que usurpa los aplausos que ellos merecen o que hace estanque de las admiraciones a que aspiraban, y así le persiguen.

Aquella ley políticamente bárbara de Atenas por la cual salía desterrado de su república el que se señalaba en prendas y virtudes porque no tiranizase con ellas la libertad pública todavía dura, todavía se observa en nuestros tiempos, aunque no hay ya aquel motivo de los atenienses; pero hay otro no menos eficaz, aunque no tan bien fundado, pues parece máxima del impío Maquiavelo, que es aborrecer al que se señala porque desluce a otros. Así sucede y así sucedió siempre.

Y si no, ¿cuál fue la causa de aquel rabioso odio de los fariseos contra Cristo, habiendo tantas razones para lo contrario? Porque si miramos su presencia, ¿cuál prenda más amable que aquella divina hermosura? ¿Cuál más poderosa para arrebatar los corazones? Si cualquiera belleza humana tiene jurisdicción sobre los albedríos y con blanda y apetecida violencia los sabe sujetar, ¿qué haría aquélla con tantas prerrogativas y dotes soberanos? ¿Qué haría, qué movería y qué no haría y qué no movería aquella incomprensible beldad,

holds sway over strength of will, and is able to subdue it with tender and enticing vehemence, what power would Divine beauty exert, with all its prerogatives and sovereign endowments? What might move, what effect, what not move and not effect, such incomprehensible beauty, that beauteous face through which, as through a polished crystal, were diffused the rays of Divinity? What would not be moved by that semblance which beyond incomparable human perfections revealed Divine illuminations? If the visage of Moses, merely from conversation with God, caused men to fear to come near him, how much finer must be the face of God-made-flesh? And among other virtues, what more to be loved than that celestial modesty? That sweetness and kindness disseminating mercy in every movement? That profound humility and gentleness? Those words of eternal life and eternal wisdom? How therefore is it possible that such beauty did not stir their souls, that they did not follow after Him, enamored and enlightened?

The Holy Mother, my Mother Teresa, says that when she beheld the beauty of Christ never again was she inclined toward any human creature, for she saw nothing that was not ugliness compared to such beauty. How was it then that in men it engendered such contrary reactions? For although they were uncouth and vile and had no knowledge or appreciation of His perfections, not even as they might profit from them, how was it they were not moved by the many advantages of such benefices as He performed for them, healing the sick, resurrecting the dead, restoring those possessed of the devil? How was it they did not love Him? But God is witness that it was for these very acts they did not love Him, that they despised Him. As they themselves testified.

They gather together in their council and say: *What do we? for this man doth many miracles.*[18] Can this be cause? If they had said: here is an evil-doer, a transgressor of the law, a rabble-rouser who with deceit stirs up the populace,

por cuyo hermoso rostro, como por un terso cristal, se estaban transparentando los rayos de la Divinidad? ¿Qué no movería aquel semblante, que sobre incomparables perfecciones en lo humano señalaba iluminaciones de divino? Si el de Moisés, de sólo la conversación con Dios, era intolerable a la flaqueza de la vista humana , ¿qué sería el del mismo Dios humanado? Pues si vamos a las demás prendas, ¿cuál más amable que aquella celestial modestia, que aquella suavidad y blandura derramando misericordias en todos sus movimientos, aquella profunda humildad y mansedumbre, aquellas palabras de vida eterna y eterna sabiduría? Pues ¿cómo es posible que esto no les arrebatara las almas, que no fuesen enamorados y elevados tras él?

Dice la Santa Madre y madre mía Teresa que después que vio la hermosura de Cristo, quedó libre de poderse inclinar a criatura alguna, porque ninguna cosa veía que no fuese fealdad, comparada con aquella hermosura. Pues, ¿cómo en los hombres hizo tan contrarios efectos? Y ya que como toscos y viles no tuvieran conocimiento ni estimación de sus perfecciones, siquiera como interesables, ¿no les moviera sus propias conveniencias y utilidades en tantos beneficios como les hacía, sanando los enfermos, resucitando los muertos, curando los endemoniados? Pues ¿cómo no le amaban? ¡Ay, Dios, que por eso mismo no le amaban, por eso mismo le aborrecían! Así lo testificaron ellos mismos.

Júntanse en su concilio y dicen: *Quid facimus, quia hic homo multa signa facit?* ¿Hay tal causa? Si dijeran: éste es un malhechor, un transgresor de la ley, un alborotador que con engaños alborota el pueblo, mintieran, como mintieron cuando lo decían; pero eran causales

they would have lied — as they did indeed lie when they spoke these things. But there were more apposite reasons for effecting what they desired, which was to take His life; and to give as reason that he had performed wondrous deeds seems not befitting learned men, for such were the Pharisees. Thus it is that in the heat of passion learned men erupt with such irrelevancies; for we know it as truth that only for this reason was it determined that Christ should die. Oh, men, if men you may be called, being so like to brutes, what is the cause of so cruel a determination? Their only response is that "this man doth many miracles." May God forgive them. Then is performing signal deeds cause enough that one should die? This "he doth many miracles" evokes *the root of Jesse, who standeth for an ensign of the people,*[19] and that *and for a sign which shall be contradicted.*[20] He is a sign? Then He shall die. He excels? Then He shall suffer, for that is the reward for one who excels.

Often on the crest of temples are placed as adornment figures of the winds and of fame, and to defend them from the birds, they are covered with iron barbs; this appears to be in defense, but is in truth obligatory propriety: the figure thus elevated cannot avoid becoming the target of those barbs; there on high is found the animosity of the air, on high, the ferocity of the elements, on high is unleashed the anger of the thunderbolt, on high stands the target for slings and arrows. Oh unhappy eminence, exposed to such uncounted perils. Oh sign, become the target of envy and the butt of contradiction. Whatever eminence, whether that of dignity, nobility, riches, beauty, or science, must suffer this burden; but the eminence that undergoes the most severe attack is that of reason. First, because it is the most defenseless, for riches and power strike out against those who dare attack them; but not so reason, for while it is the greater it is more modest and long-suffering, and defends itself less. Second, as Gracian stated so eruditely, *favors in man's reason are favors in his nature.*

más congruentes a lo que solicitaban, que era quitarle la vida; mas dar por causal que hace cosas señaladas no parece de hombres doctos, cuales eran los fariseos. Pues así es que cuando se apasionan los hombres doctos prorrumpen en semejantes inconsecuencias. En verdad que sólo por eso salió determinado que Cristo muriese. Hombres, si es que así se os puede llamar, siendo tan brutos, ¿por qué es esa tan cruel determinación? No responden más sino que *multa signa facit.* ¡Válgame Dios, que el hacer cosas señaladas es causa para que uno muera! Haciendo reclamo este *multa signa facit* a aquel *radix Iesse, qui stat in signum populorum* y al otro *in signum cui contradicetur* . ¿Por signo? ¡Pues muera! ¿Señalado? ¡Pues padezca, que eso es el premio de quien se señala!

Suelen en la eminencia de los templos colocarse por adorno unas figuras de los Vientos y de la Fama, y por defenderlas de las aves las llenan todas de púas; defensa parece y no es sino propiedad forzosa: no puede estar sin púas que la puncen quien está en alto. Allí está la ojeriza del aire, allí es el rigor de los elementos, allí despican la cólera los rayos, allí es el blanco de piedras y flechas. ¡Oh infeliz altura, expuesta a tantos riesgos! ¡Oh signo que te ponen por blanco de la envidia y por objeto de la contradicción! Cualquiera eminencia, ya sea de dignidad, ya de nobleza, ya de riqueza, ya de hermosura, ya de ciencia, padece esta pensión ; pero la que con más rigor la experimenta es la del entendimiento. Lo primero, porque es el más indefenso, pues la riqueza y el poder castigan a quien se les atreve, y el entendimiento no, pues mientras es mayor es más modesto y sufrido y se defiende menos. Lo segundo es porque, como dijo doctamente Gracián , las ventajas en el entendimiento lo son en el ser. No por otra razón es el ángel más que el hombre que porque entiende

For no other cause except that the angel is superior in reason is the angel above man; for no other cause does man stand above the beast but by his reason; and thus, as no one wishes to be lower than another, neither does he confess that another is superior in reason, as reason is a consequence of being superior. One will abide, and will confess that another is nobler than he, that another is richer, more handsome, and even that he is more learned, but that another is richer in reason scarcely any will confess: *Rare is he who will concede genius.*[21] That is why the assault against this virtue works to such profit.

When the soldiers mocked, made entertainment and diversion of our Lord Jesus Christ, they brought Him a worn purple garment and a hollow reed, and a crown of thorns to crown Him King of Fools. But though the reed and the purple were an affront, they did not cause suffering. Why does only the crown give pain? Is it not enough that like the other emblems the crown was a symbol of ridicule and ignominy, as that was its intent? No. Because the sacred head of Christ and His divine intellect were the depository of wisdom, and the world is not satisfied for wisdom to be the object of mere ridicule, it must also be done injury and harm. A head that is a storehouse of wisdom can expect nothing but a crown of thorns. What garland may human wisdom expect when it is known what was bestowed on that divine wisdom? Roman pride crowned the many achievements of their Captains with many crowns: he who defended the city received the civic crown; he who fought his way into the hostile camp received the camp crown; he who scaled the wall, the mural; he who liberated a beseiged city, or any army besieged either in the field or in the enemy camp, received the obsidional, the siege, crown; other feats were crowned with naval, ovation, or triumphal crowns, as described by Pliny and Aulus Gellius. Observing so many and varied crowns, I debated as to which Christ's crown must have been, and deter-

más; no es otro el exceso que el hombre hace al bruto, sino sólo entender; y así como ninguno quiere ser menos que otro, así ninguno confiesa que otro entiende más, porque es consecuencia del ser más. Sufrirá uno y confesará que otro es más noble que él, que es más rico, que es más hermoso y aun que es más docto; pero que es más entendido apenas habrá quien lo confiese; *Rarus est, qui velit cedere ingenio* . Por eso es tan eficaz la batería contra esta prenda.

Cuando los soldados hicieron burla, entretenimiento y diversión de Nuestro Señor Jesucristo, trajeron una púrpura vieja y una caña hueca y una corona de espinas para coronarle por rey de burlas. Pues ahora la caña y la púrpura eran afrentosas, pero no dolorosas; pues ¿por qué sólo la corona es dolorosa? ¿No basta que, como las demás, insignias, fuese de escarnio e ignominia, pues ése era el fin? No, porque la sagrada cabeza de Cristo y aquel divino cerebro eran depósito de la sabiduría; y cerebro sabio en el mundo no basta que esté escarnecido, ha de estar también lastimado y maltratado; cabeza que es erario de sabiduría no espere otra corona que de espinas. ¿Cuál guirnalda espera la sabiduría humana si ve la que obtuvo la divina? Coronaba la soberbia romana las diversas hazañas de sus capitanes también con diversas coronas: ya con la cívica al que defendía al ciudadano, ya con la castrense al que entraba en los reales enemigos, ya con la mural al que escalaba el muro, ya con la obsidional al que libraba la ciudad cercada o el ejército sitiado o el campo o en los reales; ya con la naval, ya con la oval, ya con al triunfal otras hazañas, según refieren Plinio y Aulo Gelio; mas viendo yo tantas diferencias de coronas, dudaba de cuál especie sería la de Cristo, y me parece que fue obsidional, que (como sabéis, Señora) era la más honrosa y se

mined that it was the siege crown, for (as well you know, lady) that was the most honored crown and was called obsidional after *obsidio*, which means siege; which crown was made not from gold, or silver, but from the leaves and grasses flourishing on the field where the feat was achieved. And as the heroic feat of Christ was to break the siege of the Prince of Darkness, who had laid siege to all the earth, as is told in the Book of Job, quoting Satan: *I have gone round about the earth, and walked through it,*[22] and as St. Peter says: *As a roaring lion, goeth about seeking whom he may devour.*[23] And our Master came and caused him to lift the siege: *Now shall the prince of this world be cast out.*[24]

So the soldiers crowned Him not with gold or silver but with the natural fruit of the world, which was the field of battle — and which, after the curse *Thorns also and thistles shall it bring forth to thee,*[25] produced only thorns — and thus it was a most fitting crown for the courageous and wise Conqueror, with which His mother Synagogue crowned Him. And the daughters of Zion, weeping, came out to witness the sorrowful triumph, as they had come rejoicing for the triumph of Solomon, because the triumph of the wise is earned with sorrow and celebrated with weeping, which is the manner of the triumph of wisdom; and as Christ is the King of wisdom, He was the first to wear that crown; and as it was sanctified on His brow, it removed all fear and dread from those who are wise, for they know they need aspire to no other honor.

The Living Word, Life, wished to restore life to Lazarus, who was dead. His disciples did not know His purpose and they said to Him: *Rabbi, the Jews but now sought to stone thee; and goest thou thither again?*[26] And the Redeemer calmed their fear: *Are there not twelve hours of the day?*[27]

It seems they feared because there had been those who wished to stone Him when He rebuked them, calling them thieves and not shepherds of sheep. And thus the disciples feared that if He returned to the same place — for even

llamaba obsidional de *obsidio,* que quiere decir cerco; la cual no se hacía de oro ni de plata, sino de la misma grana o yerba que cría el campo en que se hacía la empresa. Y como la hazaña de Cristo fue hacer levantar el cerco al Príncipe de las Tinieblas, el cual tenía sitiada toda la tierra, como lo dice en el libro de Job: *Circuivi terram et ambulavi per eam* y de él dice San Pedro: *Circuit, quaerens quem devoret;* y vino nuestro caudillo y le hizo levantar el cerco: *nunc princeps huius mundi eiicietur foras* , así los soldados le coronaron no con oro ni plata, sino con el fruto natural que producía el mundo que fue el campo de la lid, el cual, después de la maldición, *spinas et tribulos germinabit tibi* , no producía otra cosa que espinas; y así fue propísima corona de ellas en el valeroso y sabio vencedor con que le coronó su madre la Sinagoga; saliendo a ver el doloroso triunfo, como la del otro Salomón festivas, a éste llorosas las hijas de Sión, porque es el triunfo de sabio obtenido con dolor y celebrado con llanto, que es el modo de triunfar la sabiduría; siendo Cristo, como rey de ella, quien estrenó la corona, porque santificada en sus sienes, se quite el horror a los otros sabios y entiendan que no han de aspirar a otro honor.

Quiso la misma Vida ir a dar la vida a Lázaro difunto; ignoraban los discípulos el intento y le replicaron: *Rabbi, nunc quaerebant te Iudaei lapidare, et iterum vadis illuc?* Satisfizo el Redentor el temor: *Nonne duodecim sunt horae diei?* . Hasta aquí parece que temían porque tenían el antecedente de quererle apedrear porque les había reprendido llamándoles ladrones y no pastores de las ovejas. Y así, temían que si iba a lo mismo (como las represiones, aunque sean tan justas, suelen ser mal reconocidas), corriese peligro su vida; pero ya desengañados y enterados de que va a dar vida a Lázaro, ¿cuál es la razón que pudo mover a To-

though rebukes be just, they are often badly received — He would be risking his life. But once having been disabused and having realized that He was setting forth to raise up Lazarus from the dead, what was it that caused Thomas, like Peter in the Garden, to say *Let us also go, that we may die with him?*[28] What say you, Sainted Apostle? The Lord does not go out to die; whence your misgiving? For Christ goes not to rebuke, but to work an act of mercy, and therefore they will do Him no harm. These same Jews could have assured you, for when He reproved those who wished to stone Him, *Many good works I have shewed you from my Father; for which of those works do you stone me?*[29] they replied: *For a good work we stone thee not; but for blasphemy.*[30] And as they say they will not stone Him for doing good works, and now He goes to do a work so great as to raise up Lazarus from the dead, whence your misgiving? Why do you fear? Were it not better to say: let us go to gather the fruits of appreciation for the good work our Master is about to do; to see him lauded and applauded for His benefice; to see men marvel at His miracle. Why speak words seemingly so alien to the circumstance as *Let us also go?* Ah, woe, the Saint feared as a prudent man and spoke as an Apostle. Does Christ not go to work a miracle? Why, what *greater* peril? It is less to be suffered that pride endure rebukes than envy witness miracles. In all the above, most honored lady, I do not wish to say (nor is such folly to be found in me) that I have been persecuted for my wisdom, but merely for my love of wisdom and letters, having achieved neither one nor the other.

At one time even the Prince of the Apostles was very far from wisdom, as is emphasized in that *But Peter followed afar off.*[31] Very distant from the laurels of a learned man is one so little in his judgment that he was *Not knowing what he said.*[32] And being questioned on his mastery of wisdom, he himself was witness that he had not achieved the first measure: *But he denied him, saying: Woman, I know him not.*[33]

más para que tomando aquí los alientos que en el huerto Pedro: *Eamus et nos, ut moriamur cum eo?* . ¿Qué dices, apóstol santo? A morir no va el Señor; ¿de qué es el recelo? Porque a lo que Cristo va no es a reprender, sino a hacer una obra de piedad, y por esto no le pueden hacer mal. Los mismos judíos os podían haber asegurado, pues cuando los reconvino, queriéndole apedrear: *Multa bona opera ostendi vobis ex Patre meo, propter quod eorum opus me lapidatis?*, le respondieron: *De bono opere non lapidamus te, sed de blasphemia* . Pues si ellos dicen que no le quieren apedrear por las buenas obras y ahora va a hacer una tan buena como dar la vida a Lázaro, ¿de qué es el recelo o por qué? ¿No fuera mejor decir: Vamos a gozar el fruto del agradecimiento de la buena obra que va a hacer nuestro Maestro; a verle aplaudir y rendir gracias al beneficio; a ver las admiraciones que hacen del milagro? Y no decir, al parecer una cosa tan fuera del caso como es: *Eamus et nos, ut moriamur cum eo.* Mas ¡ay! que el Santo temió como discreto y habló como apóstol. ¿No va Cristo a hacer un milagro? Pues ¿qué mayor peligro? Menos intolerable es para la soberbia oír las reprensiones, que para la envidia ver los milagros. En todo lo dicho, venerable Señora, no quiero (ni tal desatino cupiera en mí) decir que me han perseguido por saber, sino sólo porque he tenido amor a la sabiduría y a las letras, no porque haya conseguido ni uno ni otro.

Hallábase el Príncipe de los Apóstoles, en un tiempo, tan distante de la sabiduría como pondera aquel enfático: *Petrus vero sequebatur eum a longe* ; tan lejos de los aplausos de docto quien tenía el título de indiscreto: *Nesciens quid diceret* ; y aun examinado del conocimiento de la sabiduría dijo él mismo que no había alcanzado la menor noticia: *Mulier, nescio quid dicis.*

And what becomes of him? We find that having this reputation of ignorance, he did not enjoy its good fortune, but,
rather, the affliction of being taken for wise. And why?
There was no other motive but: *This man also was with him.*[34]
He was found of wisdom, it filled his heart, he followed after
it, he prided himself as a pursuer and lover of wisdom; and
although he followed from so *afar off* that he neither understood nor achieved it, his love for it was sufficient that he
incur its torments. And there was present that soldier
to cause him distress, and a certain maid-servant to cause
him grief. I confess that I find myself very distant
from the goals of wisdom, for all that I have desired to follow it, even from *afar off*. But in this I have been brought
closer to the fire of persecution, to the crucible of torment,
and to such lengths that they have asked that study be forbidden to me.

At one time this was achieved through the offices of a
very saintly and ingenuous Abbess who believed that
study was a thing of the Inquisition, who commanded me
not to study. I obeyed her (the three some months her
power to command endured) in that I did not take up a
book; but that I study not at all is not within my power to
achieve, and this I could not obey, for though I did not
study in books, I studied all the things that God had
wrought, reading in them, as in writing and in books, all
the workings of the universe. I looked on nothing without
reflexion; I heard nothing without meditation, even in the
most minute and imperfect things; because as there is no
creature, however lowly, in which one cannot recognize
that *God made me*, there is none that does not astound reason, if properly meditated on. Thus, I reiterate, I saw and
admired all things; so that even the very persons with
whom I spoke, and the things they said, were cause for a
thousand meditations. Whence the variety of genius and
wit, being all of a single species? Which the temperaments
and hidden qualities that occasioned such variety? If I saw a

Mulier, non novi illum . Y ¿qué le sucede? Que teniendo estos créditos de ignorante, no tuvo la fortuna, sí
las aflicciones, de sabio. ¿Por qué? No se dio otra causal sino: *Et hic cum illo erat* . Era afecto a la sabiduría,
llevábale el corazón, andábase tras ella, preciábase de
seguidor y amoroso de la sabiduría; y aunque era tan *a
longe* que no le comprendía ni alcanzaba, bastó para
incurrir sus tormentos. Ni faltó soldado de fuera que
no le afligiese, ni mujer doméstica que no le quejase.
Yo confieso que me hallo muy distante de los términos
de la sabiduría y que le he deseado seguir, aunque *a
longe*. Pero todo ha sido acercarme más al fuego de la
persecución, al crisol del tormento, y ha sido con tal
extremo que han llegado a solicitar que se me prohíba
el estudio.

Una vez lo consiguieron con una prelada muy santa
y muy cándida que creyó que el estudio era cosa de
Inquisición y me mandó que no estudiase. Yo la obede-
cí (unos tres meses que duró el poder ella mandar) en
cuanto a no tomar libro, que en cuanto a no estudiar
absolutamente, como no cae debajo de mi potestad, no
lo pude hacer, porque aunque no estudiaba en los libros, estudiaba en todas las cosas que Dios crió, sirvién-
dome ellas de letras, y de libro toda esta máquina universal. Nada veía sin refleja ; nada oía sin consideración, aun en las cosas más menudas y materiales; porque como no hay criatura, por baja que sea, en que no
se conozca el *me fecit Deus* , no hay alguna que no
pasme el entendimiento, si se considera como se debe.
Así yo, vuelvo a decir, las miraba y admiraba todas; de
tal manera que de las mismas personas con quienes
hablaba, y de lo que me decían, me estaban resaltando
mil consideraciones: ¿De dónde emanaría aquella variedad de genios e ingenios siendo todos de una especie?
¿Cuáles serían los temperamentos y ocultas cualidades

figure, I was forever combining the proportion of its lines and measuring it with my reason and reducing it to new proportions. Occasionally as I walked along the far wall of one of our dormitories (which is a most capacious room) I observed that though the lines of the two sides were parallel and the ceiling perfectly level, in my sight they were distorted, the lines seeming to incline toward one another, the ceiling seeming lower in the distance than in proximity: from which I inferred that *visual* lines run straight but not parallel, forming a pyramidal figure. I pondered whether this might not be the reason that caused the ancients to question whether the world were spherical. Because, although it so seems, this could be a deception of vision, suggesting concavities where possibly none existed.

This manner of reflection has always been my habit, and is quite beyond my will to control; on the contrary, I am wont to become vexed that my intellect makes me weary; and I believed that it was so with everyone, as well as making verses, until experience taught me otherwise; and it is so strong in me this nature, or custom, that I look at nothing without giving it further examination. Once in my presence two young girls were spinning a top and scarcely had I seen the motion and the figure described, when I began, out of this madness of mine, to meditate on the effortless *motus* of the spherical form, and how the impulse persisted even when free and independent of its cause — for the top continued to dance even at some distance from the child's hand, which was the causal force. And not content with this, I had flour brought and sprinkled about, so that as the top danced one might learn whether these were perfect circles it described with its movement; and I found that they were not, but, rather, spiral lines that lost their circularity as the impetus declined. Other girls sat playing at spillikins (surely the most frivolous game that children play); I wa ed closer to observe the figures they formed, and seeing that by chance

que lo ocasionaban? Si veía una figura, estaba combinando la proporción de sus líneas y mediándola con el entendimiento y reduciéndola a otras diferentes. Paseábame algunas veces en el testero de un dormitorio nuestro (que es una pieza muy capaz) y estaba observando que siendo las líneas de sus dos lados paralelas y su techo a nivel, la vista fingía que sus líneas se inclinaban una a otra y que su techo estaba más bajo en lo distante que en lo próximo, de donde infería que las líneas visuales corren rectas, pero no paralelas, sino que van a formar una figura piramidal. Y discurría si sería ésta la razón que obligó a los antiguos a dudar si el mundo era esférico o no. Porque, aunque lo parece, podía ser engaño de la vista, demostrando concavidades donde pudiera no haberlas.

Este modo de reparos en todo me sucedía y sucede siempre, sin tener yo arbitrio en ello, que antes me suelo enfadar porque me cansa la cabeza; y yo creía que a todos sucedía esto mismo y el hacer versos, hasta que la experiencia me ha demostrado lo contrario; y es de tal manera esta naturaleza o costumbre, que nada veo sin segunda consideración. Estaban en mi presencia dos niñas jugando con un trompo, y apenas yo vi el movimiento y la figura cuando empecé, con esta mi locura, a considerar el fácil moto de la forma esférica y cómo duraba el impulso ya impreso e independiente de su causa, pues distante la mano de la niña, que era la causa motiva, bailaba el trompillo; y no contenta con esto, hice traer harina y cernerla para que, en bailando el trompo encima, se conociese si eran círculos perfectos o no los que describía con su movimiento; y hallé que no eran sino unas líneas espirales que iban perdiendo lo circular cuanto se iba remitiendo el impulso. Jugaban otras a los alfileres (que es el más frívolo juego que usa la puerilidad); yo me llegaba a contemplar las figuras que formaban; y viendo que acaso

three lay in a triangle, I set to joining one with another, recalling that this was said to be the form of the mysterious ring of Solomon,[35] in which he was able to see the distant splendor and images of the Holy Trinity, by virtue of which the ring worked such prodigies and marvels. And the same shape was said to form David's harp, and that is why Saul was refreshed at its sound; and harps today largely conserve that shape.

And what shall I tell you, lady, of the natural secrets I have discovered while cooking? I see that an egg holds together and fries in butter or in oil, but, on the contrary, in syrup shrivels into shreds; observe that to keep sugar in a liquid state one need only add a drop or two of water in which a quince or other bitter fruit has been soaked; observe that the yolk and the white of one egg are so dissimilar that each with sugar produces a result not obtainable with both together. I do not wish to weary you with such inconsequential matters, and make mention of them only to give you full notice of my nature, for I believe they will be occasion for laughter. But, lady, as women, what wisdom may be ours if not the philosophies of the kitchen? Lupercio Leonardo spoke well when he said: how well one may philosophize when preparing dinner.[36] And I often say, when observing these trivial details: had Aristotle prepared victuals, he would have written more. And pursuing the manner of my cogitations, I tell you that this process is so continuous in me that I have no need for books. And on one occasion, when because of a grave upset of the stomach the physicians forbade me to study, I passed thus some days, but then I proposed that it would be less harmful if they allowed me books, because so vigorous and vehement were my cogitations that my spirit was consumed more greatly in a quarter of an hour than in four days' studying books. And thus they were persuaded to allow me to read. And moreover, lady, not even have my dreams been excluded from this ceaseless agitation of my imagination; in-

se pusieron tres en triángulo, me ponía a enlazar uno en otro, acordándome de que aquélla era la figura que dicen tenía el misterioso anillo de Salomón, en que había unas lejanas luces y representaciones de la Santísima Trinidad, en virtud de lo cual obraba tantos prodigios y maravillas; y la misma que dicen tuvo el arpa de David, y que por eso sanaba Saúl a su sonido; y casi la misma conservan las arpas en nuestros tiempos.

Pues ¿qué os pudiera contar, Señora, de los secretos naturales que he descubierto estando guisando? Ver que un huevo se une y fríe en la manteca o aceite y, por contrario, se despedaza en el almíbar; ver que para que el azúcar se conserve fluida basta echarle una muy mínima parte de agua en que haya estado membrillo u otra fruta agria; ver que la yema y clara de un mismo huevo son tan contrarias, que en los unos, que sirven para el azúcar, sirve cada una de por sí y juntos no. Por no cansaros con tales frialdades, que sólo refiero por daros entera noticia de mi natural y creo que os causará risa; pero, señora, ¿qué podemos saber las mujeres sino filosofías de cocina? Bien dijo Lupercio Leonardo, que bien se puede filosofar y aderezar la cena . Y yo suelo decir viendo estas cosillas: Si Aristóteles hubiera guisado, mucho más hubiera escrito. Y prosiguiendo en mi modo de cogitaciones , digo que esto es tan continuo en mí que no necesito de libros; y en una ocasión que, por un grave accidente de estómago, me prohibieron los médicos el estudio, pasé así algunos días, y luego les propuse que era menos dañoso el concedérmelos, porque eran tan fuertes y vehementes mis cogitaciones que consumían más espíritus en un cuarto de hora que el estudio de los libros en cuatro días; y así se redujeron a concederme que leyese. Y más, Señora mía: que ni aun el sueño se libró de este continuo movimiento de mi imaginativa;

deed, in dreams it is wont to work more freely and less encumbered, collating with greater clarity and calm the gleanings of the day, arguing and making verses, of which I could offer you an extended catalogue, as well as of some arguments and inventions that I have better achieved sleeping than awake. I relinquish this subject in order not to tire you, for the above is sufficient to allow your discretion and acuity to penetrate perfectly and perceive my nature, as well as the beginnings, the methods, and the present state of my studies.

Even, lady, were these merits (and I see them celebrated as such in men), they would not have been so in me, for I cannot but study. If they are fault, then, for the same reasons, I believe I have none. Nevertheless, I live always with so little confidence in myself that neither in my study, nor in any other thing, do I trust my judgment; and thus I remit the decision to your sovereign genius, submitting myself to whatever sentence you may bestow, without controversy, without reluctance, for I have wished here only to present you with a simple narration of my inclination toward letters.

I confess, too, that though it is true, as I have stated, that I had no need of books, it is nonetheless also true that they have been no little inspiration, in divine as in human letters. Because I find a Debbora administering the law, both military and political, and governing a people among whom there were many learned men. I find a most wise Queen of Saba, so learned that she dares to challenge with hard questions the wisdom of the greatest of all wise men, without being reprimanded for doing so, but, rather, as a consequence, to judge unbelievers. I see many and illustrious women; some blessed with the gift of prophecy, like Abigail, others of persuasion, like Esther; others with pity, like Rehab; others with perserverance, like Anna, the mother of Samuel; and an infinite number of others, with divers gifts and virtues.

antes suele obrar en él más libre y desembarazada, confiriendo   con mayor claridad y sosiego las especies que ha conservado del día, arguyendo, haciendo versos, de que os pudiera hacer un catálogo muy grande, y de algunas razones y delgadezas que he alcanzado dormida mejor que despierta, y las dejo por no cansaros, pues basta lo dicho para que vuestra discreción y trascendencia penetre y se entere perfectamente en todo mi natural y del principio, medios y estado de mis estudios.

Si éstos, Señora, fueran méritos (como los veo por tales celebrar en los hombres), no lo hubieran sido en mí, porque obro necesariamente. Si son culpa, por la misma razón creo que no la he tenido; mas, con todo, vivo siempre tan desconfiada de mí que ni en esto ni en otra cosa me fío de mi juicio; y así remito la decisión a ese soberano talento, sometiéndome luego a lo que sentenciare, sin contradicción ni repugnancia, pues esto no ha sido más de una simple narración de mi inclinación a las letras.

Confieso también que con ser esto verdad tal que, como he dicho, no necesitaba de ejemplares, con todo no me han dejado de ayudar los muchos que he leído, así en divinas como en humanas letras. Porque veo a una Débora dando leyes, así en lo militar como en lo político, y gobernando el pueblo donde había tantos varones doctos. Veo una sapientísima reina de Sabá, tan docta que se atreve a tentar con enigmas la sabiduría del mayor de los sabios, sin ser por ello reprendida, antes por ello será juez de los incrédulos. Veo tantas y tan insignes mujeres: unas adornadas del don de profecía, como una Abigaíl; otras de persuasión, como Ester; otras de piedad, como Rahab; otras de perseverancia, como Ana, madre de Samuel   , y otras infinitas en otras especies de prendas y virtudes.

If I again turn to the Gentiles, the first I encounter are the Sibyls, those women chosen by God to prophesy the principal mysteries of our Faith, and with learned and elegant verses that surpass admiration. I see adored as a goddess of the sciences a woman like Minerva, the daughter of the first Jupiter and mistress over all the wisdom of Athens. I see a Polla Argentaria, who helped Lucan, her husband, write his epic *Pharsalia*. I see the daughter of the divine Tiresias, more learned than her father. I see a Zenobia, Queen of the Palmyrans, as wise as she was valiant. An Arete, most learned daughter of Aristippus. A Nicostrate, framer of Latin verses and most erudite in Greek. An Aspasia Milesia, who taught philosophy and rhetoric, and who was a teacher of the philosopher Pericles. An Hypatia, who taught astrology, and studied many years in Alexandria. A Leontium, a Greek woman, who questioned the philosopher Theophrastus, and convinced him. A Jucia, a Corinna, a Cornelia; and, finally, a great throng of women deserving to be named, some as Greeks, some as muses, some as seers; for all were nothing more than learned women, held, and celebrated — and venerated as well — as such by antiquity. Without mentioning an infinity of other women whose names fill books. For example, I find the Egyptian Catherine, studying and influencing the wisdom of all the wise men of Egypt. I see a Gertrudis studying, writing, and teaching. And not to overlook examples close to home, I see my most holy mother Paula, learned in Hebrew, Greek, and Latin, and most able in interpreting the Scriptures. And what greater praise than, having as her chronicler a Jeronimus Maximus, that Saint scarcely found himself competent for his task, and says, with that weighty deliberation and energetic precision with which he so well expressed himself: "If all the members of my body were tongues, they still would not be sufficient to proclaim the wisdom and virtue of Paula." Similarly praiseworthy was the widow Blesilla; also, the illustrious virgin Eustochium,

Si revuelvo a los gentiles, lo primero que encuentro es con las Sibilas, elegidas de Dios para profetizar los principales misterios de nuestra Fe , y en tan doctos y elegantes versos que suspenden la admiración. Veo adorar por diosa de las ciencias a una mujer como Minerva, hija del primer Júpiter y maestra de toda la sabiduría de Atenas. Veo una Pola Argentaria, que ayudó a Lucano, su marido, a escribir la gran Batalla Farsálica. Veo a la hija del divino Tiresias , más docta que su padre. Veo a una Cenobia, reina de los Palmirenos, tan sabia como valerosa. A una Arete, hija de Aristipo , doctísima. A una Nicostrata , inventora de las letras latinas y eruditísima en las griegas. A una Aspasia Milesia que enseñó filosofía y retórica y fue maestra del filósofo Pericles. A una Hipasia, que enseñó astrología y leyó mucho tiempo en Alejandría. A una Leoncia, griega, que escribió contra el filósofo Teofrasto y le convenció. A una Jucia, a una Corina, a una Cornelia; y, en fin, a toda la gran turba de las que merecieron nombres, ya de griegas, ya de musas, ya de pitonisas; pues todas no fueron más que mujeres doctas, tenidas y celebradas y también veneradas de la antigüedad por tales. Sin otras infinitas, de que están los libros llenos, pues veo aquella egipcíaca Catarina leyendo y convenciendo todas las sabidurías de los sabios de Egipto. Veo una Gertrudis leer, escribir y enseñar. Y para no buscar ejemplos fuera de casa, veo una santísima madre mía, Paula, docta en las lenguas hebrea, griega y latina y aptísima para interpretar las Escrituras. ¿Y qué más que siendo su cronista un máximo Jerónimo, apenas se hallaba el Santo digno de serlo, pues con aquella viva ponderación y enérgica eficacia con que sabe explicarse dice: Si todos los miembros de mi cuerpo fuesen lenguas, no bastarían a publicar la sabiduría y virtud de Paula? . Las mismas alabanzas le mereció Blesila, viuda; y las mismas

both daughters of this same saint; especially the second, who, for her knowledge, was called the Prodigy of the World. The Roman Fabiola was most well-versed in the Holy Scripture. Proba Falconia, a Roman woman, wrote elegant centos, containing verses from Virgil, about the mysteries of Our Holy Faith. It is well-known by all that Queen Isabel, wife of the tenth Alfonso, wrote about astrology. Many others I do not list, out of the desire not merely to transcribe what others have said (a vice I have always abominated); and many are flourishing today, as witness Christina Alexandra, Queen of Sweden, as learned as she is valiant and magnanimous, and the Most Honorable Ladies, the Duquesa of Abeyro and the Condesa of Villaumbrosa.

The venerable Doctor Arce (by his virtue and learning a worthy teacher of the Scriptures) in his scholarly *Bibliorum* raises this question: *Is it permissible for women to dedicate themselves to the study of the Holy Scriptures, and to their interpretation?*[37] and he offers as negative arguments the opinions of many saints, especially that of the Apostle: *Let women keep silence in the churches; for it is not permitted them to speak*, etc.[38] He later cites other opinions and, from the same Apostle, verses from his letter to Titus: *The aged women in like manner, in holy attire . . . teaching well,*[39] with interpretations by the Holy Fathers. Finally he resolves, with all prudence, that teaching publicly from a University chair, or preaching from the pulpit, is not permissible for women; but that to study, write, and teach privately not only is permissible, but most advantageous and useful. It is evident that this is not to be the case with all women, but with those to whom God may have granted special virtue and prudence, and who may be well advanced in learning, and having the essential talent and requisites for such a sacred calling. This view is indeed just, so much so that not only women, who are held to be so inept, but also men, who merely for being men believe they are wise, should be pro-

la esclarecida virgen Eustoquio, hijas ambas de la misma Santa; y la segunda tal que por su ciencia era llamada Prodigio del Mundo. Fabiola , romana, fue también doctísima en la Sagrada Escritura. Proba Falconia, mujer romana, escribió un elegante libro con centones de Virgilio, de los misterios de Nuestra Santa Fe. Nuestra reina Doña Isabel, mujer del décimo Alfonso, es corriente que escribió de astrología. Sin otras que omito por no trasladar lo que otros han dicho (que es vicio que siempre he abominado), pues en nuestros tiempos está floreciendo la gran Cristina Alejandra, Reina de Suecia, tan docta como valerosa y magnánima, y las Excelentísimas señoras Duquesa de Aveyro y Condesa de Villaumbrosa.

El venerable Doctor Arce (digno profesor de Escritura por su virtud y letras), en su *Studioso Bibliorum* excita esta cuestión: *An liceat foeminis sacrorum Bibliorum studio incumbere? eaque interpretari?* Y trae por la parte contraria muchas sentencias de santos, en especial aquello del Apóstol: *Mulieres in Ecclesiis taceant, non enim permittitur eis loqui* , etc. Trae después otras sentencias, y del mismo Apóstol aquel lugar *ad Titum: Anus similiter in habitu sancto, bene docentes* , con interpretaciones de los Santos Padres; y al fin resuelve, con su prudencia, que el leer públicamente en las cátedras y predicar en los púlpitos no es lícito a las mujeres; pero que el estudiar, escribir y enseñar privadamente no sólo les es lícito, pero muy provechoso y útil; claro está que esto no se debe entender con todas, sino con aquellas a quienes hubiere Dios dotado de especial virtud y prudencia y que fueren muy provectas y eruditas y tuvieren el talento y requisitos necesarios para tan sagrado empleo. Y esto es tan justo que no sólo a las mujeres, que por tan ineptas están tenidas, sino a los hombres, que con sólo serlo piensan que son sabios, se había de prohibir la interpretación de las

hibited from interpreting the Sacred Word if they are not learned and virtuous and of gentle and well-inclined natures; that this is not so has been, I believe, at the root of so much sectarianism and so many heresies. For there are many who study but are ignorant, especially those who are in spirit arrogant, troubled, and proud, so eager for new interpretations of the Word (which itself rejects new interpretations) that merely for the sake of saying what no one else has said they speak a heresy, and even then are not content. Of these the Holy Spirit says: *For wisdom will not enter into a malicious soul.*[40] To such as these more harm results from knowing than from ignorance. A wise man has said: he who does not know Latin is not a complete fool; but he who knows it is well qualified to be. And I would add that a fool may reach perfection (if ignorance may tolerate perfection) by having studied his tittle of philosophy and theology and by having some learning of tongues, by which he may be a fool in many sciences and languages: a great fool cannot be contained solely in his mother tongue.

For such as these, I reiterate, study is harmful, because it is as if to place a sword in the hands of a madman; which, though a most noble instrument for defense, is in his hands his own death and that of many others. So were the Divine Scriptures in the possession of the evil Pelagius and the intractable Arius, of the evil Luther, and the other heresiarchs like our own Doctor (who was neither ours nor a doctor) Cazalla. To these men, wisdom was harmful, although it is the greatest nourishment and the life of the soul; in the same way that in a stomach of sickly constitution and adulterated complexion, the finer the nourishment it receives, the more arid, fermented, and perverse are the humors it produces; thus these evil men: the more they study, the worse opinions they engender, their reason being obstructed with the very substance meant to nourish it, and they study much and digest little, exceeding the limits of the vessel of their reason. Of which the Apostle says: *For*

Sagradas Letras, en no siendo muy doctos y virtuosos y de ingenios dóciles y bien inclinados; porque de lo contrario creo yo que han salido tantos sectarios y que ha sido la raíz de tantas herejías; porque hay muchos que estudian para ignorar, especialmente los que son de ánimos arrogantes, inquietos y soberbios, amigos de novedades en la Ley (que es quien las rehúsa); y así hasta que por decir lo que nadie ha dicho dicen una herejía, no están contentos. De éstos dice el Espíritu Santo: *In malevolam animan non introibit sapientia* . A éstos más daño les hace saber que les hiciera el ignorar. Dijo un discreto que no es necio entero el que no sabe latín, pero el que lo sabe está calificado. Y añado yo que le perfecciona (si es perfección la necedad) el haber estudiado su poco de filosofía y teología y el tener alguna noticia de lenguas, que con eso es necio en muchas ciencias y lenguas, porque un necio grande no cabe en sólo la lengua materna.

A éstos, vuelvo a decir, hace daño el estudiar, porque es poner espada en manos del furioso; que siendo instrumento nobilísimo para la defensa, en sus manos es muerte suya y de muchos. Tales fueron las Divinas Letras en poder del malvado Pelagio y del protervo Arrio, del malvado Lutero y de los demás heresiarcas, como lo fue nuestro Doctor (nunca fue nuestro ni doctor) Cazalla , a los cuales hizo daño la sabiduría porque, aunque es el mejor alimento y vida del alma, a la manera que en el estómago mal acomplexionado y de viciado calor, mientras mejores los alimentos que recibe, más áridos, fermentados y perversos son los humores que cría, así estos malévolos, mientras más estudian, peores opiniones engendran; obstrúyeseles el entendimiento con lo mismo que había de alimentarse, y es que estudian mucho y digieren poco, sin proporcionarse al vaso limitado de sus entendimientos. A esto dice

I say, by the grace that is given me, to all that are among you, not to be more wise than it behoveth to be wise, but to be wise unto sobriety, and according as God hath divided to every one the measure of faith.[41] And in truth, the Apostle did not direct these words to women, but to men; and that *keep silence* is intended not only for women, but for *all* incompetents. If I desire to know as much, or more, than Aristotle or Saint Agustine, and if I have not the aptitude of Saint Agustine or Aristotle, though I study more than either, not only will I not achieve learning, but I will weaken and dull the workings of my feeble reason with the disproportionateness of the goal.

Oh, that each of us — I, being ignorant, the first — should take the measure of our talents before we study, or, more importantly, write, with the covetous ambition to equal and even surpass others, how little spirit we should have for it, and how many errors we should avoid, and how many tortured intellects of which we have experience, we should have had no experience! And I place my own ignorance in the forefront of all these, for if I knew all I should, I would not write. And I protest that I do so only to obey you; and with such apprehension that you owe me more that I have taken up my pen in fear than you would have owed had I presented you more perfect works. But it is well that they go to your correction. Cross them out, tear them up, reprove me, and I shall appreciate that more than all the vain applause others may offer. *That just men shall correct me in mercy, and shall reprove me; but let not the oil of the sinner fatten my head.*[42] And returning again to our Arce, I say that in affirmation of his opinion he cites the words of my father, Saint Jerome: *To Leta, Upon the Education of Her Daughter.* Where he says: *Accustom her tongue, still young, to the sweetness of the Psalms. Even the names through which little by little she will become accustomed to form her phrases should not be chosen by chance, but selected and repeated with care; the prophets must be included, of course, and the apostles, as well,*

el Apóstol: *Dico enim per gratiam quae data est mihi, omnibus qui sunt inter vos: Non plus sapere quam oportet sapere, sed sapere ad sobrietatem: et unicuique sicut Deus divisit mensuram fidei* . Y en verdad no lo dijo el Apóstol a las mujeres, sino a los hombres; y que no es sólo para ellas el *taceant,* sino para todos los que no fueren muy aptos. Querer yo saber tanto o más que Aristóteles o que San Agustín, si no tengo la aptitud de San Agustín o de Aristóteles, aunque estudie más que los dos, no sólo no lo conseguiré, sino que debilitaré y entorpeceré la operación de mi flaco entendimiento con la desproporción del objeto.

¡Oh, si todos—y yo la primera, que soy una ignorante—nos tomásemos la medida al talento antes de estudiar y, lo peor es, de escribir con ambiciosa codicia de igualar y aun de exceder a otros, qué poco ánimo nos quedara y de cuántos errores nos excusáramos y cuántas torcidas inteligencias que andan por ahí no anduvieran! Y pongo las mías en primer lugar, pues si conociera, como debo, esto mismo no escribiera. Y protesto que sólo lo hago por obedeceros; con tanto recelo, que me debéis más en tomar la pluma con este temor, que me debiérades si os remitiera más perfectas obras. Pero bien que va a vuestra corrección; borradlo, rompedlo y reprendedme, que eso apreciaré yo más que todo cuanto vano aplauso me pueden otros dar: *Corripiet me iustus in misericordia, et increpabit: oleum autem peccatoris non impinguet caput meum* .

Y volviendo a nuestro Arce, digo que trae en confirmación de su sentir aquellas palabras de mi Padre San Jerónimo *(ad Laetam, de institutione filiae),* donde dice: *Adhuc tenera lingua psalmis dulcibus imbuatur. Ipsa nomina per quae consuescit paulatim verba contexere, non sint fortuita, sed certa,˙ et coacervata de industria. Prophetarum videlicet, atque Apostolorum, et*

*and all the Patriarchs beginning with Adam and down to Mat-
thew and Luke, so that as she practices other things she will be
readying her memory for the future. Let your daily task be taken
from the flower of the Scriptures.*[43] And if this Saint desired
that a young girl scarcely beginning to talk be educated in
this fashion, what would he desire for his nuns and his
spiritual daughters? These beliefs are illustrated in the examples of the previously mentioned Esutochium and Fabiola, and Marcella, her sister, and Pacatula, and others
whom the Saint honors in his epistles, exhorting them to
this sacred exercise, as they are recognized in the epistle I
cited, *Let your daily task . . .*, which is affirmation of and
agreement with the *aged women . . . teaching well* of Saint
Paul. My illustrious Father's *Let your daily task . . .* makes
clear that the teacher of the child is to be Leta herself, the
child's mother.

Oh, how much injury might have been avoided in our
land if our aged women had been learned, as was Leta, and
had they known how to instruct as directed by Saint Paul
and by my Father, Saint Jerome. And failing this, and because of the considerable idleness to which our poor
women have been relegated, if a father desires to provide
his daughters with more than ordinary learning, he is
forced by necessity, and by the absence of wise elder
women, to bring men to teach the skills of reading, writing,
counting, the playing of musical instruments, and other ac-
complishments, from which no little harm results, as is experienced every day in doleful examples of perilous association, because through the immediacy of contact and the
intimacy born from the passage of time, what one may
never have thought possible is easily accomplished. For
which reason many prefer to leave their daughters unpol-
ished and uncultured rather than to expose them to such
notorious peril as that of familiarity with men, which quandary could be prevented if there were learned elder
women, as Saint Paul wished to see, and if the teaching

omnis ab Adam Patriarcharum series, de Matthaeo, Lu- caque descendat, ut dum aliud agit, futurae memoriae praeparetur. Reddat tibi pensum quotidie, de Scriptu- rarum floribus carptum . Pues si así quería el Santo que se educase una niña que apenas empezaba a ha- blar, ¿qué querrá en sus monjas y en sus hijas espiri- tuales? Bien se conoce en las referidas Eustoquio y Fabiola y en Marcela, su hermana, Pacátula y otras a quienes el Santo honra en sus epístolas , exhortán- dolas a este sagrado ejercicio, como se conoce en la citada epístola donde noté yo aquel *reddat tibi pensum*, que es reclamo y concordante del *bene docentes* de San Pablo; pues el *reddat tibi* de mi gran Padre da a enten- der que la maestra de la niña ha de ser la misma Leta su madre.

¡Oh, cuántos daños se excusaran en nuestra repú- blica si las ancianas fueran doctas como Leta, y que supieran enseñar como manda San Pablo y mi Padre San Jerónimo! Y no que por defecto de esto y la suma flojedad en que han dado en dejar a las pobres muje- res, si algunos padres desean doctrinar más de lo or- dinario a sus hijas, les fuerza la necesidad y falta de ancianas sabias a llevar maestros hombres a enseñar a leer, escribir y contar, a tocar y otras habilidades, de que no pocos daños resultan, como se experimentan cada día en lastimosos ejemplos de desiguales consor- cios, porque con la inmediación del trato y la comuni- cación del tiempo, suele hacerse fácil lo que no se pensó ser posible. Por lo cual muchos quieren más dejar bárbaras e incultas a sus hijas que no exponerlas a tan notorio peligro como la familiaridad con los hom- bres, lo cual se excusara si hubiera ancianas doctas, como quiere San Pablo, y de unas en otras fuese suce-

were handed down from one to another, as is the custom with domestic crafts and all other traditional skills.

For what objection can there be that an older woman, learned in letters and in sacred conversation and customs, have in her charge the education of young girls? This would prevent these girls being lost either for lack of instruction or for hesitating to offer instruction through such dangerous means as male teachers, for even when there is no greater risk of indecency than to seat beside a modest woman (who still may blush when her own father looks directly at her) a strange man who treats her as if he were a member of the household and with the authority of an intimate, the modesty demanded in interchange with men, and in conversation with them, is sufficient reason that such an arrangement not be permitted. For I do not find that the custom of men teaching women is without its peril, lest it be in the severe tribunal of the confessional, or from the remote decency of the pulpit, or in the distant learning of books — never in the personal contact of immediacy. And the world knows this is true; and, notwithstanding, it is permitted solely from the want of learned elder women. Then is it not detrimental, the lack of such women? This question should be addressed by those who, bound to that *Let women keep silence in the church,* say that it is blasphemy for women to learn and teach, as if it were not the Apostle himself who said: *The aged women . . . teaching well.* As well as the fact that this prohibition touches upon historical fact as reported by Eusebium: which is that in the early Church, women were charged with teaching the doctrine to one another in the temples and the sound of this teaching caused confusion as the Apostles were preaching and this is the reason they were ordered to be silent; and even today, while the homilist is preaching, one does not pray aloud.

Who will argue that for the comprehension of many Scriptures one must be familiar with the history, customs, ceremonies, proverbs, and even the manners of speaking

diendo el magisterio como sucede en el de hacer labores y lo demás que es costumbre.

Porque ¿qué inconveniente tiene que una mujer anciana, docta en letras y de santa conversación y costumbres, tuviese a su cargo la educación de las doncellas? Y no que éstas o se pierden por falta de doctrina o por querérsela aplicar por tan peligrosos medios cuales son los maestros hombres, que cuando no hubiera más riesgo que la indecencia de sentarse al lado de una mujer verecunda (que aun se sonrosea de que la mire a la cara su propio padre) un hombre tan extraño, a tratarla con casera familiaridad y a tratarla con magistral llaneza, el pudor del trato con los hombres y de su conversación basta para que no se permitiese. Y no hallo yo que este modo de enseñar de hombres a mujeres pueda ser sin peligro, si no es en el severo tribunal de un confesonario o en la distante docencia de los púlpitos o en el remoto conocimiento de los libros; pero no en el manoseo de la inmediación. Y todos conocen que esto es verdad; y con todo, se permite sólo por el defecto de no haber ancianas sabias; luego es grande daño el no haberlas. Esto debían considerar los que atados al *Mulieres in Ecclesia taceant,* blasfeman de que las mujeres sepan y enseñen; como que no fuera el mismo Apóstol el que dijo: *bene docentes.* Demás de que aquella prohibición cayó sobre lo historial que refiere Eusebio, y es que en la Iglesia primitiva se ponían las mujeres a enseñar las doctrinas unas a otras en los templos; y este rumor confundía cuando predicaban los apóstoles y por eso se les mandó callar; como ahora sucede, que mientras predica el predicador no se reza en alta voz.

No hay duda de que para inteligencia de muchos lugares es menester mucha historia, costumbres, ceremonias, proverbios y aun maneras de hablar de aquellos tiempos en que se escribieron para saber sobre qué

of those times in which they were written, if one is to apprehend the references and allusions of more than a few passages of the Holy Word. *And rend your heart and not your garments.*[44] Is this not a reference to the ceremony in which Hebrews rent their garments as a sign of grief, as did the evil pontiff when he said that Christ had blasphemed? In many scriptures the Apostle writes of succour for widows; did they not refer to the customs of those times? Does not the example of the valiant woman, *Her husband is honourable in the gates,*[45] allude to the fact that the tribunals of the judges were at the gates of the cities? That *Dare terram Deo,* give of your land to God, did that not mean to make some votive offering? And did they not call the public sinners *hiemantes,* those who endure the winter, because they made their penance in the open air instead of at a town gate as others did? And Christ's plaint to that Pharisee who had neither kissed him nor given him water for his feet, was that not because it was the Jews' usual custom to offer these acts of hospitality? And we find an infinite number of additional instances not only in the Divine Letters, but human, as well, such as *adorate purpuram,* venerate the purple, which meant obey the King; *manumittere eum,* manumit them, alluding to the custom and ceremony of striking the slave with one's hand to signify his freedom. That *intonuit coelum,* heaven thundered, in Virgil, which alludes to the augury of thunder from the west, which was held to be good.[46] Martial's *tu nunquam leporem edisti,* you never ate hare, has not only the wit of ambiguity in its *leporem,* but, as well, the allusion to the reputed propensity of hares [to bless with beauty those who dine on them]. That proverb, *maleam legens, que sunt domi obliviscere,* to sail along the shore of Malia is to forget what one has at home, alludes to the great peril of the promontory of Laconia. That chaste matron's response to the unwanted suit of her pretender: "the hinge-pins shall not be oiled for my sake, nor shall the torches blaze," meaning that she did not want to marry,

caen y a qué aluden algunas locuciones de las divinas letras. *Scindite corda vestra, et non vestimenta vestra* , ¿no es alusión a la ceremonia que tenían los hebreos de rasgar los vestidos, en señal de dolor, como lo hizo el mal pontífice cuando dijo que Cristo había blasfemado? Muchos lugares del Apóstol sobre el socorro de las viudas, ¿no miraban también a las costumbres de aquellos tiempos? Aquel lugar de la mujer fuerte: *Nobilis in portis vir eius* , ¿no alude a la costumbre de estar los tribunales de los jueces en las puertas de las ciudades? El *dare terram Deo* ¿no significaba hacer algún voto? *Hiemantes* ¿no se llamaban los pecadores públicos, porque hacían penitencia a cielo abierto, a diferencia de los otros que la hacían en un portal?

Aquella queja de Cristo al fariseo de la falta del ósculo y lavatorio de pies ¿no se fundó en la costumbre que de hacer estas cosas tenían los judíos? Y otros infinitos lugares no sólo de las letras divinas, sino también de las humanas, que se topan a cada paso, como el *adorate purpuram* , que significaba obedecer al rey; el *manumittere eum*, que significa dar libertad, aludiendo a la costumbre y ceremonia de dar una bofetada al esclavo para darle libertad. Aquel *intonuit coelum* , de Virgilio, que alude al agüero de tronar hacia occidente, que se tenía por bueno. Aquel *tu nunquam leporem edisti* , de Marcial, que no sólo tiene el donaire de equívoco en el *leporem*, sino la alusión a la propiedad que decían tener la liebre. Aquel proverbio: *Maleam legens, quae sunt domi obliviscere* , que alude al gran peligro del promonotorio de Laconia. Aquella respuesta de la casta matrona al pretensor molesto de *por mí no se untarán los quicios, ni arderán las teas,* para decir que no quería casarse, aludiendo a la ceremonia de untar las puertas con manteca y encender las teas nupciales en los matrimonios; como si ahora dijéramos: por mí no se gastarán arras ni echará bendiciones el

alluded to the ceremony of annointing the doorways with oils and lighting the nuptial torches in the wedding ceremony, as if now we would say, they shall not prepare the thirteen coins for my dowry, nor shall the priest invoke the blessing. And thus it is with many comments of Virgil and Homer and all the poets and orators. In addition, how many are the difficulties found even in the grammar of the Holy Scripture, such as writing a plural for a singular, or changing from the second to third persons, as in the Psalms, *Let him kiss me with the kiss of his mouth, for thy breasts are better than wine.*[47] Or placing adjectives in the genitive instead of the accusative, as in *Calicem salutaris accipiam*, I will take the chalice of salvation.[48] Or to replace the feminine with the masculine, and, in contrast, to call any sin adultery.

All this demands more investigation than some believe, who strictly as grammarians, or, at most, employing the four principles of applied logic, attempt to interpret the Scriptures while clinging to that *Let the women keep silence in the church*, not knowing how it is to be interpreted. As well as that other verse, *Let the women learn in silence.*[49] For this latter scripture works more to women's favor than their disfavor, as it commands them to learn; and it is only natural that they must maintain silence while they learn. And it is also written, *Hear, oh Israel, and be silent.*[50] Which addresses the entire congregation of men and women, commanding all to silence, because if one is to hear and learn, it is with good reason that he attend and be silent. And if it is not so, I would want these interpreters and expositors of Saint Paul to explain to me how they interpret that scripture, *Let the women keep silence in the church.* For either they must understand it to refer to the material church, that is the church of pulpits and cathedras, or to the spiritual, the community of the faithful, which is the Church. If they understand to be the former, which, in my opinion, is its true interpretation, then we see that if in fact it is not per-

cura. Y así hay tanto comento de Virgilio y de Homero y de todos los poetas y oradores. Pues fuera de esto, ¿qué dificultades no se hallan en los lugares sagrados, aun en lo gramatical, de ponerse el plural por singular, de pasar de segunda a tercera persona, como aquello de los Cantares: *osculetur me osculo oris sui: quia meliora sunt ubera tua vino?* . Aquel poner los adjetivos en genitivo, en vez de acusativo, como *Calicem salutaris accipiam?* . Aquel poner el femenino por masculino; y, al contrario, llamar adulterio a cualquier pecado?

Todo esto pide más lección de lo que piensan algunos que, de meros gramáticos, o cuando mucho con cuatro términos de Súmulas , quieren interpretar las Escrituras y se aferran del *Mulieres in Eclesiis taceant,* sin saber cómo se ha de entender. Y de otro lugar: *Mulier in silentio discat* ; siendo este lugar más en favor que en contra de las mujeres, pues manda que aprendan, y mientras aprenden, claro está que es necesario que callen. Y también está escrito: *Audi Israel, et tace* ; donde se habla con toda la colección de los hombres y mujeres, y a todos se manda callar, porque quien oye y aprende es mucha razón que atienda y calle. Y si no, yo quisiera que estos intérpretes y expositores de San Pablo me explicaran cómo entienden aquel lugar: *Mulieres in Ecclesia taceant.* Porque o lo han de entender de lo material de los púlpitos y cátedras, o de lo formal de la universalidad de los fieles, que es la Iglesia. Si lo entienden de lo primero (que es, en mi sentir, su verdadero sentido, pues vemos que, con efecto, no se permite en la Iglesia que las mujeres lean públicamente ni prediquen), ¿por qué reprenden a las que privadamente estudian? Y si lo entienden de lo segun-

mitted of women to read publicly in church, nor preach, why do they censure those who study privately? And if they understand the latter, and wish that the prohibition of the Apostle be applied transcendentally — that not even in private are women to be permitted to write or study — how are we to view the fact that the Church permitted a Gertrudis, a Santa Teresa, a Saint Birgitta, the Nun of Agreda, and so many others, to write? And if they say to me that these women were saints, they speak the truth; but this poses no obstacle to my argument. First, because Saint Paul's proposition is absolute, and encompasses all women not excepting saints, as Martha and Mary, Marcella, Mary, mother of Jacob, and Salome, all were in their time, and many other zealous women of the early church. But we see, too, that the Church allows women who are not saints to write, for the Nun of Agreda and Sor María de la Antigua are not canonized, yet their writings are circulated. And when Santa Teresa and the others were writing, they were not as yet canonized. In which case, Saint Paul's prohibition was directed solely to the public office of the pulpit, for if the Apostle had forbidden women to write, the Church would not have allowed it. Now I do not make so bold as to teach — which in me would be excessively presumptuous — and as for writing, that requires a greater talent than mine, and serious reflection. As Saint Cyprian says: *The things we write require most conscientious consideration.*[51] I have desired to study that I might be ignorant of less; for (according to Saint Agustine) some things are learned to be enacted and others only to be known: *We learn some things to know them, others, to do them.*[52] Then, where is the offense to be found if even what is licit to women — which is to teach by writing — I do not perform, as I know that I am lacking in means, following the counsel of Quintilian: *Let each person learn not only from the precepts of others, but also let him reap counsel from his own nature.*[53]

If the offense is to be found in the *Atenagórica* letter, was

do y quieren que la prohibición del Apóstol sea trascendentalmente, que ni en lo secreto se permita escribir ni estudiar a las mujeres, ¿cómo vemos que la Iglesia ha permitido que escriba una Gertrudis, una Teresa, una Brígida, la monja de Ágreda   y otras muchas? Y si me dicen que éstas eran santas, es verdad, pero no obsta a mi argumento; lo primero, porque la proposición de San Pablo es absoluta y comprende a todas las mujeres sin excepción de santas, pues también en su tiempo lo eran Marta y María, Marcela, María madre de Jacob, y Salomé, y otras muchas que había en el fervor de la primitiva Iglesia, y no las exceptúa; y ahora vemos que la Iglesia permite escribir a las mujeres santas y no santas, pues la de Ágreda y María de la Antigua   no están canonizadas y corren sus escritos; y ni cuando Santa Teresa y las demás escribieron, lo estaban: luego la prohibición de San Pablo sólo miró a la publicidad de los púlpitos, pues si el Apóstol prohibiera el escribir, no lo permitiera la Iglesia. Pues ahora, yo no me atrevo a enseñar—que fuera en mí muy desmedida presunción—; y el escribir, mayor talento que el mío requiere y muy grande consideración. Así lo dice San Cipriano: *Gravi consideratione indigent, quae scribimus* . Lo que sólo he deseado es estudiar para ignorar menos: que, según San Agustín, unas cosas se aprenden para hacer y otras para sólo saber: *Discimus quaedam, ut sciamus; quaedam, ut faciamus.* Pues ¿en qué ha estado el delito, si aun lo que es lícito a las mujeres, que es enseñar escribiendo, no hago yo porque conozco que no tengo caudal para ello, siguiendo el consejo de Quintiliano: *Noscat quisque, et non tantum ex alienis praeceptis, sed ex natura sua capiat consilium?* .

Si el crimen está en la Carta Atenagórica, ¿fue aqué-

that letter anything other than the simple expression of my feeling, written with the implicit permission of our Holy Mother Church? For if the Church, in her most sacred authority, does not forbid it, why must others do so? That I proffered an opinion contrary to that of de Vieyra was audacious, but, as a Father, was it not audacious that he speak against the three Holy Fathers of the Church? My reason, such as it is, is it not as unfettered as his, as both issue from the same source? Is his opinion to be considered as a revelation, as a principle of the Holy Faith, that we must accept blindly? Furthermore, I maintained at all times the respect due such a virtuous man, a respect in which his defender was sadly wanting, ignoring the phrase of Titus Lucius: *Respect is companion to the arts.*[54] I did not touch a thread of the robes of the Society of Jesus; nor did I write for other than the consideration of the person who suggested that I write. And, according to Pliny, *how different the condition of one who writes from that of one who merely speaks.*[55] Had I believed the letter was to be published I would not have been so inattentive. If, as the censor says, the letter is heretical, why does he not denounce it? And with that he would be avenged, and I content, for, which is only seemly, I esteem more highly my reputation as a Catholic and obedient daughter of the Holy Mother Church than all the approbation due a learned woman. If the letter is rash, and he does well to criticize it, then laugh, even if with the laugh of the rabbit, for I have not asked that he approve; as I was free to dissent from de Vieyra, so will anyone be free to oppose my opinion.

But how I have strayed, lady. None of this pertains here, nor is it intended for your ears, but as I was discussing my accusers I remembered the words of one that recently have appeared, and, though my intent was to speak in general, my pen, unbidden, slipped, and began to respond in particular. And so, returning to our Arce, he says that he knew in this city two nuns: one in the Convent of

lla más que referir sencillamente mi sentir con todas las venias que debo a nuestra Santa Madre Iglesia? Pues si ella, con su santísima autoridad, no me lo prohíbe, ¿por qué me lo han de prohibir otros? ¿Llevar una opinión contraria de Vieyra fue en mí atrevimiento, y no lo fue en su Paternidad llevarla contra los tres Santos Padres de la Iglesia? Mi entendimiento tal cual ¿no es tan libre como el suyo, pues viene de un solar? ¿Es alguno de los principios de la Santa Fe, revelados, su opinión, para que la hayamos de creer a ojos cerrados? Demás que yo ni falté al decoro que a tanto varón se debe, como acá ha faltado su defensor, olvidado de la sentencia de Tito Lucio: *Artes committatur decor* ; ni toqué a la Sagrada Compañía en el pelo de la ropa; ni escribí más que para el juicio de quien me lo insinuó; y según Plinio, *non similis est conditio publicantis, et nominatim dicentis* . Que si creyera se había de publicar, no fuera con tanto desaliño como fue. Si es, como dice el censor , herética, ¿por qué no la delata?, y con eso él quedará vengado y yo contenta, que aprecio, como debo, más el nombre de católica y de obediente hija de mi Santa Madre Iglesia, que todos los aplausos de docta. Si está bárbara—que en eso dicen bien—, ríase, aunque sea con la risa que dicen del conejo, que yo no le digo que me aplauda, pues como yo fui libre para disentir de Vieyra, lo será cualquier para disentir de mi dictamen.

Pero ¿dónde voy, Señora mía? Que esto no es de aquí, ni es para vuestros oídos, sino que como voy tratando de mis impugnadores, me acordé de las cláusulas de uno que ha salido ahora, e insensiblemente se deslizó la pluma a quererle responder en particular, siendo mi intento hablar en general. Y así, volviendo a nuestro Arce, dice que conoció en esta ciudad dos monjas: la una en el convento de Regina, que tenía el

the Regina, who had so thoroughly committed the Breviary to memory that with the greatest promptitude and propriety she applied in her conversation its verses, psalms, and maxims of saintly homilies. The other, in the Convent of the Conception, was so accustomed to reading the Epistles of my Father Saint Jerome, and the Locutions of this Saint, that Arce says, *It seemed I was listening to Saint Jerome himself, speaking in Spanish.*[56] And of this latter woman he says that after her death he learned that she had translated these Epistles into the Spanish language. What pity that such talents could not have been employed in major studies with scientific principles. He does not give the name of either, although he offers these women as confirmation of his opinion, which is that not only is it licit, but most useful and essential for women to study the Holy Word, and even more essential for nuns; and that study is the very thing to which your wisdom exhorts me, and in which so many arguments concur.

Then if I turn my eyes to the oft-chastized faculty of making verses — which is in me so natural that I must discipline myself that even this letter not be written in that form — I might cite those lines, *All I wished to express took the form of verse.*[57] And seeing that so many condemn and criticize this ability, I have conscientiously sought to find what harm may be in it, and I have not found it, but, rather, I see verse acclaimed in the mouths of the Sybils; sanctified in the pens of the Prophets, especially King David, of whom the exalted Expositor my beloved Father says (explicating the measure of his metres): *in the manner of Horace and Pindar, now it hurries along in iambs, now it rings in alcaic, now swells in sapphic, then arrives in broken feet.*[58] The greater part of the Holy Books are in metre, as is the Book of Moses; and those of Job (as Saint Isidore states in his *Etymologiae*) are in heroic verse. Solomon wrote the Canticle of Canticles in verse; and Jeremias, his *Lamentations*. And so, says Cassiodorus: *All poetic expression had as its source the Holy Scrip-*

Breviario de tal manera en la memoria, que aplicaba con grandísima prontitud y propiedad su versos, salmos y sentencias de homilías de los santos, en las conversaciones. La otra, en el convento de la Concepción, tan acostumbrada a leer las Epístolas de mi Padre San Jerónimo, y locuciones del Santo, de tal manera que dice Arce: *Hieronymum ipsum hispane loquentem audire me existimarem* . Y de ésta dice que supo, después de su muerte, había traducido dichas Epístolas en romance; y se duele de que tales talentos no se hubieran empleado en mayores estudios con principios científicos, sin decir los nombres de la una ni de la otra, aunque las trae para confirmación de su sentencia, que es que no sólo es lícito, pero utilísimo y necesario a las mujeres el estudio de las sagradas letras, y mucho más a las monjas, que es lo mismo a que vuestra discreción me exhorta y a que concurren tantas razones.

Pues si vuelvo los ojos a la tan perseguida habilidad de hacer versos—que en mí es tan natural, que aun me violento para que esta carta no lo sean, y pudiera decir aquello de *Quidquid conabar dicere, versus erat*— , viéndola condenar a tantos tanto y acriminar, he buscado muy de propósito cuál sea el daño que puedan tener, y no le he hallado; antes sí los veo aplaudidos en las bocas de las Sibilas; santificados en las plumas de los Profetas, especialmente del Rey David, de quien dice el gran expositor y amado Padre mío, dando razón de las mensuras de sus metros: *In moren Flacci et Pindari nunc iambo currit, nunc alcaico personat, nunc sapphico tumet, nunc semipede ingreditur* . Los más de los libros sagrados están en metro, como el Cántico de Moisés; y los de Job, dice San Isidoro, en sus Etimologías, que están en verso heroico. En los Epitalamios los escribió Salomón; en los Trenos, Jeremías. Y así dice

tures.[59] For not only does our Catholic Church not disdain verse, it employs verse in its hymns, and recites the lines of Saint Ambrose, Saint Thomas, Saint Isidore, and others. Saint Bonaventure was so taken with verse that he writes scarcely a page where it does not appear. It is readily apparent that Saint Paul had studied verse, for he quotes and translates verses of Aratus: *For in him we live, and move, and are.*[60] And he quotes also that verse of Parmenides: *The Cretans are always liars, evil beasts, slothful bellies.*[61] Saint Gregory Nazianzen argues in elegant verses the questions of matrimony and virginity. And, how should I tire? The Queen of Wisdom, Our Lady, with Her sacred lips, intoned the Canticle of the Magnificat; and having brought forth this example, it would be offensive to add others that were profane, even those of the most serious and learned men, for this alone is more than sufficient confirmation; and even though Hebrew elegance could not be compressed into Latin measure, for which reason, although the sacred translator, more attentive to the importance of the meaning, omitted the verse, the Psalms retain the number and divisions of verses, and what harm is to be found in them? For misuse is not the blame of art, but rather of the evil teacher who perverts the arts, making of them the snare of the devil; and this occurs in all the arts and sciences.

And if the evil is attributed to the fact that a woman employs them, we have seen how many have done so in praiseworthy fashion; what then is the evil in my being a woman? I confess openly my own baseness and meanness; but I judge that no couplet of mine has been deemed indecent. Furthermore, I have never written of my own will, but under the pleas and injunctions of others; to such a degree that the only piece I remember having written for my own pleasure was a little trifle they called *El sueño*. That letter, lady, which you so greatly honored, I wrote more with repugnance than any other emotion; both by reason of the fact that it treated sacred matters, for which (as I have

Casiodoro: *omnis poetica locutio a Divinis scripturis sumpsit exordium* . Pues nuestra Iglesia católica no sólo no los desdeña, mas los usa en sus Himnos y recita los de San Ambrosio, Santo Tomás, de San Isidoro y otros. San Buenaventura les tuvo tal afecto que apenas hay plana suya sin versos. San Pablo bien se ve que los había estudiado, pues los cita, y traduce el de Arato: *In ipso enim vivimus, et movemur, et sumus* , y alega el otro de Parménides: *Cretenses semper mendaces, malae bestiae, pigri* . San Gregorio Nacianceno disputa en elegantes versos las cuestiones de Matrimonio y la de la Virginidad. Y ¿qué me canso? La Reina de la Sabiduría y Señora nuestra, con sus sagrados labios, entonó el Cántico de la *magnificat* ; y habiéndola traído por ejemplar; agravio fuera traer ejemplos profanos, aunque sean de varones gravísimos y doctísimos, pues esto sobra para prueba; y el ver que, aunque como la elegancia hebrea no se pudo estrechar a la mensura latina, a cuya causa el traductor sagrado, más atento a lo importante del sentido, omitió el verso, con todo, retienen los Salmos el nombre y divisiones de versos; pues, ¿cuál es el daño que pueden tener ellos en sí? Porque el mal uso no es culpa del arte, sino del mal profesor que los vicia, haciendo de ellos lazos del demonio; y esto en todas las facultades y ciencias sucede.

Pues si está el mal en que los use una mujer, ya se ve cuántas los han usado loablemente; pues ¿en qué está el serlo yo? Confieso desde luego mi ruindad y vileza; pero no juzgo que se habrá visto una copla mía indecente. Demás, que yo nunca he escrito cosa alguna por mi voluntad, sino por ruegos y preceptos ajenos; de tal manera que no me acuerdo haber escrito por mi gusto si no es un papelillo que llaman *El sueño*. Esa carta que vos, Señora mía, honrasteis tanto, la escribí

stated) I hold such reverent awe, and because it seems to wish to impugn, a practice for which I have natural aversion; and I believe that had I forseen the blessed destiny to which it was fated — for like a second Moses I had set it adrift, naked, on the waters of the Nile of silence, where you, a princess, found and cherished it — I believe, I reiterate, that had I known, the very hands of which it was born would have drowned it, out of the fear that these clumsy scribblings from my ignorance appear before the light of your great wisdom; by which one knows the munificence of your kindness, for your goodwill applauds precisely what your reason must wish to reject. For as fate cast it before your doors, so exposed, so orphaned, that it fell to you even to give it a name, I must lament that among other deformities it also bears the blemish of haste; both because of the unrelenting ill-health I suffer, and for the profusion of duties imposed on me by obedience, as well as the want of anyone to guide me in my writing and the need that it all come from my hand, and, finally, because the writing went against my nature and I wished only to keep my promise to one whom I could not disobey, I could not find the time to finish properly, and thus I failed to include whole treatises and many arguments that presented themselves to me, but which I omitted in order to put an end to the writing — many, that had I known the letter was to be printed, I would not have excluded, even if merely to satisfy some objections that have since arisen and which could have been refuted. But I shall not be so ill-mannered as to place such indecent objects before the purity of your eyes, for it is enough that my ignorance be an offense in your sight, without need of entrusting to it the effronteries of others. But if in their audacity these latter should wing their way to you (and they are of such little weight that this will happen) then you will command what I am to do; for, if it does not run contrary to your will, my defense shall be not to take up my pen, for I deem that one affront need not

con más repugnancia que otra cosa; y **así** porque **era** de cosas sagradas a quienes (como he dicho) tengo reverente temor, como porque parecía querer impugnar, cosa a que tengo aversión natural. Y creo que si pudiera haber prevenido el dichoso destino a que nacía—pues, como a otro Moisés, la arrojé expósita a las aguas del Nilo del silencio, donde la halló y acarició una princesa como vos—, creo, vuelvo a decir, que si yo tal pensara, la ahogara antes entre las mismas manos en que nacía, de miedo de que pareciesen a la luz de vuestro saber los torpes borrones de mi ignorancia. De donde se conoce la grandeza de vuestra bondad, pues está aplaudiendo vuestra voluntad lo que precisamente ha de estar repugnando vuestro clarísimo entendimiento. Pero ya que su ventura la arrojó a vuestras puertas, tan expósita y huérfana que hasta el nombre le pusisteis vos, pésame que, entre más deformidades, llevase también los defectos de la prisa; porque así por la poca salud que continuamente tengo, como por la sobra de ocupaciones en que me pone la obediencia, y carecer de quien me ayude a escribir, y estar necesitada a que todo sea de mi mano y porque, como iba contra mi genio y no quería más que cumplir con la palabra a quien no podía desobedecer, no veía la hora de acabar; y así dejé de poner discursos enteros y muchas pruebas que se me ofrecían, y las dejé por no escribir más; que, a saber que se había de imprimir, no las hubiera dejado, siquiera por dejar satisfechas algunas objeciones que se han excitado, y pudiera remitir, pero no seré tan desatenta que ponga tan indecentes objetos a la pureza de vuestros ojos, pues basta que los ofenda con mis ignorancias, sin que los remita a ajenos atrevimientos. Si ellos por sí volaren por allá (que son tan livianos que sí harán), me ordenaréis lo que debo hacer; que, si no es interviniendo vuestros preceptos, lo que es por mi defensa nunca tomaré la pluma, porque me parece que

occasion another, if one recognizes the error in the very place it lies concealed. As my Father Saint Jerome says, *good discourse seeks not secret things,*[62] and Saint Ambrose, *it is the nature of a guilty conscience to lie concealed.*[63] Nor do I consider that I have been impugned, for one statute of the Law states: *An accusation will not endure unless nurtured by the person who brought it forth.*[64] What *is* a matter to be weighed is the effort spent in copying the accusation. A strange madness, to expend more effort in denying acclaim than in earning it! I, lady, have chosen not to respond (although others did so without my knowledge); it suffices that I have seen certain treatises, among them, one so learned I send it to you so that reading it will compensate in part for the time you squandered on my writing. If, lady, you wish that I act contrary to what I have proposed here for your judgment and opinion, the merest indication of your desire will, as is seemly, countermand my inclination, which, as I have told you, is to be silent, for although Saint John Chrysostom says, *those who slander must be refuted, and those who question, taught,*[65] I know also that Saint Gregory says, *It is no less a victory to tolerate enemies than to overcome them.*[66] And that patience conquers by tolerating and triumphs by suffering. And if among the Roman Gentiles it was the custom when their captains were at the highest peak of glory — when returning triumphant from other nations, robed in purple and wreathed with laurel, crowned-but-conquered kings pulling their carriages in the stead of beasts, accompanied by the spoils of the riches of all the world, the conquering troops adorned with the insignia of their heroic feats, hearing the plaudits of the people who showered them with titles of honor and renown such as Fathers of the Nation, Columns of the Empire, Walls of Rome, Shelter of the Republic, and other glorious names — a soldier went before these captains in this moment of the supreme apogee of glory and human happiness crying out in a loud voice to the conqueror (by his consent and order

no necesita de que otro le responda, quien en lo mismo que se oculta conoce su error, pues, como dice mi Padre San Jerónimo, *bonus sermo secreta non quaerit*, y San Ambrosio: *latere criminosae est conscientiae.* Ni yo me tengo por impugnada, pues dice una regla del Derecho: *Accusatio non tenetur si non curat de persona, quae produxerit illam* . Lo que sí es de ponderar es el trabajo que le ha costado el andar haciendo traslados . ¡Rara demencia: cansarse más en quitarse el crédito que pudiera en granjearlo! Yo, Señora mía, no he querido responder; aunque otros lo han hecho, sin saberlo yo: basta que he visto algunos papeles, y entre ellos uno que por docto os remito y porque el leerle os desquite parte del tiempo que os he malgastado en lo que yo escribo. Si vos, Señora, gustáredes de que yo haga lo contrario de lo que tenía propuesto a vuestro juicio y sentir, al menor movimiento de vuestro gusto cederá, como es razón, mi dictamen que, como os he dicho, era de callar, porque aunque dice San Juan Crisóstomo: *calumniatores convincere oportet, interrogatores docere*, veo que también dice San Gregorio: *Victoria non minor est, hostes tolerare, quam hostes vincere* ; y que la paciencia vence tolerando y triunfa sufriendo. Y si entre los gentiles romanos era costumbre, en la más alta cumbre de la gloria de sus capitanes —cuando entraban triunfando de las naciones, vestidos de púrpura y coronados de laurel, tirando el carro, en vez de brutos, coronadas frentes de vencidos reyes, acompañados de los despojos de las riquezas de todo el mundo y adornada la milicia vencedora de las insignias de sus hazañas, oyendo los aplausos populares en tan honrosos títulos y renombres como llamarlos Padres de la Patria, Columnas del Imperio, Muros de Roma, Amparos de la República y otros nombres gloriosos—, que en este supremo auge de la gloria y felicidad humana fuese un soldado, en voz alta diciendo al vencedor, como con sen-

of the Senate): Behold how you are mortal; behold how you have this or that defect, not excepting the most shameful, as happened in the triumph of Caesar, when the vilest soldiers clamored in his ear: *Beware, Romans, for we bring you the bald adulterer.*[67] Which was done so that in the midst of such honor the conquerers not be swelled up with pride, and that the ballast of these insults act as counterweight to the bellying sails of such approbation, and that the ship of good judgment not founder amidst the winds of acclamation. If this, I say, was the practice among Gentiles, who knew only the light of Natural Law, how much might we Catholics, under the injunction to love our enemies, achieve by tolerating them? And in my own behalf I can attest that calumny has often mortified me, but never harmed me, being that I hold as a great fool one who having occasion to receive credit suffers the difficulty and loses the credit, as it is with those who do not resign themselves to death, but, in the end, die anyway, their resistence not having prevented death, but merely deprived them of the credit of resignation and caused them to die badly when they might have died well. And thus, lady, I believe these experiences do more good than harm, and I hold as greater the jeopardy of applause to human weakness, as we are wont to appropriate praise that is not our own, and must be ever watchful, and carry graven on our hearts those words of the Apostle: *Or what hast thou that thou hast not received? And if thou hast received, why doest thou glory as if thou hadst not received it?*[68] so that these words serve as a shield to fend off the sharp barbs of commendations, which are as spears which when not attributed to God (whose they are), claim our lives and cause us to be thieves of God's honor and usurpers of the talents He bestowed on us and the gifts that He lent to us, for which we must give the most strict accounting. And thus, lady, I fear applause more than calumny, because the latter, with but the simple act of patience becomes gain, while the former requires

timiento suyo y orden del Senado: Mira que eres mortal; mira que tienes tal y tal defecto; sin perdonar los más vergonzosos, como sucedió en el triunfo de César, que voceaban los más viles soldados a sus oídos: *Cavete romani, adducimus vobis adulterum calvum* . Lo cual se hacía porque en medio de tanta honra no se desvaneciese el vencedor, y porque el lastre de estas afrentas hiciese contrapeso a las velas de tantos aplausos, para que no peligrase la nave del juicio entre los vientos de las aclamaciones. Si esto, digo, hacían unos gentiles, con sola la luz de la Ley Natural, nosotros, católicos, con un precepto de amar a los enemigos, ¿qué mucho haremos en tolerarlos? Yo de mí puedo asegurar que las calumnias algunas veces me han mortificado, pero nunca me han hecho daño, porque yo tengo por muy necio al que teniendo ocasión de merecer, pasa el trabajo y pierde el mérito, que es como los que no quieren conformarse al morir y al fin mueren sin servir su resistencia de excusar la muerte, sino de quitarles el mérito de la conformidad, y de hacer mala la muerte que podía ser bien. Y así, Señora mía, estas cosas creo que aprovechan más que dañan, y tengo por mayor riesgo de los aplausos en la flaqueza humana, que suelen apropiarse lo que no es suyo, y es menester estar con mucho cuidado y tener escritas en el corazón aquellas palabras del Apóstol: *Quid autem habes quod non accepisti? Si autem accepisti, quid gloriaris quasi non acceperis?* , para que sirvan de escudo que resista las puntas de las alabanzas, que son lanzas que, en no atribuyéndose a Dios, cuyas son, nos quitan la vida y nos hacen ser ladrones de la honra de Dios y usurpadores de los talentos que nos entregó y de los dones que nos prestó y de que hemos de dar estrechísima cuenta . Y así, Señora, yo temo más esto que aquello; porque aquello, con sólo un acto sencillo de paciencia, está convertido en provecho; y esto, son menester mu-

many acts of reflection and humility and proper recognition so that it not become harm. And I know and recognize that it is by special favor of God that I know this, as it enables me in either instance to act in accord with the words of Saint Agustine: *One must believe neither the friend who praises nor the enemy who detracts.*[69] Although, most often I squander God's favor, or vitiate with such defects and imperfections that I spoil what, being His, was good. And thus in what little of mine that has been printed, neither the use of my name, nor even consent for the printing, was given by my own counsel, but by the license of another who lies outside my domain, as was also true with the printing of the *Atenagórica* letter, and only a few *Exercises of the Incarnation* and *Offerings of the Sorrow* were printed for public devotions with my pleasure, but without my name; of which I am sending some few copies that (if you so desire) you may distribute them among our sisters, the nuns of that holy community, as well as in that city. I send but one copy of the *Sorrows* because the others have been exhausted and I could find no other copy. I wrote them long ago, solely for the devotions of my sisters, and later they were spread abroad; and their contents are disproportionate as regards my unworthiness and my ignorance, and they profited that they touched on matters of our exalted Queen; for I cannot explain what it is that inflames the coldest heart when one refers to the Most Holy Mary. It is my only desire, esteemed lady, to remit to you works worthy of your virtue and wisdom; as the poet said: *Though strength may falter, good will must be praised. In this, I believe, the gods will be content.*[70]

If ever I write again, my scribbling will always find its way to the haven of your holy feet and the certainty of your correction, for I have no other jewel with which to pay you, and, in the lament of Seneca, he who has once bestowed benefices has committed himself to continue; and so you must be repaid out of your own munificence, for only in

chos actos reflexos   de humildad y propio conocimiento para que no sea daño. Y así, de mí lo conozco
y reconozco que es especial favor de Dios el conocerlo,
para saberme portar en uno y en otro con aquella sentencia de San Agustín: *Amico laudanti credendum non
est, sicut nec inimico detrahenti* . Aunque yo soy tal
que las más veces lo debo de echar a perder o mezclarlo
con tales defectos e imperfecciones, que vicio lo
que de suyo fuera bueno. Y así, en lo poco que se ha
impreso mío, no sólo mi nombre, pero ni el consenti-
miento para la impresión ha sido dictamen propio, sino
libertad ajena que no cae debajo de mi dominio, como
lo fue la impresión de la Carta Atenagórica; de suerte
que solamente unos *Ejercicios de la Encarnación* y unos
Ofrecimientos de los Dolores, se imprimieron con gusto
mío por la pública devoción, pero sin mi nombre; de
los cuales remito algunas copias, porque (si os parece)
los repartáis entre nuestras hermanas las religiosas de
esa santa comunidad y además de esa ciudad. De los
Dolores va sólo uno porque se han consumido ya y no
pude hallar más. Hícelos sólo por la devoción de mis
hermanas, años ha, y después se divulgaron; cuyos asun-
tos son tan improporcionados a mi tibieza como a mi
ignorancia, y sólo me ayudó en ellos ser cosas de nuestra gran Reina: que no sé qué se tiene el que en tratando de María Santísima se enciende el corazón más he-
lado. Yo quisiera, venerable Señora mía, remitiros obras
dignas de vuestra virtud y sabiduría; pero como dijo
el Poeta:

Ut desint vires, tamen est laudanda voluntas:
hac ego contentos, auguror esse Deos .

Si algunas otras cosillas escribiere, siempre irán a
buscar el sagrado de vuestras plantas y el seguro de

this way shall I with dignity be freed from debt and avoid that the words of that same Seneca come to pass: *It is contemptible to be surpassed in benefices.*[71] For in his gallantry the generous creditor gives to the poor debtor the means to satisfy his debt. So God gave his gift to a world unable to repay Him: He gave his son that He be offered a recompense worthy of Him.

If, most venerable lady, the tone of this letter may not have seemed right and proper, I ask forgiveness for its homely familiarity, and the less than seemly respect in which by treating you as a nun, one of my sisters, I have lost sight of the remoteness of your most illustrious person; which, had I seen you without your veil, would never have occurred; but you in all your prudence and mercy will supplement or amend the language, and if you find unsuitable the *Vos* of the address I have employed, believing that for the reverence I owe you, Your Reverence seemed little reverent, modify it in whatever manner seems appropriate to your due, for I have not dared exceed the limits of your custom, nor transgress the boundary of your modesty.

And hold me in your grace, and entreat for me divine grace, of which the Lord God grant you large measure, and keep you, as I pray Him, and am needful. From this convent of our Father Saint Jerome in Mexico City, the first day of the month of March of sixteen hundred and ninety-one. Allow me to kiss your hand, your most favored

JUANA INÉS DE LA CRUZ

vuestra corrección, pues no tengo otra alhaja con que pagaros, y en sentir de Séneca, el que empezó a hacer beneficios se obligó a continuarlos; y así os pagará a vos vuestra propia liberalidad, que sólo así puedo yo quedar dignamente desempeñada, sin que caiga en mí aquello del mismo Séneca: *Turpe est beneficiis vinci* . Que es bizarría del acreedor generoso dar al deudor pobre, con que pueda satisfacer la deuda. Así lo hizo Dios con el mundo imposibilitado de pagar: diole a su Hijo propio para que se le ofreciese por digna satisfacción.

Si el estilo, venerable, Señora mía, de esta carta no hubiere sido como a vos es debido, os pido perdón de la casera familiaridad o menos autoridad de que tratándoos como a una religiosa de velo, hermana mía, se me ha olvidado la distancia de vuestra ilustrísima persona, que a veros yo sin velo, no sucediera así; pero vos, con vuestra cordura y benignidad, supliréis o enmendaréis los términos y si os pareciere incongruo el *Vos* de que yo he usado por parecerme que para la reverencia que os debo es muy poca reverencia la *Reverencia*, mudadlo en el que os pareciere decente a lo que vos merecéis, que yo no me he atrevido a exceder de los límites de vuestro estilo ni a romper el margen de vuestra modestia.

Y mantenedme en vuestra gracia, para impetrarme la divina, de que os conceda el Señor muchos aumentos y os guarde, como le suplico y he menester. De este convento de N. Padre San Jerónimo de Méjico, a primero día del mes de marzo de mil seiscientos y noventa y un años. B. V. M. vuestra más favorecida

JUANA INÉS DE LA CRUZ.

APPENDIX

The 1681 Letter
from Sor Juana to her Confessor

A Mexican religious scholar, Father Aureliano Tapia Mendez, recently discovered a letter from Sor Juana Inés de la Cruz addressed to her confessor, Father Antonio Nunez de Miranda, in the Seminary Library at Monterrey. The letter is a copy, written in early 18th century calligraphy. Internal evidence indicates that the original letter was composed about 1681 and marked the beginning of Sor Juana's confrontation with church officials, climaxing in her *Response to Sor Filotea* ten years later. Although there is a possibility that the document is a fabrication, its style and content have persuaded scholars that it is not only authentic, but that it is a discovery of major importance in understanding Sor Juana and the contemporary jealousies generated by her literary talents and achievements. Of particular interest is the revelation that Sor Juana initiated the break in her ties to her confessor, rather than *vice versa*, by refusing to give in to his efforts to force her to abandon her writing of poetry.

The full text of the letter appears in an appendix to the third edition of Octavio Paz' book, *Sor Juana Inés de la Cruz o Las Trampas de la Fe*. The following is a summary:

The 1681 letter begins with Sor Juana's assertion that various persons have told her that Father Nunez has described her conduct in conversations with them as "reprehensible." She says that rather than defend herself, she originally decided to suffer

in silence because of her "supreme veneration and filial affection" for the priest. Eventually, however, she concluded that her patience only irritated him and therefore she decided to reply directly to his criticisms.

The basis for her confessor's anger, she concluded, was the "black verses granted me by heaven." She said she had resisted writing poetry in order to please him, but there were occasions she simply could not refuse, including two *villancicos* to the Virgin, written with his permission, and the *Arch for the Church*, written, again with his permission, in response to a request voted by the full Cabildo. Sor Juana noted that two magistrates had delivered the latter request:

> Now it would be my wish that Your Reverence, with your clear judgment, put yourself in my place and consider what you would have replied in this situation? Would you answer that you could not? That would have been a lie. That you did not want to? That would have been disobedience. That you know not how? They did not ask more than I knew. That the vote was improperly taken? That would have been impudent audacity and ingratitude to those who honored me by believing that an ignorant woman knew how to do what such brilliant minds requested: then there could be nothing but to obey.

In addition to the three public works, Sor Juana mentions a *copla* or two written for a birthday, in honor of some person she esteemed, and a *loa* for the king's birthday "written at the command of His Excellency Don Fray Payo himself," and another "by order of Her Excellency the Senora Condesa de Paredes."

These works were not produced out of vanity, said her letter, for along with applause they generated unwanted envy and malice.

Women sense that men exceed them, and yet it seems that I place myself on a level with men; some men wish that I did not know so much; others say that I must know more in order to merit such approbation; elderly women do not want other women to know more than they; young women, that others make a good appearance; and both wish that I conform to the rules of their counsel; so that from all sides comes such a singular martyrdom I deem none other has ever experienced it.

Sor Juana then referred to the attention paid to her by the Spanish Viceroy and his wife, the Marquesa, saying it was unsolicited and could not be refused.

What blame is it of mine that Their Excellencies were pleased with me? And though there was no reason for their pleasure, could I deny such powerful figures?

Then she addressed the priest's objections to the amount of time and effort she spent on her studies.

My studies have not been to the harm of any person, having been so extremely private that I have not even had the direction of a teacher, but have learned only from myself and my work, for I am not unaware that to study publicly in schools is not seemly for a woman's honor, because this gives occasion for familiarity with men, and could be sufficient reason for banning public studies, and that if women may not challenge men in studies that pertain to

them alone, it is because the republic having no need of such schools for government by magistrates (from which service, for the same reason of honor, women are excluded) has not established them; but private and individual study, who has forbidden that to women? Like men, do they not have a rational soul? Shall they not enjoy the privilege of the enlightenment of letters? Is a woman's soul not as receptive to God's grace and glory as a man's? Why is she not as able to receive as much learning and science, which is the lesser gift? What divine revelation, what regulation of the church, what rule of reason framed for us such a harsh law?

Are letters an obstacle or do they lead to salvation? Was not Saint Augustine saved, Saint Ambrosius, and all the other Holy Doctors. And Your Reverence, with your learning, do you not plan to be saved?

And if you reply that a different order obtains for men, I say: did not Saint Catherine study, Saint Gertrude, my Mother Saint Paula, without harm to her exalted contemplation, and was her pious founding of convents impeded by her knowing even Greek? Or learning Hebrew? Taught by my Father Saint Jerome, to comprehend the Holy Scriptures, as the Saint himself reports? Who also, in one of his epistles, praised the supreme learning of her daughter, Blesilla—and at a very tender age, for she died at twenty?

Why do you find wicked in me what in other women was good?

With subtle sarcasm, she characterized the everyday life in the convent.

Why must it be wrong that the time I would otherwise pass in idle chatter before the grille, or in a cell gossiping about everything that happens outside and inside the house, or quarreling with a sister, or scolding a helpless servant, or wandering with my thoughts, is spent in study?

After all, she wrote, her inclination toward learning was God-given:

I have this nature; if it is evil, I am the daughter of it; I was born with it and with it shall I die.

In the balance of the letter Sor Juana challenges the priest's right to tell her what she should do, and ends up saying that if he no longer wishes to be her confessor exactly as she is, she will seek another confessor in his place.

This new letter gives deeper insights into the tenacity and determination of Sor Juana, and the fact that her later letter was not just a sudden response composed on the spur of the moment. Her resentment at the belittling of intellectual pursuits by women had been building for at least a decade.

Octavio Paz ascribes the boldness of the 1681 letter to the nun's sense of personal security at the time it was written, when she still had the support of both the Viceroy and the Bishop. It was withdrawal of the Bishop's support a few years later which triggered the more restrained wording of her 1691 *La Respuesta a Sor Filotea*.

Paz sums up his own interpretation of Sor Juana's *La Respuesta* and the newly-discovered 1681 letter with these words:

The struggles and last years of Juana Inés de la Cruz are a dramatic chapter in the history of conflict between intellectual freedom and state power, between the individual and ideological bureaucracies.

Notes

1. Minorem spei, maiorem benefacti gloriam pereunt.

2. Et unde hoc mihi? Luke, 1:43. Bracketed words have been added for clarity.

3. Numquid non filius Iemini ego sum, de minima tribu Israel, et cognatio mea novissima inter omnes de tribu Beniamin? Quare igitur locutus es mihi sermon istum? I Kings, 9:21.

4. Audivit arcana Dei, quae non licet homini loqui. II Corinthians, 12:4.

5. [St. John, 21:25.]

6. Ostende mihi faciem tuam. Exodus 33:13.

7. Quare tu enarras iustitias meas, et assumis testamentum meum per os tuum? Psalms, 49:16.

8. Ad ultimum sine periculo discat Canticum Canticorum, ne si in exordio legerit, sub carnalibus verbis spiritualium nuptiarum Epithalamium non intelligens, vulneretur.

9. Teneris in annis haut clara est fides.

10. . . . iusta, vel iniusta, timenda non est. . . .

11. . . . ad impossibilia nemo tenetur.

12. Vos me coegistis. II Corinthians, 12:11.

13. . . . privatio est causa appetitus.

14. Numquid coniungere valebis micantes stellas Pleiadas, aut gyrum Arcturi poteris dissipare? Numquid producis Luciferum in tempore suo, et Vesperum super filios terrae consurgere facis? Job, 38:31, 32.

15. In difficultatibus locorum Sacrae Scripturae ad orationem ieiunium adhibebat. Quin etiam sodali suo Fratri Reginaldo dicere solebat, quidquid sciret, non tam studio, aut labore suo peperisse, quam divinitus traditum accepisse.

16. [Don Juan Carlos Mero says that Sor Juana confused Kircher's *Magnes sive de arte magnetica* with *De magnete* by William Gilbert, London, 1600.]

17.   Quid ibi laboris insumpserim: quid sustinuerim difficultatis: quoties desperaverim: quotiesque cessaverim et contentione discendi rursus inceperim; testis est conscientia, tam mea, qui passus sum, quam eorum, qui mecum duxerunt vitam.

18.   Quid facimus, quia hic homo multa signa facit. John, 11:47.

19.   . . . radix Iesse, qui stat in signum populorum. Isias, 11:10.

20.   . . . in signum cui contradicetur. Luke, 2:34.

21.   Rarus est, qui velit cedere ingenio.

22.   Circuivi terram et ambulavi per eam. Job, 1:7.

23.   Circuit, quaerens quem devoret. I Peter, 5:8.

24.   . . . nunc princeps huius mundi eiicietur foras. John 12:31.

25.   . . . spinas et tribulos germinabit tibi. Genesis, 3:18.

26.   Rabbi, nunc quaerebant te Iudaei lapidare, et iterum vadis illuc? John, 11:8.

27.   Nonne duodecim sunt horae diei? John, 11:9.

28.   Eamus et nos, ut moriamur cum eo. John, 11:16.

29.   Multa bona opera ostendi vobis ex Patre meo, propter quod eorum opus me lapidatis? John, 10:32.

30.   De bono opere non lapidamus te, sed de blasphemia. John, 10:33.

31.   Petrus vero sequebatur eum a longe. Luke, 22:54.

32.   Nesciens quid diceret. Luke 9:33.

33.   Mulier, nescio quid dicis. Mulier, non novi illum. Luke, 22:57.

34.   Et hic cum illo erat. Luke 22:56.

35.   [The *seal* of Solomon contains triangles in its design — it is the Star of David. Possibly the ring does as well.]

36.   [Bartolomé, not Lupercio Leonardo.]

37.   An liceat foeminis sacrorum Bibliorum studio incumbere? Eaque interpretari?

38.   Mulieres in Ecclesiis taceant, non enim permittitur eis loqui. I Corinthians 14:34.

39.   Anus similiter in habitu sancto, bene docentes. Titus 2:3.

40.   In malevolam animan non introibit sapientia. Wisdom, 1:4.

41.   Dico enim per gratiam quae data est mihi, omnibus qui sunt inter vos: Non plus sapere quam oportet sapere, sed sapere ad sobrietatem: et unicuique sicut Deus divisit mensuram fidei. Romans, 12:3.

42.   Corripiet me iustus in misericordia, et increpabit: oleum autem peccatoris non impinguet caput meum. Psalms, 140:5.

43.   . . . ad Laetam, de institutione filiae. Adhuc tenera lingua psalmis dulcibus imbuatur. Ipsa nomina per quae consuescit paulatim verba contexere, non sint fortuita, sed certa, et coacervata de industria. Prophetarum videlicet, atque Apostolorum, et omnis ab Adam Patriarcharum series, de Matthaeo, Lucaque desdendat, et dum aliud agit, futurae memoriae praeparetur. Reddat tibi pensum quotidie, de Scripturarum floribus carptum.

44.   Scindite corda vestra, et non vestimenta vestra. Job, 2:13.

45.   Nobilis in portis vir eius. Proverbs, 31:23.

46.   [This is probably an error for "thundered from the left," a reference to Virgil's *Aeneid*.]

47.   . . . osculetur me osculo oris sui: quia meliora sunt ubera tua vino. Canticle of Canticles, 1:1.

48.   Psalms, 115:13.

49.   Mulier in silentio discat. Timothy, 2:11.

50.   . . . Audi Israel, et tace.

51.   Gravi consideratione indigent, quae scribimus.

52.   Discimus quaedam, ut sciamus; quaedam, ut faciamus.

53.   Noscat quisque, et non tantum ex alienis praeceptis, sed ex natura sua capiat consilium?

54.   Artes committatur decor.

55. . . . non similis est conditio publicantis, et nominatim dicentis.

56. Hieronymum ipsum hispane loquentem audire me existimarem.

57. Quidquid conabar dicere versus erat.

58. In moren Flacci et Pindari nunc iambo currit, nunc alcaico
personat, nunc sapphico tumet, nunc semipede ingreditur.

59. . . . omnis poetica locutio a Divinis scripturis sumpsit exordium.

60. In ipso enim vivimus, et movemur, et sumus. Acts, 17:28.

61. Cretenses semper mendaces, malae bestiae, pigri. Titus,
1:12.

62. . . . bonus sermo secreta non quaerit.

63. . . . latere criminosae est conscientiae.

64. Accusatio non tenetur si non curat de persona, quae produxerit illam.

65. . . . calumniatores convincere oportet, interrogatores docere.

66. Victoria non minor est, hostes tolerare, quam hostes vincere.

67. Cavete romani, adducimus vobis adulterum calvum.

68. Quid autem habes quod non accepisti? Si autem accepisti,
quid gloriaris quasi non acceperis. I Corinthians, 4:7.

69. Amico laudanti credendum non est, sicut nec inimico detrahenti.

70. Ut desint vires, tamen est laudanda voluntas: hac ego contentos, auguror esse Deos.

71. Turpe est beneficiis vinci.

*Translator's note: The Latin quotations in these notes were prepared by
consulting the textual notes of E. Abréu Gómez, Juan Carlos Merlo, and
Elías L. Rivers.*